ACROSS THE DIVIDE

WITH APPRECIATION

FOR YOUR SUPPORT AS A

CONTRIBUTING MEMBER

CAROLYN GILMAN

Introduction by JAMES P. RONDA

Lewis and Clark

ACROSS THE DIVIDE

Published by

SMITHSONIAN BOOKS

Washington and London

in association with the

MISSOURI HISTORICAL SOCIETY

St. Louis

Gilman, Carolyn, 1954–
Lewis and Clark—across the divide / Carolyn Gilman ; introduction by James P. Ronda.
p. cm.
"The companion volume to Lewis and Clark—the national bicentennial exhibition, organized and circulated by the Missouri Historical Society and presented by Emerson"—"In association with the Missouri Historical Society, St. Louis."
"Missouri History Museum, St. Louis, January–August 2004; Academy of Natural Sciences of Philadelphia, Philadelphia, November 2004–March 2005; Denver Museum of Nature and Science, Denver, May–September 2005; Oregon History Center, Portland, November 2005–March 2006; National Museum of Natural History, Smithsonian Institution, May–September 2006"—
Includes bibliographical references and index.
ISBN 1-58834-099-6 (alk. paper)—
ISBN 1-58834-095-3 (pbk. : alk. paper)
1. Lewis and Clark Expedition (1804–1806)—Exhibitions. 2. West (U.S.)—Discovery and exploration—Exhibitions. 3. West (U.S.)—Description and travel—Exhibitions. 4. Indians of North America—West (U.S.)—History—19th century—Exhibitions. 5. Indians, Treatment of—West (U.S.)—History—19th century—Exhibitions. 6. West (U.S.)—Ethnic relations—Exhibitions. I. Missouri Historical Society. II. Title.

F592.7.G55 2003
917.804'2—dc21 2002042910

British Library Cataloguing-in-Publication Data available

Printed in Singapore, not at government expense
10 09 08 07 06 05 04 03 5 4 3 2 1

SMITHSONIAN BOOKS
Caroline Newman, Executive Editor, Museum Publications
Suzanne G. Fox, Project Manager
Carol Beehler, Designer
Eric Schwass, Production Manager
D. Teddy Diggs, Copy Editor
Susan DeRenne Coerr, Index Writer
Gene Thorp, Cartographer
Julian Waters, Calligrapher

This publication has been prepared in association with the Missouri Historical Society, St. Louis.
Project Directors
Robert R. Archibald
Karen Goering
Nicola Longford

Jeff Meyer, Researcher
Joseph Carlisle, Researcher
Benjamin Cawthra, Project Manager
Diane Mallow, Registrar

Lewis and Clark: Across the Divide is the companion volume to *Lewis and Clark: The National Bicentennial Exhibition*, organized and circulated by the Missouri Historical Society and presented by Emerson. Major funding has been provided by the U.S. Congress through the National Park Service, the State of Missouri through the Missouri Lewis & Clark Bicentennial Commission, and the National Endowment for the Humanities.

EXHIBITION DATES

Missouri History Museum
St. Louis, January–August, 2004

Academy of Natural Sciences of Philadelphia
Philadelphia, November 2004–March 2005

Denver Museum of Nature and Science
Denver, May–September 2005

Oregon History Center
Portland, November 2005–March 2006

National Museum of Natural History,
Smithsonian Institution
May–September 2006

Front cover, top, and back cover: Detail, *Draught of the Falls and Portage of the Missouri*, from the journal of William Clark, 1805; front cover, bottom: Detail, *River Bluffs, 1,320 Miles above St. Louis*, George Catlin, 1832
Spine, top: *William Clark*, Charles Willson Peale, c. 1808; bottom: *Meriwether Lewis*, Charles Willson Peale, 1807
Endsheet: Bag with hell-diver bird motif and elk, pre-1841, Clatsop or Tillamook
Frontispiece: *Missouri in the Morning below Council Bluffs*, Karl Bodmer, 1833
Right: Detail, *Junction of the Yellowstone and the Missouri*, Karl Bodmer, c. 1833

The paper used in this publication meets the minimum requirements of the American National Standard for Information Sciences—Permanence of Paper for Printed Library Materials ANSIZ39.48-1984.

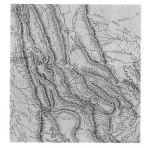

Contents

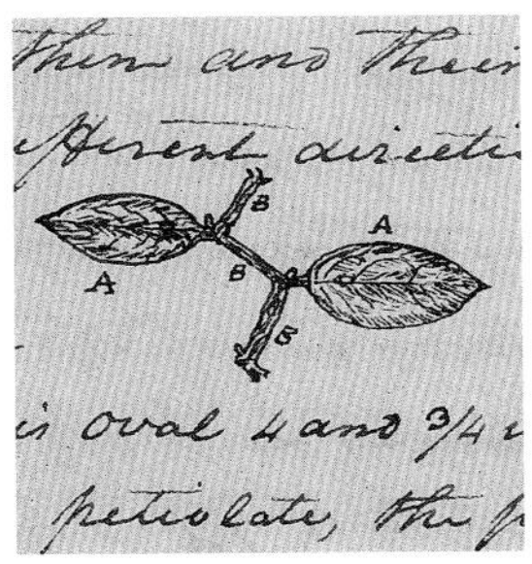

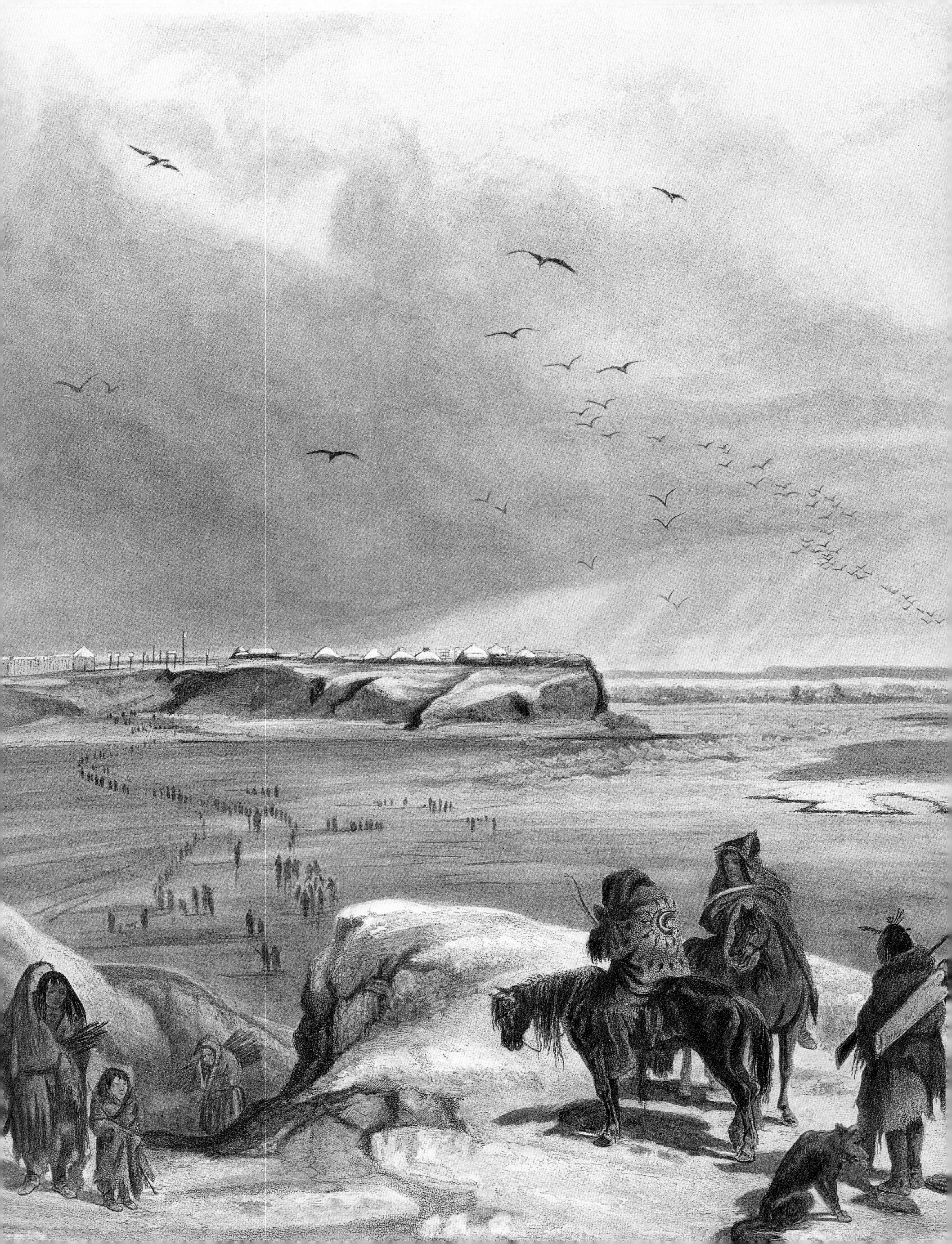

Foreword

ROBERT R. ARCHIBALD
President, Missouri Historical Society
President, National Council of the
Lewis & Clark Bicentennial

For a dozen years, I lived and worked in Montana, the state where Lewis and Clark traveled more miles than in any other of the states carved from the Louisiana Territory. Thus I can understand William Clark's impatience in the spring of 1806 as the expedition awaited the thaw that comes so late to the Bitterroot Mountains near Montana's western border. In late May, Clark began to discuss with the Nez Perce who inhabited that region the best route over those formidable mountains, which towered in frozen splendor over the low country. One of the Nez Perce drew a map, unlike any map drawn by whites, of what became the Montana-Idaho border. It was an Indian's view of his world and was not meant to depict topography and distances in precise scale. This map is a narrative of useful information based on the historical and cultural experience of a people, a diagram of the connections between generations, a guide based on those connections. It was vital, for instance, to the people who lived there and those in the expedition, to know when the grass greened up on the south sides of the hills or which parts of a river could serve as a pathway rather than present a treachery.

When I first saw this extraordinary map, I began to understand that the Lewis and Clark expedition looks in different directions: toward the East and toward the West; back to the past and into the future that is part of our past and our present; through the eyes of Lewis and Clark and the other members of the party who kept journals and through the worldview of the Native peoples, a perspective that brought as much change to the expedition as the expedition brought to that so-called empty land.

The Lewis and Clark expedition has come down to us in the twenty-first century as our very own epic, a distillation of the quintessential American dream of rediscovering a lost Paradise. In reality, the Corps of Discovery was giving the young United States its first glimpse into a land that Americans east of the Alleghenies considered empty terra incognita. Thomas Jefferson stated the intent of the Lewis and Clark mission quite clearly in his letter of instruction. Lewis was to find a "practicable water communication across this continent" and was to learn, among other things, "the names of the nations & their numbers; the extent & limits of their possessions; their relations with other tribes of nations; their language, traditions, monuments; their ordinary occupations."[1]

As Jefferson and many others knew, there were other people in the land beyond the Mississippi River. While Thomas Jefferson was gazing west over his Blue Ridge Mountains in Virginia, Indians of ancient lineage and centuries-long habitation in what Americans were calling the Louisiana Territory were looking east. Jefferson had his dreams of empire, but non-Indian Americans were about to meet another perspective, a worldview very different from their

Fort Clark on the Missouri (detail), c. 1834.
See page 112.

own but essential to the mission that the country had laid upon Lewis and Clark and their team. For without the goodwill and assistance of the Indians whose lands the United States was claiming, even the stalwart crew of the Lewis and Clark expedition could not have survived. Today's Americans can, and must, look into this meeting of different cultures as another kind of discovery by Lewis and Clark, the discovery that "foreign" peoples, their traditions, and their worldviews were of at least equal value and importance to our own familiar and parochial perspectives. Lewis and Clark themselves began to understand this concept early in their journey. Two hundred years have intervened, but the years have not diluted the lessons we can take into our own times and beyond.

The Lewis and Clark expedition, and the events and consequences it engendered, literally changed American history. But this interpretation and the overwhelming popularity of the great adventure are relatively recent. In 1836 William Grimshaw's *History of the United States* included two pages on the Lewis and Clark expedition. In his description, bears were dangerous, wild enemies to be killed. Indians were savages whose behavior was either martial and ludicrous or voluptuous and indecent. Grimshaw saw no inherent value in wilderness. The principal achievement of the expedition was the information that was gathered on the future commercial and agricultural potential of the territory encompassed within the Louisiana Purchase. Grimshaw wrote during a period of national optimism grounded in the economic growth that accompanied America's first industrial revolution, when possibilities for economic expansion sustained by an apparently infinite supply of natural resources seemed unlimited. Most Americans had neither sympathy nor time for romantic notions about unspoiled nature and Native peoples. Both were impediments to progress, which would ultimately require exploitation or extermination.

Grimshaw's perspective prevailed in the American imagination with only slight alteration through the end of the nineteenth century. In his 1890 *History of the United States of America during the Second Administration of Thomas Jefferson*, Henry Adams wrote that Lewis and Clark "were forced to pass the winter in extreme discomfort, among thievish and flea-bitten Indians, until . . . they could retrace their steps." Adams conceded that the expedition had been a good example of "American energy and enterprise," but he concluded: "They added little to the stock of science or wealth. Many years must elapse before the vast region west of the Mississippi could be brought within the reach of civilization."[2]

By the end of World War I, the frontier had receded into memory. The complexity of America's world-power status, combined with an increasingly urban landscape and the defeat and confinement of Indians to reservations, fostered a climate for non-Indian Americans to adopt a romantic and nostalgic view of Native people and the frontier wilderness while still maintaining the superiority of "civilization." Ralph Henry Gabriel's *The Lure of the Frontier*, published in 1929, reflected these attitudes. This volume elevated Lewis and Clark to heroic status and included reproductions of romanticized art by Charles M. Russell and others. Sacagawea was imbued with the status of heroine; nature was beautiful and beneficent.

In our own time, Lewis and Clark are portrayed as pioneering naturalists and proto-environmentalists. Our perspectives of the expedition are, like the others, shaped by the concerns of our own time and by our concerns about the future. Today we realize that natural resources are finite. With wilderness scarce and frontiers eliminated, we have discovered beauty and value in unspoiled nature and seek to preserve what remains. No longer confident in the superiority of the values of our own civilization, we find appeal in the very different values that defined the Indians' relationships with each other and with the planet.

Although the Corps of Discovery's extraordinary journey is worthy of commemoration, the bicentennial of the expedition is also an opportunity for productive speculation. This volume is a companion to *Lewis & Clark: The National Bicentennial Exhibition*, organized by the Missouri Historical Society, and it reflects thoughtfully on the objects, the plants, the animals, the lands, and most significantly, the indigenous peoples as they were two hundred years ago. This work evaluates the changes, the choices made, and the consequences of our predecessors' actions. Through it, we can look into ourselves and imagine the world we will leave to unborn generations.

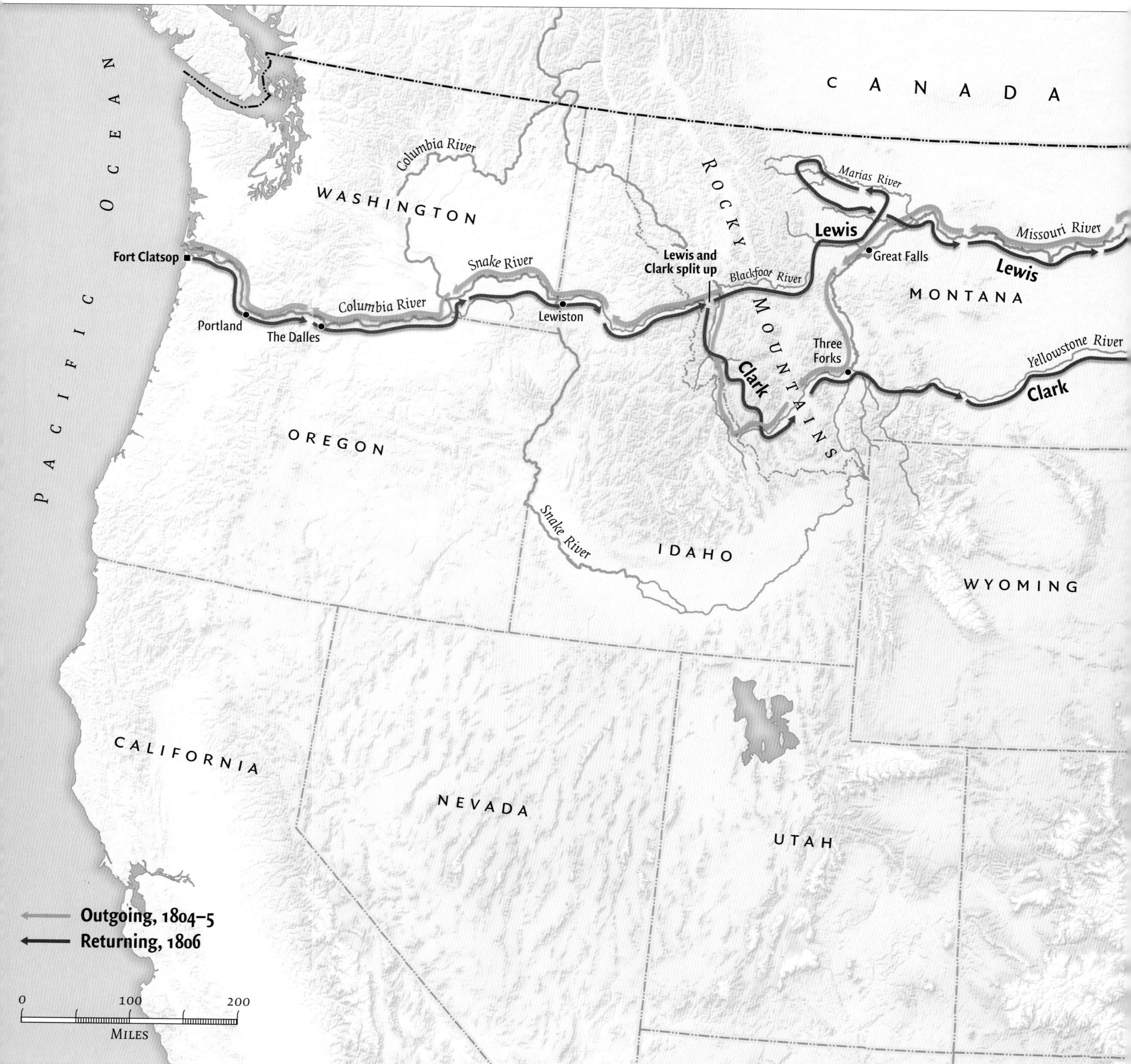
CANADA
PACIFIC OCEAN
WASHINGTON
OREGON
IDAHO
MONTANA
WYOMING
CALIFORNIA
NEVADA
UTAH
ROCKY MOUNTAINS
Columbia River
Snake River
Marias River
Missouri River
Blackfoot River
Yellowstone River
Fort Clatsop
Portland
The Dalles
Lewiston
Lewis and Clark split up
Great Falls
Three Forks
Lewis
Clark
Outgoing, 1804–5
Returning, 1806
0
100
200
Miles

Lewis and Clark reunite
NORTH DAKOTA
Fort Mandan
Bismarck
Little Missouri River
MINNESOTA
Lake Superior
MICHIGAN
Lake Michigan
WISCONSIN
SOUTH DAKOTA
Pierre
Missouri River
James River
Sioux City
IOWA
Missouri River
NEBRASKA
Omaha
Platte River
ILLINOIS
St. Louis
Kansas City
Mississippi River
COLORADO
KANSAS
MISSOURI

old man
Young man
woman
Fort Clatsop the Pacific Ocean
On the South side of the Columbia River
Thursday 30th January 1806
a bad rapid at 2 large rocks
Short Narrows
Part of the Chil luck kit te quaw
Nation of 8 large wood houses
Capt W Clarks
Ms Journal to Mo
7th April to 3 July 1805
1

The Objects of Our Journey

JAMES P. RONDA
The University of Tulsa

On a sweltering day in mid-August 1805, Captain Meriwether Lewis and the Lemhi Shoshone chief Cameahwait sat together in what Lewis described as a "little magic circle" while the American explorer slowly explained "the objects of our journey."[1]

By the time that Lewis talked with Cameahwait, the explorer knew just what he meant by that phrase. His "objects" were President Thomas Jefferson's objectives: finding the fabled Northwest Passage, making diplomatic contact with Indians in a newly expanded American empire, and conducting an initial survey of the western landscape. But Cameahwait's people—their eyes fixed on the things brought by the American expedition—remind us that the word "objects" has yet other meanings. The "objects" of the journey were its physical things: clothing, trade goods, guns, scientific instruments, and a thousand other bits and pieces that were part of the everyday life of an exploring party. Perhaps both Cameahwait and Lewis understood that at some point, those meanings merged. Certain physical objects embodied what Jefferson meant when he talked about "the objects of your journey." Flags and medals represented the ambitions of the adventuresome young Republic; guns were unmistakable reminders of the force behind all territorial expansion; and moccasin awls stood for an entire country store of items as the Industrial Revolution made its way into the West. Each object tells not one story but many. Some reveal large narratives of national aspiration or cultural survival in the face of adversity. Others offer more intimate tales of individual perseverance, suffering, or folly. But all together, they take us on a journey filled with countless stories told by many actors on a stage of continental expanse. To consider some of those emblematic objects is to know the deeper meanings of the journey.

JEFFERSON'S OBJECTS

Although Jefferson never said as much, no one more deeply influenced his exploration plans than Sir Joseph Banks. President of England's Royal Society, de facto director of the Royal Garden at Kew, and informal scientific advisor to the government, Banks was what one British explorer called "the common Center of we discoverers."[2] Banks was the patron, planner, and sometime participant in the great eighteenth-century Pacific Ocean explorations led by Captain James Cook and Captain George Vancouver. Even though Jefferson and Banks never corresponded on exploration matters, Jefferson's reading made him aware of Banks as the embodiment of global exploration. Placing exploration squarely within the Enlightenment tradition, Banks emphasized scientific inquiry, sound organization, and clearly defined goals. Carefully drafted exploration instructions were essential for success. Alert to the politics

OPPOSITE: Lewis and Clark journals, 1805–6

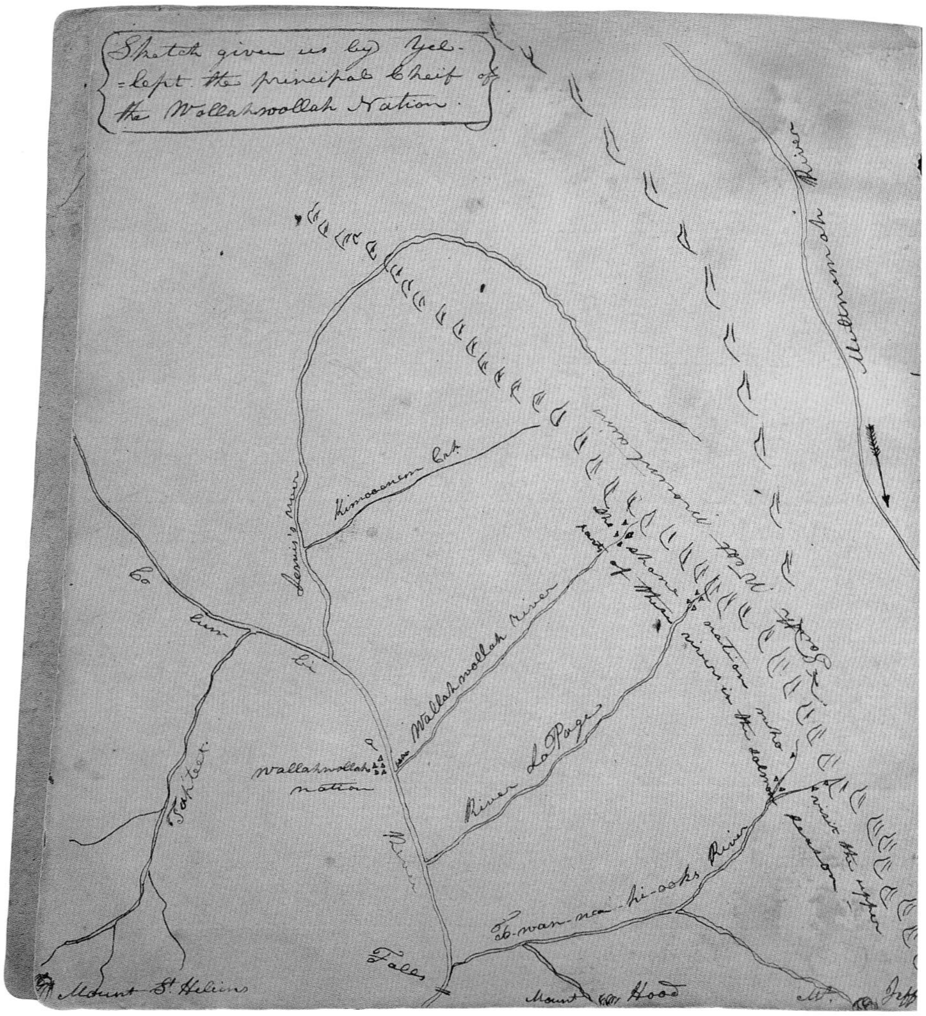

Yellept's map, 1806
This map was found in Lewis's astronomy notebook and was evidently done on paper from the notebook. Written on it is: "Sketch given us by Yellept the principal Cheif of the Wollahwollah Nation." It was probably drawn during the return journey, on or about April 28, 1806, when the explorers spent a day at Yellept's village in eastern Oregon. Reflecting Clark's geographical misconceptions, it shows the "Multnomah" (Willamette) River flowing east to west where the upper Snake should be. It also shows Mount St. Helens where Mount Adams is.

of discovery, Banks understood that exploration was always in the service of empire.

These lessons were not lost on Jefferson. Like Banks, he fashioned an exploration strategy that combined the quest for scientific knowledge with a search for wealth and power. Jefferson's first venture into exploration planning came in 1793, when he prepared instructions for André Michaux's abortive journey across the continent. It was here that Jefferson first used the words "objects of your journey."[3] That simple phrase came back to Jefferson in the spring of 1803 as he drafted instructions for Lewis. Like Banks, Jefferson believed that exploration was a systematic, intellectual activity with strategies and goals established well before making any journey. In what has become an often-quoted sentence, Jefferson made plain the expedition's central purpose. "The object of your mission is to explore the Missouri river, & such principal stream of it, as, by it's course and communication with the waters of the Pacific ocean . . . may offer the most direct & practicable water communication across this continent, for the purposes of commerce."[4] The president's intent was unmistakable. What became "the Lewis and Clark expedition" was yet another search for the ever-elusive Northwest Passage.

Both Banks and Jefferson knew that exploration in the Age of Enlightenment and Empire served many masters and pursued many objectives. Once Jefferson established the core object for Lewis and Clark, he quickly moved to define additional goals for the journey. Those ranged from discoveries in botany and zoology to matters of trade and diplomacy with Native nations. Even the quickest reading of the instructions reveals how large a presence Native people occupied in Jefferson's exploration thinking. For all sorts of reasons—some imperial and commercial and others rooted in his own inquisitive mind—Jefferson wanted his travelers to compile what amounted to the first chapters in an American encyclopedia of Native American peoples and cultures. And in all he expected they would accomplish, the president hoped Lewis and Clark could convince Native people that their new great father expected obedience in return for useful objects and a promising future.

Jefferson used the word "object" and the phrase "object of your journey" six times in his instructions for Lewis. And the president soon found the phrase convenient when describing the proposed expedition and its many objectives. Throughout the first half of 1803, as Jefferson sought advice from cabinet officers and members of the American Philosophical Society, the phrase became a kind of shorthand for what he hoped the expedition would accomplish. Lewis also quickly adopted the expression, making it part of his own exploration vocabulary. By the time Lewis wrote William Clark and formally invited him to join the expedition as coleader, the phrase was everywhere. Commenting on the legislation authorizing the journey, Lewis told Clark that "the object of this act" was to explore "the interior of the Continent of North America." After outlining his travel timetable, Lewis offered Clark a brief sketch of "the objects which it [the expedition] has in view or those which it is desirable to effect through it's means."[5]

WRITING THE OBJECTS INTO THE WEST BY PAPER, PEN, AND PRINT

The fundamental object of the expedition was clear. There might be many missions, but there was only one essential goal. When Lewis proposed a short excursion from St. Louis toward Santa Fe in the winter of 1803–4, the president sharply reminded him, "The object of your mission is single, the direct water communication from sea to sea formed by the bed of the Missouri & perhaps the Oregon."[6] Like Banks, Jefferson insisted that simply making the journey and finding the passage was not enough. As one historian has explained, "The eighteenth century believed perhaps more strongly than any other that travel makes truth."[7] But the truths revealed by travel would slip away without writing and the permanence provided by print. Enlightenment explorers and their patrons agreed that experience became useful knowledge only when recorded and then shared with a wider audience. Writing, drawing, and mapping served to fix the experience on the page and make it knowledge. As Jefferson directed Lewis, "Your observations are to be taken with great pains & accuracy, to be entered distinctly, & intelligibly for others as well as yourself." While specifically referring to astronomical observations, Jefferson's directions went well beyond matters of latitude and longitude. In an arresting suggestion, Jefferson urged Lewis to make one copy of his "other notes" on birch bark, since that material was "less liable to injury from damp than common paper."[8] Some of the objects of the journey now became the means to record it. Jefferson had put his travelers in the world of pens, paper, and ink, in the universe of compasses, chronometers, and cartography. As the explorers moved through the landscape, their pens traveled across the page, one journey imitating and inscribing the other.

At the simplest level, every writer works with tools—pen, ink, paper, and some kind of desk. Lewis knew this as he began to plan the course of his journey and the course of his writing. His early "List of Requirements" included writing paper, ink, and "4 metal Pens brass or silver."[9] By the time he left Philadelphia in the spring of 1803, the contents of his writer's toolbox had grown in size and sophistication. Lewis bought brass inkstands, more pens—both metal and quill—and a quarter pound of India ink from the druggists Gillaspy and Strong. And he took a lot of paper. The packing lists prepared in St. Louis in 1804 noted everything from blank memorandum books to many quires of lightweight post paper and common foolscap. Somewhere along the way, Lewis and Clark added two portable desks to what had become more a writer's workshop than a simple toolbox. Jefferson's questions sent the explorers into the West. Now Lewis and Clark were ready to write some answers.

The historian and documentary editor Donald Jackson once said that the journal-keepers on the Lewis and Clark expedition were "the writingest explorers of their time."[10] Those who kept logs and journals for Cook and Vancouver might have disagreed, but Jackson had a point. Submitting themselves to the discipline of the word, the pen, and the page, Jefferson's travelers wrote obsessively, taking note of small details and large events. And they wrote with different voices and in different styles. All told, the expedition had seven journal-keepers: Lewis, Clark, Sergeant John Ordway, Sergeant Charles Floyd, Sergeant Patrick Gass, Private Joseph Whitehouse, and Private Robert Frazer. Though the men often copied from each other, the surviving journals display their distinctive perspectives. Clark sometimes wrote two entries for each day, revising, editing, and pruning as he went through the day. Expedition journal-keepers wrote under difficult conditions. On a cold morning in late August 1805, both Lewis and Ordway struggled to write. As one of them noted, "The ink feizes in

Portable desk, pre-1833
The desks carried by U.S. Army officers were substantial pieces of furniture that doubled as crates for books, maps, and writing materials. Lewis and Clark each brought one, but they cached Lewis's, along with its contents ("some books, my specimens of plants minerals &c. collected from fort Mandan to that place"), at the Great Falls. Clark's desk accompanied the expedition across the Rocky Mountains, where it nearly met with disaster when the horse carrying it "Turned over & roled down a mountain for 40 yards & lodged against a tree, broke the Desk the horse escaped and appeared but little hurt."

This desk belonged to a contemporary of Lewis and Clark's: Captain Daniel Bissell, the commandant of Fort Massac, who supplied a number of the men for the expedition. Only the top part was designed to travel; it could be set on any table or countertop. It is more finely made than the desk Lewis brought to the White House from his job as army paymaster, a desk that still belongs to the Lewis family.

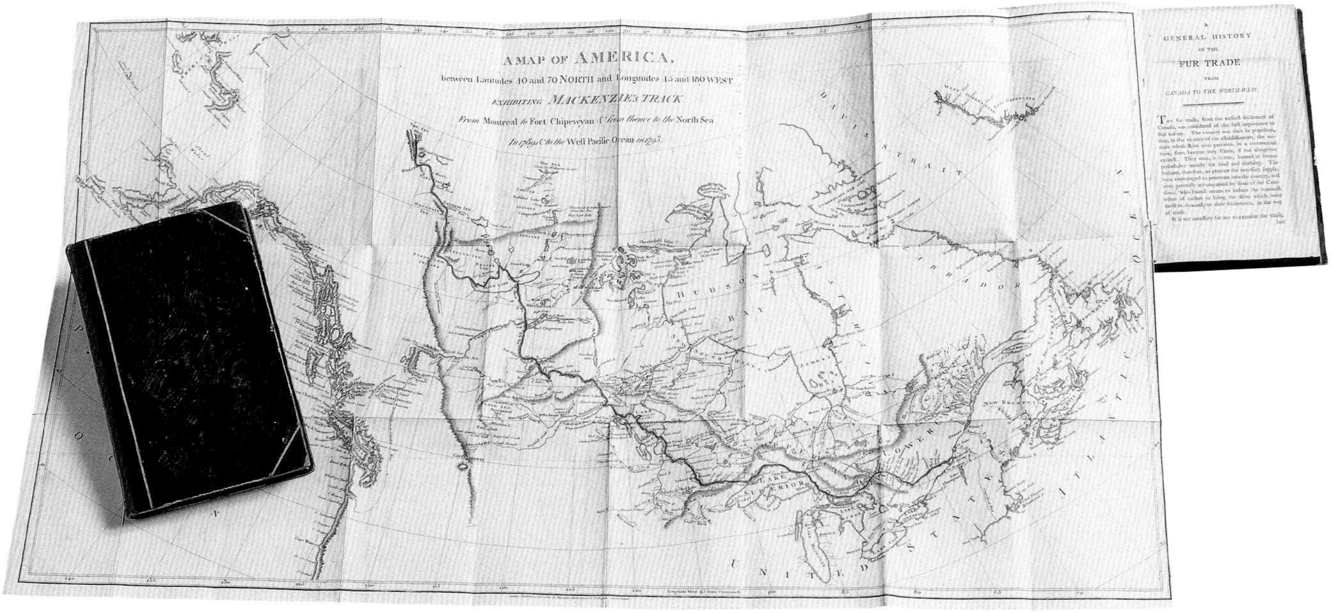

my pen."[11] A year later, as the expedition hurried down the Missouri to St. Louis, Clark found it necessary "to replenish [the] ink Stand every day with fresh ink at least 9/10 of which must evaperate."[12] Laboring over his journal while on the upper Missouri, Lewis complained, "The perogue is so unsteady that I can scarcely write."[13] When a gust of wind one July day scattered Clark's papers, he had to rely on records kept by others. Nevertheless, the expedition's writers continued to march their words across the page just as they persevered to march their way across the continent.

Alexander Mackenzie, *Voyages from Montreal, on the River St. Laurence, through the Continent of North America*, 1802
This book aroused Jefferson's alarm about British designs on the western part of the continent, thereby precipitating the expedition. The Scottish fur trader Alexander Mackenzie was the first non-Indian to cross America north of Mexico, in 1793. At the time, he was a partner in the British-Canadian North West Company, which had a network of trading posts as far west as the Canadian Rockies. After reading this book, Jefferson began to feel that the United States and Britain were in a race to establish power over the territories beyond the Mississippi. He purchased a copy for Lewis to take along on the journey.

Like the pens, ink, and paper that recorded the central object of the journey, the journals themselves have now become emblems of the passage to the Pacific. On those pages, experiences and observations became words and sentences. Often written in plain, unadorned American English, the entries seem remarkably accessible to us. But a careful reading of the expedition record is sometimes an unsettling, disconcerting experience. Expecting to find daily installments reporting the expedition's progress across the continent, modern readers confront what sometimes seems a rough jumble of information about weather, birds, plants, animals, personal health, and meetings with Native people. Now prized for their immediacy, the original journals were never meant for public scrutiny. Lewis knew as much when he sent Clark's journals from Fort Mandan to Jefferson, advising the president, "Capt. Clark dose not want this journal exposed in it's present state, but has no objection, that one or more copies of it be made by some confidential person under your direction, correcting it's gramatical errors etc."[14] Expedition writers recorded more than the bare outlines of courses and distances, what Lewis called "the daily detales of our progress."[15] The desire was to get as much on paper as possible. The eighteenth-century ideals of order, balance, and literary style could come later.

Lewis's long entry for August 20, 1805, is a good example of the journals at their complicated best—or worst. Lewis had spent nearly a week with the Lemhi Shoshone, negotiating with Cameahwait, learning about regional geography, and observing Indian life. Now Lewis quickly set down the day's events—hunting, fishing, and preparing a cache for goods left behind. He took note of Shoshone women "busily engaged all day making and mending the mockersons of our party."[16] Then, in no order, Lewis penned detailed accounts of Shoshone clothing, Indian perspectives on regional geography, and his understanding of the place the Shoshone occupied in the geopolitics of the northern plains and Rockies. We might read this journal entry as a first draft of the report Lewis knew he was expected to write at the end of the journey. As fate had it, making the transition from journal-keeper and the handwritten sheet to author and the printed page proved far more difficult than he imagined.

READING THE WEST

Every exploration venture was first a journey into the country of the mind. And on that journey, books were everywhere. As the writer Samuel Johnson told his biographer James Boswell, "A man must carry knowledge with him, if he would bring knowledge home."[17] What the eighteenth century called "voyages of discovery" were often prompted by books, shaped by books, and had their discoveries recorded and shared in books. The Lewis and Clark expedition was no exception. Jefferson's reading informed his understanding of both exploration strategy and western geography. His only published book, *Notes on the State of Virginia*, gave early expression to influential exploration ideas. Even more important, reading one particular book was the experience that jolted the president into creating the expedition.

Jefferson once told John Adams, "I cannot live without books."[18] In his ever-expanding library was a generous section devoted to geography, travel narratives, and the accounts of explorers such as Cook and Vancouver. It was to his library that Jefferson turned when writing *Notes on the State of Virginia*. That book was more than chapter-length answers to questions from an inquisitive French diplomat. After years of thinking about the nature of North American geography, Jefferson at last set down his own account of the shape of the continent.

Books taken on the expedition, 1754–1803
Lewis did not rely on his own knowledge; he brought along a substantial library of reference books and used them in writing many of the natural history entries in his journals. He kept the books in his desk during the expedition and cached some of the less useful ones at the Great Falls. This photograph shows a few volumes he is known or suspected to have had. Clockwise from bottom, they are: Patrick Kelly, *A Practical Introduction to Spherics and Nautical Astronomy* (1796); Benjamin S. Barton, *Elements of Botany; or Outlines of the Natural History of Vegetables* (1803); Richard Kirwan, *Elements of Mineralogy* (1794 and 1796); and A Society of Gentlemen, *A New and Complete Dictionary of Arts and Sciences* (1754).

What he wrote in *Notes* expressed the geographic foundation for the Lewis and Clark expedition.

Jefferson wrote an Italian correspondent that he was "a savage of the mountains of America."[19] But for all his fascination with mountains, it was rivers that captured Jefferson's attention and imagination. In chapter 2 of *Notes* he presented a comprehensive survey of Virginia's rivers. A modern reader looking at that list is soon struck by two things: each river is not merely described but judged, and the yardstick for judgment is not beauty but utility. For Jefferson, a river was important and useful to the extent that it was navigable. Looking beyond Virginia, he nominated two rivers as highways for American empire. The Mississippi was "one of the principal channels for future commerce of the country westward of the Alleghaney." But it was the Missouri and its westward course that sparked his imagination. "The Missouri is," so Jefferson confidently wrote, "the principal river, contributing more to the common stream than does the Mississippi."[20] Drawing on centuries-old images of a water highway across the continent, Jefferson put the Missouri at the center of his passage to India. And beyond the Missouri, over an easily portaged range of mountains, was the fabled River of the West. This was the "Oregon," not yet called the Columbia. Ten years after writing *Notes*, and a decade before drafting instructions for Lewis and Clark, Jefferson made his case for a river passage from Atlantic to Pacific waters. "It would seem," so he announced, "by the latest maps as if a river called Oregan interlocked with the Missouri."[21] Rivers were the plain path to the Pacific. Mountains would be no barrier to a westering nation.

But no matter how clear the imperial geography in *Notes*, there was little sign that Americans were about to venture out on these river roads. It took another book to set in motion what became "Mr. Lewis's Tour." Summer was the season for the president to escape Washington's oppressive humidity and political heat for Monticello's mountain coolness. The summer of 1802 was no exception. Writing to his New York bookseller James Cheetham, Jefferson requested a copy of Aaron Arrowsmith's newly published "Map of North America." Most important, the president wanted a copy of Alexander Mackenzie's *Voyages from Montreal*. Published in 1801, the book recounted Mackenzie's epic 1789 and 1793 journeys in search of the Northwest Passage. But it was the last few paragraphs in the final chapter that drew Jefferson's attention. In one riveting sentence, Mackenzie proposed using the Columbia River as the means to occupy the West for Great Britain. "By opening this intercourse between the Atlantic and Pacific Oceans, and forming regular establishments through the interior, and at both extremes, as well as along the coasts and islands, the entire command of the fur trade of North America might be obtained."[22] Mackenzie had more on his mind than the trade in beaver and sea otter pelts. He also urged permanent agricultural settlement in this newly minted British West. Such a plan advanced by so prominent an explorer shocked Jefferson. By 1802 he had come to believe that the future of the American republic was in the West. Now the one empire he most feared seemed poised to seize the western country and deny Americans a promising future. What became the Lewis and Clark expedition was born the summer that Jefferson read Mackenzie's work.

Books inspired the expedition and guided its course. And books were part

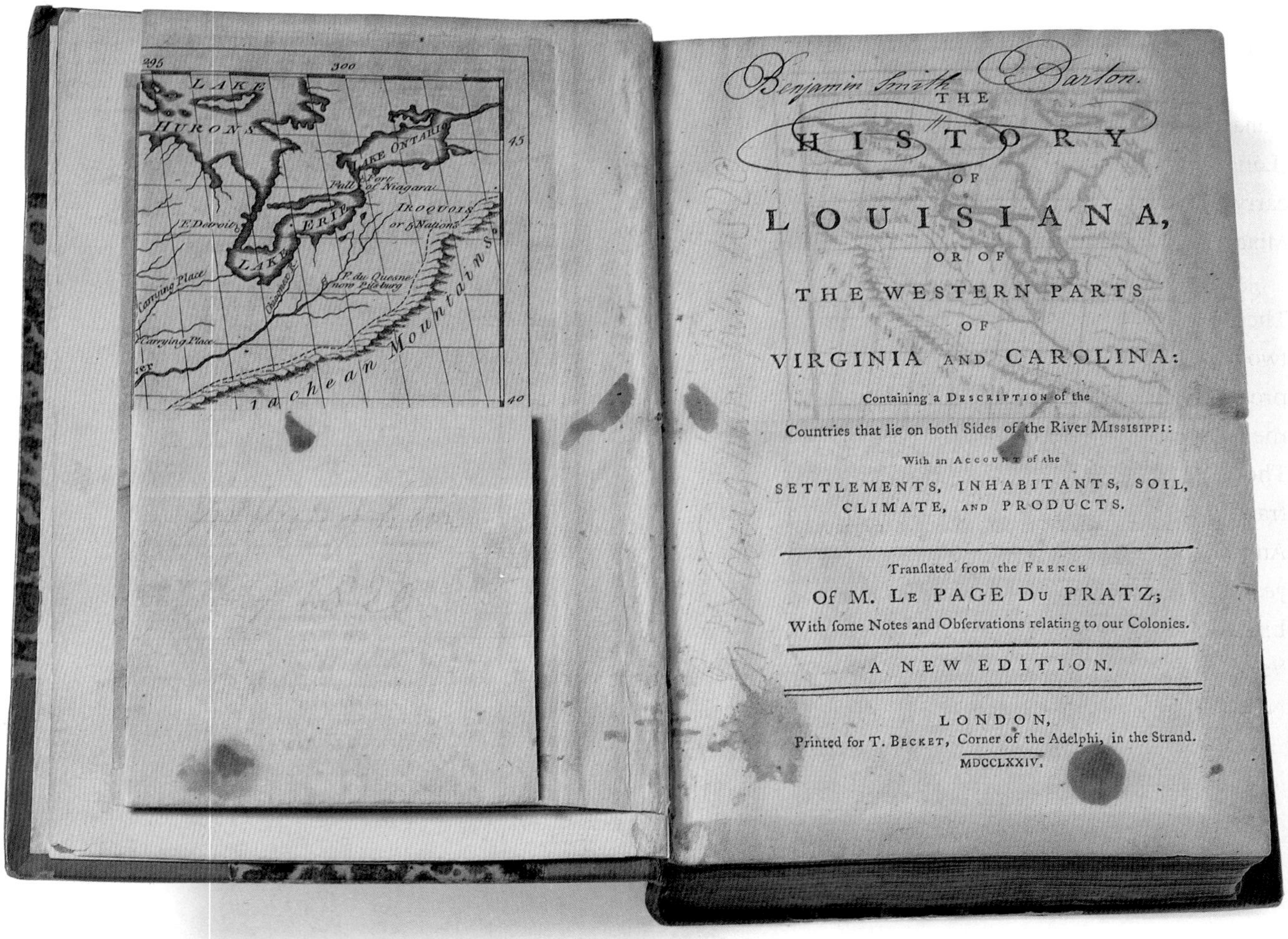

Le Page du Pratz, *The History of Louisiana*, 1774

Benjamin Smith Barton loaned this book to Lewis in 1803. Lewis returned it four years later, after carrying it to the Pacific coast and back. He wrote an inscription in the flyleaf thanking Barton for the loan: "Dr. Benjamin Smith Barton was so obliging as to lend me this copy of Monsr. Du Pratz's history of Louisiana in June 1803. it has been since conveyed by me to the Pacific Ocean through the interior of the Continent of North America on my late tour thither and is now returned to it's proprietor by his Friend and Obt. Servt. Meriwether Lewis. Philadelphia May 9th 1807."

of the baggage Lewis and Clark took into the West. While in Philadelphia, Lewis began building a modest library. The books he chose reflected the Enlightenment exploration tradition—volumes dealing with the scientific determination of geographic location, books about botany, zoology, and mineralogy, and at least one volume by a scientifically minded traveler. Predictably, most of the books were about astronomy and navigation. After consultations with the surveyor Andrew Ellicott and the University of Pennsylvania mathematician Robert Patterson, Lewis obtained a copy of Patrick Kelly's *A Practical Introduction of Spherics and Nautical Astronomy*, published in London in 1796. To aid in calculating latitude and longitude, Lewis also acquired *The Nautical Almanac and Astronomical Ephemeris*, probably one for each of the three years he planned to be traveling. He also purchased a set of tables for mathematical calculations, in this case Nevil Maskelyne's *Tables Requisite to be Used with the Nautical Ephemeris for Finding the Latitude and Longitude at Sea* (London, 1781).

Both Jefferson and Lewis worked within the intellectual tradition of natural history, a method that emphasized the collection, description, and classification of plants and animals. The eighteenth-century naturalist Gilbert White put it best: "Without system the field of Nature would be a pathless wilderness."[23] As a gifted naturalist, Lewis was especially drawn to botany. For him, nothing seemed more productive of "useful knowledge" than botany. And in Philadelphia, no one was more the academic master of American botany than Dr. Benjamin Smith Barton. Lewis talked with Barton and then spent six dollars out of his own pocket to buy a copy of Barton's *Elements of Botany* (1803). But Lewis knew he would need additional reference works, especially those keyed to the Linnaean classification system. He filled out his natural history library with John Miller's two-volume *An Illustration of the Sexual System of Linnaeus* (London, 1779) and *An Illustration of the Termini Botanici of Linnaeus* (London, 1789). Although mineralogy was not an expedition priority, Lewis did carry—and on occasion consult—a copy of Richard Kirwan's *Elements of Mineralogy* (London, 1784).

Bibliographers sometimes call such volumes "books that are not books." These works are meant to be consulted, not read. But the expedition did carry two, or perhaps even three, books that could be read for both pleasure and profit. When it came to things in print about what Jefferson called "the face of the country," there were few choices about what the explorers might acquire. There is incontrovertible evidence that Lewis and Clark took along at least one travel account, and there are hints of a second as well. The French engineer Antoine Le Page du Pratz came to Louisiana in 1718, stayed for some sixteen years surveying the lower Mississippi River, and wrote an important account of his travels. In one chapter, du Pratz summarized the explorations of Étienne Veniard de Bourgmont up the Missouri at least as far as present-day Omaha, Nebraska. Lewis and Clark would have access to far better information once they reached St. Louis, but at the earliest stages of their journey, Bourgmont's account added one more piece to their understanding of the Missouri River. Lewis borrowed Barton's copy of the English translation and later wrote the following on the flyleaf. "Dr. Benjamin Smith Barton was so obliging as to lend me this copy of Monsr. Du Pratz's history of Louisiana in June 1803. it has been since conveyed by me to the Pacific Ocean through the interior of the continent of North America on my late tour thither and is now returned to it's proprietor by his Friend and Obt. Servt. Meriwether Lewis, Philadelphia, May 9th, 1807."[24]

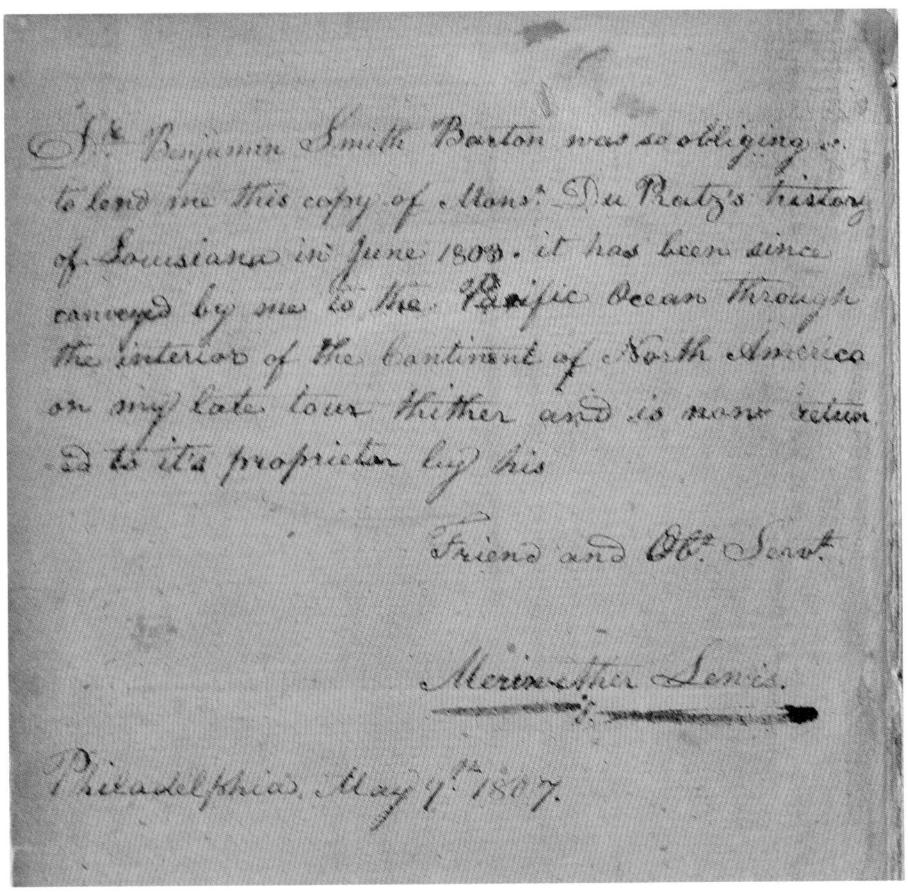
Dr. Benjamin Smith Barton was so obliging as
to lend me this copy of Monsr. Du Pratz's history
of Louisiana in June 1803. it has been since
conveyed by me to the Pacific Ocean through
the interior of the Continent of North America
on my late tour thither and is now return
d to it's proprietor by his

Friend and Obt. Servt.

Meriwether Lewis.

Philadelphia, May 9th 1807.

Inscription written by Meriwether Lewis on the flyleaf of *The History of Louisiana*, 1774

No other geographic text can be so closely associated with Lewis and Clark's journey, but there are tantalizing hints about one additional book. Because Mackenzie's *Voyages from Montreal* had set the expedition in motion and had so greatly influenced Jefferson, the president may have wanted Lewis to read it and perhaps take it along. In June 1803, as plans for the expedition were moving ahead, Jefferson wrote again to Cheetham, his bookseller. A year earlier he had wanted a copy of Mackenzie for himself; now perhaps he wanted one for Lewis. And no ordinary copy would do. Jefferson specifically did not want the English quarto edition because it was "too large and cumbersome."[25] So bulky a book might prove a burden on the way West. *Voyages from Montreal* was present at the creation of the expedition; it may have made the journey as well.

One final item filled out the expedition's library. At the end of the journey, Clark prepared a list of goods to be shipped to Louisville, Kentucky. On that list was what he described as "4 vols. of the Deckinsery of arts an[d] ciences."[26] Donald Jackson, who wrote the pioneering study of the Lewis and Clark library, believed that Clark meant Ephraim Chambers's *Universal Dictionary of Arts and Sciences*, first published in London in 1728 and issued in many subsequent editions and expansions. By 1786 it was a massive, heavily illustrated, four-folio production. Its very size probably meant that Lewis and Clark did not take Chambers's work up the Missouri and across the mountains. Instead, they probably carried a smaller, four-volume dictionary based on Chambers and commonly known as *Owen's Dictionary*.

Books were the explorers' constant companions. At least once, when a "suddon squall of wind" struck an expedition pirogue on the upper Missouri, Sacagawea put herself and her infant son in harm's way to save expedition books and papers.[27] But after 1806, the expedition journal-keepers and readers had a different relationship with the world of writing and books. Lewis and Clark had once been book consumers, readers in the world of print. Now they—and some of their traveling companions—sought to become writers, producers in the marketplace of print.

By any measure, Lewis faced a daunting task as he moved from explorer to author. He had to organize, study, and digest the expedition's massive store of journals, letters, papers, scientific specimens, and maps. Only then could he begin to write a publishable narrative. In the months after the expedition's return, Lewis took the first steps in that process. He contracted with a Philadelphia printer, parceled out scientific specimens for further study, and began to think about the engraving of maps and illustrations.

But Lewis was not alone in exploring the world of print. In October 1806—just a month after the expedition's return—Private Frazer issued a prospectus announcing his intention to publish a four-hundred-page book, complete with descriptions of western rivers, plants, animals, and "the several Indian tribes." And just to keep his readers' attention, he promised "a variety of Curious and interesting occurances" as well.[28] A month later Ordway, the expedition's senior sergeant and keeper of a detailed journal, talked with the Kentucky politician Arthur Campbell about publishing his account. Campbell told the noted geographer Jedediah Morse that Ordway's journal "had been examined and corrected by Lewis" and might "serve as an introduction" to the history of the expedition until Lewis's "larger work" appeared.[29] And at the end of the year, a third soldier entered the field as a prospective author. Private Whitehouse had also kept a journal, of which two fragmentary versions survive. Though claiming that he was "not a candidate for literary fame," Whitehouse expected that his published journal would be "received as a faithful tribute to the prosperity of [the] Country."[30]

As fate had it, these three soldier authors encountered obstacles along their paths to print. Frazer made no progress toward publication, and his original manuscript was eventually lost. Ordway's journal remained unpublished until 1916. A complete version of the surviving Whitehouse narrative did not appear in print until 1997. But a fourth soldier was successful in seeing his account through to publication. Following the common practice of the day, Sergeant Gass turned his unedited journal over to someone else—in this case, the Pittsburgh bookseller David McKeehan. McKeehan rewrote it, smoothing out the rough edges and making it an acceptable literary product. Even though McKeehan has often been criticized for his efforts, the Gass journal remains a lively, engaging book—one that rewards readers with a uniquely personal account of the journey. In late March 1807 McKeehan issued a prospectus for the Gass journal, announcing a single volume of some three hundred pages, reasonably priced at one dollar. Readers were assured that they would find "an authentic relation of the most interesting transactions during the expedition."[31] Soon after, the Gass journal appeared in print. Gass's would be the expedition's only voice in print until 1814.

Lewis's response to this publication was swift and angry. Having given Frazer initial permission to publish his account, Lewis suddenly withdrew it and publicly accused him of being a "mere" private soldier who had abandoned "good faith to the public" for "the hope of gain."[32] Lewis's denunciation of Frazer received wide newspaper circulation; although Frazer did not reply, Gass's editor surely did. In a blistering letter to Lewis, McKeehan took the explorer to task for his arrogant behavior and pompous language.[33]

Lewis had lost the race to be the first in print, but he and his Philadelphia publisher were not about to concede the entire contest. In early April 1807—very soon after the publication of Gass's journal—C. and A. Conrad and Company issued a prospectus for Lewis's official account of the expedition. Divided into three volumes and graced with maps and scientific illustrations, the published set promised a full narrative of the journey and a complete summary of the expedition's scientific accomplishments.[34] Over the next few years subscribers added their names to a growing list of Americans eager to read Lewis's grand work. And Jefferson repeatedly reminded Lewis of his duties as an author. But at the time of Lewis's death in 1809, he had made little or no progress on the manuscript. As his publishers regretfully told Jefferson, "Govr. Lewis never furnished us with a line of the M.S. nor indeed could we ever hear any thing from him respecting it tho frequent applications to that effect were made to him."[35]

With Lewis gone, Jefferson and Clark realized that the publishing burden fell on Clark. Though Clark was no backcountry illiterate, he did feel inadequate to the task of preparing the expedition report. Even by the permissive standards of the age, his spelling and syntax were uniquely his own. As he once explained to his brother Jonathan, "You must not expect either Connection grammr & good Spelling in my letters."[36] In retrospect, Clark's prose was always more vivid and compelling than Lewis's. But Clark was convinced that he needed to find someone else to organize and write the book. Over the next

John Ordway journal, 1804–6

"We have encouraged our men to keep journals," Lewis wrote Jefferson, "and seven of them do so, to whom in this respect we give every assistance in our power." Only four of the seven journals survived, either in manuscript or printed form: John Ordway's, Patrick Gass's, Charles Floyd's, and Joseph Whitehouse's. Robert Frazer also kept a journal, and probably Nathaniel Pryor did also. The last journalist is unknown.

Ordway's is the longest and most literate, but it was not published in his lifetime, since Lewis purchased it to prevent him from publishing, as Gass had done. Sergeant Ordway was a New Hampshire native who was third in command after the two captains. He was recruited from Captain Russell Bissell's company of the First Infantry at Kaskaskia. He lived in Missouri from 1809 to his death in 1817.

four years Clark worked diligently to find a suitable author and then to see the book to print. Clark finally found his author in the Philadelphia literary man Nicholas Biddle. Biddle proved energetic, hardworking, and reliable. He studied available expedition records and interviewed Clark at length, but he did little with the scientific data. What came from the printer in 1814 as *History of the Expedition under the Command of Captains Lewis and Clark* was a two-volume adventure story with some valuable geographic and ethnographic observations but far short of what either Jefferson or Lewis had hoped to accomplish. So few copies were printed that almost two years after publication, Clark still did not have a set for himself.

FINDING THE WAY WEST

By the time Biddle's *History* appeared, Lewis and Clark were old news. In a strange twist, the map that accompanied the book had a far greater impact than the book itself. Engraved by Samuel Lewis and based on Clark's 1810 master map kept in St. Louis, what came to be called the Lewis and Clark Track Map is widely acknowledged as the most significant cartographic accomplishment of the expedition. Like so many other maps of the American West, this one held on to some old illusions while proclaiming new geographic discoveries. And no illusion had a tighter grip on the imagination than the hope of finding the water communication between the Atlantic and the Pacific. The map kept alive the enduring dream of the Northwest Passage by tracing the course of the ghost river Multnomah flowing southeast from the Columbia near present-day Portland, Oregon, to the western edge of the Rockies. At the same time, Clark portrayed a West far more topographically diverse and complex than Jefferson ever imagined. With firsthand experience to guide him, Clark knew that the Rockies consisted of a tangle of mountain ranges and that western rivers were not the navigable highways so essential to Jefferson's imperial geography. And as an act of political imagination, the map advanced an American imperial and expansionist agenda—one that sometimes acknowledged an Indian presence while ignoring Spanish and British claims in the West.

For Lewis and Clark, maps were a way to impose order and predictability on the landscape. This was an order of lines and grids, a surveyor's vision of the earth. Fundamental to that vision was the reckoning of latitude and longitude. Without being able to determine position on that invisible framework of lines, Enlightenment explorers believed that all maps would be mere guesswork. Jefferson put that passion for precise position at the center of the expedition when he directed his explorers to "take careful observations of latitude and longitude, at all remarkeable points."[37] Whereas the method for ascertaining latitude had long been known, what was called "the longitude problem" had only recently been solved. John Harrison's invention of the chronometer, and the development of smaller, more portable timepieces, made establishing position on lines of longitude possible. The chronometer became the embodiment of the spirit of geometry.

In Philadelphia few objects were more important for Lewis to acquire than a reliable chronometer. The task of finding a suitable chronometer probably fell to Israel Whelan, the hardworking Purveyor of Public Supplies. The

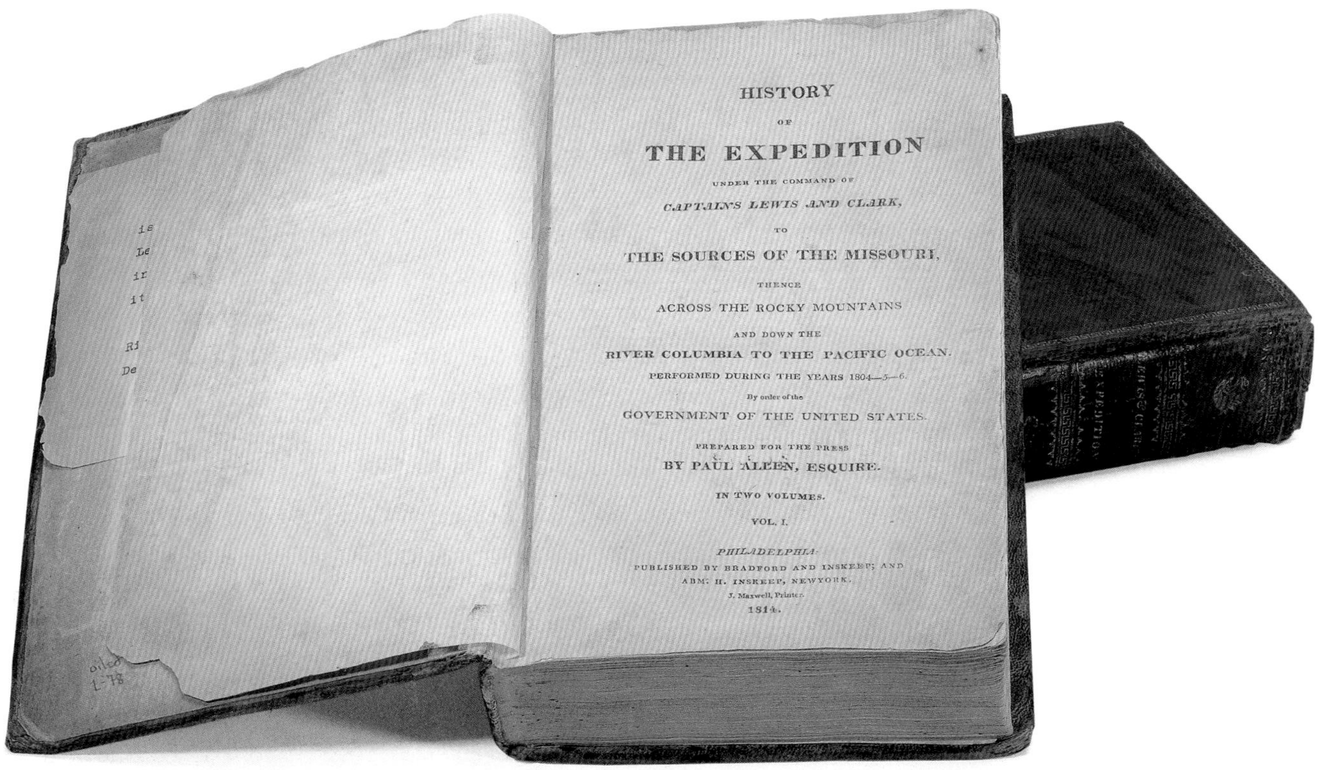

History of the Expedition under the Command of Captains Lewis and Clark, 1814
The only authorized book about the expedition was a paraphrase of the journals. It was written by Nicholas Biddle but edited and brought to publication by an obscure Philadelphia literary man named Paul Allen, whose name was the only one to appear on the title page. The bankruptcy of the original publisher delayed its appearance until 1814. Lewis never saw the book, but his mother and siblings did. This copy was owned by the Lewis family. A note in it from 1931 says that it had "been in the possession of the family since it was published."

search took Whelan to Thomas Parker, a watch and clock maker. Parker provided "1 Gold Chronometer and keys for winding" at a cost of $250.75. But to be useful in the field, the pocket chronometer needed to be adjusted and placed in a protective box. That work was done by Henry Voigt, another Philadelphia clock maker. What finally came to Lewis was something the explorer described as a timepiece set in a "small case" with a mechanism built "on the most improved construction."[38] More than any other object, the chronometer signaled that Lewis and Clark were part of the Enlightenment exploration enterprise.

Like many other objects on this journey, Lewis's chronometer was more than bits of cleverly crafted metal and glass. It represented a whole cluster of cultural values about location, precision, and possession. And it came to have almost a life of its own. Jefferson recognized that chronometers could be fragile, sometimes temperamental devices. Writing to his friend William Dunbar, the president worried that "a thousand accidents might happen" to the timepiece and "thus deprive us of the principal object of the expedition, to wit, the ascertaining the geography of [the] river."[39] And just as Jefferson guessed, a "thousand accidents" did befall the chronometer. Throughout the journey the timepiece slowed down, stopped, and otherwise behaved in mysterious ways. And it didn't help that at least once Lewis forgot to wind the instrument. On one windy April day in 1805, soon after the expedition left Fort Mandan, Lewis discovered that the chronometer would run for a few minutes and suddenly stop. "I can discover," he complained, "no radical defect in her works, and must therefore attribute it to the sand, with which, she seems plentifully charged, notwithstanding her cases are double and tight."[40]

As early as August 1804 Lewis had become so exasperated with the chronometer that he wrote, "This day the Chronometer stoped again just after being wound up; I know not the cause, but fear it procedes from some defect which it is not in my power to remedy."[41] Lewis's efforts to lubricate the chronometer with bear's grease probably did little to make it run more reliably. Near the end of the journey Lewis was almost ready to believe that the device was haunted by some unfriendly spirit, surely a strange fate for an object that exemplified the ideal of rational inquiry. As Lewis explained in a revealing note, "As if the fates were against me my chronometer from some unknown cause stoped today."[42] But perhaps his most unsettling experience with the troubled timepiece came in May 1806 as the expedition spent weeks with the Nez Perce Indians before recrossing the Bitterroot Mountains. Eager to protect the chronometer against the wet spring weather and for "greater security," Lewis put it in a fob, or deep pocket. One morning Lewis awoke to find the chronometer fully soaked. "It seems a little extraordinary that every part of my breechies which were under my head, should have escaped the moisture except the fob where the time peice was." When Lewis opened the fob, he "found it nearly filled with water."[43] Just as the star-crossed chronometer had once drawn sand and alkali dust, it now appeared to magically attract water.

"THE FACE OF THE COUNTRY"

Journals, maps, and scientific instruments—all these objects were the means to define and record what Jefferson called "the face of the country." The land, and the rivers that ran through it, became an object to be experienced and studied.

The president and his explorers did not lack the ability to appreciate what we might see as majestic or beautiful western landscapes. Like all travelers, however, Lewis and Clark viewed the world through eyes conditioned by cultural values and years of personal experience. Perhaps more important, they headed west not to stand in awe at sublime grandeur but to document a useful landscape. Fertile soil was more important than what Lewis famously described as "seens of visionary inchantment."[44] The British writer Arthur Young put it best: "Agriculture is beyond all doubt the foundation of every other art, business, or profession."[45] Like their Enlightenment contemporaries, Lewis and Clark held nature up to the yardstick of utility. Usefulness was the essential measure of all things, whether it be the agricultural potential of the land or the navigability of a river. That measure did not rule out other kinds of aesthetic appreciation, but it did make every landscape description something more than a mere account of western wonders.

Lewis and Clark had a landscape vision shaped by eastern experiences and an Atlantic sensibility. Forests and meadows, farmsteads and villages, were all part of that landscape world. Navigable rivers, clearly defined seasons, and a dominant green color were other features of that face of the country. The great open sweep of the plains challenged that vision in every way. Here was a boundless sea of grass with only fringes of cottonwoods along a scattering of creeks. On the Fourth of July 1804—around present-day Doniphan, Kansas—Clark set his mind to describing the prairie world. At first he noted the obvious things—or those things obvious to someone rooted in a world of farms and plantations. Wood and fresh water were nearby, and beyond the trees lay "one of the most butifull Plains" Clark had ever seen. But "butifull" did not necessarily mean aesthetically pleasing in the way a modern tourist might see an expanse of tallgrass prairie today. Clark was quick to note that the big bluestem grass stretching to the horizon was "well calculated for the sweetest and most norushing hay." But for all his determination to domesticate the prairie, Clark could not escape its seductive charm. Sounding much like a Romantic poet, he wrote, "Nature appears to have exerted herself to butify the Senery by a variety of flours raising Delicately and highly flavered rasised above the Grass, which Strikes & profumes the Sensation and amuses the mind." All this prompted Clark to conclude the journal entry with a remarkable meditation on the meaning of such a landscape. The prairie had beauty and utility all mixed together, but no one—so it seemed to Clark—was there to either use or appreciate it. He admitted that the entire scene put his mind "into Conjecterng the cause of So magnificent a Senerey in a Country thus Situated far removed from the Sivilised world to be enjoyed by nothing but the Buffalo Elk Deer & Bear in which it abounds & [here the page is torn] Savage Indians."[46] Enjoyment meant use, and use was inevitably connected to commercial agriculture. Here was land as object. Unsettled by it all, Clark could only imagine a time when grass would be hay and trees might be timber. Only then might beauty and utility be appreciated by "Sivilised" eyes.

Clark was not alone in trying to sort out the meanings of a plains landscape. At the end of March 1805, as the expedition prepared to leave Fort Mandan for points west, Lewis wrote his mother, Lucy Marks, a letter filled with observations and judgments about the northern plains. Although he had seen the country mostly from the edges of the Missouri River, Lewis felt ready to pronounce the region "one of the fairest portions of the globe." And with future American settlement in mind, the explorer declared that nowhere else in the universe was there "a similar extent of country, equally fertile, well watered, and intersected by such a number of navigable streams." Lewis admitted that all of this had come as a surprise to him. Evidently he had been told, or had simply assumed, that the country up the Missouri was "barren, steril and sandy." But "on the contrary," he told his mother: "I found it fertile in the extreem." Yet a puzzle remained, and it was all about trees. For the explorers and their eastern contemporaries, trees were a visible sign of soil fertility. A country without trees was not merely deficient in wood for building or fuel; such a landscape probably could not sustain traditional Euro-American agriculture as well. The plains seemed to have everything an American farmer wanted except trees, "truly a very serious [objection]." Here was a prairie mystery—fertile soil but few trees. Ever the astute naturalist, Lewis concluded, "This want of timber is by no means attributeable to a deficiency in the soil to produce it, but ows it's orrigine to the ravages of the fires, which the natives kindle in these plains at all seasons of the year."[47] Lewis was at least partly right. Fire—whether deliberately set or caused by lightning—was one of the fundamental forces that shaped the grassland environment.

On the plains Lewis and Clark were caught between new terrain realities and old landscape vocabularies. In the second year of travel, as the expedition moved from the upper Missouri to the northern Rockies and on to the Pacific, the tension between Jefferson's dream of the West as the Garden of the World and the reality of the quite different regional lands and climates became even more pronounced.

Lewis described a plains Eden for his mother. Had the president seen that letter, it would simply have verified what he wanted to believe about the West. In the months after leaving Fort Mandan, Lewis continued to see paradise everywhere he looked. Early in May 1805 the expedition was on the upper Missouri in present-day Roosevelt County, Montana. There Lewis saw "immense quantities of buffaloe in every direction." What surprised him was how gentle and unafraid these animals seemed. "The bull buffaloe particularly will scarcely give way to you. . . . they viewed me for a moment as something novel and then very unconcernedly continued to feed."[48] Here was a country without fear, an Eden before the fall of Adam and Eve. A month later, near the confluence of the Missouri and Marias Rivers, Lewis discovered an even more complete western paradise. After a brief reconnaissance up the Marias, the explorer wrote one of the most vivid and Romantic passages in the entire expedition record: "It [the Marias River] passes through a rich fertile and one of the most beatifully picteresque countries that I ever beheld, through the wide expance of which, innumerable herds of living anamals are seen, it's borders garnished with one continued garden of roses, while it's lofty and open forests, are the habitation of miriads of the feathered tribes who salute the ear of the passing traveler with their wild and simple, yet s[w]eet and cheerfull melody."[49]

Rose gardens, lofty forests, gentle buffalo, and tribes of birds instead of Indians—this was the West as Jefferson's Garden of the World. For most of the nineteenth century, the garden image continued to be the dominant American view of the West. Settlers, land speculators, and government officials all shared that optimistic vision. But not everyone on the expedition saw north-central

River Bluffs, 1,320 Miles above St. Louis, 1832
This scene was painted by George Catlin south of Sioux City, Iowa, near the present Omaha Indian Reservation.

Montana in quite the same way. Seeing is always more than a physical, optical act. It is also perception, understanding, and evaluation. Clark and Ordway shared a common woodland and farming past. Looking at the upper Missouri, they saw a very different face than the one revealed to Lewis. In May 1805 the expedition was on the river around present-day Fergus County, Montana, still some days from Lewis's rose garden. From the river the travelers could see what seemed a harsh, inhospitable country with steep hills and little plant and animal life. Copying each other, Clark and Ordway both put the following in their journals: "This country may with propriety . . . be termed the Deserts of America, as I do not Conceive any part can ever be Settled as it is deficent in water, Timber & too Steep to be tilled."[50] Historians have often attributed the "West-as-Desert" idea to the army explorer Stephen H. Long and his memorable phrase "the Great American Desert." But it is plain that some on the Lewis and Clark expedition were quite ready to use a word like "desert" to describe those western areas that did not quite match the vision from Monticello.

For Lewis and Clark, the land of the West was what the author Willa Cather a century later called "the great fact." But Jefferson's explorers were part of an exploration era dominated by epic surveys of the Pacific Ocean. It was the Pacific that sparked the imagination not only of explorers and their patrons but also of British Romantic poets such as William Wordsworth, Samuel Taylor Coleridge, and Robert Southey. When Lewis and Clark saw the ocean—and even before, when they dreamed of seeing it—they too were challenged and inspired by its vast distances and tempestuous power. As the land had become an object, so the ocean drew Clark's attention. Clark was the expedition's most geographically thoughtful journal-keeper. In early November 1805, the expedition was within the Columbia River estuary. Thinking this was the ocean, Clark composed a simple but memorable journal entry: "Great joy in camp we are in View of the Ocian, this great Pacific Octean which we been So long anxious to See."[51] With few words, Clark explained how the explorers understood themselves, their journey, and the ocean as an object of desire. Jefferson's dreams of an empire for liberty in the West were always important, but in the day-to-day reality of hard traveling, it was the hope of reaching the ocean that kept the anxious company moving on.

Whatever landscape he found himself in, Clark always sought out some defining mark, some piece of terrain that might represent both the country and the expedition's experience in it. But on this gray November day, with the broad Columbia stretching out before him, Clark could find no such landmark. What drew him instead was sound—the sound of the river and the ocean. Listening to what he could not see, Clark imagined he could hear "the roreing or noise made by the waves brakeing on the rockey Shores."[52]

But sound, especially sound without sight, was not enough for those "anxious" to see the ocean firsthand. The object of desire demanded a personal encounter. Despite cold, wet, and uncomfortable days on the river, the longing to see the ocean did not diminish. On November 17 Clark organized a party to journey to the ocean, to venture to the edge of the continent and experience what they had only imagined. The following day several expedition members made their Pacific pilgrimage. Clark reported that his men were "much Satisfied with their trip beholding with estonishment the high waves dashing against the rocks and this emence ocian."[53]

Early in December 1805 Clark tried yet again to capture the emotional geography of the ocean. Often quoted, these lines are Clark at his best, struggling to deal with a part of geographic reality at once powerful, strange, and alluring: "The emence Seas and waves which breake on the rocks & Coasts to the S[outh]W[est]. & N[orth]W[est] roars like an emence fall at a distance, and this roaring has continued ever Since our arrival in the neighbourhood of the Sea Coast . . . Since we arrived in Sight of the Great Western; (for I cannot Say Pacific) Ocian as I have not Seen one pacific day Since my arrival in its vicinity, and its waters are forming [foaming] and petially [perpetually] breake with emenc waves on the Sands and rockey Coasts, tempestous and horiable."[54]

From the plains to the Pacific, Lewis and Clark sought to make western landscapes fit eastern expectations. At the Great Falls of the Missouri, Lewis threw up his hands in despair at the task, wishing he had the ability of an artist or the talent of a poet to capture what seemed beyond the reach of his pen and journal. Like all travelers, Lewis and Clark experienced landscape encounters that were both liberating and deeply frustrating. Lewis looked at the treeless plains, noted the fertile soil, considered the role of fire, and momentarily abandoned what had been conventional wisdom about the plains. But illusion and desire remained constant companions as the explorers tried to sketch the face of the country. Lewis kept finding Jefferson's garden, whereas Clark and Ordway saw the "Deserts of America." Perhaps Cather was right when she observed that like the rest of the West, the plains formed not a country but instead the materials from which a country might be made.

TOKENS OF POSSESSION, OBJECTS OF DESIRE

On the day the Corps of Discovery left St. Louis, Clark predicted that the expedition's "road across the Continent" would take it through a "multitud of Ind[ian]s."[55] Like Jefferson, Lewis and Clark knew that the West was not an empty place. Indian country was home to thousands of people. The expedition's Indian missions inevitably involved objects of all kinds—everything from guns and peace medals to clothing and trade goods. Gifts of all sorts were required for safe passage on the road across the continent. Such gifts represented not only national political power but the growing presence of American commercial influence as well. Behind every object, whether a peace medal or a fancy-dress coat, was a story with many voices and meanings.

In early May 1806 the expedition camped with Nez Perce friends before attempting to cross the snow-choked Bitterroot Mountains. A year earlier Lewis and Clark had struck up friendships with several important Nez Perce chiefs. Even though the Nez Perce homeland was beyond the boundaries of the Louisiana Purchase, Lewis and Clark decided now was the time to formalize relations between the tribe and the American republic. As always, Lewis and Clark imagined that Indian families, clans, and villages were part of a unified political entity and that certain men spoke for all on every occasion. In an impressive meeting, Hohastillpilp (Red Grizzly) and Tunnachemootoolt (Broken Arm) were given peace and friendship medals. "We explained to them," wrote Lewis, "the desighn and the importance of medals in the estimation of the whites as well as the red men who had been taught their value."[56] When Lewis and Clark gave medals to the Nez Perce chiefs, the American explorers were part of a venerable diplomatic tradition linking Euro-Americans and Native nations. Long before the American republic issued its first peace medal in 1789, Spain, France, and Great Britain had used medals as an essential part of their Indian diplomacy. Indians expected medals, and Euro-American negotiators always came prepared to deliver them. Among the bales and packages of Indian gifts gathered by Lewis and Clark were medals of several sorts of grades. The most prominent were those bearing the profile of Jefferson. In preparing his lists of Indian gifts, Clark made it clear that principal chiefs would receive the largest medals and that lesser dignitaries and warriors might be given smaller ones. For Lewis and Clark, political leadership was all about rank and authority. The larger the medal, the more important was the man.

The Jefferson peace and friendship medals were minted with images now widely recognized and often reproduced. On one side was Jefferson in profile, clearly identifying the American president as the new "great father," replacing crowned heads like Britain's George III or Spain's Charles IV. The other side of the medal showed a crossed pipe and tomahawk, two hands clasped in a sign of unity, and the words "peace and friendship." So that none might miss the message of the hands and who was the dominant partner in the relationship, one cuff was from a military uniform coat whereas the other, presumably Native, hand had a studded wristband bearing the imprint of an American eagle. When medals were struck for the James Madison administration, the eagle cuff vanished and the Native hand showed only a bare wrist, making the distinction between civilized power and savage simplicity even stronger.

Lewis and Clark also carried medals minted in England for the second

Peace medal, 1801
This medal was probably given by Lewis and Clark to a member of the Palus tribe. It was found in an archaeological excavation of a canoe burial near the mouth of the Palouse River in Washington in 1964. Washington State University, which conducted the excavation, returned the medal to the Nez Perce Tribe, which now owns it. This was the smallest size of Jefferson medal.

Washington administration. Known as the "season" medals, these displayed three domestic scenes originally sketched by the noted American artist John Trumbull. The scenes are important because they reveal in visual terms key elements in federal Indian policy. That policy was increasingly described by government agents as "civilization"—the notion that Native people would abandon traditional ways and beliefs to become farmers like their white neighbors. Native men would follow the plow while women would stay at home to pursue the domestic arts of spinning, weaving, and child rearing. With all of these changes, government agents assumed that lands no longer needed for hunting would be available for white settlers. The season medals depict the evolutionary scheme of social and economic development common in Jefferson's intellectual circle, one that saw all societies moving from grazing to farming and domestic delight. In proper sequence, the first medal portrays a shepherd, his flock, and a cow and calf; the second shows a farmer sowing wheat while another plows the ground; the third is an interior with women spinning and weaving while a young child rocks an infant in a cradle. The season medals expressed what Lewis and Clark often told Native people: accepting American sovereignty meant peace and prosperity. The images on the season medals were to be the shape of the future.

Like so many of the other objects carried by the expedition, medals spoke with many different voices. For Lewis and Clark, the medals represented national power and American sovereignty. Giving medals meant "making chiefs," even if such chiefs often spoke only for themselves. The medals—along with flags, certificates, and other official items—were a way for American diplomats like Lewis and Clark to impose order on what seemed to them a chaotic Indian political universe. Medal sizes indicated rank and importance, values essential in the political world Lewis and Clark inhabited. An Indian wearing a medal symbolized a bloodless conquest, an ally and client in future negotiations and conflicts. The connection Lewis and Clark made between medals and the exclusive sovereignty of the United States became clear at Fort Mandan when the explorers complained about a Canadian trader they believed was distributing British flags and medals. François-Antoine Larocque—the trader in question—wrote that the Americans "look'd upon those things as the Sacred Emblem of the attachment of the Indians to their country."[57] Clark, always a careful observer of diplomatic ritual, made the case for an American understanding of medals. Writing about a meeting with a Cathlamet chief on the Columbia River, Clark reported, "We gave him a Medal of the Small Size which appeard. to please him verry much; and will I hope have a favourable tendincy, in as much as it will attach him to our interest, and he probably will harang [harangue] his people in our favor."[58]

Almost a decade before Lewis and Clark made their way west, Secretary of War James McHenry noted the widespread use of medals in relations with eastern Indians and observed, "My poor Indians are very clamourous for their medals."[59] Lewis and Clark found that most western Indians were also eager to possess American medals. Indians on the Missouri River already had Spanish or British medals and flags and willingly added American ones to their collections. But it is plain that these objects embodied a wholly different set of meanings in Indian country. Many Native leaders expected medals as marks of respect and distinction. Medals were signs of connection to powerful outsiders as well as conduits of spirit power, linking the wearers to whites and their vast stores of goods. Medals were also understood as emblems of personal accomplishment given by one group of warriors to another. The ceremonies that always attended the giving and getting of medals were an important part of Native sensibility. When Clark and Lewis Cass prepared a report on Indian affairs and diplomacy in 1829, American agents were reminded that medals were to "be presented with proper formalities, and with an appropriate speech, so as to produce a proper impression upon the Indians."[60] Such rituals gave the medals and their new owners special place in a world shaped by the language of gesture, dance, and sacred objects.

Whereas many chiefs and prominent men readily accepted the medals, if not the meanings that Lewis and Clark intended, at least one Cheyenne chief was not ready to wear the likeness of Jefferson around his neck. His fear about the medal and what it might bring is a revealing moment in the expedition story. Near the end of August 1806, as the expedition made its way down the Missouri River to St. Louis, Lewis and Clark met a group of Cheyenne visiting and trading at the Arikara villages. Most of the day was taken up talking with the Mandan chief Sheheke-Shote, the Arikara chief Grey Eyes, and the Cheyenne chief about peace between the Mandan and the Arikara. As the day grew longer and hotter, the Cheyenne thoughtfully invited Clark to his teepee. Once settled into camp, Clark offered the chief a small Jefferson medal. To the captain's surprise, the chief seemed genuinely frightened by the prospect of receiving such a gift. In order not to offend Clark, the Cheyenne ordered a buffalo robe and some meat given to the explorer along with the rejected medal. What came next was a telling explanation. "He [the chief] knew," Clark recalled later, "that the white people were all *medecine* and that he was afraid of the midal or any thing that white people gave to them."[61]

Clark's immediate problem was how to persuade an important Cheyenne to accept a peace medal—an object seen as something potentially dangerous. Clark evidently repeated the now-familiar story of the great father and his good wishes for his red children, all represented in the medal itself. This time the effort worked, and soon the Cheyenne wore the medal. Clark was satisfied, but just how long the chief kept the president around his neck is anybody's guess. And the Cheyenne chief was not alone in believing that expedition goods could convey dangerous forces. The Hidatsa worried that flags and medals given to them by Lewis and Clark could carry "bad medicine to them and their children." Alexander Henry the Younger heard that the Hidatsa gave those items to their enemies "in hope the ill-luck would be conveyed to them."[62]

Not every medal around every Native neck promised peace and friendship. At one moment on the journey, a peace medal became an emblem for bloodshed and death. In late July 1806 Lewis led a small scouting party to explore the course of the Marias River in present-day north-central Montana. On July 26 Lewis and his men met a group of Piegan Blackfeet in the valley of the Two Medicine River. Having heard about the well-armed Blackfeet and their ties to the Canadian traders, Lewis feared trouble. Hoping to make peaceful contact, he inquired if there were any chiefs in the party. Told there were three, Lewis offered a medal, a flag, and a handkerchief as gifts. Later that evening around the campfire, Lewis astounded his Piegan visitors by telling them that the Americans would soon be trading with neighboring tribes. Trade meant guns, and more guns surely threatened the place the Blackfeet enjoyed on the plains.

But large questions of the balance of power in Indian country seemed far away the next morning when several young Piegan attempted to make off with expedition horses and guns. The morning exploded in confusion and violence as Reubin Field stabbed one Indian while Lewis shot another. It was the single most violent moment during the expedition. What Lewis did before leaving the Two Medicine killing ground gave the event an even more terrible meaning. After taking the sacred amulets from the Indian shields and burning their weapons, Lewis hung a peace medal around the neck of a dead Piegan so "that they might be informed who we were."[63] A peace medal had become a calling card for empire. The promise of "peace and friendship" so boldly stamped on the medal now seemed all about violence and hostility.

It would be tempting to see peace medals and Native American pipes as rough cultural and diplomatic equivalents—each symbolizing power and authority in the rituals of council and treaty talk. And certainly some American diplomats and policymakers made that connection. The earliest medals from the Washington administration depicted an Indian smoking a pipe while an American diplomat reached out to touch it. By the time of the Jefferson presidency, peace medals featured the crossed pipe and tomahawk above clasped hands. But a thoughtful look at those times when Native Americans and Euro-Americans met for diplomatic exchanges makes it clear that medals and pipes inhabited two quite different realms of meaning, realms that sometimes overlapped but remained distinct. As Lewis and Clark made their way through Indian country—the realm of the pipe—they encountered the pipe in its many forms and faces.

On the simplest level, smoking the pipe meant creating a friendly atmosphere for social visiting. Again and again over two and a half years of travel, Lewis and Clark met Native people who simply came "to Smoke a friendly pipe."[64] Clark quickly grasped the personal meaning of such visits, explaining that smoking a pipe was "the greatest mark of friendship and attention."[65] The social pipe did not exclude the possibility of a diplomatic exchange of some sort, but social smoking did not require the complex pipe rituals that were always part of a formal council. The "friendly pipe" was one more way to create some common ground, a way to reach across the cultural divide. When Clark and his Mandan friend Black Cat smoked together, they shared a moment made possible by the pipe.[66]

Long before heading up the Missouri, Lewis and Clark knew that pipes and the rituals surrounding them were at the heart of Native American diplomatic protocol. Decades of experience had taught first European and then American negotiators that pipes and their ceremonies were a fundamental part of every council. If Lewis and Clark failed to understand every nuance of the ritual, they did appreciate its central place in formal relationships. Clark summed up his own grasp of that importance when he wrote: "The pipe is the Semblem of peace with all, The different nations have their different fashions of Dilivering and receiving of it—The party delivering generally Confess their Errors & request a peace, the party receiving exult in their Suckcesses and receive the Sacred Stem."[67] The pipe ritual aimed at clearing the air, quieting the mind, and making a space for peace. Smoking sacred pipes united the

Pipe, c. 1800–50

Smoking, both before and after meals, was part of the hospitality offered to guests in Plains Indian homes. When the Mandan chief Four Bears entertained George Catlin, he did not eat with the guest but sat "deliberately charging and lighting the pipe which is to be passed around after the feast is over."

This pipe could have been collected by Lewis and Clark, since it was among artifacts from Peale's Museum, to which Lewis and Clark donated fourteen pipes. Flat- or ovoid-stemmed pipes like this were not used for diplomatic pipe ceremonies at this date; Catlin called them "ordinary pipes, made and used for the *luxury* only of smoking; and for this purpose, every Indian designs and constructs his own pipe." However, pipes of this style may have been used as tribal and clan pipes and were definitely used, as Catlin put it, by a host to "pledge his friends." The technique of wrapped quillwork used on the stem has been called the earliest form of pipe decoration. It was primarily associated with Mississippi Valley and Great Lakes tribes but was also used by the Dakota on the eastern plains.

social and the diplomatic, the personal and the official. All who took part in the ceremony saw the pipes, smoked them, and felt the calming effects of the tobacco itself. The presence of the pipe and the ritual words associated with smoking created a common experience for all participants. And from that common experience could come a shared space for peace.

Lewis and Clark experienced pipes as social objects, as diplomatic objects, and as gifts. The American explorers returned from the West with a number of pipes given to them as presents. Those pipes were not "collected" as part of the expedition's ethnographic mission, although they have sometimes been interpreted in that way. Instead, expedition journals make it plain that these objects were gifts. At the end of an important council with the Yankton Sioux in late August 1804, one of the chiefs "presented the pipe" to the explorers.[68] Having concluded a long series of negotiations with the Americans about peace with his Shoshone neighbors, the Nez Perce chief Broken Arm produced two pipes. Clark wrote, "He said [one] was as a present to me [and] the other he intended to Send to the Shoshones."[69] But perhaps the most notable pipe gift came from Cameahwait. Clark received not only one of Cameahwait's names but a pipe as well.[70]

Lewis and Clark came into a West already familiar with the sound of gunfire. At the beginning of the nineteenth century, Native people were no strangers to guns. From the Missouri River to the Pacific coast, Indians had guns, knew what it meant not to possess them, and above all, wanted more guns. No object carried by the expedition attracted more attention than firearms. Whereas Lewis's air gun was a great curiosity that "much astonished" some Indians, there was nothing novel about the muskets and rifles the explorers proudly displayed and used almost every day. The very presence of the Americans and their guns seemed to promise the possibility that Native people might become owners of such powerful weapons.

By Native standards, the Lewis and Clark expedition was a large, well-armed party of travelers. Guns were an essential part of the Lewis and Clark infantry company on the move. Lewis's earliest estimate of travel expenses included funds for "Arms & Accoutrements extraordinary." Guns put meat in the explorers' cooking pots. As Lewis reported to his mother, "Our guns have furnished us an ample supply."[71] Guns were also for personal protection, whether against real hazards posed by dangerous animals or against imagined threats from supposedly hostile Indians. But perhaps most significant, expedition guns were a visible and audible sign of national power. President Jefferson once told an Indian delegation representing Missouri River tribes, "We are strong, we are numerous as the stars in the heavens, & we are all gun-men."[72] The message was unmistakable. Guns spoke with the voice of power, and

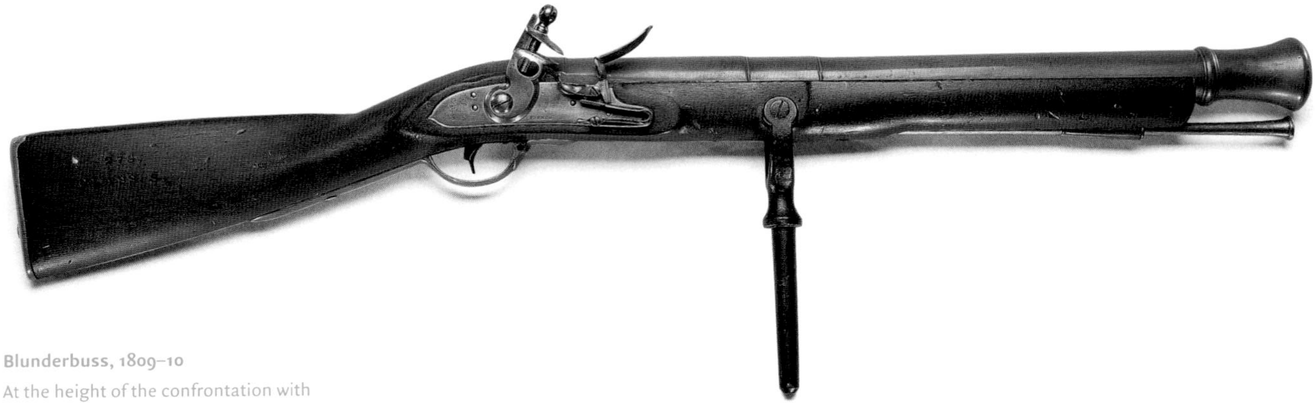

Blunderbuss, 1809–10

At the height of the confrontation with the Teton Sioux, Ordway reported: "Capt. Lewis . . . ordered every man to his arms. the large Swivel loaded immediately with 16 Musquet Ball in it the 2 other Swivels loaded well with Buck Shot, Each of them manned." The "2 other Swivels" were both blunderbusses like this one. Alternately called "blunderbuts" by Clark and "bluntderbushes" by Lewis, the weapons were used for crowd control. They may have been mounted on the stern of the keelboat in 1804, but they were transferred to the pirogues the next year. They were cached at the Great Falls but were recovered on the way back and used to announce the party's arrival at St. Charles: "We Saluted the Village by three rounds from our blunderbuts and the Small arms of the party." This one was from the Washington Navy Yard and was probably used as a wall piece or boat gun.

power demanded obedience. When Lewis and Clark gave the Hidatsa chief Le Borgne one of the expedition's swivel guns, Clark made a point of telling him that the gun "had anounced the words of his great father to all the nations" the explorers had seen.[73]

Few weapons in the expedition's arsenal more fully embodied the voice of force and authority than the blunderbuss. The explorers carried two of these "thunder guns." With their short stocks, stubby barrels, and wide-mouthed muzzles, there was nothing attractive about these guns. Their workmanship was simple, and their purpose was direct—maximum killing at minimum range. Like the shotguns carried by some frontier peace officers, the blunderbuss was intimidating in its blunt appearance and threat of deadly force at close range. Lewis and Clark never fired their blunderbusses at Native people but instead employed them in an equally dramatic way. Blunderbusses were discharged to announce the arrival of the expedition at an Indian camp or town. The voice of the blunderbuss spoke in flame and smoke, echoing Jefferson's words about "gun-men" and the new American order in the West.

The seventeenth-century English essayist Sir Francis Bacon once said that printing, gunpowder, and the compass changed the shape of the world. Firearms certainly created a new world in Indian country. Along with horses, guns transformed Native life. Warriors ranged farther, inflicted more harm on enemies, and intimidated neighbors who lacked guns. Firearms also became potent symbols of status and prestige. Denied guns by Spanish frontier policy, the Lemhi Shoshone had few firearms. It is thus little wonder that Cameahwait's war name meant "black weapon owner."[74] Cameahwait and Black Cat, two of the most articulate Native leaders who met with Lewis and Clark, understood what it meant to have guns or to be without them. Black Cat once reminded Clark that the St. Louis trader John Evans had promised guns and ammunition but had failed to keep those promises. Would the new great father in Washington do any better? At a council in late October 1804, promises of intertribal peace and prosperity were everywhere. Such words seemed to imply not just iron pots and bright cloth but guns as well. Trying to imagine what this all might mean, Black Cat conjured up a world made safe by American weapons in Mandan hands. "I believe what you have told us in Council," he said, "& that peace will be general, which not only givs me pleasure, but Satisfaction to all the nation, they now Can hunt without fear, and our womin Can work in the fields without looking every moment for the enimey."[75]

But no one made a more explicit and eloquent statement about guns, security, and prosperity than Cameahwait. The Lemhi people lived in a perpetually dangerous world, surrounded by well-armed and aggressive enemies.

Lewis counted only three guns among the Lemhi, hardly sufficient to defend against Blackfeet, Hidatsa, or Atsina raiders. Eager to obtain Shoshone horses, Lewis and Clark promised guns as soon as American traders could make it to Lemhi country. In a speech filled with compelling images, Cameahwait sketched out the shape of the future once his people had firearms. "If we had guns, we could then live in the country of buffaloe and eat as our enimies do and not be compelled to hide ourselves in these mountains and live on roots and berries as the bear do."[76] As an arms race spread throughout the West, Cameahwait was sure that more guns would mean a better life for his beleaguered people.

Among all the objects taken on the Lewis and Clark journey, none were more various in size, shape, color, and purpose than those Lewis listed simply as "Indian Presents." Mostly purchased from Philadelphia suppliers, with additional St. Louis acquisitions, the trade goods destined for Native hands put Jefferson's travelers squarely in a time-honored practice. For generations, visitors to Indian country had brought stocks of European manufactured goods. This was the bounty of the Industrial Revolution come to the West. Fur traders brought guns, ironware, and alcohol in exchange for beaver pelts and deer skins. Diplomats and soldiers packed stores of beads, blankets, and tobacco to win allies or seal treaties. And missionaries often carried objects such as magnets, compasses, and clocks to represent the blessings of Christianity and Western civilization.

The expedition's Indian presents were always meant to be more than simple gifts from weary travelers to wary hosts. Lewis and Clark expected the gifts would be payment in exchange for food and horses. There was much to buy, and Native sellers were such skilled bargainers that near the end of the journey, Lewis complained that his stock of gifts had been reduced to "a mear handful."[77] The American explorers did not consider themselves to be merchants like the Canadian traders whom they met at the Knife River villages or the maritime fur traders who frequented the northwest coast. But the goods the expedition spread out for Native people represented the contents of a grand general store, all revealing the wonders of the Industrial Revolution.

Those objects made plain an expedition object: to locate suitable places for "mutual emporiums" and then redirect trade away from British and Canadian companies and into American hands. Lewis and Clark also knew that the goods were essential as diplomatic tools and as signs of respect. On the road across the continent, tolls had to be paid, and trade goods were the appropriate currency. Years of experience had taught the earth lodge people to expect appropriate gifts. When Lewis and Clark did not meet those expectations, there was confusion and edgy resentment. With his usual tact, Black Cat put it this way: "When the Indians of the Different Villages heard of your Comeing up they all Came in from hunting to See, they expected Great presents. they were disappointed, and Some dissatisfied—as to my Self, I am not much So, but my Village are."[78] Some of these presents were given in exchange for more intimate pleasures. During the Fort Clatsop winter, some members of the expedition eagerly exchanged metal goods for sexual favors. As the supply dwindled, Lewis and Clark took drastic action. "We divided Some ribin between the men of our party to bestow on their favourite Lasses." Clark hoped that this plan would "Save the knives & more valueable articles."[79]

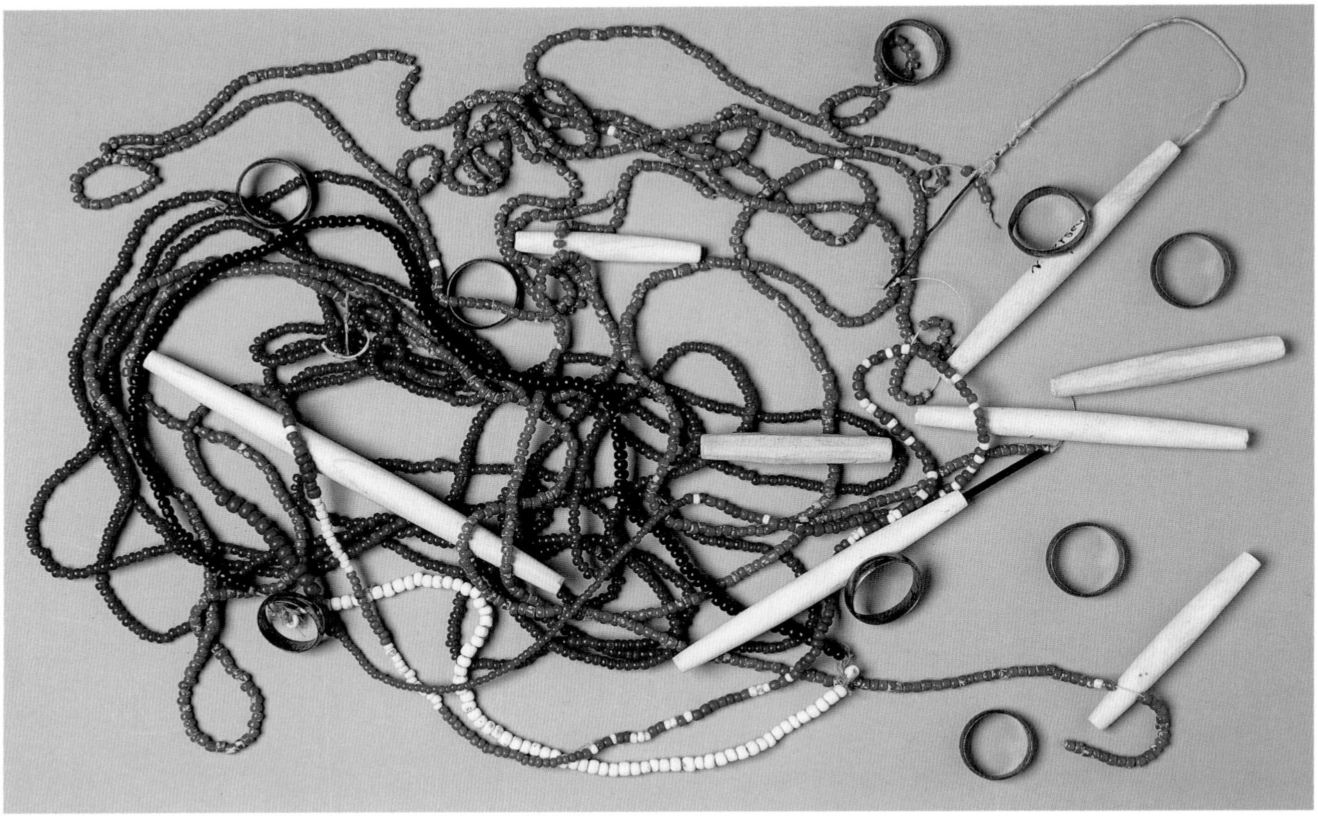

Trade goods, 1800s

Among the wide variety of Indian trade goods Lewis purchased in Philadelphia were seventy-two silver rings, seventy-three bunches of assorted beads, and a total of eleven and one-half pounds of other beads—white, sky-blue, yellow, red, green, and garnet. Lewis did not learn about the demand for the long tubular ornaments called "hair pipes" until he got to St. Louis, where he was still seeking a source for them in May 1804. Apparently he found them, because twenty-four were listed in the baling invoices.

These rings are copper or brass and are typical of the plain band rings sold in the Indian trade for two hundred years. They came from Montana. These beads, known as pony beads, were the most popular size and style traded from the late 1700s to mid-1800s, though these examples were not collected until the 1850s. Handmade bone and shell hair pipes had been used on the plains since prehistoric times, though they were later mass-produced in a New Jersey factory. At this date, they were strung singly in the hair; only later were they used on breastplates.

Even the quickest look at the invoices prepared in Philadelphia and the packing lists compiled in St. Louis reveals a remarkable variety of trade goods. There were textiles of all kinds and grades, beads of many colors, and a bewildering array of hardware. Some of that hardware would be familiar to anyone who haunts the aisles of modern home-improvement stores: wire, brads, awls, curtain rings, knives, and strips of brass and iron. Other objects fit a modern sense of gift, including ivory combs, mirrors, rings, broaches, lockets, and earrings. Now that most Americans no longer make their own clothing, the textiles bound for Indian country seem the most exotic objects of all. Lewis and Whelan, the purchasing agent, gathered up yards of red flannel, pieces of silk ribbon, strips of striped fabric tape, and all the necessary sewing supplies including needles and thimbles.

Perhaps the most useful way to sort out all these objects is to look at them as Native people did. Ordway captured some sense of the Indian perspective when he commented on trade at Fort Mandan. Indians like Black Cat and his wife brought corn and beans and in return sought "looking Glases Beeds buttens, or & other kinds of articles pleasing to the Eye."[80] What the Mandan and their neighbors wanted were luxury goods. The prosperous earth lodge people could afford to trade for things to decorate themselves and their clothing. Jewelry, colored beads, vermilion cosmetic paint, hawk bells, and ready-made calico shirts were among the luxuries that Lewis and Clark offered. The message was clear. Trade with the Americans would bring more goods of greater variety than the Canadians could ever supply. Each silver ring and every bright mirror had a meaning that was both personal and national.

Luxury goods "pleasing to the Eye" were an essential part of the exchange between explorers and Indians. But many of the goods that Lewis and Clark took along as Indian presents were objects better understood as necessities. The Missouri River peoples already had considerable experience with the products of the Industrial Revolution. Northwest coast Natives like the Clatsop increasingly incorporated those items into their daily lives. A Clatsop story tells it best. A trading vessel became grounded on the Columbia River bar and broke up. The Clatsop quickly salvaged iron, copper, and brass from the wreck. When Indians living farther up the Columbia heard the news, they hurried to trade. As the Clatsop storyteller explained, "The people [the upriver Indians] bought this and the Clatsop became rich."[81]

It was not just metal that captured the Native market. Intrigued by the textiles offered in the maritime fur business, the Clatsop and their neighbors called the maritime fur traders "pah-shis´h-e-ooks," the cloth men. Indians throughout the West recognized that some objects of Euro-American manufacture were perhaps superior to those traditionally used. Knives, pairs of scissors, fire steels, fish spears, and textiles of all sorts were adopted into Native life. Metal itself became something of a necessity. Lewis and Clark carried strips of sheet iron, knowing that Indians would cut them up for arrow points and hide scrapers. Like the luxury goods, the necessities expressed commercial and political messages. Each knife or needle was a reminder that Indians were increasingly part of a global trading system. That system offered luxuries but also sold necessities at a price set by distant suppliers. The Mandan who eagerly sought sharp-edged iron arrow points were now dependant on faraway iron workers and hardware dealers.

Just as Native people adopted European goods into the patterns of their daily life, so did they adapt many of those same objects to uniquely Native uses. Sheet iron was cut to make arrow points; brass wire was twisted and shaped into jewelry; thimbles were pierced at the top and made into pendant earrings; discarded gun barrels were flattened to make hide scrapers. And then there were the corn mills. At Jefferson's direct request, the expedition took along hand-operated corn grinders as gifts for Indians. Like peace medals or guns, these machines expressed a number of messages. Jefferson surely understood the corn mill as emblematic of the entire federal policy to civilize Indians by making them into Euro-American farmers. According to this view, Indians would abandon hunting, plant corn, and use the mill to grind the corn into meal. The device represented not only farming but the division of labor envisioned by Jefferson. Like the images on the Washington season medals, Indian men were to plant the crops and follow the plow—perhaps while Indian women did the grinding.

Following presidential orders, Lewis and Clark took the corn mills up the Missouri to demonstrate for the earth lodge people. In October 1804 Lewis and Clark gave one grinder to the Arikara and a second to the Mandan. Clark was pleased to report that the Indians "appeared delighted" with the mills.[82] But though the earth lodge people might have been "delighted," they were not about to abandon more traditional ways of pounding corn into meal. Female labor for such a task was plentiful, whereas the metal in the grinders was scarce. The Mandan promptly redefined the corn mill, seeing it not as an agricultural machine but as a convenient supply of metal. When the trader Alexander Henry the Younger saw the remains of the mill in 1806, he found that some of its parts had become arrow points and hide scrapers. The largest part of the mill was attached to a wooden handle to fashion a pounder for making grease from buffalo bones. Like many other trade goods, the corn mill had moved from one world of meaning to another.

When Lewis made his "List of Requirements" in the spring of 1803, he included clothing of all sorts and styles. These were obvious necessities for a long journey of discovery. But Lewis also knew that clothing was part of the encounter and discovery process itself. The explorers wore military clothing. At the same time, uniform coats and hats were put aside as gifts for chiefs and prominent warriors. The men in Lewis and Clark's infantry company set out on their western tour of duty wearing the proper uniforms prescribed for the U.S. Army. Those uniforms, with their symbols of national power, were the visible sign of what Jefferson meant when he told Lewis that Americans were now the "sovereigns of the country."[83] Uniforms, badges of rank, and all sorts of military accoutrements were a reminder that the expedition marched through the West as the advance guard of an American empire.

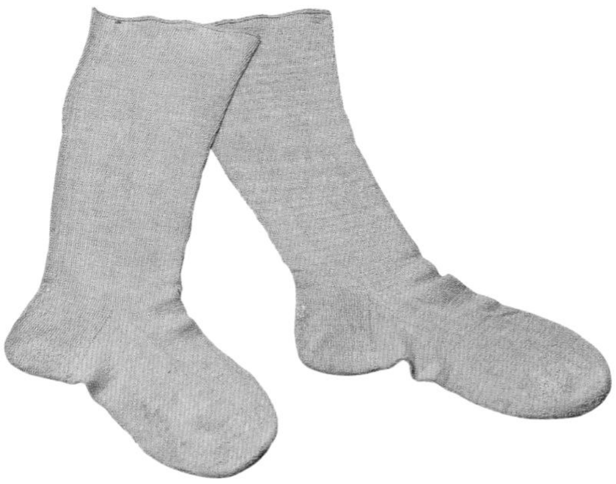

Socks, early 1800s
Joseph Whitehouse commented on the hardship experienced by several men who had no socks while crossing the Rocky Mountains in the snow. The socks worn by those men who still had them probably looked like this pair from Stonington, Connecticut. They have been darned at the heels and toes.

But underneath those uniform hats, coats, and trousers were simple things like woolen socks. A pair of woolen socks from the Lewis and Clark period has survived to remind us of a painful moment on the expedition's way west. In September 1805 the Corps of Discovery struggled over the Lolo Trail in present-day northern Idaho. Their path was blocked by deep snow, twisted undergrowth, and steep hillsides. On Monday morning, September 16, the explorers awoke to find themselves covered with snow. Private Whitehouse, one of the expedition journal-keepers, recalled the scene in vivid detail: "Some of the men without Socks raped rags on their feet, and loaded up our horses and Set out without any thing to eat, and proceeded on. could hardly See the old trail for the Snow."[84]

Perhaps members of the expedition sensed that in some way their identity was connected to what they wore. Putting on the uniforms of the Republic, they became the embodiment of the nation. And as those uniforms wore out and fell to tatters, the travelers put on the style of the West in the form of buckskin and moccasins. Whether in dressing more like Indians these men crossed the boundary from one cultural identity to another remains a lively question. When Lewis and his men were with the Lemhi Shoshone in mid-August 1805, they wore overshirts "of the Indian form" and became "so[o]n completely metamorphosed" into "complete Indian[s]."[85]

If Lewis thought that for a moment that his identity had been transformed by wearing Indian clothing, Native people had even stronger things to say about the power that Euro-American clothing offered to them. Presenting Indian leaders and their families with clothing had long been part of frontier diplomacy. Military-style coats, shirts, and hats were offered to prominent men while their wives and children were given shirts, leggings, breechclouts, and gartering. Native people quickly became quite discerning about the quality of those gifts. Indians on the Missouri were critical of Spanish goods, preferring the higher-quality English ones. Knowing how important clothing was in diplomacy and trade, Lewis and Clark procured a large stock of appropriate items. The baling lists Clark prepared in St. Louis reveal an astounding range of clothing and textiles, all arranged by tribe and all graded according to the rank or place of each potential recipient. Fancy red "chief's coats," hats, plumes, blue breechclouts, red leggings, white and calico shirts, and bunches of gartering—Lewis and Clark were not to be outdone in any fashion contest for the loyalty of Native people.

Indians expected that clothing would be part of the gift-giving whenever Euro-Americans came to visit, trade, or hold diplomatic talks. Some of the clothing distributed by Lewis and Clark went simply as gifts, without any ritual or ceremony; other times, the goods were traded for food. Now and again there was a mutual exchange of clothing as a sign of gratitude and goodwill. When the expedition was with the Nez Perce in mid-May 1806, Lewis and Clark rewarded the young men who brought in the party's horses with ribbon, wampum, and vermilion. In return, one man gave Lewis "a hansome pare of legings."[86] Not to be outdone, Broken Arm gave Clark his leather shirt. And to keep the balance, Broken Arm received a linen shirt in return.

But nowhere was clothing more important than in formal diplomatic meetings. For Lewis and Clark, dressing chiefs and prominent men in officers' coats and cocked hats was one more means to establish American authority in a visible way. The captains' speech to the Oto in early August 1804 made it clear that coats and hats, "such as he [President Jefferson] dresses his war chiefs with," were signs of a new political order.[87] Indians viewed the clothing as objects properly owed to them. After a council with the Yankton Sioux in late August 1804, Lewis and Clark named Shake Hand as "First Chief" and gave him an impressive array of military-style clothing. The response of Tar-ro-mo-nee (Turning Rock) suggests a Native American understanding of clothing and its symbolic meanings: "I am verry glad you have made this man [Shake Hand] our great chief, the British & Spaniards have acknowledged him before but never Cloathed him. you have Cloathed him."[88] Ar-ca-we-char-chi (Half Man), the Yankton whom Lewis and Clark made "Third Chief," was even more blunt: "You have Dressed him and I like it."[89]

But not every act of "Cloathing" went smoothly. On at least one occasion, the various kinds and qualities of clothes sparked considerable resentment among Indian men. Soon after meeting with the Lemhi Shoshone, Clark gave coats to two "under Chiefs." Of course, Lewis had given Cameahwait a far fancier outfit that included a uniform coat, shirt, and scarlet leggings. The "under Chiefs" noted the distinction and said that their gifts were simply not enough. As Clark laconically noted, the two were "not well Satisfied that the first Chief was dressed so much finer than themselves."[90]

HEARING THE OBJECTS

Today, we take in the Lewis and Clark expedition experience with our eyes. We read the men's journals, glance at their maps, and look at the objects that made up the expedition community's daily life. We see the objects but do not hear them. Taken out of human hands and lives, they have fallen silent. And because they are silent, a large part of our past falls silent as well. Lewis and Clark made their journey through a rich, complex, often noisy soundscape. There were the sounds of nature—wind and rain, the song of a bird, the snorting of a buffalo, and the whinny of a horse. There were the sounds of work—men making canoes, men laboring at a blacksmith's forge, and that remarkable moment when Lewis heard Nez Perce women pounding roots, a sound that reminded him of a nail factory. All along the way there were the sounds of a young mother and her child. And there were the many sounds of music. Native American musicians played and sang, accompanied by the sound of feet moving in steps on age-old dance grounds. The expedition's own music makers added to the soundscape. Pierre Cruzatte's fiddle joined with sounding horns and tambourines to fill the air with memories of home in distant places.

Carpentry tools, early 1800s
Anticipating the need to construct winter quarters, Lewis purchased a hand saw, a shingling hatchet, cut nails, and many other tools from the hardware merchants Harvey and Worth in Philadelphia. He picked up felling axes at Fort Fayette. The tools pictured here all come from the Philadelphia area.

We sometimes imagine the Lewis and Clark expedition as part of a grand American adventure story. In our mind's eye, we see Jefferson's intrepid travelers marching through a brightly colored West, moving from one mountaintop experience to another. But in its life as a human community, the expedition shaped its days to the patterns of work. Every moment of high adventure and great drama was matched by long days of backbreaking labor and tedious work. There were piles of wood to cut, huts to build, clothes to mend, and guns to repair. The sounds of the explorers' lives were the sounds made by tools—by hammers and saws, felling axes, and drawing knives.

The work was done by hand and muscle, not by the tireless efforts of piston or motor. And those hands grasped tools of all sorts and uses. Clark once observed that the expedition packed along "Tools of every description."[91] Some remain familiar to us even if most Americans no longer work with hammers and saws or labor at the forge. In Philadelphia, Lewis and Whalen began the business of filling the expedition's toolbox. Lewis and Clark lived in a world of wood and metal. Their tools reflected that. There were tools that are still familiar today for cutting, shaping, and joining wood: axes, saws, planes, and chisels. Others, like a cooper's howel or a drawing knife, seem to belong to another time. But whereas wood could be sawed and joined, metal needed to be worked at the forge with hammer and tongs. So the expedition's toolbox held all the items of the blacksmith's trade: several kinds of vises, files, and a bellows. The Fort Mandan smithy did a booming business repairing guns and forging war axes. Such work led the Hidatsa chief Le Borgne to observe that the expedition had "only two sensible men among them—the worker of Iron, and the mender of Guns."[92]

We need to imagine these tools in the hands of those who did the work. And part of that imagining is hearing the sounds: the wheeze of a bellows breathing at John Shields's forge; the squeal of an auger twisting into unseasoned wood; the rhythmic rip and cut of a whipsaw being pulled back and forth by Clark's slave York and Private Whitehouse; the bite and chop of axes felling trees for forts named after Native neighbors; the tap of a hammer fixing a bit of bent metal on a gun; the long sigh of a cooper's howel drawing off curls of wood shavings from barrel staves. With practiced eyes and a deft touch, expedition workers transformed wood and metal into the objects of daily life.

During the expedition, soundscape work sounds provided the rhythm; the melody came from music. On their way west, Jefferson's travelers made music and found music all along the "road across the continent." At almost every meeting with Native people were moments of song and dance. One evening with the Yankton Sioux in late August 1804 was especially memorable. After a day of diplomacy with the chiefs Weuche and White Crane, it was time to celebrate. At dark a blazing fire was built in the center of camp. Into the firelight came Sioux in gaudy paint to dance and to sing of their great feats in battle and the chase. Music came from a drum whose deerskin head was a gift from Lewis. While drummers beat out a powerful rhythm, other Yankton kept time with deer-hoof rattles. Later, Ordway recalled the sights and sounds of the Calumet Bluff spectacle: "It always began with a houp & hollow & ended with the Same, and in the intervales, one of the warries [warriors] at a time would rise with his weapen and Speak of what he had done in his day, & what warlike actions he had done."[93] Perhaps instructed by the interpreter Pierre Dorion and his son, members of the expedition threw the dancers gifts of tobacco, knives, and hawk bells.

When the Corps of Discovery was not being entertained by Indian musicians and dancers, the explorers created their own song and dance routines. Cruzatte was the party's principal fiddler; more than once, expedition journal-keepers noted, "All muche pleased with the violin."[94] Among Lewis's Philadelphia purchases were four tin sounding horns, soon to become the expedition's brass section. And somewhere along the way the Lewis and Clark musicians acquired a tambourine. The Corps of Discovery traveling band made its joyful noise to celebrate holidays, revive weary spirits, and impress Native visitors.

The music the expedition played had many parts for many voices. Some of those were for grand events and ceremonial occasions. Not every arrival and departure at an Indian village was signaled by a blast from a blunderbuss's mouth. When the expedition pulled out of the Arikara villages in October 1804, Ordway recalled that the event was marked by "the fiddle playing & the horns Sounding."[95] New Year's Day 1805 at Fort Mandan was celebrated by the Corps of Discovery band in full voice. The sounding horns blared, the fiddle whined, and the tambourine beat out a jingling rhythm, all to the delight of the Mandan audience. Music and dance also came at the end of a stretch of hard work. On a windy day in late April 1805, the expedition was at the confluence of the Missouri and Yellowstone Rivers in present-day North Dakota. It had been an exhausting time on a twisted part of the river. The captains wrote that the men were ready to rest and recover: "In order to add in some measure to the general pleasure which seemed to pervade our little community, we ordered a dram to be issued to each person; this soon produced the fiddle, and they spent the evening with much hilarity, singing & dancing, and seemed as perfectly to forget their past toils, as they appeared regardless of those to come."[96]

Music also provided some common ground and shared experience for the American explorers and Native people. Indians seemed especially drawn to Cruzatte's fiddle and the spectacle of expedition members dancing with each other. At The Dalles on the Columbia, "the nativs requested the party to dance which they very readily consented and Peter Cruzat played on the Violin."[97] When Lewis completed initial negotiations with Cameahwait, he "directed the

Fiddle, 1795–1811
On Christmas 1804 Whitehouse wrote, "The Men then prepared one of the Rooms, and commenced dancing, we having with us Two Violins & plenty of Musicans in our party." The two violinists were Pierre Cruzatte and George Gibson. The journals frequently mentioned the men dancing to fiddle music. On the Columbia, the fiddle played an important diplomatic role by entertaining apprehensive villagers and putting them at ease. "Peter Crusat played on the violin and the men danced which delighted the nativs, who Shew every civility towards us," Clark wrote at The Dalles.

fiddle to be played and the party danced very merily much to the amusement and gratification of the natives."[98] Music and dance sometimes helped bridge the cultural divide as Indian spectators became participants in the Lewis and Clark road show. Visiting some Tenino Indians on the return journey up the Columbia, Lewis and Clark "had the violin played." Lewis added: "Some of the men danced; after which the natives entertained us with a dance after their method."[99]

But the most memorable moment of musical encounter and exchange came in late April 1806 as the expedition spent time with the Walula in present-day eastern Washington State. Earlier in the day Clark and the principal chief Yellept exchanged gifts—an "elegant white horse" for Clark and Clark's own sword and some ammunition for the chief. That evening some three hundred Indians came calling at the American camp. To honor their visitors, the Corps of Discovery put on its customary music and dance program. When the expedition performers were finished, Yellept stood and made a remarkable request. As Ordway understood it, Yellept insisted that the Walula would "be lonesome" when the Corps left. The chief then asked to hear one of the American "medicine songs." In Yellept's world, songs were associated with spirit power. Perhaps he thought that the songs sung by the powerful strangers meant the same thing. Yellept hoped his people could learn one of the expedition's songs and at the same time teach Lewis and Clark one of theirs. All of that, so Yellept explained, "would make them glad." The expedition camp now became a makeshift music school. The Lewis and Clark chorus sang two songs, "which appeared to take great affect" on the Indians. While the Americans sang, the Walula "tryed to learn Singing [along] with us with a low voice." Yellept responded to all this with a second speech, each word repeated by a prominent warrior "that all might hear." Then it was time to dance. What began as a dance exclusively for Indians soon involved the explorers as well. "They wished our men to dance with them," Ordway recalled. "So we danced among them and they were much pleased, and Said they would dance day and night untill we return."[100] And so music and dance spread out that night, embracing Natives and strangers in a time of harmony and good cheer.

OUR JOURNEYS AND THEIRS

In the American book of memory, few chapters have attracted more popular attention than the one written by the Lewis and Clark expedition. Thanks in large part to the Lewis and Clark Bicentennial, reminders of the expedition are everywhere. There are hundreds of Lewis and Clark books on the market—everything from Gary Moulton's magnificent multivolume scholarly edition of the expedition's journals to cookbooks, coloring books, and trail guides. There are Corps of Discovery videos, television documentaries, an IMAX movie, and Internet Web sites beyond counting. Each year sees more Lewis and Clark conferences, museum exhibitions, and visitor centers.

But in all of this—whether celebration, commemoration, or just plain exploitation—we run the risk of missing the central meanings and objects in the Lewis and Clark story. Even more important, we stand to lose our chance to connect the Lewis and Clark chapter to the larger, richer, deeper stories in our past and in our present. At the risk of cultural heresy, we should ask: Lewis and Clark, who cares, why bother?

A Snow Landscape with Buffalo, 1854
"Last night was excessively Cold," Clark wrote on January 10, 1805. "The murkery this morning Stood at 40° below 0." Cold weather did not stop the relentless need for food. "Big White . . . Came and informed us that a large Drove of Buffalow was near and his people was wating for us to join them in a Chase," Clark wrote. "Capt. Lewis took 15 men & went out joined the Indians, who were at the time he got up, Killing the Buffalows on Horseback with arrows which they done with great dexterity, his party killed 14 Buffalow, *five* of which we got to the fort. . . . three men frost bit badly to day." George Catlin, the artist of this painting, spent the years 1830–32 in St. Louis and the West, returning in 1834, 1835, and 1836. This, however, is thought to be a studio painting.

A thoughtful look at the expedition story offers at least four reasons why this particular American story should continue to occupy a large space in our national memory. First, it is a story—or, rather, a series of stories told by many actors and narrators. Human beings are storytellers; we explain our lives to ourselves and others in story form. We do that as individuals, as families, and as a nation. Even when life is in tatters, we stitch the fragments together and make a story. We might think about the American West as a storied place—a place of many narratives and of countless layers of meaning and experience like the stories in some grand building. What happened to Jefferson's Corps of Discovery is a great story, one filled with energy and forward motion. It has wonderful settings, memorable action, and a remarkable cast of characters speaking with many voices and in many languages. The Lewis and Clark story offers drama, adventure, struggle, failure, disappointment, and an enduring set of sweeping consequences. It is at heart a tellable story. And as the distinguished psychiatrist and writer Robert Coles says, we are all "called by stories." Stories reach out to us, and then the best of them ask us to respond. Good stories prompt us to consider our own stories and to then share those stories with others as they share theirs with us.

Second, this is no ordinary story. There are American stories beyond counting. Why has this one captured our imagination in so profound and enduring a way? Perhaps it is because this is a story about a journey. If Americans are a story-telling people, we are also a nation of journey makers. Some of the oldest Native American stories are about journeys. Journeys brought Africans and Europeans to eastern North America. Journeys took Americans west by way of the Oregon Trail and the transcontinental railroad. Journeys took Chinese women and men across the Pacific to California, Idaho, and Wyoming. Journeys took—and continue to take—Spanish-speaking men and women to a place they properly call el Norte. And in the twentieth century the journeys of African Americans from the rural South to the urban North remade the racial, cultural, and political map of the United States. We are a people on the road, whether the road be the Trail of Tears, Route 66, or the Interstate Highway System. We talk about "Home Sweet Home" and little houses on the prairie, but it is the lure of the road and the promise of the journey that still holds many of us. Lewis and Clark gave us our first national road story. Willa Cather once said that there are only two or three great human stories and that we keep repeating them over and over again. One of those stories is the journey story. Telling the Lewis and Clark journey story not only puts us on the American road but also clears a space so that we can share our own journey stories with others.

Third, although we are rightly drawn to Lewis and Clark because their experiences tell a story about a compelling journey, there is surely more. The Lewis and Clark expedition is sometimes cast as an alien army rolling west, an invading force out of *Apocalypse Now.* Think again. We might consider the expedition as a human community, a community as diverse as any in America today. Lewis understood this when he described the expedition as a family and "a little community." Look at this community closely. Here are people of many racial, ethnic, cultural, and social backgrounds. Consider York, Clark's slave and fellow adventurer. Pay attention to Pierre Cruzatte, the one-eyed, fiddle-playing engagé of French and Omaha ancestry; his world was as complex as ours. Here is Private John Potts, born in Germany, a miller by trade, a soldier perhaps by necessity, a man heading for a violent death at the hands of the Blackfeet in 1808. Sacagawea, a Shoshone woman who spent her formative years with the Hidatsa, was part of that community too, as was Jean-Baptiste Charbonneau, her child of mixed Shoshone-French ancestry. Do the simple categories of red, white, and black really make any sense in so various a community? Pause and listen to what that community sounded like: William Clark's Virginia-Kentucky accents, John Ordway's New Hampshire twang, George Drouillard's Shawnee-flavored French, and the cries and first words from a child brought up in a linguistic Tower of Babel. What could be more American than this? The Lewis and Clark story puts us on a journey with a distinctively American community. And then we see that community move through the lands and lives of other communities in a West already called home by thousands of Native people.

Finally, this is a remarkably accessible story. We can still float part of the upper Missouri and marvel at Lewis's "seens of visionary inchantment." We can still stand at Lemhi Pass and see the distant Bitterroot Mountains. We can still hike parts of the Lolo Trail. We can still visit the Knife River Villages and Fort Clatsop. This is what the novelist Henry James called "the visitable past." But there is a dangerous fantasy at work here. Driving the Lewis and Clark trail does not guarantee seeing the Lewis and Clark West. Such a trip is at best a diverting, educational, and probably memorable American vacation. But the hard, irreducible truth is that much of Lewis and Clark's West is either gone or profoundly transformed. We've dammed the rivers, plowed the plains, and laced the sky with high-tension wires. Whatever we might think about two centuries of change, the western landscapes of 1804 and 2004 are profoundly different. And it is not just the physical West that has changed. Modern Americans see and understand the landscape differently than did Lewis and Clark. We look at the Rockies, and thanks to artists such as Albert Bierstadt and Thomas Moran, we wonder at their beauty. Sergeant Gass looked at the mountains and called them a "desert."

Although the Lewis and Clark story is an accessible one, gaining this access involves more than taking a day trip to an expedition site. The distinguished exploration scholar Donald Jackson once said that Lewis and Clark were the "writingest" explorers in American history. The expedition journal-keepers wrote page after page about everything from bison to thunderstorms, from tribal politics to river currents, from mountain ranges to prairie plants. Some of that writing is dull, plodding stuff recording miles traveled and campsites set up. But there are also passages of the most marvelous, flashing prose when the West comes alive, leaps the abyss of time, and dances for us across the page. And all of it, whether dull or delightful, is written in a language we can understand. The expedition journals are not jargon-encrusted scientific reports prepared for a few specialists. We can read Lewis and Clark's words. And if we have sufficient imagination, we can in some way march with them on their way across the West. Even more compelling, we can sometimes get off the boats, climb up on the bank, and join the Native people watching as the travelers approach. The objects of our journey change, but the passion to be on the road endures. We continue to gather the objects and tell the story.

ONE Imagining America

One old man . . . dreamt: he saw strange people, they spoke to him, and showed him everything. . . . He said: "Soon all sorts of strange things will come. No longer [will things be] as before; no longer . . . shall we use these things of ours. . . . White people with mustaches on their faces will come from the east. Do you people be careful!

—WISHRAM PROPHECY, AS TOLD BY SOPHIA KLICKITAT[1]

Possessing a chosen country, with room enough for our descendants to the hundredth and thousandth generation . . . what more is necessary to make us a happy and prosperous people?

—THOMAS JEFFERSON[2]

In 1803 North America was poised on the brink of transformation. In the west, the Wishram lived prosperously under the fluted black cliffs and wrinkled hills of the Columbia Plateau. They had already survived what seemed like ceaseless change. First, the Snake Indians to the south had started using horses to stage long-distance raids on the wealthy riverside communities, and all thoughts turned to war and defense. Then, a more terrifying enemy invaded: disease that killed so cruelly no prayers could stop it. Corpses soon outnumbered the living, villages were reduced to ghost towns, and ominous skeletal images haunted the imaginations of Wishram artists. Next, neighboring tribes began to bring objects of inexplicable origin to the trading festivals where Plateau people mingled. Out of the mystery of the times, new prophets arose, foretelling events to come. The millenial Prophet Dance, or Waashani religion, swept through the Columbia River tribes till they all knew that the world was about to change.[3]

In the East, the Virginians lived prosperously on rich, slave-tilled plantations by the sleepy rivers of the Tidewater and Piedmont. They also thought they had been through epochal change. They had just emerged from a war of independence from

Sculpture of a human figure, prehistoric
The Wishram and related tribes who lived around The Dalles of the Columbia River were prolific sculptors in the basalt rock that abounded there, using distinctive art styles of ancient lineage. This effigy, made by pecking and grinding the basalt with a harder stone, shows stylistic similarities to the carved wooden house-posts produced by Chinookan tribes farther downriver. Its meaning is unknown.

Great Britain and the invention of a constitutional government. They belonged to a fractious, disunified collection of peoples trying to knit themselves into a new sort of nation. They had no inkling that their society was on the edge of transformation into the modern age. But out of the changes they had endured, they too had bred prophets. And some prophets are able to bring about the futures they foretell.

For years, Thomas Jefferson had wanted to send an exploring expedition west. In 1783 he had proposed such an adventure to the Revolutionary War hero George Rogers Clark. In 1786 he supported the abortive ambitions of the world traveler John Ledyard. In 1792 it was the naturalist André Michaux. But Jefferson's election to the presidency in 1800 finally gave him the power to carry out his desires. This time, he turned to his young fellow Virginians Meriwether Lewis and William Clark to execute a grand plan: to cross the continent on a voyage of discovery.[4]

"Explorers," wrote the historian William Goetzmann, "as they go out into the unknown, are 'programmed' by the knowledge, values, and objectives of the civilized centers from which they depart."[5] By and large, explorers discover what they have been sent to find and see what they are prepared to see. Lewis and Clark were no different. They did not wish to be; theirs was a mission of reinvention—not just seeing new things but seeing things in new ways.

But there were older perspectives on the land they were about to cross and the people they would encounter. Today, those perspectives are difficult to reconstruct, at least in part because the vision of Lewis and Clark was so vivid, and their descriptions were so compelling, that they erased from the public mind what had gone before. To historians who followed, it was as if the West began with Lewis and Clark.

Much has been written about the expedition's encounter with the American landscape. In this book, the focus will be on the human landscape. Here, we will explore the mental currents and the conceptual mountains that Lewis and Clark crossed. The recurring question will not be "What did they see?" but instead "What *didn't* they see?" For though we know well the terrain they traversed (or think we do), America's native landscapes of culture remain as alien to most of us today as they were to Lewis and Clark. Our task, then, is the same as theirs: to meet people different from us in mind and time, and learn to know them.

GEOGRAPHIES OF THE MIND

The Lewis and Clark expedition began in the mind of Thomas Jefferson. He had never set foot beyond the Blue Ridge Mountains, but no matter. From books and travelers' tales, Jefferson had imagined the West—not just the West that was but the West that was to be—more vividly than anyone else alive. But still he craved facts. In 1801 he offered his cousin's stepson, a young army captain named Meriwether Lewis, a position as his private secretary. "Your knolege of the Western country, of the army and of all it's interests & relations has rendered it desireable . . . that you should be engaged in that office," he wrote. Living together in the unfinished White House "like two mice in a church," Lewis and Jefferson hatched an ambitious scheme. Together with "ten or twelve chosen men, fit for the enterprize and willing to undertake it," Lewis would ascend the Missouri River and find "the most direct & practicable water communication across this continent for the purposes of commerce."[6]

Page 50: ***Thomas Jefferson* (detail), 1805**
Lewis's journal called Jefferson "the author of our enterprize." Charles Willson Peale's son Rembrandt painted this portrait of Jefferson while Lewis was at Fort Mandan in January 1805. Jefferson was sixty-one years old and had just been reelected to the presidency. The portrait was displayed at Peale's Museum on March 3, 1805, on the eve of Jefferson's second inauguration. Later, portraits of both Lewis and Clark would be displayed there as well.

Bust of Thomas Jefferson, 1789
This sculpture by the French artist Jean-Antoine Houdon was one of the most famous of Jefferson and served as the model for his likeness on Indian peace medals and the U.S. nickel coin. The original was made in Paris during the time Jefferson served there as minister plenipotentiary to France. During his lifetime Jefferson purchased several plaster copies, of which this is one. He gave it to David Rittenhouse, the Philadelphia astronomer and mechanical genius who preceded him as president of the American Philosophical Society.

Theodolite of Thomas Jefferson, 1778
Jefferson's love of precision instruments and Euclidean geometry reflected the Enlightenment view that measurement and mathematics would reveal the underlying architecture of the universe. He took an active, but not always practical, role in planning the expedition. His love of state-of-the-art technology led him to recommend a theodolite like this one, by the famed English instrument-maker Jesse Ramsden. It was one of his treasured possessions because it measured both horizontal and vertical angles, thus taking the place of both a surveyor's compass and a sextant in surveying and in measuring latitude and longitude. His recommendation that Lewis take one on the journey was vetoed by men of more experience. Lewis explained, "They think it a delicate instrument, difficult of transportation, and one that would be very liable to get out of order." It was replaced on Lewis's equipment list by a sextant and a surveyor's compass, both tried-and-true technologies.

Later, when William Clark heard about the plans for the expedition, he called Jefferson "that great Chaructor the Main Spring of its action." His clockwork metaphor would have appealed to Jefferson. Clockwork, with its mechanical precision and predictability, not only was the focus of every eighteenth-century technophile's desires but also was the guiding metaphor of the age. Ever since Sir Isaac Newton's laws of motion had proved that mathematics could perfectly predict the paths of the planets, European intellectuals had thought of the universe as a perfect clockwork set in motion by God. Nature's laws seemed so regular and reasonable that only diligent observation was needed to discern them. "A patient pursuit of facts, and a cautious combination and comparison of them, is the drudgery to which man is subjected by his Maker, if he wishes to attain sure knowledge," Jefferson wrote. Measurement, compilation, and classification of observed facts made up the methodology that led to truth. No intuition, revelation, secret knowledge, or correct doctrine was necessary. The world held no mysteries, only insufficient data. It was such an optimistic and egalitarian belief system that its adherents began to believe they had not just discovered a powerful new way of understanding the world: they had discovered the *correct* way.[7]

The expedition was to be deeply imbued with Enlightenment rationalism. Jefferson's vision for it was not based on the model of exploration offered by Sir Francis Drake or Hernando Cortés; it was based on that of Captain James

George Vancouver, *A Voyage of Discovery to the North Pacific Ocean, and Round the World*, 1798 and **Lewis's tracing from Vancouver's map, 1803**
The British Royal Navy had long since been to the Pacific coast where Lewis was headed. The Columbia River, though discovered and named by the Boston sea captain Robert Gray in 1792, was first mapped and explored by Englishmen under Captain George Vancouver. They named Mount St. Helens and Mount Hood for members of the British government. Lewis and Jefferson hoped that the Columbia would prove to be the fabled "River Oregan," rumored to connect with the headwaters of the Missouri River. Vancouver's book was scarce in America, but in May 1803 Lewis found a copy in Philadelphia and made "some sketches taken from Vancouver's survey of the western Coast of North America." This shows one of his tracings resting on the map. The book itself, Lewis thought, was "both too costly, and too weighty," for him "either to purchase or carry."

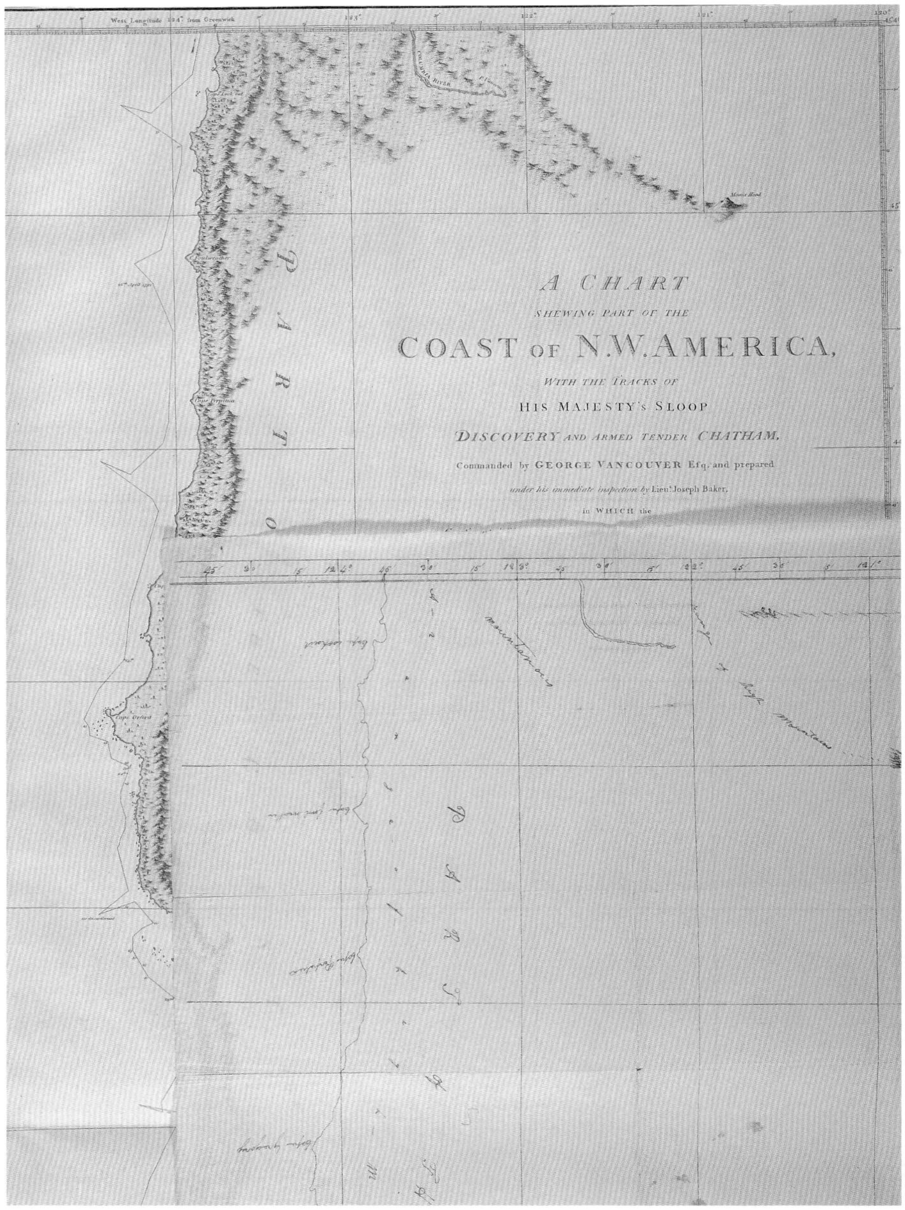

Cook of the British Royal Navy, whose sober and scientific reports had set a new standard for authoritative investigation of the unknown. In the tradition of the Royal Society of London, Lewis and Clark would set out not to discover marvels but to familiarize the unknown through the methods of quantification, classification, and dispassionate description. And yet, even before it started, their mission was shaped by other factors—political rivalry, wishful thinking, and ideology. All helped form the preconceptions that Lewis and Clark carried with them into the West and shaped what they saw there.

When Jefferson sat down to form a mental image of the West, he turned to books. In fact, it was a book that pushed him into action. In 1801 a British fur trader named Alexander Mackenzie published an account of his voyage to the Pacific Ocean. The first non-Indian to cross the continent north of Mexico, Mackenzie concluded his journal with a plan of how the fur trade might be organized to monopolize the commerce of the western tribes. The essay was aimed at his former employers, the North West Company, whom he had left in a snit; but it was Jefferson who took alarm. The British still ruled Canada; if they had designs on the territory west of the Mississippi, the nascent United States would be surrounded on two sides by an acrimonious former colonial

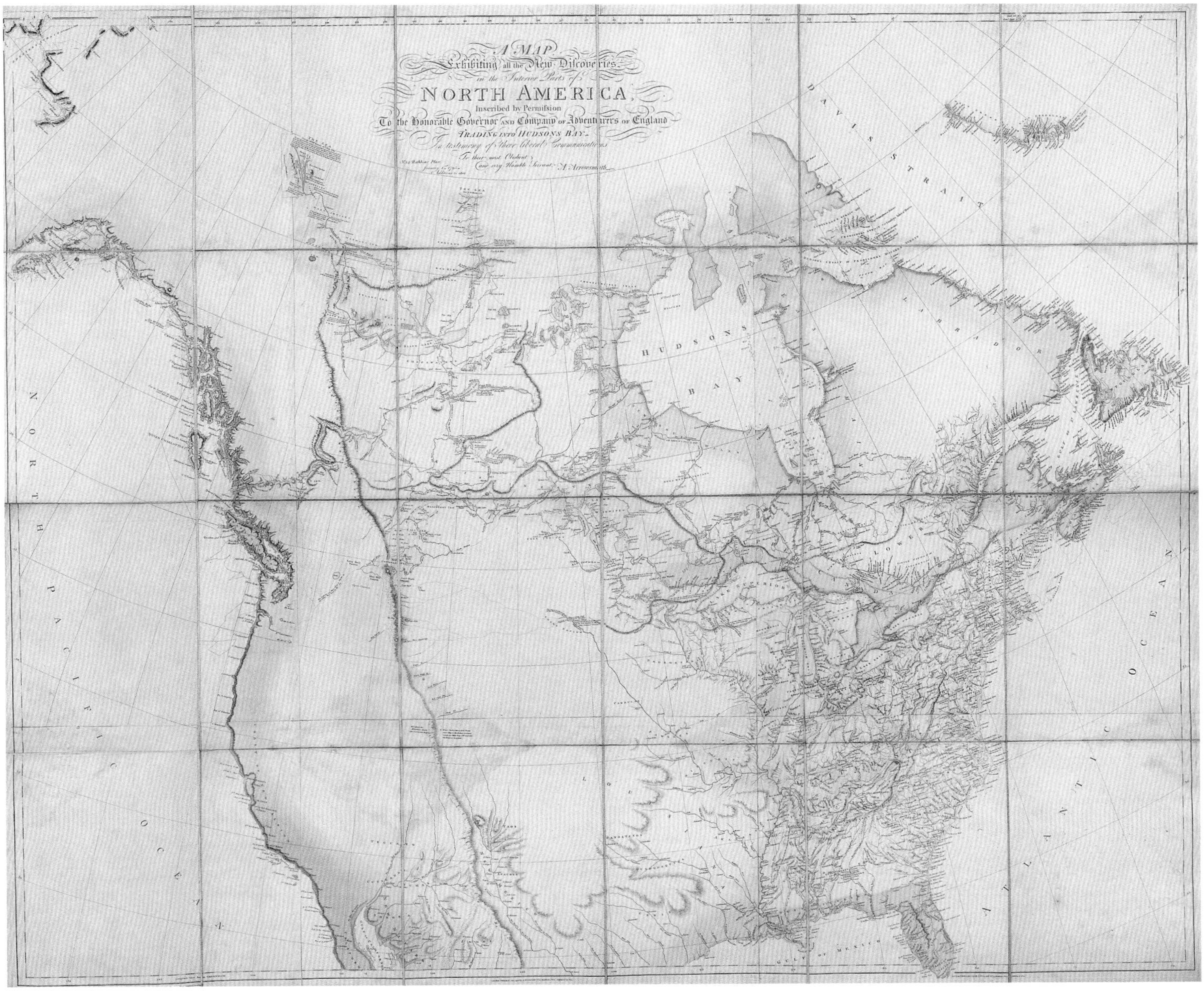

power with enormous commercial capital. Jefferson decided to assert a claim on the West by duplicating Mackenzie's feat.

This chain of events reflects Jefferson's first preconception about the West: that it was a stage for the geopolitical ambitions of European nations. For centuries, the European convention of claiming portions of western North America like animals marking territory had mainly affected only other Europeans, just as bear territories are respected only by other bears. The actual inhabitants of the land continued to rule their own societies and control the trade and travel of visiting Europeans as they always had. In the year Jefferson read Mackenzie's book, the United States claimed (without really controlling) most of the territory east of the Mississippi, minus Florida; west of the Mississippi, Spain administered the scattered towns and trade but had secretly ceded the Louisiana Territory, including the watershed of the Missouri, to France. The west coast was claimed variously by Spain, Britain, and Russia. To the north, the redcoats lurked. Thus, when Jefferson looked west, he saw a gameboard of European boundaries that seemed like the most important aspect of the land. How little impact such imaginary boundaries had on the ground, his explorers were soon to learn. And yet, Lewis and Clark would con-

Aaron Arrowsmith, *A Map Exhibiting all the New Discoveries in the Interior Parts of North America*, 1802
This British map has been called "the single most important item of cartographic data available to Jefferson and Lewis." The geography of Canada was well known, thanks to the efforts of British fur traders. But south of the border was a blank filled with a major misconception: that the Rocky Mountains were a single line of "low ridges." Jefferson had a copy of the 1802 edition as early as March 1803, but he ordered another copy from the New York bookseller James Cheetham on June 17, 1803, presumably for Lewis to take on the expedition. Clark seems to have used Arrowsmith's map for the basis of his 1805 map of the West, drawn at Fort Mandan; and Lewis wrote of looking at Arrowsmith's map on June 8, 1805, at the mouth of the Marias River.

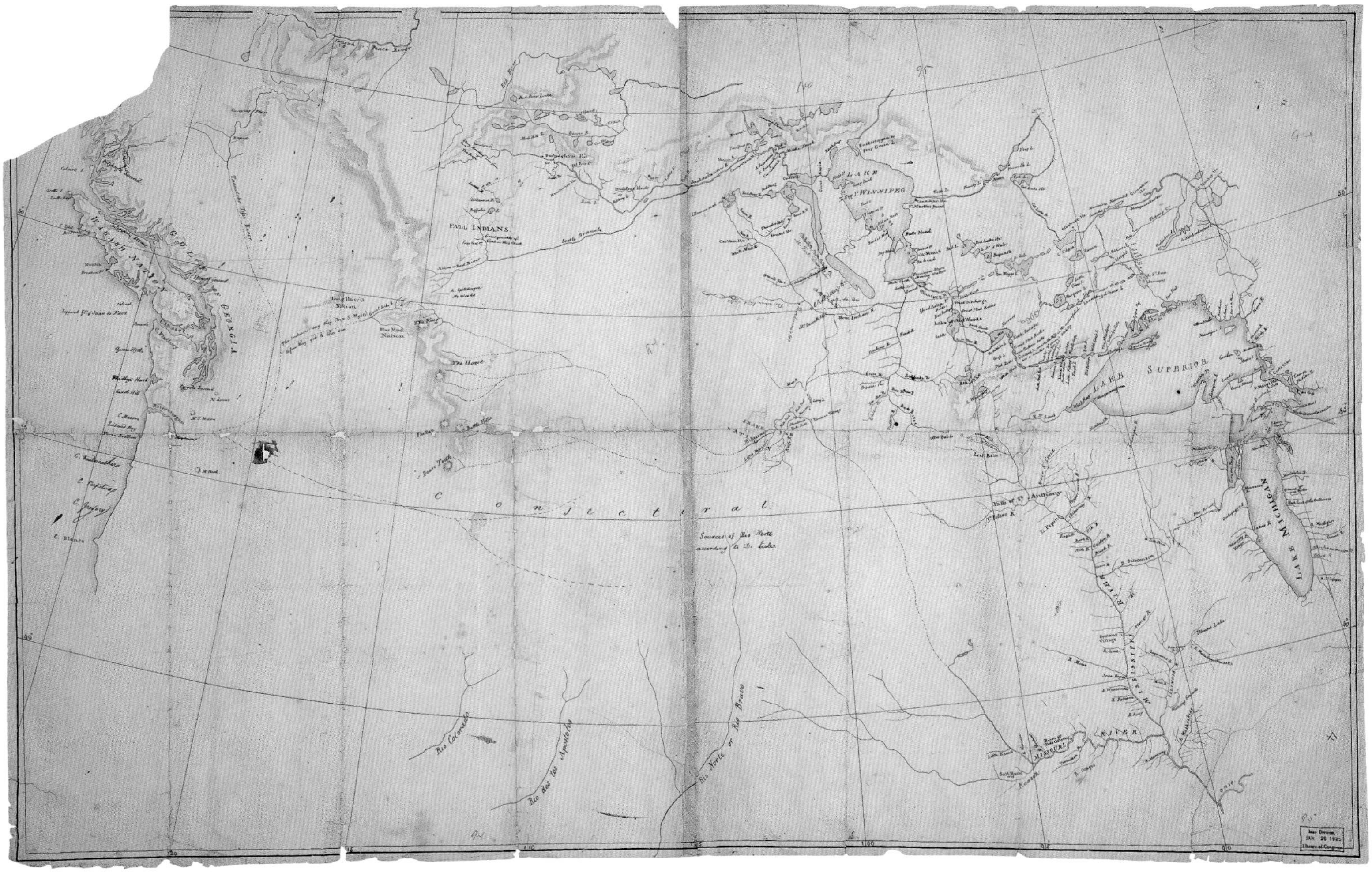

Nicholas King, map of western North America, 1803

This map was drawn in the spring of 1803 to summarize current knowledge of the West for Lewis, who took it on the expedition. Albert Gallatin, the secretary of the treasury, supervised its creation by the government cartographer Nicholas King. Gallatin wrote: "I have requested Mr. King to project a blank map to extend from 88 to 126° West longitude from Greenwich & from 30° to 55° north latitude. . . . In this I intend to insert the course of the Mississipi as high up as the Ohio from [Andrew] Ellicot's, the coast of the Pacific from [James] Cook & [George] Vancouver, the north bend of the Missouri . . . from the three maps of [Aaron] Arrowsmith & from that of [Alexander] Mackenzie." At Fort Mandan, Lewis added the locations of various British fur posts in Canada.

tinue to follow the dictates of geopolitics, even when their actions seemed self-defeating from any other point of view.

A second set of preconceptions about the West related to its geography. Here also Jefferson's ideas had a long lineage. For centuries, Europeans had sought a water route across North America, the fabled Northwest Passage. At first, they imagined this to be a sea route, then a chain of lakes, and finally a pair of rivers—one flowing east, the other west, connecting near their sources, where a short portage would make it possible to ship goods across the continent. The fabled River of the West even had a name—"Oregan." This river theory suited Jefferson, since a sea lane would have made it possible for European commerce to bypass the United States, but a river could be the conduit of settlement as well as trade. In 1792 the theory received a boost from another British explorer, George Vancouver, who visited the west coast and mapped the estuary and lower course of a great river, the Columbia, flowing into the Pacific from the east. The Missouri had to be the other link in the passage; three centuries of geographers could not be wrong.[8]

Supporting the Northwest Passage theory were two other geographical concepts: "the pyramidal height of land" and "symmetrical geography." The pyramidal height of land was a mythical spot in the West where all the major rivers of the continent had their sources. From this commanding height, armchair explorers imagined it would be possible to travel north, south, east, and west by river. Symmetrical geography projected onto the West what was known of the East. Reasoning from known to unknown, geographers assumed resemblances: between the Missouri and the Ohio, the Rockies and the Appalachians, the Columbia and the Potomac. In their minds, the West became a rough mirror image of the East, only better. Symmetrical geography must have appealed to the architect of Monticello, since symmetry was one of the guiding principles of neoclassical aesthetics. If the beauty of Euclidean geometry reflected God's mind, it was only reasonable to assume that the continent would also obey rules of symmetry.

In 1803 this collection of geographical concepts was compiled into a map for Lewis's use by the government mapmaker Nicholas King. King's map combined some of the most accurate geographical information available and wishful thinking. It had the width of the continent correct because the longitudes of the west and east coasts had been measured with precision, thanks to the Royal Navy. But instead of showing the Rockies as an unbroken north-south chain, it portrayed intermittent hills that ended a little south of today's Canadian border, complying with Jefferson's description of them as "highlands" rather than mountains. A branch of the Columbia interlocked with a southern branch of the Missouri, illustrating the president's claim that the Missouri offered "continued navigation from it's source, and, possibly with a single portage, from the Western Ocean."[9]

Lewis and Clark internalized the implications. Symmetrical geography led them to believe that the Missouri would be relatively short and navigable, the mountains would be green and rolling, and the Columbia would flow in a valley through them. The pyramidal height of land was so strongly embedded in their minds that even when they stood at the source of the Missouri, deep in the Rockies, they could barely believe their eyes that the Columbia was not just over the next hill. Lewis even called the Lemhi River the Columbia until reality set in. After they returned, Lewis still reported to Jefferson that, just beyond the lands they had explored, there was a place where the Willamette and Colorado had their sources in the same height of land. The myth had receded but not died.[10]

A third preconception was the pure quintessence of Jefferson: the West would be a garden. Like generations of Europeans, Americans saw their El

Animals, plants, and people of Louisiana, 1758

In trying to form a picture of Louisiana Territory, Jefferson found a major source of information in Le Page du Pratz's *Histoire de la Louisiane*, where these quaint illustrations first appeared. Du Pratz's book belonged to a genre of booster books aimed at prospective settlers and investors, and its illustrations showed exotic but rich products of the land. It led Jefferson to imagine Louisiana as an abundant garden where the Natives lived in a state of nature.

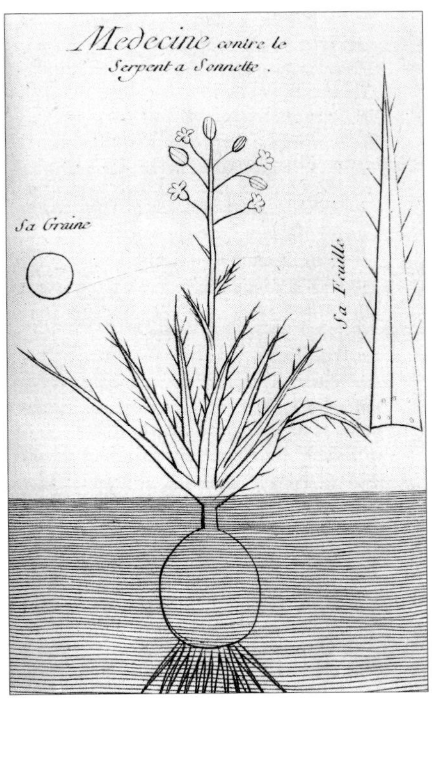

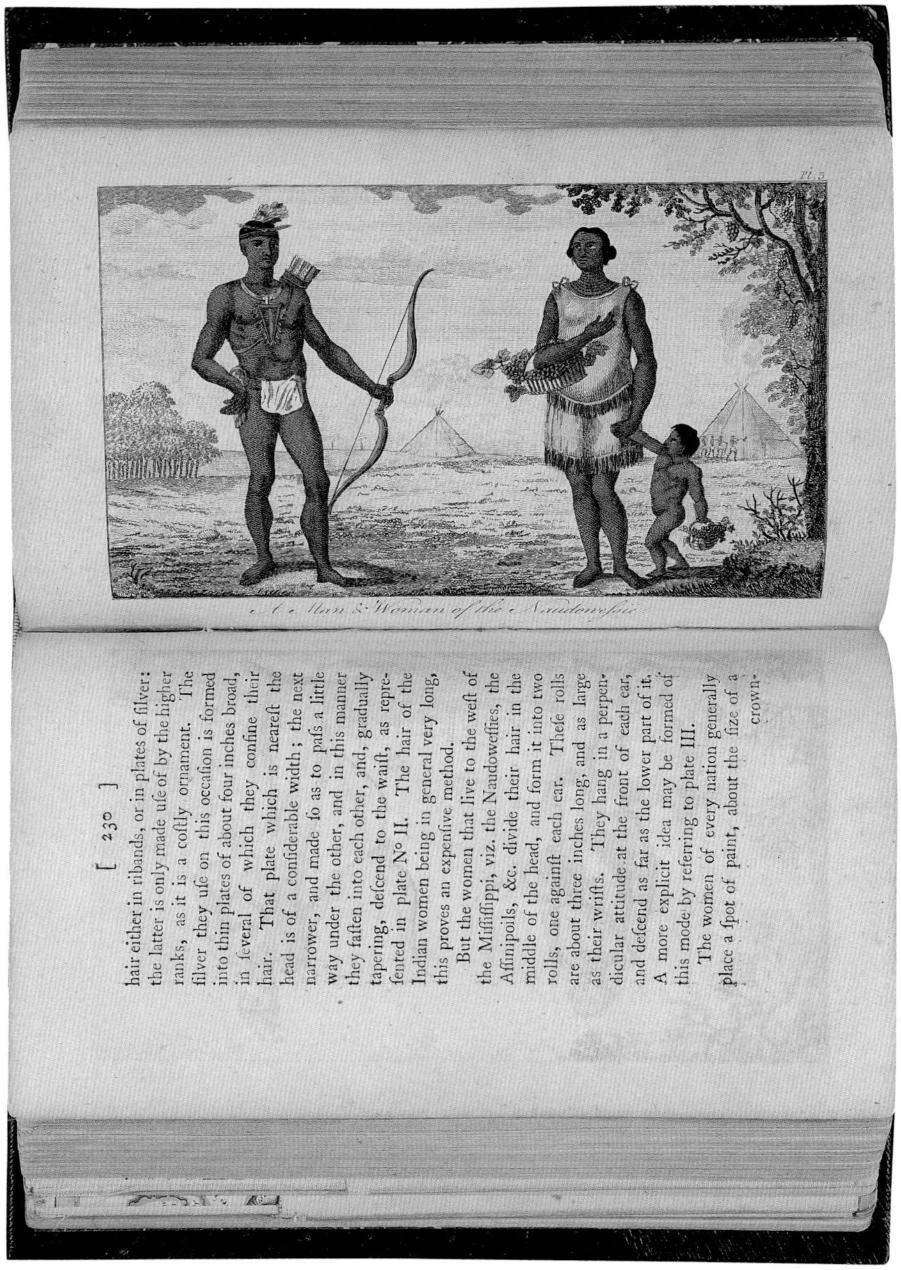

Jonathan Carver, *Travels through the Interior Parts of North America in the Years 1766, 1767, and 1768*, 1781

Carver's work, a best-selling travel book, described the West as a place that would provide "all the necessaries of life for any number of inhabitants." Carver popularized the concept that somewhere in the West was a spot where a single portage would lead to the headwaters of the "four most capital rivers of the Continent of North America, viz. the St. Lawrence, the Mississippie, the River Bourbon [Nelson], and the Oregan, or the River of the West." The book also helped form Jefferson's impression of the western Indians. Here he learned about the immense power of the Sioux, whom Carver called the Naudowessie.

Dorado in the West; but they did not look for mountains of gold or rubies. They did not fill the blank maps with imagined unicorns or pygmies. Their images reflected their hopes: fertile soil, a gentle climate, hordes of grazing beasts, easy river transportation, streams for mills, low rolling mountains, and useful minerals like lead and salt. It was an agrarian Eden they sought. And that was what Jefferson promised them. Ignoring British sources that saw the interior as cold and inhospitable, and Spanish ones that warned of "great waste lands" that were "full of sand dunes and rocks," Jefferson formed his picture of Louisiana from French sources written to promote settlement. The West, he claimed, would "yield an abundance of all the necessaries of life, and almost spontaneously; very little labor being required in the cultivation of the earth." The Great Plains were there only because the soil was "too rich for the growth of forest trees." If Lewis could not discover the Passage to India, he needed to find this other ancient dream, the Garden of the World.[11]

Jefferson's most paradoxical preconception about the West related to its residents: to him, the land was simultaneously full and empty. There were Indians there; no one doubted that. In fact, the Indians were at the forefront of the expedition's mission. In his instructions to Lewis, Jefferson put Indian relations right after geographical discovery in order of importance, and he wrote a laundry list of questions about tribal cultures. Natural history came after ethnography. When Lewis summarized the objectives of the expedition for Clark, five of the nine points he listed concerned the Indians.[12]

The importance of Indians in the mission was a pragmatic reflection of reality. No matter which European country claimed the West, Jefferson knew who actually controlled it. But Indians occupied two separate, and mutually exclusive, images in Jefferson's mind. First, there were the "merciless Indian Savages" of the Declaration of Independence. This image was formed thirty years before, in the bloody conflicts of the Ohio Valley, when American squatters and Indian residents had clashed over land. In 1763 Britain had attempted to prevent more atrocities and bloodshed by protecting the Indians—and, not incidentally, the profits from their trade—against the incursions of aggressive settlers. The Crown drew a boundary along the Appalachian Mountains and forbade settlement west of it. Although the ploy did not work, this defense of Indian rights was one of the fiery issues that led to the Revolution. One of the freedoms Americans fought for was the freedom to take Indian land. Not surprisingly, the most militant Indians had fought decisively for Britain in the war—in the Ohio Valley against George Rogers Clark, as well as on the Great Lakes. By 1803 the problem of forming a policy regarding these former combatants had landed in Jefferson's lap.[13]

At the same time, Jefferson had another image of Indians. They might be savages, but they were *our* savages, and he leaped to their defense when the French naturalist Comte de Buffon asserted that they were stunted and degen-

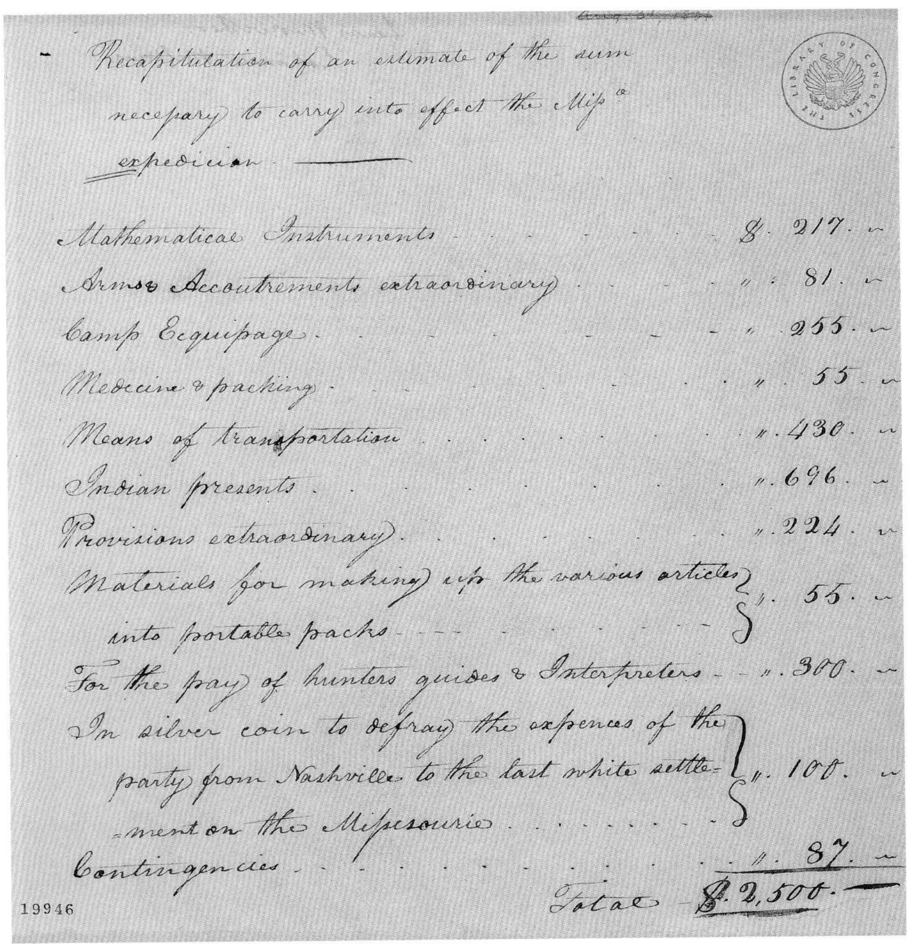
Recapitulation of an estimate of the sum necessary to carry into effect the Missa expedition

Mathematical Instruments	$. 217.
Arms & Accoutrements extraordinary	" . 81.
Camp Equipage	" . 255.
Medecine & packing	" . 55.
Means of transportation	" . 430.
Indian presents	" . 696.
Provisions extraordinary	" . 224.
Materials for making up the various articles into portable packs	" . 55.
For the pay of hunters guides & Interpreters	" . 300.
In silver coin to defray the expences of the party from Nashville to the last white settlement on the Missisourie	" . 100.
Contingencies	" . 87.
Total	$. 2,500.

19946

Lewis's estimate of expenses, 1803
Like any federal project, the expedition had to have a budget. In this document, Lewis proposed a bargain expedition costing only $2,500. This was probably a deliberate underestimate to get a first appropriation from Congress. His ploy worked. Lewis then proceeded to exceed his budget by 1,420 percent. The final bill was more than $38,000, but Congress paid it anyway.

Patent chamber lamp, early 1800s
Lewis took along a variety of lighting devices, from the low-tech (candles and candle molds) to the latest invention, shown here. In his list of requirements, Lewis specified "patent chamber lamps & wicks." He probably meant this style of oil lamp, called "Miles's Patent Agitable Lamp." In 1787 the Englishman John Miles patented a type of burner for whale oil lamps that prevented the oil from spilling, even if the lamp tipped over. The name "chamber lamp" was applied to any lamp with a saucer base and a finger loop for carrying. Lewis purchased two lamps for twenty-five cents each, from the tinsmith Thomas Passmore.

erate. "They are formed in mind as well as in body, on the same module with the 'Homo sapiens Europaeus,'" Jefferson wrote defensively.[14] Influenced by thinkers (starting with John Locke and Montesquieu) who traced the origin of culture to environment, and believing that species were perfectly adapted to the geographies they inhabited, Jefferson could hardly denigrate the Indians without denigrating the continent that had produced them—the continent on which he placed all his hopes for the future. Instead, he tended to see in Indians some of the traits he hoped the American environment would produce in his own race—love of freedom, bravery, independence, and nobility. All that was lacking from them was the "civilizing" influence of an agrarian lifestyle, a blessing he hoped soon to bestow on them.

Indians might provide a noble clay from which to shape an American Adam, but Jefferson did not imagine this would happen in one day. The West was important because it bought time. Jefferson had given up on peaceful coexistence with tribes east of the Mississippi. His plan was to "remove" them (a gentle euphemism) into the Louisiana Territory, which would become a giant Indian reservation, while white settlers from the United States filled up the eastern half of the continent. Hundreds or thousands of years in the future, when a growing population would produce a need for western land, the Indians would be welcome to "incorporate" with white Americans.[15]

There was a place reserved for Indians in Jefferson's future America, but the price of their ticket was assimilation. They were to achieve "the benefits of our government" by giving up their cultures and their ethnic identities and adopting Euro-American values and lifestyles. Thus, wrote Jefferson, "their history may terminate." He expected this "final consolidation" to be a peaceful and voluntary transition: as soon as the Indians gave up hunting for agriculture, they would "prove to themselves that less land & labour" would maintain them "in this, better than in their former mode of living." Moreover: "When they shall cultivate small spots of earth, and see how useless their extensive forests are they will sell."[16]

Make no mistake, Jefferson's West was not to be a diverse or multicultural land. It was more like the Serbian view of an ethnic homeland: "a people speaking the same language, governed in similar forms, and by similar laws; nor can we contemplate with satisfaction either blot or mixture in that surface." As for those who held out, he wrote: "We shall be obliged to drive them, with the beasts of the forest into the Stony mountains."[17]

Set of dental tools, mid-1800s
Along with medical supplies, Lewis purchased "1 Set Teeth Inst[rument]s. small" for $2.25. They may have looked like this set, which contains forceps, lancets, a blowpipe, a director, curved and straight bistouries, a dental elevator, and various blades and scalpels. Also shown is a pair of tooth keys for pulling teeth. Lewis did not record whether he used his dental tools.

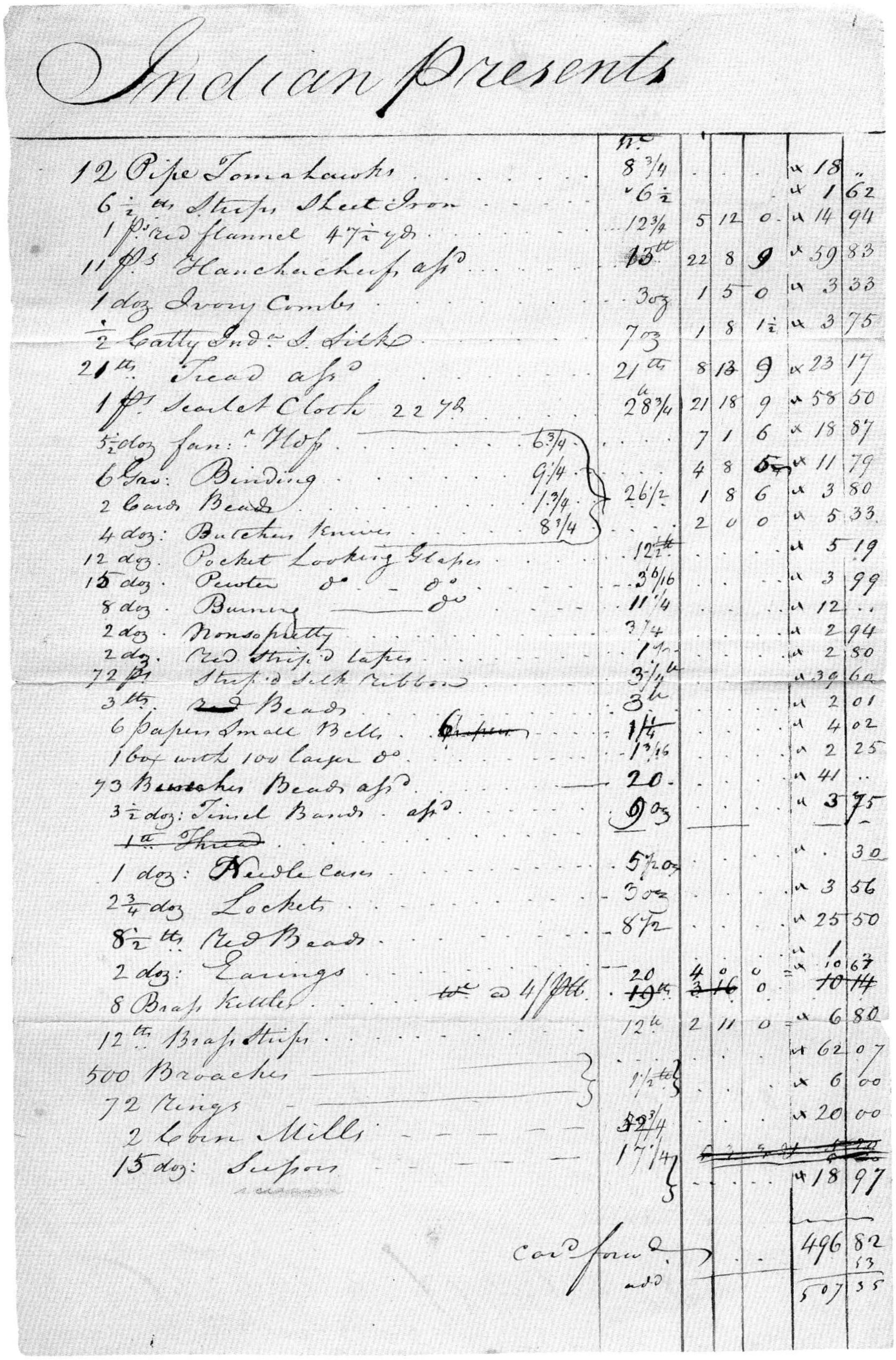

Indian Presents

		lb	£	s	d	$	cts
12 Pipe Tomahawks		8 3/4				18	..
6 1/2 lbs Strips Sheet Iron		6 1/2				1	62
1 ps red flannel 47 1/2 yds		12 3/4	5	12	0	14	94
11 ps Handkerchiefs ass'd		15 lb	22	8	9	59	83
1 doz Ivory Combs		3 oz	1	5	0	3	33
1/2 Catty Ind. S. Silk		7 oz	1	8	1 1/2	3	75
21 lbs Tread ass'd		21 lb	8	13	9	23	17
1 ps Scarlet Cloth 22 yds		28 3/4 lb	21	18	9	58	50
5 1/2 doz fan: Hdfs	6 3/4		7	1	6	18	87
6 Gro: Binding	9 1/4		4	8	5	11	79
2 Cards Beads	1 3/4	26 1/2	1	8	6	3	80
4 doz: Butcher Knives	8 3/4		2	0	0	5	33
12 doz. Pocket Looking Glasses		12 1/2 lb				5	19
15 doz. Pewter do - do		3 6/16				3	99
8 doz. Burning — do		11 1/4				12	..
2 doz. Nonsopretty		3 1/4				2	94
2 doz. Red Striped tapes		1				2	80
72 ps Striped Silk ribbon		3 1/4 lb				39	60
3 lbs ~~Red~~ Beads		3 lb				2	01
6 papers Small Bells ~~6 paper~~		1 1/4				4	02
1 box with 100 larger do		1 3/16				2	25
73 Bunches Beads ass'd		20				41	..
3 1/2 doz: Tinsel Bands ass'd		9 oz				3	75
~~1 lb Thread~~						.	30
1 doz: Needle cases		5 1/2 oz				3	56
2 3/4 doz Lockets		3 oz				25	50
8 1/2 lbs Red Beads		8 1/2				1	
2 doz: Earings		20	4	0	0	10	67
8 Brass Kettles wt @ 4/ p lb		~~19 lb~~	~~3~~	~~16~~	0	~~10~~	~~14~~
12 lbs Brass Strips		12 lb	2	11	0	6	80
500 Broaches		1 1/2 lb				62	07
72 Rings						6	00
2 Corn Mills		~~52~~ 3/4				20	00
15 doz: Scissors		17 1/4				18	97
Carried forward						496	82
add							53
						507	35

Summary of purchases, 1803
The summary of Lewis's purchases by the purveyor of public supplies was eight pages long, of which this is only one. Indian presents represented the largest expenditure, both on Lewis's budget and on his bills. Despite this, the supply was inadequate. Though the Corps added to the supply before leaving St. Louis, there were still not enough to take the men to the Pacific and back. Indian presents not only had to purchase goodwill and passage through tribal territories but also had to buy food, horses, labor, and information.

Trade kettle, early 1800s
Lewis purchased fourteen brass kettles from Benjamin Harberson & Sons. He designated eight of them as Indian presents and six as camp equipage. After returning from the expedition, he wrote that nests of camp kettles were among the goods most prized by the Indians: "Brass is much preferr'd to Iron, tho both are very useful to the Indians size from 1 to 4 gallons." The North West Company, which imported kettles like this in nested sets, already knew this. This kettle is typical of ones mass-manufactured in Great Britain for the Indian trade in the early nineteenth century. The sheet-metal lugs with turned-down ears, the copper rivets, and iron bail are all characteristic of that date.

This, then, was Jefferson's attitude toward Indians: benevolent rhetoric veiling a steely ruthlessness. In the same year that he exhorted Lewis and Clark to put their energies to "extending & strengthening the authority of reason & justice among the people around them," he also wrote Governor William Henry Harrison: "We have only to shut our hand to crush them."[18]

So Indians were an inextricable part of the West. And yet, at the same time, the West was an empty land—not so much physically as symbolically. Beyond the sunset and the Blue Ridge lay a place of Jefferson's imagining, untainted by Old World history and corruption, a geography of transformation and rebirth. On this unstoried land, as on a blank page, a new people could inscribe new narratives. Mankind could return to nature and start over, building up a society from first principles—only this time they would get it right.

The discovery of this national landscape of renewal was the least articu-

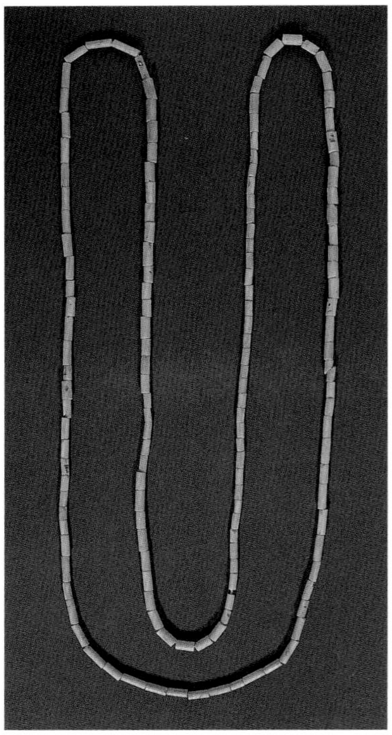

Wampum, c. 1800–50

Based on his knowledge of Ohio Valley tribes, Lewis listed "5 lbs. White Wampum" among his requirements for the trip. It was a blunder, because tribes west of the Mississippi did not use wampum. Lewis and Clark were reduced to explaining it as a Euro-American symbol; among the Nez Perce Clark wrote, "I deckorated the Stem of this pipe with blue ribon and white wampom and informed the Chief this was the emblem of peace with us."

"Wampum" refers to small cylindrical beads made from the shell of the whelk (which produced white beads) and the quahog clam (purple). Handcrafted by Native peoples from prehistoric times, by Lewis's day wampum was mechanically drilled in quantities for the Indian trade. Strung into belts, wampum had symbolic diplomatic meanings for eastern tribes. Lewis and Clark donated some wampum to Peale's Museum. This strand is from the collection that included that museum's artifacts.

lated, but most pressing, mission of the Lewis and Clark expedition. The question that underlay every other was, "What sort of nation is this going to be?" The urgency of this question stemmed from the precarious state of the new republic. In 1803 the United States was little more than a set of legal documents and a miscellaneous and factionalized populace. The election of 1800 had been ruinously divisive. The country had little of the glue that generally binds nations together—a shared ethnicity, history, culture, or even race. It had few national institutions or arts. The prospect of westward expansion worried many public figures because when geographic distance and regionalism were added to the other forces of disunity, the result might tear apart the whole ragtag construction.[19]

Looking for the future of the nation, Jefferson gazed into the crystal ball of the land. He had good scientific justification for doing so. He was deeply influenced by Locke, who had written that character is formed by the imprint of natural surroundings on the senses. Morality developed from natural law through this process of sensory impressions. Later philosophers added arguments about the influence of climate, habitat, and subsistence on the societies of mankind. The power of environment was such that people were virtual transcripts of the land in which they lived. In the nature-versus-nurture debate that raged as much then as now, Jefferson was a committed nurture man—only it was Nature that did the most important nurturing.[20]

In Jefferson's mind, there was a hierarchy of lifestyles and at the top was the yeoman farmer's. Rural life, he believed, produced the democratic virtues of discipline and independence, whereas cities encouraged debauchery, cupidity, and corruption. Because Jefferson equated democracy with an agrarian nation, it was essential that his explorers find in the West "an immensity of land courting the industry of the husbandman." Nothing less than the national character was at stake: would the landscape of America foster virtuous, self-reliant landholders to carry on the democratic tradition, or would degraded, servile serfs be produced? "Our governments will remain virtuous for many centuries," Jefferson wrote, "as long as they are chiefly agricultural; and this will be as long as there shall be vacant lands in any part of America."[21]

When Jefferson instructed his emissaries to study "the character of the country," he was by implication asking them to find the character of the people who would inhabit it. This was a journey freighted with urgency: Lewis and Clark would be traveling into the nation's future and bringing back news of it to the American oracle who had sent them. It can be argued that this was the only part of their mission in which Lewis and Clark succeeded unequivocally. The Northwest Passage proved to be illusory; their expectations of negotiating peace and commerce with the Indians collapsed; their scientific findings were never published. But in discovering a unifying national narrative, they succeeded beyond their grandest expectations.

PACKING EQUIPMENT, PACKING PRECONCEPTIONS

The preparations Lewis made during the spring of 1803 were focused on gathering equipment and gathering information. He and Jefferson had originally imagined a small expedition. Jefferson consistently referred to it as a party of about ten men. Once Congress had given its approval, Lewis's first stop for supplies was at the U.S. arsenal at Harper's Ferry, Virginia (now West Virginia).

View of Several Public Buildings, in Philadelphia, 1790

This engraving, based on a sketch by Charles Willson Peale, shows the intellectual nerve center of Philadelphia, where Lewis consulted the leading minds of the nation. The artist was looking northeast across the open space behind the statehouse, now called Independence Hall. The fourth building from the left is Philosophical Hall, which housed the American Philosophical Society, and the middle one is the statehouse, where Peale's Museum occupied the upstairs chambers. The interweaving of institutions of learning and government was characteristic of the young nation's rationalist inventors.

There, he requisitioned only fifteen rifles, a number dwarfed by the eventual component of over forty men for the first leg of the trip, thirty-three in the "permanent company." His purchases of clothing and supplies were similarly frugal.

After leaving Harper's Ferry, Lewis went first to Lancaster, Pennsylvania, and then to Philadelphia, to get what has been described as a crash course in the scientific skills of an Enlightenment explorer. Here, the bargain-basement scale of the plan again became apparent. Whenever Captain Cook staffed an exploring expedition, he included artists, surgeons, and eminent scholars from the Royal Society of London; the United States did not put a single scientist on the payroll. In his letters to the men of learning deputized to train Lewis, Jefferson was apologetic: Lewis was "not regularly educated," but he possessed "a great mass of accurate observation." Besides, he added: "It was impossible to find a character who to a compleat science in botany, natural history, mineralogy & astronomy, joined the firmness of constitution & character, prudence, habits adapted to the woods, & a familiarity with the Indian manners & character, requisite for this undertaking."[22]

The Long Room, Interior of Front Room in Peale's Museum, 1822

Peale arranged his collection of natural specimens in a gridwork, classified according to the Linnaean system. Viewers could thus see relationships and hierarchies that were obscured in the natural setting. This sketch was started by Charles Willson Peale as a study in perspective, using a device called a "painter's quadrant" to map converging sight lines. His son Titian Ramsay Peale completed it by adding the watercolor details. The room it shows is the second-floor room, which extended across the entire Chestnut Street side of the statehouse.

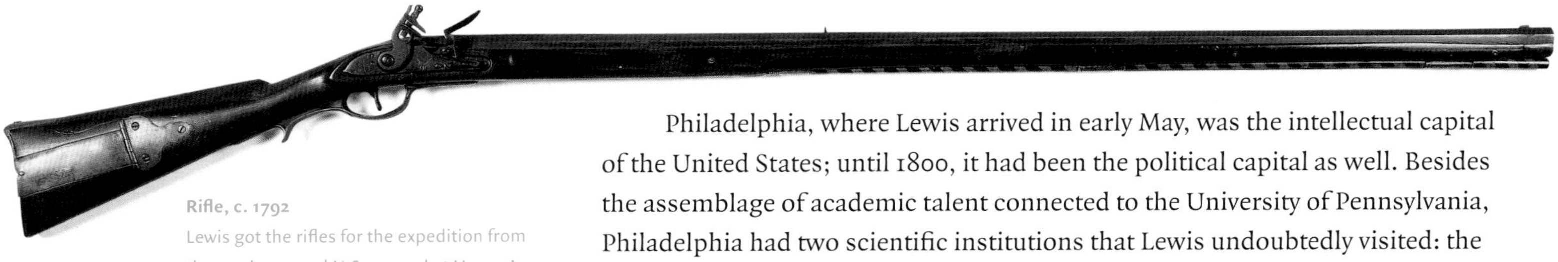

Rifle, c. 1792
Lewis got the rifles for the expedition from the newly opened U.S. arsenal at Harper's Ferry, Virginia (now West Virginia). For years it was believed that he used the elegant Model 1803 Harper's Ferry rifle, but recent research has proved this to be impossible: the first prototype of that gun was not produced until the fall of 1803, and production on it did not begin until the spring of 1804. What he used instead were 1792 rifles that were stored at the arsenal and that had been produced by private gunmakers on contract with the federal government. These were guns he was quite familiar with, since they had been produced for Anthony Wayne's campaign and probably had been used by the Chosen Rifle Company when both Lewis and Clark served in it. Lewis had the gunmakers at Harper's Ferry recondition the guns, probably by replacing the locks, and he had extra locks and parts produced.

All known surviving examples of the 1792 contract rifle have been refitted with a Harper's Ferry 1812 lock, apparently so that they could be used in the War of 1812. This one has an illegible maker's mark but has been attributed, on stylistic grounds, to George F. Fainot, one of the gunmakers who carried out the 1792 contract.

Philadelphia, where Lewis arrived in early May, was the intellectual capital of the United States; until 1800, it had been the political capital as well. Besides the assemblage of academic talent connected to the University of Pennsylvania, Philadelphia had two scientific institutions that Lewis undoubtedly visited: the American Philosophical Society and Peale's Museum. Located in adjoining buildings, these institutions represented the nation's aspirations to participate in the intellectual life of Europe.

The American Philosophical Society was the U.S. answer to the Royal Society. It could trace its origins back to 1743, when Benjamin Franklin proposed an association of "Virtuosi or ingenious Men residing in the several Colonies" to meet periodically and present papers, published after 1771 in its *Transactions*. Jefferson had been elected the society's president in 1797 and remained so until 1815. Its library and meeting rooms occupied Philosophical Hall, next to the statehouse in Philadelphia. When Lewis and Clark returned, this would be the institution that Jefferson would designate to house their journals for the use of researchers. The journals remain there today.[23]

Peale's Museum was the creation of one of the most remarkable Renaissance men of early America, Charles Willson Peale. He was first an accomplished artist, but he was also an inventor, naturalist, mastodon excavator, and public educator. Together with his seven sons—including Raphaelle, Rembrandt, Rubens, and Titian Ramsay—he created in his museum one of the premier scientific and educational institutions of early America. After 1802 Peale's Museum took over the upstairs rooms of the statehouse, where the Declaration of Independence had been hammered out.[24]

Any visitors who came to Peale's Museum expecting the bizarre and miscellaneous collections of the early cabinets of curiosities would have been disappointed. Peale's objective was openly didactic: to make sense of the natural world by ordering it into a comprehensible system. The museum's encyclopedic collection of zoological specimens was arranged into a gridwork of boxes

Swivel gun, mid- to late 1700s
Mounted on the keelboat was a swivel gun, a small cannon that fired balls weighing one to one and a half pounds. Besides its usual use for salutes and signaling, it was almost used once in anger, in the near confrontation with the Teton Sioux on September 25, 1804: "The large Swivel [was] loaded immediately with 16 Musquet Ball in it." The gun was not fired, however. The swivel gun was probably mounted on a wall of Fort Mandan in the winter of 1804–5. It was cached at the Great Falls in June 1805 and then recovered in August of the following year. Since it "could no longer be Serveceable . . . as it could not be fireed on board the largest Perogue," the captains gave it as a gift to the Hidatsa chief Le Borgne (One Eye). This one is a British-made swivel gun found on the site of Fort William Henry on Lake George, New York, and may date to the French and Indian War.

Pocket pistols, late 1700s
Lewis purchased "1 Pair Pocket Pistols, Secret Triggers" for ten dollars from Robert Barnhill, Philadelphia. Pistols with secret triggers were usually French or British and came in a case; thus they could be called case pistols. The triggers folded in flush with the underside of the pistol until the flintlock hammer was cocked, when the triggers popped out. This was to prevent the trigger from catching on clothing when being drawn from a pocket and made it possible to carry the pistol loaded at half cock for swift action. These handguns were loaded by unscrewing the barrel, placing the powder and ball into the chamber, then replacing the barrel.

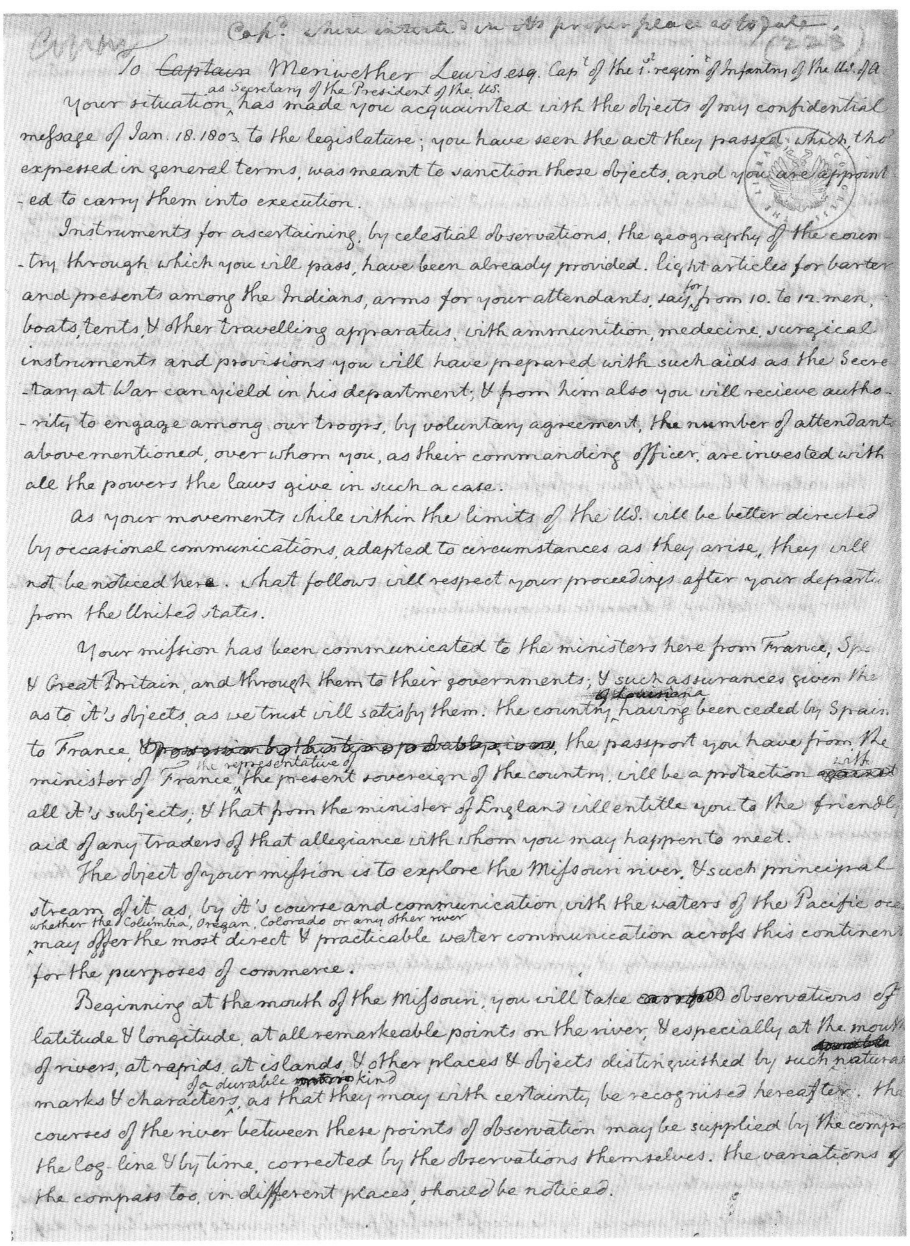

Copy Capt. [illegible] inserted in its proper place as to date (228)

To ~~Captain~~ Meriwether Lewis esq. Capt. of the 1st. regim. of Infantry of the U.S. of A

Your situation as Secretary of the President of the U.S. has made you acquainted with the objects of my confidential message of Jan. 18. 1803. to the legislature; you have seen the act they passed, which, tho' expressed in general terms, was meant to sanction those objects, and you are appointed to carry them into execution.

Instruments for ascertaining, by celestial observations, the geography of the country through which you will pass, have been already provided. light articles for barter and presents among the Indians, arms for your attendants, say for from 10. to 12. men, boats, tents, & other travelling apparatus, with ammunition, medecine, surgical instruments and provisions you will have prepared with such aids as the Secretary at War can yield in his department; & from him also you will recieve authority to engage among our troops, by voluntary agreement, the number of attendants abovementioned, over whom you, as their commanding officer, are invested with all the powers the laws give in such a case.

As your movements while within the limits of the U.S. will be better directed by occasional communications, adapted to circumstances as they arise, they will not be noticed here. what follows will respect your proceedings after your departure from the United states.

Your mission has been communicated to the ministers here from France, Sp[ain] & Great Britain, and through them to their governments; & such assurances given them as to it's objects, as we trust will satisfy them. the country of Louisiana having been ceded by Spain to France, ~~[illegible]~~ the passport you have from the minister of France, the representative of the present sovereign of the country, will be a protection with all it's subjects; & that from the minister of England will entitle you to the friendly aid of any traders of that allegiance with whom you may happen to meet.

The object of your mission is to explore the Missouri river, & such principal stream of it as, by it's course and communication with the waters of the Pacific ocean, whether the Columbia, Oregan, Colorado or any other river may offer the most direct & practicable water communication across this continent for the purposes of commerce.

Beginning at the mouth of the Missouri, you will take ~~careful~~ observations of latitude & longitude, at all remarkeable points on the river, & especially at the mouths of rivers, at rapids, at islands, & other places & objects distinguished by such natural marks & characters of a durable kind, as that they may with certainty be recognised hereafter. the courses of the river between these points of observation may be supplied by the comp[ass] the log-line & by time, corrected by the observations themselves. the variations of the compass too, in different places, should be noticed.

Jefferson's instructions, 1803
This famous document was Jefferson's blueprint for the expedition. In its mix of commercial, scientific, and imperial agendas, it also served as the model for subsequent explorations sponsored by the United States. Two copies survive: Jefferson's rough draft (shown here) and his letterpress copy of the original sent to Lewis.

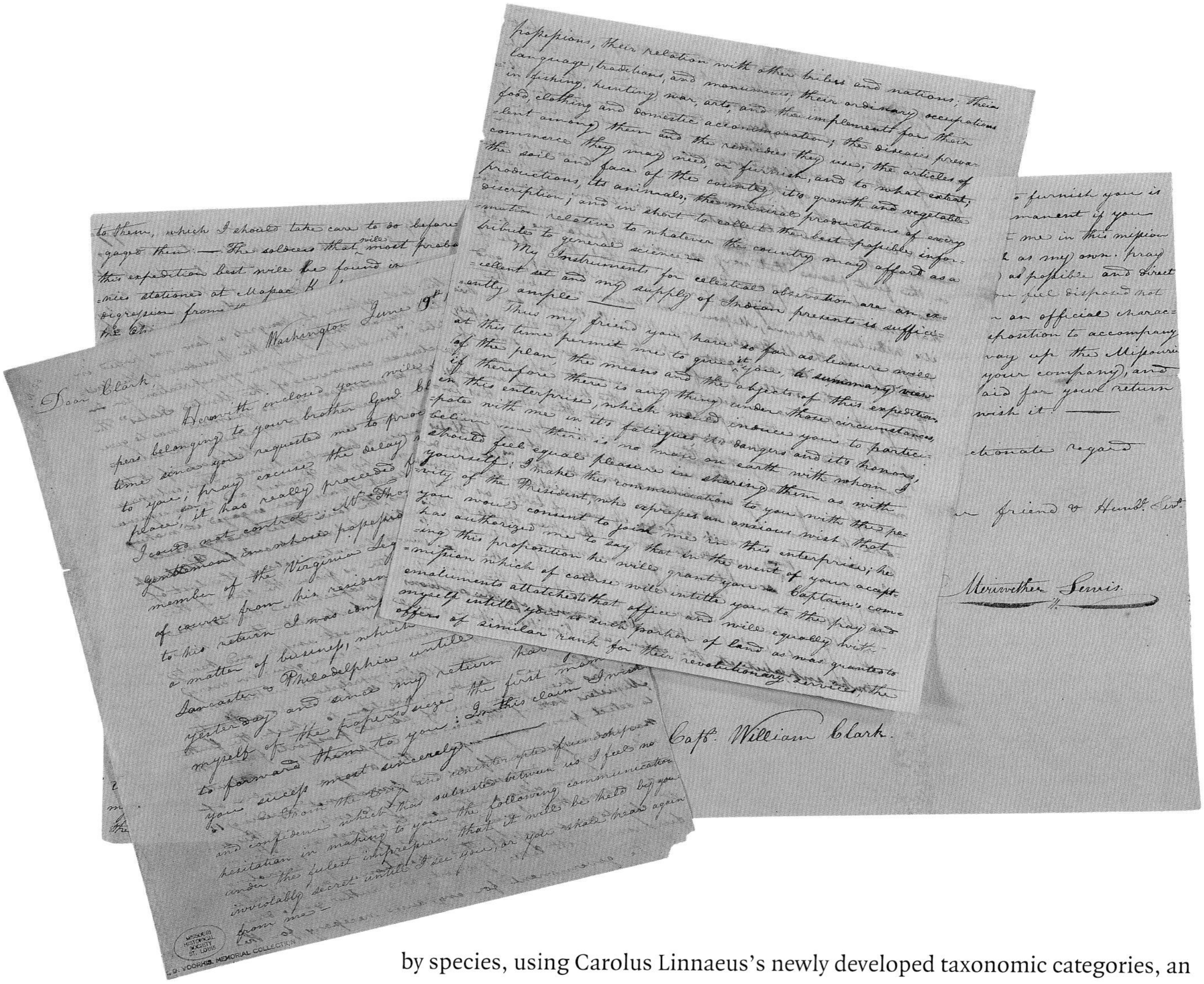

Letter from Lewis, inviting Clark to join the expedition, 1803

The historian Donald Jackson called this letter "one of the most famous invitations to greatness the nation's archives can provide." Written on June 19, 1803, it informed Clark of the expedition and offered him a captain's commission to join. Because the letter revealed the secret of the expedition's destination, Lewis spent the first page talking about routine matters and brought up his real purpose inside.

by species, using Carolus Linnaeus's newly developed taxonomic categories, an organizing scheme that naturalists were using in a project as ambitious as the human genome project today: to inventory and classify every plant and animal on earth. Visitors to Peale's Museum could not escape the impression that species were well-defined, separate categories; that they were arranged in an orderly progression of orders, phyla, and genera; and that those categories were fundamental and unchanging. In short, it appeared that there was a wondrously rational system behind creation, just waiting to be discovered. The extent to which the organizing system was arbitrarily imposed for the convenience of researchers and could easily have been replaced by a different system probably never occurred to anyone but the specialists.

Peale's Museum was a three-dimensional expression of the great project of Enlightenment science: to comprehend the natural world through rational inquiry. The objective was to gather data without respect to any theory, since following theories would distort the information; eventually, patterns would emerge. (Of course, the underlying theory that the world was rationally organized didn't count.) The upshot of this grand project would be, according to the charter of the American Philosophical Society, to "let Light into the nature of Things" and, ultimately, reveal the underlying purpose of creation. The project led instead to the theory of evolution, but that is another story.

The American Philosophical Society and Peale's Museum linked American intellectuals to a cultural movement that was based in Europe but that would soon affect the entire globe, for better or worse. It was a universalist, egalitarian, individualist, rational, progressive, and materialist mindset.

South East Corner of Third, and Market Streets. Philadelphia, 1799
This engraving by William and Thomas Birch shows one of the busy commercial corners of Philadelphia where Lewis did his shopping. He visited the shops of Thomas Leiper, Edward Shoemaker, Benjamin Harberson, John and Charles Wister, and William Chancellor on Market Street and the shops of Christian Denckla, Thomas Parker, and David Jackson on Third.

Science was to be its universal language, transcending race, nation, and creed—as the neutral choice of Latin for its nomenclature indicated. America's version of Enlightenment science was pragmatic; the colonists' emphasis was always on "useful knowledge," and the American Philosophical Society encouraged research on topics like ship pumps, stoves, peach blight, dyes, and street lighting as well as on more abstract subjects. The fact that the major institutions of the American Enlightenment were housed in the same building in which the Constitution had been born was no coincidence. The United States

Miniature of George Rogers Clark, 1832
Two years after the death of George Rogers Clark, "The Hannibal of the West," John Wesley Jarvis painted a portrait of him in his prime, wearing his Revolutionary War uniform. This was William's copy, painted by George Catlin. In the war, William's elder brother captured the towns of Kaskaskia and Cahokia on the Mississippi and Vincennes on the Wabash, thus driving the British from the Kentucky frontier. He earned little but fame for his deeds. Though his campaign was authorized by the governor of Virginia, Thomas Jefferson, after the war the state refused to reimburse his expenses, leaving him impoverished and embittered. In 1783 George, who grew up in Albemarle County, was Jefferson's first choice to lead a western exploring expedition, but he apparently declined to undertake more adventures on Jefferson's behalf.

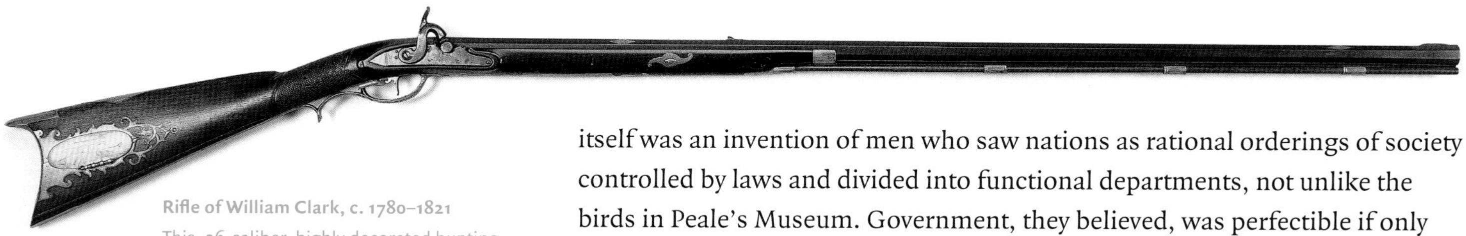

Rifle of William Clark, c. 1780–1821
This .36-caliber, highly decorated hunting rifle belonged to Clark and represents his deep roots in the Ohio Valley frontier. It is marked "Jn° Small Vincennes" for its maker, "Colonel" John Small, who was the gunsmith at Fort Pitt during the American Revolution and is said to have been one of George Rogers Clark's men in the capture of Vincennes in 1778. The gun was originally a flintlock but was later converted to percussion. It has a silver patchbox and inlays with Revolutionary War iconography: a flying angel (symbolizing Fame) blowing a trumpet and holding a staff with a Liberty cap; and an eagle with spread wings, thirteen stars, and "The Spirit of Seventy-Six" in script.

Clark had a .36-caliber hunting rifle with him on the expedition, as his statement that the balls were one hundred per pound shows. He called it his "small rifle," or "small gun." At Fort Clatsop, he used it to shoot two brants from forty yards; the Indians "came around examined the Duck looked at the gun the Size of the ball which was 100 to the pound and Said in their own language *Clouch Musket, wake, com ma-tax Musket* which is, a good Musket do not under Stand this kind of Musket &c." There is no direct evidence to indicate this rifle was taken on the expedition.

itself was an invention of men who saw nations as rational orderings of society controlled by laws and divided into functional departments, not unlike the birds in Peale's Museum. Government, they believed, was perfectible if only more ingenious and logical thought could be applied to devising mechanisms impervious to the failures and corruptions of human beings. Knowledge was to be the great leveler and the best defense against tyranny. When he was elected president of the American Philosophical Society, Jefferson wrote wryly of his "ardent desire to see knowledge so disseminated through the mass of mankind, that it may at length reach the extremes of Society, beggars, and kings."[25]

Lewis spent most of May 1803 absorbing the advice of the learned men who frequented Peale's Museum and Philosophical Hall: the astronomer and mathematician Robert Patterson; the botanist and ethnographer Benjamin Smith Barton; the anatomist Caspar Wistar; the physician Benjamin Rush; and the surveyor Andrew Ellicott. On their recommendations, he assembled an eclectic reference library of books to take on the expedition.

But Lewis did not spend all his time bookishly. He was often out on the bustling streets, buying equipment. Philadelphia was also a commercial hub; its wharves were lined with visiting ships, and its shops displayed goods from around the world. Lewis's purchase records, preserved by diligent federal clerks, portray an expedition with aspirations to be a demonstration of state-of-the-art technology, despite its limited budget.

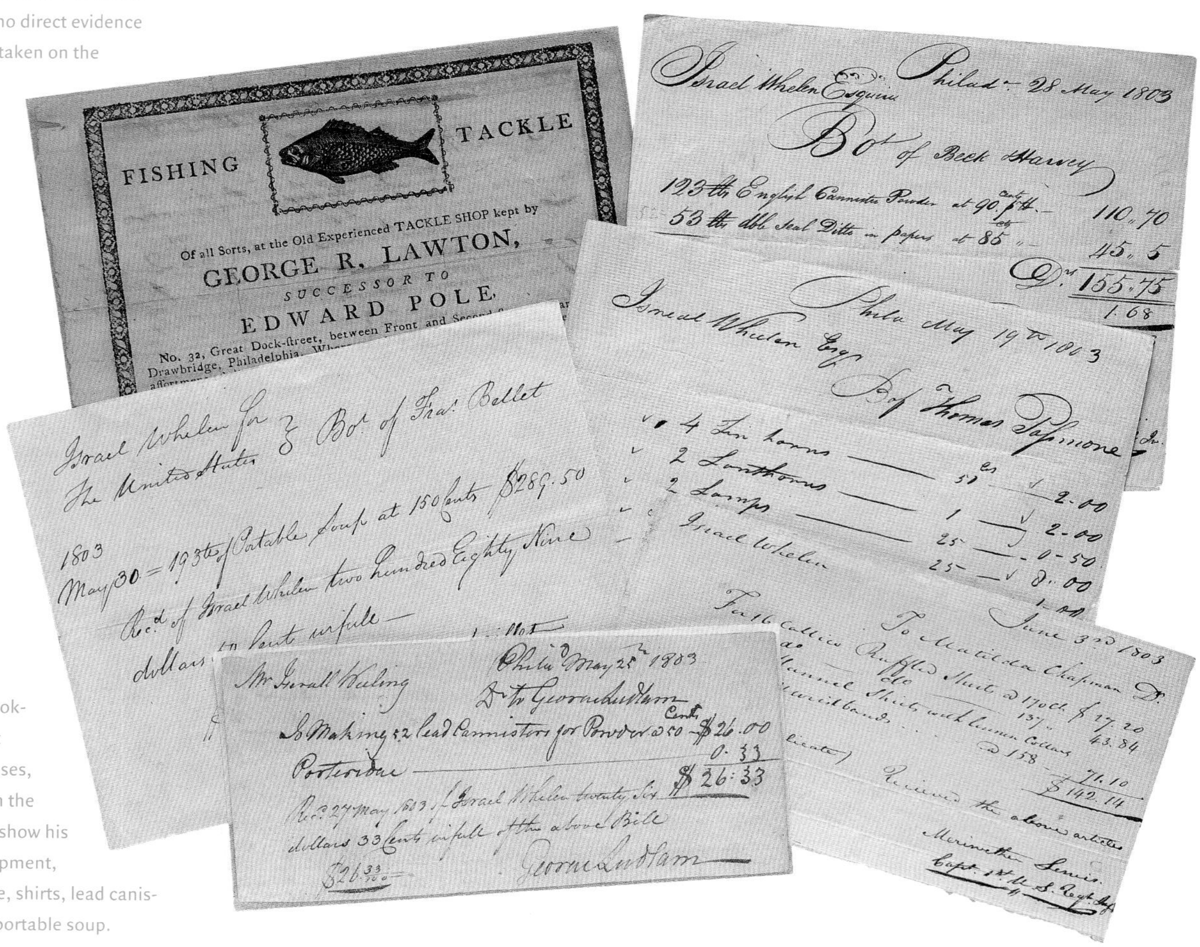

Receipts for purchases, 1803
To satisfy government bookkeepers, Lewis had to get receipts for all his purchases, and they are still on file in the National Archives. These show his purchases of fishing equipment, gunpowder, soap, tinware, shirts, lead canisters for gunpowder, and portable soup.

The hand of Jefferson and the scientific advisors can be seen in the list of "Mathematical Instruments" that Lewis purchased. These instruments included the latest in high-tech navigational and surveying equipment, packed into a custom-made box. Lewis's army background came to the fore in his purchases of arms and supplies. He armed the party not only with rifles and muskets but also with a small cannon, blunderbusses, and pistols—enough to send a message about U.S. military power. But even here he could not resist some gadgets, such as pocket pistols with secret triggers and an experimental air gun. Under "Camp Equipage" is listed not only practical things like spoons and tumblers but also patent chamber lamps and an invention he called "portable soup"—a dried mix that could be easily kept and transported in the field but that proved so unpopular with the men that it was used only for starvation rations. He would travel west with a pharmacopoeia of medicines, surgical and dental instruments, and a complete carpentry shop. But the most expensive category of purchases was "Indian Presents." To entice the Indians away from British traders, the expedition needed to be a traveling trade show of superior American goods. Here, Lewis's limited knowledge of the western tribes' needs and tastes led to some guesswork. Sometimes—as with kettles, knives, and rings—he guessed correctly. Other times—as with wampum and "knitting pins"—his guesses were wrong.

The list is a graphic reminder that Lewis expected this to be a water journey. Except for the "single portage" from the Missouri to the Columbia, he never expected to have to carry all this tonnage. The equipment list explains, as does nothing else, his later panicky search for horses to transport the expedition across the Rockies. The equipment list also reflects the various motives that were propelling the planning of the expedition: commerce, empire, and science.

As Lewis scoured the shops of Philadelphia for concrete tools to accomplish those missions, Jefferson explained the motives to Congress, the cabinet, and foreign diplomats, describing the expedition differently depending on the audience. Requesting funds from a frugal Congress, Jefferson noted that the expedition, like a trade delegation, would be good for business. The West, he pointed out, was a huge untapped market full of customers. For centuries, British and French companies had made fortunes trading manufactured goods for Indian products, and U.S. citizens wanted to compete. The expedition would "have conferences with the natives on the subject of commercial intercourse, [and] get admission among them for our traders." The Constitution gave Congress authority over interstate commerce, which justified an appropriation "for the purpose of extending the external commerce of the U.S.," the code language in which the expedition might be described. Almost as an afterthought, Jefferson added that the project "should incidentally advance the geographical knowledge of our own continent."[26]

Meriwether Lewis, c. 1803
According to Lewis family legend, Meriwether Lewis sent this life-size portrait to his mother at Locust Hill, Albemarle County, before setting out on the expedition in 1803. It is by the French artist Charles Balthazar Julien Févret de Saint-Mémin, who toured the eastern United States making portraits. To capture the life-sized image, Saint-Mémin used a device called a physiognotrace; then, with the help of a pantograph, he reduced the likeness onto an engraver's plate and printed as many copies as the sitter ordered. His use of mechanisms convinced Enlightenment America that his portraits were more objective, and therefore more accurate, than those produced with an artist's subjective style and imagination. Lewis was so pleased with Saint-Mémin's work that he sat twice for the artist.

Telescope of Meriwether Lewis, c. 1800
This elegant telescope embodied the love of technology that Lewis and Jefferson shared. Made by the British instrument-maker William Cary, it incorporated the latest optics in its two-element achromatic objective lens, magnifying thirty-six times with a field size of one degree (about fifty feet at one thousand yards). Fully extended, the telescope is almost five feet long, but it collapses to a compact fifteen inches. Called a ship's-master style for its popularity with naval officers, it is a refracting terrestrial telescope—made for viewing faraway objects during the day but not for nighttime celestial observations. It consists of five brass drawtubes and an outer tube of mahogany with a leather wrap.

Lewis's family believed he took this telescope on the expedition, but there is no documentation supporting this claim. He frequently mentioned his "spy-glass" on the expedition but did not describe it.

Watch of Meriwether Lewis, 1796–97
Lewis had a watch with him on the expedition, and this could be it. One of the expenses he incurred in Philadelphia was for "Cleaning a Silver Secont Watch." Two years later, in what is now Williams County, North Dakota, he wrote: "My pocket watch, is out of order, she will run only a few minutes without stoping. I can discover no radical defect in her works, and must therefore attribute it to the sand, with which, she seems plentifully charged, notwithstanding her cases are double and tight." He later tried, unsuccessfully, to trade the watch to an Indian for an otter skin.

This English-made silver watch has a second hand (the small dial at the twelve o'clock position) and a double case, matching his descriptions. On the rim is a tiny metal lever for stopping the works, which would have been useful for synchronizing the watch with a chronometer. The watch was wound with a key. There is no maker's name on the movement, but the initials "ML" are lightly scratched on it in script. Inside the outer case is a circle of paper with a vine motif painted on it in watercolor.

Inside the cabinet, Jefferson's tone was different. The West was no longer just a market but was also a stage for imperial expansion. Albert Gallatin, the secretary of the treasury and the man for whom Lewis would later name a branch of the Missouri, wrote Jefferson that "the future destinies of the Missouri country" were of "vast importance" because that land would be "settled by the people of the U. States." To that end, he added: "Preventing effectually the occupying of any part of the Missouri country by G[reat] B[ritain], seems important." Indians did not figure in Gallatin's imperial calculus, even temporarily. "The great object to ascertain is whether from its extent & fertility that country is susceptible of a large population," he wrote.[27]

The story was again very different when Jefferson spoke to the French and British ministers to get passports for Lewis. Now, it was an expedition "entirely of a scientific nature"; the British chargé d'affaires reported that Jefferson was "ambitious in his character of a man of letters and of science, of distinguishing his Presidency by a discovery." It was "in no shape his wish to encourage commerce . . . with any Indian tribes."[28]

All three descriptions of the expedition were true, as far as they went. When Jefferson wrote up instructions for Lewis on June 20, the commercial, imperial, and scientific motives were interwoven. Empire was useless unless it could profit the colonial power. Commerce could not thrive without military strength to keep peace and enforce laws. Science was in the service of both. It would be wrong to say one was the "true" motive. They all were.

THE MEN OF THE CORPS OF DISCOVERY

Lewis set out for the west on July 4, 1803. He crossed the mountains to Pittsburgh and then traveled down the Ohio River, assembling his team on the way. His first decision, made back in June, had been unusual: he had offered

***Newfoundland Dog*, 1803**
Lewis brought along his dog Seaman, whom he described as "of the newfoundland breed very active strong and docile." Newfoundlands were a popular breed among sporting men in the early nineteenth century and were eulogized by Lord Byron as "in life the firmest friend, The first to welcome, foremost to defend." Seaman lived up to Byron's recommendation, functioning as a hunter of squirrels, beaver, and even deer and as a watchdog in camp. He was much admired by the Indians for his "segacity." The breed's appearance has changed since the eighteenth century, as this engraving by John Scott, from *The Sportsman's Cabinet*, shows. Seaman's fate is unknown; the last mention of him occurs near the Great Falls on the return journey, when Lewis described him howling from the torture of the mosquitoes.

THE PRESIDENT OF THE United States OF AMERICA,

To all who shall see these presents Greeting:

Know Ye, That reposing special Trust and Confidence in the Patriotism, Valour, Fidelity and Abilities of [illegible] I have nominated, and by and with the Advice and Consent of the SENATE, do appoint him [illegible] in the service of the UNITED STATES: [illegible]

He is therefore carefully and diligently to discharge the duty of [illegible] by doing and performing all manner of things thereunto belonging. And I do strictly charge and require all Officers and Soldiers under his Command, to be obedient to his Orders as [illegible] And he is to observe and follow such Orders, and Directions, from time to time, as he shall receive from me, or the future President of the United States of America or the General, or other superior Officers set over him, according to the Rules and Discipline of War. This Commission to continue in force during the Pleasure of the President of the United States, for the time being.

Given under my Hand, at [illegible] this [illegible] day of [illegible] in the Year of our Lord One Thousand [illegible] Hundred and [illegible] and in the [illegible] Year of the Independence of the United States.

By Command of the PRESIDENT of the UNITED STATES of AMERICA.

[illegible]

[illegible]

Engraved by I. Draper

Commission of Meriwether Lewis, 1802

Lewis was made a captain in the First U.S. Infantry in 1800, two years before he received this grand document signed by Jefferson and adorned with republican symbols such as the liberty cap in the lower left. By the time he received this, Lewis was already on leave from the army and serving as Jefferson's private secretary. One of his first tasks at the White House was informing the president on the political views of the officers' corps, which had been packed with Federalists by the previous administration.

William Clark, c. 1810
Clark's nephew testified that this portrait was "the one that he and everyone who knew him considered his best likeness." It was probably painted after Clark's return from the expedition. Multiple copies were made for members of the Clark family.

his old army friend, William Clark, a co-captaincy with rank and responsibilities "in all respects [to] be precisely such as my own."[29]

To understand what led to Lewis's extraordinary offer, it is necessary to go back to 1795. In that year, Captain Clark was commanding an elite unit of rifle sharpshooters on the Ohio frontier when a problem recruit was transferred to his unit. The young ensign had just been court-martialed for verbally attacking an officer in a drunken rage, then challenging him to a duel. The commanders must have thought Clark could handle the fellow, maybe even shape him up. The ensign was Meriwether Lewis, and his disciplinary transfer marked the beginning of one of the great friendships of history.[30]

The two men had much in common. Both were members of the Virginia gentry from Albemarle County, as was Jefferson—though the large Clark family had moved to the Kentucky frontier when "Billy" was a child. Clark had joined the army at nineteen, Lewis at twenty. Both owned slaves. Though they had served together for only six months, they kept in touch; Lewis referred to their "long and uninterupted friendship and confidence."[31]

Yet there were many ways in which they were different. Clark, a middle child from a large, close family, was fated always to be the steady, responsible one, cleaning up the messes left by brilliant, self-destructive associates. He had grown up in the shadow of his older brother George Rogers Clark, the heroic "Hannibal of the West" who had won the Ohio Valley from the British in the Revolution. Eager to distinguish himself as something more than the brother

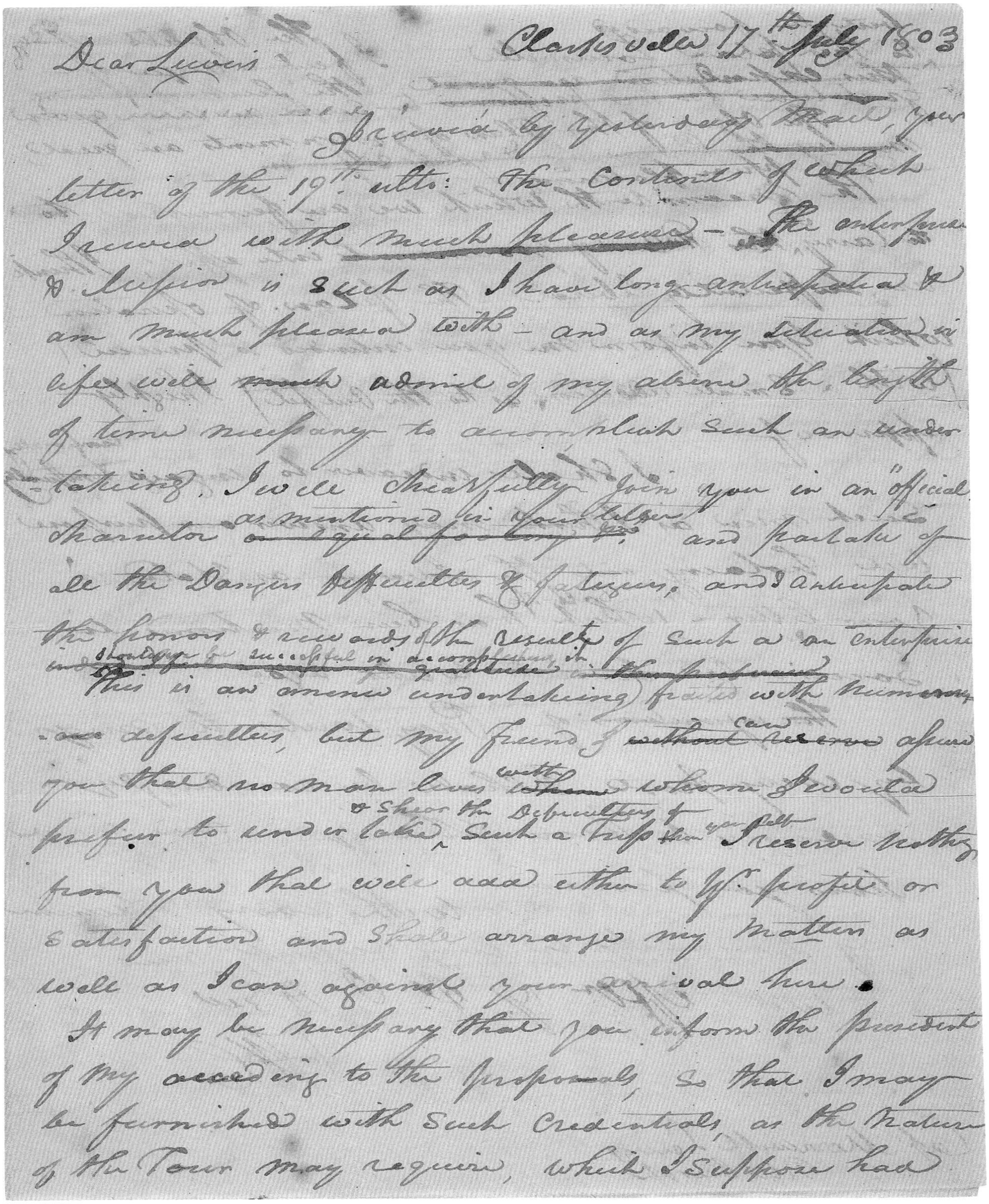

Dear Lewis   Clarksville 17th July 1803

I receiv'd by yesterdays Mail, your letter of the 19th ulto. the Contents of which I received with much pleasure— The enterprise & Mission is such as I have long anticipated & am much pleased with— and as my situation in life will admit of my absence the length of time necessary to accomplish such an under-taking. I will chearfully join you in an "official Charrector as mentioned in your letter, and partake of all the Dangers Difficulties & fatigues, and I anticipate the honors & rewards of the result of such an enterprise

This is an immense undertaking fraited with numerous difficulties, but my friend I can assure you that no man lives with whom I would prefer to undertake & Share the Difficulties of Such a trip than your self. I reserve nothing from you that will add either to yr. profit or Satisfaction and Shall arrange my matters as well as I can against your arrival here.

It may be necessary that you inform the president of my acceding to the proposals, so that I may be furnished with Such Credentials, as the Nature of the Tour may require, which I suppose had

of a legend, William had joined the U.S. Army; but despite fighting in the Battle of Fallen Timbers, he found glory elusive. By 1796, George was deeply indebted and alcoholic, and William quit the army to settle his brother's affairs. It was a thankless task, but in performing it, William got to know Jefferson—who, as the revolutionary governor of Virginia, held more than a little responsibility for George's financial troubles.

William Clark was four years older than Meriwether Lewis; he was a more experienced officer and a keen judge of people and situations. He was even less regularly educated than Lewis—and self-conscious about it. Charles Willson Peale thought him "too diffident of his abilities" on that score. But his earthy

Letter of Clark to Lewis, joining the expedition, 1803

Clark was so eager for his acceptance to reach Lewis that he sent at least three letters. This is his rough draft. "I will chearfully join you . . . and partake of the dangers, difficulties, and fatigues, and I anticipate the honors & rewards of the result of such an enterprise, should we be successful in accomplishing it. . . . but My friend I do assure you that no man lives whith whome I would perfur to undertake Such a Trip &c. as your self."

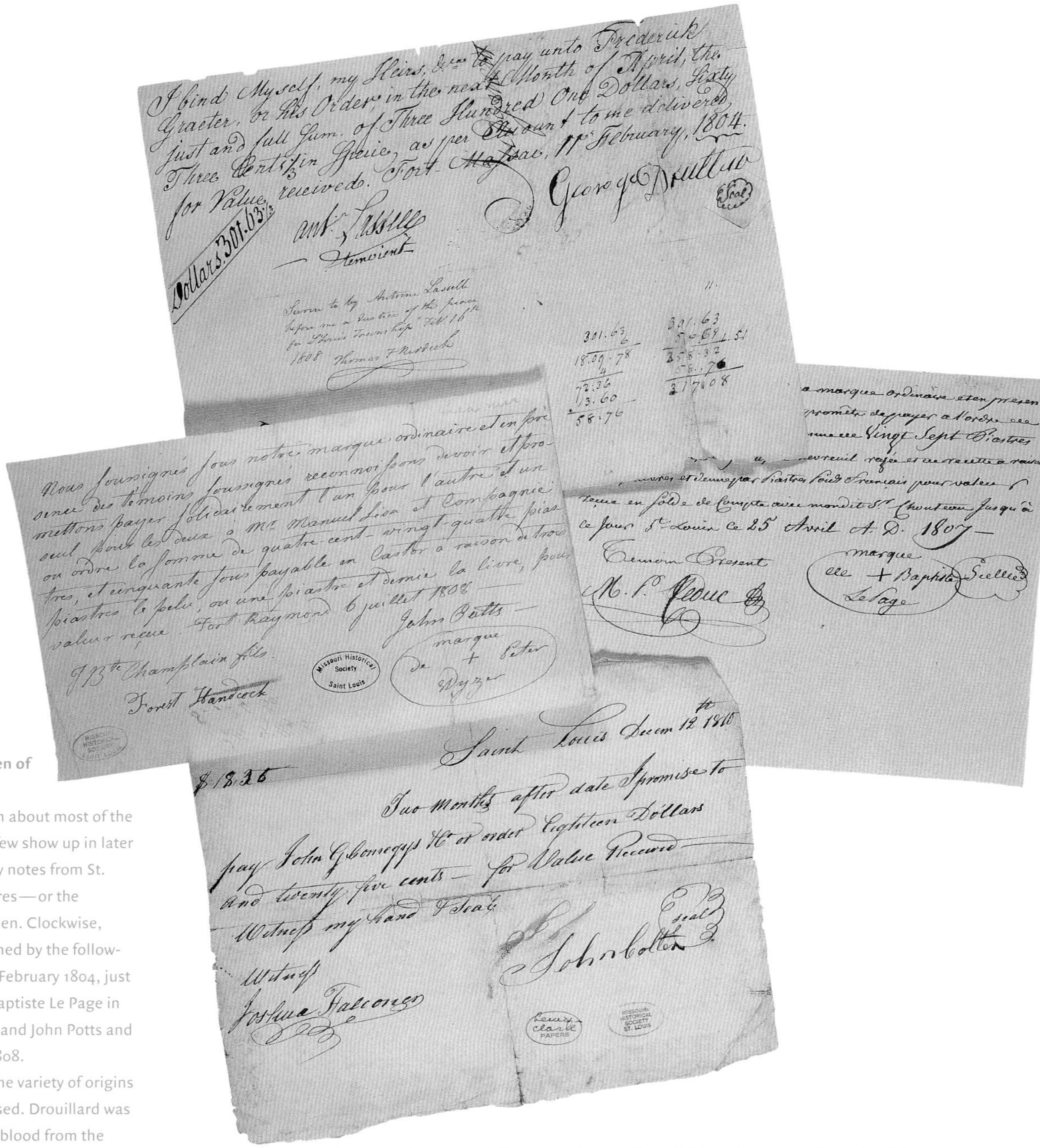
I bind Myself, my Heirs, &c to pay unto Frederik Graeter, or his Order in the next Month of April, the just and full Sum of Three Hundred One Dollars, Sixty Three Cents in Specie, as per Account to me delivered, for Value received. Fort Massac, 11th February, 1804.

George Drouillard (Seal)

Dollars 301.63

Ant. Lasselle
Temoin

Nous soussignés sous notre marque ordinaire et en présence des témoins soussignés reconnoissons devoir et promettons payer solidairement l'un pour l'autre et un seul pour les deux à Mr Manuel Lisa et Compagnie ou ordre la somme de quatre cent vingt quatre piastres, et cinquante sous payable en Castor a raison de trois piastres la pelu, ou une piastre et demie la livre, pour valeur reçue Fort Raymond 6 juillet 1808

John Potts
marque de + Peter Wyzer
J B Champlain fils
Forest Hancock

Témoin Présent
marque de + Baptiste Lesage

Saint Louis Decem 12th 1810
$18.25
Two Months after date I promise to pay John G Comegys & Co or order Eighteen Dollars and twenty five cents — for Value Received
Witness my hand & Seal
John Colter (seal)
Witness
Joshua Falconer

Documents signed by men of the Corps, 1804–10
Remarkably little is known about most of the men in the Corps; only a few show up in later records. These promissory notes from St. Louis contain the signatures—or the marks—of some of the men. Clockwise, from the top, they are signed by the following: George Drouillard in February 1804, just before setting out; Jean Baptiste Le Page in 1807; John Colter in 1810; and John Potts and Peter Wyzer [Weiser] in 1808.

These men represent the variety of origins that the Corps encompassed. Drouillard was a French-Shawnee mixed-blood from the Cape Girardeau district of Missouri; Le Page was a French-Canadian who had been living among the Cheyenne in the Black Hills; Potts was a German immigrant, and Weiser was a native Pennsylvanian, both serving as infantry soldiers from different units; and Colter was one of the "nine young men from Kentucky." Two of them—Le Page and Weiser—were illiterate. Drouillard outranked the rest, being paid for his professional skill as an interpreter, but afterward he seems to have fared badly in the shifting legal and class structure of the newly American Mississippi Valley, for he was in and out of legal trouble. All of these men earned their livings in the fur trade after the expedition; Drouillard, Potts, and probably Weiser were killed by the Blackfeet near Three Forks in 1810, and Colter barely escaped the same fate. Colter became the first Euro-American to explore the Yellowstone Park region, and he contributed to Clark's geographical information on that area. Le Page's later life is unknown.

observations and fractured spelling hid a sharp and logical intellect. He was far more the Enlightenment rationalist than Lewis. He wrote in an early diary: "Man cannot make principles; he can only discover them. The most formidable weapon against errors of every kind, is Reason." Reason was a weapon he deployed frequently.[32]

By contrast, Lewis was a more complex story. His cousin described him unflatteringly, as family members often will: "stiff and without grace, bowlegged, awkward, formal, and almost without flexibility. His face was comely and by many considered handsome. It bore to my vision a very strong resemblance to Buonaparte. . . . He was always remarkable for perseverance, which in the early period of his life seemed nothing more than obstinacy." Not everyone thought Jefferson had chosen well by putting him in charge. The St. Louis businessman Manuel Lisa described him as "a very headstrong, & in many instances an imprudent man," and Levi Lincoln, the attorney general, wrote Jefferson with cautious tact, "From my ideas of Capt. Lewis he will be much more likely, in case of difficulty, to push too far, than to rec[e]de too soon." When Clark joined the expedition, Secretary of War Henry Dearborn gave an almost audible sigh of relief: "Mr. W. Clark's having consented to accompany

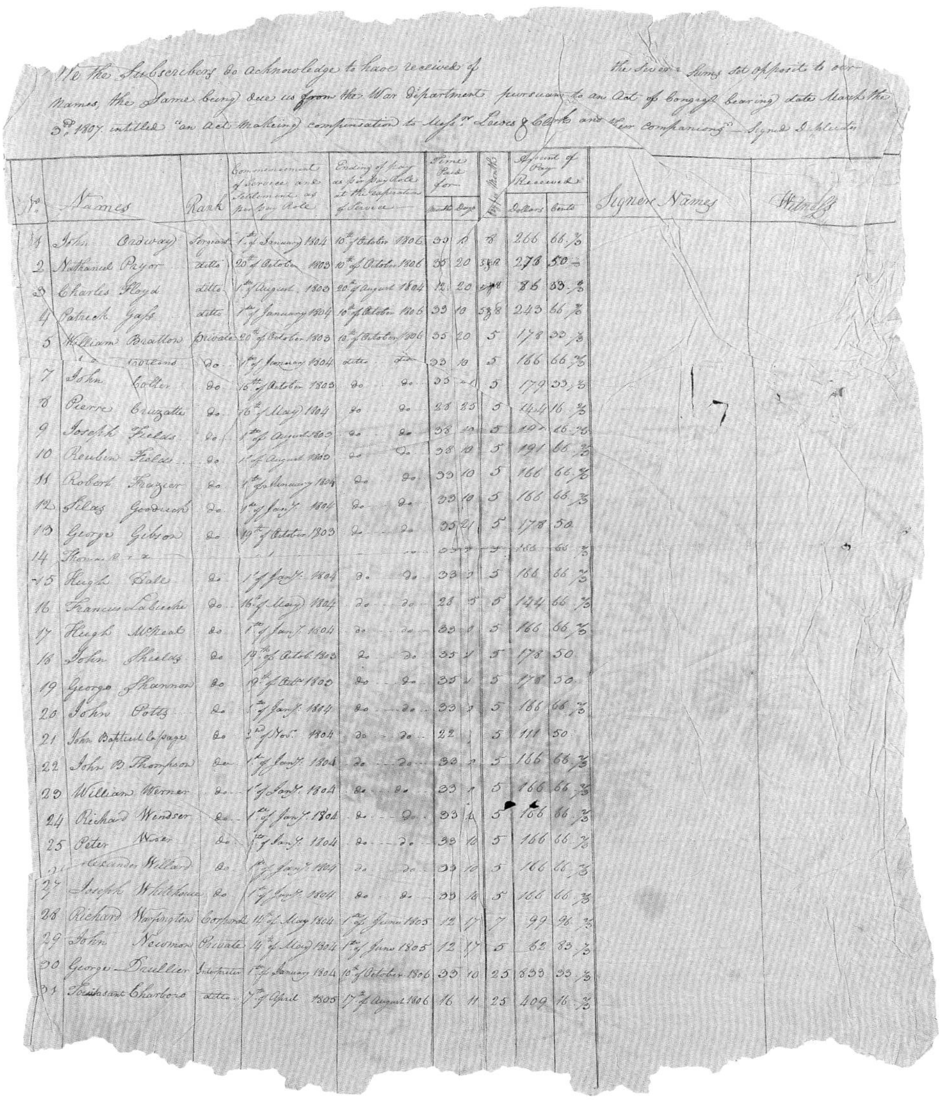

We the Subscribers do acknowledge to have received of   the Several Sums set opposite to our Names, the Same being due us from the War Department pursuant to an Act of Congress bearing date March the 3rd, 1807 intitled "an Act making compensation to Messrs. Lewis & Clark and their Companions" Signed Duplicates

No.	Names	Rank	Commencement of Service and Settlement as per Pay Role	Ending of Pay as per Pay Role at the expiration of Service	Time Paid for: Months	Time Paid for: Days	Pay per Month	Amount of Pay Received: Dollars	Amount of Pay Received: Cents	Signers Names	Witness
1	John Ordway	Sergeant	1st of January 1804	10th of October 1806	33	10	8	266	66 2/3		
2	Nathaniel Pryor	ditto	20th of October 1803	10th of October 1806	35	20	5 8/12	278	50		
3	Charles Floyd	ditto	1st of August 1803	20th of August 1804	12	20	[illegible]	86	33 1/3		
4	Patrick Gass	ditto	1st of January 1804	10th of October 1806	33	10	5 8/12	243	66 2/3		
5	William Bratton	private	20th of October 1803	10th of October 1806	35	20	5	178	33 1/3		
[illegible]	[illegible] Collins	do	1st of January 1804	ditto	33	10	5	166	66 2/3		
7	John Colter	do	15th of October 1803	do	35	[illegible]	5	179	33 1/3		
8	Pierre Cruzatte	do	16th of May 1804	do	28	25	5	144	16 2/3		
9	Joseph Fields	do	1st of August 1803	do	38	10	5	[illegible]	66 2/3		
10	Reubin Fields	do	1st of August 1803	do	38	10	5	191	66 2/3		
11	Robert Frazier	do	1st of January 1804	do	33	10	5	166	66 2/3		
12	Silas Goodrich	do	1st of Jany. 1804	do	33	10	5	166	66 2/3		
13	George Gibson	do	19th of October 1803	do	35	21	5	178	50		
14	Thomas [illegible]				33	[illegible]	5	166	66 2/3		
15	Hugh Hall	do	1st of Jany. 1804	do	33	[illegible]	5	166	66 2/3		
16	Francis Labiche	do	16th of May 1804	do	28	5	5	144	66 2/3		
17	Hugh McNeal	do	1st of Jany. 1804	do	33	[illegible]	5	166	66 2/3		
18	John Shields	do	19th of Octob. 1803	do	35	[illegible]	5	178	50		
19	George Shannon	do	19th of Octr. 1803	do	35	[illegible]	5	178	50		
20	John Potts	do	1st of Jany. 1804	do	33	[illegible]	5	166	66 2/3		
21	John Baptiest Lepage	do	2nd of Novr. 1804	do	22	[illegible]	5	111	50		
22	John B. Thompson	do	1st of Jany. 1804	do	33	[illegible]	5	166	66 2/3		
23	William Werner	do	1st of Jany. 1804	do	33	[illegible]	5	166	66 2/3		
24	Richard Windser	do	1st of Jany. 1804	do	33	[illegible]	5	166	66 2/3		
25	Peter Wiser	do	1st of Jany. 1804	do	33	10	5	166	66 2/3		
[illegible]	Alexander Willard	do	1st of Jany. 1804	do	33	10	5	166	66 2/3		
27	Joseph Whitehouse	do	1st of Jany. 1804	do	33	10	5	166	66 2/3		
28	Richard Warfington	Corporal	14th of May 1804	1st of June 1805	12	17	7	99	96 2/3		
29	John Newman	Private	14th of May 1804	1st of June 1805	12	17	5	62	83 1/3		
30	George Drullier	Interpreter	1st of January 1804	10th of October 1806	33	10	25	833	33 1/3		
31	Touissant Charbono	ditto	7th of April 1805	17th of August 1806	16	11	25	409	16 2/3		

Roster of men, 1807
This document is one of several prepared by Lewis and Clark for getting the expedition members' pay from the government. It lists only the adult male members of the "permanent party," who went all the way to the Pacific and back. Another contingent of soldiers and boatmen went as far as Fort Mandan and returned with the keelboat.

Capt. Lewis . . . adds very much to the ballance of chances in favour of ultimate success."[33]

Jefferson heard none of this. He later eulogized Lewis as a man of "courage undaunted, possessing a firmness & perseverance of purpose which nothing but impossibilities could divert . . . honest, disinterested, liberal, of sound understanding and a fidelity to truth." And yet, Jefferson also saw a darker side: "While he lived with me in Washington, I observed at times sensible depressions of mind." In fact, Lewis was moody and introspective, given to self-dramatization in his journals, as solitary as Clark was gregarious, but a far more astute observer and capable of extraordinary insight. Intellectually, he was much closer than Clark to the emerging sensibility of the Romantic era.[34]

Clark's reaction to the invitation did not leave Lewis guessing about his feelings. "My friend I join you with hand & Heart and anticipate advantages which will certainly derive from the accomplishment of so vast, Hazidous and fatiguing enterprize," Clark wrote back. He heartily approved of Lewis's plans, and suggested only "a Small addition as to the outfit." By the time they set out, that small addition would quadruple the size of the expedition.[35]

The rest of the Corps assembled around the two leaders as they traveled down the Ohio. Lewis and Clark agreed they wanted no "Gentlemens sons," who would not be "accustomed to labour." Lewis warned from Pittsburgh, "Much must depend on a judicious scelection of our men . . . outherwise they

Razor and brush, late 1700s or early 1800s
Keeping up standards of appearance was necessary to enforce military discipline and to maintain a distance from other residents of the West, so the captains almost certainly required the men to shave. The razors earned mentions only when they wore out and were traded to the Indians; one man traded his for a woven hat on the Columbia, Clark gave a razor to the Clatsop chief Coboway, and Robert Frazer sold his for two Spanish dollars on the return trip. Brushes were not mentioned but could have been used with the twelve pounds of Castile soap they brought on the trip.

Finger-woven sash, late 1700s to early 1800s
Several members of the Corps, notably George Drouillard and Pierre Cruzatte, belonged to a unique cultural group of the frontier: the métis or mixed-bloods, who lived with one foot in each society, Indian and European. In over a century of habitation, the French of the Mississippi and Ohio Valleys had intermarried and blended with the tribes, borrowing traits from them and creating a new culture that was neither wholly Indian nor wholly French. They had their own dress and art styles. This type of sash, called *ceinture fleché* (arrow pattern), is often associated with the métis of the Great Lakes and Mississippi Valley. It is made using an ancient hand-braiding technique. In the early nineteenth century, high-status métis men like Drouillard sometimes wore sashes with frock coats, either underneath or over the coat. This one is from the collection that included the Peale's Museum artifacts.

will reather clog than further the objects in view." He had no need to worry; Clark's judgment proved reliable.[36]

The men came from several sources. First to sign up were nine Kentucky backwoodsmen, mostly recruited by Clark; they proved to be some of the most valuable members of the expedition, and all went on to the Pacific. From Forts Massac and Kaskaskia came a mix of soldiers from infantry and artillery regiments. On the Mississippi the expedition added some French boatmen to paddle the pirogues. Then there were two civilian employees: George Drouillard, the interpreter from an old and prominent Shawnee-French family; and York, Clark's African American slave.[37]

What kind of person would sign up for such a project? There is no easy answer because the Corps, like the nation, was widely varied in ethnicity, education, wealth, and background. They were young—mostly in their twenties or

Man's shirt, 1785–1800
Lewis wanted thirty shirts of flannel and "Strong linnen" but was able to get only calico (cotton) with ruffles and flannel with linen collars and cuffs. The shirts worn with uniforms were undoubtedly white, but fatigue shirts were a variety of colors and patterns. Once, Lewis spoke of wearing a yellow flannel shirt, and at another time, he bought a horse for "an old checked shirt." On the return trip the men eagerly purchased linen shirts from the first trader they met to replace their leather clothing. This plain shirt is of middling-quality linen. Its pattern is typical of the late eighteenth century: a square of fabric gathered at the neck and reinforced at the shoulders, with gussets at the neck and under the sleeves and with full sleeves gathered at the shoulder and cuff. The high collar was meant to be folded over a stock.

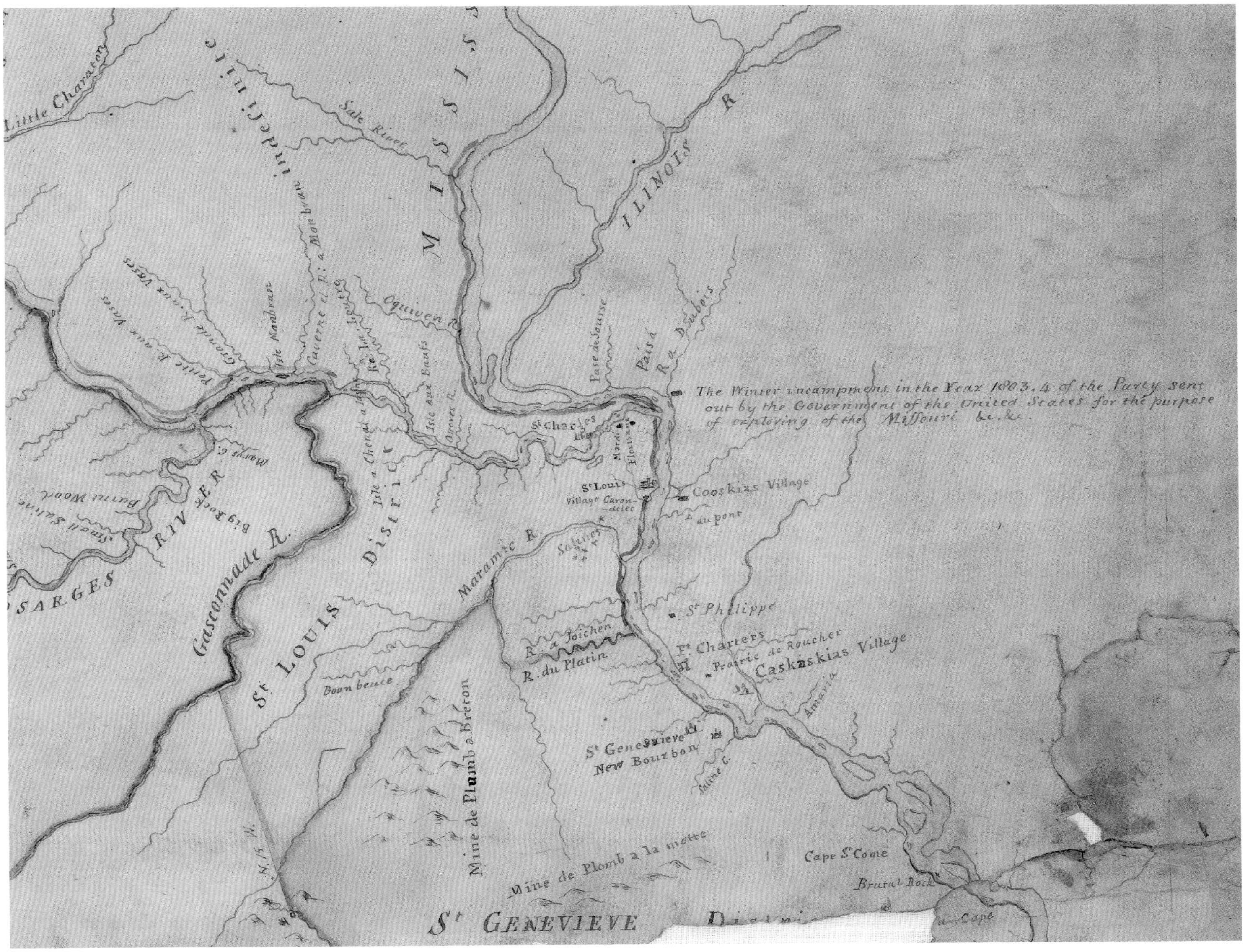

early thirties—though George Shannon was only eighteen and John Shields was thirty-four. Only two (York and Shields) were married. The majority came from Kentucky and Pennsylvania, but there were also Yankees, such as John Ordway and Alexander Willard. Patrick Gass was of Irish ancestry. Two of them—John Potts and Peter Weiser—spoke German. At least four of the permanent party spoke French. Two (Joseph and Reubin Field) were brothers, and two (Nathaniel Pryor and Charles Floyd) were cousins. Some wrote serviceable prose in their journals; others were illiterate. In sum, they were what Lewis wanted: "good hunters, stout, healthy, unmarried men, accustomed to the woods, and capable of bearing bodily fatigue in a pretty considerable degree."[38]

Map of the region along the Mississippi River (detail), 1803
The Mississippi was the western boundary of the United States when Clark drew this map of the area where they wintered. This was part of a larger map summarizing geographical information gathered in St. Louis. In 1803 the Missouri River entered the Mississippi opposite the small stream called Rivière Dubois (now named Wood River), where the Corps established winter quarters. Today, the Missouri has shifted three miles farther south. Lewis sent the original of this map to Jefferson on May 18, 1804, and it is sometimes called "Lewis and Clark's Map of 1804." Lewis described it as "A Map of a part of Upper Louisiana, compiled from the best information that Capt. Clark and myself could collect, from the Inhabitants of Saint Louis, haistily corrected by the information obtained from the Osage Indians lately arrived at this place."

POLITICAL WINTER

Lewis's original plan had been to travel several hundred miles up the Missouri before camping for the winter, but delays related to the building of the keelboat prevented him from reaching St. Louis until early December, though he rode ahead of the main party. His first act was to visit the lieutenant governor, who administered Upper Louisiana for Spain. Charles Dehault Delassus had, as yet, received no official word of the transfer of Louisiana to the United States; though he received Lewis "with much politeness," he said that his orders "forbad his granting . . . permission at this time to asscend the Missouri river."

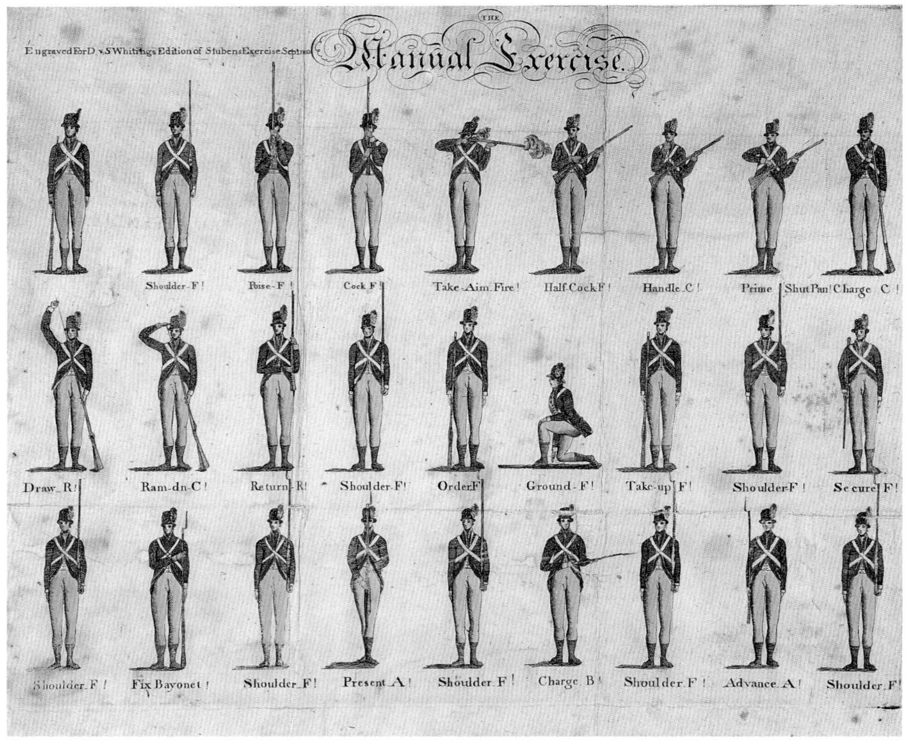

The Manual Exercise, 1803

Much of the men's time at Camp Dubois was spent in infantry drills. Daily parades, like athletic team practices, developed skills, solidarity, and discipline. The captains also used the parade, when everyone was assembled, to read orders and make announcements. Later, the men would perform these drills before Indian audiences. The instructions come from the 1803 edition of Baron Von Steuben's *Regulations for the Order and Discipline of the Troops of the United States*, a training manual originally developed by the Prussian military instructor for George Washington's troops during the Revolution; it remained the army's official military manual through the War of 1812. The uniforms shown match the style used in 1803.

Map of the Mississippi Country, 1804

In December 1803 Lewis first met the probable maker of this map: Antoine Soulard, the surveyor-general of Upper Louisiana for the Spanish government. Lewis noted that Soulard was "very friendly" and added: "He gave me many unqualifyed assurances of his willingness to serve me." However, when Lewis started to copy a census document, the Frenchman stopped him. Lewis gave Soulard's explanation: "The jealousy of his gouvernment was such, that if it were known that he had given me permission to copy an official paper, that it would injure him with his government." By the next spring, when news of the Louisiana Purchase was public, Soulard became more relaxed and shared several maps with Lewis, probably including this one. It shows the village of St. Louis.

Since it was late in the year anyway, Lewis gracefully agreed to camp for the winter on the American side of the Mississippi.[39]

The keelboat and Clark arrived in St. Louis soon after, "under Sales & Cullers. . . . the admiration of the people were So great, that hundreds Came to the bank to view us." The men went several miles north to build their winter quarters near a small stream named Rivière Dubois, where they could look across to the mouth of the Missouri emptying its muddy western waters into the Mississippi. The spot was good for discipline, being "Clear of the means of Corruption" at St. Louis. There, they worked on the drills and skills—particularly marksmanship—that would turn the motley crew of recruits into a functioning team.[40]

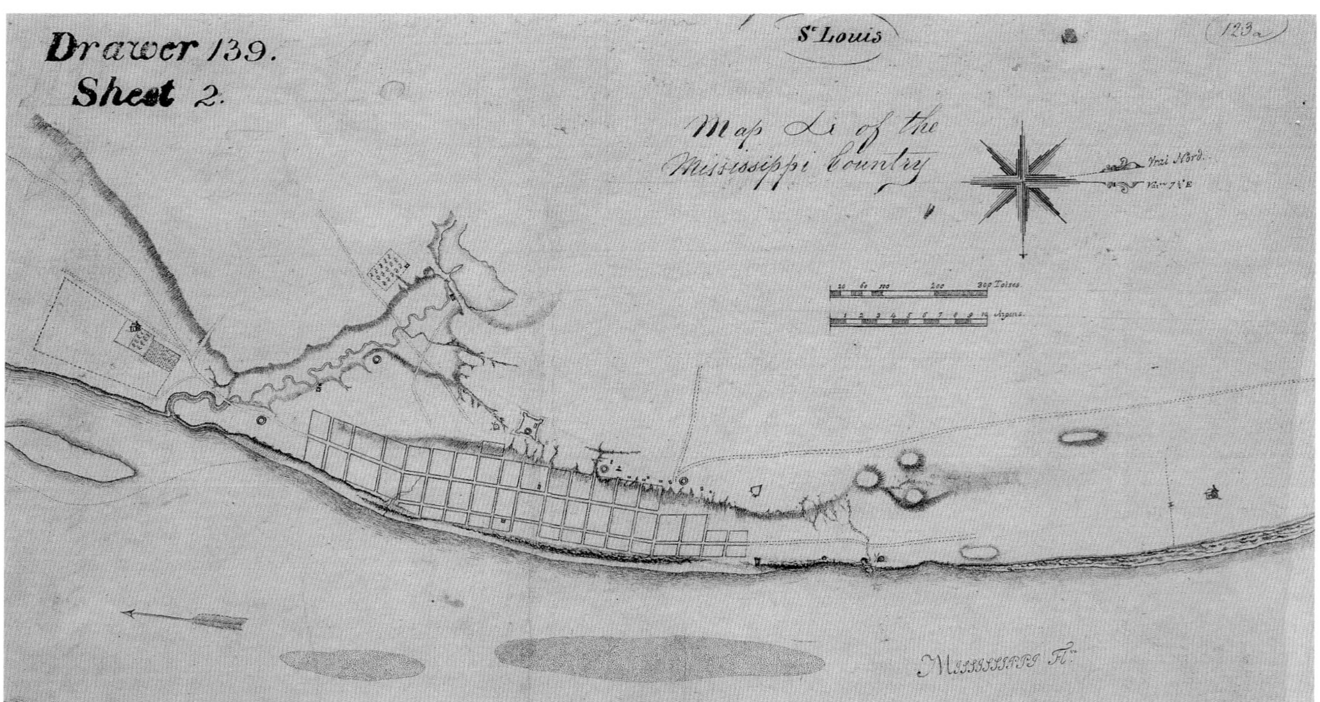

Dinnerware and books from St. Louis, c. 1761–1815
The elite of St. Louis entertained Lewis and Clark over the winter of 1803–4. When in town, they both stayed in the three-story stone mansion of Pierre Chouteau, the son of the town's founder and a leading merchant who had made his fortune monopolizing the fur trade of the Osage Indians. These dishes and salt cellar all belonged to either Pierre Chouteau or his brother Auguste and date to an early enough time for Lewis and Clark to have used them. The napkin on which they rest belonged to Nicolas Jarrot, a trader from Cahokia who translated for Lewis and Clark. The books belonged to the libraries of the lieutenant governor, Charles Dehault Delassus, and the town's doctor, Antoine Saugrain, an aristocratic Parisian royalist refugee who also entertained the American visitors. The books show the depth of intellectual life in the remote outpost, for they cover the topics of philosophy, natural history, and medicine.

The fleshpots of St. Louis were not very deep, but the captains enjoyed them that winter nonetheless. The town was laid out like a rural French village, with the houses clustered on the riverbank, surrounded by some dilapidated fortifications and with long, narrow farm fields stretching out behind. The best houses were three-story, pillared mansions of stone, but more common were wood ones with peaked roofs and wide, shady porches on all four sides. Lewis and Clark alternated visiting the town, to keep an officer always in charge at Camp Dubois, having learned by experience that bedlam broke out when they were both gone. While the men sawed boards and packed salt pork in kegs, the officers drank French wine and attended balls with ladies in Paris fashions.[41]

Lewis, the ardent young republican who had once addressed his own mother as "Citizen," saw St. Louis as a fossil of *ancien régime* society, and he was not far from wrong. It was a highly stratified world where authority was unquestioned. "These people are so much accustomed to elude the eye of dispotic power, that . . . they move more as tho' the *fear of the commandant*, than *that of god*, was before their eyes," Lewis observed. His main mission in St. Louis was gathering information, and he naturally fell under suspicion of being a spy. That did not prevent his being entertained in the upper echelons of St. Louis society, which were as educated and cosmopolitan as those of New Orleans or Montreal.[42]

The news that came that winter changed everything. It arrived in mid-February: Napoleon had sold the Louisiana Territory to the United States. It was the new nation's first venture into colonialism. When the news had broken in the East, the public reaction had been mixed; Caspar Wistar reported that his Philadelphia circle thought it "the most important & beneficial transaction

Spanish medal and sword, pre-1787 and 1777
This silver medal with a relief bust of King Carlos III of Spain, who reigned from 1759 to 1788, was presented to Charles Dehault Delassus, the last lieutenant governor of Upper Louisiana, whose duty it was to turn over the territory to the United States. Though he was appointed by Spain, Delassus was a Flemish refugee from the French Revolution, praised for his "most elegant manners" and his "pleasing and winning address." The sword is of the type used in Louisiana between 1774 and 1804 by the Spanish infantry. The blade is stamped "POR EL REY CARLOS III" and "YNFANTª Tº 1777," identifying it as the product of the Toledo arsenal established by Carlos III in 1761.

which has occurred since the declaration of Independence, & next to it, most like to influence or regulate the destinies of our Country." But other thoughtful people feared that an imperial United States was not sustainable as a democracy. Becoming a colonial power would, they feared, either require an undesirably strong central government or fracture the union on geographic lines. They were both right and wrong; westward expansion vastly increased the power of the federal government, and the question of whether to extend slavery into the West would eventually tear the union apart. But both would happen much differently than they imagined.[43]

The reaction in St. Louis was also mixed, but the citizens nevertheless put on a good show, which Clark described to his brother. Captain Amos Stoddard, commandant of Kaskaskia, arrived on February 24, 1804, to represent both France and the United States and was "ascorted into town by about 20 Citizens." Delassus received him and set the date of March 9 for the formal transfer to take place. That night the officers dined with Delassus, "a most Sumpcious Dinner, & a large Compy. a great Deel of formality and parade was displayed." On the day when the formal transfer of Upper Louisiana took place, Meriwether Lewis signed the document as a witness.[44]

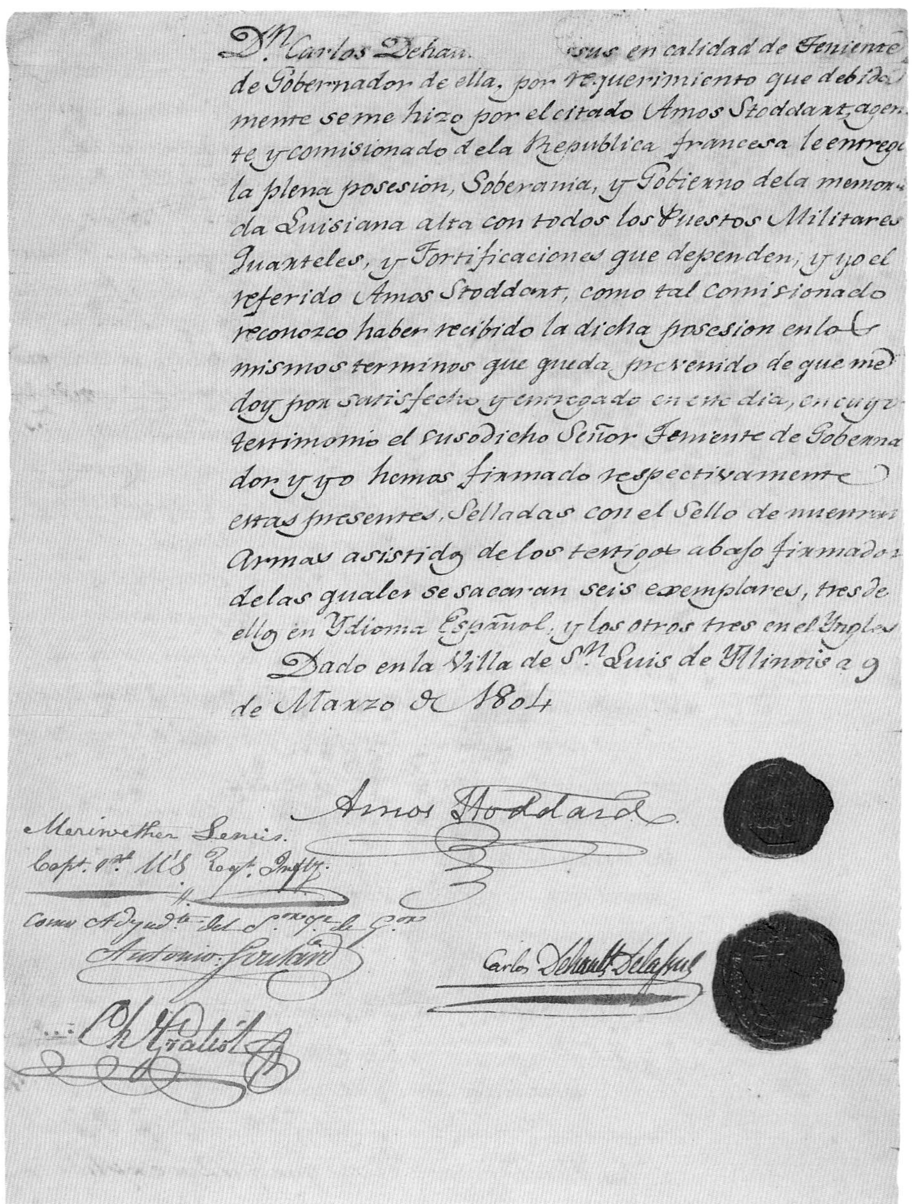
Dn Carlos Dehau... ssus en calidad de Teniente
de Gobernador de ella, por requerimiento que debida-
mente se me hizo por el citado Amos Stoddart, agen-
te y comisionado de la Republica francesa le entregé
la plena posesion, Soberania, y Gobierno de la memora-
da Luisiana alta con todos los Puestos Militares
Quarteles, y Fortificaciones que dependen; y yo el
referido Amos Stoddart, como tal Comisionado
reconozco haber recibido la dicha posesion en los
mismos terminos que queda prevenido de que me
doy por satisfecho y entregado en este dia, en cuyo
testimonio el susodicho Señor Teniente de Gobernador y yo hemos firmado respectivamente
estas presentes, Selladas con el Sello de nuestras
Armas asistido de los testigos abajo firmados
de las quales se sacaran seis exemplares, tres de
ellos en Ydioma Español, y los otros tres en el Ingles
Dado en la Villa de Sn Luis de Ylinois a 9
de Marzo de 1804

Amos Stoddard

Meriwether Lewis.
Capt. 1st U.S. Regt. Infty.

Como Ayudte del Sr Tente de Gor
Antonio Soulard

Carlos Dehault Delassus

Ch. Gratiot

Louisiana Purchase transfer document, 1804

Though the treaty had been ratified by the U.S. Congress in October 1803, the formal transfer of Louisiana took place in two stages. Lower Louisiana was transferred in New Orleans in December 1803, and Upper Louisiana was transferred in its capital, St. Louis, the following March 9. This is the back of the document that signed over the Missouri Valley first from Spain to France and then from France to the United States. Meriwether Lewis signed as a witness.

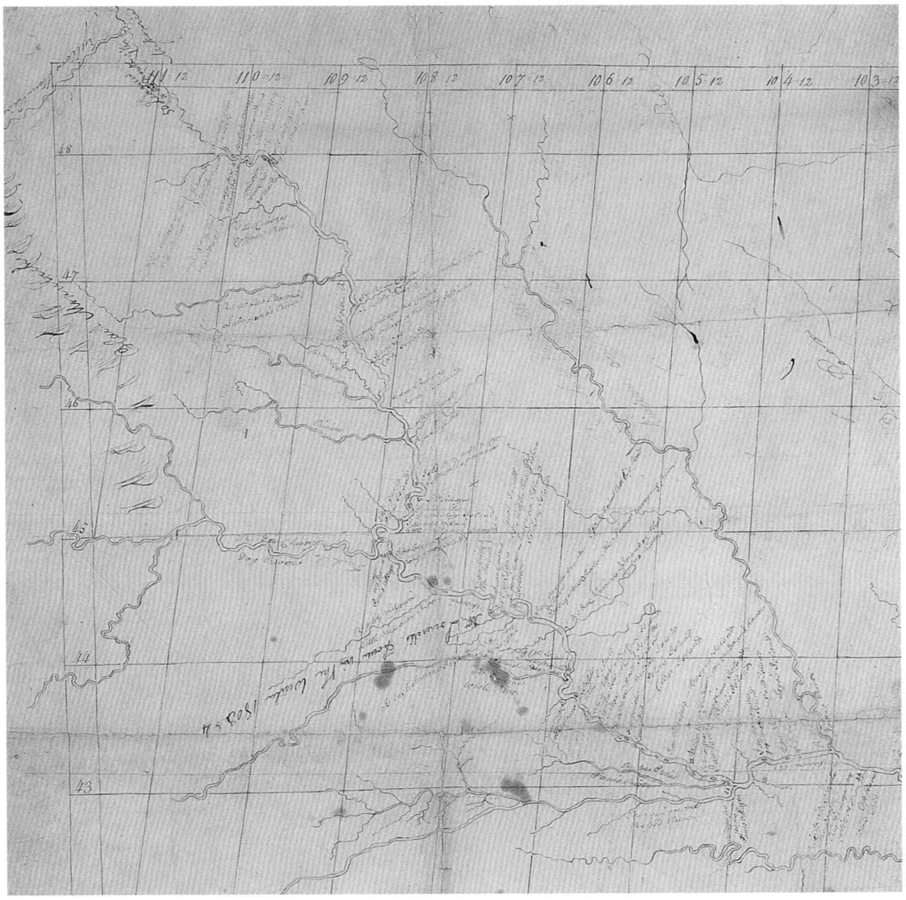

Map of the Missouri River (detail), 1797
If Lewis ever thought the Missouri was unexplored, this map would have set him straight. It was sent to Clark in November 1803 by William Henry Harrison, governor of Indiana Territory, and Lewis described it to Jefferson as "a map of the Missouri river, from it's mouth to the Mandane nation." This detail shows the part of the river roughly from Omaha north. It was drawn by James Mackay or John Evans, entrepreneurs who explored the Missouri in 1795–97 in order to "ascertain the discovery of the Pacific Sea." Evans spent the winter with the Mandan, and from their information he mapped the Missouri as far as the Three Forks. Lewis and Clark took this map on the expedition, and Clark followed their progress on it, writing in the English names of the rivers as they traveled.

The change of regimes opened the floodgates of information. Lewis and Clark laid their hands on one map, by the fur traders James Mackay and John Evans, that showed the Missouri in exquisite detail as far as the Mandan villages north of present Bismarck, North Dakota. Another map, though less detailed, showed the Yellowstone River, the Great Falls, and the southward bend of the Missouri as far as the Three Forks. Suddenly, the West that had seemed so speculative from Monticello came into sharp focus—all but the people.

The Louisiana Purchase changed the mission of the Corps of Discovery. Now the Corps members were not just explorers seeking information but were representatives of a foreign power "taking possession" of the land. On January 22, Jefferson wrote Lewis with supplemental instructions. "Being now become sovereigns of the country, without however any diminution of the Indian rights of occupancy . . . It will now be proper you should inform those through whose country you will pass . . . that henceforward we become their fathers and friends, and that we shall endeavor that they shall have no cause to lament the change."[45]

That too would turn out differently than expected.

TWO Learning Diplomacy

In all your intercourse with the natives, treat them in the most friendly & conciliatory manner which their own conduct will admit.

—THOMAS JEFFERSON TO MERIWETHER LEWIS[1]

"Honored Parence," young Sergeant John Ordway wrote his family in Hebron, New Hampshire, "I now embrace this oppertunity of writing to you once more to let you know where I am and where I am going. . . . I am now on an expidition to the westward, with Capt. Lewis and Capt. Clark. . . . We are to ascend the Missouri River with a boat as far as it is navigable and then to go by land, to the western ocean, if nothing prevents &c. . . . This party consists of 25 picked Men . . . and I am So happy as to be one of them. . . . I and all the party are if we live to Return, to Receive our Discharge . . . if we chuse it."[2]

At four o'clock in the afternoon on May 14, 1804, some forty-eight men in three boats crossed the Mississippi, so recently the western boundary of the United States, and entered the Missouri River. The boats rode low with about thirty tons of supplies and equipment, enough to fill three modern semitrailers. But their heaviest load consisted of the hopes of Thomas Jefferson.

One of the president's last missives to Lewis had turned up the pressure a notch. "The enquiries are perpetual as to your progress," he wrote. Only the rancorous political opposition scoffed at the expedition and "would rejoice in it's failure." He added: "I hope you will . . . be the living witness of their malice and folly. . . . assure all your party that we have our eyes turned on them with anxiety for their safety & the success of their enterprize."[3]

Despite the reminder that Jefferson's political future rode with him, Lewis's spirits were high as he set out from St. Louis on horseback to join the rest of the party at the French town of St. Charles some twenty-three miles up the Missouri. "After bidding an affectionate adieu to my Hostis . . . and some of my fair friends of St. Louis," he wrote, "we set forward to that village in order to join my friend companion and fellow labourer Capt. William Clark who had previously arrived at that place with the party destined for the discovery of the interior of the continent of North America."[4]

A five-day delay at St. Charles gave them a chance to rearrange the boats' cargo, reinstate discipline, and enjoy the entertainment of the citizens. Clark privately summed up the town, "This Village Contns. about 100 houses, the most of them Small and indefferent and about 450 inhabitents Chiefly French, those people appear pore, polite & harmonious." The final departure of the Corps was festive, according to Private (soon to be Sergeant) Patrick Gass: "At 4 o'clock in the afternoon we left this place under a salute of three cheers from the inhabitants, which we returned with three more and a discharge of three guns."[5]

Compass, 1803
This was either one of the "3 Brass pocket Compasses" or the "Silver plated pocket Compass" Lewis bought from Thomas Whitney in Philadelphia. Lewis carried a compass on his frequent solitary excursions away from the river. He used it with the lid fully open so that the small upright arms with slits lined up to take readings on distant landmarks. At some point, the bottom was broken in half and repaired with two brass plates. It was passed down in the family of Captain Robert A. McCabe, a "fine, jolly" army man who got to know Clark later in life.

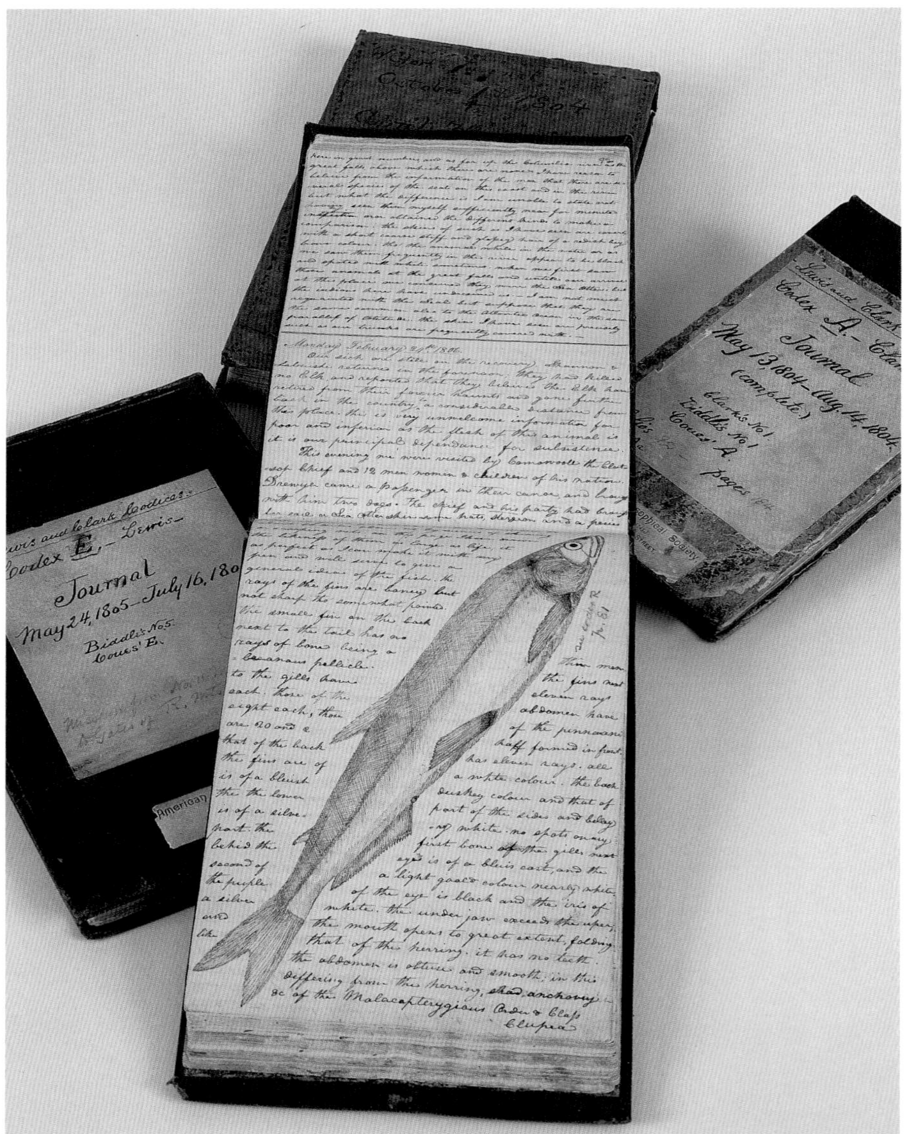

Journals of Lewis and Clark, 1804–6
Lewis and Clark kept their journals in small notebooks bound in red Morocco leather, brown suede, and marbled cardboard. The notebooks hinge at the top, like steno pads. Jefferson had instructed, "Several copies . . . of your other notes should be made at leisure times, & put into the care of the most trustworthy of your attendants, to guard, by multiplying them, against the accidental losses to which they will be exposed." Accordingly, two copies of many of the journals survive. Lewis and Clark did not write separate journals but collaborated and copied from each other; however, Clark's terse, factual entries are often easy to distinguish from Lewis's literary, descriptive ones. Lewis went for long periods without writing, including most of the upriver journey in 1804; when he sent those volumes to Jefferson, Lewis wrote, "Capt. Clark dose not wish this journal exposed in it's present state, but has no objection, that one or more copies of it be made by some confidential person under your direction, correcting it's gramatical errors &c." The labels were put on the covers by the historian Elliott Coues in the 1890s.

Page 82: *Sioux Dog Feast* (detail), 1832–37. See page 105.

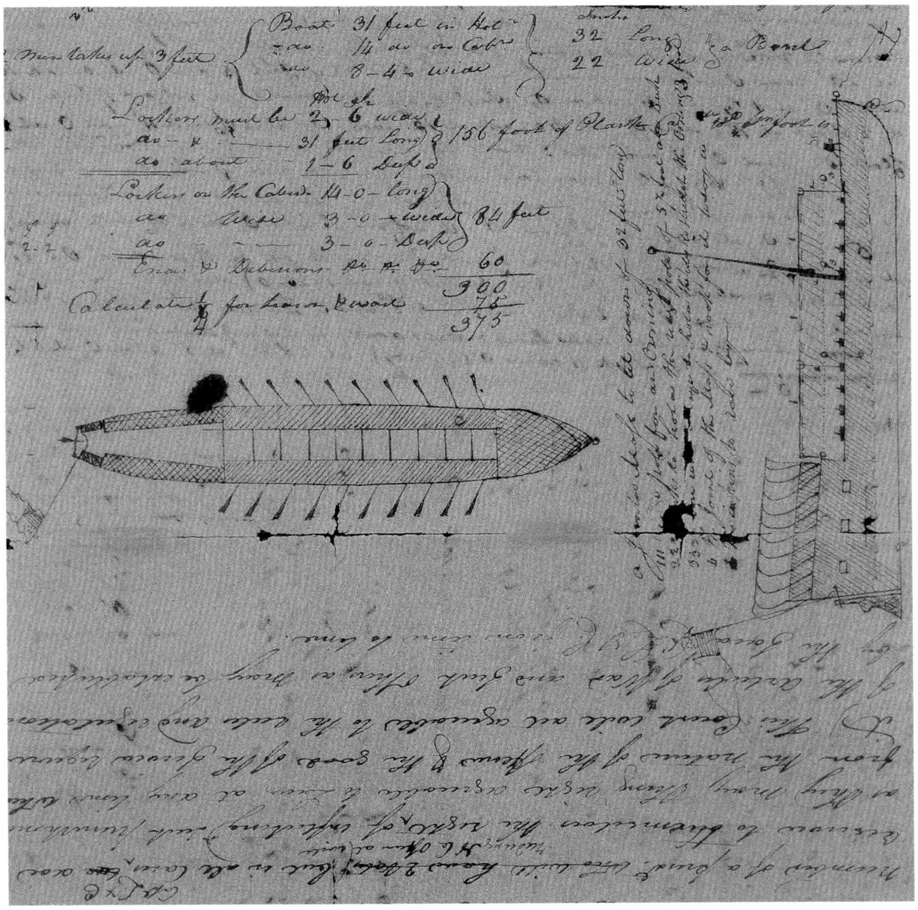

Sketch of the keelboat, 1804
The size of the keelboat made one observer doubt that Lewis was "able to fully accomplish the object of his mission." Thomas Rodney, who met Lewis on the Ohio, wrote: "His vessel fitted with very nice and comfortable accommodations with great stores of baggage . . . will be very heavy to go up against the stream. . . . This will be the cause of great delay." Clark apparently drew this sketch, the only contemporary image of the keelboat, to figure out square footage for sleeping and lockers. Built by shipwrights in Pittsburgh, the vessel was 55 feet long with an 8-foot 4-inch beam and a 3-foot draft. It originally had two masts, but one was broken and removed before the Corps started up the Missouri. When there was no wind, the boat was propelled by twenty-two oars, poles, or a tow rope. The expedition was rarely able to make more than ten miles a day in the keelboat.

***Snags on the Missouri*, 1833**
"Lined with Snags as far as we could See down," Clark described the Missouri River on July 14. The channel was still hazardous with sunken timber when Karl Bodmer painted it twenty-nine years later.

Keg and canteen, c. 1800 and 1778
"Some punishment of two men *Hall & Collins* for takeing whiskey out of the Barrel last night," Clark recorded on June 29. He noted that juries of the other men were always "verry ready to punish Such Crimes." In Philadelphia, Lewis purchased 6 iron-bound kegs (like this one for cider), each containing five gallons of strong spirit wine, and in St. Louis, he added at least another 18 kegs of whiskey. In all, the boat lading included at least 123 kegs containing pork, flour, corn, salt, and hog's lard as well as alcohol. On the Pacific, having run out of liquor, the men reused some of the iron-bound kegs to pack salt they made. None of their kegs survive.

Each man would have been outfitted with a canteen. This one is not army issue, but expedition members who furnished their own equipment may have owned ones similar to it.

As they traveled up the Missouri River, Lewis and Clark saw largely what their expectations had prepared them to see: a land of bounty and beauty, practically preformed into farms. The lower river was already dotted with French villages and American homes; on May 23 they passed the settlement of the frontiersman Daniel Boone, who had beaten them to the Missouri by five years. As cultivated land fell behind, they still saw a pastoral Eden: "Leek Green Grass, well calculated for the sweetest and most norushing hay—interspersed with Cops [copses] of trees, Spreding ther lofty branchs over Pools Springs or Brooks of fine water. Groops of Shrubs covered with the most delicious froot is to be seen in every direction, and nature appears to have exerted herself to butify the Senery."[6]

But the Missouri soon demolished the image of easy river navigation that had induced them to bring the large keelboat. The upriver journey was hazardous with snags and sandbars, swift currents, and collapsing banks. Only a few days out, they came to "a Verry bad part of the River Called the Deavels race ground." The two pirogues—thirty- to forty-foot wooden canoes, at least one propelled by skillful French boatmen—passed through safely, but the unwieldy "barge," or keelboat, was caught in the current and nearly overturned. That was only the beginning of their problems. On June 9 Clark wrote a typical entry: "We had like to have Stove our boat, in going round a Snag her Stern Struck a log under Water & She Swung round on the Snag, with her broad Side to the Current. . . . This was a disagreeable and Dangerous Situation, particularly as immense large trees were Drifting down and we lay imediately in their Course, . . . by the active exertions of our party we got her off in a fiew Mints. without engerey [injury]."[7]

The men, forced to haul the heavy boat by towlines and poles, gave the officers disciplinary troubles, recorded in a series of courts-martial. The Corps has often been compared to a community that mirrored the larger nation, but it

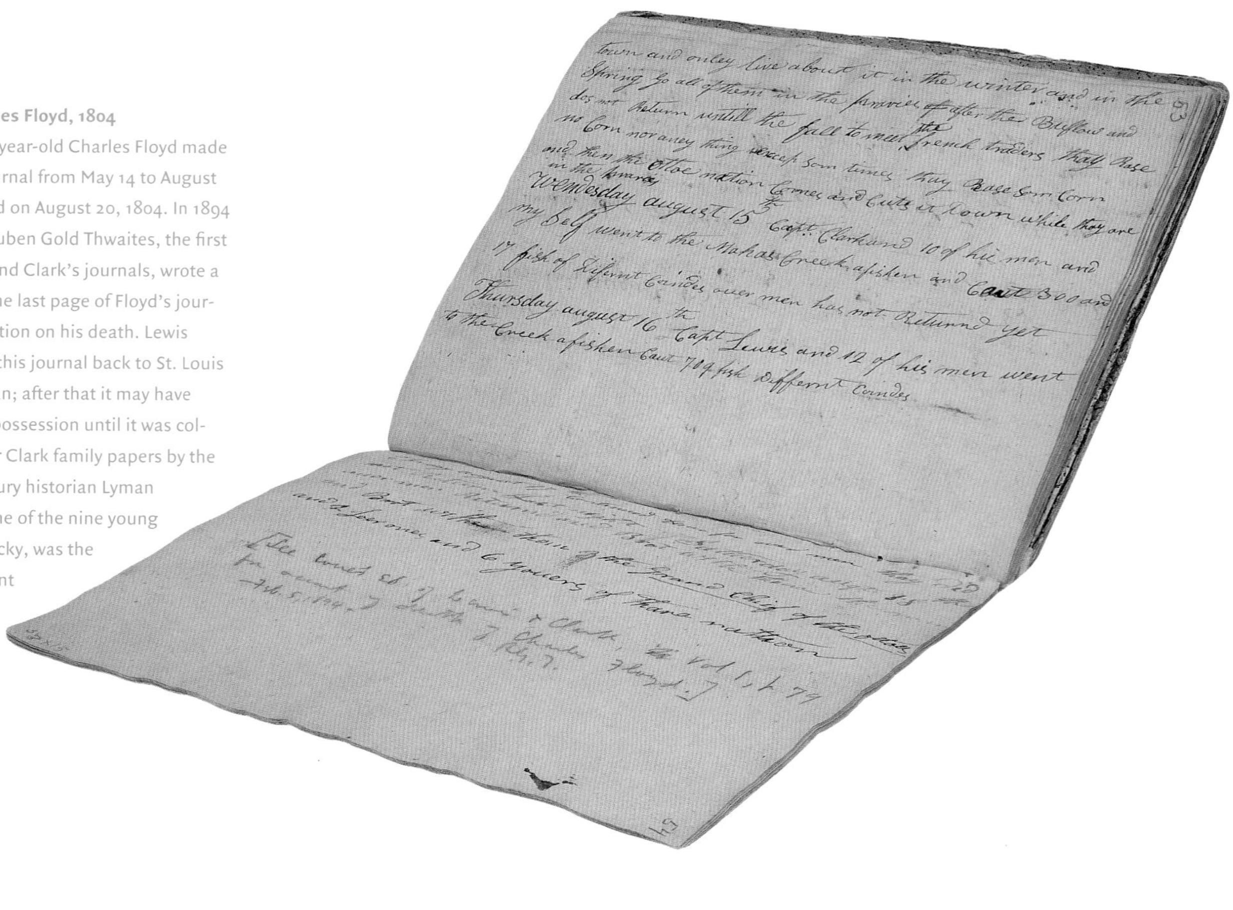
town and onley live about it in the winter and in the
Spring go all of them in the pirarie after the Buflow and
do not Return untill the fall to meet the French traders that Rase
no Corn nor aney thing else Som times they Rase Som Corn
and then the Otoe nation Comes and Cuts it down while they are
in the pirarie
Wednesday august 15th Capt. Clark and 10 of his men and
my Self went to the Mahas Creek afishen and Caut 300 and
17 fish of Diferent Cindes over men has not Returned yet
Thursday august 16th Capt Lewis and 12 of his men went
to the Creek afishen Caut 709 fish different Cindes

Journal of Charles Floyd, 1804
The twenty-two-year-old Charles Floyd made entries in his journal from May 14 to August 18, 1804. He died on August 20, 1804. In 1894 the historian Reuben Gold Thwaites, the first editor of Lewis and Clark's journals, wrote a pencil note on the last page of Floyd's journal, giving a citation on his death. Lewis apparently sent this journal back to St. Louis from Fort Mandan; after that it may have been in Clark's possession until it was collected with other Clark family papers by the nineteenth-century historian Lyman Draper. Floyd, one of the nine young men from Kentucky, was the cousin of Sergeant Nathaniel Pryor.

was not egalitarian or democratic. Military rank and hierarchy were clearly laid out and strictly enforced according to the regulations of the articles of war. The captains' orders were laws with no appeal; enforcing them were three sergeants and a corporal, each of whom commanded a squad, or mess, of privates. Absence without leave, insubordination, falling asleep on guard, drunkenness, and stealing whiskey were all promptly punished, usually with a sentence of fifty to one hundred lashes. When one disgruntled soldier deserted, the captains sent a party to arrest him, ordering that "if he did not give up Peaceibly to put him to Death."[8]

In general, Clark marveled at the men's good health; their complaints were limited to boils, "Tumers," and dysentery. But on August 19 their good luck changed. "Sergt. Floyd was taken violently bad with the Beliose Cholick and is dangerously ill," Clark wrote. "We attempt in Vain to releive him, I am much concerned for his Situation. . . . nature appear exosting fast in him every man is attentive to him (york pr[ticular]ly)." All their efforts were useless; the sergeant probably had appendicitis, incurable in those days. The next day "Sergt. Floyd . . . expired, with a great deel of composure, haveing Said to me before his death that he was going away and wished me to write a letter—we

Floyd's Grave, Where Lewis and Clark Buried Sergeant Floyd in 1804, 1832
Floyd's grave remained a landmark well into the 1830s, when George Catlin made this painting. Clark described the burial spot as "a high round hill over looking the river & Countrey for a great distance." The grave marker was cedar, with Floyd's name, title, and death date branded into it with Lewis's branding iron. The original grave eroded away, and the bones were moved in 1857 to another spot, still marked, near present Sioux City, Iowa.

Buried him to the top of a high round hill over looking the river & Countrey for a great distance. . . . we buried him with all the honors of War, and fixed a Ceeder post at his head with his name title & Day of the month and year. . . . this desceased man . . . had at All times given us proofs of his impatiality Sincurity to ourselves and good will to Serve his Countrey."[9]

The Missouri had turned north, and the travelers had passed into a new type of landscape, the broad open expanses of the Great Plains. Their garden imagery was succeeded by Lewis's descriptions of "rich pleasing and beatiful" land full of "immence herds of Buffaloe deer Elk and Antelopes." In glowing Jeffersonian terms, Lewis reported that the plains were "one of the fairest portions of the globe."[10]

Everything about the plains seemed larger than life, including the weather. Storms swept across the flat land with terrifying power. "At half past Seven, the atmispr. became Sudenly darkened by a black and dismal looking Cloud," Clark wrote. "The Storm which passd over an open Plain from the N.E. Struck the our boat on the Starbd. quarter, and would have . . . dashed to peces in an Instant, had not the party leeped out on the Leward Side and kept her off with the assistance of the ancker & Cable. . . . the waves Dashed over her windward Side. . . . In this Situation we continued about 40 Minits. when the Storm Sudenly Seased and the river become Instancetaniously as Smoth as Glass."[11]

They did not neglect the scientific investigations that might shed light on the usefulness of the country. The Missouri Valley was rumored to contain mineral resources such as lead mines and mountains of salt, and the captains were on the lookout for them—a little too incautiously at times. On August 22 they came across a bluff that "Contained alum, Copperas, Cobalt, Pyrites; a alum rock Soft & Sand Stone. Capt. Lewis in proveing the quality of those minerals was near poisoning himself by the fumes & tast of the *Cabalt* which had the appearance of Soft Isonglass— . . . Capt Lewis took a Dost of Salts to work off the effects of the Arsenic."[12]

Another long-standing rumor held that a volcano on the upper Missouri was responsible for the pumice and slag found on the banks as far south as the Osage River. On September 14 Clark "walked on Shore with a view to find an

Mineral specimens, collected 1804–5
These are the only remnants of sixty-eight mineral specimens collected along the lower Missouri River and sent back to Jefferson in 1805, "with a view of their being presented to the Philosophical society of Philadelphia, in order that they may . . . be examined or analyzed," as Lewis wrote. Here they are arranged (clockwise from upper left) in the most likely order of discovery: a fossil from a Cretaceous fish named *Xiphactinus*, found by Patrick Gass across from the mouth of Soldier River, Iowa; selenite or gypsum specimens probably found south of Calumet Bluffs near Yankton, South Dakota; pumice "Found Floating on the river Missouri"; and slag from burning coal strata near Fort Mandan, a specimen that Lewis erroneously identified as lava. The pumice and "lava" specimens represent the last nail in the coffin of a long-standing theory that there were volcanoes on the Missouri River. At Fort Mandan, Clark performed an experiment to prove that pumice could be created by burning coal beds; he burned some earth in a furnace and transformed it into pumice.

Prairie Dog Village, 1866
The first prairie dog the explorers saw up close was "cooked for the Capts dinner." The next one had a more illustrious fate: captured and kept alive through the winter, it was shipped to Thomas Jefferson in the spring of 1805, along with four live magpies and a live prairie grouse. Lovingly cared for by a succession of handlers, the rodent and one magpie survived the four-thousand-mile, four-month voyage via New Orleans to Washington, D.C. The bemused White House major domo reported to Jefferson that he had put them "in the room where Monsieur receives his callers." There they spent several weeks greeting startled visitors of state before being shipped to Peale's Museum in Philadelphia. They survived at least until January 12, 1806, when Charles Willson Peale reported to Jefferson, "The Marmot sleeps and the Magpie chatters a great deal." The naturalist George Ord, the first scientist to identify the prairie dog as a species (which he named *Arctomys ludovicianus*), based his description on the preserved specimen in Peale's Museum. This scene was originally sketched by George Catlin in 1832.

old Vulcanio, Said to be in this neighbourhood by Mr. J. McKey of St. Charles." He wrote, "I walked on Shore the whole day without Seeing any appearance of the Villcanoe." In fact, Clark would eventually prove that the origin of both the rocks and the rumors lay in burning coal beds under the sedimentary hills of present-day North and South Dakota.[13]

Strange wildlife also attracted their attention. During this summer they caught their first sights of the pronghorn antelope, the mule deer, and the coyote, all of which they promptly shot to collect skins and skeletons to send back east. Their first encounter with prairie dogs, which they called "barking squirrels," led to an even more ambitious collecting project. "Capt Lewis & my Self . . . discovered a Village of Small animals that burrow in the grown," Clark wrote on September 7. "The Village of those animals Cov[er]s. about 4 acrs of Ground . . . and Contains great numbers of holes on the top of which those little animals Set erect make a Whistleing noise and whin allarmed Slip into their hole." This discovery brought the entire expedition to a halt. As Gass told it, "Having understood that the village of those small dogs was at a short distance from our camp, Captain Lewis and Captain Clarke with all the party, except the guard, went to it; and took with them all the kettles and other vessels for holding water; in order to drive the animals out of their holes by pouring in water; but though they worked at the business till night they only caught one of them." Clark recorded, with typical precision, that they emptied the equivalent of five barrels of water into the holes without filling them.[14]

Ten days later, Lewis studiously recorded: "One of the hunters killed a bird of the *Corvus genus* and order of the pica. . . . the beak is black, and of a convex and cultrated figure. . . . it note is not disagreeable though loud—it is twait twait twait." The bird, on which he lavished over a page of description and measurements, was the magpie—a species well-known in Europe but

Sketch of the magpie, 1810–11
This is the magpie that Lewis sent back to Jefferson; it was painted either from life or from the preserved specimen. The ornithologist Alexander Wilson, who drew this sketch, called the magpie "a very beautiful specimen, sent from the Mandan nation, on the Missouri, to Mr. Jefferson, and by that gentleman to Mr. Peale of this city, in whose museum it lived for several months, and where I had an opportunity of examining it." He noted, "The color of its plummage is very splendid, being glossy green dashed with blue and bright purple." Magpie was a prominent character in Mandan mythology and the hero of the Mandan flood story.

never before identified in North America. Later, they were able to capture four magpies, which they kept in a cage through the winter, along with the single live prairie dog they had managed to collect. In the spring, they sent the small menagerie back to Jefferson.[15]

TOOLS OF DIPLOMACY

> Children . . . the great Chief of the Seventeen great Nations of America, whose cities are as numerous as the stars of the heavens, and whose people like the grass of your plains . . . could consume you as the fire consumes the grass of the plains . . . but it is not the wish of your great father to injure you.
>
> —MERIWETHER LEWIS[16]

> My Father—Listen to what I say I had an English medal when I went to See them, I went to the Spanoriards they give me a meadel and Some goods, I wish you would do the Same for my people.
>
> —THE SHAKE HAND, YANKTON, AS TRANSCRIBED BY CLARK[17]

Of the Indians, they saw little at first. The powerful Osage were off to the south, the Omaha were hunting buffalo. Fourteen members of the Oto and Missouri tribes listened to Lewis's elaborate speeches at Council Bluffs. In early September the Corps met cordially with about seventy Yankton Sioux.[18]

They had expected wilderness, so they never questioned the empty landscape. But in fact, they were traveling through the desertion left by an unimaginable tragedy. The wildlife was so abundant in part because the people were all gone. Starting almost twenty-five years before, a series of smallpox epidemics had rolled through this land with a higher mortality rate than that of the Black Death in Europe. The disease depopulated whole towns, wiped out clans, and decimated political and cultural leaders. Before 1780, the tributaries of the Missouri had been crowded with the thriving villages of farmers like the

Omaha, Ponca, Pawnee, and Iowa, thousands strong. By 1804, the banks were dotted with ghostly ruins.

The emptiness left by the smallpox was a stage set for the westward expansion of other peoples. But Euro-Americans were not the first to discover this. In the late eighteenth century, the westernmost Sioux—a nation of seven divisions speaking three dialects of the Lakota language—had moved onto the plains from the prairies and woodlands by the Mississippi, riding on a transportation revolution: horses. Spreading north from the Spanish settlements in the Southwest, horses for the first time provided a way to cross the immense distances of the West, hauling products and gear. The Sioux seized the opportunity, transforming themselves from corn farmers into mounted buffalo hunters and long-distance traders. They discovered fearsome new military strategies relying on cavalry and firearms. In only a few generations, they left behind their villages of bark houses for portable tipis and a mobile lifestyle perfectly matched to the once-uninhabitable plains. That lifestyle was what protected them. Far less affected by contagious disease than the village Indians, the swift-traveling bands of the Sioux expanded as their rivals perished. Lewis and Clark walked into the results of this recent shift of power.[19]

Relying on outdated sources, Jefferson had thought that the expedition would be too far west to meet any Sioux; but just in case, he wrote, "On that nation we wish most particularly to make a friendly impression, because of their immense power." The test of those instructions did not come until the end of September, when the traveling soldiers came upon two large camps of the Brulé band of the Teton division of the Sioux nation, camped near the mouth of the Bad River.[20]

Missouri in the Morning below Council Bluffs, 1833

Clark found the view from Council Bluffs "the most butifull prospect of the River up & Down and the Countrey . . . which I ever beheld; The River meandering the open and butifull Plains, interspursed with Groves of timber, and each point Covered with Tall timber, Such as willow Cotton Sun Mulberry, Elm, Sucamore, Lynn & ash." In his imagination, Clark populated the landscape with a fort, trading posts, and a village. John Ordway concurred: "I think it is the Smothest, & prittyest place for a Town I ever Saw." In 1819 the U.S. Army fulfilled Clark's prophecy by locating a fort about one mile north of Council Bluffs.

***Omaha Man*, 1833**
The Omaha, who once ruled their stretch of the Missouri River under their great chief Blackbird, had declined in power. Clark wrote, "The ravages of the Small Pox . . . has reduced this Nation not exceeding 300 men and left them to the insults of their weaker neighbours. . . . I am told whin this fatal malady was among them they Carried ther franzey to verry extroadinary length, not only of burning their Village, but they put their *wives* & Children to *D[e]ath* with a view of their all going together to Some better Countrey." The Omaha that Lewis and Clark met were mostly war prisoners of the Sioux. This portrait was made by Karl Bodmer.

OPPOSITE: ***Sioux Encamped on the Upper Missouri, Dressing Buffalo Meat and Robes*, 1832**
The tipis depicted here were the portable housing that made the mobile Sioux lifestyle possible. Clark called them "of a Conic form Covered with Buffalow Roabs Painted different Colours and all Compact & hand Somly arranged, covered all round an orpen part in the Center for the fire. . . . each Lodg has a place for Cooking detached, the lodges contain 10 to 15 persons." George Catlin, who painted this scene, wrote that the Sioux moved camp six to eight times in a summer.

For four days they met together. Twice they smoked together in peace. Twice, arrows were drawn, guns were cocked, and people almost died. At the end of the tense encounter, Clark confessed to feeling "verry unwell . . . for the want of Sleep."[21] To understand why it went so badly, one needs to look from two viewpoints—that of the men on the river and that of the people on the bank.[22]

When the Teton looked around them, they saw a land ruled by Native tribes, of which they were the preeminent military and commercial power. In 1804 they controlled a strategic territory straddling the Missouri. Their livelihood depended not just on the buffalo but on a three-way trade between the horsemen of the western plains, the farmers of the river valleys, and the traders at the British posts on the Des Moines, Minnesota, and Red Rivers. The Sioux had no intention of losing their lucrative position as suppliers and middlemen.[23]

By ancient Indian custom, rivers were not open roads for anyone: they belonged to the people who controlled their banks. Like European nations, tribes claimed the right to charge importers of goods and to stop arms shipments to their enemies—though inexperienced traders often called these rights "pillage" and "extortion" rather than "duties." When Lewis and Clark arrived, the Teton saw a huge boat full of weapons and goods passing up their river to arm their enemies and enrich their trading rivals. They needed to make it clear that they would not allow this without a heavy tax.

Horse effigy pipe bowl, pre-1839
The animal that allowed the Sioux to invent a new lifestyle figured prominently in their art. This artifact, one of the earliest known Plains Indian pipes depicting a horse, was collected by George Catlin around 1832. It has been identified as Teton Sioux. Catlin said the pipe to which it belonged was "made and used for the *luxury* only of smoking; and for this purpose, every Indian designs and constructs his own pipe." It originally had an ornamented flat stem.

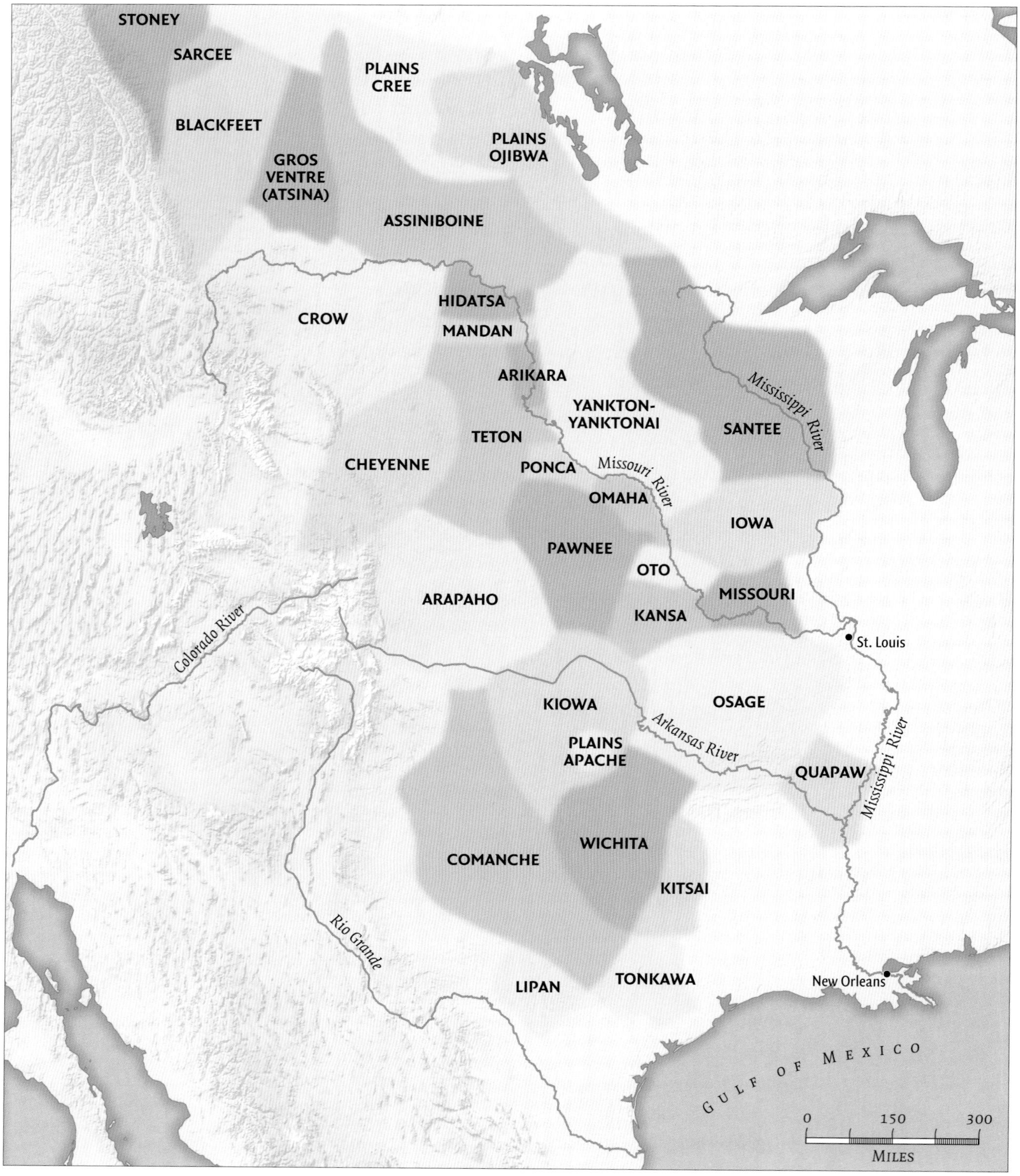

The Two Plains
When the expedition met the Teton Sioux, each side was maneuvering against enemies outside the other's mental world. To the Sioux, power on the plains was divided among themselves, the village tribes (Pawnee, Arikara, Mandan, Hidatsa), and the western nomads (Cheyenne, Arapaho, Comanche). Europeans were minor players manipulated by powerful tribes. To the Americans, power was divided among themselves, Great Britain, and Spain. The Indians were pawns manipulated by European superpowers.

When Lewis and Clark looked around them, they saw a land dominated by European nations—the British to the north and the Spanish to the south. Representing the interests of the United States, they had several goals to achieve. They didn't want Sioux land—yet. Instead, they wanted to announce the sovereignty of the United States, solicit Sioux allegiance, and "clear the road" for traders from St. Louis. The United States needed to establish peace and security on the plains so that they could go about their real objective: making money and driving the British out of business in the West. To achieve that, they had to make allies of the Sioux.

But the Sioux had fought for the British in the Revolutionary War, and

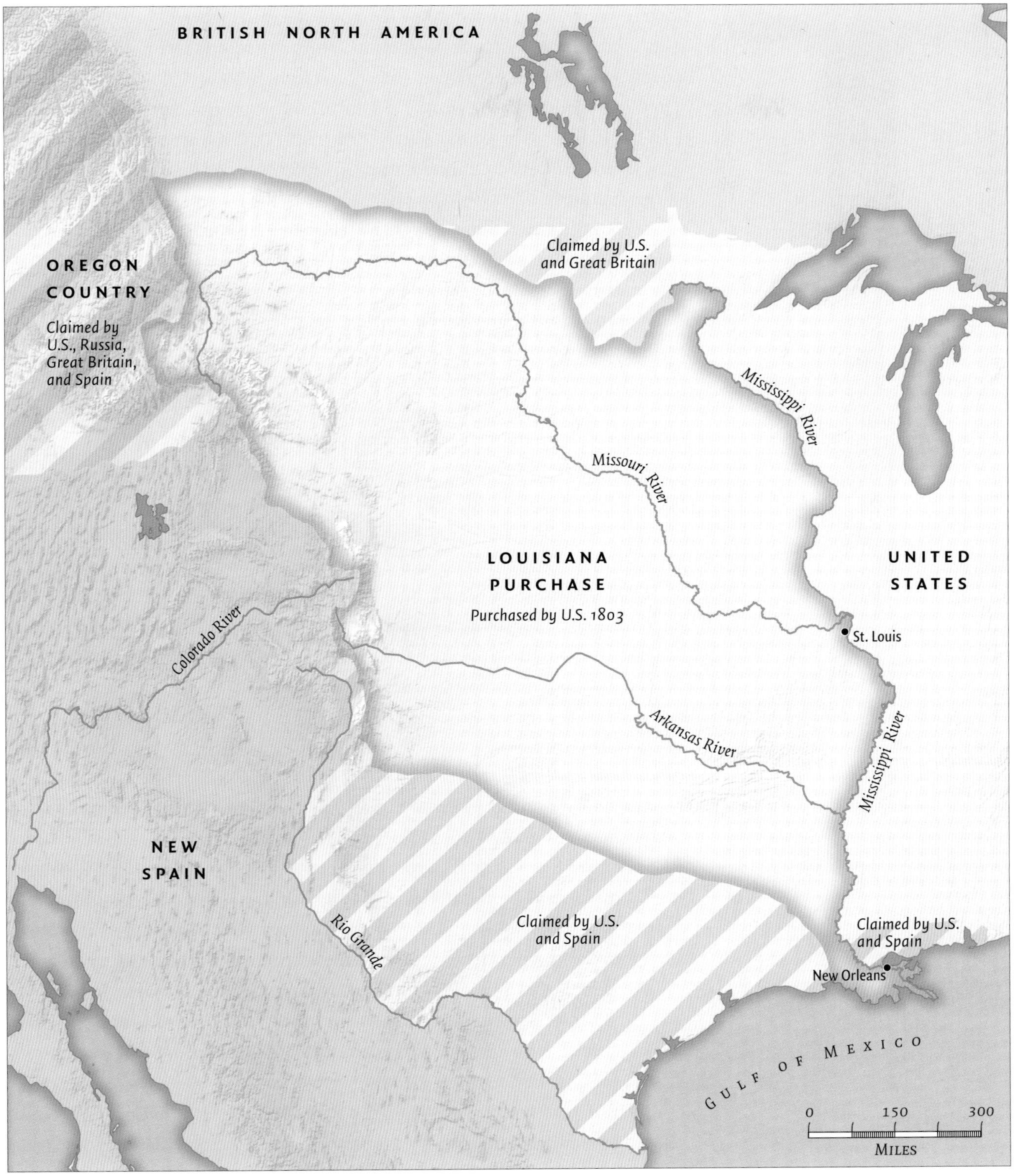

now they did a profitable business with British traders. When the two captains asked the Sioux to allow free passage for American traders and to stop making war, their requests went against Sioux interests, alliances, customs, and pride.

Lewis and Clark came prepared to use diplomatic protocols developed from over two centuries of negotiations between Indians and Europeans. In U.S. law, Indian tribes were defined as foreign nations, no different from France or Spain, and the mechanisms for dealing with them were the same: treaties negotiated by diplomats and ratified by Congress. But the rituals and symbols of European diplomacy did not always translate. When Lewis had met with Lieutenant Governor Delassus in St. Louis, their speeches made use of flowery courtesies. The symbols they employed were papers—orders, passports, commissions, treaties—and indicators of position like uniforms and medals. When Lewis prepared to meet the Teton, he expected no less formality. "On those occasions," he wrote, "points of etiquet are quite as much attended to by the Indians as among scivilized nations." But the symbols were different ones, hybrids unique to Indian-European diplomacy and belonging wholly to neither culture.[24]

From the outset there were a few problems. In North America there were several Native diplomatic traditions, and Lewis was familiar only with eastern customs, most highly developed between the British and Iroquois but also used in relations with Algonquian-speaking tribes. The eastern tradition used symbols like wampum belts and was adapted from the Iroquois Condolence ceremony. The western tradition revolved around the calumet, a pipe of diplomacy, and was probably based on an ancient adoption ceremony. Consequently, Lewis was like a diplomat in the wrong country.[25]

The other problem ran deeper. In Europe, diplomatic relations were between legal entities—nation-states—and not between individuals. The agreements reached were secular and impersonal. But Indian diplomatic tradition grew out of deeply emotional ceremonies held to mourn the dead or create new ties of kinship. The bonds invoked were sacred personal obligations, and the individual honor of the participants was at stake. Anyone who broke custom was contemptible, unprotected by sacred powers. When two parties interact with such different assumptions, the danger of misunderstanding is intense.

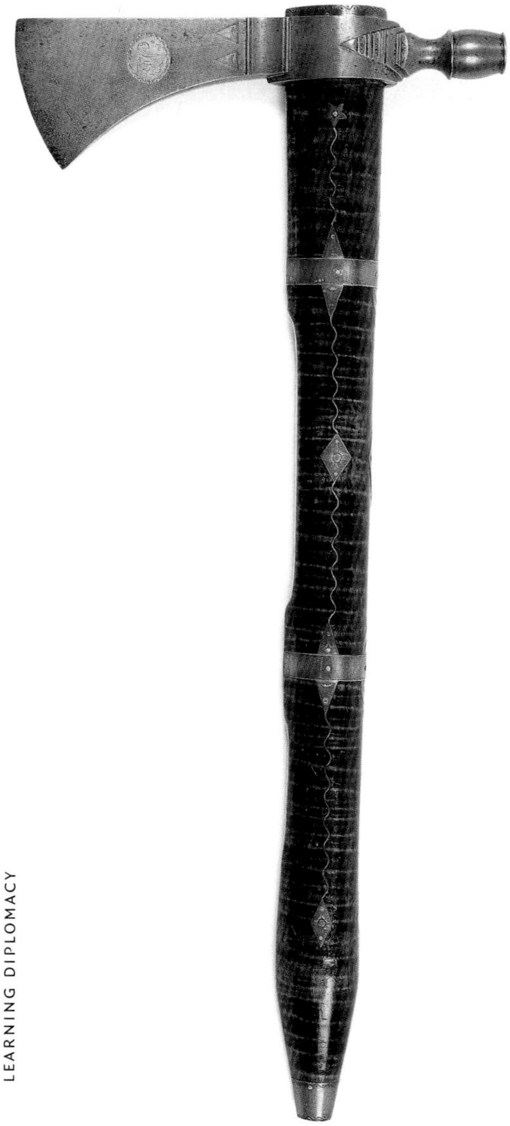

Pipe tomahawk of Meriwether Lewis, c. 1809

The pipe tomahawk combined one emblem from each culture: the Indian pipe of peace and the European ax of war. It symbolized the choice that underlay every meeting of the two cultures. An artifact unique to the American frontier, the pipe tomahawk was not used by either Indians or Europeans before 1700, but it was adopted by soldiers of both during the eighteenth century. Decorated ones like this were "presentation tomahawks" reserved for diplomatic gifts and high-status individuals.

This is almost certainly the pipe tomahawk that Lewis had with him at his death in 1809; it was described in documents as "One Tomahawk—handsomely moun[te]d." Both officers and enlisted men carried pipe tomahawks on the expedition, but it is not known if Lewis owned this one at the time.

SEPTEMBER 25: FOUR STRATEGIES

On the first day of meetings with the Teton, Lewis and Clark tried four time-tested strategies: making chiefs, kinship speech, gifts, and a parade of power. "The commanding officers," wrote Gass on the first day of meetings with the Teton, "made three of them chiefs." They accomplished this feat by presenting medals, flags, hats, and uniform coats to leading men.[26] Making chiefs was an attempt to create a permanent central authority with whom the United States could deal in the future. But the act went against the grain of Indian custom.

All of European diplomacy assumed that the other nation was hierarchically organized, with a clear difference between rulers and subjects and with a central authority that could make commitments for all. Among Europeans, these were safe assumptions. Among Indians, they were not. Europeans adapted to many Indian customs, but not this one. To them, hierarchy seemed both rational and natural, and they expended much effort enforcing it, both in their own society and on others. By 1804, Europeans had spent two centuries trying to change the decentralized nature of Indian society, and Lewis inherited that tradition.

Lakota society was a web of overlapping, shifting realms of authority. Power was distributed among the *otiyotipi* (council of old men), the many warrior and sacred societies, heads of families, holy men, pipe owners, and chiefs. Leaders might change according to circumstances; the same band could have different chiefs in war, peace, hunting, and camp. All were subject to the laws of custom. Communal decisions were reached by discussion and persuasion, and leaders could not compel obedience; anyone who disagreed was free to leave and form another camp. "When a man was not pleased with his camp or his people," said Bad Bear, a Lakota, "he set up his tipi far away from the camp. . . . if many joined him, then he became a chief of influence." With such individualistic customs, tribes had no unified policies toward European nation-states. Each family group (*tiyospaye*) was free to set its own.[27]

This individualistic arrangement drove Europeans crazy. It was impossible to reach an agreement that everyone would honor. Lewis and Clark clearly understood the situation. "The power of the chief," Clark wrote, "is rather the influence of character than the force of authority." And so their first step was to bolster the authority of Teton chiefs so that the men could represent the band in decisions.[28]

Captains Lewis & Clark Holding a Council with the Indians, 1810
Clark described the scene at the Teton encounter: "Raised a Flagg Staff and formed an orning & Shade . . . to Council under." Later, Patrick Gass's book about the expedition depicted a council with this woodcut. The uniforms are accurate; the Indian togas are not. The person next to Lewis is probably the translator.

But often, making chiefs backfired. Unlike Europeans, who were taught to respect the office even when they disliked or disagreed with the person in it, Indians traced power to the person rather than the title. Designating the wrong person as chief brought disrepute to the title rather than power to its holder. As a Lakota named Charles Garnett later explained: "A chief's authority depended on his personality and his ability to compel others to do his will, and if he were successful in his undertakings, followers were apt to flock to him. . . . If he were weak or cowardly . . . his people deserted him, and he became a person of little consequence, though he might be the head chief of the tribe." Euro-American honors then became objects of ridicule.[29]

The other danger of making chiefs was one that Lewis and Clark walked right into. They thought of the Brulé Teton as one group, but in fact there were two. The camps, led by Black Buffalo and The Partisan, had an uneasy relationship, and the two chiefs were rivals in the midst of a dispute over their relations with the Omaha and the Ponca. Honors presented to Black Buffalo could easily offend The Partisan, and vice versa. The visitors were unknowing pawns in a power struggle they barely understood, and meddling could hardly help but make it worse.[30]

The second strategy they tried was kinship speech. "C[aptain]. L[ewis].

Gorget, 1783–84

Since the seventeenth century, European nations had passed out military insignia to designate officers of their Indian allies. The gorget, a ceremonial remnant of medieval armor, was still worn around the neck by British officers in the eighteenth century and was used as a diplomatic gift. This one, engraved with the totemic animals of the British monarchy—a lion and a unicorn—was passed down in the family of the St. Louis fur trade magnate Pierre Chouteau, who supplied Lewis and Clark's expedition and took an Indian delegation to Washington, D.C., at Lewis's request. This gorget was said to have been worn by an English officer killed by Indians.

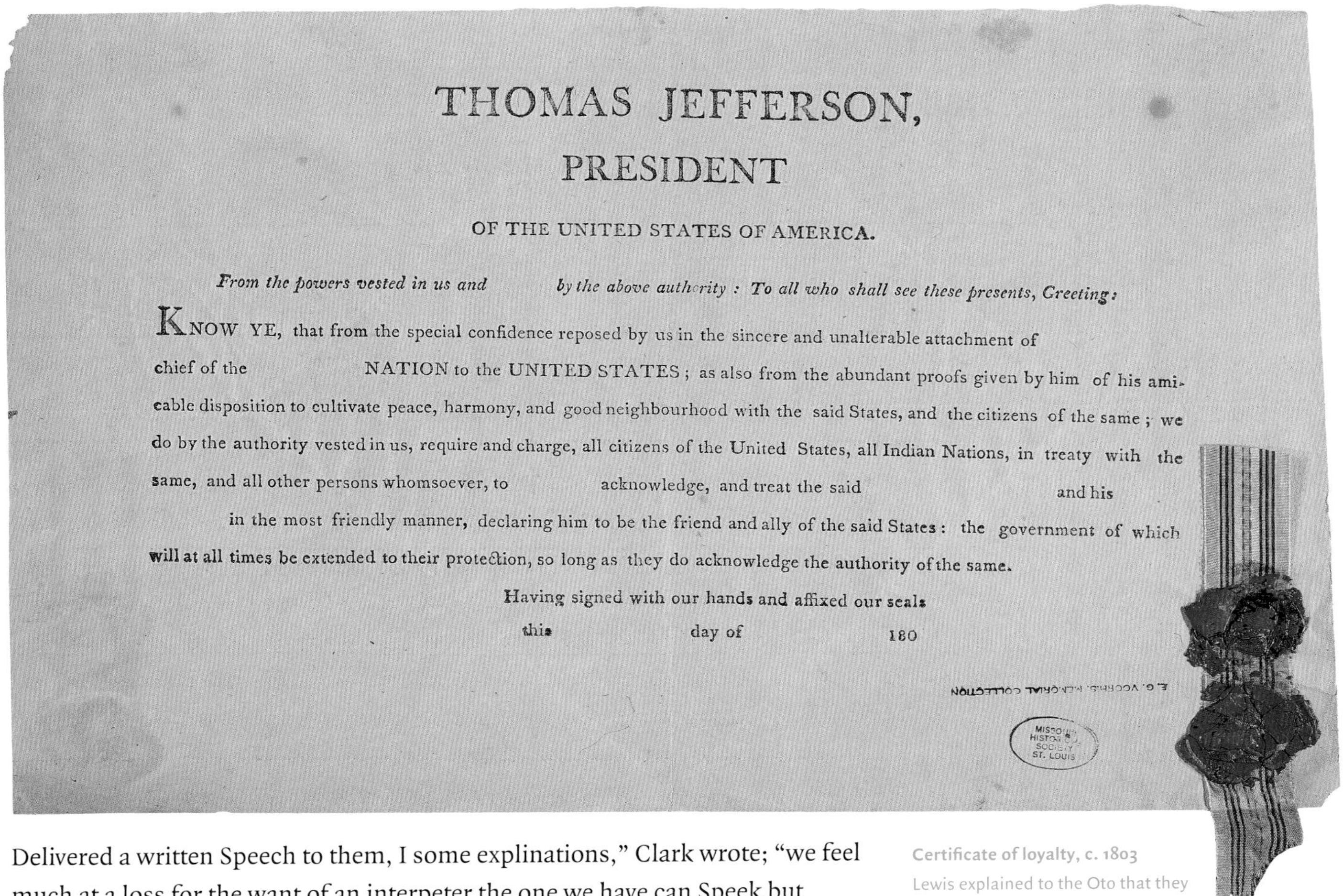

THOMAS JEFFERSON,

PRESIDENT

OF THE UNITED STATES OF AMERICA.

From the powers vested in us and *by the above authority : To all who shall see these presents, Greeting:*

KNOW YE, that from the special confidence reposed by us in the sincere and unalterable attachment of chief of the NATION to the UNITED STATES; as also from the abundant proofs given by him of his amicable disposition to cultivate peace, harmony, and good neighbourhood with the said States, and the citizens of the same; we do by the authority vested in us, require and charge, all citizens of the United States, all Indian Nations, in treaty with the same, and all other persons whomsoever, to acknowledge, and treat the said and his in the most friendly manner, declaring him to be the friend and ally of the said States: the government of which will at all times be extended to their protection, so long as they do acknowledge the authority of the same.

Having signed with our hands and affixed our seals this day of 180

Certificate of loyalty, c. 1803
Lewis explained to the Oto that they needed these certificates "In order that the commandant at St. Louis, as well as your great father, and all his chiefs may know . . . that you have opened your ears to your great father's voice." Lewis and Clark brought along so many of these blank certificates to give out to leading Indian "soldiers" that they ended up with extras, like this one from Clark's papers. One reason may have been the Indians' lack of appreciation for the reverence that Euro-Americans bestowed on slips of paper; when a disappointed Oto gave his certificate back, the captains "rebuked the [tribe] verry roughly."

Delivered a written Speech to them, I some explinations," Clark wrote; "we feel much at a loss for the want of an interpeter the one we have can Speek but little." In fact, their translation problems went even deeper than they knew.[31] Lewis's speech was full of the special rhetoric that whites used to address Indians. Over and over, he addressed them as "children." In reply, elderly chiefs called him "father." But the terms meant different things to the different speakers.

In the Indian diplomatic language where the terms originated, they conveyed not condescension or abasement but kinship. When two people, even ones of different tribes, "had a good heart toward [one] another," they might formalize their relationship in an adoption ceremony that made them kin. Different standards of behavior were expected of kin (*owepi* in Lakota) and of non-kin (*oyate unma*, other-people). Kinship was based not just on biology but also on behavior; relatives were people who acted like relatives. The adoption ceremony could create ties—and obligations—as strong as those created by any blood relation. By accepting an adoptive (or *hunka*) relationship, a person took on a long list of responsibilities: to aid his *hunka* in war and love; to care for his horses, wife, and children; to share possessions; and many more. "If a *Hunka* were hungry or naked and another *Hunka* knew this, he would give the hungry one something to eat, even if he had to take it out of his mouth," said John Blunt Horn, a Lakota. In the metaphorical language of the adoptive relationship, men addressed each other as "*hunka*" (ancestor) and "*ate*" (father), though they might be more like brothers. Even women used the same words, because it was a ceremonial relationship.[32]

Much of the ritual of intertribal diplomacy was aimed at creating an adoptive kinship between two groups. So when a visiting captain said "children," what the Indian audience heard was that he desired an adoptive relationship—

Certificate of loyalty, 1796
The true message of a certificate was aimed at other Europeans, since the paper marked its Indian owner as an ally. At each change of power, the new colonial power tried to gather up its predecessor's emblems. Lewis urged the Missouri River Indians to give up "all the flags and medals which you may have received from your old fathers the French and Spaniards," since the new great father did not tolerate "those emblems of attachment to any other great father but himself." In 1816 Clark confiscated this old Spanish certificate from its recipient, Mabaga, probably to replace it with an American one, thereby affirming U.S. sovereignty.

a solemn personal commitment to take on the obligations of a *hunka ate*, or adoptive father. If he then violated that promise, the reaction was forceful. Little Wound summarized: "You are a sham, and . . . disease and hardships will come upon you."[33] On the other hand, when the Lakota words for "father" and "child" were translated into English, the meanings changed, and paternalism took the place of promises.[34]

The third strategy Lewis and Clark tried was gifts. To tribes across North America, gifts were the universal language of goodwill. No alliance could exist without the generosity and sincerity they symbolized. In European society, leaders gained prestige by possessing many riches; in Indian society, they gained honor by giving them away. If the captains had really been soliciting a long-term relationship, giving everything away would have caused them no hardship, since they could have counted on their new friends to honor them by giving back as much or more over the long run.

Lewis and Clark brought as many goods as their tight budget would permit to "brighten the chain of friendship." The articles served a double purpose: to create goodwill and to advertise the products of American traders. To the latter end, the gifts were as carefully chosen as a salesman's samples.[35]

Among the gifts was a special category of symbolic objects: medals, flags, uniforms, and certificates. The Euro-Americans regarded these objects with profound respect because they were icons of national allegiance and conveyed nuances of political meaning that did not always translate. "When you accept his [the Great Father's] flag and medal," Lewis told the Indians, "you accept

TOP FOUR: **Jefferson peace medals and U.S. dollar, 1801 and 1803**
Lewis and Clark's medals came in five sizes, in order to designate five "ranks" of chief. Such a hierarchy reflected their own social system better than the Indians'. European powers had been recognizing Indian leaders with medals for decades, and the tokens were valued, a later Indian agent said, as "badges of power . . . and trophies of renown." Given knowledgeably, they could reinforce existing power structures. Used unwisely, they imposed hierarchy where none existed, subverted Indian leadership systems, and created dissention and rivalry. U.S. emissaries on the Mississippi found that the Corps' lavish distribution of medals "played the devil and all" with tribal relations, since eastern tribes felt slighted.

Lewis and Clark took at least eighty-nine medals, all of silver, on the expedition. They included three sizes of medal (all the same design) struck for Thomas Jefferson, three designs of medal (all the same size) struck for George Washington, and U.S. silver dollars, which they occasionally used as the smallest size of medal. None of the medals shown here is known to have been used by Lewis and Clark.

LOWER THREE: **Washington medals, 1798**
Lewis and Clark had more Washington medals than any other kind. These are often called "season" medals from the mistaken impression that they represent seasonal activities. The designs, by the artist John Trumbull, were visual homilies depicting the lifestyles that the U.S. government wanted Indians to adopt: a man sowing wheat; a farmer guarding domestic animals; a woman spinning cloth.

therewith his hand of friendship, which will never be withdrawn from your nation as long as you continue to follow the councils which he may command his chiefs to give you." The Teton, knowing how the visitors revered flags, respectfully displayed two Spanish flags in Lewis and Clark's honor.[36]

But the gift-giving backfired for the expedition. Even before setting out, Clark worried that their stock of gifts was "not as much as . . . necssy for the multitud of Inds. tho which we must pass." He was right. According to Sergeant John Ordway, the Teton "did not appear to talk much untill they had got the goods, and then they wanted more, and Said we must Stop with them or leave one of the pearogues with them." In a society where a man's status depended on his generosity, Jefferson's emissaries had lost face through stinginess.[37]

The last strategy Lewis and Clark tried was a parade of power. The soldiers erected a flagpole and ran up the flag. Wearing their bright blue and red dress uniforms, with their guns cleaned and ready, the men paraded to the orders of the sergeants, then stood for review by the commanding officers. Then, as Ordway wrote: "2 Guns was fired from our bow peace. The colours displaying &-C—Each man of our party Gave the 4 men of Band a peace of Tobacco."[38] After all the ceremonies came a demonstration of "Such Curiossities as was Strange to them"—the air gun, telescope, and compass, which never failed to give the Americans the impression that they had amazed and awed their guests. It was entertainment with a message.[39]

To the Petit Voleur, or Wear-ruge-nor, the great Chief of the Ottoes, to the Chiefs and Warriors of the Ottoes, and the Chiefs and Warriors of the Missouri nation residing with the Ottoes—

Children.— Convene from among you the old men of experience; the men, on the wisdom of whose judgement you are willing to risk the future happiness of your nations; and the warriors, to the strength of whose arms you have been taught to look for protection in the day of danger.— When in Council tranquilly assembled, reflect on the time past, and that to come; do not deceive yourselves, nor suffer others to deceive you; but like men and warriors devoted to the real interests of their nation, seek those truths, which can alone perpetuate its happiness.—

Children.— Commissioned and sent by the great Chief of the Seventeen great nations of America, we have come to inform you, as we go also to inform all the nations of red men who inhabit the borders of the Missouri, that a great council was lately held between this great chief of the Seventeen great nations of America, and your old fathers the french and Spaniards; and that in this great council it was agreed that all the white men of Louisiana, inhabiting the waters of the Missouri and Mississippi should obey the commands of this great chief; he has accordingly adopted them as his children and they

> Oh Spirit of the Skies, we offer this smoke to you, cause the spirits we have invoked to listen to us.
>
> —BAD WOUND'S PIPE PRAYER[40]

> Spirits
> Earth
> All over
> Every one, as many as there are
> I am related to
> *Mitaku oyasin.*
>
> —WORDS OF A PIPE CEREMONY[41]

In the next two days, the Teton replied with four strategies of their own. On September 26, the Teton took the diplomatic lead. Clark said: "I was met by about 10 well Dressd. yound men who took me up in a roabe Highly a decrated and Set me Down by the Side of their Chief . . . in a large Council House. . . . under this Shelter about 70 men Set forming a Circle. . . . a plac of 6 feet Diameter was Clear and the pipe of peace raised on Sticks under which there was Swans down Scattered."

He then witnessed one of the holiest ceremonies of the Lakota. He did not understand the invocation summoning "all my relations" to witness. He did not mention a hush of reverence falling as Black Buffalo filled and lit the pipe, but we can be sure it was there. Though the ceremony was charged with meaning, he recorded only the outward motions. "The Great Chief . . . with Great Solemnity took up the pipe of peace . . . & after pointing it to the heavins the 4 quarter of the Globe & the earth, lit it and . . . presented the Stem to us to Smoke."[42]

To virtually all tribes between the Mississippi and the Rockies, pipes were sacramental vessels and conduits of communication with natural powers. Some pipe ceremonies were secret and private, but the ones seen by whites were rites of social communion that adopted outsiders into the very heart of tribal culture. The Lakota had been using the pipe ceremony to create kinship with Europeans since the 1670s and had probably used it long before to forge relations with other tribes. In the early days, the ritual seems to have grown out of one in which bereaved parents adopted a war prisoner in place of their dead child. It symbolized not just adoption but the reincarnation of the dead in the person of the European visitor. The ceremony began with mourning, after which the adoptee was ritually brought to life and welcomed back into the family. Clark's ride to the council chamber in a robe may have symbolized a passage through death. If so, he did not understand it.[43]

OPPOSITE: **Talk of Capt. Lewis to the Oto nation, 1804** All along the Missouri River, Lewis used the same speech announcing the imminent empire of the United States. "Your old fathers the french and Spaniards have gone beyond the great lake towards the rising Sun, from whence they never intend returning. . . . the great chief of the Seventeen great nations of America, has become your only father." This copy is the speech he delivered at Council Bluffs to the Oto and Missouri.

Air gun, c. 1803
Lewis's air gun has never been found. It was a type designed by the Austrian gunmaker Bartolomeo Girandoni, a repeating gun with a breech-loading attachment that made it possible for him to fire twenty-two rounds straight, in an era when conventional guns had to be reloaded between each shot. An eyewitness said, "All the balls are put at once into a short side barrel and are then droped into the chamber of the gun one at a time by moving a spring; and when the triger is pulled just so much air escapes out of the air bag which forms the britch [breech] of the gun as serves for one ball. It is a curious peice of workmanship not easily discribed."

Lewis never used his air gun for hunting or defense; it was a technological novelty, part of the performance the Corps delivered to impress Indian tribes with the superiority of U.S. power. Joseph Whitehouse described such a scene: "Captain Lewis took his Air Gun and shot her off, and by the Interpreter, told them that there was medicine in her, and that she could do very great execution, They all stood amazed at this curiosity; Captain Lewis discharged the Air Gun several times, and the Indians ran hastily to see the holes that the Balls had made. . . . at finding the Balls had entered the Tree, they shouted a loud at the sight."

Calumet pipe, late 1700s to mid-1800s

This pipe may have been given to Lewis and Clark as a record of the sacred commitment of brotherhood that they had undertaken by smoking it. At least twice, tribes presented a pipe to Lewis and Clark at the end of a ceremony so that they would never forget the event. It is not known which tribe this pipe is from or what promise the pipe once witnessed.

Clark wrote that Teton pipes were "of red earth—the stem is of ash highly decorated with feathers hair & porcupine quills, & about 4 or 3 feet long." The calumet was the oldest and most symbolic style of pipe used in North America. It had been used to mediate relations with Euro-Americans since at least the 1670s. Although the stem decorations were symbolic, the meanings often originated in visions or myth, so no generalizations can be made. The bowl was often made of a red stone now called catlinite, found in a quarry in southwestern Minnesota. According to the Lakota in the 1830s, all the people of the world once took refuge there from a universal flood and were transformed into stone; bowls of catlinite were literally formed from the flesh of their ancestors.

The pipe itself summoned sacred powers, harmonized the spirits of those who smoked, and sealed agreements. It was improper to fill a pipe bowl with the fingers; the tobacco was pressed in with a tamper. Often, each pinch of tobacco was offered to a part of creation—the wingeds, the four-legged peoples, the growing peoples, the water, the Thunder Beings. After every form of creation had been mentioned, the pipe held in it the entire universe. The smoke was a visible prayer that called all the powers to witness the binding of those who smoked together. George Sword, a Lakota born in about 1847, explained: "The spirit in the smoke will soothe the spirits of all who thus smoke together and all will be as friends and all think alike. When the Lakotas smoke in this manner, it is like when the Christians take communion."[44]

Every act in a pipe ceremony had meaning. The bed of down that Clark noticed under the pipe was a nest, representing the world made for the dwelling place of all the people. The pipe was referred to as a living thing, with a body (the stem) and a head (the bowl), but it was not brought to life till the stem and bowl were joined. It was never lit with a flame, but instead with a coal from the council fire that held the *ton*, or spiritual essence, of the sun; "what is done in its presence is solemn and binding." The celebrant offered the pipe first to the four directions, the sky, and the earth, then passed it "sun-wise" (clockwise) around the circle. Participants smoked it "in the Indian way: one whiff at a time, then pass it to another." The ash was never discarded on the ground, where it might be trod on and dishonored; it was burned up in the fire or carefully buried. At the end, the pipe itself might be given to one of the participants as the tangible record of the kinship created in the ceremony and the responsibilities that kinship entailed. As Euro-Americans used treaty papers to remember, so Indians used pipes.[45]

Just as the captains had used special language to manipulate the Indians, so too did the Teton use speech as their second strategy. They were so effective that Lewis and Clark took their words at face value. At one tense moment when conflict seemed imminent, the Teton chief Black Buffalo made a startling statement: "he was Sorry to have us Go for his women and children were naked and poor and wished to Git Some Goods." The next day an elder of the powerful tribe made a speech "requesting us to take pity on them."[46]

The men were using a type of speech as ancient and ritualized as the courtesies of European diplomats. Its purpose was to show the speaker's humble and deserving nature and to shame the other side into cooperation. Though such language predated their meeting with Europeans, the Sioux had used it to influence whites since the 1600s. In Indian society, humility was an essential attribute of leadership, and pity speech was used to respectfully address powerful entities, both human and nonhuman. The Teton could not know that Europeans preferred arrogance and pride in their leaders and called Indian pity speech "begging." But it often had the desired effect.[47]

Sioux Dog Feast, 1832–37
In 1832 the traveling artist George Catlin met the Teton Sioux on the Missouri and participated in a council almost identical to the one Lewis and Clark experienced. It included a speech that used the same rhetorical devices: "My father, I hope you will have pity on us, we are very poor"—after which the speaker heaped gifts on the visitors and gave a sumptuous feast. Catlin interpreted the dog feast as "a truly religious ceremony," in which the host "sees fit to sacrifice his faithful companion to bear testimony to the sacredness of his vows of friendship, and invite his friend to partake of its flesh, to remind him forcibly of the reality of the sacrifice, and the solemnity of his professions."

Feast bowl, pre-1865
Sharing food was an indispensable part of the ceremonial gift exchange that accompanied intertribal diplomacy. The foods were often symbolic, with the dog meat presented to Lewis and Clark by the Teton being one example. Bowls depicting eagles, like this one, were widely used in feasts and public ceremonies. The raised portion of the rim opposite the head represents the eagle's tail.

Belt, early 1800s
Clothing, especially decorated clothing, was often part of the gift exchange between Indian tribes and Euro-American negotiators. Lewis and Clark presented "chiefs' coats" (military uniform coats) to the Sioux, and the two captains may have received pieces of clothing in return. This could be one of those pieces. Among the Sioux, Clark noted that both men and women wore belts, or "girdles": the men wore "a girdle round the waist of dressed Elk Skin or if it can be obtained of cloth . . . about one inch wide," into which they tucked the tops of their leggings, their breech cloth, and their pipe bags. After returning, the explorers donated two belts to Peale's Museum. This one came from the collection that included the Peale's Museum artifacts.

Saber of William Clark, c. 1808
Twice during the Teton encounter the captains drew their swords: Clark when a chief's "insults became So personal and his intentions evident to do me injurey"; and Lewis to cut the mooring line of the keelboat. Americans' willingness to use their swords had earned them the name "Long Knives" among the eastern tribes, and the Mandan gave Lewis the same name because he "wore a broad sword." Later, the Lakota *akicitapi*, or camp marshals, would adopt an American-style sword as one of their emblems of authority.

Clark wore this sword as brigadier general of the Louisiana Territorial Militia, a post he assumed in 1808. It is of a style popular from the late eighteenth century through the War of 1812. The blade is ornately engraved with floral and patriotic motifs, including an eagle, thirteen stars, and "E Pluribus Unum," but it was likely made in England for export. Its knuckle bow has been broken off.

Third, the soldiers had given gifts, and the Teton had no intention of letting their guests leave without reciprocal gifts. Mainly, they gave food: several hundred pounds of fat buffalo meat, then two sumptuous feasts. Visitors to the Teton in similar circumstances received headdresses, shirts, leggings, necklaces, moccasins, and pipes as tokens of friendship. By custom, if a guest admired a piece of clothing or furnishing, the owner gave it to him, and the gift reflected honor on the giver. All their finery and wealth circulated freely among the tribe and between tribe and allies.[48]

Finally, the Teton also had an answer to the expedition's parade of power. In the evening of September 26, "all was cleared away & a large fire made in the Center, Several men . . . assembled and began to Sing & Beat—The women Came forward highly decerated with the Scalps & Trofies of war of their fathes Husbands & relations, and Danced the war Dance."[49] The explorers thought the dance was in their honor, but scalp dances were generally performed after the return of a successful war party, and this one may have celebrated a recent victory against the Omaha. The women held up the newly captured scalps, suspended on sticks, while the men danced around the women and recounted their deeds. The respect paid to the scalps satisfied the angry spirits of the slain and honored the victorious warriors. Lewis and Clark could not have missed the message of Teton military power.[50]

SEPTEMBER 28: CONFRONTATION

> The Lakotas are superior to all others of mankind.
>
> —RED HAWK[51]

> These are the vilest miscreants of the savage race, and must ever remain the pirates of the Missouri, until such measures are pursued, by our government, as will make them feel a dependence on its will for their supply of merchandise.
>
> —WILLIAM CLARK[52]

The first day, September 25, had ended badly. Clark wrote: "The 2d Chief was very insolent. . . . his justures were of Such a personal nature I felt my Self Compeled to Draw my Sword, at this motion Capt. Lewis ordered all under

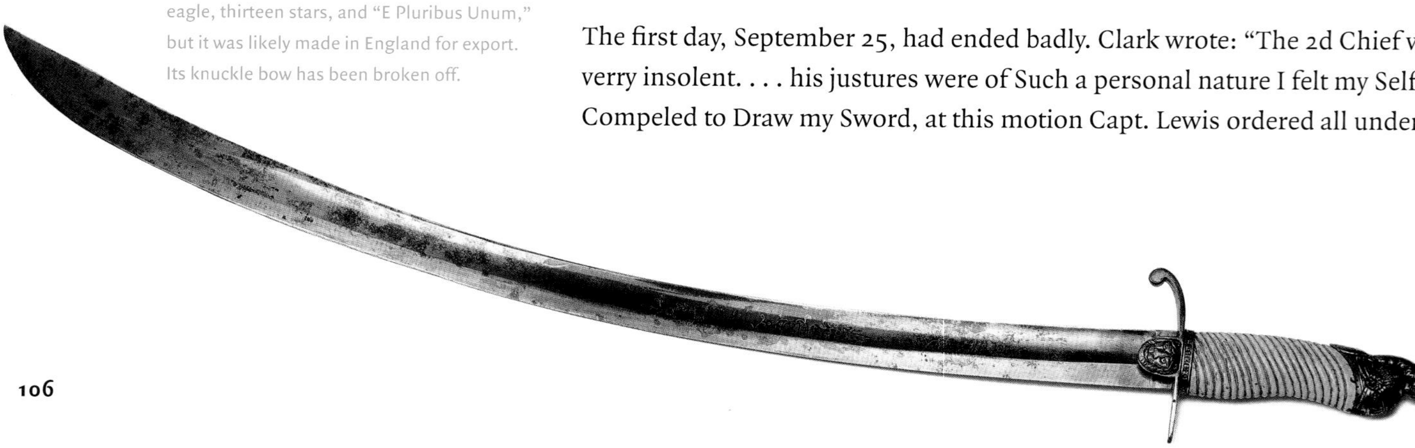

arms in the boat. . . . I felt my Self warm & Spoke in verry positive terms. Most of the warriers appeared to have ther Bows Strung and took out their arrows." After an exchange of threats, Clark wrote, "I offered my hand to the . . . Chief who refusd to recve it."[53]

The last day was even worse. Problems arose as they prepared to leave. Ordway wrote: "Some of the chiefs were on bord insisting on our Staying. . . . about 200 Indians were then on the bank. Some had fire arms. Some had Spears . . . and all the rest had Bows and Steel or Iron pointed arrows. . . . Capt. Lewis . . . ordered the Sail hoisted. . . . their warrie[r]s caught hold of the chord and tyed it faster than before. Capt. Lewis then appeared to be angerry." Gass thought Lewis "was near giving orders to cut the rope and to fire on them."[54]

But the chief Black Buffalo, who had performed the pipe ceremony, stepped in to offer a face-saving compromise. If Lewis would give the young

Scalp Dance, Sioux, 1832
Almost thirty years after Lewis and Clark's visit, George Catlin portrayed a dance similar to the firelit evening performance that the Corps witnessed. Sergeant John Ordway was entranced by the sight: "The Squaws formed on each Side of the fire & danced and Sang as the drumm and other ratles &.C. were playing. they danced to the center untill they met, then the rattles Shook and the houp was Given. then the Squaws all fell back to their places. when the mens music Seaced the womens voice Sounded one part of the tune delightful. then the other Music would commence again."

Gun stock war club, pre-1841
The warriors attending the Yankton chief who held a council with Lewis and Clark were armed with "a War Club & Speer each, & Dressed in feathurs." This formidable weapon was collected by the U.S. Army in 1841, but the style goes back to the seventeenth century. The club's outline was modeled on the shape of a European gun stock. Both Catlin and Bodmer illustrated them, and Prince Maximilian collected one very like this on the Missouri in 1833.

Knife and sheath, c. 1820–40
This rare and early style of sheath, covered with whole bird quills, is sometimes attributed to the Santee Sioux, but two examples in European collections are from the Missouri River valley. This one was owned by John Varden, the proprietor of the Washington Museum, who acquired much early Plains Indian material, including items from Clark's museum after its dissolution in 1838.

Quiver, pre-1839
Clark described the Yankton Sioux as armed mainly with bows and arrows, "and verry much deckerated with porcupine quills." This quiver embroidered with dyed quillwork in thunderbird motifs may have been the type of thing he was seeing. It was collected by the artist George Catlin, who is often rumored to have acquired material from Clark, whom he visited and painted. However, Catlin would have had ample opportunity to collect this quiver in his own travels up the Missouri in 1832.

men some tobacco, they would allow the boats to leave. At first Lewis refused. Clark wrote, "After much difucelty—which had nearly reduced us to hostility I threw a Carot of Tobacco to 1s Chief." To make sure that yielding produced the right effect, he then "Spoke So as to touch his pride" and "took the port fire from the gunner" in preparation for firing the cannon on the assembled crowd. But he did not need to light the fuse. "The Chief gives the Tobaco to his Soldiers & he jurked the rope from them and handed it to the bows man." The Corps sailed away "under a gentle breeze of wind."[55]

In the end, neither the expedition nor the Teton achieved their goals. The Corps had not promoted peace, initiated friendly relations, or "cleared the road" for American traders. The Teton had not extracted the toll payment they wanted. But at least everyone escaped without bloodshed. Unknown to Clark or Lewis, it may have been the divisions among the Teton that saved the Corps from attack. Black Buffalo might never have intervened to let them leave if The Partisan had not opposed it. This would not be the last time that Euro-Americans would benefit unwittingly from the internal politics of a tribe.

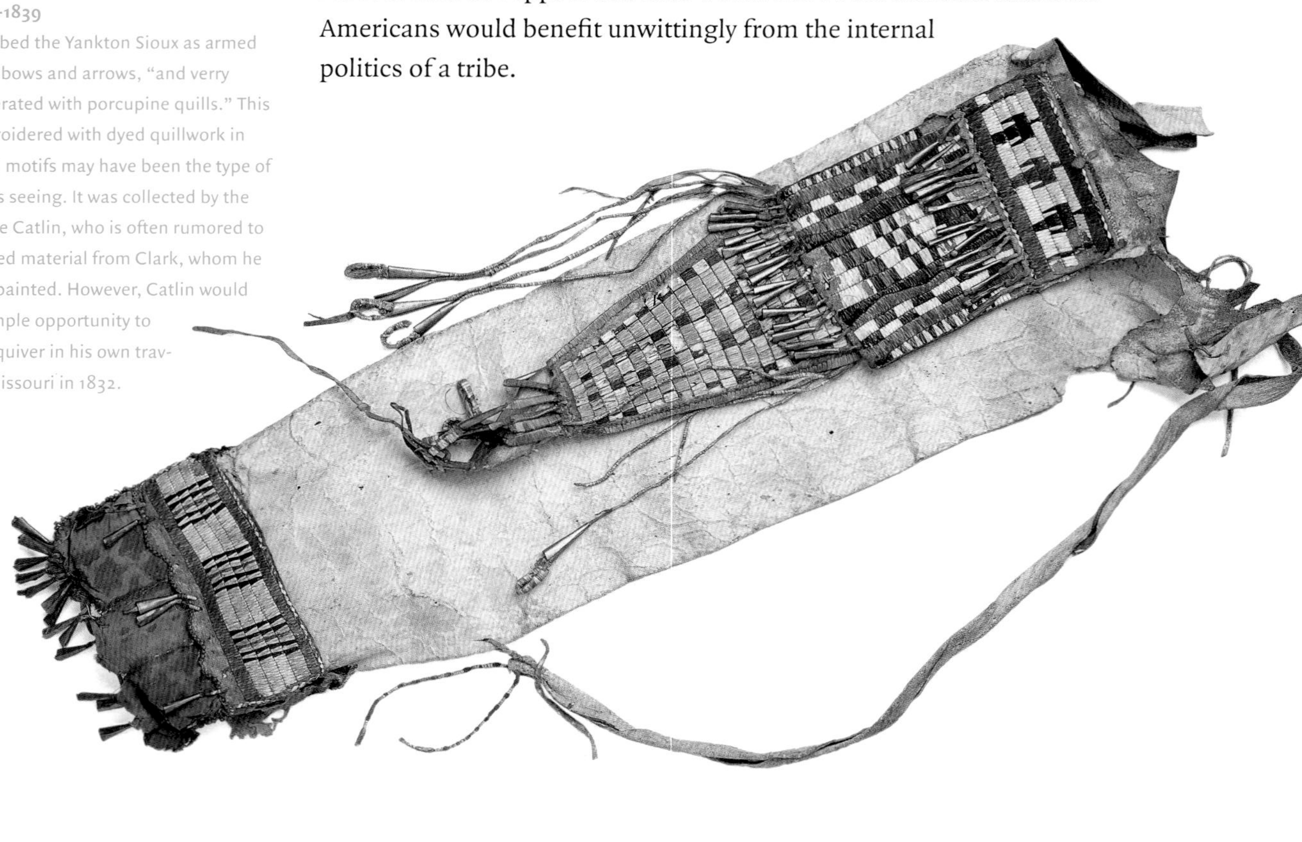

Buffalo robe, c. 1780–1825
This robe doubtless looks much like the one Lewis and Clark sent to Jefferson, showing a battle fought by the Sioux and the Arikara against the Mandan and the Hidatsa. Although it has often been published as that robe, there is no evidence to prove such a claim. It could, however, be one of the many other robes collected by Lewis and Clark.

Thought to have been painted by at least two warriors, this robe depicts military exploits in a very early and abstract style. The recurring warfare between the Sioux, Arikara, Mandan, and Hidatsa was a favorite subject of Missouri Valley art. Clark may have seen battle paintings from both sides; among the Teton, he was carried to the feast on an "elegent painted B. Robe"; and later the Mandan leader Black Cat presented him with a "highly decoraterd" robe. Sioux and Mandan military prowess was an underlying message of both incidents.

Unable to strike a deal with the Teton, Lewis and Clark adopted another plan: to persuade the upriver tribes—Arikara, Mandan, and Hidatsa—to make peace with each other and ally against the Sioux. They wanted a pro-American opposition to the pro-British Sioux. Had they looked carefully at one of the objects they had collected, it would have told them how hard this might be.

In 1805, they sent Jefferson a buffalo robe depicting a battle "faught 8 years since" between the Sioux and Arikara allied on one side against the Mandan and Hidatsa on the other. It reflected an existing pattern of alliances and animosities that trumped the few gifts given and speeches made by Lewis and Clark. The tribes could not change their policies to suit a passing troop of American soldiers.[56]

Arrows (detail), early to mid-1800s
Lewis and Clark collected Indian weapons to document the various tribes' potential strength in warfare and needs for trade, as well as for the novelty of the souvenirs. Having identified the Sioux as the most dangerous potential opponents to U.S. expansion, they donated a "great number" of arrows from "different Tribes of the Saux [Sioux]" to Peale's Museum. These arrows could be some of their donations. They had good opportunities to observe Teton weapons; on September 25 Clark noted with great clarity that the warriors surrounding him during a confrontation "had their bows Strung & guns Cocked."

These arrows illustrate the transitional styles Lewis and Clark might have seen, when metal was scarce and older styles were still in use. The tips of these are bone, chalcedony, quartz, and hand-cut iron. Iron points had been available from traders for decades, and Indian artisans were adept at making them from salvaged sheet iron.

THREE A World of Women

The treatment of women is often considered as the standard by which the moral qualities of savages are to be estimated.

—*HISTORY OF THE EXPEDITION UNDER THE COMMAND OF CAPTAINS LEWIS AND CLARK*[1]

After the tension of the encounter with the Sioux, the next leg of the trip was pleasantly uneventful. The only challenges worthy of note were the sandbars, which were "So noumerous, that it is impossible to discribe them." The weather, as if making up for the hard times, was "Calm and pleasant."[2]

Close to what is now the border of North and South Dakota, the men of the Corps of Discovery came upon a new tribe, the Arikara, who called themselves the Sahnish. It was the expedition's first exposure to a different, and much older, style of Plains Indian life. Long before the arrival of horses or the Sioux, village-dwelling agricultural tribes had populated the broad river valleys of the Great Plains. Living in densely packed, fortified towns of earth lodges, these tribes farmed the fertile bottomlands and made seasonal forays onto the plains to hunt buffalo—at first on foot, later by horseback.

The three village-dwelling tribes that Lewis and Clark met—the Arikara, the Mandan, and the Hidatsa—were related to one another only in lifestyle, not in origin or language. The Arikara had split off from the Pawnee farther south. In the eighteenth century they had been lords of the Missouri, controlling traffic up and down the river.

Arikara Village, 1866
"This Village is Situated about the Center of a large Island near the L[arboard]. Side & near the foot of Some high bald uneaven hills," Clark wrote. "The Isld. is covered with fields, where those people raise their Corn Tobacco Beens &c. &c. Great numbers of those People came on the Island to See us pass."

The Arikara villages near the Grand River in present-day South Dakota were formed of earth lodges, the dome-shaped permanent homes of all the Missouri Valley tribes. Patrick Gass, the expedition's carpenter, explored the lodges and wrote a detailed description of their construction. What he did not know was that women were the ones who had the sacred right to lay them out and supervise their construction. This engraving is from an 1832 painting by George Catlin.

But smallpox epidemics in 1780–82 and 1801–2 had reduced them from thirty-two villages to three. When Lewis and Clark arrived, the demoralized remnants of the tribe were split by factions; as a trader living with them put it, there were too many "captains without companies." Their situation left them disorganized and vulnerable to the powerful Sioux.[3]

To many Euro-Americans of that era, agriculture marked the dividing line between savagery and civilization. Because they farmed, the village tribes seemed more "advanced" than the nomadic tribes. Lewis and Clark, still smarting from their treatment by the Sioux, readily accepted the Arikara Indians' complaints that they were peaceful people tyrannized and oppressed by their neighbors. The American captains spent much of the fall of 1804 trying to pro-

Fort Clark on the Missouri, c. 1834
By the time this image was made, the Mandan had moved their village of Mitutanka (which Clark spelled "*Mar-too-ton-ha*") two miles downriver, but it still looked much the same. Fort Clark, an American Fur Company post named for William Clark, was built there in the late 1820s. This winter view looking northwest shows the village across a frozen slough. The northeast bank, where Fort Mandan once stood, is to the right.

Page 110: *Dance of the Mandan Women* (detail), c. 1833. See page 124.

mote an alliance that would pit the farmers of the valley against the horsemen of the plains. What they did not understand was how crucial the Sioux were to the economy of the river valley. Hated though the Sioux might have been for acts of war, they were also like long-distance truckers bringing trade goods and buffalo products to the commercial fairs that the village tribes hosted each summer. One trader portrayed the complex relationship: "The Ricaras and this Sioux nation live together peacefully. The former receive them in order to obtain guns, clothes, hats, kettles, clothes, etc., which are given them in exchange for their horses. They humor them through fear and to inevitably overpower them."[4]

The visit with the Arikara seemed "all tranquillity." The captains made an effort to impress their hosts with "Some account of the Magnitude & power of our Countrey which pleased and astonished them verry much." The Arikara diplomat Kakawissassa played along, saying, "If you want the road open no one Can provent it, it will always be open for you." And yet there must have been undercurrents that Lewis and Clark did not pick up. Three years later it would be the Arikara, not the Sioux, who would close off river navigation—and shoot off Corps member George Shannon's leg—in a gambit to gain back their former commercial power.[5]

To the Arikara, the captains' efforts to impress them were overshadowed by other novelties. "Many Came to view us all day," Clark wrote. "Those Indians wer much astonished at my Servent, They never Saw a black man before, all flocked around him & examind. him from top to toe, he Carried on the joke and made himself more turibal than we wished him to doe . . . telling them that before I cought him he was wild & lived upon people, young children was verry good eating . . . &c. &c."[6] In Clark's summary, the Arikara were "Durtey, Kind, pore, & extravigent pursessing national pride. not beggarley re[ce]ive what is given with great pleasure, Live in worm houses large and built in an oxigon form. . . . Those people express an inclination to be at peace with all nations."[7]

It took the expedition less than a month to reach their next destination. On October 26 Clark wrote: "We came too and Camped . . . about 1/2 a mile below the 1st. Manddin Town. . . . Soon after our arrival many men womin & Children flocked down to See us."[8] The group of towns where they had arrived,

Shehek-Shote's village, 1900
The layout of a traditional Mandan village was both symbolic and practical. At the center was an open plaza for religious and civic performances. In it stood the Ark of the First Man, symbolizing the structure that Lone Man built to save his people from a world-spanning flood. Inside the ark stood a sacred cedar post, painted red to symbolize Lone Man's body. North of the ark stood the ceremonial lodge, a towering structure where crowds could attend observances. Its south-facing entryway was flanked by votive poles. Earth lodges formed a circle around the plaza, with the most prominent families of designated clans living in the central circle.

The Mandan artist I-ki-ha-wa-he (known as Sitting Rabbit or Little Owl) was painting from memory and the accounts of elders when he drew this depiction of the village at the site where the town of Deapolis was later built. This was probably the original site of Shehek-Shote's village.

Eh-toh'k-pah-she-pée-shah, Black Moccasin, Aged Chief, 1832
Whereas the Mandan welcomed the expedition, the Hidatsa were more skeptical. Visiting in the summer of 1806, the British fur trader Alexander Henry found that the Hidatsa "were disgusted at the high-sounding language the American captains bestowed upon themselves and their own nation, wishing to impress the Indians with an idea that they were great warriors, and a powerful people who, if exasperated, could crush all the nations of the earth."

Twenty-seven years later, Eh-toh'k-pah-she-pée-shah, or Black Moccasin, was the only Hidatsa to remember Lewis and Clark's visit, and his memories were kinder than contemporary accounts. The artist George Catlin wrote, "He inquired very earnestly for 'Red Hair' and 'Long Knife' (as he had ever since termed Lewis and Clarke), from the fact, that one had red hair (an unexampled thing in his country), and the other wore a broad sword." At the time of this painting, Black Moccasin was believed to be over one hundred years old. "His voice and his sight are nearly gone; but the gestures of his hands are yet energetic and youthful, and freely speak the language of his kind heart," Catlin said.

and where they would spend the winter, had a population of about three thousand—larger than St. Louis, where they had wintered the previous year. It was a cluster of five fortified earth-lodge towns located near the mouth of the Knife River, across from present-day Washburn, North Dakota. Two of the towns were inhabited by members of the Mandan tribe. The other three towns had been founded by people who called themselves Awatixa, Awaxawi, and Hidatsa, but European visitors lumped them all together under a variety of names: Minitaree, Gros Ventre, and Big Bellies. Today they are known as Hidatsa.[9]

Captain Clark & His Men Building a Line of Huts, 1810
Patrick Gass's book about the expedition showed the framework of Fort Mandan as a structure of Escherlike impossibility. The artist intended to show rows of barracks forming two sides of a triangle. The visiting North West Company trader François-Antoine Larocque wrote that the fort was "constructed in a triangular form, ranges of houses making two sides, and a range of amazing long pickets, the front. The whole is made so strong as to be almost cannon ball proof. The two ranges of houses do not join one another, but are joined by a piece of fortification made in the form of a demi circle that can defend two sides of the Fort, on the top of which they keep sentry all night; the lower parts of that building serves as a store." When finished, each of the two sides of the fort contained four rooms measuring fourteen feet square with plank ceilings, lofts insulated with grass and clay, and slanting shed roofs. The outer walls were eighteen feet high.

Trade goods from Shehek-Shote's village, late 1700s and early 1800s
The manufactured goods of Europe were plentiful in Mitutanka, the village across from Fort Mandan. They came mostly from Canada via the North West Company and its competitors. The site of the first village named Mitutanka yielded bushels of late-eighteenth-century trade goods when it was destroyed by a gravel pit in 1958–60. These examples were picked up by a local collector. Any of them could have been seen by Lewis and Clark. Clockwise from upper right: beads (including seed, pony, bugle, and pigeon-egg), fishhooks, buttons, a flintlock hammer, lead shot, gun flints, three gun parts (lock plate, gun worm, and serpent side plate), and arrow heads.

The Mandan and the Hidatsa spoke separate languages and had different origins. Although Mandan origin stories say they came from the south, they had lived since time immemorial at the mouth of the Heart River, opposite present-day Bismarck, North Dakota. At the peak of their power in the mid-1700s, the Mandan had been numerous enough to have five divisions and three major dialect groups. That all changed with the smallpox. After the epidemic of 1780–82, the remnants of the tribe moved upriver to join the Hidatsa for mutual defense.[10] The Hidatsa said they had originated to the north and east, but by the time Lewis and Clark met them, they had adopted the corn-planting, earth lodge-dwelling Missouri Valley lifestyle of the Mandan and even shared with their neighbors some ceremonies and religious practices.

The Corps' first impressions were positive. Clark admired the architecture and fortifications: "This village is Situated on an eminance of about 50 feet above the Water in a handson Plain it Containes houses in a kind of Picket work. the houses are round and Verry large Containing Several families, as also their horses." Private Joseph Whitehouse, who also wrote a journal, admired the people: "The Mandan Indians are in general Stout, well made Men; and they are the lighest coulour'd Indians I ever saw. . . . They behaved extreamly kind to the party . . . and to appearance are a very Industrious sett of people."[11]

The soldiers soon set about building a fort to house them over the winter. Clark chose a spot south of the villages and across the river from most of them—isolated for privacy and defense but close enough to socialize and buy supplies. In late November, as the weather grew "raw and Cold," Clark recorded: "We this day moved into our huts, which are now completed. This place, which we call Fort Mandan, is situated in a point of low ground, on the north side of the Missouri, covered with tall and heavy cottonwood. . . . The latitude by observation is 47° 21′ 47″, and the computed distance from the mouth of the Missouri is 1,600 miles."[12]

That autumn, the explorers met some people who would figure prominently in their lives over the winter and thereafter. First, there was the chief of Mitutanka, the village closest to Fort Mandan. They called him "The Big Man or *Sha-ha-ca*," but his Mandan name was Shehek-Shote, or White Coyote. Traders nicknamed him Big White for his corpulence. He welcomed the newcomers hospitably but warned them, "If we eat you Shall eat, if we Starve you must Starve also."[13]

Indians were not the only company for the members of the expedition. If any of the travelers had expected an isolated aboriginal village, they were soon

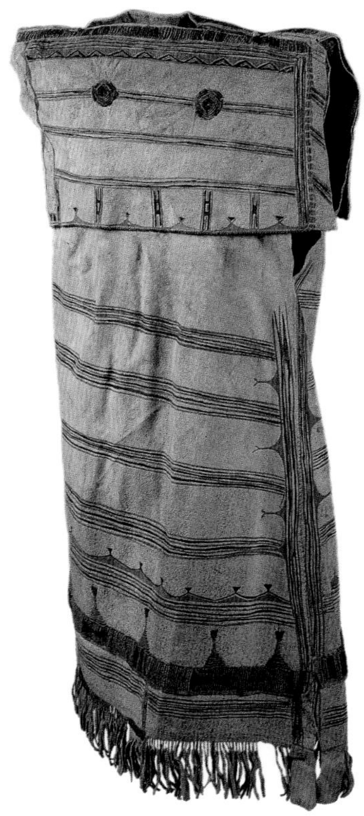

Side-fold dress, late 1700s to early 1800s
Clark never mentioned what Sacagawea wore, but he described Mandan women's dress as "a Shift of the Antelope or big horn animal, fringed & decerated with Blue Beeds Elk tusks & pieces of red Cloth." This dress is made in a rare and early style associated with Northern Plains Indian tribes. It is called a side-fold dress because it is made of two hides, one folded at the side and the other at the top to form a yoke flap. For years this dress and another like it at the Peabody Museum were thought to have been collected by Lewis and Clark, but there is no evidence that Clark or Lewis donated any women's clothing to Peale's Museum. Clark did mention acquiring two dresses, which he gave to his brother and to First Lady Dolley Madison.

disabused. There were already quite a few white men living with the Mandan and Hidatsa. Two competing British companies—the Hudson's Bay Company and the North West Company—had employees stationed there, and a variety of *gens libres*, or freelancers, also called the villages home. We know the names of fourteen who were there in 1804–5.[14]

The presence of so many white men was a testimony to the importance of the Knife River villages as a hub of trade. The Mandan were at the intersection of three trade routes. From the west, the Crow brought products of mountain tribes such as the Nez Perce and Shoshone; from the southwest, the Sioux, Cheyenne, and Arapaho came with products of the plains and Spanish settlements; from the north, the Cree and Assiniboine brought subarctic goods and the wares of Canadian traders. The Mandan themselves raised corn and horses to sell. Each summer they hosted grand trade fairs where feasting, dancing, horse racing, courting, and gambling combined with commerce. They profited enormously from their position as shopkeepers and middlemen, marking up the price whenever the products changed hands.[15]

Significantly, most of the traders at the Knife River villages that winter came from Canada, where the Mandan had been accustomed to turning for the goods of Europe. Lewis and Clark brought hints of a new opportunity: trade goods from the south, possibly at cheaper prices. Competition among European traders always benefited the Indians, for it drove down prices. The Mandan must have scented a shift in the winds of commerce, and they treated the messengers cordially. The British traders had less reason to be cordial. Lewis and Clark brought them a clear statement of U.S. policy: America was in favor of free trade, and foreign companies were

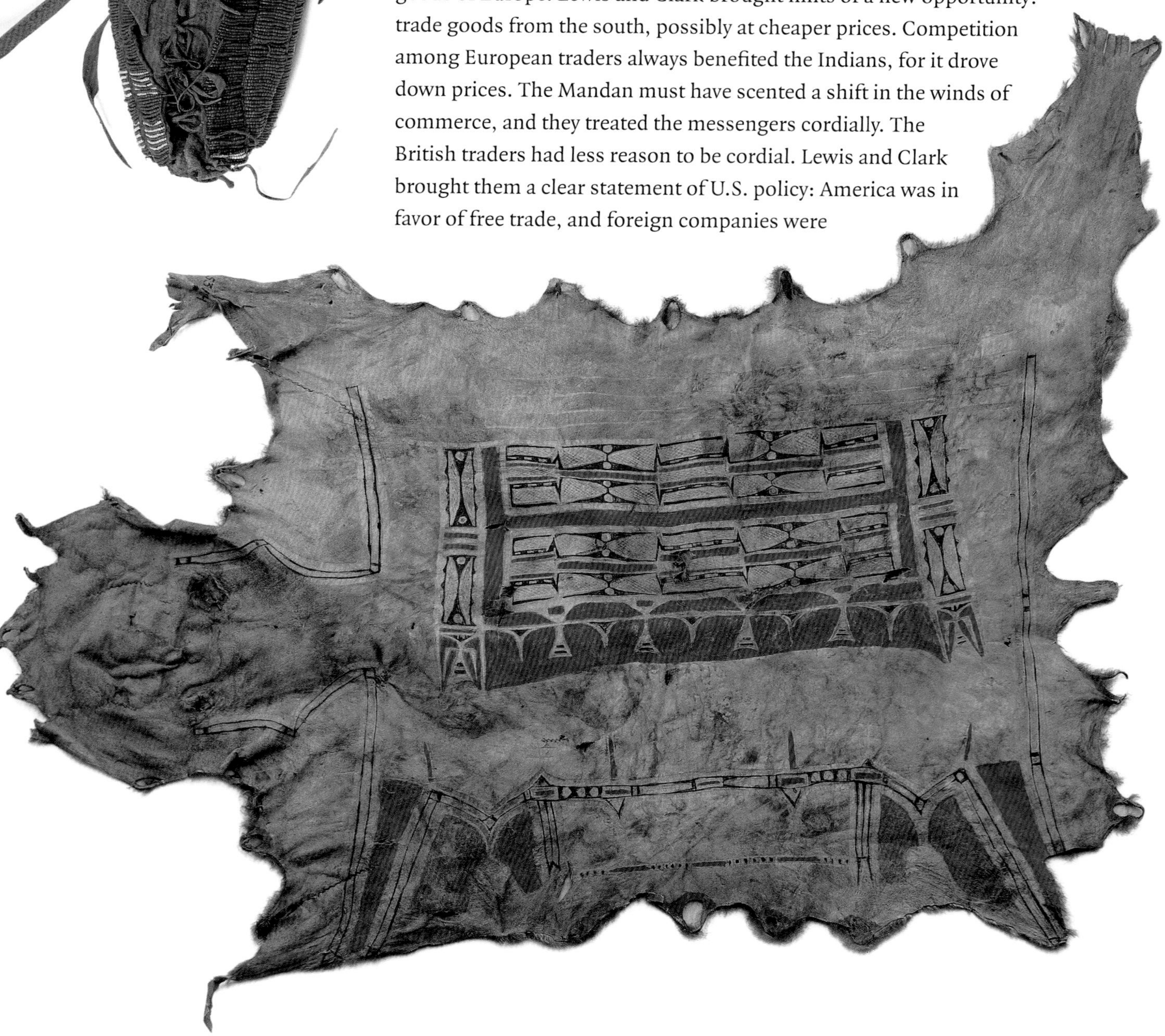

Rattlesnake tails and necklace, 1800s
To maintain the stereotype that Indian women had less difficulty giving birth than did white women, Lewis had to ignore Sacagawea's experience. At the birth of her son in February 1805, he wrote, "This was the first child which this woman had boarn, and as is common in such cases her labour was tedious and the pain violent." The interpreter René Jusseaume suggested giving her some ground rattlesnake tail, a cure that was used by the Choctaw of Louisiana and that he may have learned on the Mississippi. "Having the rattle of a snake by me I gave it to him and he administered two rings of it to the woman. . . . Whether this medicine was truly the cause or not . . . I was informed that she had not taken it more than ten minutes before she brought forth." Despite this observation, Lewis later sweepingly asserted, "It is a rare occurrence for any of them to experience difficulty in childbirth."

OPPOSITE, TOP: **Beaded baby carrier, c. 1800–25**
No one knows how Sacagawea carried her baby on the expedition: in a cradleboard, as was the custom of Shoshone women, or in a folded cloth sling, as many Hidatsa women carried their infants. This carrier, one of the earliest cradleboards from a Rocky Mountain tribe, was almost certainly collected in 1825 by the army officer George C. Hutter. It has been attributed to the Crow, who were an offshoot of the Hidatsa, but it is of a style used throughout the Rocky Mountains and the plateau and shows stylistic resemblances to early Shoshone and Nez Perce work.

OPPOSITE, BOTTOM: **Box and border robe, early 1800s**
Box and border robes were worn by women. To Plains Indian tribes, the bison was associated with earth and the maternal forces that give rise to life. This style of robe was a visual affirmation of the bison's sacred power. The border represented the body of the buffalo. The box (always placed asymmetrically) was an abstract reference to its vital organs. The thin parallel lines often placed opposite the box were said to represent the childbearing stage of a woman's life; the life-lines were sometimes punctuated by tufts separating them into "hills" or stages of life. The head was worn over the left shoulder. This robe may be from the Peale's Museum collection, to which Lewis and Clark donated several robes.

welcome to compete on U.S. soil, but they were not welcome to undermine U.S. sovereignty or to interfere with U.S. tribal relations.

The traders who left the best record of Lewis and Clark were two young, well-educated men of the North West Company: François-Antoine Larocque and Charles Mackenzie. Eager for company and conversation, the traders soon called on their neighbors. "Was very politely received by Captains Lewis and Clarke and passed the night with them," Larocque wrote on November 29. "Their party . . . are sent by Government for the purpose of exploring the North West countries to the Pacific Ocean, so as to settle the boundary line . . . likewise to make it known to the Indians on the Missouri and adjacent country, that they are under the Government of the Big Knives. . . . In short, during the time I was there a very grand plan was schemed, but its being realized is more than I can tell."[16] Mackenzie was more jaundiced. "Captain Lewis could not make himself agreable to us," he wrote. "He could speak fluently and learnedly on all subjects, but his inveterate disposition against the British stained, at least in our eyes, all his eloquence. Captain Clarke was equally well informed, but his conversation was always pleasant, for he seemed to dislike giving offence unnecessarily."[17]

The traders that Lewis and Clark got to know best were not employees of any company. René Jusseaume lived among the Mandan, and Toussaint Charbonneau lived among the Hidatsa, both of them picking up odd jobs from the companies and doing freelance trading on a small scale. The captains immediately hired them as translators. "A french man by Name Chabonah," Clark wrote on November 4, "wished to hire & informed us his 2 Squars were Snake [Shoshone] Indians, we engau him to go on with us and take one of his wives to interpet the Snake language."[18] And so Charbonneau's family moved into some huts adjacent to Fort Mandan.

It was the captains' first introduction to the pregnant teenage girl whose name would become associated with theirs in the years to come. Had they been told that Sacagawea would appear on a U.S. coin before either of them, they would have been incredulous—particularly considering that she was never a

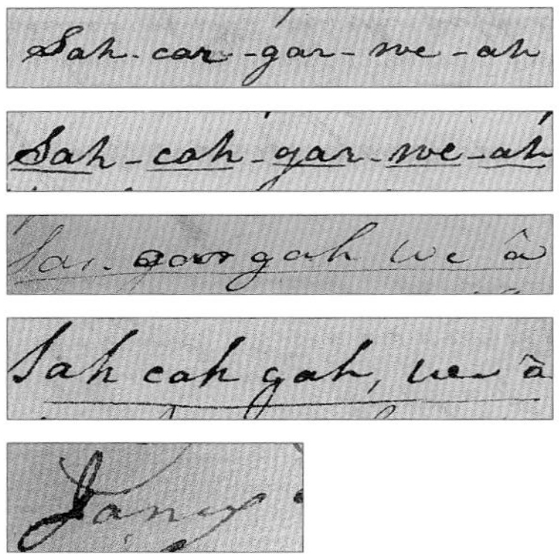

Spellings of Sacagawea's name, 1804–6
Lewis and Clark never settled on how to spell Sacagawea's name or even on what to call her. She appears in the journals as "the interpreters wife" or "the Indian woman" or "the squaw" (*squaw*, an eastern Algonquian term for "woman," originally had no derogatory meaning). Clark, who was apt to give people nicknames, rechristened her "Janey." The best-known spelling, "Sacajawea," was never used by the captains; when compiling their journals for publication in 1814, the ghostwriter Nicholas Biddle inexplicably invented that spelling. In recent years the origin and the meaning of her name have become controversial; most historians believe it is Hidatsa and means "Bird Woman," the translation that Lewis and Clark gave (in Hidatsa, *tsakaka* = bird, *wea* = woman). Some Shoshone speakers believe the name is Shoshone, but translations vary widely.

U.S. citizen. In fact, the most remarkable thing about Sacagawea is how little is known of her. The void of information has been filled in by legend and controversy. Lewis and Clark recorded that she was a Shoshone girl who had been captured by the Hidatsa in a war raid before she had reached the age of puberty. Back in the Knife River villages, her captors "sold her as a slave" to Charbonneau, who had another Shoshone wife from a more southern division of the tribe. The captains gave her name (in various spellings) as Sacagawea, which they translated "Bird Woman," its Hidatsa meaning. During the course of the expedition, they mentioned her seventy-three times: Lewis praised her "fortitude and resolution," and Clark noted her "patience truly admirable."[19]

Some time after the expedition, Sacagawea and her husband moved to St. Louis to take up Clark's offer to raise and educate their son, Jean Baptiste. When the child was baptized in 1809, the priest left a blank where the mother's name should have been and described her as "Sauvagesse de la nation des Serpents." By 1811, the couple had given up on St. Louis and decided to move back to the plains. A traveler who met Sacagawea on the way gave a fuller description of her than either Lewis or Clark. She was "a good creature, of a mild and gentle disposition." Like many Indian wives of traders, she was balanced between two worlds: "greatly attached to the whites, whose manners and dress she tried to imitate, but she had become sickly, and longed to revisit her native country." One year later a trader at Fort Manuel on the Missouri recorded the death, from a "putrid fever," of Charbonneau's unnamed wife. He wrote, "She was a good and the best Women in the fort, aged abt 25 years she left a fine infant girl." In about 1828, Clark also recorded that she was dead.[20] These constitute all the contemporary references to Sacagawea. Almost all have been denied or contradicted.

For years the Hidatsa have protested that Sacagawea was not Shoshone but was one of their ancestors captured in a raid and raised among the Shoshone. The Shoshone deny that her name was Hidatsa and have given various Shoshone translations, the most famous of which is "Boat Launcher." The Wind River Shoshone dispute that she died in 1812 and believe instead that she lived to old age on the Wind River Reservation. The Lemhi Shoshone disagree, either accepting the 1812 death date or maintaining that she moved back to the Rocky Mountains to live with her own family.[21] We can be reasonably sure of one thing: like many other women of the frontier, Sacagawea had to adapt to a fluid identity that made it possible for her to step across boundaries of culture—from Shoshone to Hidatsa, from Hidatsa to French-Canadian, from French-Canadian to American. Her adaptability was a kind of border-crossing at which women were often particularly adept.

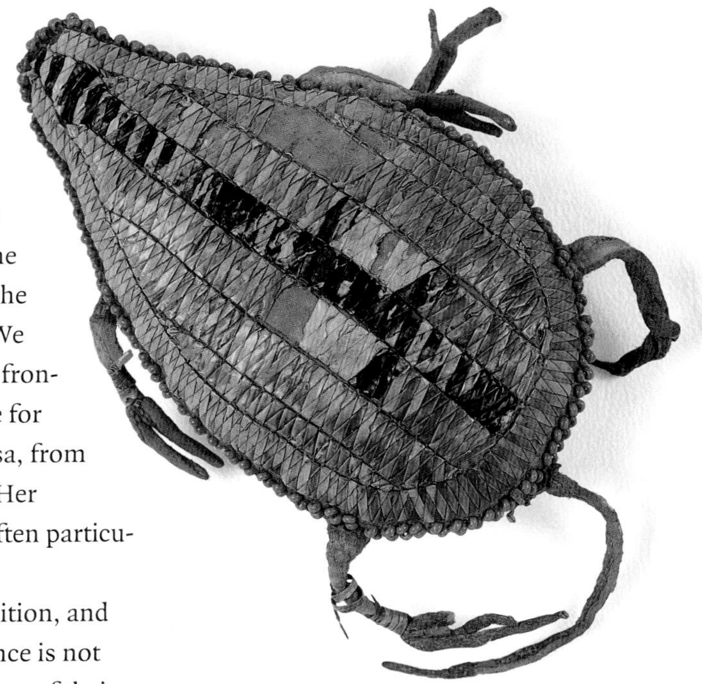

Umbilical bag, mid-1800s
When a Mandan child was born, the mother saved the umbilical cord and sewed it into a decorated case for her child to keep throughout life. The case was often shaped like a lizard, frog, or turtle, animals with a protective power over women and children. The turtle, in particular, was intimately connected with women's power, having influence over conception, birth, infancy, and women's health. "The turtle is a wise woman," young girls were taught. "She hears many things and says nothing. . . . Her skin is a shield. An arrow cannot wound her."

Women barely figure in the voluminous journals of the expedition, and when they appear, they are rarely named as individuals. Their absence is not surprising: simply to speak to Sacagawea, the captains had to get one of their bilingual men to translate a question into French for her husband, who then translated the question into Hidatsa for her. Barriers of gender separation made it even more difficult to speak to other women. But that did not stop the explorers from drawing sweeping conclusions about Indian women's lives. And what the explorers left out cast as long a shadow down the years as what they put in.

A WORLD OF WOMEN

> The women . . . being viewed as property & in course Slaves to the men have not much leisure time to Spear.
>
> —WILLIAM CLARK[22]

> We Hidatsa women were early risers in the planting season. It was my habit to be up before sunrise, while the air was cool, for we thought this the best time for garden work. . . . We thought that the corn plants had souls, as children have souls. . . . We cared for our corn in those days, as we would care for a child.
>
> —BUFFALO BIRD WOMAN, HIDATSA[23]

Lewis and Clark traveled through a world full of women, yet for the most part, they saw only other men. When they did see women, they decried what seemed like oppression. "The Mandans Minit[aree]s &c. treat their women as subservient," Clark noted. The women "do the drugery as Common amongst Savages." Among the Sioux, the women seemed to him like "perfect Slaves to the men, as all Squars of nations much at war, or where the womin are more noumerous than the men." This was the expedition's main discovery about Plains Indian gender relations.[24]

It was not a new discovery. In fact, Thomas Jefferson had stated this widespread belief as early as 1785: "The [Indian] women are submitted to unjust drudgery. This I believe is the case with every barbarous people. . . . The stronger sex imposes on the weaker. It is civilization alone which replaces

OPPOSITE: ***The Travellers Meeting with Minatarre Indians near Fort Clark*, c. 1833**
This aquatint by Karl Bodmer is the only image thought to show Toussaint Charbonneau, Sacagawea's husband. It depicts an occasion on which Charbonneau (third from right) served as a Hidatsa (Minatarre) translator for visiting dignitaries, as he had done for Lewis and Clark twenty-nine years earlier. Lewis called Charbonneau "A man of no peculiar merit," and he was frequently the subject of irritated journal entries about his incompetence, laziness, and beating of his wife. At the time Lewis and Clark met him, Charbonneau was about thirty-six years old and working as a freelance trader among the Hidatsa, though intermittently employed by the North West Company.

women in the enjoyment of their natural equality." But during the course of Lewis and Clark's journey, they would encounter a variety of gender roles, and they would be forced to modify simple assumptions. In many respects, the status of women rose as the men traveled west. Passing through the Plateau tribes, Clark noted a more egalitarian attitude,[25] and on the Pacific coast, it came as an almost unpleasant shock that the women were "permitted to speak freely before them, and sometimes appear[ed] to command with a tone of authority." Forced to account for the variation, Lewis developed the astute theory that the status of women was linked to their economic role. "Those nations treat their old people and women with most difference [deference] and rispect where they subsist principally on such articles that these can participate with the men in obtaining them."[26] Many modern anthropologists would agree.

And yet, the captains could not let go of their first conclusions. Even the commanding Chinookan women were "compelled"—they never chose—"to geather roots, and assist them in taking fish, [and] . . . perform every species of domestic drudgery." Observing them, Lewis confidently echoed Jefferson's assertion that "our women [are] indebted to civilization for their ease and comfort."[27] Generations of readers would accept the implication that Indian women could only benefit from Euro-American civilization.

But was it that simple? Because Lewis and Clark could rarely speak to anyone but men, they could not know that for Native women, as for their non-Indian sisters, power and powerlessness were intertwined. On the plains, men and women lived strictly separate lives and spent much of their time apart. They had separate duties in society and separate religious organizations, and they even spoke different versions of their own languages. As in the United States, in Indian society there was conflict and disrespect between the sexes, including

Hideworking tools, late 1700s to late 1800s
The skilled work of producing fancy clothing was a source of both income and prestige to Indian women. When women stood up to recite their accomplishments in public gatherings, what they mentioned was the number of robes and shirts they had made.

A hideworker used the flesher (upper left) for removing the bits of flesh adhering to a green hide. After the hide had been soaked and wrung out, she removed the hair and evened out the hide's thickness with the scraper (top right). With the awls (lower right), she poked holes to thread sinew through when sewing seams or applying quillwork. The Mandan used both bird and porcupine quills, which had to be soaked and flattened before use, for which the bone quill-flattener (lower left) was used. Embroiderers often kept their dyed quills sorted in cases like this one (center), made from the bladder of a large animal. Since porcupines were associated with the sun, some quillworkers felt that they were trapping the rays of the sun onto the garments they made.

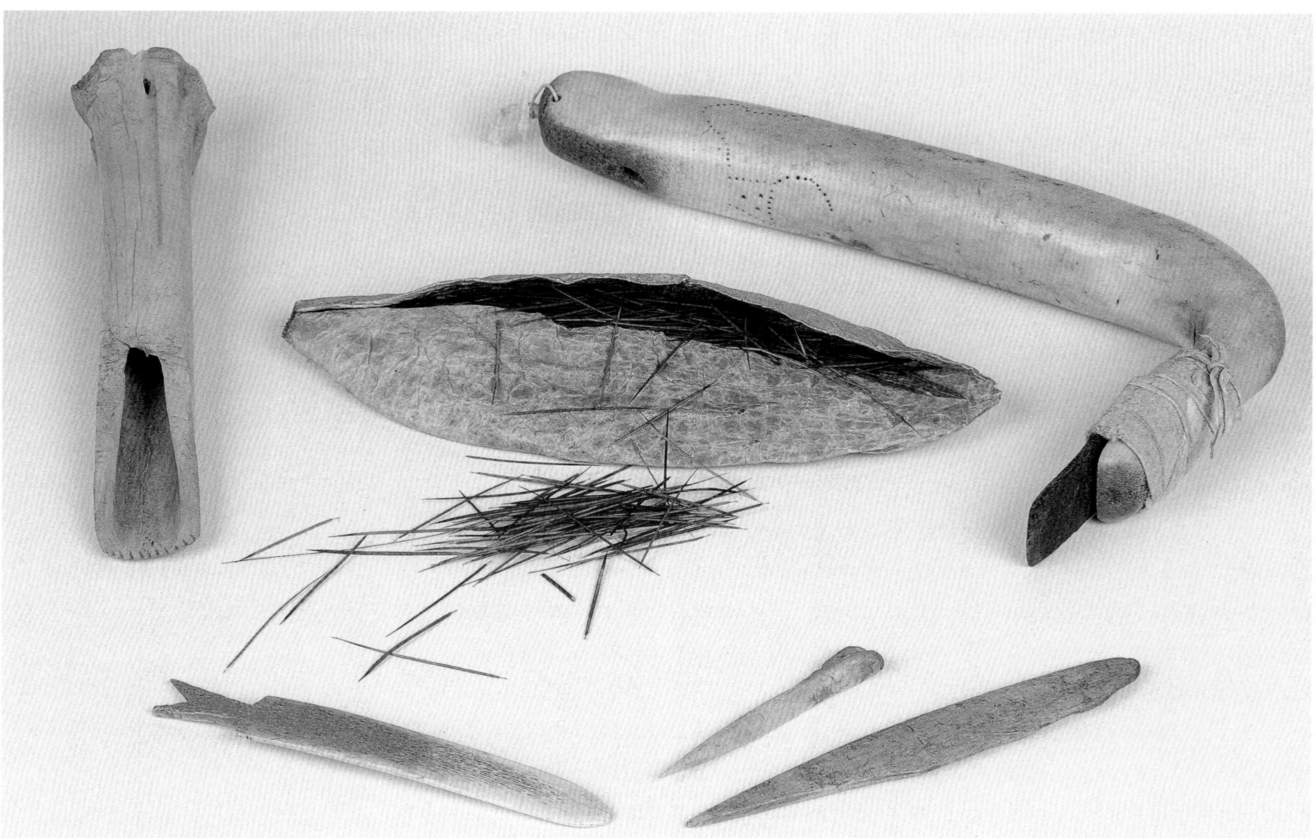

Jeune Indienne, 1807
This may be the only surviving portrait of an Indian woman whom Lewis and Clark met on the expedition. She has been identified as Yellow Corn, the wife of Shehek-Shote. Charles B. J. F. de Saint-Mémin drew her while she was touring Washington, D.C., with the delegation led by Shehek-Shote, whom Lewis accompanied back to the East in 1806. One eyewitness, Augustus John Foster, described Yellow Corn at a performance of Indian rope dancers in Washington: she "sat by her husband with whom she talked in a whisper. . . . She had pretty features, a pale yellowish hue, bunches of ear-rings and her hair divided in the middle, a red line running right across from the back part of the fore-head—tho' no paint was on the face." Henry Brackenridge, who met her after her return to the Mandan villages, said she had "a good complexion and agreeable features."

the domestic violence and ribald talk that Lewis and Clark themselves recorded. Men wielded public power and the power of violence. Nevertheless, for Indian women, separation did not necessarily mean subservience. Their roles complemented men's, requiring mutual reliance and cooperation. Their responsibilities even gave them secret sources of influence. In many ways, Mandan women would have been shocked at the status of women in Virginia.[28]

One woman who got a chance to judge the difference in status was named Yellow Corn. She was the wife of Shehek-Shote, the chief of the Mandan village closest to the spot where the expedition wintered. Her husband held a public position dealing with war and diplomacy, and Lewis and Clark often crossed the river to speak to him in his earth lodge. What they did not know was that the house he lived in and the food he ate belonged to Yellow Corn and her family. The chief's children traced their descent through their mother's line, and belonged to her clan. With others of her age group, Yellow Corn was a member of women's societies that exercised sacred power over growing things, and she had the right to purchase knowledge of female mysteries like pottery and housebuilding. Officially, she had no say in public policy, but she influenced men through persuasion and criticism.[29] When Lewis and Clark invited Shehek-Shote to go with them to meet the president, Yellow Corn insisted on going. The captains were not pleased, but she got her way. Along with her young child, she toured the east coast and met Jefferson. But for Lewis and Clark, she remained a cipher: they never even recorded her name.[30]

Pot, 1700s

The creation of pottery was a secret skill belonging to a few women who passed it on only to worthy young apprentices who paid them for the knowledge. Not just techniques but also sacred histories and songs pertaining to pottery were passed on this way. When knowledgeable old women died in epidemics, skills like pottery making were often lost.

This pot is from On-a-Slant, a Mandan village that was abandoned after the smallpox epidemic of the 1780s. It is of a style called Knife River ware, made between 1500 and 1845. Lewis and Clark collected two pots of this general style but barely mentioned their use. In 1806 Alexander Henry wrote that Mandan pots were made "of different sizes, from five gallons to one quart. In these vessels nothing of a greasy nature is cooked, every family being provided with a brass or copper kettle for the purpose of cooking flesh. . . . They assured us that any kind of flesh cooked in those earthen pots would cause them to split." Catlin added that the "strong and serviceable" Mandan pots were "manufactured by the women of this tribe in great quantities, and modelled into a thousand forms and tastes."

SOURCES OF POWER

> All those near relatives of mine . . . are bound to me like the threads of the spider-web.
>
> —BEAR'S ARM, HIDATSA, QUOTING CHARRED BODY[31]

Like other Mandan women, Yellow Corn had sources of power that were often invisible to outsiders. The most important ones were children, work, sisterhood, and love. The bonds of family affection were as strong in a Mandan village as in Virginia, but there were differences. In Euro-American society, children belonged to their father's family, and inheritance passed from father to son. It was not so with the Mandan and the Hidatsa. These tribes were matrilineal—children belonged to their mother's family and inherited their clan from her. Since children belonged to a clan different from that of their father, all the important ties and duties of clan membership—as well as discipline—were taught by their mother's relations. Religious rites, property, and social status all passed from mother (or mother's brother) to child.[32]

A Mandan household often consisted of a group of sisters, all married to the same man. Women never had to leave their homes: when a couple married, the man came to live in his wife's earth lodge, moving in with her parents and sisters. Children brought up in such a lodge called all their mother's sisters "mother" as well, and if their mother died, the sisters became responsible for her children. As a result, it was inconceivable for a woman to lose custody of her children.

Even among the patrilineal Sioux, where women's status was lower, their rights over their children up to the age of puberty were uncontested. If a couple separated or if the husband sold his wife, gave her away, or abandoned her, she kept the children. It did not stop a Lakota man from asserting: "His woman (*tawicu*) was his property. . . . He might dispose of her at his will." But if he acted on that belief, he might pay the price of losing his children.[33]

The tenderness of Indian women's relationship to their children and grandchildren was embodied in the things they made, from toys to clothes to cradles. Unlike men, women could also call on special powers to protect their

Agricultural tools, c. 1914

Women's agricultural tools were full of symbolism. The Hidatsa made rakes from deer antlers in memory of the deer who raked the garden of Old Woman Who Never Dies. Hoes made from the shoulder bones of bison symbolically linked the fecundity of the herds to the other main food, corn. Digging sticks were found in the bundle of Sacred Woman. Baskets used to haul in the harvest were made with a sacred technique that had to be purchased by a daughter from her mother.

This rake, hoe, digging stick, and basket were created in the early twentieth century by members of a Hidatsa family as replicas of the ones that women had used in traditional gardens. Women were seldom separated from their digging sticks; Sacagawea brought one on the expedition and used it to dig up roots.

Food samples and replicas, early 1900s
"Great numbers of indians of all discriptions Came to the fort many of them bringing Corn to trade," Clark wrote on December 23, 1804. Throughout the winter, Mandan women kept the expedition fed, and these are some of the foods they sold (clockwise, from bottom left): four varieties of corn (flint, red flour, society, and blue flour), *tipsin* (prairie turnip), white and orange pumpkin, black green squash, and red and black beans. These are all indigenous varieties. *Tipsin* was also called *pomme blanche* and *pomme des prairies* by French Canadians.

children, for their songs and dreams reached beings with an interest in their welfare. On children's clothes, symbols of those powers warned away less friendly forces.

The women's work that Clark condemned as "drudgery" was the most important source of Native women's power. They *did* work hard, but it gave them economic control. Unlike Euro-Americans, Plains Indians believed that the products of a woman's labor belonged to her, not to her husband. Even though a man might shoot a buffalo, the hide belonged to the woman who tanned it. All the things she made from the tanned hide—clothes, bags, even the tipi—belonged to her as well, unless she gave them away.[34]

Mandan and Hidatsa women guarded the secrets of skilled craftwork as jealously as medieval guilds in Europe. The secrecy kept prices high and reinforced women's control over the commodities they produced, but that was not why they guarded the knowledge; they did so out of respect. "Basket makers would not let others see how they worked," said the Hidatsa Buffalo Bird Woman, "because if another wanted to learn how to make baskets she should pay a good price for being taught." A mother trained her daughter to value knowledge by encouraging her to give a present for each skill. The price for learning sacred skills like pottery was especially high, because that included songs and rituals given to humans by supernatural beings. "If one did it [a craft] who had no right he or some of his friends would get hurt," said Buffalo Bird Woman.[35]

The basis of the Mandan and Hidatsa tribes' great wealth was the surplus of corn they sold to traders and other tribes. The scale of their agriculture was captured by the fur trader Alexander Henry, who rode between the villages in 1806: "Upon each side were pleasant cultivated spots, some of which stretched up the rising ground on our left, whilst on our right they ran nearly to the Missouri. In those fields were many women and children at work, who all appeared industrious. . . . The whole view . . . had . . . the appearance of a country inhabited by a civilized nation."[36] It was women who owned and worked the fields, with their sisters and daughters, and who guarded the ripening corn from birds and boys. Women kept the seed and danced to lure the corn spirits back each spring. Women processed and preserved the food so that it would last through the winter, and they prepared it into meals. And yet, no aspect of women's work caused more confusion for visitors from the East.

Mortar and pestle, pre-1913
For centuries, Mandan and Hidatsa women had been doing the backbreaking work of grinding their corn in mortars like this, sunk into the floor of the earth lodge. The pestle was held with the weighted end up. They used the ground corn in mushes, soups, and stews.

Corn mill, late 1700s
The corn mills brought by the expedition must have looked something like this English hand mill for grinding coffee, corn, or beans. Lewis and Clark did not present it to the Mandan women, whose role it was to grind corn. Instead, they gave it to the men, who promptly dismantled the mill to turn it into gender-appropriate arrow points.

Dance of the Mandan Women, c. 1833
The White Buffalo Cow Society was composed of women past the age of menopause. The society traced its origin to the buffalo, who left a child of their own with the Mandan tribe as a promise for their return. Each winter they came back in the shape of women to visit their child and dance. When the White Buffalo Cow Society reenacted this event, they brought the blizzards that drove the buffalo, looking for shelter, into the valleys, where they could be hunted. The dance was held during the shortest days of the year. When word went out that the ceremony was about to commence, the whole village observed quiet order. Dogs were taken into the lodge, hunting was prohibited, and women cut no wood. Such was the power of the White Buffalo women that even mentioning the society during the wrong time of year could bring an early frost.

Euro-Americans also divided labor by gender, but differently: to them, farming was the work of men and slaves. Seeing women in the fields, white men often concluded that they were slaves as well. European preconceptions about gender roles made it difficult for them even to see what the Indians were doing as agriculture. Gender-role blindness also led to a comic blunder by Lewis and Clark. Hoping to introduce the Indians to mechanized agriculture, they presented a corn mill to the Mandan men, failing to take into account that grinding corn was a woman's job. The Mandan men later reduced the corn mill to arrow barbs. Weapons were more appropriate gifts for men than food processors; had the mill been given to women, the result may have been different.[37]

Incomprehension and disapproval of Indian work roles did not stop the Corps of Discovery from relying on women's labor. Over the winter they bought countless bushels of corn to eat and to take upriver in the spring of 1805. But in the long run, Clark was prophetic. As the market economy reached west, women's control was eroded by traders who dealt with men for commodities produced by women. First, men "took charge" of the small furs prized by traders and of the proceeds from their sale.[38] Later, other aspects of women's work came under new rules. When Lewis and Clark compensated Sacagawea for her services, they did not pay her: they paid her husband. It was a taste of things to come.

Sisterhood was another source of power for Indian women, but it was one that Lewis and Clark never discovered. On the plains, men and women had

Courting flute, late 1800s
Music was as important in Indian courtship as it is today. A visitor to the Mandan villages in 1806 wrote: "The custom here is to barricade the doors of the huts during the night and not admit the young men. The latter therefore employ the night in addressing love songs to their mistresses." To put women in the right mood, Lakota men played flutes carved in the shape of birds with conspicuous courtship behaviors and calls, like the crane or snipe. Played correctly, the courting flute could produce music that was irresistible to women.

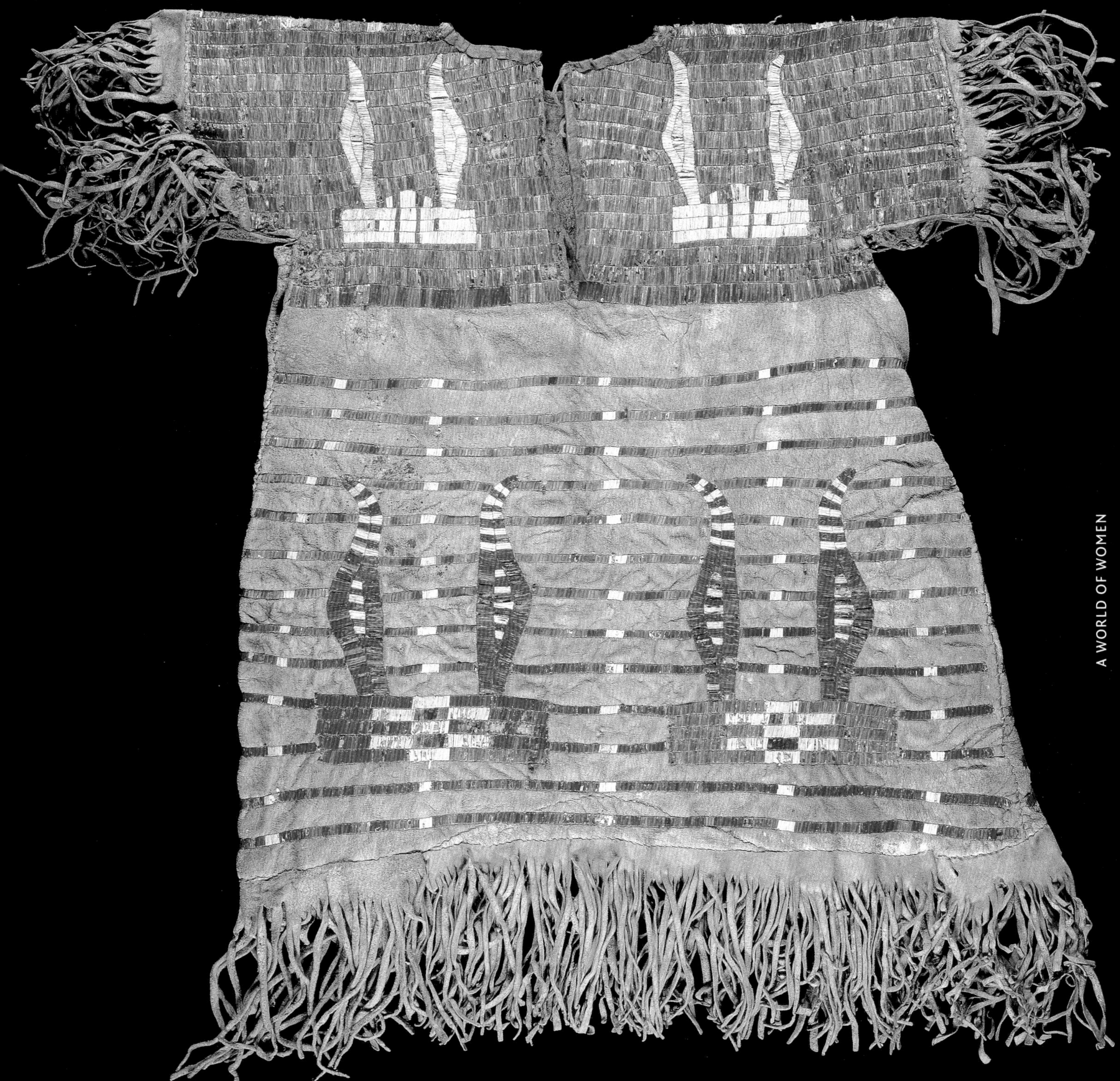

Child's dress with elk design, pre-1903
The quillwork design on this dress is usually thought to symbolize the supernatural power of the elk. The elongated horns of a bull elk were associated with the Elk Dreamers Society of the Lakota but were also found on baby carriers. The man who dreamed of the bull elk received mystical powers to entrance women.

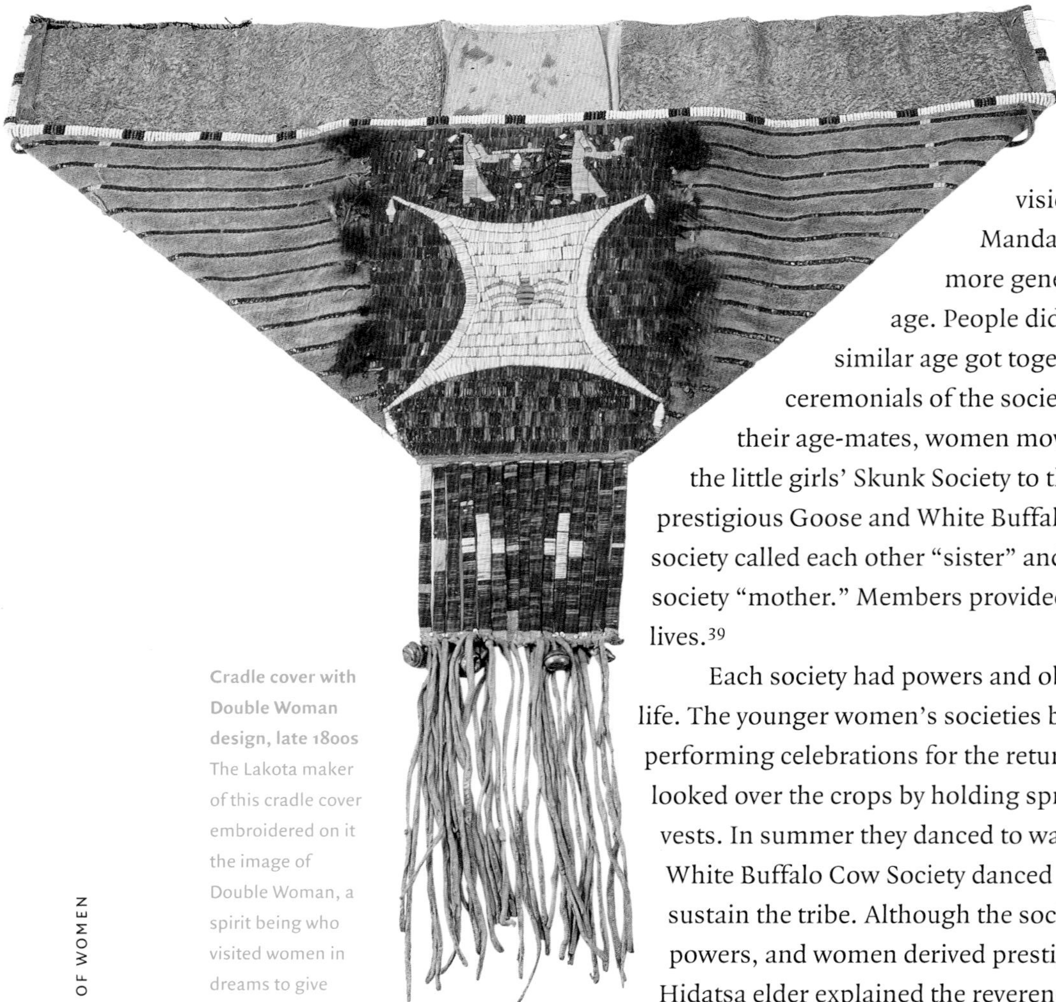

Cradle cover with Double Woman design, late 1800s The Lakota maker of this cradle cover embroidered on it the image of Double Woman, a spirit being who visited women in dreams to give them supernatural powers, including artistic skill and seduction. Here, Double Woman is depicted as two women joined by a cord. Each woman is shown in two colors to emphasize her dual nature. Below Double Woman is a spiderweb. Iktomi, the spider, was a cunning trickster whose web had "catching-power." A woman who had dreamed of Double Woman could perform a ceremony that called on the power of the spider to bring good fortune to her child. She then had the right to mark the child's belongings with a spiderweb symbol. This cradle cover may have belonged to such a child.

separate social and religious organizations. Among the Lakota, membership in societies was often limited to those who had dreamed or received visions from a particular source. But in the Mandan and Hidatsa villages, membership was more general. There, societies were organized by age. People did not join as individuals; all the girls of a similar age got together to purchase the songs, regalia, and ceremonials of the society from the generation above them. With their age-mates, women moved up the scale through their lives: from the little girls' Skunk Society to the River Society or Enemy Society, to the prestigious Goose and White Buffalo Cow societies. Members of a women's society called each other "sister" and called the women of the next-older society "mother." Members provided mutual support throughout their lives.[39]

Each society had powers and obligations related to a different aspect of life. The younger women's societies brought their village success in war by performing celebrations for the return of a war party. The Goose Society looked over the crops by holding springtime rites that ensured good harvests. In summer they danced to ward off drought and grasshoppers. The White Buffalo Cow Society danced in winter to draw the buffalo close and sustain the tribe. Although the societies were not sacred, they had great powers, and women derived prestige and social standing from them.[40] A Hidatsa elder explained the reverence in which they were held: "This society of old women was . . . inspired by the spirits of the mysterious women who live everywhere on the earth. . . . They appear in many forms, sometimes as animals, sometimes even as little children. Wherever they wish to go they can travel to in no time, just like thought. *Wa-hu-pa Wi-a,* Mysterious woman, they are called."[41]

Another potent source of female power lay in sexual attraction. For Plains Indian women, love was ruled by tradition and mystery. The Lakota believed that when a girl reached sexual maturity, changes occurred: "A *tonwan* [spiritual essence] possesses her which gives her the possibility of motherhood and makes her *wakan* [holy] and this *tonwan* . . . [is] very powerful for either good or evil as it may be used." Forces of disorder and irrationality lurked near women between puberty and marriage and could make approaching them dangerous.[42]

Men were not without powers of their own. A young man who had distinguished himself in war or hunting was eligible to look for a marriage partner, and he often called on the supernatural for help. The bull elk was considered the master of power over females. A man who dreamed of the elk received its mystical ability to attract women. He might exercise that power through music, dancing, love potions, or charms, and he had the right to wear elk-horn symbols on his possessions.[43]

But men were not the only aggressors in love. Double Woman, or Anog Ite, could give women the power of seduction over men. According to Lakota elders, she "was like a woman with two faces. One face was very beautiful, and the other very ugly. . . . She would lure hunters away with her beautiful face, and when she had them in her embrace she would turn her horrid face to them and frighten them out of their senses." The woman who dreamed of Double Woman could cause all men near her "to become possessed. . . . So the people are very afraid of her. . . . Whoever dreams in this way seems to be crazy . . . but then everything she makes is very beautiful." According to a modern Lakota scholar, Double Woman "represents a dualism in which a moral choice must be made. . . . the dreamer must choose between the life of reckless fun and sexuality or the life of modesty."[44]

According to Clark, the men of the Corps needed no aid from the elk, since they "found no difficulty in getting women."[45] Tales of Native licentiousness were a staple of travel narratives, and the journal-keeping men knew that their readers would miss the tales if omitted, so hints of sexual escapades abounded. The only love medicine used by the Corps was mercury, with which Lewis dosed the men who contracted venereal disease.

But every exchange between the expedition and the Native tribes required translation, and sex was no exception. Sexual mores were a perpetual source of misunderstanding. The men of the Corps were constantly on the lookout for sexual partners, but often when they found willing women, their reactions were judgmental. To Missouri Valley tribes, sex could be a way of fulfilling sacred obligations of hospitality, a way of transferring supernatural power, and a way of incorporating strangers into kinship and trade networks. Men who offered their wives to the visitors for one of those reasons were scrupulously rejected by the captains, despite the ill will it caused. When the women themselves made overtures, the journals called them "lechous" and "lude." But the captains did not demand from their men the chastity that they criticized Indian women for lacking. Lewis wrote:

> "To prevent this mutual exchange of good officies altogether I know it impossible to effect, particularly on the part of our young men whom some months abstanence have made very polite to those tawney damsels."[46]

Cradle cover, late 1800s
Plains Indian women often worked symbols of sacred power into the objects they created for themselves and their children, as a kind of visual prayer. The Lakota woman who made this quillwork hood used the images of animals that watched over the well-being of her child: the spider (symbolized by the four-sided "web") and the lizard. To the Lakota, the fact that bullets pass through webs without harming them was evidence of the spider's protective power. The four-sided design evoked the four directions, home of the thunder powers to which the spider was allied.

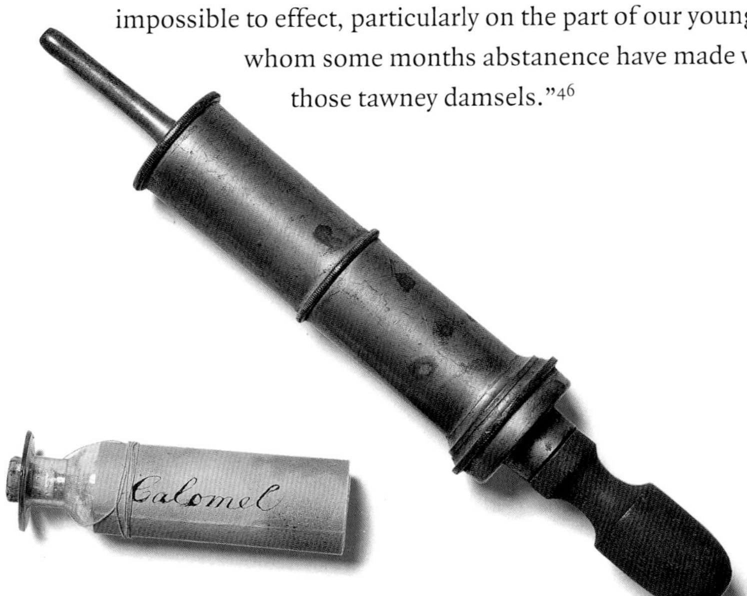

Calomel bottle and urethral syringe, late 1700s to early 1800s
Lewis took the precaution of bringing the standard remedies for venereal disease, and he began treating the men in January 1805. Calomel, or mercurous chloride, was a tasteless powder used primarily as a purgative. Incorporated into a salve, it was used to treat syphilis by applying it directly to lesions. Lewis was confident of its efficacy, writing in 1806, "I cured him [Goodrich] as I did Gibson last winter by the uce of mercury." It almost certainly had little effect: the "cures" were natural remissions.

When venereal disease resulted in urinary blockage, standard treatment called for irrigation of the urethra with a caustic solution and lukewarm water. On Lewis's list of requirements for the medical equipment of the Corps were "4 Pewter Penis Syringes" to perform this operation. He bought them from the Philadelphia druggists Gillaspy & Strong for a dollar total.

THE WOMEN THEY LEFT BEHIND

Lewis and Clark saw a huge contrast between the downtrodden Indian women and the women of their own culture. Lewis idealized women of his race, writing once of "the pure celestial virtues and amiable qualifications of that lovely fair one."[47] Women of the upper classes in Virginia had an easier life than did Indian women, and undoubtedly few plantation mistresses would have chosen to exchange places.

Yet Virginians of the time did not think it proper for even elite women to have much power. A woman of Virginia could not vote, hold public office, or serve on juries. She could make a contract or sue in court only under special circumstances. Marriage was a mixed blessing: to be without a husband often meant poverty, but when a woman married, her property became her husband's. Her children belonged to their father's family, and a divorced or widowed woman risked losing custody. As in Indian society, women's and men's work was segregated. And yet, Virginian women had some of the same informal powers that Indian women had—through children, work, religious authority, and love. Such powers were often invisible to men.[48]

Meriwether Lewis's most enduring relationship with a woman was that with his mother, Lucy Marks. Though she came from the landowning class of

Lucy Marks, c. 1830
Lucy Meriwether Lewis Marks (1752–1837) was described as having "refined features, a fragile figure, and a masterful eye." Legends of her handiness with a shotgun—against both animals and invading British soldiers—propagated down the generations through her family.

Spectacles of Lucy Marks, c. 1830
According to family tradition, these are the spectacles that Lucy Marks wore in her portrait.

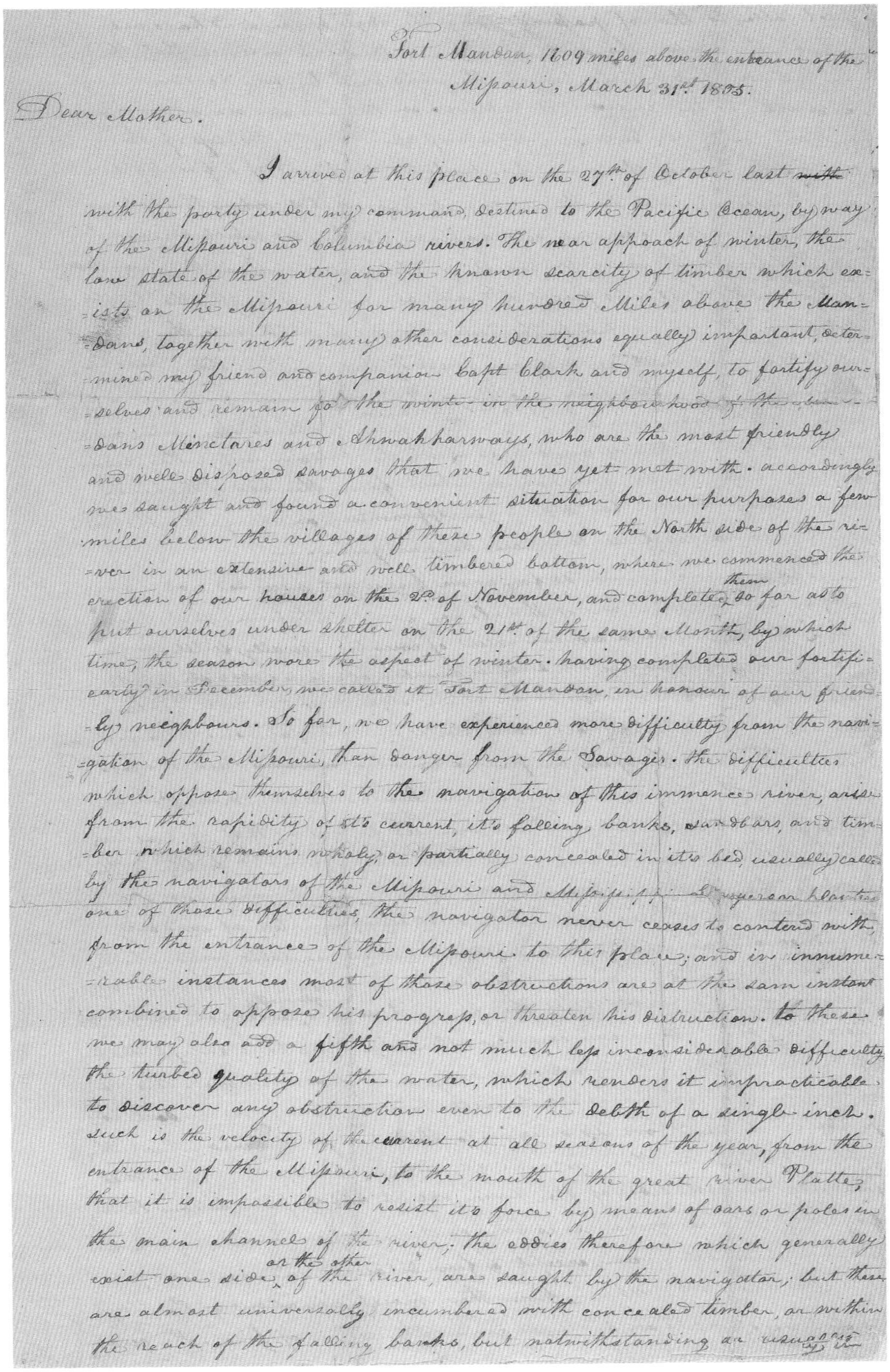
Fort Mandan, 1609 miles above the entrance of the Missouri, March 31st 1805.

Dear Mother.

I arrived at this place on the 27th of October last ~~with~~ with the party under my command, destined to the Pacific Ocean, by way of the Missouri and Columbia rivers. The near approach of winter, the low state of the water, and the known scarcity of timber which exists on the Missouri for many hundred Miles above the Mandans, together with many other considerations equally important, determined my friend and companion Capt Clark and myself, to fortify ourselves and remain for the winter in the neighbourhood of the Mandans Minetares and Ahwahharways, who are the most friendly and well disposed savages that we have yet met with. accordingly we sought and found a convenient situation for our purposes a few miles below the villages of these people on the North side of the river in an extensive and well timbered bottom, where we commenced the erection of our houses on the 2d. of November, and completed them so far as to put ourselves under shelter on the 21st. of the same Month, by which time, the season wore the aspect of winter. having completed our fortifi- early in December, we called it Fort Mandan, in honour of our friendly neighbours. So far, we have experienced more difficulty from the navigation of the Missouri, than danger from the Savages. the difficulties which oppose themselves to the navigation of this immence river, arise from the rapidity of it's current, it's falling banks, sandbars, and timber which remains wholy, or partially concealed in it's bed, usually called by the navigators of the Missouri and Mississippi [illegible] one of those difficulties, the navigator never ceases to contend with, from the entrance of the Missouri to this place; and in innumerable instances most of those obstructions are at the same instant combined to oppose his progress, or threaten his distruction. to these we may also add a fifth and not much less inconsiderable difficulty, the turbid quality of the water, which renders it impracticable to discover any obstruction even to the debth of a single inch. such is the velocity of the current at all seasons of the year, from the entrance of the Missouri, to the mouth of the great river Platte, that it is impossible to resist it's force by means of oars or poles in the main channel of the river; the eddies therefore which generally exist one side or the other of the river, are sought by the navigator; but these are almost universally incumbered with concealed timber, or within the reach of the falling banks, but notwithstanding are usually [illegible]

Letter of Meriwether Lewis to Lucy Marks, 1805
From Fort Mandan, Lewis wrote to his mother to let her know that he was safe, well, and having a good time. "So far," he wrote, "we have experienced more difficulty from the navigation of the Missouri, than danger from the Savages." After assuring her that he was going to reach the Pacific Ocean by summer, he wrote, "Give yourself no uneasiness with rispect to my fate, for I assure you that I feel myself perfectly as safe as I should do in Albemarle." Though Meriwether left his mother's home at age thirteen, the two always kept in touch by mail. Many of his letters to her survive; hers do not.

Virginia, she had "spartan ideas" and "a good deal of the autocrat" about her, according to those who knew her. And yet she was "kind without limit" and full of "activity beyond her sex." At seventeen, she married her cousin William Lewis, a man of "hypocondriac affections," or what today we would call depression. After ten years, four children, and a revolution, he died, and she married John Marks, a relative of Jefferson's by marriage. She outlived her second husband as well, retiring to her practice of herbal medicine and her prized library of books.[49]

Because of the laws of primogeniture, Lucy lost guardianship of her oldest son, Meriwether, when her first husband died. It was not that anyone doubted her fitness; it was simply because the eight-year-old boy was heir to the Lewis estate that his father's family had to be in charge of his upbringing and property—including the property that Lucy was living on. And so Lucy's

Julia Hancock Clark, c. 1810
Julia's family nicknamed her "Judy," and tradition held that Clark named the Judith River in Montana for her, thinking her name was Judith. "She is verry domestuc," Clark wrote of her in 1809. "Stays at home and works, when She finds herSelf loneson . . . takes a little cry and amuses herself again with her domestuc concerns." When the novelist Eva Emory Dye interviewed family members in 1901–4, they reported that Julia "was as famous for her excessive neatness, and scrupulous care as a hostess . . . in the Mansion of the Governor of Missouri, as in her beautiful suburban home."

OPPOSITE: **Notebook of Julia H. Clark, 1808–20** and **Locket with hair of Julia and Mary Clark, c. 1820**
Julia used one of the leftover journal books from the expedition to keep her household accounts and inventories. Ill with tuberculosis, she made this list of household belongings before returning to her parents' home in Virginia to recover. She never returned.

Like many other families of their day, the Clarks saved locks of their loved ones' hair. This locket contains strands from Julia and her daughter Mary, who died the next year.

husband's brother Nicholas Lewis became the boy's guardian. She did not lose actual custody of her son for another five years. By then, she had remarried and thus had lost all claim to the Lewis estate.[50]

The death of her second husband in 1791 brought on more complications. Lucy was the executrix of John Marks's estate, which she managed till their sons were old enough to inherit it; but her hands were somewhat tied because a man had to represent her in suits or contracts related to the property. And so the "masterful" Lucy enlisted her young son Meriwether, assigning him the power of attorney to represent her. She still had authority, but she had to exercise it invisibly, through male proxies.[51]

If a matriarch of Lucy's standing had little control over her children and property, a younger and less experienced woman was that much more dependent. Such was the case of Julia Hancock, the most important woman in William Clark's life. Clark family legend said that when William saw the young Julia Hancock at her family's Virginia plantation in 1801, he decided to marry her. If so, he was prescient, because she was only ten years old. After returning from the expedition in 1806, Clark's first visit—even before he went to Washington—was to her family to fix the date of their wedding. "I have made an attacked most vigorously," he wrote Lewis with soldierly jocularity. "We have come to terms, and a delivery is to be made first of January [. . .] when I shall be in possession highly pleasing to my self." Julia had just turned sixteen when they married.[52]

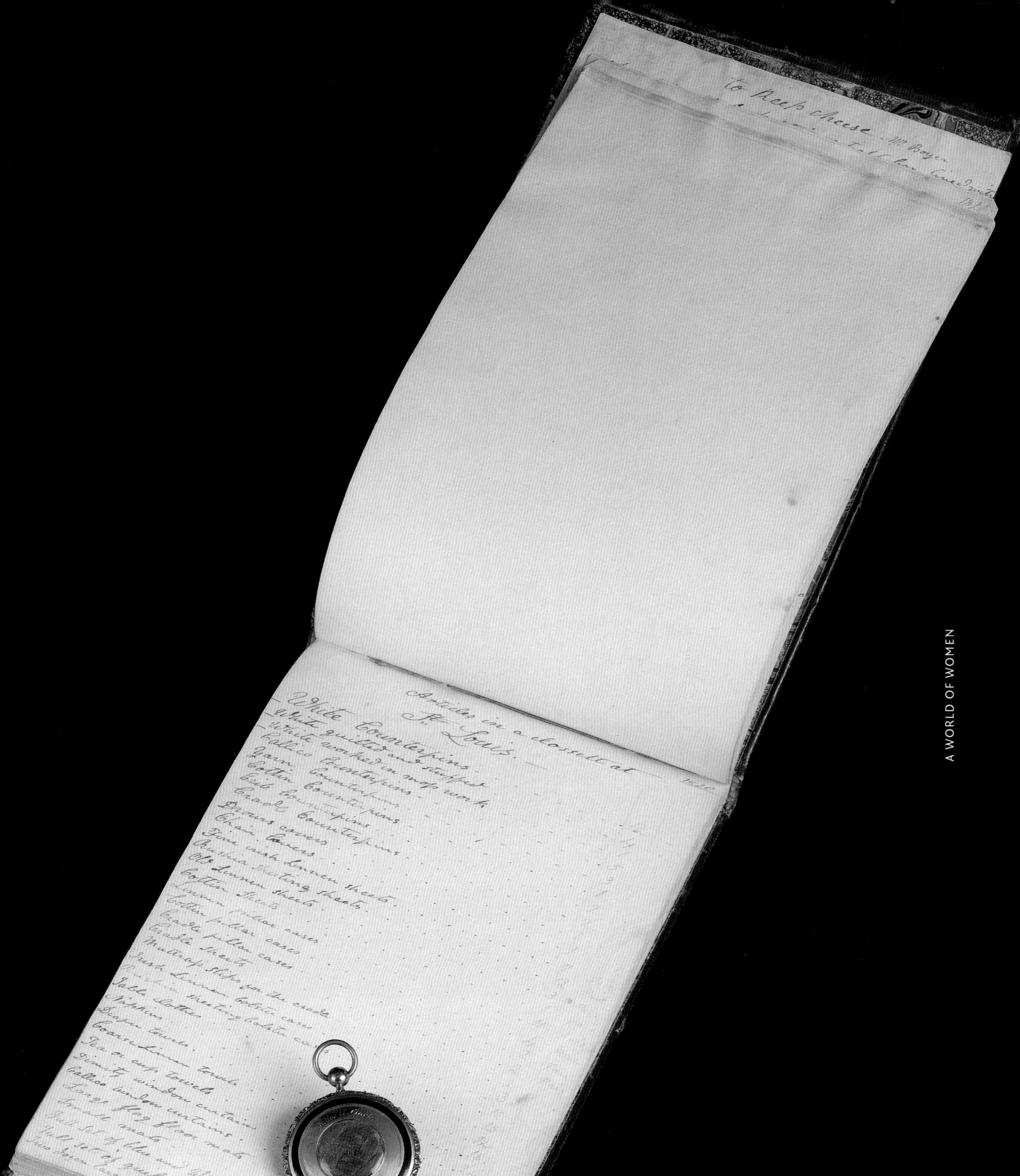
To keep cheese
Articles in a clossett at
St. Louis
White Counterpins
White quilted and stuffed
White worked in mop work
Callico Counterpins
Yarn Counterpins
Cotton Counterpins
Cradle Counterpins
Chair covers
Fine irish Linnen sheets
Cotton sheets
Linnen Sheets
Cotton pillow cases
Cradle pillow cases
Cradle sheets
Table clothes
Napkins
Diaper towels
Coarse Linnen towels
Tea or cup towels
Dimity window curtains
Callico window curtains

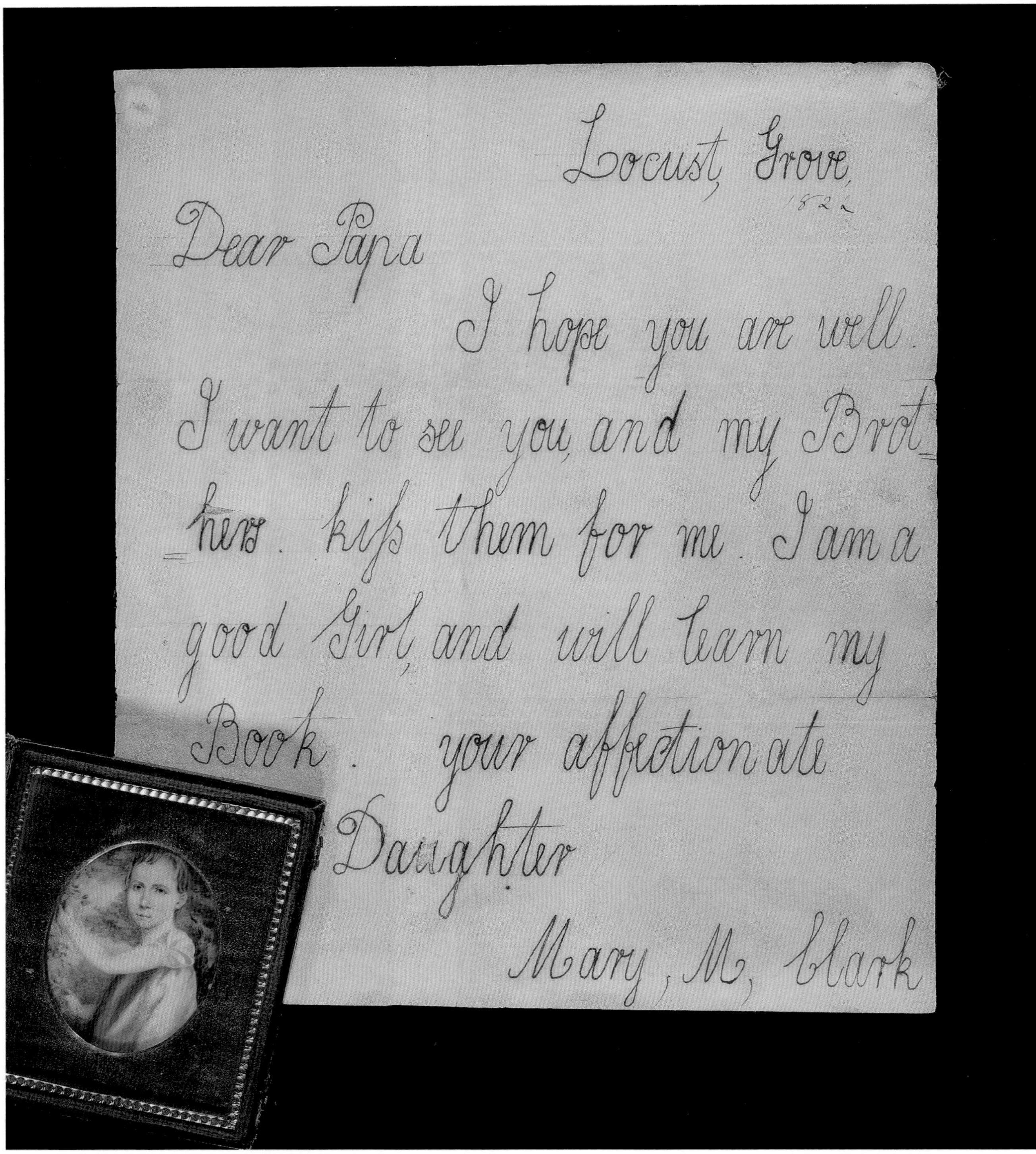

Locust Grove,
1822

Dear Papa

I hope you are well. I want to see you, and my Brot-hers. kiss them for me. I am a good Girl, and will learn my Book. your affectionate Daughter

Mary, M, Clark

Letter from Mary Margaret Clark to Papa, 1821 and **Miniature of Mary M. Clark, pre-1821**
The Clarks' only daughter was born in 1814 and inherited her father's famous red hair. After Julia's death, Mary lived with relatives in Virginia and Louisville, from where she sent this letter to her father in St. Louis. She died soon after. The letter was still in Clark's papers when he died in 1838.

Julia had privileges that most women of her day could not expect. She grew up in a wealthy household, surrounded by slaves. She was well educated, owning volumes of Shakespeare and writing more legibly than her husband. And yet her marriage followed some customs that a Mandan woman might have found demeaning. Both Virginian and Mandan women married young, around age fifteen to seventeen. Their husbands were often older; the twenty-two-year difference between William and Julia was not unusual in either culture and made for a relationship as much like father and daughter as husband and wife. If they belonged to prominent families, girls could not decide on their marriage partners; that was a matter of negotiation between parents. But there the similarities ended. In Mandan society, a suitor offered rich gifts of horses and goods, and girls boasted about how much had been given for them, since it was a public affirmation of their value to the family. In Virginia, it was the girl's family who paid to get daughters off their hands; Julia brought a groaning boatload of slaves and furnishings to set up house with her new husband. A Mandan girl stayed in her parents' home, surrounded by a supportive family; a Virginian girl had to move to her husband's home. In Julia's case, that meant an eight-hundred-mile trek westward to St. Louis, where she was isolated from family and friends and was utterly dependent on her husband's kindness.

As far as we know, Julia was never discontent with her marriage. As the wife of a prominent man, she managed two large houses, entertained official visitors, and set the social and material standards of St. Louis society. It was essential work, but it did not meet Lewis's criterion of adding to the family's subsistence, so it gave her little economic power. Family letters recorded little of her life other than pregnancy and ill health. In ten years, she had five children. She was dead at twenty-eight. Clark then married her cousin.

Children, work, sisterhood, and love worked as powerfully for Julia and Lucy as for Sacagawea and Yellow Corn. They were not direct powers but worked only through their influence on men. But if Lewis and Clark thought Indian women would gladly assume the rights and roles of Virginia women, they might have been surprised.

CLARK 19th Novr 1805
Chin nook R
Cape Disapointment
S 88° W 11 m
Point Adams
Round
S 41° W 7 m
6 Encamped from 16th to 25th Novr 18
Chinnook old Villa

FOUR Depictions of the Land

You will endeavor to inform yourself, by enquiry, of the character . . . of the country.

—THOMAS JEFFERSON TO MERIWETHER LEWIS[1]

The Mandan marked the passage of seasons with a continual series of ceremonies and celebrations. At the earliest sign of spring, members of the women's Goose Society assembled to welcome the water birds back from the south, for they brought the corn spirits to renew the gardens. In May the community gathered for the Corn Ceremony to bless the seed. Throughout the warm months, the Goose Society continued to meet, and the celebration of Old Woman Who Never Dies brought rain and good growing conditions.

In summer the grandest ceremony of all, the Okipa, reenacted the most ancient myths surrounding the creation of the world and ensured an abundance of buffalo. Fall brought a harvest festival and Eagle-Trapping rites. In winter the Red Stick, Snow Owl, and White Buffalo Cow ceremonies called the winter buffalo. Rites associated with war and healing, such as the Small Hawk, People Above, Shell Robe, and Bear ceremonies, could be held at any time of year. When there was not a celebration going on in the Mandan villages, there was almost sure to be one in the Hidatsa towns just to the north.[2]

The men at Fort Mandan also celebrated holy days in the winter of 1804. On Christmas, they got some privacy by asking the Indians not to visit them because "it

Winter Village of the Minatarres, c. 1833 The summer villages of the Hidatsa (Minatarre) were on the flat terraces of the river valley, but during winter the people moved into settlements in the shelter of the wooded bottomlands. The men at the left are playing with ice gliders. Karl Bodmer made the sketch on which this aquatint is based when he spent the winter of 1833–34 at the Knife River Villages. The village shown contained about eighty households.

Tin horn, 1800s
The "Sounden horn" the men used for New Year's merrymaking was probably similar to this peddler's horn. Lewis called the horns "Tin blowing Trumpets" on his list of requirements, and he purchased four of them for fifty cents each from the tinsmith Thomas Passmore in Philadelphia. The Corps used them frequently for summoning missing men, announcing arrivals and departures, and making military signals.

Page 134: William Clark, Map of Columbia River near the mouth (detail), 1805. See page 155.

was a Great medician day with us." As Sergeant John Ordway described it, their celebration was anything but religious: "We fired the Swivels at day break & each man fired one round. our officers Gave the party a drink of Taffee [ratafia, an alcoholic drink]. we had the Best to eat that could be had, & continued firing dancing & frolicking dureing the whole day."[3]

New Year's Day was even more sociable. Sixteen of the men got the commanders' permission to visit the village across the river. Ordway was one of them. "Carried with us a fiddle & a Tambereen & a Sounden horn. as we arived at the entrence of the vil. we fired one round then the music played. loaded again. then marched to the center of the vil, fired again. then commenced dancing. a frenchman danced on his head and all danced around him." By the time Clark arrived, he found the villagers "much pleased at the Danceing of our men." He noted, "I ordered my black Servent to Dance which amused the Croud verry much, and Some what astonished them, that So large a man Should be active &c."[4]

It was not the last time they would use music and revelry as an ice-breaker and social lubricant. Their tactics

generally worked, but not always. Behind their backs, one Mandan grumbled to the British traders about American parsimony, since all their noisemaking did not include the Mandan custom of gifts: "It is true they have ammunition, but they prefer throwing it away idly than sparing a shot of it to a poor Mandane."[5]

Any hard feelings could not have lasted long. A few nights later the Mandan reciprocated by inviting the soldiers to the Red Stick ceremony. The white men viewed it with the same baffled incomprehension that the Mandan might have felt at a Christmas ceremony, and for the same reason—they did not know the sacred stories and events that the ritual commemorated. And so the soldiers recorded only the lurid, superficial aspects of this "curious Custom," as Clark called it. "The young men . . . [each] go to one of the old men with a whining tone and *request* the old man to take his wife (who presents necked except a robe) and —— (or sleep with him). . . . all this is to cause the buffalow to Come near So that They may kill thim." Unknown to Clark, only men possessing rights to pray to the buffalo bulls could participate in this ceremony, which was overseen by the owner of the Earthnaming bundle. The older men impersonated the buffalo bulls and transmitted sacred buffalo power to their clan "sons" through their wives. Bear's Arm, a Hidatsa, said of a celebrant, "His prayers were supposed to show that by giving the ceremony he was responsible for the welfare of all the people."[6]

As the temperature sank to forty degrees below zero, the men's activities were curtailed. "We did nothing but git wood for our fires," Ordway wrote one cold day. "Our Rooms are verry close and warm . . . but the Sentinel who Stood

The Interior of the Hut of a Mandan Chief, c. 1833
Clark wrote: "Their Houses (also Cald. Lodges) are built in a Circular form of different Sises from 20 to 70 feet Diameter and from 8 to 14 feet high, Supported with 4 pillars Set in a Squar form near the Center near the hight of the hut. . . . The Mandans & Minnetarras & live in 2. 3 & 4 families in a Cabin, their horses & Dogs in the Same hut." The artist George Catlin was more descriptive: "The lodge . . . was a room of immense size, some forty or fifty feet in diameter, in a circular form, and about twenty feet high—with a sunken curb of stone in the centre, of five or six feet in diameter and one foot deep, which contained the fire over which the pot was boiling." When he sketched this, Karl Bodmer was standing in the back of the house looking toward the door, which was hidden by a partition. It was the home of Dipäuch, an old and respected man.

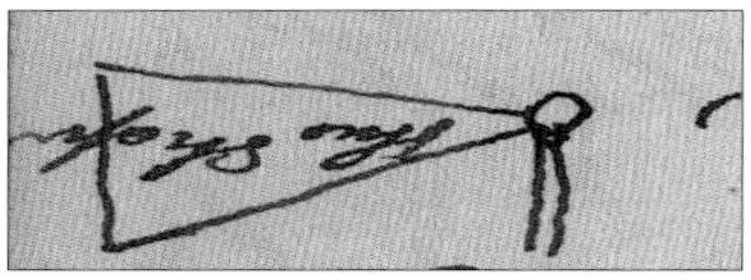

Sketch of a Mandan battle ax, 1805 and **Missouri war ax, pre-1870** This type of battle ax, later known as the Missouri war ax, was favored at the time of the expedition's arrival; it was the style produced by the Fort Mandan forge. Introduced in the late eighteenth century, it was most popular with tribes along the lower Missouri River but was found as far east as the Sauk and Fox and as far west as the Comanche. Lewis described it as "formed in a very inconvenient manner." He explained, "It is fabricated of iron only, the blade is extreemly thin. . . . the great length of the blade of this ax, added to the small size of the handle renders a stroke uncertain and easily avoided." Because the ax blades were rarely sharpened or edged in steel, and because they were structurally weak, these weapons may have served mainly as fashion accessories. Regardless, they were a godsend to the Corps: "The blacksmith's have proved a happy reso[ur]ce to us in our present situation as I believe it would have been difficult to have devised any other method to have procured corn from the natives. the Indians are extravegantly fond of sheet iron."

out in the open weather had to be relieved every hour all this day." The captains routinely recorded instances of frostbite.[7]

They spent some of their time promoting the U.S. objective of quelling intertribal conflict in order to create a better climate for commerce. When a Hidatsa chief informed them of his intention to take a war party against the Shoshone the next spring, Clark tried to dissuade him by appealing to the profit motive. "We advised him to look back at the number of nations who had been distroyed by war . . . observing . . . that by being at peace and haveing plenty of goods amongst them & a free intercourse with those defenceless nations, they would get on easy terms a great Number of horses."[8]

And yet their message of peace was continually undermined by their own actions. One day, they heard a rumor that a large party of Sioux was nearby and had ambushed five Mandan men. Clark "thought it well to Show a Disposition to ade and assist them against their enimies." Accordingly, he mustered twenty-three armed men, marched across the frozen river, flanked the town, and came up behind it, causing the residents to be "a littled allarmed at the formadable appearance of [the] party." The chiefs strove to pacify Clark. "My father the Snow is deep and it is cold," one leader said diplomatically. "If you will go with us in the Spring after the Snow goes off we will raise the Warriers." They thanked him anyway, Clark said, for the "fatherly protection." The troops then "Paraded & Crossed the river. . . . the Snow So deep, it was verry fatigueing arrved at the fort after night."[9]

As if bellicose displays were not enough, the Corps soon found itself in the position of selling arms. The food the men had brought from St. Louis was gone, and they needed to stock up on Mandan corn for the next leg of their journey west. They had few trade goods to spare. In this dilemma, they hit on the solution of using their small set of blacksmith tools to repair guns and make tomahawks for the upcoming war season. In January their carpenter, Patrick Gass, recorded that "all hands [were] employed in cutting wood, to make charcoal" for the forge. "The blacksmith makes war-axes, and other axes to cut wood; which are exchanged with the natives for corn, which is of great service to us." It was, in fact, the one thing they did that won the grudging respect of one skeptical Hidatsa chief. "Had I these white warriors in the upper plains," the chief told the British traders, "my young men on horseback would soon do for them, as they would do for so many 'wolves,' for . . . there are only two sensible men among them, the worker of iron and the mender of guns."[10]

The most important thing Lewis and Clark did over the winter was to gather information. Tirelessly they questioned their hosts about the way west: where the rivers ran, how to cross the mountains. But often the answers were to a different question than the one they had asked. Interviewing the Indians for geographical information, they soon came up against some unfamiliar assumptions about knowledge, space, and land.

SHEHEK-SHOTE MAKES A MAP

One such interview, with Shehek-Shote, happened on a clear January day, when it was twenty-two degrees below zero. "The Big White Chef of the Lower Mandan Village, Dined with us, and gave me a Scetch of the Coutrey as far as the high mountains," Clark wrote.[11] It was a scene that would be repeated many times over the next two years: Lewis and Clark sitting by the fire with a knowledgeable older man, smoking, eating, and taking notes while he told them the geographical information they sought.

They were far from the first Euro-Americans to rely on Indian geographical knowledge; as early as 1680, Father Louis Hennepin had praised the cartographic skills of a Sioux chief: "With a Pencil, [he] mark'd down on a Sheet of Paper, which I had left, the Course that we were to keep for four hundred Leagues together. In short this natural Geographer described our Way so exactly, that this Chart served as well as my Compass could have done." In fact, unknown to Lewis and Clark, they were already following Indian information. A Blackfeet named Ackomokki had given Peter Fidler of the Hudson's Bay Company a map of the Rocky Mountains; this map had been conveyed back to England, where the cartographer Aaron Arrowsmith had incorporated the information into the map of North America that Jefferson and Lewis had used to plan the expedition. Because the captains had a copy of Arrowsmith's map at Fort Mandan, they may have shown it to Shehek-Shote, thus bringing the information almost full circle.[12]

The copy of Shehek-Shote's map that survives today is drawn on paper, but that may not have been the original medium. Native cartographers drew maps several ways for Lewis and Clark. The Shoshone Cameahwait created a

Anvil, c. 1809
This U.S. Army surplus anvil was brought to Fort Henry at Three Forks, Montana, in 1810 by the party of Andrew Henry and Pierre Menard, sent by the Missouri Fur Company to erect a trading post. John Colter and George Drouillard were members of the party, which was the same one that returned Shehek-Shote to his home. The anvil was abandoned at the site when Henry left in the fall of 1810. In 1867 James Aplin picked it up to use in his blacksmith shop, and it was passed down through various local residents of the Three Forks area. Sometime before August 1807 Lewis held a public auction in St. Louis to sell the "Sundry Rifles, Muskets, powder horns, Shot pouches, Powder, Lead, Kettles, Axes, & other public property remaining on hand at the termination of the Expedition." It has been suggested that this anvil could have been purchased at that sale by members of the Missouri Fur Company, in which both Lewis and Clark had a financial interest. This is plausible but cannot be proved.

***Shehek-Shote*, 1807**
Shehek-Shote (also known as Sheheke and Shahaka) was the principal chief of Mitutanka, the Mandan village closest to Fort Mandan. Alexander Henry, a British fur trader who visited in the summer of 1806, found him "very attentive and polite" and noted that he was flying the U.S. flag given to him by Lewis and Clark. Shehek-Shote was "brow-beaten" by other chiefs, "although he was the only one decorated with a silver medal of the United States." When the Corps returned from the Pacific, Shehek-Shote went with them to the East, where he met Thomas Jefferson. In 1807 he was in Philadelphia, where the French artist Charles B. J. F. de Saint-Mémin made this portrait. An attempt to return him to his home later in 1807 was turned back by the Arikara, and it was not until 1809 that he rejoined his people. He was described by Henry M. Brackenridge as "a fine looking Indian, and very intelligent . . . a man of a mild and gentle disposition . . . rather inclining to corpulency, a little talkative, which is regarded amongst the indians as a great defect; add to this, his not being much celebrated as a warrior; such celebrity can alone confer authority and importance."

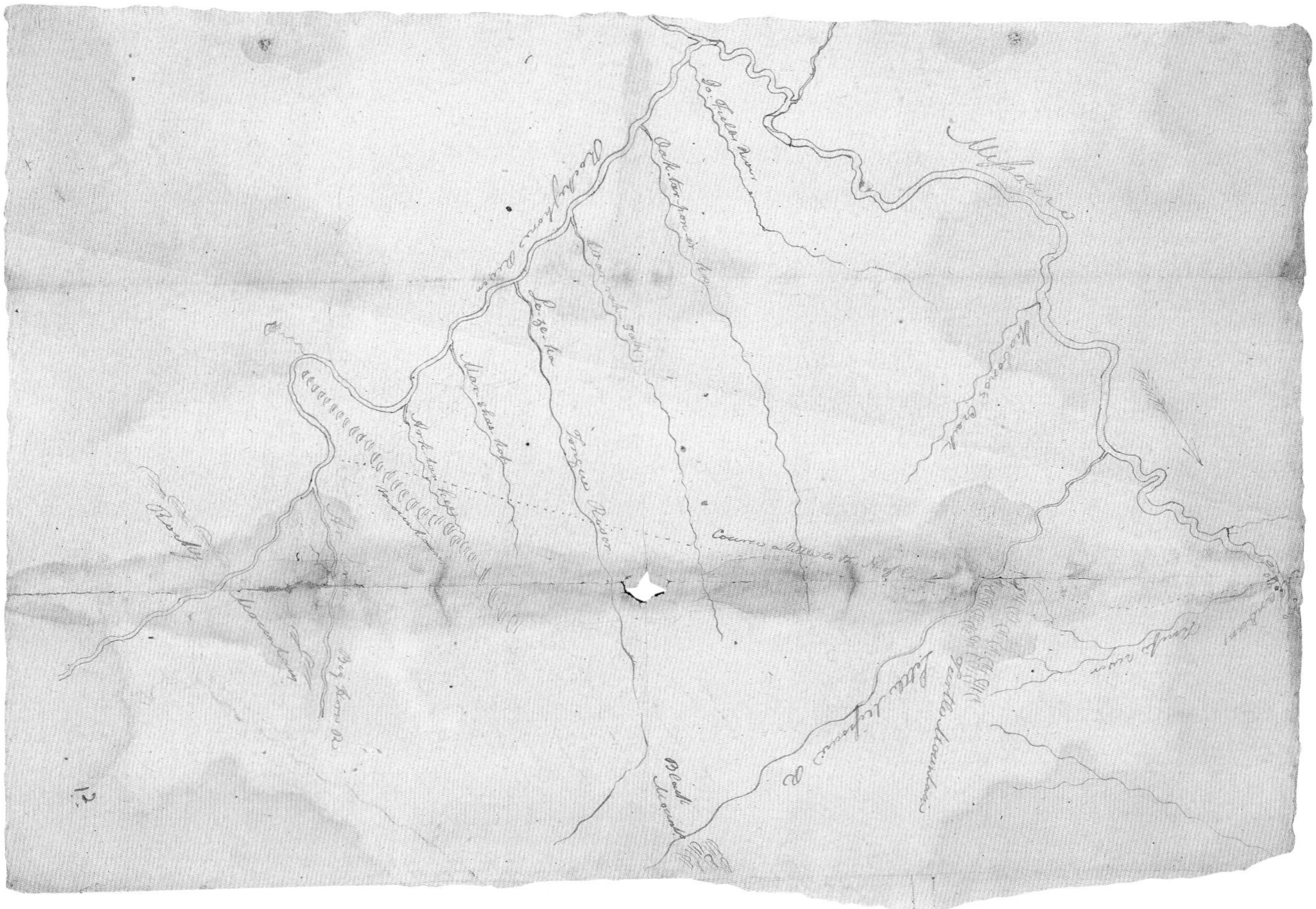

Shehek-Shote's map, 1805
The original of this map may have included information such as the route of Shehek-Shote's war party, the location of camps attacked, and pictographs for the accomplishments of the raid. If these details were ever present, Clark left them out when he recopied the map. The Missouri River is in the upper right, and the Yellowstone ("Rochejhone") and the Little Missouri flow into it from the southwest. Shehek-Shote's name (which means White Coyote) may suggest that he served as a scout, a role in which men took on the persona of Coyote, the crafty traveler.

three-dimensional map in the dirt to show mountain ranges around the Continental Divide. The Nez Perce Twisted Hair drew a map "on a white Elk Skin," and the lower Chinookans used charcoal on a mat. Clark sometimes copied these impermanent maps on paper, and sometimes he seems to have given the pen and ink directly to the Indians, later writing in captions and names himself. Information also traveled the other way: Lewis drew a map of the continent on a skin for the Nez Perce.[13]

Reflecting his culture's respect for paper, Clark carefully preserved many of the Indian maps he copied or collected. But nowhere did he save the verbal component that went with those maps. In this omission, he reflected the most fundamental mistake that Euro-Americans made about Indian maps: thinking that the visual component stood alone. In fact, these were not maps in the European sense. They were journey charts—graphs created to illustrate stories. Narrative was the technique that Native Americans used to pass on information, because it preserved accuracy; even geographical information was tied to story, and whatever did not relate to the story was left out.

Although Clark gave no description of the verbal component of Shehek-Shote's map, we can try to reconstruct it from what Mandan and Hidatsa men of a later generation said. The first thing Shehek-Shote probably did was to recite the credentials that gave him the right to pass on information. In an oral society, this was a crucial step toward authenticating the accuracy of information, and it preceded any form of teaching. Unlike Clark, Shehek-Shote did not have the right to pass on other people's knowledge—only his own. A person could earn the right to teach knowledge in only two ways: by purchasing it formally from its original owner or by experiencing the actual event. Hearsay was looked down on. "A person who tells the stories without seeing the places, should anyone see the account, will be laughed at," said the Mandan elder Crow's Heart. Discouraging the use of hearsay prevented the spread of rumor and misinformation.[14]

Shehek-Shote's credentials were probably a list of the war parties in which he had participated. Preparing for war was the way most Plains Indian men learned geography. When a group of young men decided to go on a raid into a country unknown to them, the older men assembled to instruct the warriors. A participant described one such scene: "All being seated in a circle, a bundle of sticks was produced, marked with notches to represent the days. Commencing with the stick with one notch, an old man drew on the ground with his finger, a rude map illustrating the journey of the first day. The rivers, streams, hills, valleys, ravines, hidden water-holes, were all indicated with reference to prominent and carefully described landmarks." The young warriors learned the information well because their lives might depend on it.[15]

When they passed on geographical knowledge, the warriors almost always framed it as a recital of what they had actually seen and the context in which they had seen it. Years later, the Hidatsa leader Poor Wolf drew a map of much the same territory as was portrayed in Shehek-Shote's map; in addition to showing the rivers, he drew the route his war party had followed, the layout of the battlefield, pictographs symbolizing the enemies conquered, and the route by which the victors had brought the captured horses home to the Knife River villages. Long after Poor Wolf, Crow's Heart, a Mandan, gave a narrative meant

Map of "Lewis's River" and "Clark's River," 1806
Like a sketch on a placemat, this sheet preserves evidence of the process that Clark went through to get Indian maps. This rough draft may have been drawn by some Nez Perce men Clark was consulting on geography or may have been copied by him from sketches drawn on skin or dirt. It is stained with the food and drink they were eating, and it was burned by the rim of a hot kettle someone set down on it. Clark later redrew the map in a more European style (see "Chopunnish map," p.144). It was "given by Sundery Indians of the Chopunnish [Nez Perce] Nation together."

to go with a map. He offered the kind of detailed information that Shehek-Shote might have passed on with his map. Describing a trip through land near the border between North Dakota and Montana, Crow's Heart mentioned "a nice-looking butte called Children's-home where spirit children live; from thence come the children born into the tribe. From there on is another butte called Where-they-find-blue-clay because here one finds blue clay with pockets of red and yellow ochre. The next hill is Buffalo Den. People say that when a heavy fog lies on this hill, when it lifts there are always buffalo to be seen. The next butte is called Home-of-the-rain. When the Indians go on hunting parties it seems as if it was always raining there."[16]

Only a little information of this sort survived Clark's editing. Later, Clark combined Shehek-Shote's information with that of a Hidatsa warrior and drew the latter's warpath on the map as a dotted line—the same convention that Plains Indians used to indicate journey routes. Other, more subtle aspects of the map also reflect its origin: the rivers are spaced with diagrammatic regularity and shown as nearly straight lines. The distances, when compared with those on a modern map, seem distorted. In fact, by European measures, it is not a very accurate map. But to judge it by European standards misses the point. Shehek-Shote was not trying to draw a European map. He used different cartographic conventions—ones suited to the purpose of the map and to its creator's concepts of time, space, and travel.

HOW TO READ AN INDIAN MAP

Indian maps were not intended to be naturalistic representations of the landscape. They were visual narratives. Native cartographers did not portray the land as an abstract thing, a pattern to be measured onto the surface of a sphere. They showed what people *did* with the land. Each map was a diagram of a human-landscape interaction—a journey or a battle or a mythic act. Because the maps showed information related to time and subjective experiences, they were unlike the maps that Lewis and Clark were used to.[17]

The most confusing difference was that Indian maps used a temporal rather than a spatial scale, showing travel time, not distance. Each day's travel would be drawn the same size, even though one day's journey through hard terrain might cover only ten miles, whereas a day of easy traveling might cover forty or fifty. Space was distorted in order to show time more accurately. This was quite functional in planning war raids, as the explorer Giacomo Beltrami wrote less than twenty years after Lewis and Clark: "They can fix on their maps the precise time requisite to attack an enemy's post."[18]

Another convention that caused endless confusion was that Indian maps showed routes and not necessarily physical landforms. Sometimes a route might combine travel on a river, across a portage, along a trail, and down another river. An Indian mapmaker would not always differentiate between the river and the land travel, because his purpose was to show a journey, not landscape. Looking at such maps, Europeans often thought rivers flowed across mountain ranges and imagined other topographic impossibilities.

Indians traced rivers differently than did Europeans. A European trying to decide which branch was the river and which was the tributary looked at hydrology—the amount of water flowing in each branch. The one with the larger flow was the main river. An Indian making the same decision would ask

Shirt and **Leggings, 1830s**
On formal occasions when he wanted to evoke his war record, Shehek-Shote may have worn clothing resembling this. This suit of Mandan clothes could be from the George Catlin collection; its style is appropriate to that date. Bodmer painted Pehriska-Ruhpa (Two Ravens), a Hidatsa, wearing leggings strongly resembling these in 1833. The decoration on the leggings is of dyed quills wrapped around horsehair, a technique rarely seen after the 1830s. The fringe on the shirt is horsehair, but the fringe on the leggings includes human hair.

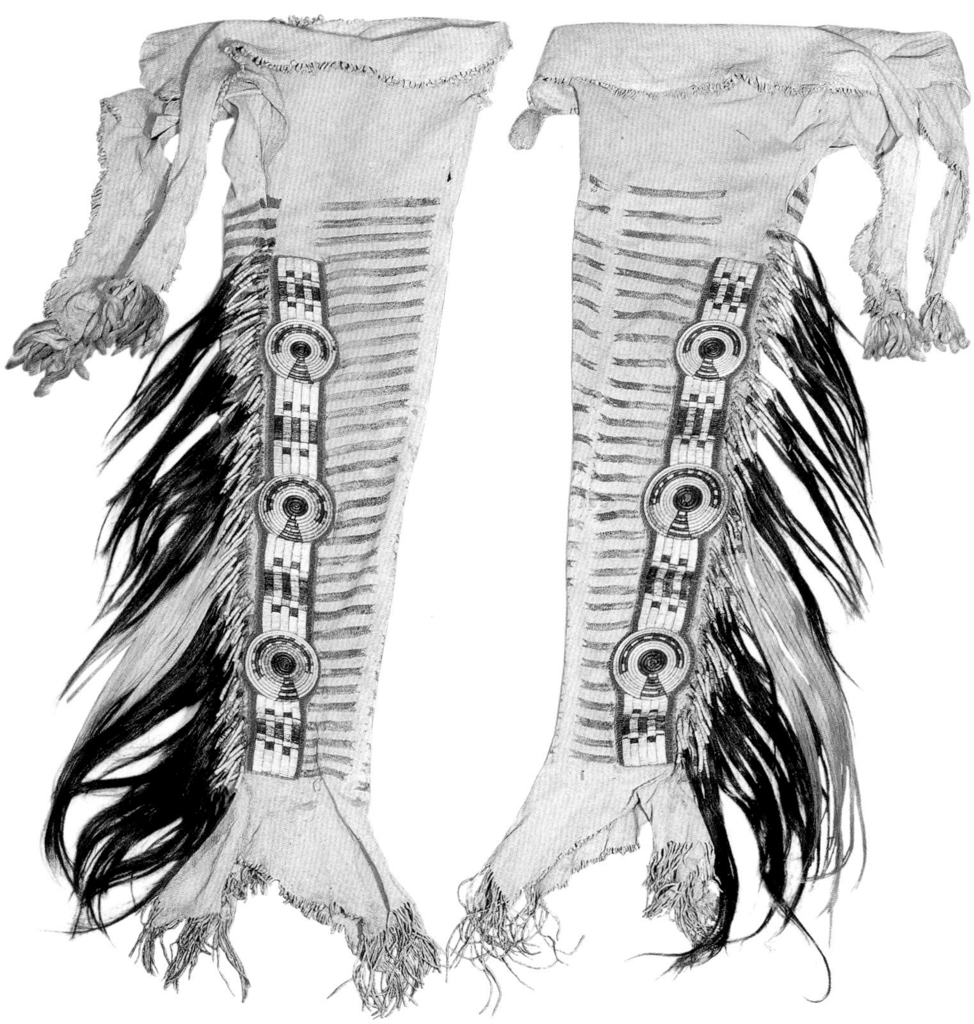

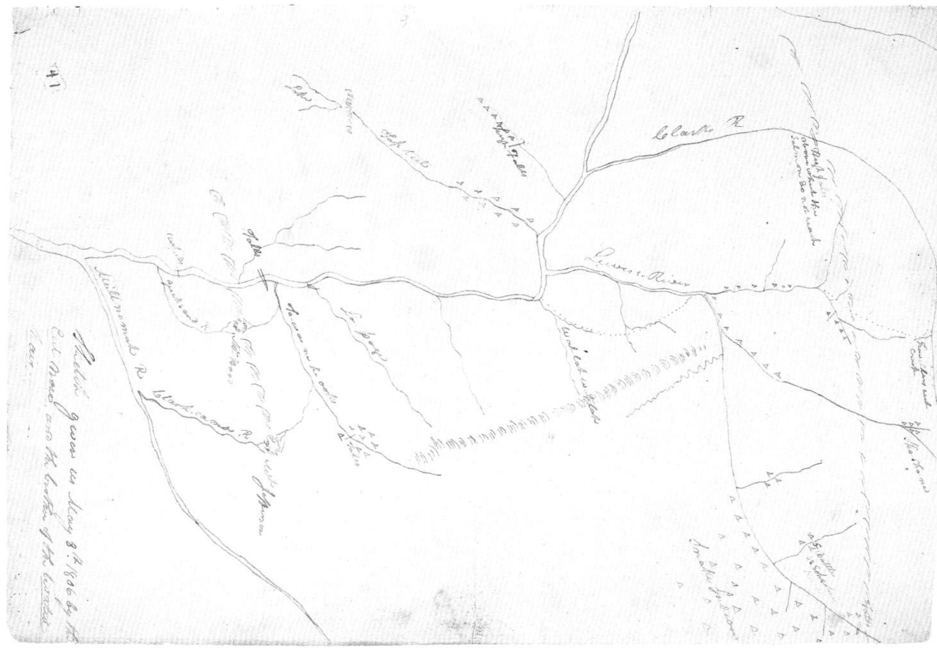

Cut Nose's map, 1806
Indian maps showed distance in travel time rather than in measured space. The journey up the Columbia to the Snake River was made difficult by numerous waterfalls and rapids; north of there, the trip was easy. On this map, the easy journey between "Lewis's River" (the Snake) and "Clark's River" (the Spokane) is greatly compressed, whereas the hard part below that section is stretched out. Space is distorted to depict travel time more accurately. The river that forms a right angle is the Columbia. The entire state of Washington ought to fit between Lewis's River and Clark's River.

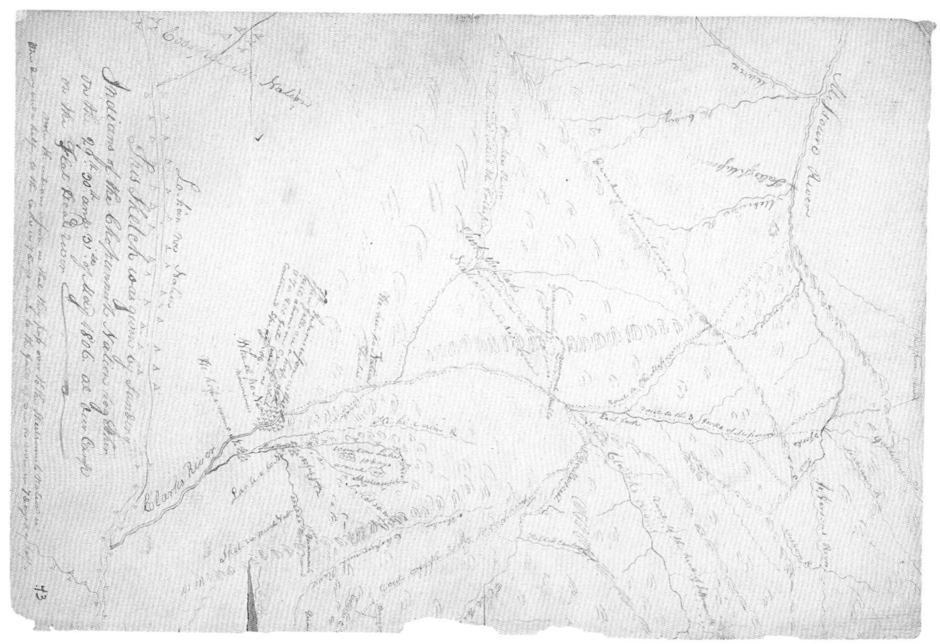

Chopunnish map, 1806
Indian maps show routes where European maps show rivers. If a route went up a tributary or included a portage, it was still shown as if it were the river. This elaborate map of a river that Clark never saw but still named for himself is based on a misunderstanding. "Clark's River" is today regarded not as one river but as three: the Spokane, the Clark Fork, and the Bitterroot. They do not connect directly; Indian travelers cut across land from the upper Spokane to Lake Pend Oreille. It was a *route*, not a *river*, but Clark mapped it as a continuous waterway. The Columbia is at the left side, and the Missouri is at the right.

which branch went to a place he wanted to go. That branch was the river, regardless of hydrology. As a result, many waterways regarded as a single unit by Indians are now mapped as a chain of tributaries.

Indian maps disregarded other European conventions. North was not always at the top, and directions were not always absolute or oriented to cardinal points but might vary within the map. The size of features showed their relative importance, not their size in nature. Rivers were not shown naturalistically, because their twists and turns made little difference to the traveler in a canoe. Tributaries appeared as straight lines spaced evenly because an Indian traveler did not need to know how far apart they were; he merely needed to count how many he passed before turning. The result was an abstract and diagrammatic rendition of a river system, not a representational one.

The conventions used in Indian maps were so well suited to conveying information about the travel experience that some are still used today. Modern subway maps also distort space to represent time more accurately. They are

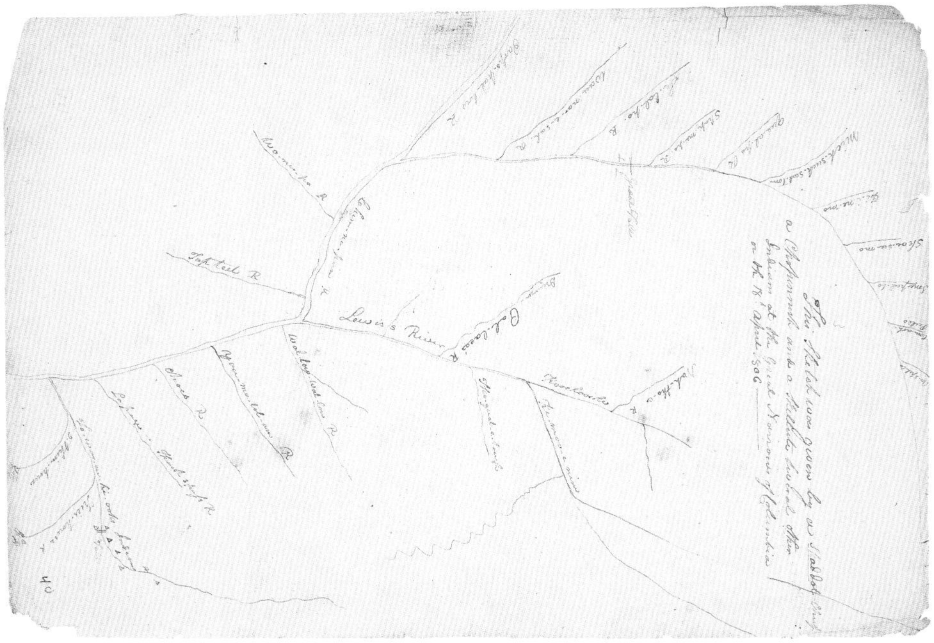

Skaddot map, 1806
Indian mapmakers portrayed rivers in a diagrammatic, not a representational, style. Here rivers are shown as nearly straight lines, spaced without regard to actual distance. Traveling by river was like traveling on a road: as long as you knew how many corners to pass, you didn't need to know the twists and turns of the streambed. This map also shows the name of the Columbia changing on its way north, first to "Chum-na-pum," then to "Parps-pal-low." Tribes seldom named rivers as single systems, the way Europeans did. To them, the river's identity changed as it passed through the land of different tribes. This was originally true of the Mississippi and Missouri as well as the Columbia. On this map, the river that starts at the top, makes a right angle and flows off the left margin is the Columbia.

only casually oriented to cardinal directions. They omit irrelevant information like the difference between aboveground and underground travel or the twists and turns of the tunnel. Instead, they show a schematic diagram with evenly spaced stations, much as Indians showed rivers. These conventions allow the compression of an enormous amount of usable information into a small space.

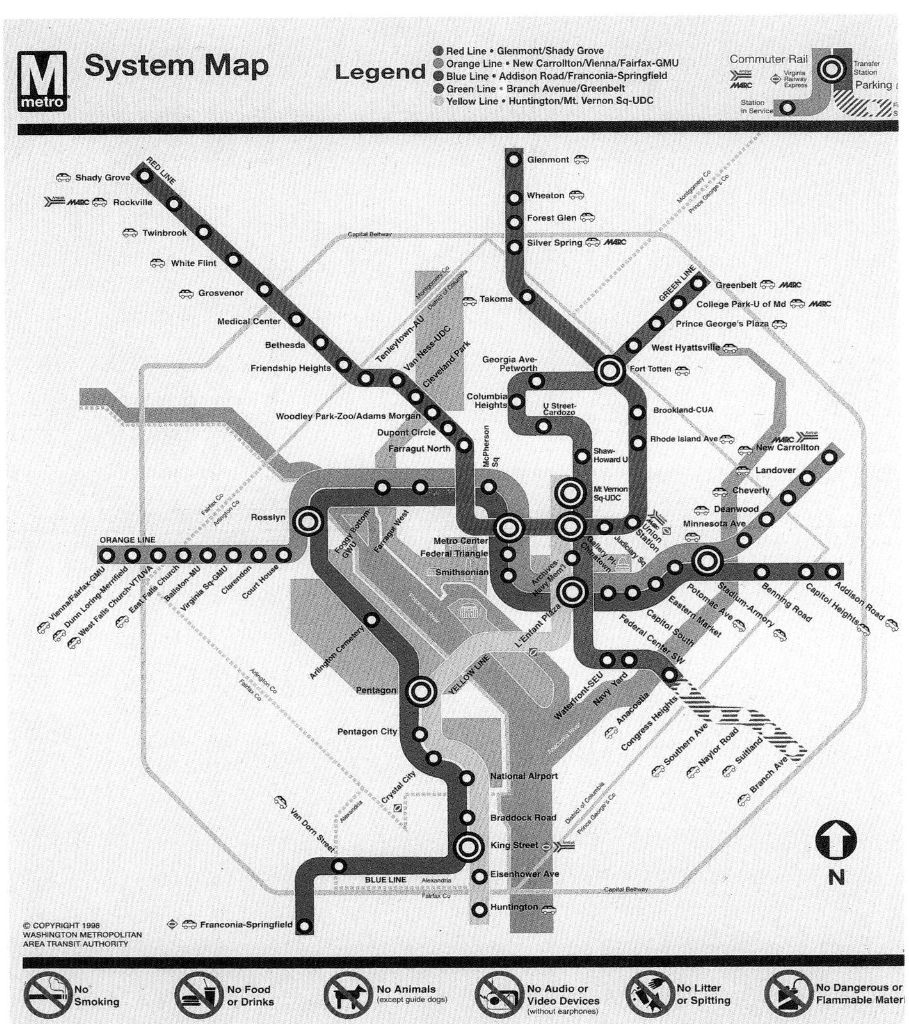

Subway map of Washington, D.C.
Rapid-transit maps use some of the same rules as Indian maps: they distort space to enhance clarity, and they show rivers and routes in diagrammatic style. They do not try to portray the twists and turns of the tunnel realistically. Instead, they show the traveler's experience.

Despite their functionality, the alien conventions of Indian maps probably misled Lewis and Clark several times. The technique of counting distance by travel time may have contributed to their confusion about the northern tributaries of the Missouri, which almost led them astray at the Marias River. On the way back, when they asked the Nez Perce if there was another way across the Rockies, the information they received caused Clark to map a water route called "Clark's River." Not only was it not a practical route—it would have taken them hundreds of miles out of their way—but it did not even follow what they would have considered a river. Today it is mapped as a chain of rivers—the Spokane, Clark Fork, and Bitterroot—interrupted by a portage.

The most dangerous mistake was misinterpreting omission. Try as they might, Lewis and Clark could not learn anything from the Mandan or the Hidatsa about the source of the Missouri, the goal of their journey. The reason was that the Missouri dead-ended one hundred arduous miles from the nearest pass across the Rocky Mountains. The Indians never went there because it was not on the way to anywhere. But so sure were the captains of the geography they had brought from Monticello that they put the Indians' silence down to ignorance.

A GRIDWORK WORLD

> True time of observtn. as Shewn by the Chro[nome]tr. A.M. h8 m38 S10.7 True apparent time of observation A.M. as deduced from Mean Time by the application of the Equation of time with its sighn changed—h8 m38 S18 Distance of [sun]'s and [moon]'s nearest limbs at the time of this observation. [sun] East 66° 20′ 31.7″ Estimated Greenwich time of the Observation h15 m15 S57.7
>
> —MERIWETHER LEWIS[19]

> In winter, when the moon shines very brightly, the people all go out, plainly she is seen; they never point her out to one another with their fingers. It is a bad sign, a great frost will take place; the moon would become ashamed if pointed at.
>
> —WISHRAM SAYING[20]

When Lewis and Clark said "map," they meant something quite different from what the Indians meant. To Euro-Americans, mapping was a matter of measurement. The objective of a Euro-American cartographer was to make a "realistic" picture of how the land would look from above, if the observer were abstracted from the earth and placed in a God's-eye position. At the time, this was purely a thought experiment. Today, satellites can actually do what mapmakers only dreamed of—and their photographs have shown us how faulty those imaginings were. Real pictures show complex, braided waterways with indistinct boundaries obscured by changing vegetation—not the neat, clean lines of maps. But it is the simplification of maps that makes them so persuasive. They tame the messiness of nature and make it seem more understandable than it is.

In Europe, cartographers had greatly refined their science by concentrating on representing just two types of information that could be accurately measured: distance and direction. Once determined, these factors never changed. To achieve accuracy in representing them, cartographers adapted a system from

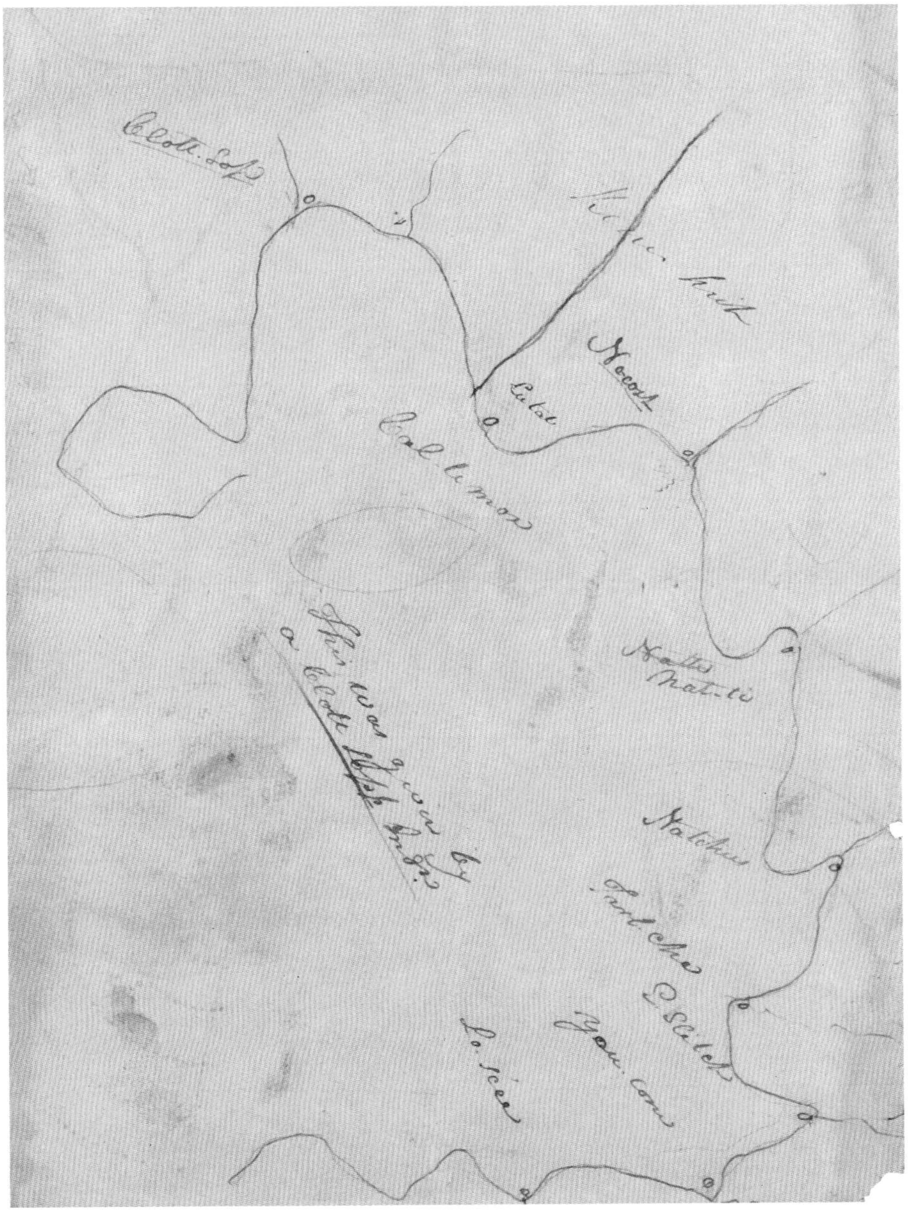

Clatsop map, 1806

This map of the Oregon coast, drawn by a "Clott Sopp" Indian and labeled by Clark, shows the Indian approach to two cartographic principles: direction and size of landmarks. Direction was not absolute and was not oriented to the cardinal points. North was not always at the top, and directions might vary within a single map, as here. Today we think of the Oregon coast as a straight north-south line. This mapmaker showed it as an arc, in order to fit more of it on the paper. Our viewpoint is from above; his is from within the landscape.

The size of a mapped feature showed its importance, not its size in nature. The bays along the Oregon coast are relatively small, but to an ocean traveler in a canoe, they were the most important feature of the coast. This map exaggerates the bays. It also shows them peopled with villages, which is what gave them importance to the mapmaker.

Renaissance art: the gridwork. By measuring landforms and graphing them onto paper, square by square, they could translate the horizontal surface of earth into a vertical perspective that accurately showed distance and direction. The gridwork ensured uniform and systematic results because it kept scale and orientation consistent. Geometry—particularly trigonometry—was crucial for making the necessary measurements. To achieve measurability, cartographers excluded information related to variables such as time, subjective experience, weather, and even animals, plants, and people—though the last could be added once the landscape was accurately determined.

Lewis and Clark used two gridwork systems, on different scales. On a local scale, Clark used a grid to make daily maps of the river's course and the party's path. But the explorers also needed to measure their location on a global scale. Jefferson had not sent them west to guess where they were. On the contrary, they were participants in an ambitious Enlightenment project to map every point on earth according to a universal system of location—the grid of latitude and longitude. It was an elegant system. With the globe divided into a net of imaginary lines, a person had to know only two coordinates—distance north or south of the equator and distance east or west of the prime meridian

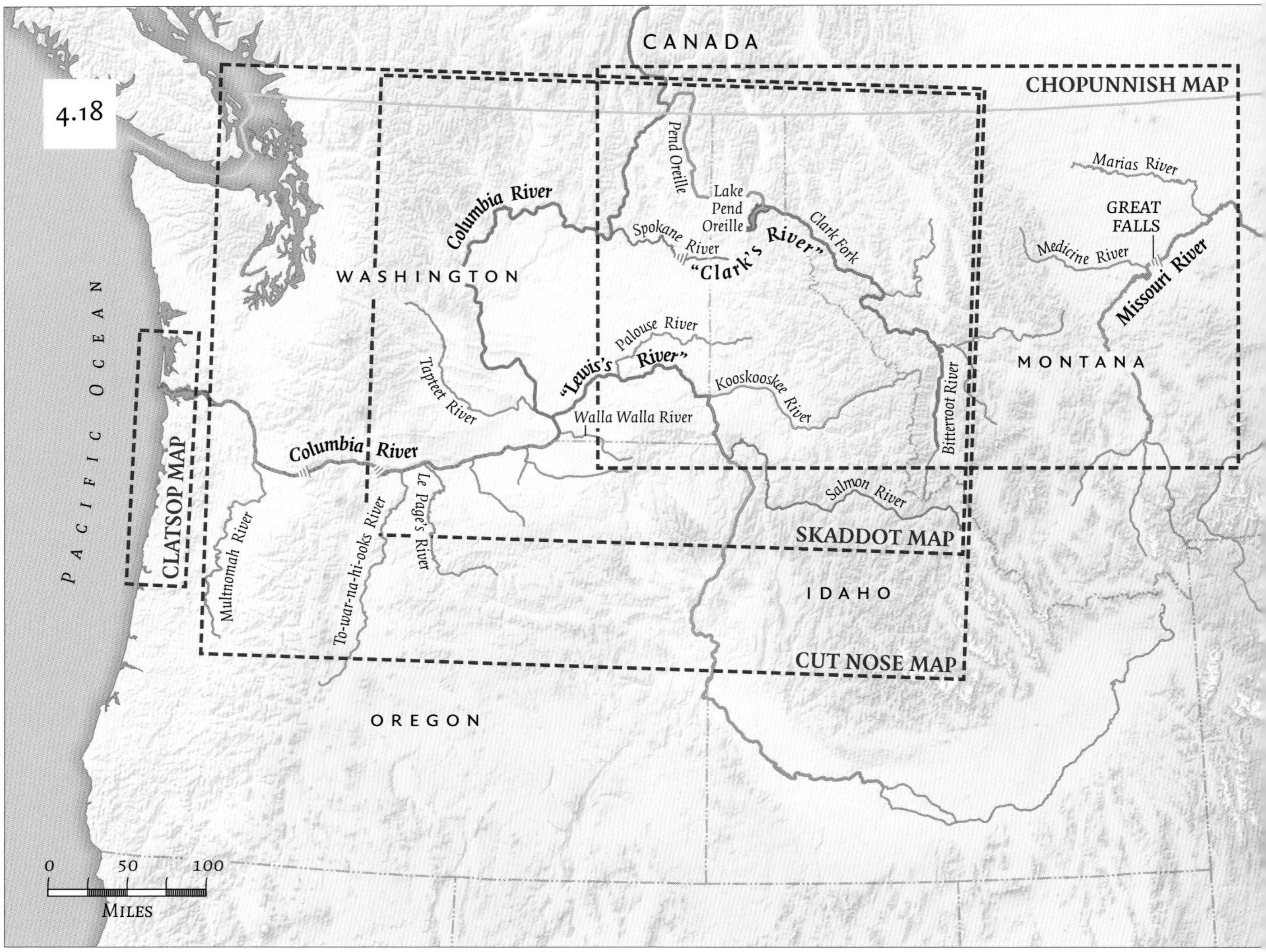

Map of the Columbia, Snake, and "Clark's River"
This gives a European view of the territory mapped by the Indian maps shown on the preceding pages.

running through Greenwich, England—to pinpoint his or her exact location anywhere on the globe. No one would ever be lost again.

The devil was in the details. Finding one's latitude and longitude was fiendishly difficult because to do so, a traveler had to measure current position relative to something outside of Earth—the sun or stars. But Euro-Americans had been strongly motivated to invent clever ways of measuring location, in order to make long-distance navigation possible by sea and the accurate marking of boundaries possible on land. By Lewis and Clark's time, the science of celestial navigation was highly refined, and the technophilic Lewis used the latest methods.

Latitude—distance north of the equator—was relatively easy to find. Theoretically, all Lewis had to do was measure the height of the sun above the horizon at noon. Practically, this was not so easy. On land, determining where the horizon is can be difficult because trees and hills obscure it. To solve this problem, Lewis had brought a device called an artificial horizon—usually just a tray of water with a sheet of reflective mica on the surface. Measuring the angle between the sun and its reflection in the mica yielded exactly twice the angle between the sun and the horizon. But even when he found the measurement, he had to correct for things that threw it off: the tilt of Earth (which varies according to season), the refraction of the sun's rays by the atmosphere, the height of the observer, and so forth. Despite these complications, Lewis's latitude readings were usually correct to within a fraction of a degree.[21]

No one thought measuring longitude was easy. The key to finding one's distance west of Greenwich was timekeeping. Today we have time zones to correct for the fact that noon comes at different times as one travels east and west. Of course, time does not really vary in hour-long units; it changes gradually and continually. If you travel ten miles west for lunch, noon actually comes slightly later. Because the time of day varies a predictable amount for every mile traveled west, in theory all you need to know is what time it is at Greenwich and what time it is where you stand. By comparing the two times, you can work out the distance.

For Lewis, there were just two problems: finding Greenwich time and finding local time. Local time was easier. To determine when noon came, Lewis (and sometimes Clark) measured "equal altitudes"—taking the height of the sun at some time before noon, then timing when the sun arrived at the exact same altitude after noon. The readings could then be averaged to arrive at the time of local noon.

Finding Greenwich time was harder. In Lewis and Clark's day, seagoing ships brought along extraordinarily accurate chronometers, set to Greenwich time, so that they could compare their local time to it. Lewis and Clark had no such luxury. A naval chronometer was as large as a toaster and far more temperamental, so they brought a pocket chronometer, their single most expensive piece of equipment. It was constantly stopping. But even without the chronometer set to Greenwich time, they could still measure longitude, if only

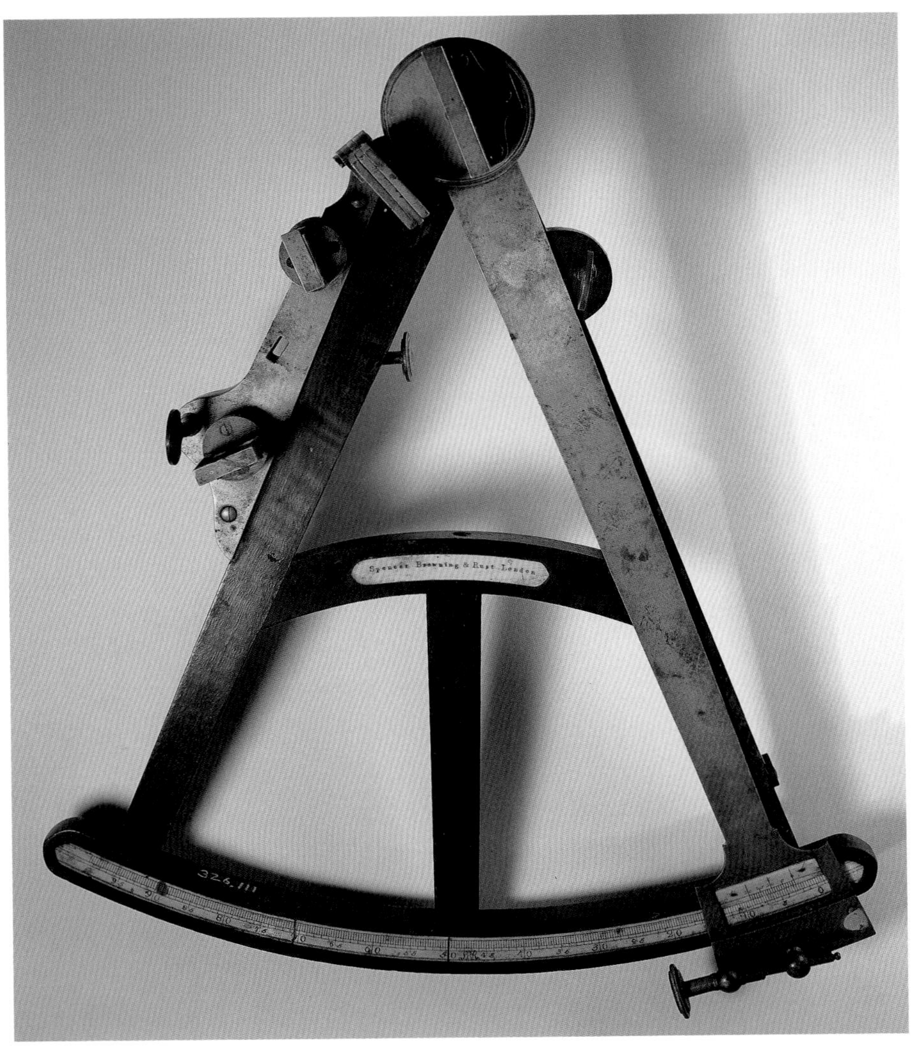

Octant, c. 1800
Lewis bought his octant (which does not survive) from Thomas Whitney for twenty-two dollars. He called it both "Tangent screw Quadrant" and "Hadleys Quadrant with Tangt Screw." The tangent screw is on the bottom of the moveable index arm. He described it as "A common Octant of 14 Inches radius, graduated to 20′, which by means of the nonius [Vernier] was devisbile to 1′, half of this sum, or 30″ was perceptible by means of a micrometer. This instrument was prepared for both the *fore* and *back* observation." He more often used it for back observation, which was done when the celestial object was too high for the octant to read the angle directly. It was also occasionally used to impress the Indians as "Great Medicines." The vernier is the scale inscribed on the window of the index arm.

Sextant, late 1700s or early 1800s

The octant and the sextant were both devices for measuring angles, the sextant being slightly more accurate. Lewis and Clark used them most frequently to measure the sun's height in order to find their local time and latitude. The instruments could also be used to measure vertical heights like the Great Falls. A number of Jefferson's scientific instruments were purchased from the maker of this sextant. Lewis bought his sextant (which does not survive) from Thomas Whitney for ninety dollars and paid seven dollars extra for attaching the microscope to the index arm. He described it as "a brass Sextant of 10 Inches radius, graduated to 15′ which by the assistance of the nonius [Vernier] was devisible to 15″; and half of this sum by means of the micrometer could readily be distinguished. . . . she was also furnished with three eye-pieces, consisting of a hollow tube and two telescopes one of which last reversed the images of observed objects."

they could observe some astronomical event that happened at a precise time and that was either observed or predicted at Greenwich. By measuring the local time of its occurrence, they could find their distance west. Lewis tried this with a lunar eclipse at Fort Mandan, but weather interfered. When eclipses were not handy, he used a technique called "lunar distances," which measured the moon's movement against the stars as a kind of clock. Unfortunately, the mathematical calculations necessary to find the longitude from these observations made by Lewis were so tedious that they were not completed until a computer could take on the task in the year 2000. Almost two hundred years after he made the measurements, Lewis's longitude readings proved to have an average error of thirty-five minutes (about thirty miles at latitude 40°), which was standard for the day.[22]

Despite all the expense and effort that went into celestial observations, Clark did not end up using them much in making his maps of their route. Instead, he used an older and less high-tech method called "dead reckoning." The key was good record-keeping. Each day as they traveled, Clark wrote down whenever they changed direction and how far they traveled on each bearing, using no more than a compass and a watch. To find the speed of the boat, he used a log line and reel. After a few days, he would transfer his readings onto a gridwork map on which each square represented a set distance. A journal nota-

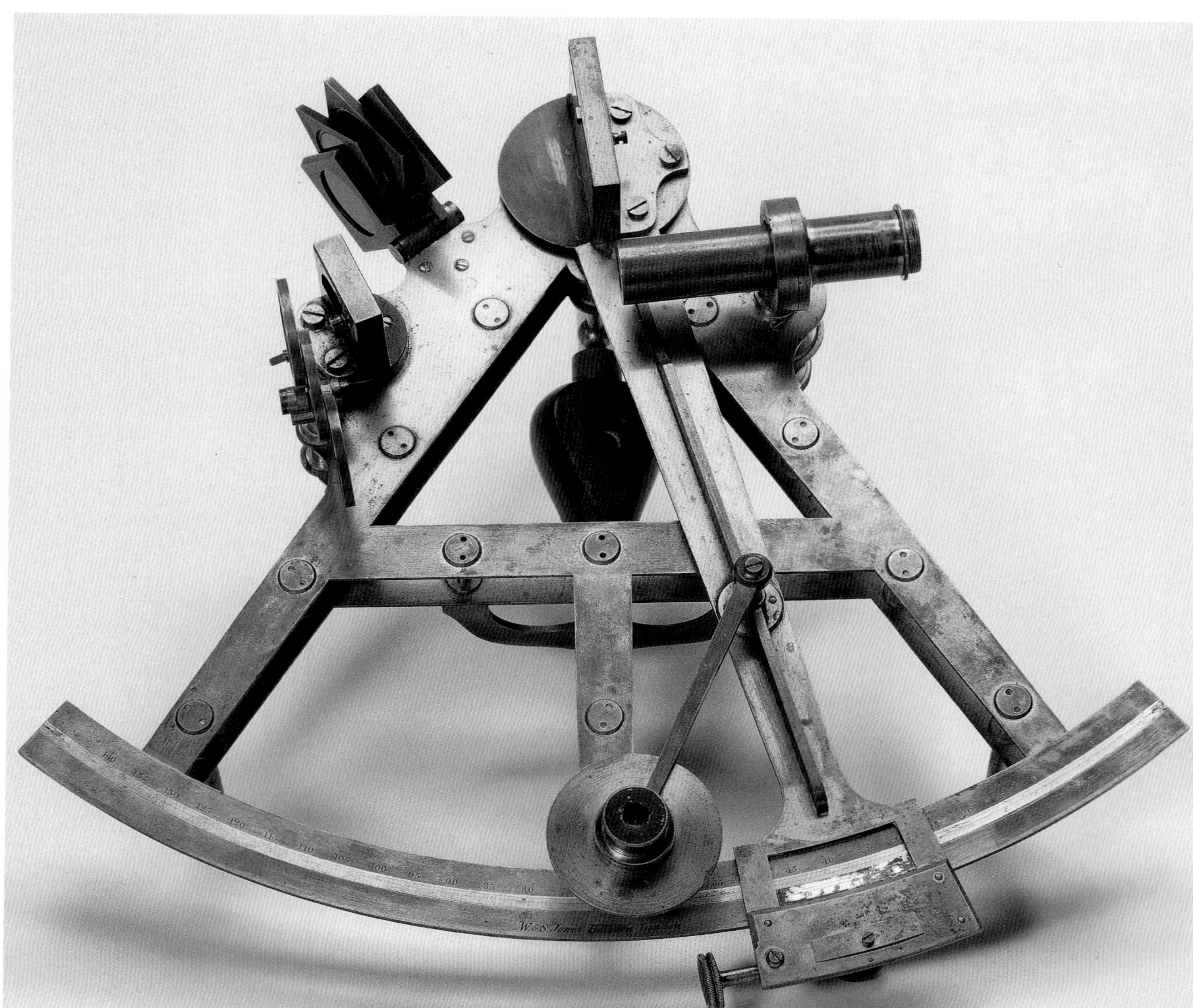

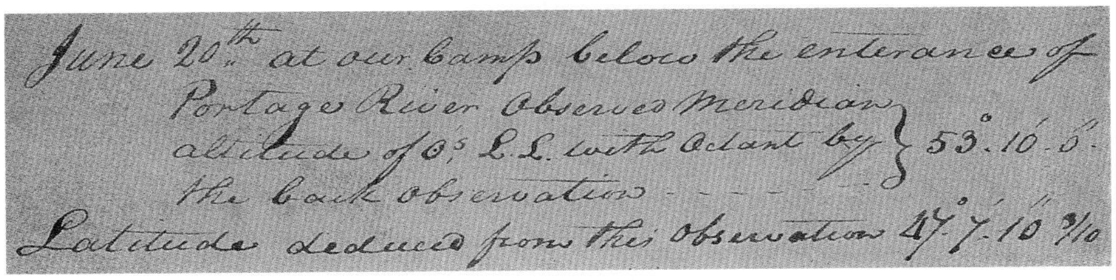
June 20th at our Camp below the entrance of Portage River Observed Meridian altitude of ☉'s L.L. with Octant by the back observation } 53°.10'.0.
Latitude deduced from this Observation 47°7'.10 3/10

Latitude reading, 1805
When the expedition paused at major landmarks, Lewis took latitude readings by measuring the angle of the sun above the horizon at noon, or "meridian altitude." Here, Clark copied down Lewis's measurement on the sun's lower edge, or lower limb ("L.L."). He then adjusted the reading for factors such as the earth's declination or tilt and refraction through the atmosphere, to arrive at the corrected number, 47° 7′ 10.3″. The actual latitude of the Great Falls is about 47° 30′ 6″.

tion of "3 miles N 30° W" became a line on the map, laid out with a protractor and ruler. During the winters, Clark assembled all his route maps and transferred the information onto a master map, reducing the scale with an engineer's drawing tools.

The Euro-American system of mapping worked superbly at what it set out to do: represent the scale and orientation of topographic features. Such maps also transformed their users' perceptions, making the land an abstract object of study. Maps also altered the very reality they were meant to represent. Surveying technology made it possible to draw boundaries more accurately than ever before—boundaries between nations, states, and private owners. It made the landscape into something that could be measured, divided, and commodified. As Lewis and Clark traveled west, surveyors were busy laying out the old Northwest Territory into a neat Euclidian gridwork for private ownership, as if to make the land conform to its cartographic image. Possession of land would no longer be determined by custom, memory, or usage but by mathematics and the stars.

LANDSCAPES OF THE PAST AND FUTURE

> I walked on Shore with the Indian Chief [Piahito]. . . . This Chief tells me of a number of their Treditions about Turtles, Snakes, &. and the power of a perticiler rock or Cave on the next river which informs of everr thing none of those I think worth while mentioning.
>
> —WILLIAM CLARK[23]

If Euro-American maps revealed their makers' perceptions of the landscape, so did Indian maps. One of the holiest objects of Mandan spiritual life, the namesake of the Sacred Robe bundle, was "a map of the world." At the center of the world was the Missouri River. It was depicted as a giant snake. At its southern end lay the hole in the ground from which the Mandan people and the corn spirits had emerged in the ancient past. They had climbed up a vine from the underground land where they had both originated and from which the corn still came forth each spring. Since that time, the history of the Mandan had been a centuries-long journey up the river, always leaving behind their past in the ruins of former villages and the sites of battles and ancestral tales. When a Mandan died, his or her spirit returned downriver along the path the tribe had followed.[24]

The Sacred Robe was lost when the earth lodge of its last owner burned. But in 1905 a historian named Orin G. Libby approached a Mandan man named Sitting Rabbit or Little Owl (I-ki-ha-wa-he) to create something similar. For archaeological purposes, Libby wanted a map that located old Mandan village sites that lay along the Missouri River. But what Sitting Rabbit did was much more significant. He drew a map that showed the river valley as an embodiment of Mandan myth and history.[25]

Pocket chronometer, 1807–8
At $250, the chronometer was the single most expensive piece of equipment that Lewis purchased for the voyage. It was a wonder of technology: a watch so accurate that, if properly cared for, it could be set to Greenwich time and vary at a predictable rate, so that a simple comparison of local noon to Greenwich noon would yield the longitude. Unfortunately, Lewis and Clark were never able to use it that way. Even before they set out, their chronometer showed a distressing propensity to stop for no reason; each time, they had to go through the tedious process of redetermining the local time. Later, Lewis forgot to wind it, got it wet, dried it with feathers, and oiled the works with bear's grease—not exactly recommended treatment for the delicate instrument. As long as it ran, they did not reset the chronometer but simply kept track of how far off it was as their local time changed. When it stopped, Lewis tended to reset it as close as possible to local time. The original chronometer does not survive; this one matches what we know of it.

Stars Names.	Days	Noon.	III^h.	VI^h.	IX^h.	Midnight.	XV^h.	XVIII^h.	XXI^h.
		D. M. S.	D. M. S.	D. M. S.	D. M. S.	D. M. S.	D. M. S.	D. M. S.	D. M. S.
α Pegasi.	17	- - -	- - -	- - -	- - -	66. 57. 2	65. 26. 38	63. 56. 6	62. 25. 22
	18	60. 54. 28	59. 23. 25	57. 52. 17	56. 21. 1	54. 49. 40	53. 18. 12	51. 46. 43	50. 15. 14
	19	48. 43. 43	47. 12. 16	45. 40. 51	44. 9. 33	42. 38. 22			
α Arietis.	19	- - -	- - -	- - -	- - -	83. 14. 44	81. 35. 43	79. 56. 25	78. 16. 50
	20	76. 36. 57	74. 56. 47	73. 16. 20	71. 35. 37	69. 54. 38	68. 13. 23	66. 31. 53	64. 50. 9
	21	63. 8. 9	61. 25. 54	59. 43. 26	58. 0. 45	56. 17. 50	54. 34. 43	52. 51. 25	51. 7. 56
	22	49. 24. 16							
Aldebaran.	22	81. 52. 2	80. 9. 9	78. 26. 6	76. 42. 55	74. 59. 33	73. 16. 3	71. 32. 27	69 48. 44
	23	68. 4. 54	66. 20. 58	64. 36. 59	62. 52. 56	61. 8. 50	59. 24. 42	57. 40. 33	55. 56. 25
	24	54. 12. 17	52. 28. 10	50. 44. 8	49. 0. 12	47. 16. 20	45. 32. 34	43. 49. 0	42. 5. 38
	25	40. 22. 28	38. 39. 35	36. 56. 59	35. 14. 44	33. 32. 51			
Pollux.	25	- - -	- - -	- - -	- - -	74. 50. 51	73. 4. 30	71. 18. 9	69. 31. 50
	26	67. 45. 33	65. 59. 18	64. 13. 6	62. 26. 57	60. 40. 51	58. 54. 51	57. 8. 55	55. 23. 3
	27	53. 37. 17	51. 51. 37	50. 6. 2	48. 20. 32	46. 35. 8			
The Sun.	25	- - -	- - -	120. 27. 44	118. 48. 11	117. 8. 38	115. 29. 5	113. 49. 33	112. 10. 1
	26	110. 30. 31	108. 51. 2	107. 11. 36	105. 32. 11	103. 52. 49	102. 13. 30	100. 34. 14	98. 55. 1
	27	97. 15. 51	95. 36. 45	93. 57. 43	92. 18. 45	90. 39. 52	89. 1. 3	87. 22. 18	85. 43. 38
	28	84. 5. 3	82. 26. 33	80. 48. 9	79. 9. 50	77. 31. 37	75. 53. 29	74. 15. 27	72. 37. 32
	29	70. 59. 42	69. 22. 0	67. 44. 24	66. 6. 55	64. 29. 33	62. 52. 18	61. 15. 10	59. 38. 10
	30	58. 1. 18	56. 24. 34	54. 47. 59	53. 11. 32	51. 35. 14	49. 59. 5	48. 23. 5	46. 47. 14
	31	45. 11. 33	43. 36. 2	42. 0. 41	40. 25. 31	38. 50. 32			

Chart from *The Nautical Almanac and Astronomical Ephemeris*, 1804

The *Nautical Almanac* contained tables that allowed the navigator to determine the locations in the sky of the sun, moon, planets, and many stars for Greenwich time on any day of the year for which that edition was valid. It was published for several years in advance by the Commissioners of Longitude in London. Although John Garnett started publishing a U.S. edition in 1803, the 1804 and 1805 volumes were not available in time for Lewis to use them, so he must have had the English edition, shown here. It was probably from this book that he knew of the predicted lunar eclipse that he tried to observe at Fort Mandan.

Sitting Rabbit's map is a hybrid creation. Libby provided him with a base map and asked him to follow it, so the structure is non-Indian. But Sitting Rabbit added sites and symbols of the Mandan world as they had been passed down to him. Some he labeled in Mandan, and some the reservation missionary labeled in English. The most significant sites he did not label. They were indicated only with cryptic pictographs that would have been easily understandable to someone with a knowledge of Mandan mythology but that the uninformed could not decipher.

In societies that have no system of writing, the sense of history is often geographic rather than temporal. Literate societies think of history as a chronicle: a long linear sequence of events that get farther away—and less relevant—as they recede into the past. Nonliterate societies use the landscape as their history book; they tell stories connected to places, stories in which sequence is unimportant. In Sitting Rabbit's map, the Missouri Valley itself is a symbolic history rich with past events, both human and supernatural. It has the same density of meaning that the Holy Land has for Christians, Jews, and Muslims.

In October 1804 Lewis and Clark came through part of the Missouri Valley later shown on Sitting Rabbit's map. They did not have a Mandan guide, but they had an Arikara one named Piahito. Piahito made an attempt to explain what they were seeing, but Clark did not think the stories worth recording. Using Sitting Rabbit's map, we can today try to reconstruct what Piahito might have said.

On October 16 they passed a small tributary on the west side without giving it a name. The Mandan called it Turtle Fall Creek because, in his work as creator, the culture hero Lone Man made four turtles, but one got away and slipped into this creek. The turtle now supports the dry land and prevents it from sinking. Holy Corral Creek, which Clark probably called Torch Creek, just beyond on the other side, was a place where the Mandan lured buffalo for hunting with the supernatural assistance of beings called the Two Men.[26]

South of the Cannonball River, Clark mapped nothing, but Sitting Rabbit drew two shapes resembling corncobs that the missionary labeled "snowshoes." This may have been a mistake or a deliberate deception, because the Mandan well knew that the Cannonball River was the winter home of the corn spirits. Here lived the Old Woman Who Never Dies. "Of all female life on earth I am head," she said. "Cold and blizzard I subdue. . . . I make whatever I plant to grow." Every fall the water birds guided the corn spirits south to her lodge. She kept them through the winter and sent them north in the spring. She also had a summer home farther upriver.[27]

On October 18 the expedition passed a series of prominent bluffs on the west side, where they found ruins Clark labeled as old fortifications. To the Mandan, one of these was Bird Bill Butte. When a great flood had covered the world, this was the only spot that rose above the water. Magpie had tried to warn the people the flood was coming, but they didn't listen. Magpie and his mother, Corn, and his four brothers, the buffalo, tried to swim for Bird Bill Butte. Only Magpie and Spring Buffalo made it, with their mother, an ear of corn, tied around the buffalo's neck. They founded a village there. Sitting Rabbit called it Eagle Nose Village; it was probably among the ruins Clark saw.[28]

On October 20 the expedition camped across from the mouth of the Heart River. Had they gone up it that evening, they would have come to Heart Butte, also called Heart of the Land. This was the site of creation, and the center of Earth. To the Mandan, the Missouri River was the remnant of the primordial water and was the dividing line between two types of creation. In the beginning, the whole earth was covered with water. The first being, Lone Man, found himself walking on top of the waves. As he wandered, wondering where he had come from, he met First Creator, who was also Coyote. The two of them asked a mud-hen to dive down and bring up some earth so that they could create land. First Creator made the land west of the river; it was rugged and contained buffalo, sheep, mule deer, antelope, and rattlesnakes. Lone Man made the east side. It was flat and dotted with lakes and contained white men. They argued over who had done a better job. Heart Butte was where they stood.[29]

Boat compass, early 1800s

A compass mounted on gimbals that kept it level was essential for measuring the direction of the river channel. Clark or one of the men had to keep a close eye on the compass and note all changes in course to make daily maps of the river. Lewis bought a "Brass Boat Compass," probably much like this one, from Thomas Whitney for $1.50.

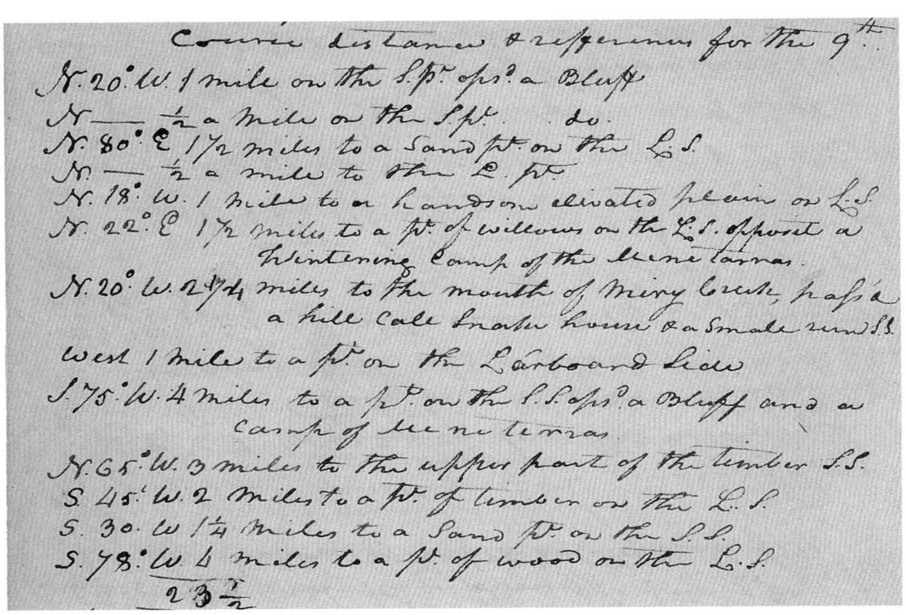

Course distance & refferences for the 9th.
N. 20° W. 1 mile on the S. pt. opsd. a Bluff
N.— ½ a mile on the S. pt. do.
N. 80° E 1½ miles to a Sand pt. on the L.S.
N.— ½ a mile to the L. pt.
N. 18° W. 1 mile to a handsom elivated plain on L.S.
N. 22° E 1½ miles to a pt. of willows on the L.S. opposit a Wintering Camp of the Menetarras.
N. 20° W. 2¾ miles to the mouth of Miry Creek, pass'd a hill Call Snake house & a Smale run S.S.
West 1 mile to a pt. on the Larboard Side
S. 75° W. 4 miles to a pt. on the S.S. opsd. a Bluff and a camp of Menetarras.
N. 65° W. 3 miles to the upper part of the timber S.S.
S. 45° W. 2 miles to a pt. of timber on the L.S.
S. 30. W 1¼ Miles to a Sand pt. on the S.S.
S. 78° W. 4 miles to a pt. of wood on the L.S.
23½

List of courses and distances, 1805

Every step of the way, Clark kept a tally of how far they had traveled and in what direction. He took down this list in his journal on April 9, just after leaving Fort Mandan. He was traveling along the part of the Missouri between the present towns of Stanton and Garrison, North Dakota. The river no longer exists here; it has been inundated by Garrison Dam, which forms Lake Sakakawea.

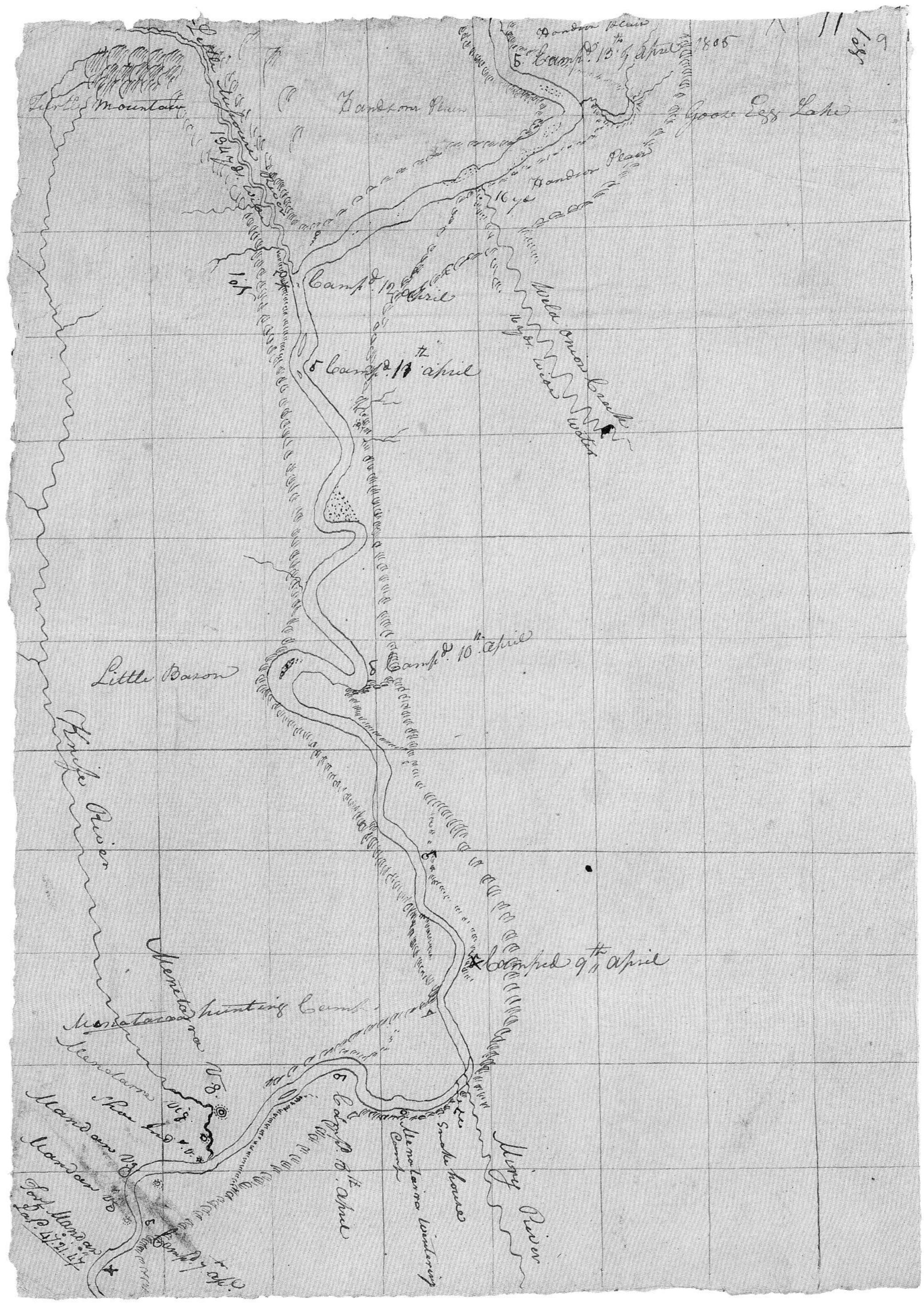

Route map, 1805
Using his lists of courses and distances, Clark mapped the river onto a grid in which every square equaled a given number of miles. This map shows the Missouri from the Mandan-Hidatsa villages to the bend above the Little Missouri and incorporates the courses and distances Clark collected on April 9. North is to the right.

Around the mouth of the Heart River, Clark marked a number of ruins. These were the remains of the Heart River Villages, which the Mandan considered their true home. The smallpox epidemic of 1780–82 had forced them to move north. On the night of October 24 the expedition camped near a stream that the Mandan knew as Charred Body Creek. Sitting Rabbit marked this site with the picture of a bow and arrow. Charred Body came down from the sky in the shape of an arrow and struck the earth so hard that he was buried and could not get loose. An evil spirit who lived in the creek had flaming moccasin tops and set the arrow on fire. Charred Body made a spring and loosened the earth to free himself. The Mandan said the spring would flow as long as the world lasted. The men of the Corps may have drunk from the eternal spring and never known it. All Clark marked was their campsite.[30]

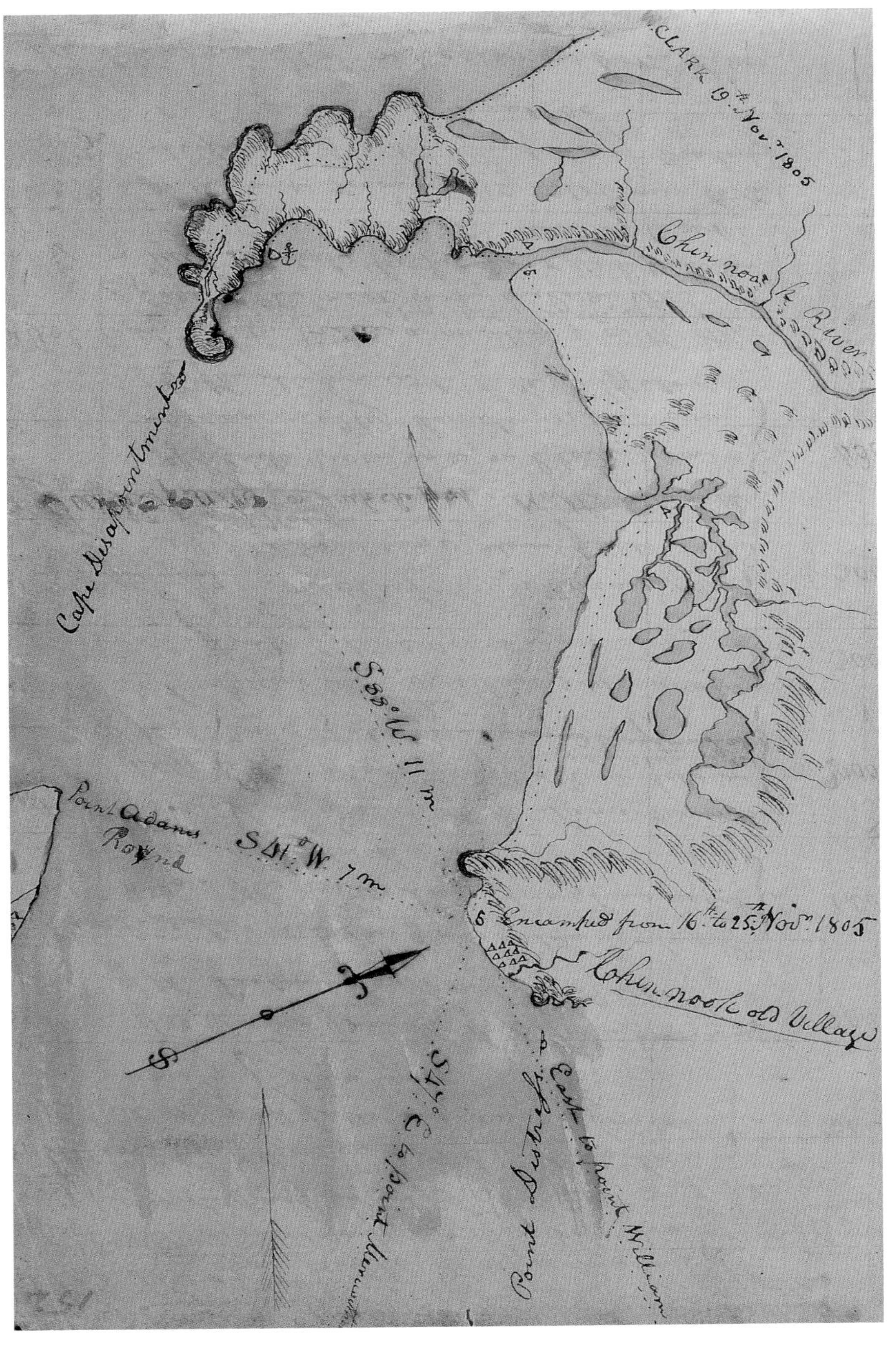

Surveyor's compass, c. 1817

The surveyor's compass was used not only to find north but also to measure horizontal angles. By locating a landmark or the rising sun in the crosshair of the slit on the upright arms, Lewis could measure how many degrees the object was from the north, where the needle pointed (an angle called *azimuth*). He described his compass as "A circumferentor, circle 6 Inches diameter, on the common construction." He added: "By means of this instrument adjusted with the sperit level, I have taken the magnetic azimuth of the sun and pole Star. It has also been employed in taking the traverse of the river." Clark lost the "circumferenter" in a flash flood in June 1805. Ordway commented, "The Compass is a Seerious loss, as we have no other large one." Found buried in mud the next day, it was washed off, and Clark continued to use it. It does not survive today. Lewis purchased his compass from the Philadelphia instrument-maker Thomas Whitney, the maker of this compass. Although this one is dated later, the design of surveyors' compasses did not change much, so Lewis's probably looked much like this. His cost $23.50.

Map of Columbia River near the mouth, 1805

Clark made this map with the surveyor's compass during the time they were camped at Chinook Point on the north shore of the Columbia estuary. He was measuring the bearings of different landmarks by sighting them through the slits in the upright arms of the compass, in order to work out the width of the estuary. North is to the right.

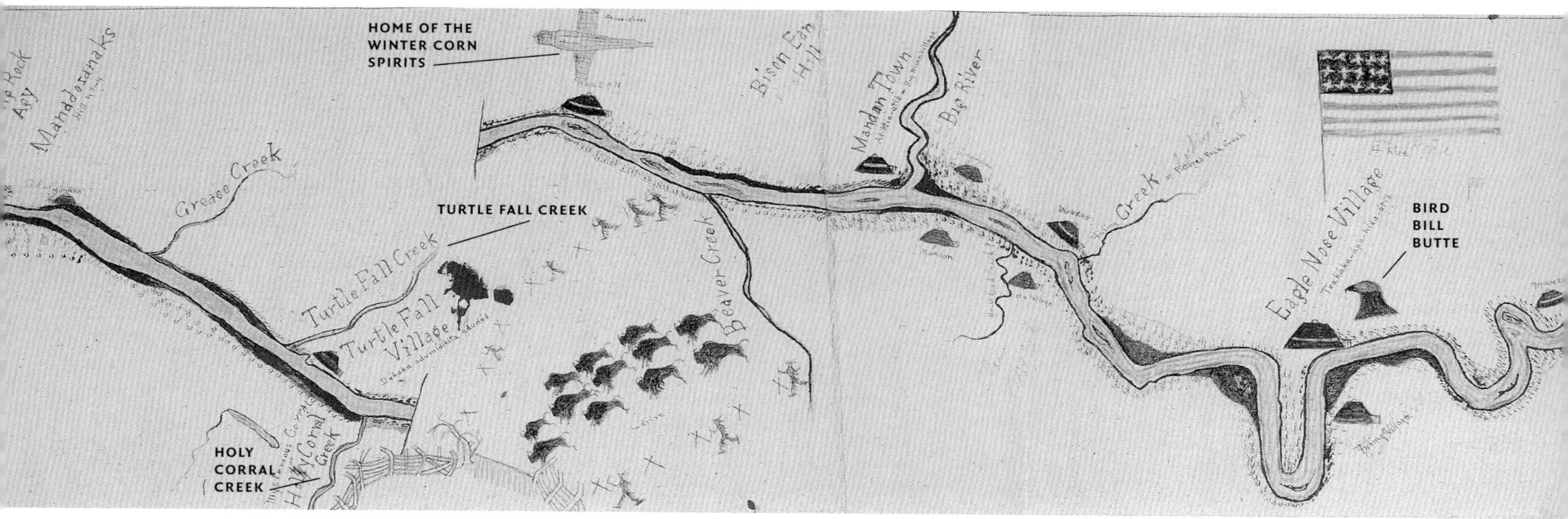

Sitting Rabbit's map of the Missouri River (detail), 1906–7
This is a portion of Sitting Rabbit's map of the Mandan world. The Missouri River was the heart of his map, just as it was the heart of the tribe's world. He named the historic sites of his ancestors and encoded in pictographs the locations of mythic events. The whole map is more than twenty-three feet long and shows the Missouri through the entire state of North Dakota, from the Standing Rock Reservation to the Yellowstone River.

On October 26 they arrived at the five Knife River Villages, where Lewis and Clark met the Mandan and Hidatsa and where the tribes would live until another smallpox epidemic in 1837 drove them north again and reduced them to one village.

Clark's map of this stretch is emptier than Sitting Rabbit's because Clark was not attempting to show the layers of history and meaning surrounding every stream and hill. To him, the valley looked uninhabited, so he renamed the landmarks from his own observations. Unintentionally, he had begun to erase the Mandan presence and to remake the land from his own experiences.

Piahito was not the only one who gave Clark an opportunity to learn—an opportunity that Clark missed. Over and over, the journals record tantalizing hints that Indian people tried to communicate their sense of the living landscape to the explorers. At first, the captains' reaction was scorn at Indian "superstitions." After being told that mysterious beings dwelled at Spirit Mound in South Dakota, the officers made a hot overland trek just to prove there was a rational explanation for the stories. Clark concluded that the wind drove insects to seek shelter in the lee of the hill, attracting birds who fed on them. This, he concluded, was "Suffi[ci]ent proof to produce in the Savage mind a Confident belief of all the properties which they ascribe it." Later, when he heard of a medicine stone the Mandan visited to learn the future, he did not even need to see it to conclude that the stone "no doubt has Some mineral qualtites effected by the Sun."[31]

But Clark's rationalist perspective was not the only view. In fact, Euro-Americans *did* personalize and seek lessons in the land; they just confined such thoughts to modes like literature and landscape painting. It was Lewis, the proto-Romantic, who left the best examples. Standing on a cliff above the Great Falls of the Missouri the next year, while the rock beneath him shuddered with the force of the water, Lewis had a peculiarly modern reaction: he wished he had a camera. What he wanted was not a modern camera but a device of his era, a camera obscura. It made no permanent image but merely projected the view onto a screen, making the landscape flat and square like a painting. By inserting a mechanism between the observer and reality, the camera obscura ostensibly made the scene more impartial and objective. Lewis felt that by looking at such an image, he might be able to describe or sketch the scene, which was too overwhelming to convey in its full three-dimensional reality.[32]

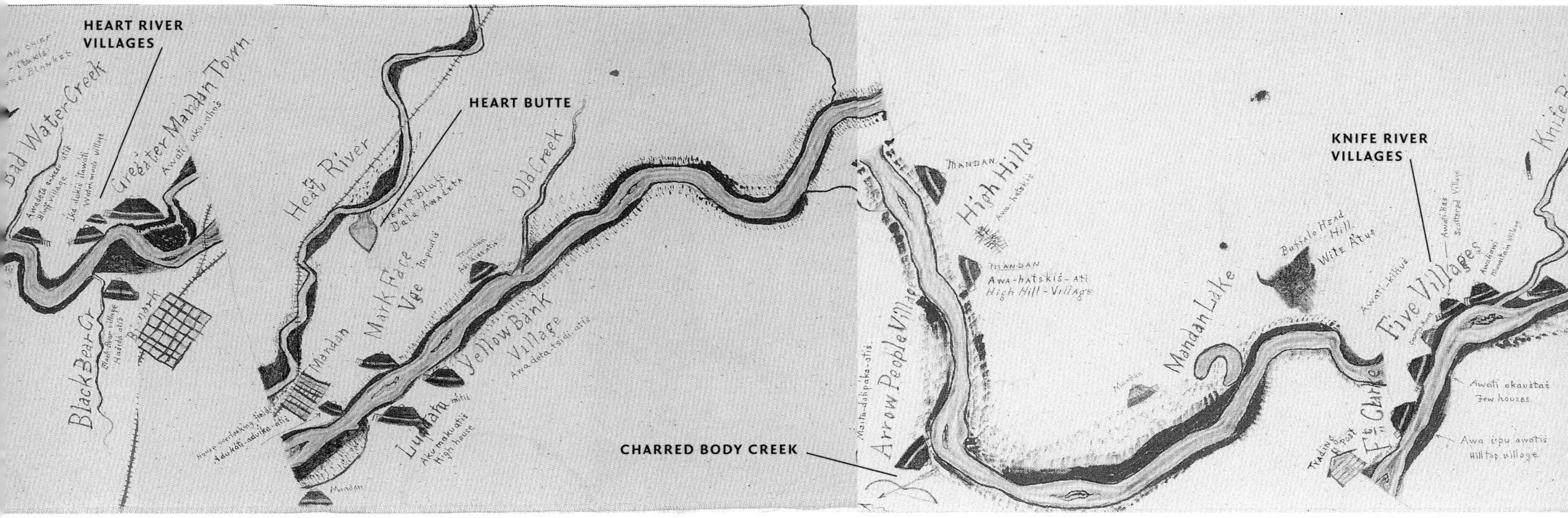

Even without the camera obscura, Lewis framed the scene before him in his mind. Just as today we cannot help but see landscapes through a lens formed by images from photography and television, he saw them through a lens formed by images from European art and literature.[33] In the late eighteenth century, English writers on aesthetics, like Edmund Burke, classified natural phenomena according to the emotions they evoked in the observer. The principal categories were the "sublime" and the "beautiful." Beautiful landscapes were light, uniform, pastoral, and pleasing. They evoked cheerful and harmonious reactions. Sublime landscapes were "dark, uncertain, confused, [and] terrible." They produced thrilling emotions of terror and awe. The prototype of the beautiful landscape was seen in the French art of Claude Lorrain; the Italian painter Salvator Rosa typified the sublime.[34]

In the summer of 1805 Lewis classified landscapes he passed through according to aesthetic quality. The Marias River was beautiful, "garnished with one continued garden of roses." The Great Falls of the Missouri, on the other hand, was sublime. "A precipice of at least eighty feet . . . formes the grandest sight I ever beheld. . . . projecting rocks below receives the water in it's passage down and brakes it into a perfect white foam which assumes a thousand forms in a moment sometimes flying up in jets of sparkling foam. . . . scarcely formed before large roling bodies of the same beaten and foaming water is thrown over and conceals them." In this moment, Lewis explicitly evoked European landscape art: "I wished for the pencil of Salvator Rosa . . . that I might be enabled to give to the enlightened world some just idea of this truly magnifficent and sublimely grand object, which has from the commencement of time been concealed from the view of civilized man."[35]

This passage perfectly expressed the enterprise of discovery as Lewis understood it. Discovery consisted of fitting the landscape into the framework of European intellectual traditions, something only an informed man of refined sensibilities could do. Discovery immeasurably expanded the meaning of the landscape by placing it in the context of a thousand years of European literature and thought. But it also diminished meaning, for Lewis edited away all non-European thought and, in the process, mentally reduced a complex reality to a square image of two dimensions.

Lewis probably never even knew that Indians also had a tradition of landscape painting—partly because it was practiced almost entirely by women and

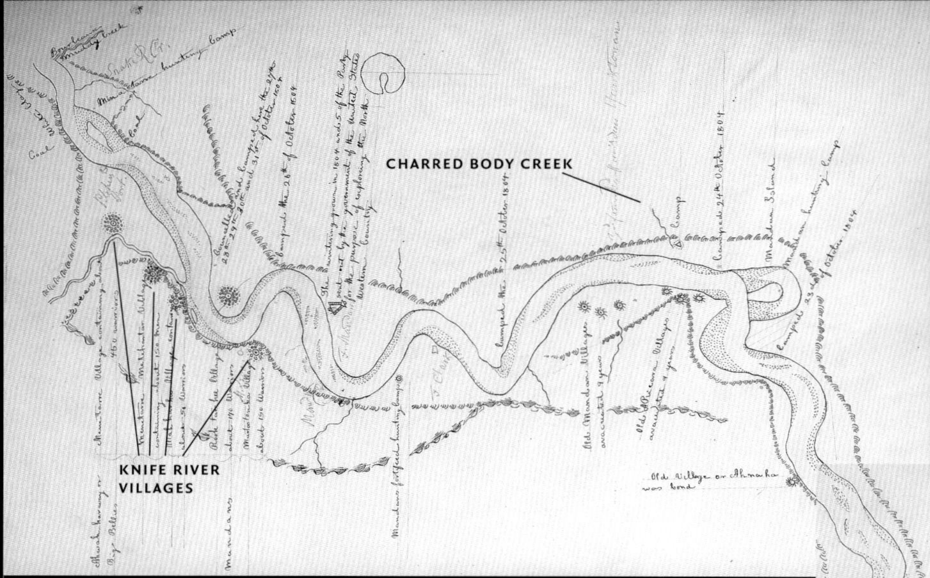

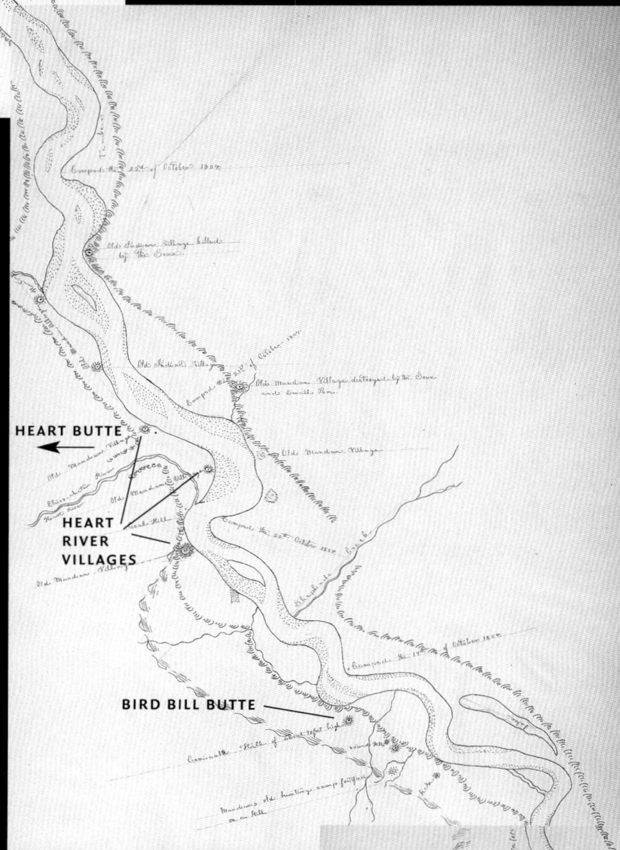

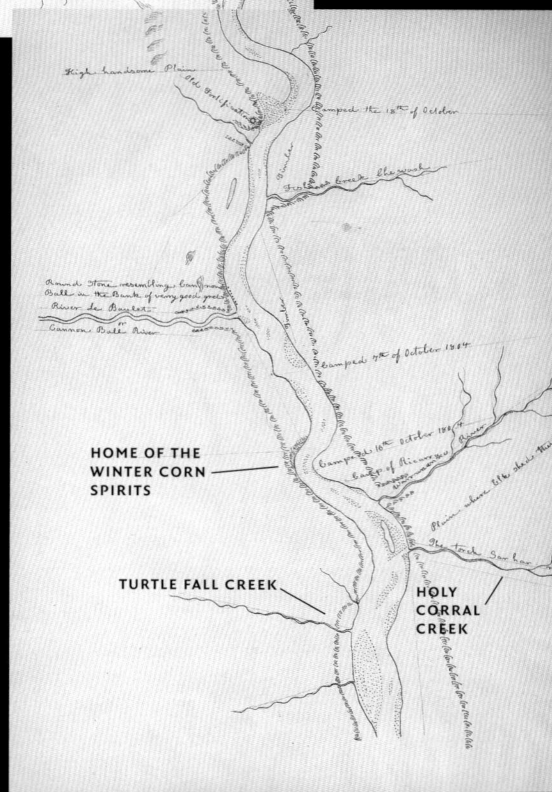

Clark's route maps of the Missouri River, 1833

The type of information that Sitting Rabbit mapped was not the purpose of scientific cartography. When Clark came through the heart of the Mandan homeland, he mapped the landscape and the physical evidence of Indian habitation—the ruined villages and fortifications—but not the cultural evidence. Clark's 1804 route maps of the lower Missouri have been lost. However, in 1833 the German Prince Maximilian of Wied-Neuwied stopped in St. Louis to visit Clark on the way up the Missouri River, and Clark asked his nephew Benjamin O'Fallon to copy the maps. Maximilian took these copies back to Germany, where they were preserved. They are now the only record of Clark's cartography on the lower river.

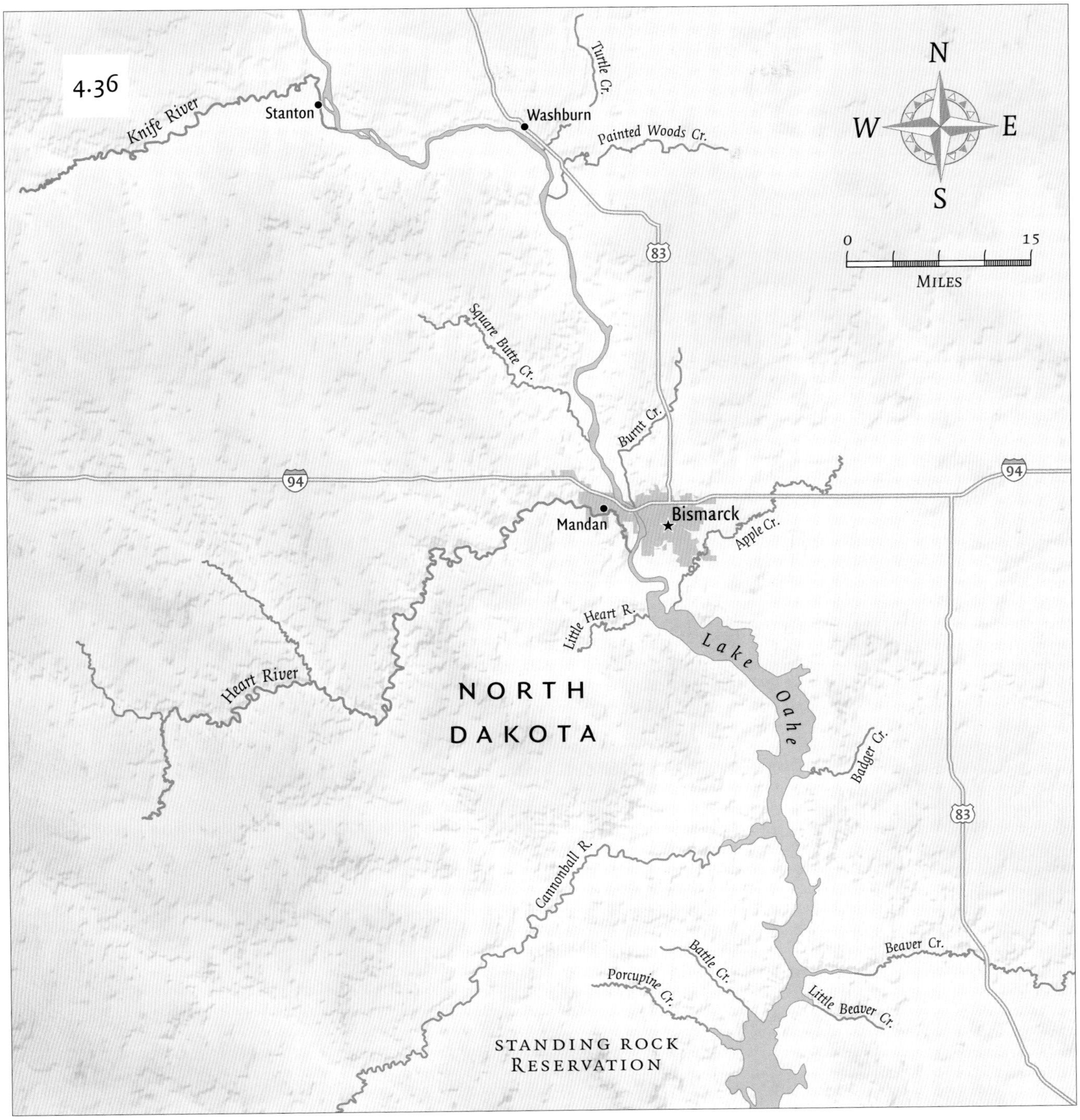

partly because the results were so unlike the representational art of Europe. The rawhide containers called parfleches were the usual canvases on which Indian women painted landscapes. Europeans interpreted the results as abstract geometric designs, but their meanings were richly symbolic. The triangles, stripes, and diamonds symbolized mountains, caves, paths, streams, and sky. No two people meant exactly the same thing by using a design; interpretations were personal and not meant to be read by others. Multiple layers of symbolism were possible, since all things on Earth corresponded to other things, and the deepest Indian thought was a search for those correspondences. The spine represented the path of the sun; the sun represented the eagle's feathers. A color represented "all objects having those colors," so a red shape could be berries, earth, and flame at the same time—since, on a deeper level, the realities of those things were all the same.[36]

The symbolism of the landscape painting only reflected the symbolism of

Map of the Missouri River
Today, the map of the Missouri River has changed once again. The names that Lewis and Clark gave the creeks and hills have mostly been erased and replaced by names given by white settlers. At each stage of history, the names and important landmarks change, and the previous stage is forgotten.

Rocky Landscape with a Hunter and Soldiers, late 1600s
Salvator Rosa was known for his dramatic depictions of the "sublime" landscape. Jefferson, who may have learned of Rosa through reading Horace Walpole, put one of Rosa's paintings on a list of artworks that he hoped to acquire copies of. Lewis was probably familiar with Rosa only through printed reproductions and literary sources.

the landscape. A hill was not simply a hill; it might represent (and, on a deeper level, *be*) the sacred hill from which the buffalo entered the world. A path did not lead over land alone; it also led through life. Plains Indian parfleche paintings had no backgrounds; even the blank spaces meant something. The same was true of their land.

Lewis's openness to the mystical and subjective sensibilities of Romanticism made him a less skeptical observer than Clark. As the landscape made inroads on his mind, he reacted with sentiments of wonder and awe. Around the Great Falls, he recounted a series of "novel occurrences": mysterious booming sounds that he was "at a loss to acount for," strangely sentient behavior by animals, freakish weather. It all contributed to an atmosphere he

Parfleche with landscape design, c. 1900
The old woman who painted this design on a rawhide bag told the collector, Alfred Kroeber: "It represents the land as it is, as nearly as it can be represented." She said that the red areas on the edges symbolize a red bank along a stream. The unpainted spaces next to them are sand. The triangles are a hill with green grass at the top and yellow earth at the bottom. In the center, the vertical stripe represents a trail. The trail is red in the middle and white at the ends because "a road cannot be alike in all its length." It leads to the place where the bag opens. The rectangular shape of the design represents the earth.

Landscape with the Marriage of Isaac and Rebekah ("The Mill"), 1648

In Lewis's day, the painter Claude Lorrain was so famous that he was known simply as "Claude." This work, which ostensibly illustrates the biblical story of the marriage of Isaac and Rebecca, is typical of the idealized pastoral landscapes for which Lorrain was famous. With its tame greenswards and dancing rustics, it typifies the "beautiful" landscape. His art was so popular that a device named a "Claude Lorrain glass" was invented. It slightly distorted and tinted a real landscape so that the scene would resemble a painting. Lacking a glass, people like Lewis could perform the same feat in their imaginations.

described as one of "inchantment." In naming the nearby Medicine River, he wrote respectfully of the Indian concept of medicine as "something that eminates from or acts immediately by the influence or power of the great sperit; or that in which the power of god is manifest by it's incomprehensible power of action." He had come a long way from his earlier scoffing at Spirit Mound.[37]

Even Clark had a different attitude by the time they returned down the river. In 1804 he had dismissed the Mandans' "little Indian aneckd[o]ts," but in 1806, as he was traveling downriver with Shehek-Shote, he listened to the chief's stories and recorded a long account of Mandan creation and history. By then, the river had become interwoven with the explorers' own stories and perceptions, and perhaps they were willing to see it less as a problem in navigation and engineering and more as a homeland.[38]

CLARK MAKES A MAP

"I imploy my Self drawing a Connection of the Countrey from what information I have recved," Clark wrote at Fort Mandan on January 5, 1805. The map he was working on was a hybrid. Below Fort Mandan, it was based on his route maps and Lewis's astronomical observations. West of there, it incorporated Shehek-Shote's map almost unchanged, as well as the information from the unnamed Hidatsa warrior whose route was shown as "War Path of the Big Bellies [Hidatsa]." He also used Ackomokki's map transmitted to him via Arrowsmith and "information . . . from Indians collected at different times and entitled to some credit." As a result, it showed Indian perceptions mapped onto a European gridwork.[39]

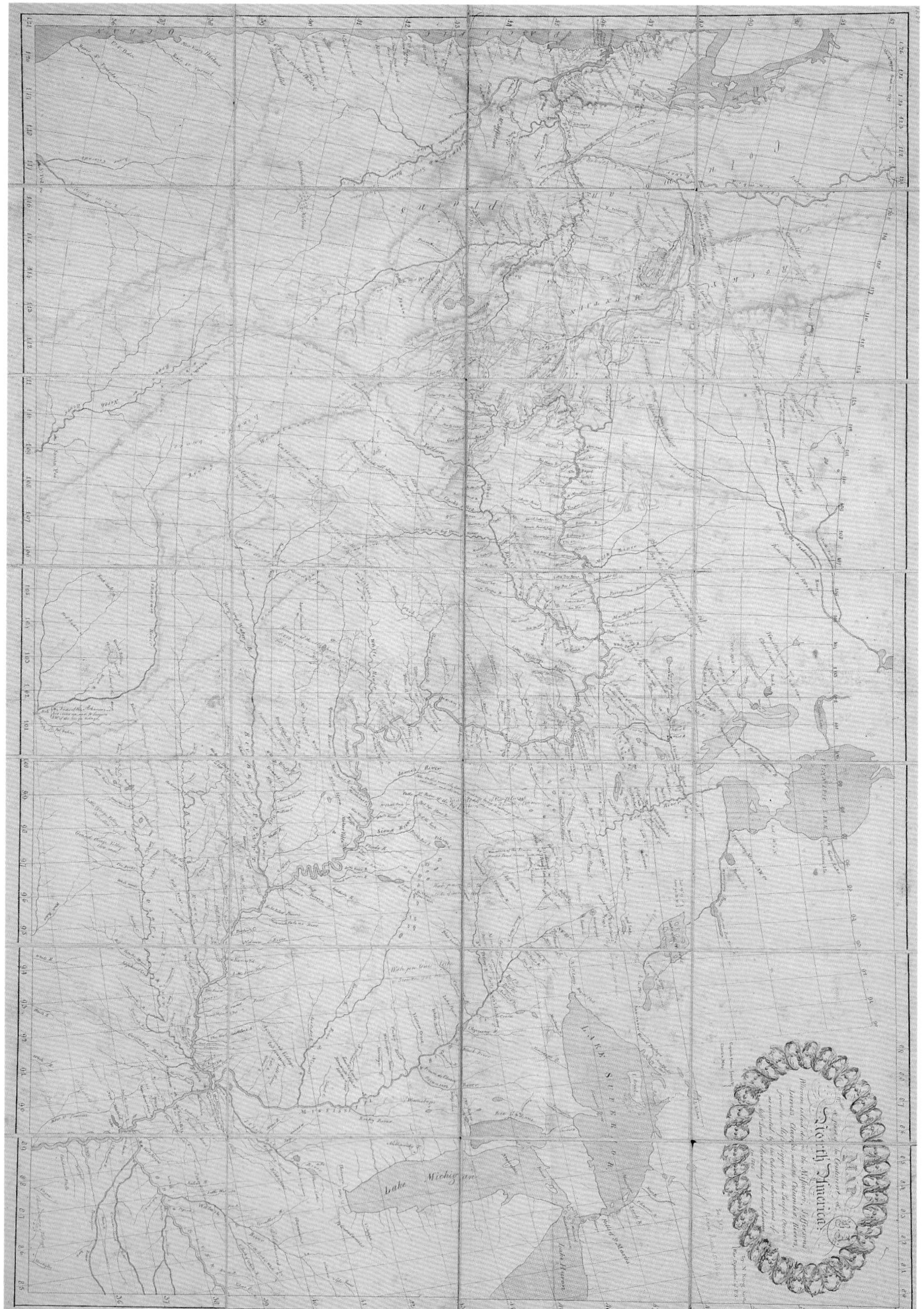
MAP
North America

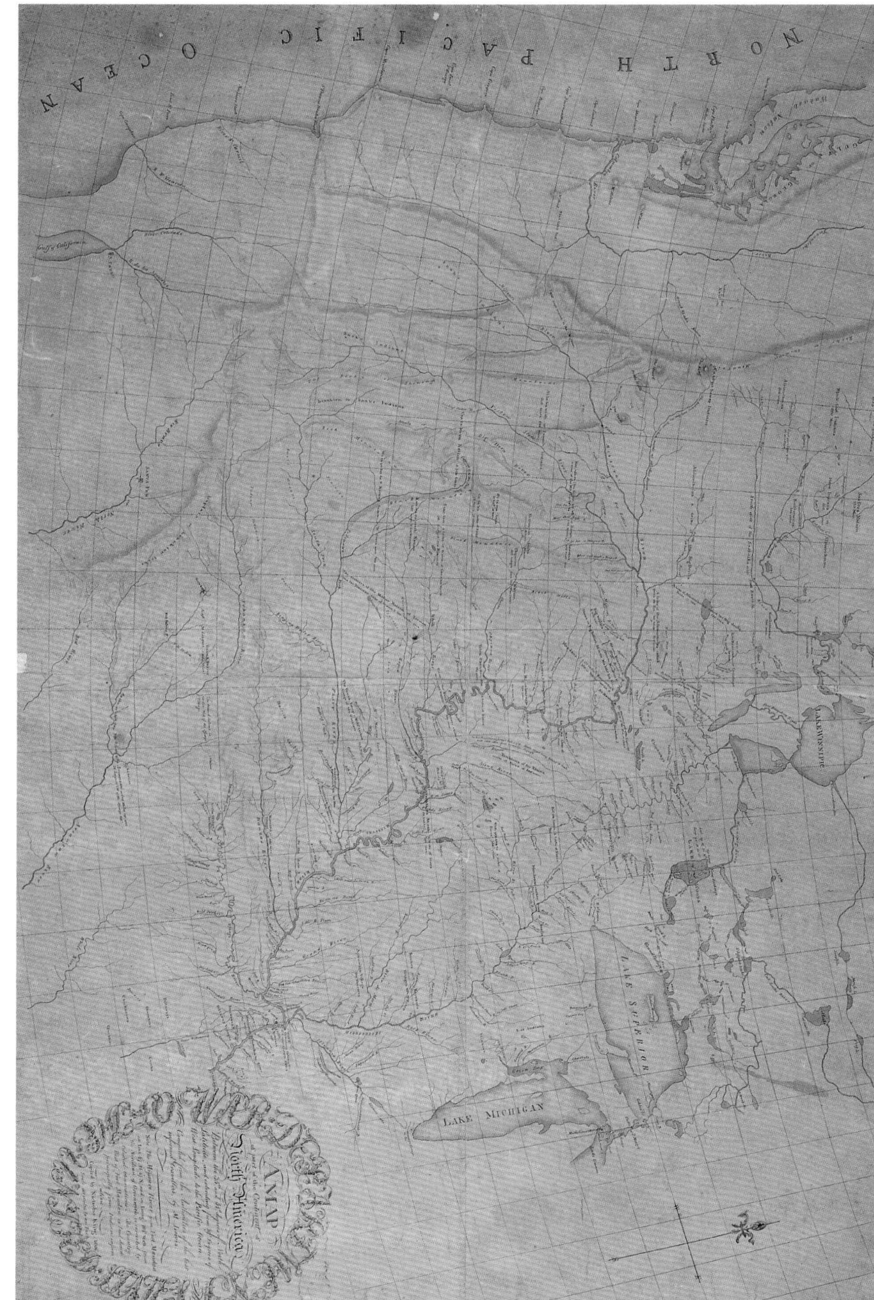
NORTH PACIFIC OCEAN
LAKE SUPERIOR
LAKE MICHIGAN
A MAP
North America

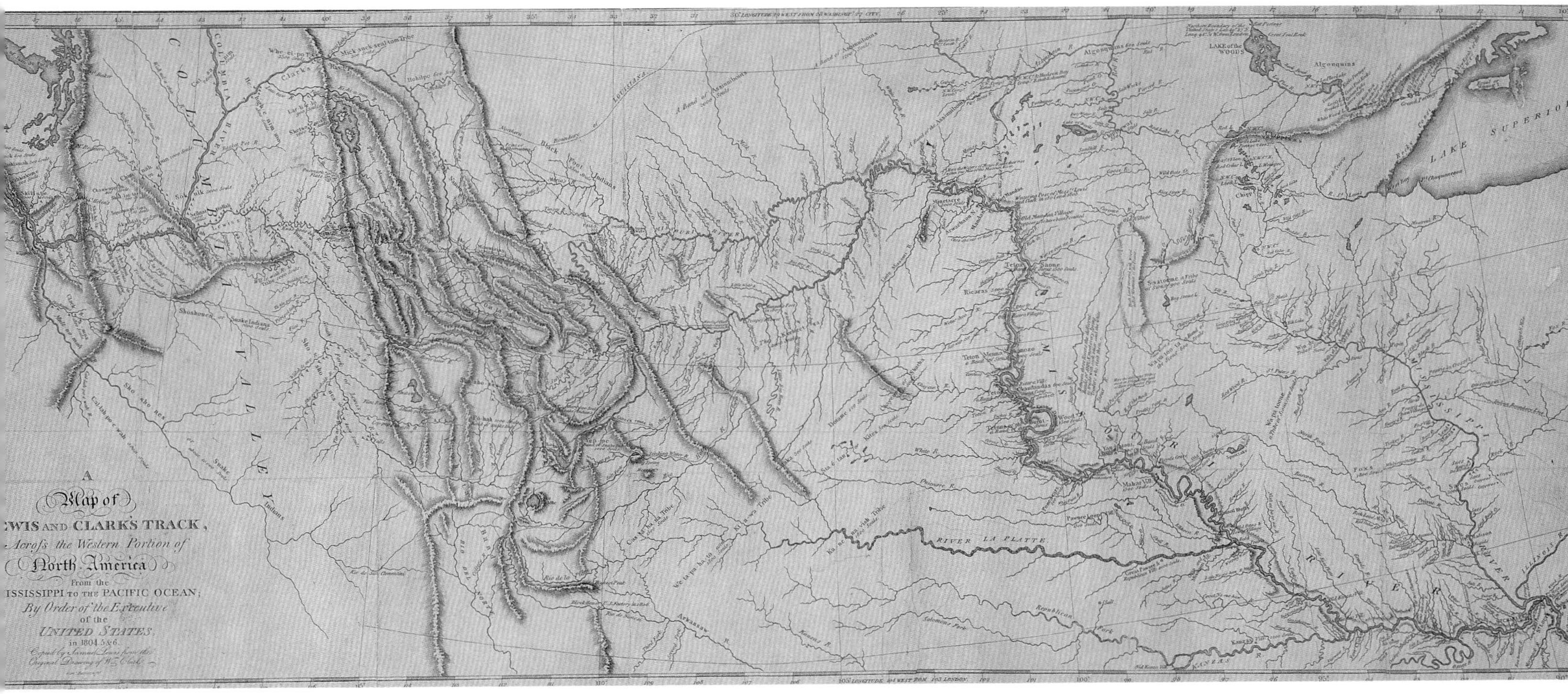

The map he drew after returning from the expedition was revised to reflect his new perception of the land. For the first time, it showed the Rockies correctly as a series of ranges and distinguished them from the Cascades. It corrected the course of the Missouri, Yellowstone, and Columbia Rivers and identified the Snake as a major western waterway. Along the path the expedition had followed, the Indian contributions were replaced by Clark's own observations, using Euro-American methods of cartography. In the places where the expedition had not gone, some Indian information remained. When Clark's map was finally published eight years after the expedition's return, it focused on the slice that had been mapped by Euro-American methods. It is an undisputed masterpiece of cartography and was tremendously influential in forming eastern images of the West. But it is not a value-neutral document.

Clark's map of 1814 showed the western half of the continent as a unit, providing an image of a United States that went all the way to the Pacific. It showed rivers and mountains with names like Jefferson and Madison, making U.S. claims to the land seem patriotically ordained. It showed vast open tracts where only a single boundary existed—that between the United States and Great Britain. It emphasized interlocking river routes, implying a ready-made transportation system giving access to huge stretches of arable country. All of these features carried political messages that the public embraced, as opinion turned from cautious and isolationist in 1803 to exuberantly expansionist by the 1820s.

It is worth considering what the map left out. Missing was the social and symbolic landscape the Indians saw, the stage of events. Missing were Indian names, towns, trade routes, hunting territories, and sacred sites. The tribes themselves were represented, since they were still a force to be reckoned with. But any sense that they *inhabited* the landscape was erased. The map showed what Jefferson wanted: an essentially empty land, open and ready for settlement.

A Map of Lewis and Clark's Track, 1814
This is the version of Clark's map that most people saw; it was published with the journals eight years after the expedition's return. Comparing it with other maps of North America, one historian called it "one of the most influential ever drawn." The cartographer, Samuel Lewis (no relation to Meriwether), focused on the part mapped by Euro-American methods.

OPPOSITE, TOP: **A Map of Part of the Continent of North America, 1805**
This is a copy of the map that Clark drew at Fort Mandan. Below the Mandan villages, it is based on Clark's own surveys; west of there, it is based on a combination of Indian information and European maps. Although two copies of the map survive at the Library of Congress and the National Archives, neither is in Clark's hand; they are both copies made by Nicholas King, a government cartographer. This is the copy archived at the Library of Congress.

OPPOSITE, BOTTOM: **A Map of Part of the Continent of North America, 1806**
This map shows the explorers' view of the country after their return. At Fort Clatsop, Clark "compleated a map of the Countrey" through which they had been passing. Lewis wrote Jefferson that he had only one "general map" that he was "unwilling to wrisk by the Mail"; he probably hand-carried it to Washington. Whether this is a copy of the Fort Clatsop map or a later one is a source of debate, since it incorporates information discovered on the return voyage in 1806, particularly information on the Yellowstone River.

FIVE Animal Encounters

Sometimes men say that they can understand the meaning of the songs of birds. I can believe this is true . . . for these creatures and man are alike the work of a greater power.

—CHASED BY BEARS[1]

Lewis loved the drama of setting out. The day the Corps departed from Fort Mandan, he compared himself to Christopher Columbus and Captain James Cook. "Entertaing as I do, the most confident hope of succeading in a voyage which had formed a da[r]ling project of mine for the last ten years, I could but esteem this moment of my departure as among the most happy of my life." He continued: "We were now about to penetrate a country at least two thousand miles in width, on which the foot of civillized man had never trodden; the good or evil it had in store for us was for experiment yet to determine, and these little vessells contained every article by which we were to expect to subsist or defend ourselves."[2]

The "little vessells" were the white and red pirogues and six dugout canoes constructed in the spring at Fort Mandan. On April 7 the explorers bade farewell to the keelboat, which turned back to St. Louis with a crew of soldiers, crates and barrels full of scientific specimens, journals, and letters home. Lewis's letter to Jefferson was buoyant with optimism. "We . . . expect to reach the Pacific Ocean, and return, as far as the head of the Missouri, or perhaps to this place before winter," he wrote. "Every individual of the party are in good health, and excellent sperits; zealously attatched to the enterprise, and anxious to proceed."[3]

Rocky Mountain sheep horn, 1805
Clark sent home a collection of souvenirs, including three sheep horns, to his family via the keelboat in 1805. At that time, he had not yet seen the Rocky Mountain sheep; the horns had been purchased from the Mandan. After shooting some of the animals, he sent an additional four horns to his family in 1806. This one was passed down in the family of Clark's sister Fanny and was associated with the expedition. When Lewis described the sheep in 1805, he called the horns "compressed, bent backwards and lunated; the surface swelling into wavy rings which incircleing the horn continue to succeed each other from the base to the extremity." He noted, "The horn is of a light brown colour; when dressed it is almost white extreemly transparent and very elastic."

The crew he praised was now thirty-three strong. It was still a mix of Kentucky woodsmen, soldiers, and French-Indian trappers, plus one African American, one Shoshone woman, a baby, and a Newfoundland dog. With fewer men and more trust between them, the military discipline eased, though it never disappeared. As they departed past the Mandan villages, then the Hidatsa ones, onto the upper Missouri, they quickly settled into a routine of eating, traveling, and sleeping. "When we halted for dinner the squaw busied herself in serching for the wild artichokes which the mice collect and deposit in large hoards," Lewis recorded on the second day. "This operation she performed by penetrating the earth with a sharp stick. . . . she procurrd a good quantity of these roots. The flavor of this root resembles that of the Jerusalem Artichoke."[4]

The landscape around them was a badland of high buttes and eroded gullies. "Immence quantities of sand . . . is driven by the wind from the sandbars," Lewis complained on April 24. "So penitrating is this sand that we cannot keep any article free from it; in short we are compelled to eat, drink, and breath it very freely." A week later, it was the inclement northern weather that earned a remark from Clark: "This morning about Sunrise began to Snow . . . a verry extroadernaley Climate, to behold the trees Green & flowers Spred on the plain, & Snow an inch deep . . . Ice freesing to the Ores."[5]

Soon they celebrated reaching the confluence of the Yellowstone and the Missouri on the present-day border of North Dakota and Montana. Lewis man-

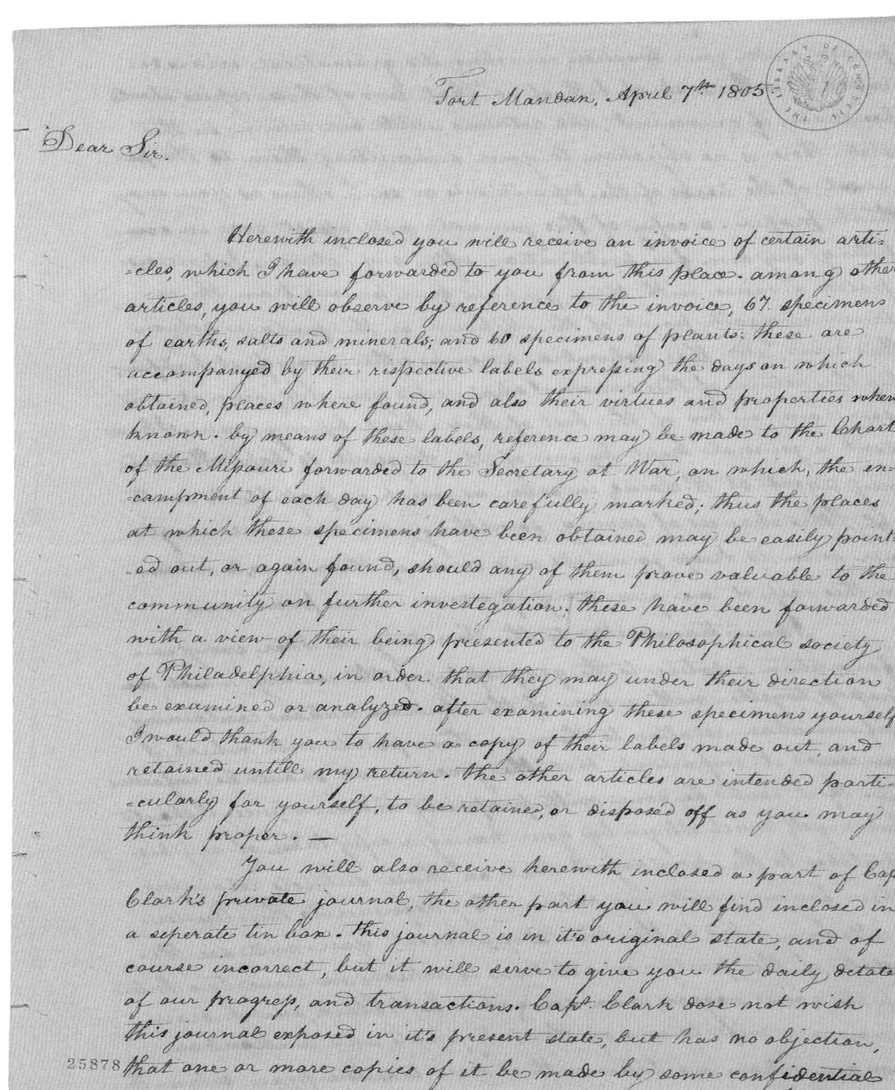

Fort Mandan, April 7th 1805

Dear Sir.

Herewith inclosed you will receive an invoice of certain arti-cles, which I have forwarded to you from this place. among other articles, you will observe by reference to the invoice, 67. specimens of earths, salts and minerals; and 60 specimens of plants: these are accompanyed by their rispective labels expressing the days on which obtained, places where found, and also their virtues and properties when known. by means of these labels, reference may be made to the Chart of the Missouri forwarded to the Secretary at War, on which, the en-campment of each day has been carefully marked; thus the places at which these specimens have been obtained may be easily point-ed out, or again found, should any of them prove valuable to the community on further investegation. these have been forwarded with a view of their being presented to the Philosophical society of Philadelphia, in order that they may under their direction be examined or analyzed. after examining these specimens yourself, I would thank you to have a copy of their labels made out, and retained untill my return. the other articles are intended parti-cularly for yourself, to be retained, or disposed off as you may think proper. —

You will also receive herewith inclosed a part of Capt. Clark's private journal, the other part you will find inclosed in a seperate tin box. this journal is in it's original state, and of course incorrect, but it will serve to give you the daily detales of our progress, and transactions. Capt. Clark dose not wish this journal exposed in it's present state, but has no objection,

 that one or more copies of it be made by some confidential person,

Letter to Jefferson from Lewis at Fort Mandan, 1805
Lewis was sanguine about the journey ahead in this letter, written before leaving Fort Mandan. He predicted that they would travel twenty to twenty-five miles a day, that the crossing of the mountains would be "easy and expeditious," and that they would reach the Pacific and return in the same year. None of these predictions came true. To publicize this rosy picture of the expedition, Jefferson immediately had the letter printed and forwarded to Congress, along with Clark's information on the Indian tribes of Louisiana.

Page 164: *Buffalo and Elk on the Upper Missouri* (detail), 1833. See page 172.

Junction of the Yellowstone and the Missouri, c. 1833
When he made this watercolor, Karl Bodmer may have been standing on the same hill from which Lewis described the mouth of the Yellowstone River. Bodmer, however, did not see the green Arcadian valleys Lewis described.

aged to conjure an agrarian paradise out of this rugged land, describing "wide and fertile vallies formed by the missouri and the yellowstone rivers, which . . . disclose their meanderings for many miles in their passage through these delightfull tracts of country."[6]

The year before, when their attention had been focused on getting the unwieldy keelboat up the river, the pirogues had given them few problems; now that changed. The white pirogue, on which they had loaded all the most valuable papers and instruments, was so plagued by accidents that Lewis began to joke that it was "attended by some evil gennii." On May 14 a "sudon squawl of wind" upset the pirogue. As the translator Toussaint Charbonneau flailed helplessly, "crying to his god for mercy," the more cool-headed bowsman, Pierre Cruzatte, "threatened to shoot him instantly if he did not take hold of the rudder," while Sacagawea "caught and preserved most of the light articles which were washed overboard." The pirogue was saved, though "filled within an inch of the gunwals." A week later the captains rewarded "the Indian woman" by naming a tributary of the Missouri "Sâh-câ-gar me-âh or bird woman's River, after our interpreter the Snake woman."[7]

They consistently underestimated how far they had to go. On May 26 Lewis saw what he took to be the outliers of the Rockies, when he was actually more than one hundred miles from them. "I felt a secret pleasure in finding myself so near the head of the heretofore conceived boundless Missouri," he wrote, "but when I reflected on the difficulties which this snowey barrier would most probably throw in my way . . . it in some measure counterballanced the joy I had felt. . . . but as I have always held it a crime to anticipate evils I will believe it a good comfortable road untill I am compelled to beleive differently."[8]

"Perogue of 8 Tuns," 1804

The only sketch of the pirogues is this doodle by Clark, not drawn to scale; they were actually much longer in relation to the width. Pirogues were boats up to forty feet long and four feet wide, with carved sides and flat, often plank, bottoms. One of the Corps pirogues was propelled by six oars, the other by seven. They had rudders and masts and were often sailed—although with no keel, they were apt to tip over. The white pirogue also had an awning so that its occupants could sit in the shade. The "8 tuns" in Clark's caption refers to the amount of lading it could hold.

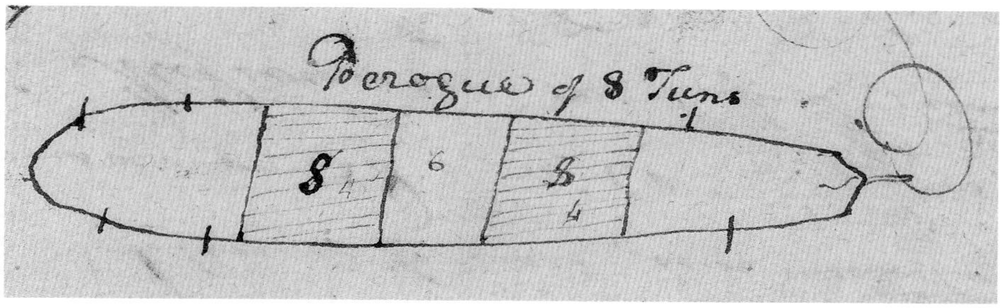

The men were already beginning to believe differently. As the river grew shallower and more rapid, the days of easy sailing were past. "The men are compelled to be in the water even to their armpits, and the water is yet very could," Lewis wrote. "Draging the heavy burthen of a canoe and walking ocasionally for several hundred yards over the sharp fragments of rocks . . . their labour is incredibly painfull and great, yet those faithfull fellows bear it without a murmur."[9] As they passed into central Montana and the rain shadow of the Rockies, Patrick Gass's pragmatic assessment of the land was damning—"the most dismal country I ever beheld; nothing but barren mountains on both sides of the river, as far as our view could extend."[10]

At last not even Lewis could pretend it looked fertile and Arcadian. But he still found redeeming value in its "romantic appearance." His adjectives changed. Instead of lauding the harmony and order of the pastoral landscape, he now praised the grandeur and sublimity of vistas that could be a fitting future home for a noble, lofty-minded people. When they came to the white cliffs of the Missouri, he wrote lyrically of the "thousand grotesque figures" worn by erosion into the sandstone bluffs, "which with the help of a little immagination . . . represent eligant ranges of lofty freestone buildings, having their parapets well stocked with statuary." He added, "As we passed on it seemed as if those seens of visionary inchantment would never have and end."[11]

View of the Stone Walls, 1833

Like Lewis, the artist Karl Bodmer was fascinated by the white castles formed by erosion along a stretch of the Missouri in Montana. Patrick Gass wrote: "We passed some very curious cliffs and rocky peaks, in a long range. . . . They seem as if built by the hand of man, and are so numerous that they appear like the ruins of an ancient city."

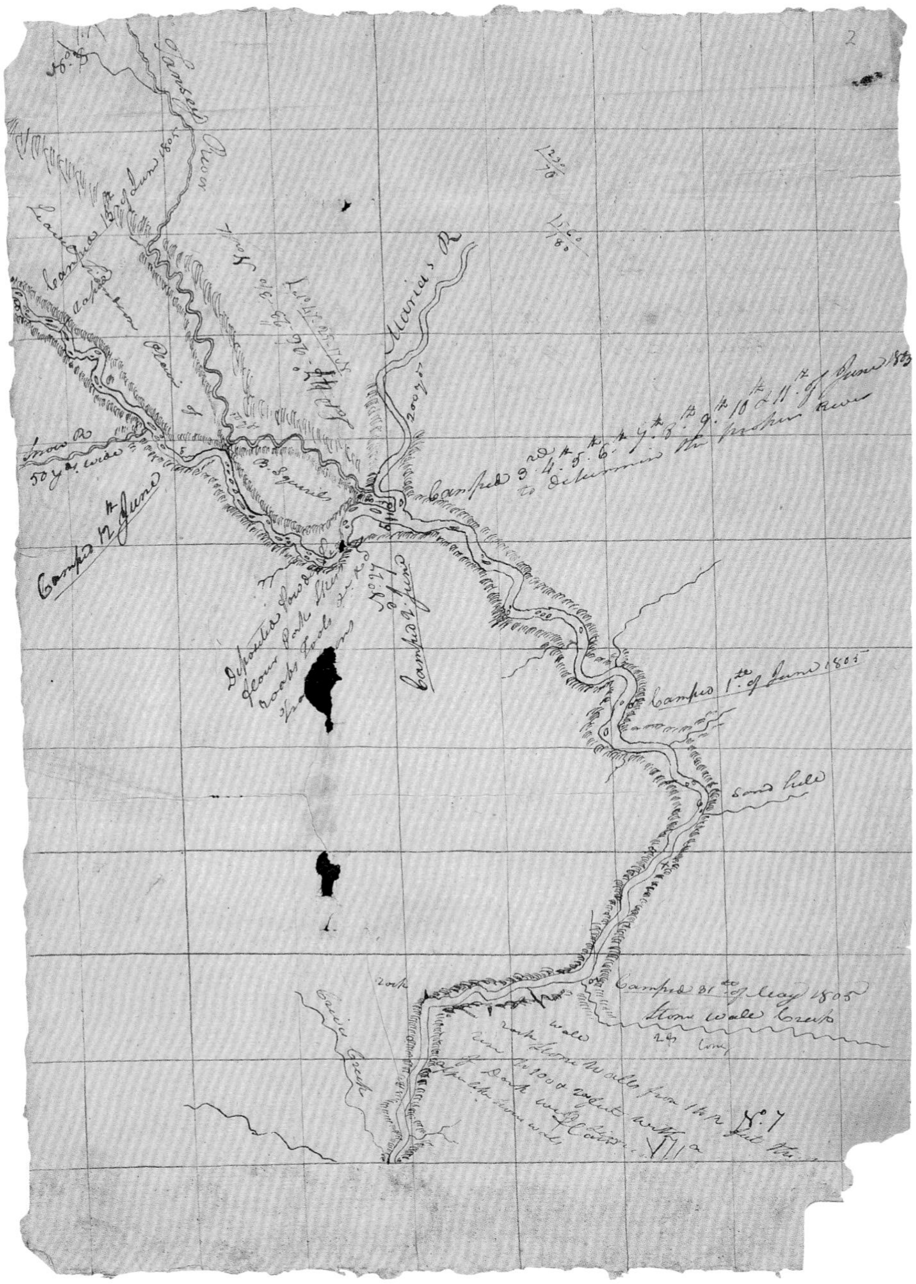

Route map of the Marias River, 1805
Clark drew this map to summarize the scouting they performed in nine days while camped at the Marias River. Lewis described the Marias hyperbolically as "a noble river; one destined to become . . . an object of contention between the two great powers of America and Great Britin . . . and . . . one of the most interesting brances of the Missouri in a commercial point of view." He was wrong on both counts.

No matter how romantic, nationalism was still a factor in all their observations. Throughout April and May, they had been skirting the northernmost boundary of the United States, where Louisiana butted up against Great Britain. They kept a sharp eye out for major rivers flowing in from the north in hopes that the watershed of the Missouri would extend into valuable fur lands. Early in June, they came on the most promising north branch yet. In fact, this rain-swollen fork (the Marias River) was so large that it was difficult to tell which branch to take.

"To mistake the stream at this period of the season . . . might defeat the expedition altogether," Lewis wrote. "The party with very few exceptions have already pronounced the N. fork to be the Missouri. . . . Capt. C. and myself concluded to set out early the next morning with a small party each, and . . . satisfy ourselves of the one, which it would be most expedient for us to take." Lewis took the north fork, Clark the south; both came to the same conclusion. Six days later, they were back at the forks, studying their maps. The best ones showed a great waterfall in the Missouri, after which the river passed through a chain of mountains and bent southward. "Today we examined our maps . . .

Falls of the Missouri, 1868
This may be Rainbow Falls, the third in the series that make up the Great Falls. Clark called it the "Handsom" falls, and Lewis characterized it as "*pleasingly beautifull*, while the other was *sublimely grand*." The artist, Alfred E. Mathews, was standing on the north side, from where Lewis also first viewed the falls. In 1910 this fall was obliterated by the Rainbow Dam.

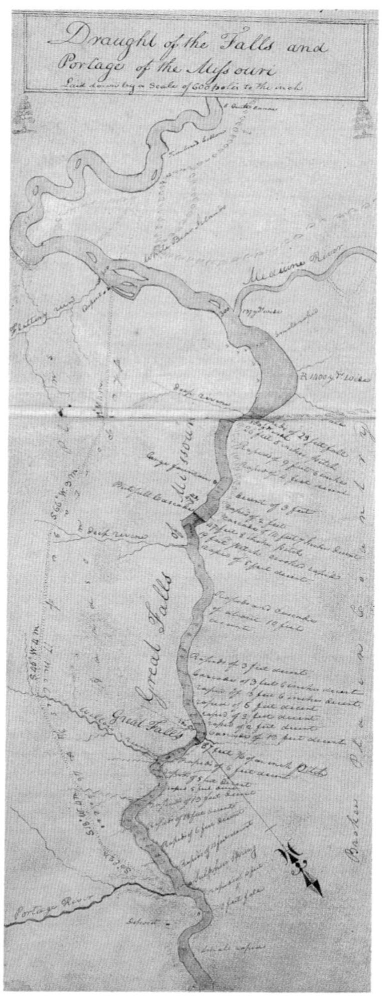

Draught of the Falls and Portage of the Missouri, 1805
While Lewis struggled to encompass the grandeur of the falls by describing them in his journal, Clark conquered them by diagram. "I employ my Self drawing a Copy of the river to be left at this place for fear of Some accident in advance," Clark wrote on July 4, 1805. This map was drawn in a two-page spread of his journal. The portage route is shown on the left (south) side of the river.

and fully settled in our minds the propryety of addopting the South fork," Lewis wrote. "The party . . . being still firm in the beleif that the N. Fork was the Missouri . . . they said very cheerfully that they were ready to follow us any wher we thought proper to direct but that they still thought that the other was the river."[12]

Perhaps second-guessing his own decision, Lewis scouted on ahead of the main party, looking for the "great waterfall." Their maps from St. Louis showed it; the Hidatsa had told them exactly where to find it. On June 13 he wrote: "My ears were saluted with the agreeable sound of a fall of water and . . . I saw the spray arrise above the plain like a collumn of smoke . . . which soon began to make a roaring too tremendious to be mistaken for any cause short of the great falls of the Missouri."[13] Lewis's initial reaction to the falls was shaped by established literary conventions for the first sight of any natural wonder by a European of polished sentiment. He filled his journal with descriptions of the "ravishing prospect" of a "beautifull cascade."[14] But soon, practicalities took over. The waterfall itself was no surprise. What did come as a surprise was that a second fall lay beyond the first—then a third, and a fourth, and a fifth. The "Great Falls" were not one obstruction but many, and the only way around was an arduous, eighteen-mile portage.

When Lewis returned to break the bad news to the rest of the crew, he discovered another problem. "Found the Indian woman extreemly ill. . . . this gave me some concern as well for the poor object herself, then with a young child in her arms, as from the consideration of her being our only dependence for a friendly negociation with the Snake Indians on whom we depend for horses." Faced with the alarming prospect of crossing the mountains with a motherless baby on their hands, both Clark and Lewis used all their medical skills. Lewis's diagnosis of "an obstruction of the mensis" and Clark's dark hint that "if She dies it will be the fault of her husband" suggest that she may have suffered a miscarriage. A combination of mineral water and opium pulled her through.[15]

As Sacagawea convalesced, the men began hauling the tons of boats and baggage around the falls. They rigged makeshift wagons, using their masts as axles. Even so, it was hard going over the hilly terrain. "The men has to haul with all their Strength wate & art," Clark wrote; "maney times every man all catching the grass & knobes & Stones with their hands to give them more force in drawing on the Canoes & Loads, and notwithstanding the Coolness of the air in high presperation and every halt, those not employed in reparing the Cou[r]se; are asleep in a moment, maney limping from the Soreness of their feet . . . but no man Complains all go Chearfully on."[16]

John Ordway gave the perspective of those supposedly uncomplaining men. "The men mended their mockisons with double Soles to Save their feet from the prickley pear (which abound in the plains) and the hard ground. . . . one pair of good mockins will not last more than about 2 days. will ware holes in them the first day and patch them for the next." But the labor was not without moments of levity. "The wind blowing steady from the South east, We hoisted sail in our largest Craft (or Canoe) which assisted us as much, as 4 Men hawling," wrote Joseph Whitehouse. Ordway added whimsically, "This is Saleing on dry land in everry Since of the word."[17]

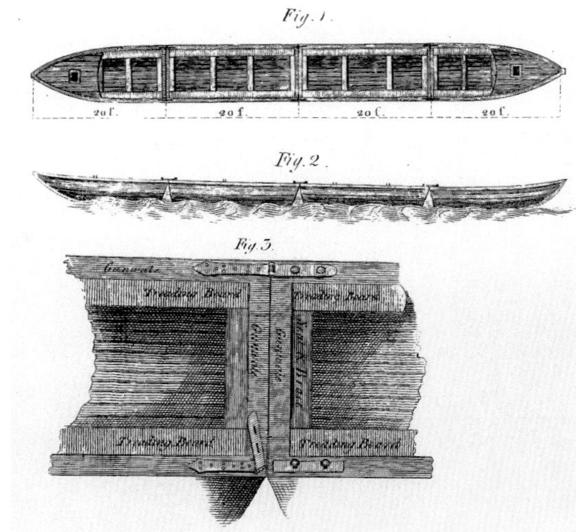

Engraving of a modular boat, 1799
Lewis was not the only one devising ingenious schemes for boats made in detachable sections. This plan for an experimental canal boat was published in the American Philosophical Society's *Transactions* for 1799, where Lewis easily could have seen it.

Lewis's iron boat was a wrought-iron framework that assembled with screws into eight sections, each four feet long. Put together, it measured 36 feet long, 4½ feet wide, and 26 inches deep, "in shape like a Ships Yawl." As in this illustration, the prow and stern were both curved, and the body of the boat was semicylindrical in cross-section. The hull was covered with twenty-eight elk skins and four buffalo skins, and the inside and gunwales were lined with wood slats. Lewis estimated that it would have held eight thousand pounds of cargo, if it had only stayed afloat.

Even the weather seemed determined to block their progress. One day, Clark, York, Charbonneau, and Sacagawea were walking the portage under the shade of Clark's umbrella. "I perceived a Cloud which appeared black and threaten imediate rain. . . . we took Shelter...[in] a Deep rivein. . . . the rain fell like one voley of water . . . and gave us time only to get out of the way of a torrent of water which was Poreing down the hill in the rivin with emence force tareing every thing before it takeing with it large rocks & mud, I . . . Scrambled up the hill pushing the Interpreters wife (who had her Child in her arms) before me. . . . I Scrcely got out before it raised 10 feet deep with a torrent which [was] turrouble to behold." At the same time, Ordway was with a group of men hauling baggage over the trail. "The Shower met us and our hind extletree broke in too we were obledged to leave the load Standing and ran in great confusion to Camp the hail being So large . . . we were much bruuzed . . . one [man] knocked down three times, and others without hats or any thing about their heads bleading and complained verry much."[18]

Lewis spent much of the time at the upstream end of the portage. "Myself I assign the duty of cook," he wrote. "I collected my wood and water, boiled a large quantity of excellent dryed buffaloe meat and made each man a large suet dumpling by way of a treat." But his main focus was on cooking up a visionary project—a collapsible wrought-iron boat frame they had hauled all the way from Harper's Ferry, where it had been made. Lewis had designed this "novel peice of machinism" to improve on the age-old technology of the Indian canoe. He intended to substitute his invention for the white pirogue, thinking it would be lighter to carry across the inevitable portage to the Columbia.[19]

In April, Lewis had informed Jefferson that the iron boat was "in a situation which will enable us to prepare it in the course of a few hours." He was thinking only about the iron framework and was optimistically dismissing the hull—the most important part of any boat. When they actually started work on June 21, only three men were assigned to the boat. A week later, there were six. By July 3, he wrote: "We employed all hands." Still the boat was not done.[20] It was not until July 9, after eighteen days of hard work, that they launched the vessel the men had christened "the Experiment." At first, "she lay like a perfect cork on the water." But after a few hours, Lewis was forced to admit "she leaked in such manner that she would not answer." He wrote, "I need not add that this circumstance mortifyed me not a little."[21]

A mistake about the western landscape was at the heart of Lewis's miscal-

Buffalo and Elk on the Upper Missouri, 1833
To both Indians and Europeans, the herds of buffalo symbolized the bounty of the land. Near the Great Falls, Lewis wrote: "I overlooked a most beatifull and level plain of great extent . . . in this there were infinitely more buffaloe than I had ever before witnessed at a view." Karl Bodmer suggested the same overflowing abundance in this watercolor.

culation. When designing the boat, he had imagined they would be traveling through a boreal forest where birchbark and pine pitch would abound. Bark and wood, he wrote, were "reaidily obtained . . . at all seasons of the year, and in every quarter of the country." When he instead found himself assembling the boat in a treeless plain, he substituted skins and tallow for the hull, materials the Indians could have told him would not work. They too had made boats from buffalo skins for centuries, but they never used more than a single skin, to avoid the seams that sank Lewis's invention. His endearingly American faith that technological ingenuity could trump experience wasted precious days.[22]

The passage of time was making Lewis uneasy. But it was not the only disturbing thing about the month at the Great Falls. "I have scarcely experienced a day since my first arrival in this quarter without experiencing some novel occurrence among the party or witnessing the appearance of some uncommon object," Lewis wrote. Among the "prodegies of this neighbourhood," none was more baffling than the behavior of the animals that thronged around the falls.[23]

All that year the men had been commenting on the abundance and tameness of the wildlife. "We can send out at any time and obtain whatever species of meat the country affords in as large quantity as we wish," Lewis wrote on May 8. In their journals, the West was a Peaceable Kingdom, a natural Eden disturbed only by man: "The buffaloe Elk and Antelope are so gentle that we pass near them while feeding, without apearing to excite any alarm among them, and when we attract their attention, they frequently approach us more nearly to discover what we are. . . . we killed three cows and a calf . . . took their tongues and a part of their marrow-bones only."[24]

The explorers' reaction to animals was complex. They used multiple strategies—measurement and classification, romantic personification, and killing—to comprehend and control what they saw. In the closest personal encounters, scientific detachment fell away and they reacted with awe and wonder. The Indians would have understood.

Specimen of Lewis's woodpecker, 1806[?]
On July 20, 1805, Lewis wrote: "I saw a black woodpecker today about the size of the lark woodpecker as black as a crow. I indevoured to get a shoot at it but could not. it is a distinct species of woodpecker; it has a long tail and flys a good deel like the jay bird." It was not until the following spring at Camp Chopunnish that he was able to write a full description, after the men "killed and preserved several of them." This may be one of those specimens. It comes from the Peale's Museum collection.

Europeans were not the only ones who collected bird skins. To the Lakota, the woodpecker's feathers "put the individual . . . in a position to speak to the Thunder." To evoke this power, many tribes used its skin and beak on pipes and headdresses, and in medicine bundles.

SPIRITS AND SPECIES

> Other objects worth of notice will be . . . the animals of the country generally, & especially those not known in the U.S.
>
> —JEFFERSON'S INSTRUCTIONS TO LEWIS[25]

The Euro-American creation story defined mankind's relationship with animals. The Creator gave the first man the right of naming all the animals and granted him "dominion over . . . every living thing that moveth upon the earth." The story expresses the sharp and fundamental division that Europeans felt between nature and mankind.

In the eighteenth century, European naturalists were busy reenacting Adam's role in the creation by giving every creature on earth a new name. They were using a system consisting of Latin binomial nomenclature. Under this system, invented by the Swedish taxonomist Carolus Linnaeus, each animal was assigned two names: the unique name designating its species and a second name indicating the genus it fell into. The name thus classified the animal as well as identified it. Like Adam, naturalists gained a sense of intellectual dominion from the act of naming. Once an animal was assigned a place in the classificatory gridwork, it had been "discovered."

Sketch of mountain quail and Lewis's woodpecker, 1806
Charles Willson Peale made these sketches from specimens brought back by Lewis and deposited in Peale's Museum for study by researchers. Lewis is credited as the discoverer of both birds; he described the quail on April 7, 1806, and the woodpecker on May 27, 1806. These sketches may have been made for inclusion in the natural history volume of Lewis and Clark's travels—a work that never appeared. Peale wrote after Lewis's death, "It was the request and particular wish of Captain Lewis made to me in person that I should make drawings of each of the feathered tribe as had been preserved, and were new."

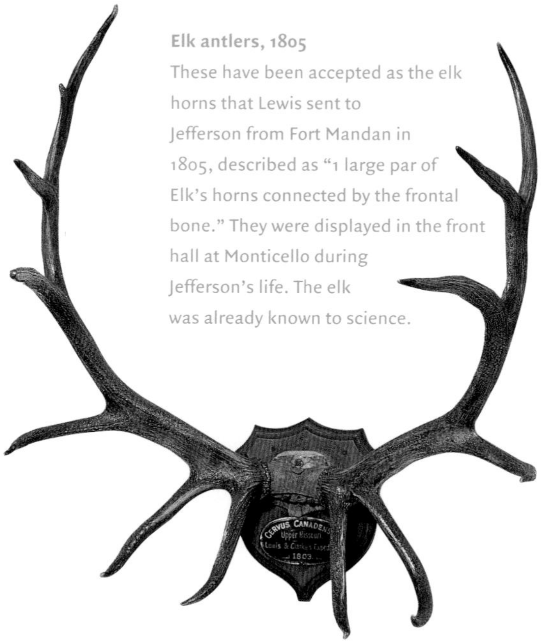

Elk antlers, 1805
These have been accepted as the elk horns that Lewis sent to Jefferson from Fort Mandan in 1805, described as "1 large par of Elk's horns connected by the frontal bone." They were displayed in the front hall at Monticello during Jefferson's life. The elk was already known to science.

The Linnaean system reflected the Enlightenment view that nature conformed to an underlying organizational scheme as regular as celestial mechanics. The "Great Chain of Being," formed whole at the creation, neither decayed nor developed but was stable and orderly. Species did not change or disappear. Thomas Jefferson was following the most current science of his day when he imagined the West as a land where noble animals like the mammoth and megalonyx still roamed free.

Linnaeus chose an organizing principle curiously similar to that of European society: hierarchy. He even used pseudo-social terminology, as if nature mirrored the well-ordered state. The largest category was the Kingdom. Under that came the Phylum, then the Class, the Order, the Family, the Genus, and the Species. The system encouraged its users to think of each species as a discrete category, forever assigned to its place. No revolutions would disturb the immut-able order of the animal kingdom or threaten mankind's position at the top.

There are any number of ways animals could have been organized into a classification system: by what they eat, where they live, or how they behave, to name a few. The Linnaean system chose anatomy, a category that could most easily be based on systematic, uniform criteria reached through objective observation and measurement. The underlying assumption—that animals similar in form are most closely related—served its users well until DNA analysis began to reveal how misleading anatomy could be as a guide to relationship. Today the hierarchy is under constant revision.[26]

Even in Lewis and Clark's time, there was already one chink in the armor of the Great Chain of Being: the concept that animals adapted to their environment. It was a proto-evolutionary notion that introduced change into the stasis of the Great Chain. The study of American wildlife was crucial to the theory of environmental adaptation. French taxonomists, notably the Comte de Buffon, had asserted that the supposed lack of large animals in North America showed that wildlife had adapted to an inclement environment. Jefferson had devoted most of his only book to refuting this notion. At least one of the specimens sent to him by his explorers—a magnificent rack of elk antlers with no other obvious scientific value—may have been intended as a rude gesture to Buffon.

Bighorn sheep, 1819–20
Lewis expressed amazement at the sight of bighorn sheep on a "nearly perpendicular clift . . . on the fase of this clift they walked about and bounded from rock to rock with apparent unconcern where it appared . . . that no quadruped could have stood, and from which had they made one false step the[y] must have been precipitated at least a 500 feet." These animals were already known in the East, but Lewis and Clark brought back more complete information on them. Titian Ramsay Peale and Samuel Seymour, who accompanied Stephen H. Long's exploring expedition in 1819, were the first Euro-American artists to portray the plains. Peale drew this and the next two sketches during that expedition.

Although historians have credited Lewis and Clark with the "discovery" of a long list of animals, the explorers did not in fact name any new species; that task was for specialists. But it was part of their mission to collect enough information so that men of learning could name and classify the animals they had seen. Since the crucial information was anatomy, when Lewis and Clark were functioning as Enlightenment observers, their attention was on physical characteristics. They measured each part, described markings, boiled down carcasses to study bone structure, and when possible, preserved the skins. Their descriptions, like the illustrations made by wildlife artists who followed them onto the plains, attempted to isolate the unique characteristics of each species. Though by necessity they described individual animals, they looked for normal, representative specimens to serve as models for the whole species. Unlike earlier explorers, they were not seeking the monstrous or unusual. They sought an abstract ideal: the typical.[27]

American Antelope, 1819
At first Lewis and Clark called antelopes "goats," but they gradually adopted the term "antelope." Clark described the antelope as "Keenly made, and . . . butifull." Lewis wrote, "We found the Antelope extreemly shye and watchfull. . . . I had this day an opportunity of witnessing the agility and superior fleetness of this anamal. . . . it appeared reather the rappid flight of birds than the motion of quadrupeds." The captains had a skin stuffed in order to send it back to Washington. They have been credited with the discovery of the antelope.

One moment in which Lewis acted as Enlightenment observer occurred in June 1805, at the Great Falls. "When I awoke from my sleep today I found a large rattlesnake coiled on the leaning trunk of a tree under the shade of which I had been lying," he wrote. In this alarming situation, he took two actions. "I killed the snake and found that he had 176 scuta on the abdomen and 17 half formed scuta on the tale." His first impulse—to physically control, by killing the snake—was almost instantly followed by his impulse to intellectually con-

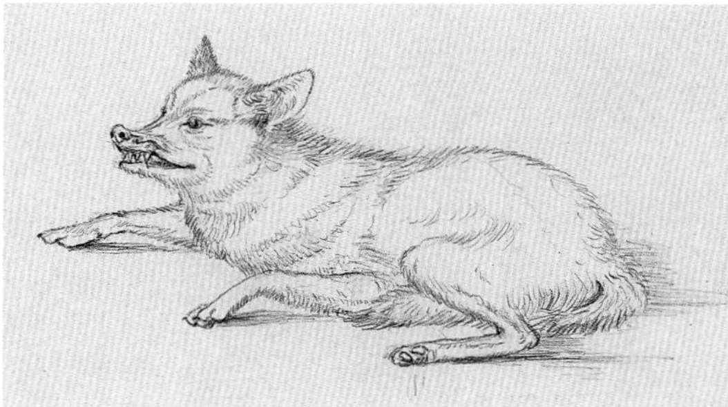

Coyote, 1819
Coyotes were new to the explorers, and the men vacillated between calling them wolves and foxes. "I killed a Prarie Wollf," Clark wrote on September 18, 1804, "about the Size of a gray fox bushey tail head & ear like a wolf, Some fur." Once they got a good look at one, they realized that it was, in fact, a distinct animal. Among Indians from the Mandan to the Nez Perce, Coyote was the mythic trickster who created all living beings but who was constantly humiliated by his own schemes.

trol, by quantifying and measuring the snake. By the time he recorded the results, he had detached himself not only from the danger but from the snake as well. From fearsome predator, it had turned into a mere object of study.[28]

But Lewis was also a contemporary of the poets Percy Shelley, Lord Byron, and Samuel Taylor Coleridge, and he showed the influences of the nascent Romantic era, which sought transcendent truth in nature through subjective reaction, not detached objectivity. On the Marias River he listened, with sentiment that the nature poet William Wordsworth might have recognized, to the song of "a small bird which in action resembles the lark," characterizing it as both "sweet" and "plaintive" and remarking, "These larks as I shall call them add much to the gayety and cheerfullness of the scene." Animals also evoked the mystical and gothic sensibilities of Romanticism. On June 14, his second day at the Great Falls, the threatening behavior of a succession of animals "wore the impression . . . of inchantment." He wrote: "For a moment I thought it might be a dream. . . . all the beasts of the neighbourhood had made a league to distroy me."[29]

Enlightenment science had made significant breakthroughs in identifying and classifying animals. None of it could have happened without a rigorous separation of observable fact from anthropomorphic lore. But the ancient emotional connection to animals, though now cordoned off into literature and art, still lived in the Euro-American psyche.

NONHUMAN PEOPLES

> No man can succeed in life alone, and he can not get the help he wants from men; therefore he seeks help through some bird or animal which Wakantanka sends for his assistance. Many animals have ways from which a man can learn a great deal.
>
> —SIYA'KA[30]

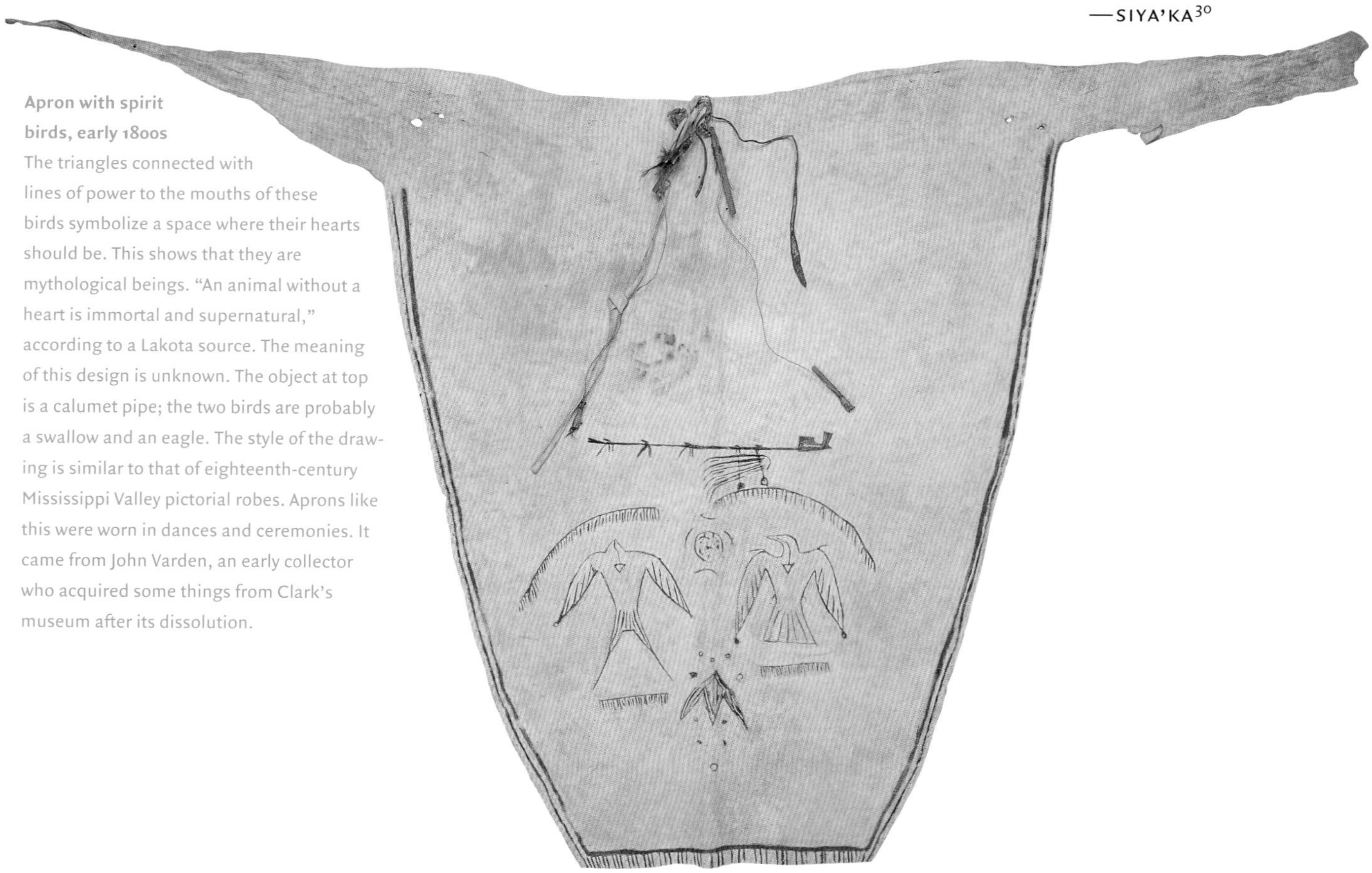

Apron with spirit birds, early 1800s
The triangles connected with lines of power to the mouths of these birds symbolize a space where their hearts should be. This shows that they are mythological beings. "An animal without a heart is immortal and supernatural," according to a Lakota source. The meaning of this design is unknown. The object at top is a calumet pipe; the two birds are probably a swallow and an eagle. The style of the drawing is similar to that of eighteenth-century Mississippi Valley pictorial robes. Aprons like this were worn in dances and ceremonies. It came from John Varden, an early collector who acquired some things from Clark's museum after its dissolution.

The native men and women of the plains were in constant conversation with their world. Keenly attuned to the nuances of weather, growing things, and animal behaviors, they saw the purposeful action of consciousness all around them. Their sense of "personhood" extended far beyond humans. Animal people, plant people, sky people—all communicated and interacted with humans. They were beings in their own right.

In fact, humans were the younger siblings of the natural world. In most Northern Plains Indian creation stories, humans were recent arrivals. Before them, there had been a long, ancient beginning time in which animals had not yet solidified into their present shapes or languages. In this mythic time, animal forms and human forms were fluid and interchangeable. Because they were older than humans, animals possessed a primordial wisdom and had much to teach. They intersected the worlds of the sacred and the everyday and provided a conduit between those worlds.[31]

There were several ways in which animals acted as teachers. Indian children were taught to practice intense observation of animals, to know their habits and minds. This was partly a practical skill, for the hunter who achieved identity with the quarry was a better provider. But just as important, only by such study could a person learn right living. "Let a man decide upon his favorite animal and make a study of it," Brave Buffalo, a Lakota holy man, said around 1914. "Let him learn to understand its sounds and motions. The animals want to communicate with man, but . . . not . . . directly—man must do the greater part in securing an understanding." Animal behavior was like a sacred text—to be studied, interpreted, and analyzed for meaning.[32]

Animals also helped humans in more formal ways. Almost every tribe that Lewis and Clark met practiced the vision quest, in which adolescents (mostly boys) sought a spirit guardian to guide them through life. The animal who appeared in the vision became their sponsor, and the human being gradually became like that animal in skills, personality, and morals. A vision often gave men or women the right to name themselves or others after their guardian or to wear emblems of that animal. A Lakota elder warned: "Only those who have accomplished much are entitled to wear the buffalo horns; only those who have much power to do mysterious things are entitled to wear hawk's feathers and only those who are very cunning are entitled to wear the weasel skins. . . . to do so without the right is contemptible."[33]

Bird war club, pre-1840
Birds had powers that could protect and enhance the warrior. "The eagle, hawk, swallow, dragon-fly, all possess great speed in flight and ability to strike swiftly and surely," said John Blunt Horn, "and they seem to bear a sort of charmed life before bullets, arrows, hail and lightning, for one does not find them killed or injured by these forces." This object, made from an elk antler, was collected by George Catlin. It is identified as Sioux, but Bodmer and Maximilian also saw bird war clubs of elk antler among the Atsina and Assiniboine.

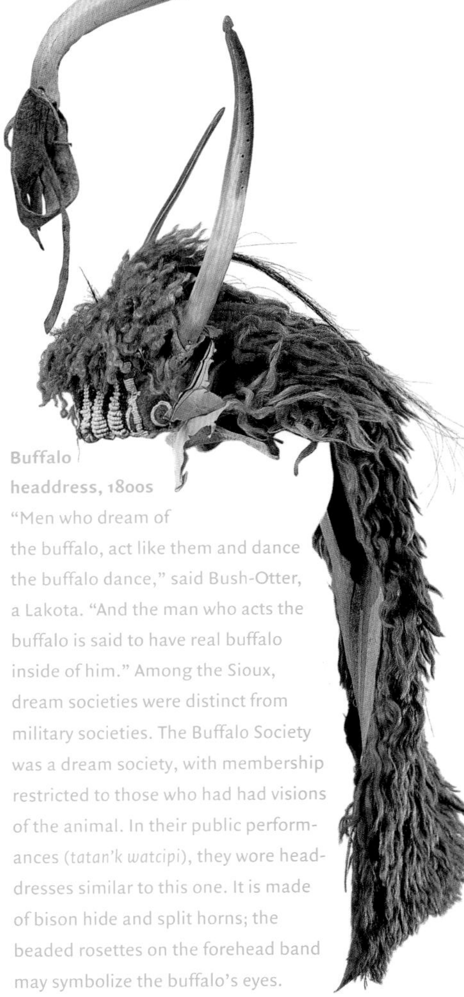

Buffalo headdress, 1800s
"Men who dream of the buffalo, act like them and dance the buffalo dance," said Bush-Otter, a Lakota. "And the man who acts the buffalo is said to have real buffalo inside of him." Among the Sioux, dream societies were distinct from military societies. The Buffalo Society was a dream society, with membership restricted to those who had had visions of the animal. In their public performances (*tatan'k watcipi*), they wore headdresses similar to this one. It is made of bison hide and split horns; the beaded rosettes on the forehead band may symbolize the buffalo's eyes.

Buffalo effigy pipe, pre-1872
In very early times, stone buffalo effigies resembling this one were used to attract the animals in "medicine hunts." However, this sculpture in catlinite serves as a pipe bowl, with the smoke hole in the buffalo's hump. Its stem was carved in a spiral. It has been called "a masterpiece of Plains Indian carving" and may have been created as a diplomatic presentation pipe. Very few naturalistic buffalo effigy pipes survive from such an early date.

Bag with buffalo design, late 1800s
"If a man sees a Buffalo in his boy vision, he should paint the picture of a buffalo on his shield and on his tipi," said Little Wound, a Lakota. This bag may have belonged to a man who had received a dream vision of the buffalo. The reverse side has an X pattern symbolizing the four directions. The stylized treatment of the buffalo head is an early form of Plains Indian art.

Elk courting flute, pre-1889
Among the Lakota, young men in pursuit of women sought the assistance of elk medicine. The courting flute was used to mimic the bugle of the bull elk in mating season. The instrument is played like a recorder; the sound, generated by a reed, comes out of the elk's mouth. According to the Santee, the courting flute was first given to a poor young man who wanted to court the chief's daughter. In a dream, two elks appeared in the form of handsome men and gave him a flute along with instructions to play among the lodges at night. When the young man did so, all the women in the village rose and followed him.

To some favored individuals, animals appeared in visions, instructing them to perform ceremonies or form societies. Often, all the camp or village inhabitants whose visions had shown them the same animal formed the membership. They were then entitled to perform songs and rituals, and wear regalia, that evoked the power and protection of the animal. The human visionary was only the spokesperson for the animal spirit.

The most intimate interaction humans had with animals was in hunting. In this act too, the difference between the Indian and the European attitudes was pronounced. At a Mandan lodge during the winter of 1804–5, some men of the Corps observed a ritual act that was closely related to hunting. "When they had done eating," Whitehouse said, "they gave a bowl of victuls to a buflows head which they worshiped, & Sd. Eat this So that the live ones may come in that we may git a Supply of meat." Gass attributed this to "superstitious credulity," but Whitehouse conceded, "Most of them have Strange & uncommon Ideas . . . but quick & Sensible in their own way & in their own conceit."[34]

To understand what Whitehouse and Gass saw at the lodge, one needs to realize that the Plains Indians did not believe hunting was a mark of human superiority over animals. On the contrary, it was a mark of animal generosity. No animal could be killed unless it consented to give its life graciously so that humans could survive. Before setting out, a hunter would address the animal in prayer with a respectful and humble tone, explaining that he and his family were needy and deserving. When the animal presented itself to be killed, the hunter expressed thanks by treating the animal's body with respect and by giving offerings. European hunters relied on technology; Indian hunters relied on persuasion.[35]

It was not the buffalo skull the Indians worshipped, as Whitehouse believed—although the Lakota said: "The Spirit of the *Tatanka* [buffalo] dwells in the skull of the buffalo. It is with it in the lodge." Rather, it was that spirit they honored—the invisible, numinous aspect that was the true bison, of which individual bison were only projections. "Each animal has its own Master Spirit which own all the animals of its kind," said Raining Bird, a Montana Cree. "It is just like a large family." The Mandan were maintaining a relationship with that spirit.[36]

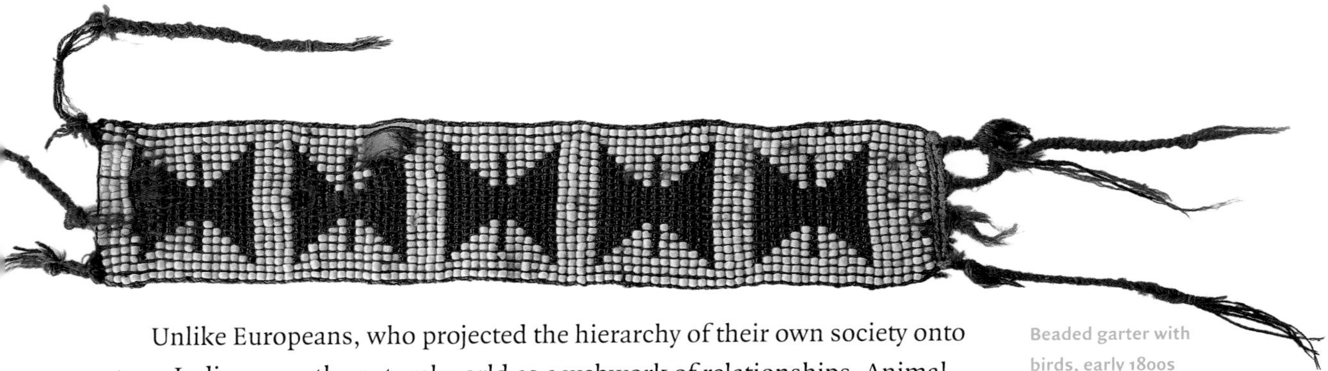

Beaded garter with birds, early 1800s
Indian art portrayed an animal's inner essence, not its physical form. The Woodland or eastern Plains Indian artist who wove this garter abstracted the bird to a geometric symbol. The artist was not portraying an individual bird but the universal spirit of birdness. This artifact from Peale's Museum could have been collected by Lewis and Clark. They donated "A handsome Belt worn by the Saux as a garter."

Unlike Europeans, who projected the hierarchy of their own society onto nature, Indians saw the natural world as a webwork of relationships. Animal people who shared with and helped humans ranked as kin and were addressed as "grandfather" or "brother." A few examples that Lewis and Clark encountered—buffalo, elk, and birds—give the flavor of those relationships. "The spirit of *Tatanka* [buffalo] cares for the family," said Takes the Gun, a Lakota born in the nineteenth century. "It cares for the little children. It cares for the hunters. It cares for the growing things. . . . It cares for everything that has young."[37] The buffalo, which provided food, clothing, and shelter for so many Plains Indian tribes, was a model of fecundity, generosity, maternal care, and industry. It was often associated with women, but a man who saw a buffalo in his vision was upright and prosperous: "He will be a successful hunter. . . . He will get the woman he wishes for his wife." Little Wound, also Lakota, said: "The Buffalo gives all game to the Lakotas. He is pleased with those who are generous and hates those who are stingy." The famous twentieth-century Lakota holy man Black Elk said that the buffalo represented the earth, which gives rise to all life. The herds were said to come from underground and to mysteriously disappear there again when displeased.[38]

The elk had different powers. He was the master seducer. The bull elk's ability to bugle so that the cow was irresistibly drawn to him showed that he possessed a mysterious power over females. The elk could teach humans who dreamed of him to practice those arts. Shooter, a Lakota, called elk "the emblem of beauty, gallantry, and protection." The elk's teeth, which "remain after everything else has crumbled to dust," were an emblem of long life and were often used to decorate children's clothing.[39]

"The most important of all the creatures are the wingeds," said Black Elk, "for they are nearest to the heavens. . . . Their religion is the same as ours." The Lakota classified flying insects in the same family as birds. Winged beings saw everything that happened on earth. Of all the wingeds, eagles were the most potent, and their feathers gave power and beauty to ceremonial and battle regalia.[40] Siya'ka, a Lakota, expressed a religious message he learned from winged things: "The birds and insects which I had seen in my dream were things on which I knew I should keep my mind and learn their ways. . . . They are not all on the earth, but are *above* it. My mind must be the same."[41]

Grizzly bear headdress, pre-1881
This headdress, formed of the upper skull of a grizzly, belonged to a Teton Lakota man named Bear Head. Headdresses like it were worn only by men with bear power and were used in curing ceremonies or in dances held in preparation for a bear hunt. Catlin painted aspiring Lakota bear hunters wearing headdresses and bearskins in a dance accompanied by a "song to the *Bear Spirit*," which "holds somewhere an invisible existence, and must be consulted and conciliated. . . . All, with the motions of their hands, closely imitated the movements of that animal." He also saw a grizzly bear headdress and skin worn by a bear medicine man during the terrifying performance of a healing ceremony.

HUNTING THE BEAR

> The bear . . . has a soul like ours, and his soul talks to mine in my sleep and tells me what to do.
>
> —BEAR WITH WHITE PAW[42]

> When the Indians are about to go in quest of the white [grizzly] bear . . . they paint themselves and perform all those superstisious rights commonly observed when they are about to make war uppon a neighbouring nation.
>
> —MERIWETHER LEWIS[43]

Bear effigy pipe bowl, pre-1830s
To Plains Indians, the bear embodied terrible anger but also deep wisdom about curing. "We consider the bear as chief of all the animals in regard to herb medicine," said the Lakota Two Shields. "If a man dreams of a bear he will be expert in the use of herbs for curing illness." The carving on this pipe probably represented the bear's role as teacher and transmitter of power. At least three pipe bowls of this design were collected by non-Indians: Duke Paul of Württemberg, George Catlin, and General Stephen Watts Kearny, who acquired this one, possibly in 1825. All three of these men were associated with Clark and his museum of Indian artifacts. The tribal identifications of the pipes were Pawnee, Osage, and Sioux; but it is likely that all were by the same artist, who was most likely Pawnee.

> In the evening, the most of the corps crossed over to an island, to attack and rout its monarch, a large brown [grizzly] bear, that held possession and seemed to defy all that would attempt to besiege him there. Our troops, however, stormed the place, gave no quarter, and its commander fell. Our army returned the same evening to camp without having suffered any loss on their side.
>
> —PATRICK GASS[44]

Among Northern Plains Indians, no animal was hunted with more respect than the bear. Of all the animals, bears were most closely related to humans—to the point that some Plains Indian tribes, like the Cheyenne and the Arapaho, would not eat bear meat because doing so was too much like cannibalism.[45] Bears were the wise elders of the animal people. They were masters of plant lore, healing, and the mystical arts. Because they dug roots and dwelt in caves and dens, they were associated with the earth and underground powers. They had power even over death, because each winter they passed through a deathlike state and were resurrected from the grave in the spring.

The bear's physical body was not the real object of a bear hunt. Rather, the hunter sought the fearsome power of the bear, and the struggle was as much moral and mental as physical. In many tribes, bear hunters would not use guns or bows but only hand weapons like clubs and spears. If the bear did not consent to give his life because the hunter was undeserving, no gun would be of use anyway. Conquering a bear was an act of bravery equivalent to killing an enemy in battle. Cheyenne men counted coup on bears, and Assiniboine warriors included bears in their recitals of conquered enemies. Bear-claw necklaces represented the heroism and spiritual power of the bear slayer. Men had to earn the right to wear them.[46]

Grizzly bear claws, c. 1780–1825
These two claws, drilled for stringing on a cord, may be all that remains of a bear claw necklace given to Peale's Museum by Lewis and Clark. Lewis wrote that among the Shoshone, "the warriors or such as esteem themselves brave men wear collars made of the claws of the brown bear which are also esteemed of great value and are preserved with great care. these claws are ornamented with beads about the thick end near which they are peirced through their sides and strung on a throng of dressed leather and tyed about the neck commonly with the upper edge of the tallon next the breast or neck but sometimes are reversed."

Much of what we know today about bear hunting by Northern Plains tribes comes from the Cree, who lived just across the border in Canada. More southerly tribes may have had less elaborate customs. A Cree bear hunt started with dreams and divinations to learn the mood of the spirits and to get special knowledge of use in the hunt, such as songs, the design of weapons, or contents of a medicine bundle. The hunter then contacted the bear spirit through prayers and dreams, asking for its gift of life and addressing it with honorific names like "grandfather." Before setting out, the hunter took a steam bath to purify himself physically and spiritually, and he cleansed his clothing and

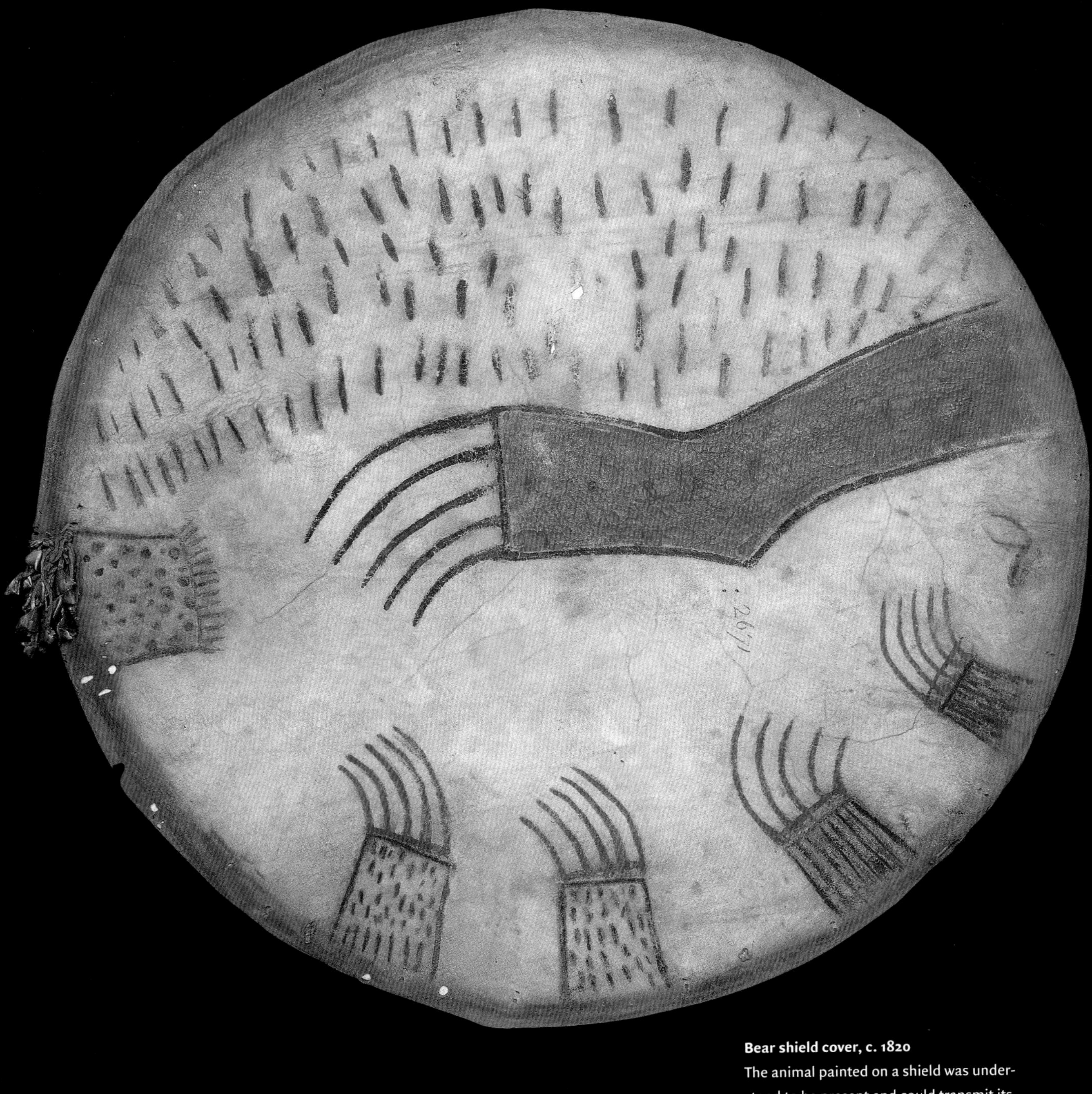

Bear shield cover, c. 1820
The animal painted on a shield was understood to be present and could transmit its power to observers. This shield evoked the bear's power to protect its owner in battle. The short black lines at the top may represent a hail of bullets, which the bear's paw blocks. The owner of one bear shield said that "the claws of the bear were on every side to protect him," hence he was not hurt in the battle. This upper Missouri shield was part of the War Department's collection.

Captain Clark and His Men Shooting Bears, 1810
In this woodcut published with Patrick Gass's journal of the expedition, the men appear to be safely in charge.

equipment. After the bear was killed, he asked its forgiveness and decorated its body in honor of the sacrifice it had made. The bear's bones were treated with respect and were never given to dogs, so that the bear would return to life again. A Cree explained: "We do [these rites] to keep from starving . . . we do them because it pleases the bears, it makes them want to be killed by us. . . . We do these things because it is the proper way to behave toward an animal that is making a gift of its life."[47]

Before he had seen a grizzly bear, Lewis scoffed at the Indians' "formidable account of the strength and ferocity of this anamal." He attributed their awe to "their bows and arrows and the indifferent guns with which the traders furnish[ed] them." He was confident in the power of superior American technology, even after encountering two small grizzlies. He wrote, "The Indians may well fear this anamal . . . but in the hands of skillfull riflemen they are by no means as formidable or dangerous as they have been represented."[48]

That attitude lasted five days. Then the soldiers encountered "a most tremendious looking anamal, and extreemly hard to kill notwithstanding he had five balls through his lungs and five others in various parts." Though the size and roaring of the animal had "staggered the resolution" of the men, the explorers tried to regain some control by measuring it: "8 Feet 7 1/2 Inches from the nose to the extremety of the hind feet, 5 F. 10 1/2 Inch arround the breast, 1 F. 11 I. arround the middle of the arm, & 3 F. 11 I. arround the neck." The next day, Lewis wrote, "I find that the curiossity of our party is pretty well satisfyed with rispect to this anamal."[49]

But the bears were not done with the Corps. Several hairsbreadth escapes followed, and Lewis began referring to the bears respectfully as "gentlemen." On June 14 it was his turn. He had just shot a buffalo and was watching it die when he realized that a grizzly had crept up on him "within 20 steps." He described the encounter: "I drew up my gun to shoot, but at the same instant recolected that she was not loaded. . . . it was an open level plain, not a bush within miles . . . in short there was no place by means of which I could conceal myself. . . . I had no sooner terned myself about but he pitched at me, open mouthed and full speed, I ran about 80 yards and found he gained on me fast, I then run into the water . . . about waist deep, and faced about and presented the point of my espontoon, at this instant . . . he sudonly wheeled about as if frightened, declined the combat on such unequal grounds, and retreated." Shaken, Lewis waded out of the river, speculating on the bear's motivation for

The Bear Pursueing His Assailant, 1813
This sketch, published in an unauthorized 1813 book about Lewis and Clark by William Fisher, may have illustrated Lewis's closest encounter with a grizzly.

sparing him. He concluded that its reasons were "misterious and unaccountable."[50] Generations of Indians had come to the same conclusion about bears.

When both Indians and Europeans looked into animal eyes, they saw themselves reflected back. Their assumptions about animals mirrored their assumptions about themselves and their societies. Indian and European observations were equally astute, in their separate ways. But as the members of the Corps of Discovery traveled west, their experiences changed who they were, making it ever harder to maintain the scientific detachment so easy in the East. The land invaded the orderliness of their mental grids, and they reacted with the same awe and wonder as the Indians.

SIX Crossing the Divide

They say that . . . he that acquires a good and great name during his lifetime is always remembered and lamented. This fame can be attained only by formal bravery in some great action at war.

—ALEXANDER HENRY ON PLAINS INDIANS[1]

"I begin to be extremely impatient to be off as the season is now waisting a pace," Lewis wrote on June 30. After covering several hundred miles each month in April and May, the Corps of Discovery had spent a whole month going only eighteen miles around the Great Falls. Lewis was not the only one anxious about this critical delay. "We all believe that we are about to enter on the most perilous and dificuelt part of our Voyage," Clark wrote.[2]

On July 4, with most of the labor of the portage behind them, the men celebrated. "It being the 4th of Independence we drank the last of our ardent Spirits except a little reserved for Sickness," John Ordway wrote. "The fiddle put in order and the party amused themselves dancing all the evening untill about 10 oClock in a Sivel & jovil manner." It was the last relaxation they would have for a long time.[3]

They set out again on July 15. Four days later, the first range of the Rocky Mountains loomed ahead. The river cut through them in a dramatic gorge they called Gates of the Mountains. "These clifts rise from the waters edge on either side perpendicularly to the hight of 1200 feet," Lewis wrote. "Every object here wears a dark and gloomy aspect. the tow[er]ing and projecting rocks in many places seem ready to tumble on us."[4] Beyond the first barrier of mountains, the river bent south, flowing

Gates of the Mountains, 1868

When they reached the Gates of the Mountains, Lewis wrote: "This evening we entered much the most remarkable clifts that we have yet seen. . . . the river appears to have forced it's way through this immence body of solid rock . . . and where it makes it's exit below has thown on either side vast columns of rocks mountains high." The name that Lewis and Clark gave to this gorge of the Missouri, north of present-day Helena, was still its name in 1867 when Alfred E. Mathews made the sketch for this lithograph. Both name and gorge remain today.

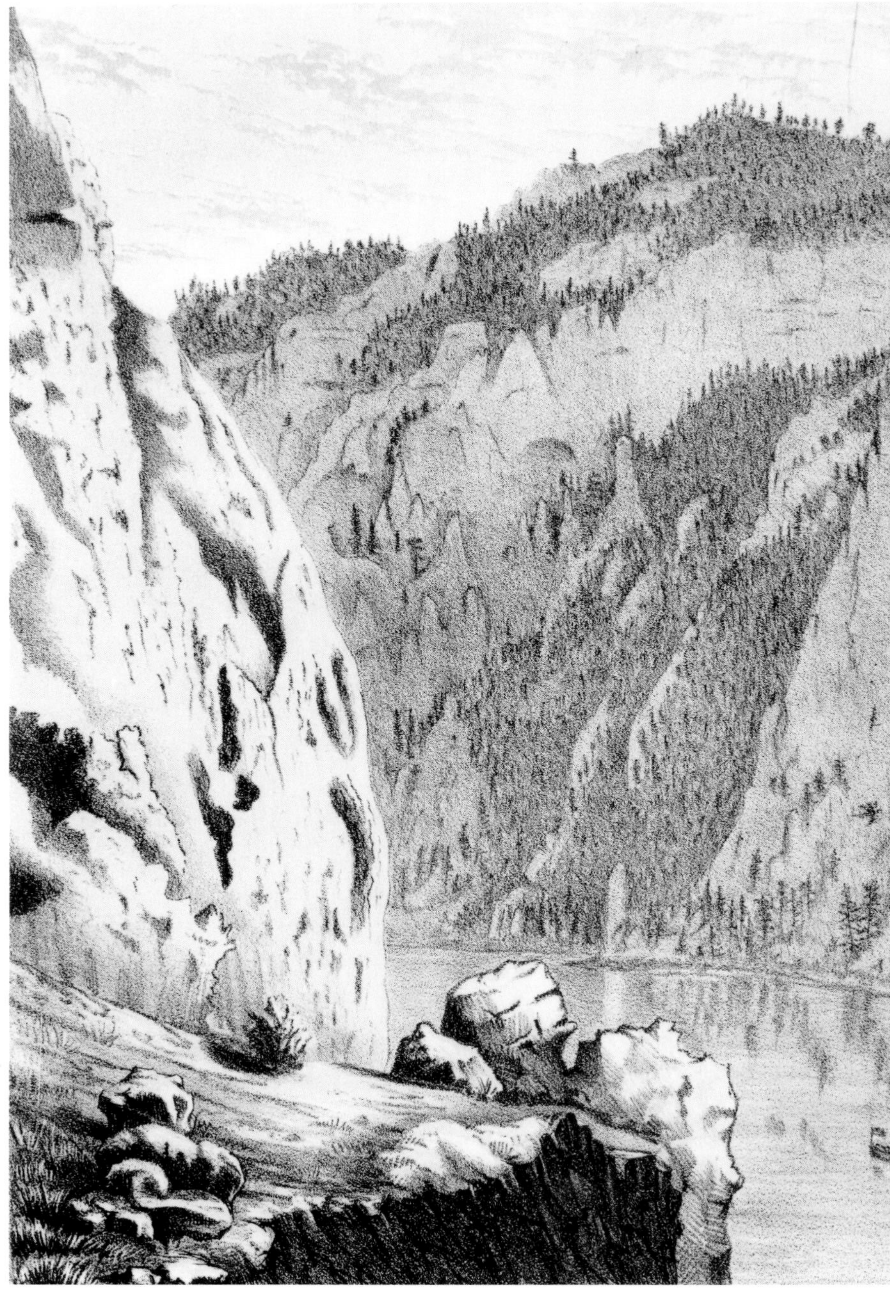

The Three Forks, 1868

The "large flocks of Mountain Sheep or Ibex and antelopes" that John Ordway saw on the plain around the Three Forks were gone by the time Alfred E. Mathews made this lithograph. Today, the Missouri is thought to begin at the Three Forks. The tributaries that join there have retained the names Lewis gave them—the Jefferson, the Madison, and the Gallatin. Lewis optimistically declared, "It is impossible that the S. W. fork [Jefferson] can head with the waters of any other river but the Columbia."

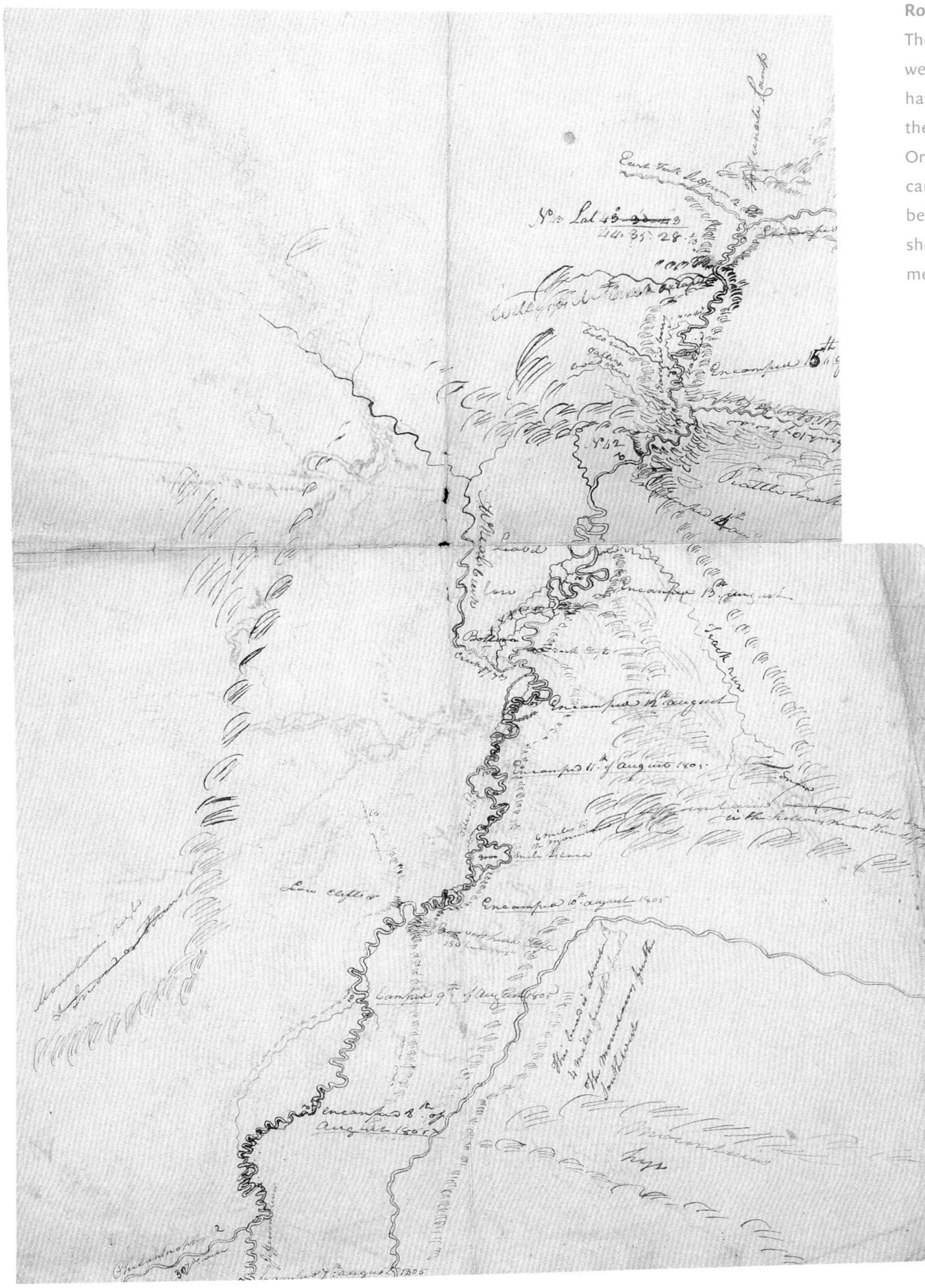

Route map of Jefferson River, 1805
The excruciating twists and bends of the river were documented by Clark in this map. "We have to double man the canoes and drag them over the Sholes and rapid places," Ordway wrote. The tons of baggage in the canoes made it impossible to leave them before getting packhorses. Camp Fortunate, shown at the top, was where the Corps finally met the Shoshone.

through a "beautifull and extensive plain . . . bounded by two nearly parallel ranges of high mountains which have their summits partially covered with snow." Unknown to the men of the Corps, if they had struck out overland rather than following the river south, they could have shortly reached the pass they would arrive at two months later. Instead, obedient to instructions and still confident that the Missouri connected with the Columbia near its source, they followed the river toward the mountain cul-de-sac from which it sprang.[5]

It was three months since they had seen anyone other than themselves, and they knew how badly they needed information. All their hopes were pinned on meeting the Shoshone, from whom they could get both guidance and horses. Fearing that the tribe would mistake them for enemies and flee, they split into two parties—one going ahead by land to search for help, the other following by water. Despite this precaution, they soon had the feeling of being watched by unseen observers. "About 10 A.M. we saw the smoke arrose as if the

Page 184: *Shoshonee, Wind River* (detail), 1837. See page 189.

country had been set on fire," Lewis wrote. "The natives . . . had unperceived by us discovered Capt. Clark's party or mine, and had set the plain on fire to allarm the more distant natives . . . *thinking it their enemies Blackfoots* and fled themselves further into the interior of the mountains."[6]

Travel grew increasingly hard. The group on foot had to contend with prickly pear cactus and burrs. "These barbed seed penetrate our mockersons and leather legings and give us great pain untill they are removed," Lewis wrote. "My poor dog suffers with them excessively, he is constantly binting and scratching himself as if in a rack of pain." The contingent in the canoes had it no easier, as the current grew swift and the river shallow. Because "the men complain of being much fortiegued," Lewis even broke the rules that exempted officers from any physical labor. "I occasionly encourage them by assisting in the labour . . . and have learned to *push a tolerable good pole* in their fraize [phrase]." A more effective encouragement came from Sacagawea. "The Indian woman recognizes the country and assures us that this is the river on which her relations live. . . . this peice of information has cheered the sperits of the party."[7]

At the end of July they reached the Three Forks, where the Missouri divided into smaller branches. "Arived at the three forks of the Missourie," Ordway wrote, "which is in open view of the high Mountains covered in Some places with Snow. . . . we expected to have found the Snake nation of Indians at this place, but . . . perhaps they are gone over the mountains to the Columbian River on the other Side to fish."[8] The absence of the Indians was a blow to Lewis's hopes. "We begin to feel considerable anxiety with rispect to the Snake Indians," he brooded in his journal. "If we do not find them or some other nation who have horses I fear the successfull issue of our voyage will be very doubtfull. . . . we are now several hundred miles within the bosom of this wild and mountanous country . . . without any information with rispect to the country not knowing how far these mountains continue, or wher to direct our course to pass them."[9]

The expedition pitched its tents on the very spot where Sacagawea's family had been camped when she had been taken captive by the Hidatsa five years earlier. With no sign of the Shoshones he wanted to see, Lewis grew peevish toward the one he could see. "*Sah-cah-gar-we-ah* o[u]r Indian woman was one of the female prisoners taken at that time; tho' I cannot discover that she shews any immotion of sorrow in recollecting this event, or of joy in being again restored to her native country; if she has enough to eat and a few trinkets to wear I beleive she would be perfectly content anywhere."[10]

They spent several days at the forks, partly to take its latitude and longitude and partly to rest. "We have a lame crew just now, two with tumers or bad boils on various parts of them, one with a bad stone bruise, one with his arm

Telescope of Meriwether Lewis, c. 1790
Lewis was carrying his "spye-glass" at the Continental Divide, and he used it to spot a Shoshone man on horseback two miles away; the magnification was sufficient to show him details of the man's arms, dress, and horse bridle. In his "haist" to signal the man, he dropped the telescope on the ground and had to send George Drouillard and John Shields back to fetch it. The Lewis family owned this English telescope until 1972 and believed it went on the expedition. Lewis frequently mentioned his "spye-glass" but did not describe it.

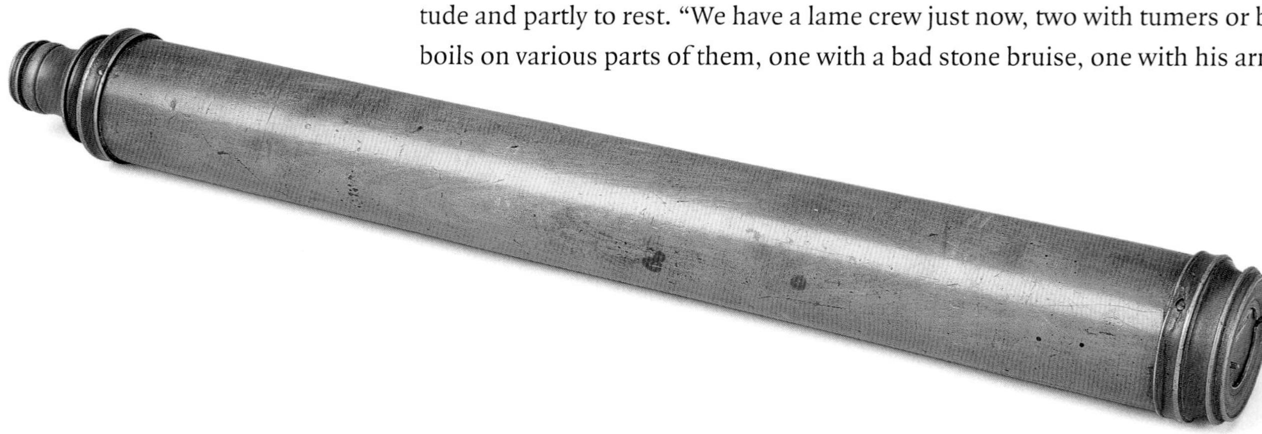

Shoshonee, Wind River, 1837
The first Shoshone Lewis saw was "mounted on an eligant horse without a saddle, and a small string which was attatched to the underjaw of the horse which answered as a bridle." The first artist to portray the Shoshone Indians in detail, Alfred J. Miller, met them more than thirty years after Lewis and Clark. Traveling on the Oregon Trail, Miller encountered a more southern branch who had wholly adopted the Plains lifestyle that the northern Shoshone practiced only part of the year. Cameahwait's people still mixed elements of their Great Basin past, such as brush lodges called *coni-gani* and grass basketry, with the tipis and parfleches of their adopted lifestyle.

accedently dislocated but fortunately well replaced, and a fifth has streigned his back by sliping and falling backwards on the gunwall of the canoe." Even Clark was "very sick with a high fever on him," and Lewis solicitously "prevailed on him to take a doze of Rushes pills . . . and to bath his feet in warm water and rest himself."[11]

During the delay, Lewis exercised the explorer's role of renaming the branches of the Missouri, imbuing the landscape with American dominion. "We called the S.W. fork, that which we meant to ascend, Jefferson's River in honor of that illustrious personage Thomas Jefferson *the author of our enterprize.* the Middle fork we called Madison's River in honor of James Madison, and the S.E. Fork we called Gallitin's River in honor of Albert Gallitin [Gallatin]." Later, when the Jefferson also branched, he named the tributaries Philosophy, Wisdom, and Philanthropy for the attributes of his patron.[12]

As they continued south up the Jefferson River, Lewis scanned the landscape critically. "The mountains are extreemly bare of timber and our rout lay through the steep and narrow hollows . . . exposed to the intense heat of the midday sun without shade or scarcely a breath of air . . . the nights are so could that two blankets are not more than sufficient covering."[13]

The going got no easier as the Jefferson dwindled, then split, and the men headed up the present-day Beaverhead River, still going south. The men began to grumble. "Passed over rapids worse than ever," Ordway wrote. "It is with difficulty & hard fatigue we git up them Some of which are allmost perpinticular 3 or 4 feet fall. . . . the currents So rapid we were oblidged to hall by the bushes, and Some places be out in the water where we could Scarsely kick our feet for the rapidity of the current. . . . the party much fatigued and wish to go

Omaha man demonstrating robe language, c. 1905
These are three from a series of nine photographs showing messages that Plains Indian men conveyed through the use of their robes. The one on the left shows a man in a hesitant state of mind, not having decided how to act. The middle one shows an orator about to address his people with an admonition. The last one shows anger. "Stung by sudden wrong or injury, the man grasps the edges of his robe and hastily draws it up over his head, thus withdrawing from observation. The rousing of his anger has made him intensely conscious of his personality." Even in the twentieth century, robes were "an extension of an Indian man's status and feelings," wrote Bob Block, an Osage. "They define a person's means and are a part of his personal wealth." Luther Standing Bear added in 1933 that robes were "worn with the significance of language."

by land." Joseph Whitehouse's experience was even worse: "One canoe got up Set and everry perticle of the loading got wet. . . . I was in the Stern when She Swang & jumped out to prevent hir from turning over but the current took hir round So rapid that caught my leg under hir and lamed me & was near breaking my leg."[14]

At last Lewis could bear the tortuous progress of the boats no longer. "As it is now all important with us to meet with those [Shoshone] people as soon as possible, I determined to proceed tomorrow with a small party to . . . pass the mountains to the Columbia; and down that river untill I found the Indians."[15]

TRANSLATIONS

When Lewis left behind the rest of the expedition and set out with three men to find the Shoshone, he did not know he would soon need to cross two divides. The first divide was geographical: the Continental Divide separating the waters of the Atlantic and Pacific Oceans. Reaching it was a moment of mixed triumph and dismay. Lewis wrote first of the triumph. "4 miles further the road took us to the most distant fountain of the waters of the mighty Missouri in surch of which we have spent so many toilsome days and wristless nights. thus far I had accomplished one of those great objects on which my mind has been unalterably fixed for many years, judge then of the pleasure I felt in all[a]ying my thirst with this pure and ice cold water." McNeal, one of the men with him, "exultingly stood with a foot on each side of this little rivulet and thanked his god that he had lived to bestride the mighty & heretofore deemed endless Missouri."[16]

But almost before Lewis had a chance to savor the moment, he made a chilling discovery. Over the hill beyond the Divide lay not the Columbia River—not the green slopes leading down to a western Tidewater, as Jefferson's geography had led him to expect—but "immence ranges of high mountains still to the West of us with their tops partially covered with snow." After all their toil, they had barely reached the beginning of the mountains. And summer was nearly gone.[17]

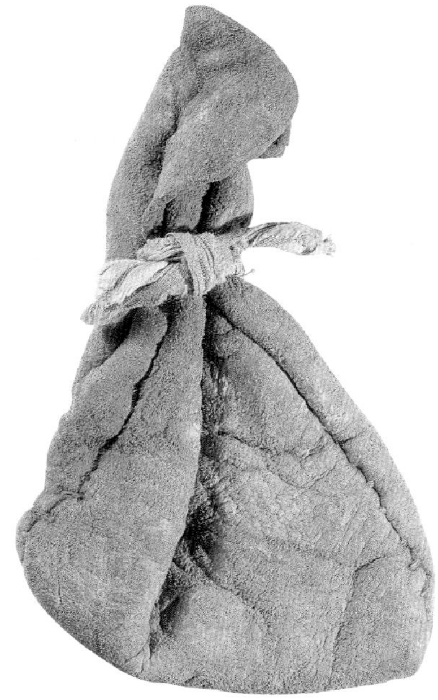

Group of gifts, 1800s

In Lewis's first attempts to communicate with the Shoshone, he used "some b[e]ads a looking glas and a few trinkets." This shows articles like those he had brought: a trade mirror, beads, and a bag of vermillion paint. Lewis's mirrors were pewter; this one is of silvered glass and wood and was collected from a Shoshonean tribe in Utah. The beads are of the early-nineteenth-century style that Lewis might have used, but these come from the Mandan villages. The paint bag is Shoshonean and is stained red from the vermillion it once carried. Trade vermillion was imported from China and used by Plains tribes for both cosmetic and ceremonial purposes.

The only way ahead lay over another divide. This one was cultural. Across barriers of language, custom, and history, Lewis would need to reach out and ask for help.

"I discovered an Indian on horse back about two miles distant coming down the plain toward us," Lewis wrote on August 11. "With my glass I discovered from his dress that he was of a different nation from any that we had yet seen, and was satisfyed of his being a Sosone. . . . I was overjoyed at the sight."[18]

But the explorer immediately faced a problem: his translator, Sacagawea, was miles behind with the boats, and neither he nor his three companions spoke Shoshone. He had come prepared with only a single word: *tab-ba-bone*, which he believed to mean "white man" but which modern-day Shoshone speakers either do not recognize or do not agree on. In this critical moment, language failed Lewis as a mode of communication, and he had to resort to other means. Fortunately for him, language in Indian societies extended beyond the purely verbal. It included space and movement—how one stood, wore clothes, gestured, performed ritual, made facial expressions, and exchanged objects. Unfortunately for Lewis, the messages conveyed by such means were sometimes no more translatable than words.[19]

His first recourse was to a blanket. "Unloosing my blanket from my pack, I mad[e] him the signal of friendship . . . which is by holding the mantle or robe in your hands at two corners and then throwing [it] up in the air higher than the head bringing it to the earth as if in the act of spreading it, thus repeating three times. this signal of the robe has arrisen from a custom among all those nations of spreading a robe or skin for ther gests."[20] The symbol he had chosen was an evocative one. Native Americans conveyed many messages with robes, from purposes and moods to roles in society, by the way they wore and gestured with them. But in this case, the signal "had not the desired effect." Lewis explained: "He suddonly turned his ho[r]se about, gave him the whip leaped the creek and disapeared. . . . with him vanished all my hopes of obtaining horses."

What went wrong? One possible explanation may lie in a set of photographs taken years later of an Omaha man who demonstrated for an anthropologist the subtleties of Plains Indian robe language. The body language of the

Omaha man was not European. For example, Euro-Americans had no qualms about displaying anger in public; anger was how they got their way. In Plains Indian society, by contrast, leadership was signified by a man's ability to control his emotions and stay calm. Men who grew angry in public hid their faces with their robes in a gesture more eloquent and intimidating, to those who knew how to read it, than any amount of Euro-American bluster. If Lewis mistook any such subtleties, or conveyed one thing through his unconscious body language and another through his robe gesture, it may have made the message as incomprehensible as his crying out *tab-ba-bone!*[21]

Having missed their chance to communicate with the lone rider, Lewis and his party continued to walk westward. The day after crossing the divide, they again encountered Indians. "We had not continued our rout more than a mile when we were so fortunate as to meet with three female savages. . . . they

Flag, c. 1808

Lewis and Clark brought three sizes of flags for presentation to tribal leaders: one large, several of the second size, and at least nineteen small ones—although "small" is relative, since they probably measured nine by nine feet (the large ones being nine by sixteen). None of the Lewis and Clark flags survive, so it is unknown what style they had; designs were not standardized. This flag is one possible style. It was said to have been captured by the Ojibway Indians of Manitoulin Island, Lake Huron, during the War of 1812, but it could also have been a presentation flag. The bunting field of fifteen red and white stripes was used from 1795 to 1818. The blue canton bearing a painted eagle and seventeen stars (for the seventeen states prior to the admission of Louisiana in 1812) is similar to one painted by Christopher Gullergey, a Danish immigrant artist residing in Philadelphia, making Gullergey the probable artist and most likely dating this flag to 1808 or 1809.

appeared much allarmed but . . . seated themselves on the ground, holding down their heads as if reconciled to die."[22] This time, Lewis tried the universal language of gifts. "I took the elderly woman by the hand and raised her up. . . . I gave these women some beads a few mockerson awls some pewter looking-glasses and a little paint. . . . I now painted their tawny cheeks with some vermillion which with this nation is emblematic of peace." Whether or not Lewis was right about the symbolism of vermillion, the language of gifts worked. The women "appeared instantly reconciled," and Lewis prevailed on them to lead him to the Shoshone camp.

But they had gone only two miles when they "met a party of about 60 warriors mounted on excellent horses who came in nearly full speed." In this risky moment, when any slip could have resulted in disaster, Lewis tried yet another symbol with great resonance to his own culture: a flag. In a single expressive square of cloth, the flag wove together messages about his national identity, his mission, his republican beliefs, and his wishes.

He had been trying to show the flag to the Shoshone for several days. Previously, he had "fixed a small flag of the U'S. to a pole which I made McNeal carry. and planted in the ground where we halted or encamped." Once before he had unfurled it to show, without success. Now, he "advanced towards them

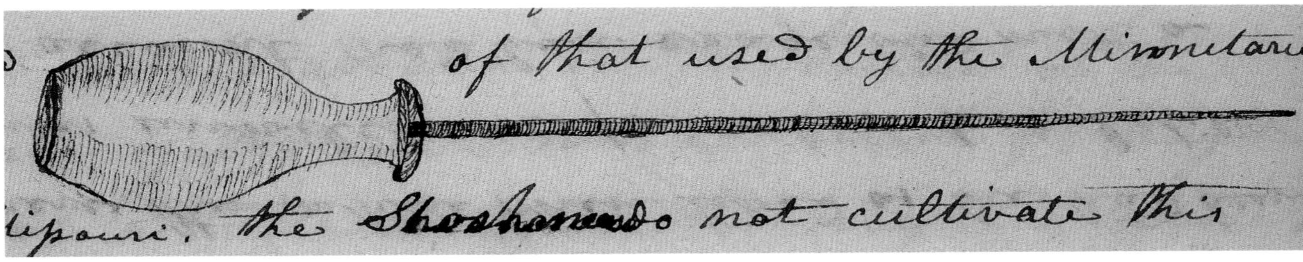

of that used by the Minnetares
the Shoshones do not cultivate this

Sketch of a Shoshone pipe, 1805
This is Lewis's sketch of Cameahwait's pipe. It was a straight pipe, the earliest style of pipe used in North America. Unlike an elbow pipe, the bowl and stem did not meet at an angle; the tobacco was stuffed in the end of the tube. It was "made of a dense simi-transparent green stone very highly polished about 2½ inches long and of an oval figure. . . . a small piece of birned clay is placed in the bottom of the bowl to seperate the tobacco from the end of the stem and is of an irregularly rounded figure not fitting the tube purfectly close in order that the smoke may pass."

with the flag," but it was the gifts that continued to do the talking. "The women . . . informed them who we were and exultingly shewed the presents which had been given them. . . . The principal chief Ca-me-âh-wait made a short speach to the warriors. I gave him the flag which I informed him was an emblem of peace among whitemen and now that it had been received by him it was to be respected as the bond of union between us."[23]

Gestures of greeting came next. "These men then advanced and embraced me very affectionately in their way which is by puting their left arm over you wright sholder . . . while they apply their left cheek to yours and frequently vociforate the word *âh-hi´-e, âh-hi´-e* that is, I am much pleased. . . . we wer all carresed and besmeared with their grease and paint till I was heartily tired of the national hug." As strange as this greeting seemed to Lewis, shaking hands seemed as strange to a Crow chief met by the trader François Larocque in the same year, 1805. "When we offered to shake hands with this great man, he did not understand the intention, and stood motionless until he was informed that shaking hands was the sign of friendship among white men: then he stretched forth both his hands to receive ours." But even stranger to Indians was the facial expression of smiling, not part of most Native American greetings; in fact, Euro-American smiling seemed improper and ridiculous to many tribes.[24]

The burden of communication then passed to the Shoshone. They continued to use symbolic objects, but they chose ones from their own culture, and the messages were often as opaque to Lewis as the flag had been to the Indians. As soon as the men reached the Shoshone camp, they "were seated on green boughs and the skins of Antelopes. . . . The chief next . . . began a long cerimony of the pipe. . . . [He] lit his pipe at the fire kindled in this little magic circle, and standing . . . uttered a speach of several minutes in length at the conclusion of which he pointed the stem to the four cardinal points of the heavens. . . . he . . . repeated the same c[e]remony three times, after which he pointed the stem first to the heavens then to the center of the magic circle smoked himself with three whifs and . . . then held it to each of the white persons and then gave it to be consumed by his warriors." Despite the photographic detail of Lewis's observations, the rich symbolism and the religious meaning of the ceremony were lost on him.[25]

Another message was conveyed by the etiquette surrounding moccasins. "They . . . pulled of[f] their mockersons before they would receive or smoke the pipe. this is a custom among

Moccasins, pre-1860
Lewis described Shoshone dress as indistinguishable from early-nineteenth-century Plains Indian attire. These moccasins are made in the same soft-soled, side-fold style as Shoshone moccasins. "The mockerson is formed with one seem on the outer edge of the foot is cut open at the instep to admit the *foot and sewed up behind. in this rispect they are the same with the Mandans.* they sometimes ornament their mockersons with various figures wrought with the quills of the Porcupine." These are from the upper Missouri and were collected by Lieutenant G. K. Warren of the Corps of Topographical Engineers in the 1850s.

them as I afterwards learned indicative of a sacred obligation of sincerity in their profession of friendship . . . as much as to say that they wish they may always go bearfoot if they are not sincere; a pretty heavy penalty if they are to march through the plains of their country. . . . this we complyed with.”[26]

“I now explained to them the objects of our journey,” Lewis wrote. “The means I had of communicating with these people was by way of Drewyer [George Drouillard] who understood perfectly the common language of jesticulation or signs which seems to be universally understood by all the Nations we have yet seen.” Lewis had probably brought his high opinion of the powers of sign language with him. Thomas Jefferson himself had transmitted the first systematic study of sign language, by William Dunbar, to the American Philosophical Society in 1801. In that paper, Dunbar made a claim that formed one of Lewis's axiomatic expectations: “Almost all the Indian nations living between the Mississippi, and the Western American ocean, understand and use the same language by signs, although their respective oral tongues are frequently unknown to each other.” And yet a later comparison of the signs recorded by early explorers, who had observed their use among diverse tribes, showed almost no agreement on the signs for basic terms like *chief, day, dead, fear, woman,* and *yes.* The sign-language vocabulary was largely confined to concrete objects and practical verbs, not concepts like sovereignty or exploration. Even Lewis conceded, “This language is imperfect and liable to error.” But perhaps hesitant to contradict scholarship with experience, he added that the errors were “much less so than would be expected.” He noted, “The strong parts of the ideas are seldom mistaken.”[27]

SHOSHONE CHIEF MANY NIGHT SNOW EACH OTHE[R]

Sign language gestures, 1881
A fur trader on the Missouri in 1806 wrote: “Sign-language serves as interpreter in every affair of importance. . . . They hold conferences for several hours, upon different subjects, during the whole of which time not a single word is pronounced upon either side, and still they appear to comprehend each other perfectly well.” In 1880 Tendoy, then chief of the Lemhi Shoshone, spoke in sign language with an Apache when both were visiting Washington, D.C. An ethnologist took notes on the signs they used. This shows some of Tendoy's Shoshone signs. He was descended from Cameahwait's family.

So whether George Drouillard's Shawnee sign language actually conveyed “the objects of our journey” to the Shoshone may be doubted. But whatever it did convey must have satisfied them. Lewis wrote: “The Indians entertained us with their dancing nearly all night. . . . I was several times awoke . . . by their yells but was too much fortiegued to be deprived of a tolerable sound night's repose.” Now that he had found the Shoshone, he felt that a huge obstacle had been overcome.[28]

He was mistaken. There were still cultural mountains ahead.

METAMORPHOSES

The white strangers had wandered into the Shoshone camp at a particularly bad time for the band. Cameahwait's people were the very northernmost offshoot of a large tribe that had been expanding into new territory over the previous century, and they lived the precarious life of all residents of a frontier. The ancient homeland of the Shoshone was to the south, in the harsh desert coun-

Snake Indians Migrating, c. 1837
Constant movement was a part of Shoshone existence. Each year Cameahwait's people left behind the buffalo plains and crossed the Rocky Mountains to live on the resources of the salmon streams. Other versions of this painting by Alfred J. Miller identify the Indians as Pawnee, but the mountain landscape suggests that the Snake (Shoshone) identification is more correct.

try of the Great Basin in Nevada and Utah, where they had lived for centuries on the margins of survival. The acquisition of horses had changed their lives, drawing some of them east onto the plains of Wyoming, others northwest into the plateau country of Oregon, and others north into Idaho. The northernmost Shoshone had established their homes along the spine of the Rockies, like a wedge between the Plains Indian culture of the Crow on the east and the salmon-fishing culture of the Nez Perce on the west. Living on a boundary, they became accomplished at self-transformation.

Jefferson had charged his explorers to learn "the names of the nations" in the West—never an easy task but particularly hard in the case of the northern Shoshone, who had different names for themselves at different times of year. All Shoshone divisions were known for what they ate or where they lived. To the south lay the *tuba-dika* (pine nut eaters), *wara-rika* (eaters of ryegrass seed), and *kuembe-rika* (squirrel eaters). In the Sawtooth Mountains lived the *tuku-rika* (sheep eaters). But Cameahwait's people were *agai-dika* (salmon eaters) in the spring and summer and *kutsun-dika* (buffalo eaters) in the fall and winter. When they changed names, they changed lifestyles as well, transforming from fishermen who built weirs and dug camas roots to mounted hunters who pursued the herds with powerful elkhorn bows. Later, whites would give them the name of Lemhi Shoshone, a term from the Book of Mormon.[29]

"Our people were in continual fear," a Shoshone man later remembered of this time in the band's history. "During our excursions for buffalo, we were frequently attacked by [the Blackfeet], and many of our bravest warriors fell victims to the thunder and lightning they wielded. . . . The great chief of our tribe [said] . . . 'The lips of our women are white with dread, there are no smiles on the lips of our children. . . . let us fly to the mountains, let us seek their deepest recesses . . . unknown to our destroyers.'"[30]

Hiding was exactly what they were doing when Lewis came into their camp. Mere weeks before, they had been camped on the Missouri River when Blackfeet raiders, whom they called Pahkees, had swept down on them. Fleeing from attack, the Shoshone had been forced to abandon most of their food and possessions and take refuge in the mountains. But to stay safely hidden was to

Parfleche, 1800s
Among the Shoshone, Lewis saw dried roots stored by being "foalded in as many parchment hides of buffaloe." Parfleche was made by cleaning and sizing rawhide so that it had a smooth, paintable surface. The brightly decorated containers were used by most Plains Indian tribes as saddle bags and suitcases for storing food, clothing, and other valuables. The simple geometric design of this Shoshone one is typical of that tribe's styles.

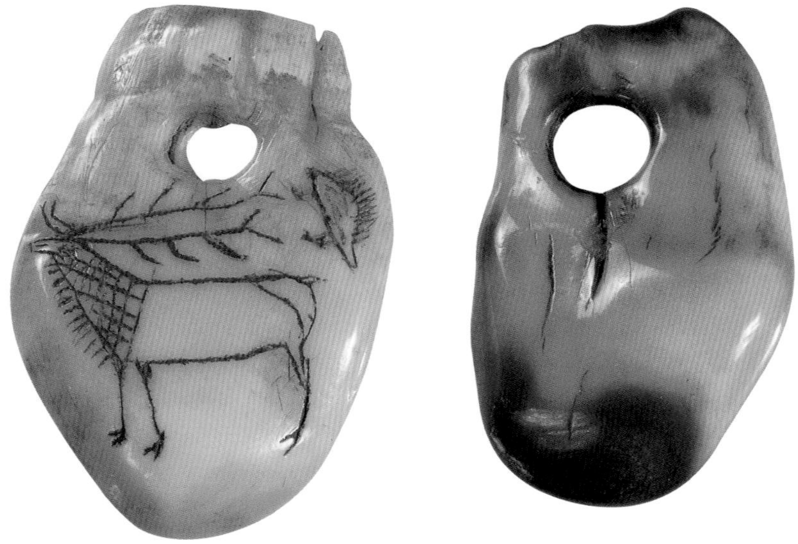

Elk teeth, 1800s

The Shoshone were so impoverished and vulnerable that when a party under Clark surprised an isolated family, the desperate parents "offered every thing they possessed (which was verry littl) to us. . . . The first offer of theirs were Elks tuskes from around their Childrens necks." Like other Plains Indian tribes, the Shoshone gave elk teeth to their children because the two ivory tusks in an elk "remain after everything else has crumbled to dust. These teeth will last longer than the life of a man, and for that reason the elk tooth has become the emblem of long life." Lewis said, "The tusks of the Elk are pierced strung on a throng and woarn as an orniment for the neck, and is most generally woarn by the women and children." These may be Shoshone.

starve, so they were cautiously preparing to venture back into the Missouri Valley to hunt buffalo when Lewis arrived.

Observing the strange, well-armed visitors, many in the Shoshone band saw treachery. Lewis had barely fallen asleep before rumors started circulating that he and his men "were in league with the Pahkees and had come on in order to decoy them into an ambuscade."[31] But Cameahwait saw more: a possible new future for his people. He must have been a remarkable leader. Later, Clark described him as "a man of Influence Sence & easey & reserved manners," who appeared "to possess a great deal of Cincerity." He was also a long-range strategic thinker. Europeans, he knew, were the source of the firearms that gave the surrounding tribes such an advantage over the isolated Shoshone. Pinned in the mountains by "bloodthirsty neighbours," the members of his band were like refugees in their own land. Clark later described Cameahwait, "with his ferce eyes and lank jaws grown meager for the want of food," saying that his band's desperation "would not be the case if we had guns, we could then live in the country of buffaloe and eat as our enimies do and not be compelled to hide ourselves in these mountains and live on roots and berries."[32]

It was an uncertain situation that Lewis woke to the next morning. He needed to persuade the Shoshone to venture back across the Divide to where the Blackfeet might wait and to delay their hunting long enough to help the Corps carry its equipment over the pass. Sensing their suspicion, he worried that if he lost their trust, "they would immediately disperse and secrete themselves in the mountains where it would be impossible to find them." If that happened, he added: "We should be disappointed in obtaining horses, which would . . . defeat the expedition altogether."[33] And so he promised them a caravan of wonders: loads of merchandise to barter for horses, a man who was black and had short curling hair, a woman of their own nation who would explain everything in Shoshone. He even "told them that . . . whitemen would come to them with an abundance of guns and every other article necessary to their defence and comfort."[34]

But it was not enough. To win the trust of the Shoshone, Lewis had to enter their mental world. It was not easy. Over the next few days, he crossed the cultural divide and pulled back several times. At each crossing, he encountered a barrier of mental resistance. He wrote of feeling offended, threatened, bewil-

Ihkas-Kínne, Siksika Blackfeet Chief, 1833
Although this man is Blackfeet, he is wearing the same type of "tippet" or mantle that Cameahwait gave to Lewis. Lewis described it as "the most eligant peice of Indian dress I ever saw." It was made from five-inch-wide strips of otter skin cut from the back fur of two or more animals, with a head and tail on either end. The otter fur was decorated with "the shells of the perl oister." Unlike this one, Cameahwait's was fringed with 140 whole ermine skins formed into rolls. Among the Piegan in the 1780s, an otter-skin mantle decorated with abalone shell was a civil chief's "insignia of office," worn by the chief's son only when he was acting for the chief.

dered, and disgusted with himself. In the end, he was left with an uncomfortable uneasiness about his own identity. They were all signs of the profound transformation he was having to make.

At first, Cameahwait was cautious and his warriors reluctant to set out. To persuade the chief, Lewis used a concept common to both societies: military honor. But he spoke not like a Euro-American commander whose orders were obeyed; instead, he used the words of an Indian war leader rallying the young men to follow him: "I still hoped that there were some among them that were not affraid to die, that were men and would go with me."

It was an astute use of the idiom of war. "I soon found that I had touched him on the right string," Lewis said. Cameahwait mounted his horse and

Captain Meriwether Lewis in Shoshone regalia, 1807

Charles B. J. F. de Saint-Mémin may have painted this in Washington, D.C., or Philadelphia in January or March 1807, shortly after Lewis returned from the West. When Lewis gave the costume to Peale's Museum, Charles Willson Peale changed the assemblage by replacing the rifle with a calumet donated by Lewis and Clark, to support his pacifist views. He wrote, "My object in this work is to give a lesson to the Indians who may visit the Museum, and also to shew my sentiments respecting wars." The original museum label read in part: "This mantle, composed of 140 Ermine skins was put on Captn. Lewis by *Comeahwait* their Cheif. Lewis is supposed to say, Brother, I accept your dress—It is the object of my heart to promote amongst you, our Neighbours, Peace and good will. . . . Possessed of every comfort in life, what cause ought to involve us in War? . . . If any differences arise about Lands or trade, let each party appoint judicious persons to meet together & amicably settle the disputed point." Peale added, "I am pleased when ever I can give an object which affords a moral sentiment to the Visitors of the Museum."

Payouska, Chief of the Great Osages, 1804 The uniform coats that the Corps presented to the most prominent Indian chiefs probably looked like the one worn by this man, the leader of the Osage delegation Lewis dispatched to Washington, D.C., from St. Louis in 1804. His name is often given as Pawhuska. He wears an officer's coat, epaulettes, two gorgets, and a peace medal. A contemporary newspaper account described him "dressed in a laced blue coat, and corresponding under vestments, wore a cocked hat, and had a handsome sword by his side." Dressing chiefs in uniform was intended to attach them to the cause of the United States.

addressed his warriors, using the same words Lewis had used: "he hoped there were some of them who heard him were not affraid to die with him." Soon, despite the lamentations of the women, all the men of the village had set out to follow Cameahwait and Lewis.[35]

But having stepped momentarily into the role of a tribal war leader, Lewis soon pulled back. None of them had eaten much in days, and Lewis, for one, was "hungary as a wolf." As they were riding back across the Divide, Drouillard killed a deer. The Shoshone warriors "ran in tumbling over each other like a parcel of famished dogs each seizing and tearing away a part of the intestens . . . the kidnies the melt [spleen] and liver and the blood runing from the corners of their mouths." The sight jolted Lewis back into an aloof, judgmental stance. "I viewed these poor starved divils with pity and compassion. . . . I really did not untill now think that human nature ever presented itself in a shape so nearly allyed to the brute creation."[36]

The feeling of alienation did not last long. As they neared the headwaters of the Missouri, where Lewis expected Clark and the boats to be waiting, Cameahwait became apprehensive that Lewis was leading them into a trap. In

War shirt, pre-1819

"Scalp shirts and official feathers are worn only at great public functions," said a Lakota elder in 1911. "The hair on the scalp shirt is obtained from scalps of the enemy or they purchase it from other members of the tribe." This shirt with human hair fringes chronicles the record of a fearsome contemporary of Lewis and Clark's, a war leader who counted coup on two armed enemies and killed thirty-four. The front and the back are both filled with icons of enemy warriors killed with a lance. Some icons have distinguishing marks such as a shield, sash, or headdress. The shirt was probably collected by Roderick McKenzie, the cousin of the explorer Alexander Mackenzie, who was a partner in the Canadian North West Company. It has been identified as both Crow and Mandan, but it generally matches Lewis's description of the Shoshone shirt, which he called "a commodious and decent garment." He described two sorts of neck treatment: "left square at top," like this one, or decorated with "the tails of the animals of which they are made and which foald outwards." Shoshone shirts were made of antelope, bighorn, or elk skin.

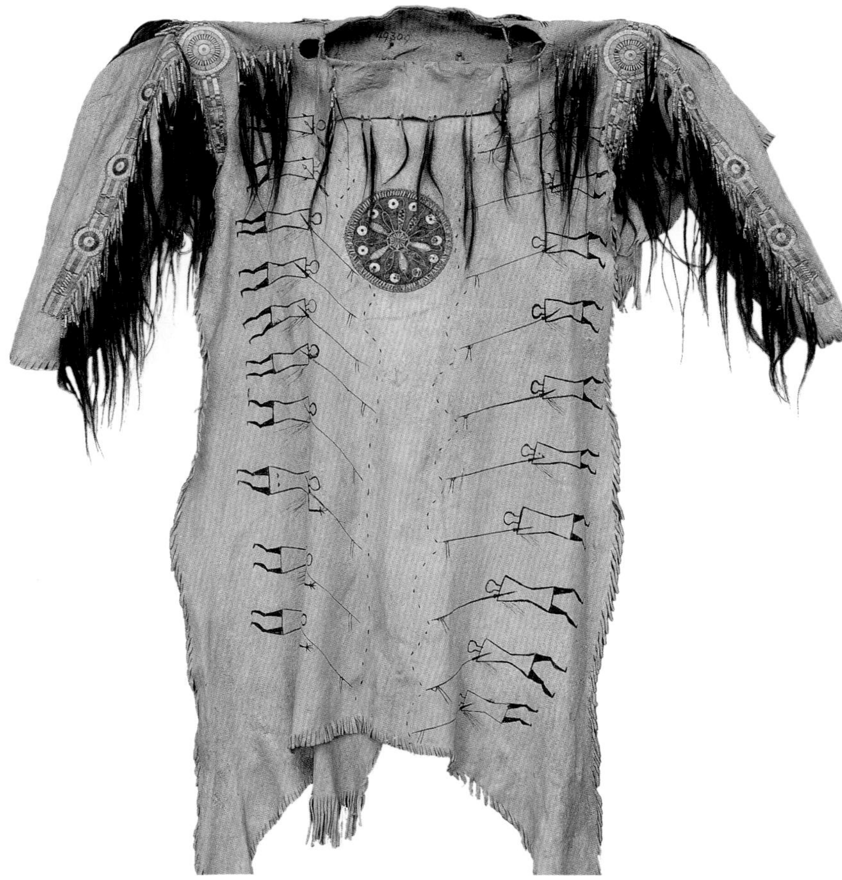

Leggings, mid-1800s

These leggings were made to go with a painted war shirt and are fringed with human hair. Lewis and Clark donated to Peale's Museum a pair of Sioux leggings "ornamented with the hair & scalps taken by the Indian who wore it, and marked with stripes shewing the number he had scalped." That pair is now lost but must have looked much like this. Lewis described Shoshone leggings and Clark described Sioux ones in some detail. In both tribes, leggings were made of antelope skin and were held up by tucking the tops under a belt. They were made "to cover the buttock and lap before in such a manner that the breechcloth is unnecessary." The sides were "deeply fringed and ornimented. sometimes this part is ornimented with little fassicles of the hair of an enimy whom they have slain in battle."

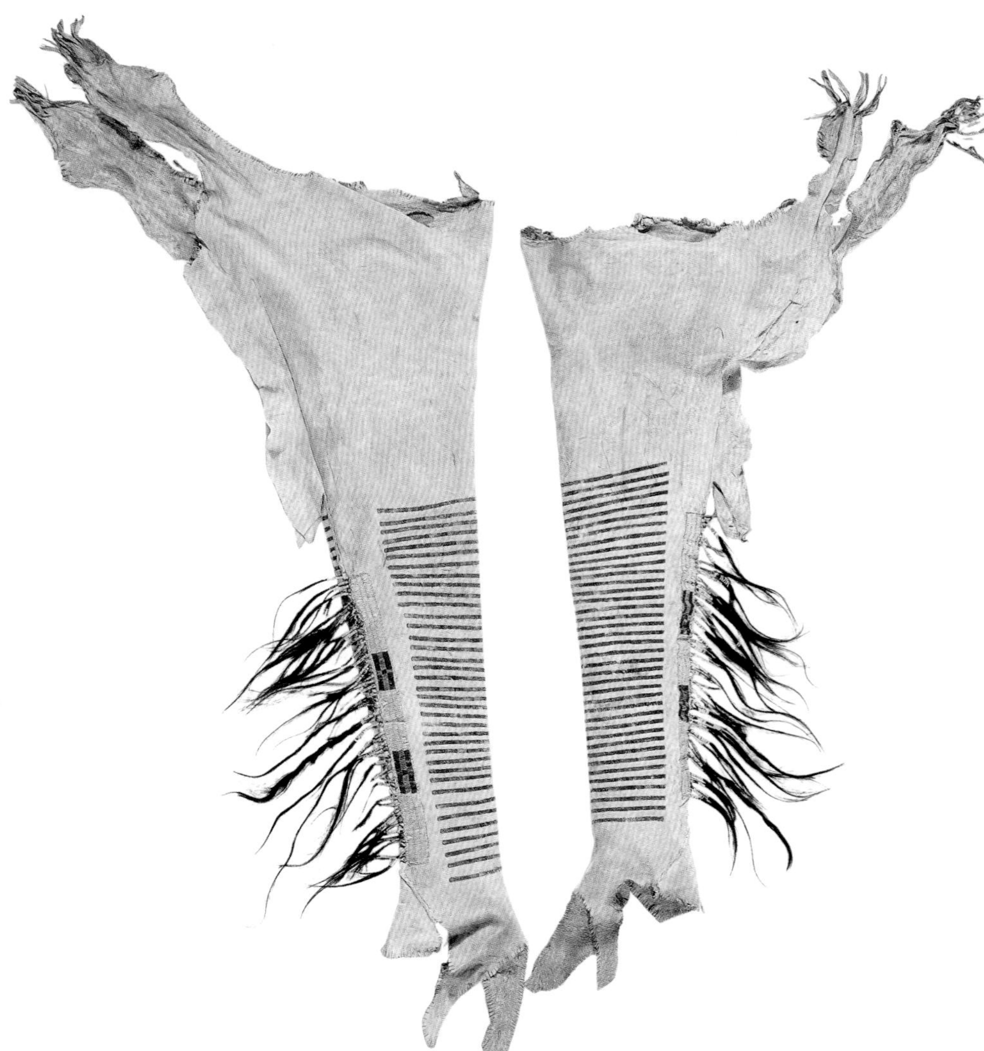

this moment of uncertainty, the chief hit on an idea: to symbolically transform the strangers into Shoshone men. It turned into a double transformation. "The Chief with much cerimony put tippets about our necks such as they t[h]emselves woar," Lewis wrote. "To give them further confidence I put my cocked hat with feather on the chief and my over shirt being of the Indian form my hair deshivled and skin well browned with the sun I wanted no further addition to make me a complete Indian in appearance the men followed my example and we were so[o]n completely metamorphosed."[37]

The exchange of clothing was a critical moment in establishing trust between the Corps and the Shoshone. Symbolically, Lewis and Cameahwait had done more than wear each other's garments: they had exchanged identities. In Plains Indian custom, a warrior's clothing incorporated a complex code about his deeds and achievements. To give away a piece of clothing was to give away part of himself. Lewis seems to have sensed the profundity of Cameahwait's gesture, however subconsciously. The ties of mutual dependence, and Cameahwait's trust and friendship, had changed him. He had become, in some sense, "a complete Indian."

The sincerity of his transformation was put to the test at once. When they reached the place where Lewis had promised the canoes would be waiting, no one was there. Clark and the crew had not yet arrived. Somehow, Lewis had to keep the Indians from leaving. Though he had told Cameahwait that "among whitemen it was considered disgracefull to lye," he now "had recource to a stratagem . . . which . . . set a little awkward": he lied. Pretending that a note he himself had left was a message from Clark, he announced that the party was nearby. He wrote of his mood that night: "My mind was in reallity quite as gloomy . . . as the most affrighted indian but I affected cheerfullness to keep the Indians so. . . . I slept but little." Fortunately, no one discovered that he had repaid Cameahwait's trust with deceit. The canoes arrived the next day, and "all appeared transported with joy."[38]

It is hard to cross a cultural divide and come back unchanged. A week of metamorphoses had left Lewis feeling uncertain of who he was—or ought to be. On the evening of his thirty-second birthday, August 18, he looked inward, questioning his life. "I reflected that I had as yet done but little, very little indeed, to further the hapiness of the human race. . . . I viewed with regret the many hours I have spent in indolence, and . . . resolved in future to redouble my exertions and . . . live for *mankind*, as I have heretofore lived *for myself*."[39]

1804 Infantry captain's uniform, reproduced 2002
The U.S. Army was so small at the time of the expedition that no complete uniforms, and very few components, survive. This reproduction was assembled using information from records in the National Archives. It portrays a captain in the full-dress uniform of the 1st U.S. Infantry Regiment (to which Lewis belonged) in about 1804.

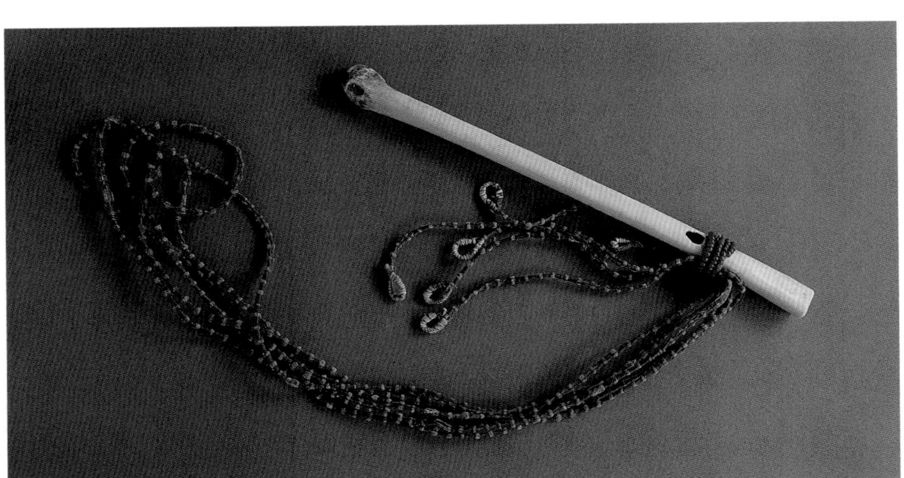

Eagle bone whistle, early 1800s
Whistles like this, often called war whistles, were worn in battle and in the ceremonies of men's associations such as the Mandan Dog Society and the Lakota Miwatani Society. Later, they were used in the Sun Dance. Ceremonial whistles could be made of goose, crane, or swan bones, but war whistles were most often made of eagle bone. Catlin said: "A chief or leader carries this to battle with him, suspended generally from his neck, and worn under his dress. This little instrument has but two notes, which are produced by blowing in the ends of it. The note produced in one end, being much more shrill than the other, gives the signal for battle, whilst the other sounds a retreat." However, Indian sources suggested it was used to appeal to eagle power to confuse the enemy. This is probably the "Bone War Whistle" collected on the Missouri River by George C. Hutter in 1825 and donated to Peale's Museum in 1828.

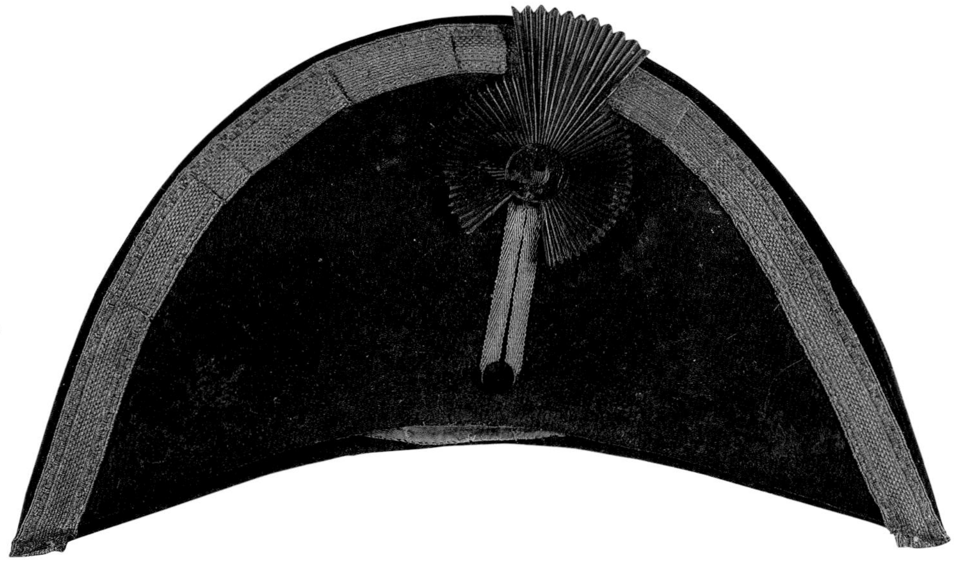

Chapeau de bras, 1795–1815
Hats were symbols of social class in civilian society and of rank in the military. Gestures made with the hat expressed gradations of deference. The military salute, originally a broad sweeping gesture of removing the hat, combined with a bow, had by 1801 been simplified into the motion of touching the hat brim with the flat of the hand. This hat style—known as the bicorne, the cocked hat, or the chapeau de bras—was reserved for officers. It is made with wide brims turned up to form flaps called the cock (on the front) and the fan (rear), with a cap or crown in the center. It is designed to be compressed flat for carrying under the arm, hence the name, which translates as "arm hat." There is a socket for a plume behind the cockade. This is probably a militia hat.

In the years after, Lewis returned again and again to the moment when he, however temporarily, became an Indian. All the way across the Rockies to the Pacific Ocean, and all the way back, he transported the otter-skin mantle Cameahwait had given him. When he got back to Philadelphia, he assumed again his Shoshone regalia and had himself painted as an Indian warrior. Eventually he gave the entire suit of clothes to Charles Willson Peale's museum, where it was mounted on a wax likeness of him, memorializing forever that moment when his identity as a white man had wavered.

Lewis was not the only one to experience a blending of identities on the frontier. It happened to whole groups of people, and the borrowing went both ways. The meeting of Indians and Europeans was not always a story of conflict and conquest; it was also a story about mutual dependence, accommodation, communication, and creativity. In the place where cultures met, a "middle ground" developed, with its own rules, languages, and customs—and even its own art and objects that were neither Indian nor white but a mixture of both. This middle ground was a rich hybrid of cultures that might not have vanished if only enough white Americans had followed Lewis's first halting steps into the Indian world and had endured the change that process requires and inspires.

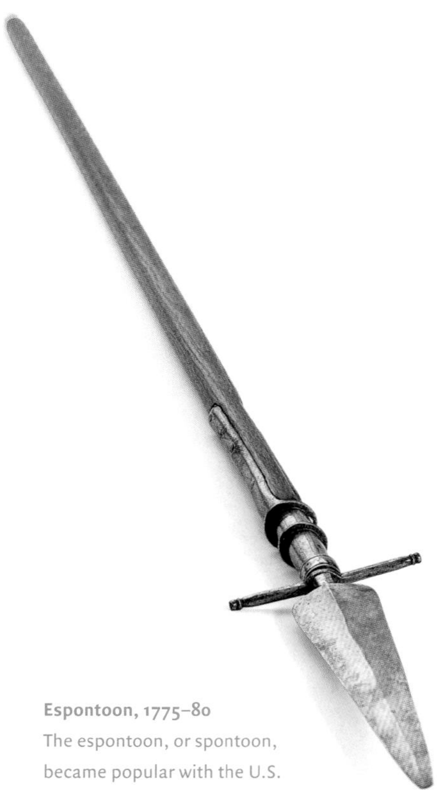

Espontoon, 1775–80
The espontoon, or spontoon, became popular with the U.S. Army during the Revolutionary War when it was used by officers as a badge of rank and as a fighting weapon. There was an attempt to standardize the American spontoon in 1778, but a number of different patterns remained. Lewis mentioned using the spontoon as a walking stick, a weapon, and a gun rest. He even used his spontoon to stabilize himself to prevent a fall down a precipice.

DRESSED IN COURAGE

> To clothe a man falsely is only to distress his spirit.
>
> —LUTHER STANDING BEAR[40]

> Every able-bodied boy was taught that he should become a warrior, not only in order to defend himself and his people against hostile persons, but to get honor. . . . When one had accomplished such things, he was entitled to certain decorations and privileges, and he could compose songs in honor of himself which the women would sing.
>
> —BAD BEAR, LAKOTA[41]

Throughout Lewis's encounter with the Shoshone, physical objects acted as communicators and translators, but no objects were more eloquent than clothing. To wear another's clothing is an intimate act that connects people on a deeply physical level. But clothing also conveys explicit messages about the wearer through formal codes. And no type of clothing was more overtly symbolic than the soldier's. In both cultures, warriors revealed who they were and what they had accomplished—in sum, expressed their identity—through dress.

Military heroism was a concept that needed no translation. As a soldier, Lewis instantly understood the Indian system of status through great deeds symbolized with insignia. "Bravery is esteemed the primary virtue," he wrote; "nor can any one become eminent among them . . . without some ware-like achievement." It was the same virtue—undaunted courage—that Jefferson would praise in Lewis when he wrote the explorer's obituary.[42]

Lewis believed that military success was the only route to political power in Plains tribes. He told the story of a young Mandan man who objected to the idea of intertribal peace. Lewis explained the Mandan's concern: "If they were in a state of peace with all their neighbours what the nation would do for Cheifs? . . . taking as granted that there could be no other mode devised for making Cheifs but that which custom had established through the medium of warlike acievements." A Mandan traveler in the United States might have come to the same conclusion by observing how men like George Washington, Alexander Hamilton, and Meriwether Lewis had achieved political prominence through their military service. But in both cultures, political achievement was more complicated than that. Mandan men needed a powerful clan, ownership of sacred bundles, prominence in men's societies, wealth, eloquence, and other sources of power to rise to the status of chief. So did Euro-American men.[43]

Warriors everywhere experienced the words of a Lakota man's song: "I am living in uncertainty." Risking life was the price they paid; honor and fame were their rewards. Soldiers of Lewis and Clark's generation lived by a complex code of honor defended through duels both verbal and physical. "Honors & rewards" were Clark's stated motivations to join the expedition, and he used a hunting rifle on whose patchbox was engraved a flying angel with a trumpet, symbolizing Fame.[44] Plains Indian men had the same ambitions, though their means of achieving and expressing those goals were different. Shooter, a Lakota, described the attributes of the ideal man: "He has the strength and

Split-horn bonnet, c. 1875–85
Split-horn bonnets were "worn only by the bravest of the brave; by the most extraordinary men in the nation," according to Catlin. The maker split a buffalo horn end to end, then took a third of the horn and shaved it thin. He then attached the horns to the cap so that they fell back or forward as the wearer moved his head, "giving a vast deal of expression and force of character, to the appearance of the chief who is wearing them." Ribbons and horsehair attached to the horn tips intensified the effect. Such headdresses were worn only for the visits of other chiefs, at celebrations of a war victory, at public festivals, or on war parties, where they served as a "symbol of power." This Mandan or Hidatsa one is early in style but late in date, substituting cow horns for buffalo; the ermine trailer is made using the same technique as the fringe on Lewis's Shoshone tippet.

Bear claw necklace, mid-1800s
Lewis wrote among the Shoshone: "The warriors or such as esteem themselves brave men wear collars made of the claws of the brown bear which are also esteemed of great value and are preserved with great care. these claws are ornamented with beads about the thick end near which they are peirced through their sides and strung on a throng of dressed leather and tyed about the neck commonly with the upper edge of the tallon next the breast or neck but sometimes are reversed. it is esteemed by them an act of equal celebrity the killing one of these bear or an enimy, and with the means they have of killing this animal it must really be a serious undertaking."

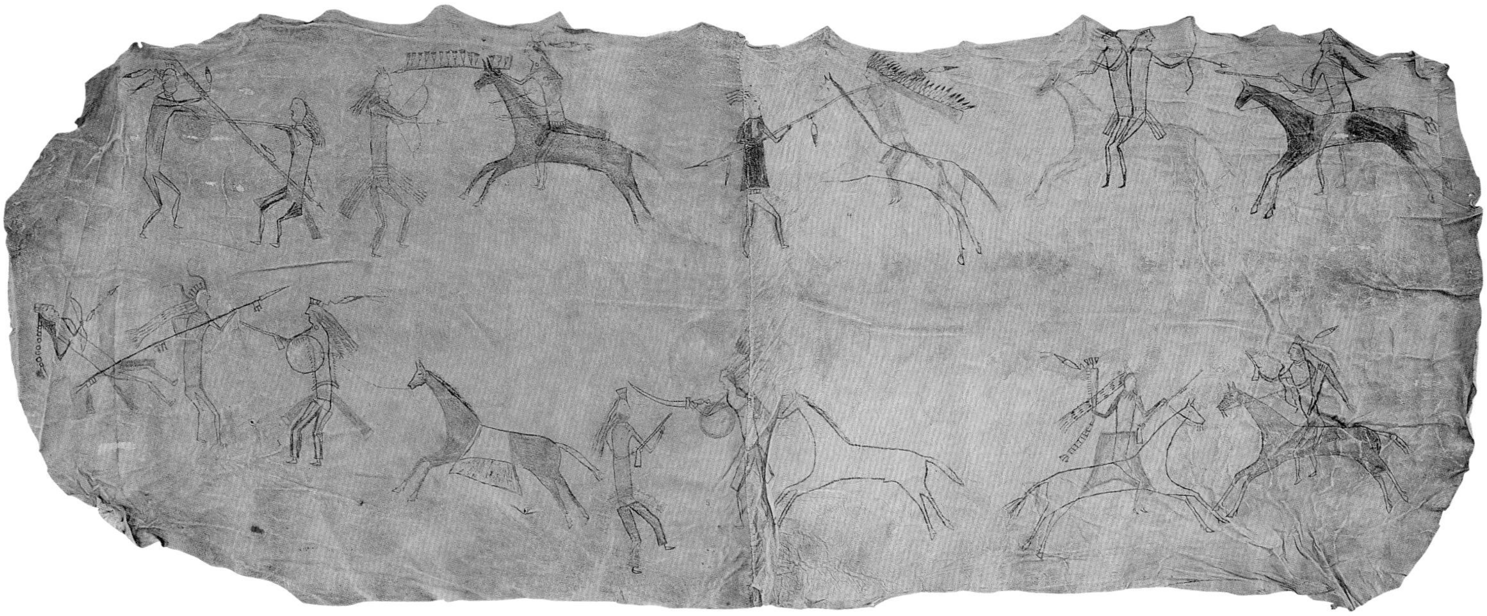

War robe of Chief Washakie, pre-1897
Washakie was a one-year-old child living with the Salish of Montana when Lewis and Clark encountered his people. After his Salish father's death, his Shoshone mother took him to live with her family in Wyoming. There he achieved the war honors shown on this robe and rose to become the chief of the Wind River Shoshone. He led his tribe during the transition to reservation life; he died in 1900. He painted approximately ten war robes, and his son Charlie Washakie painted twice as many depicting his father's exploits. This one was painted on two cured deer hides. Lewis wrote that Shoshone robes were "woarn . . . loosly thrown about their sholders, and the sides at pleasure either hanging loose or drawn together with the hands." They were "formed most commonly of the skins of Antelope, Big-horn, or deer, dressed with the hair on, tho' they prefer the buffaloe when they can procure them."

ability to accomplish his aims. He is brave to defend himself and others and is free to do much good. He is kind to all, especially to the poor and needy. The tribe looks to him as a defender, and he is expected to shield the women." Iron Tail put it differently: "The ambition of an Indian is principally to be high among his fellow men, to be superior to them in killing enemies, stealing horses, owning a fast horse, belonging to societies, having many wives." Those were the accomplishments that brought honor.[45]

Both Indians and Euro-Americans created artifacts to embody honor and fame. Plains Indian men wore their fame on their backs in the form of painted skin robes displaying their achievements. Washakie, the great nineteenth-century chief of the Wind River Shoshone, was one example. In the diagrammatic battle scenes of Washakie's painted robe, individuals were distinguished not by their faces but by their costumes, hairstyles, or equipment that symbolized tribal affiliation, society membership, and past deeds. Enemies were often reduced to mere disembodied guns or arrows. Events happened not in a landscape but in a symbolic realm of deeds. The sum of the exploits shown was the measure of the man's worth.[46]

A different image of heroism appeared in a painting that would have been familiar to Lewis and Clark through its wide circulation in print form: Benjamin West's 1771 *The Death of General Wolfe*. Like the Shoshone war robe, West's painting tells the story of a heroic event. In 1759, at the height of the French and Indian War, James Wolfe had led a British-American assault on the French on the Plains of Abraham outside Quebec. The painting shows the general, fatally wounded in the battle, dying just as a messenger brought the news that the enemy was retreating and the British army had won the battle. Poignantly, Wolfe could win victory and suffer death at the same moment because he had achieved transcendent glory. His Christlike pose and uplifted eyes suggested both expiatory sacrifice for the nation and triumph over death—not through faith but through fame. This was a morally uplifting image that military men of Lewis and Clark's generation aspired to, just as Shoshone youths aspired to painted robes portraying their own deeds.[47]

The similarities between Washakie and Wolfe are striking, but there were differences as well, and they ran deeper than art styles. In Euro-American culture, war was conducted by nation-states for strategic ends: to conquer territory or subjugate enemy states. Wolfe could honorably achieve his nation's victory while sacrificing his own, but not the other way around. On the plains, warfare could also be conducted for conquering territory and other tribes, but individual achievement was not subordinate to those goals. Men went to war to test their bravery and spiritual power as well as to defend their people. The honor of a coup went not to the man who killed the enemy but to the first one to demonstrate bravery by striking the dead body with something held in his hand. Going into battle without weapons or fighting while tethered to a stake in the ground was more admired than achieving a utilitarian victory from superior numbers, tactics, or weapons—though victory by any means was celebrated.[48]

Both Indian and Euro-American men went into battle dressed in regalia that symbolized their deeds and status. The leader of a plains war party was often distinguished by a painted shirt that detailed his war record and by leggings with horizontal stripes symbolizing vanquished enemies. On such war shirts, the contours of the animal skin were often left intact as a sign of respect to the animal, so that it would lend its qualities to the wearer. The most powerful shirts were fringed with locks of human hair that symbolized enemy scalps but that could be given by relatives and supporters to represent the man's

The Death of General Wolfe, 1770
The innovation that made the work of the American artist Benjamin West famous was to show heroism in the present day, not in an idealized classical or biblical past. The dress, hairstyles, and equipment are accurately depicted, but the posing and composition reflect the theatrical conventions of history paintings. The background tells the story of the attack on Quebec, dividing it into a sequence of exploits in much the same way as war robes did.

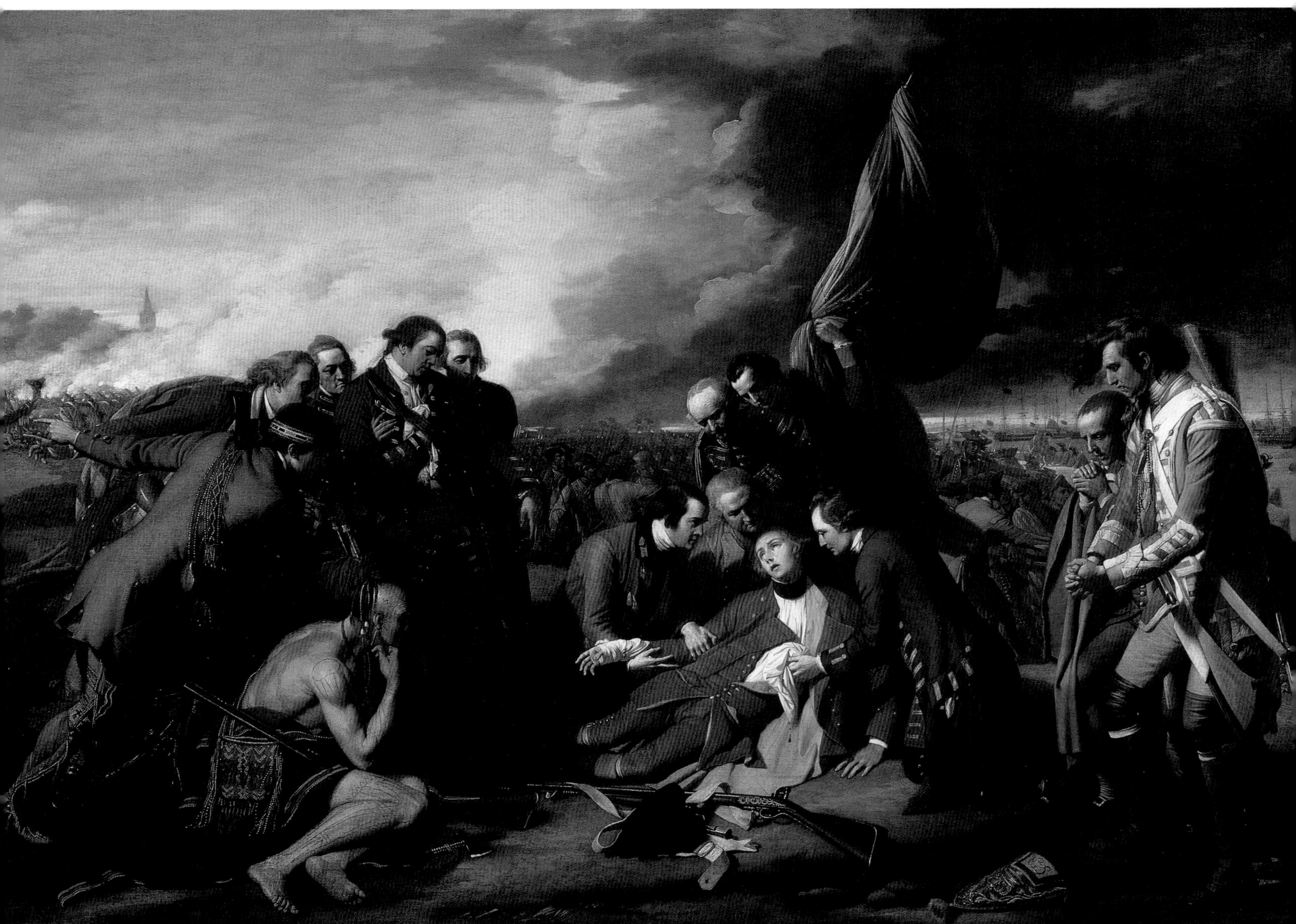

Feather war insignium, mid-1800s
Lewis and Clark donated several eagle-tail feathers used for "ornimental and war-like dresses" to Peale's Museum, where this feather may have originated. Among the Teton Sioux, Clark told his ghostwriter Nicholas Biddle, men wore a *"Calumet [eagle] feather adorned with porcupine quills & fastened to the top of the head & falls backwards,"* but he did not mention that the feathers were symbols of achievement in war. Eagle-tail feathers like this one, white with black tips, were reserved for the most distinguished warriors. Thunder Bear said in 1912: "A Lakota who has done deeds of desperate daring in the presence of an enemy is entitled to wear a quill from the tail of the eagle notched at its sides. This should be worn dangling from the forelock or the pierced ear."

Cockade and eagle, early 1800s
Cockades were hat decorations originally worn in colors that identified the adherents of a lord or his party. In early-eighteenth-century England, Hanoverians wore black cockades and Jacobites wore white ones. To American soldiers, they were signs of national allegiance and carried patriotic symbols, of which the eagle was most important. The standing orders for the 1st Regiment of Infantry, 1802, specified that an officer's dress include a "Cockade to be of Black Ribband and an Eagle." Eagles were silver, like this one, for infantry officers and gold for artillery.

responsibilities to his relations. "To don . . . a scalp shirt . . . indicates intention to do an act of bravery," said Thunder Bear, a Lakota. "To habitually wear it indicates a brave who has done a notable act of bravery. To wear it temporarily indicates a position of responsibility that may be dangerous."[49]

The soldiers of Lewis and Clark's troop wore clothing designed not to advertise their individual deeds but to obliterate their differences and make them uniform. Their clothing symbolized the fact that in battle, they acted not as individual warriors but as a coordinated group following orders. There were differences in their uniforms, but the differences reflected organization rather than individuality. The Corps included men of both infantry and artillery regiments, distinguished by the color of the buttons and piping on the uniforms (gold and yellow for artillery, silver and white for infantry) and by the design of the hats. The officers, who were obliged to provide their own uniforms and equipment made to a specified design, were distinguished from the men by showy decorations like crimson sashes, engraved swords, and sword knots (a tassel attached to the hilt, made in symbolic colors). The army lavished effort on designing and specifying the details of uniforms, knowing the psychological impact they had.[50]

Battle leaders in both cultures used implements to differentiate themselves from soldiers. A Plains Indian war chief often carried a decorated whistle made from the wing or leg bone of an eagle. Although the whistle could be used to signal advance or retreat, its more important function was to speak to the thunder power by emulating the piercing cry of an eagle. Euro-American officers rallied their troops with more pragmatic tools. Lewis carried a tall spear, called an "espontoon," that dated back to the Roman legions, when commanders raised tall standards or pikes so that foot soldiers could locate them in battle. Lewis never used the espontoon in battle, but it proved handy as a gun rest and grizzly-bear spear, and it instantly identified him as an officer.[51]

The dress of war always included headgear. Though artists have portrayed Lewis and Clark in everything from Revolutionary tricorne hats to coonskin caps, the prescribed military hats of the day were cylindrical top hats for the enlisted men and a bicorne hat called a *chapeau de bras* for the officers. The enlisted men's hats were decorated with a strip of bearskin arching over the top from front to back. The officers' hats sported sunburst symbols of silk ribbon, called cockades, and tall feather plumes. Upright feathers were also symbolic to Indian warriors, though at this date the famous eagle feather war bonnets were not yet common. The most honored men wore split-horn headdresses covered with ermine skins, suggesting both the power of the buffalo and the quickness and sharp observation of the weasel.[52]

All warriors used symbols and insignia on their regalia, but again there were subtle differences. Whereas Euro-Americans wore symbols of rank, Northern Plains Indian men wore symbols of the deeds that had earned them honor with their peers. There was a formal system for classifying and comparing such deeds—a typology of action of far more significance to Native peoples than the classification of animals or plants that Euro-Americans favored. Lewis cataloged these "distinguishing acts" among the Shoshone: killing and scalping an enemy, killing a grizzly bear, leading a successful war party, stealing the horses of an enemy. The Lakota had a complicated feather code for indicating such deeds. According to Thunder Bear, any man who had fought in battle

Epaulettes of William Clark, 1808
According to his family, Clark purchased these on being appointed brigadier general of the Louisiana Territorial militia.

could wear an eagle tail feather suspended from his hair, clothing, or implements. Killing or striking an enemy with a war club or stick earned a warrior an eagle feather fastened upright to the hair. A wound in battle earned an upright eagle feather colored red. Killing a renowned enemy earned an eagle feather suspended from the ear. Various ways of trimming and coloring the feathers indicated different things.[53]

Other kinds of insignia worn by Indian men were the material manifestations of spirit powers. Amulets, shields, and other protective devices captured and intensified the vision of the wearer, bringing supernatural forces to bear on the battle. Lewis described the creation of a Shoshone battle shield as "a cerimony of great importance," and he understood that its "protecting power" lay not just in its mechanical ability to repel arrows. In fact, the painted design

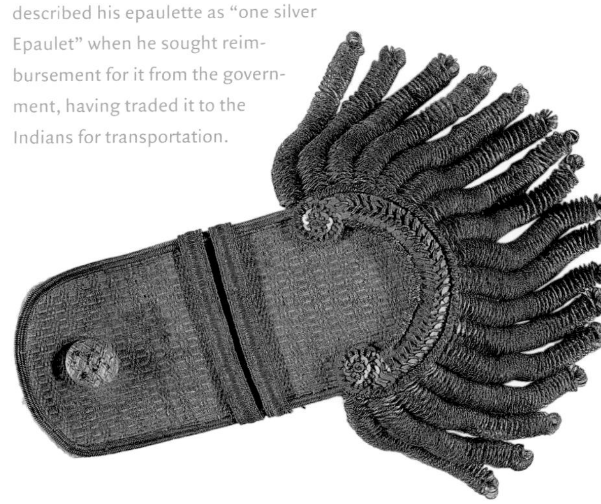

Epaulette, c. 1804–8
In all but color, this is the style of epaulette worn by Lewis and Clark on the expedition. Epaulettes were first used to designate rank by the Continental Army during the Revolutionary War. In 1783 silver lace epaulettes were prescribed for infantry officers and gold for artillery. An order from the War Department in 1799 provided a system for identifying rank by the placement and number of epaulettes worn. Lewis described his epaulette as "one silver Epaulet" when he sought reimbursement for it from the government, having traded it to the Indians for transportation.

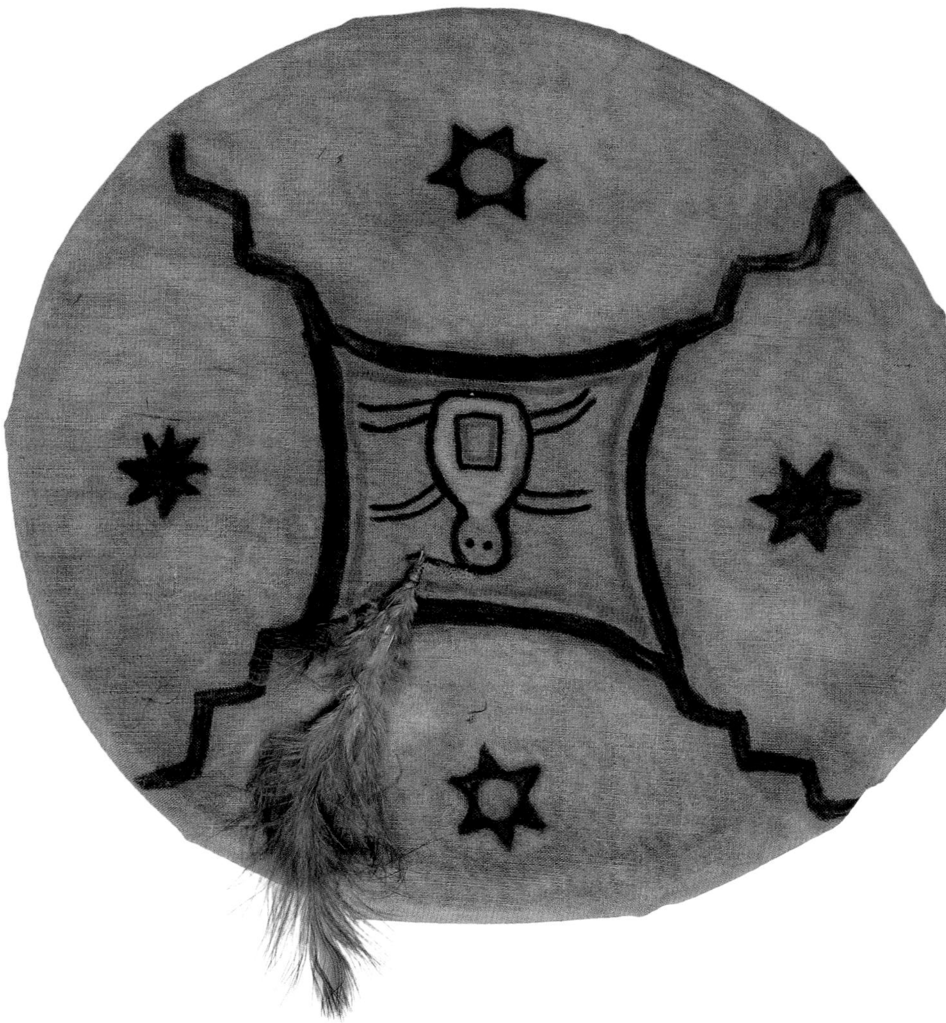

Dance shield, pre-1885
The style of shield Lewis saw among the Shoshone was "formed of buffaloe hide, perfectly arrow proof." He added, "This is frequently painted with varios figures and ornamented around the edges with feather and a fringe of dressed leather." This shield of painted cloth stretched over a hoop of willow was a model used in dances and ceremonies to symbolize the rawhide shield that a warrior carried into battle. It replicates the most important part of the shield—its design. To Lakota men, the spiderweb was a cosmological sign because of the spider's close association with thunder. The four-cornered web symbolized the structure of the cosmos, divided into the four directions where the four winds and four thunders made their homes. The thunderbolts indicated the web's supernatural character. The spiderweb was protective because hail and bullets passed through it without harming it.

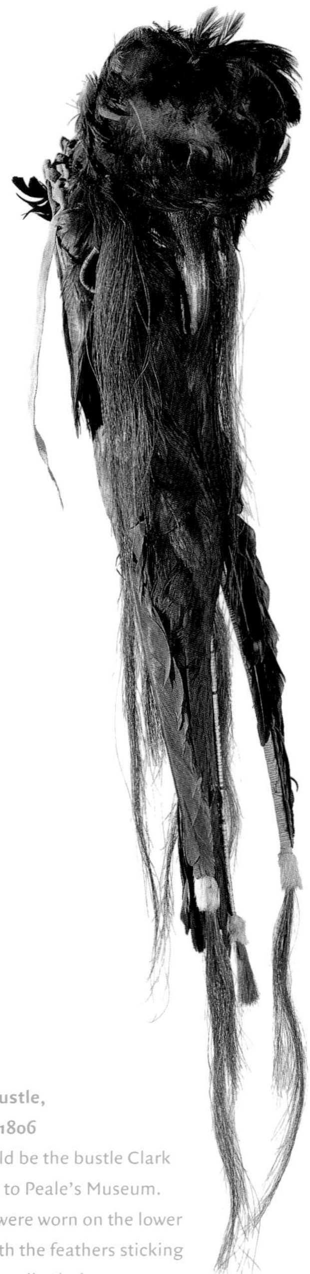

Raven bustle,
c. 1780–1806
This could be the bustle Clark donated to Peale's Museum. Bustles were worn on the lower back, with the feathers sticking out like a tail. Clark sent an artifact like this one to Jefferson in 1807, along with mammoth bones from Big Bone Lick. Jefferson inventoried it as "a Sioux dress for the head & hips when on duty as a souldier or police man." This may be that bustle or another that Peale accessioned into the museum in 1809 as "A Dress made of Crow or Raven Skins, worn by the Police Officiers of the Saux, nation."

and the animal parts that were suspended from the shield were its most important aspects, for they summoned the warrior's spiritual patron.[54]

Euro-American insignia were just as prolific but had come to symbolize national affiliation, rank, and unit. Shoulder belt-plates (ovals of metal attached to the white leather belt that suspended the bayonet) and cockade eagles (small cast-metal insignia attached to the decorations on the hat) were pewter for infantry, brass for artillery, and silver or gold for officers. Both were made in the richly symbolic form of an eagle. To the soldier, the eagle symbolized the United States. The Indians viewed the symbol differently. A later visitor to the Teton observed, "The United States emblem of the eagle with outstretched claws, holding arrows and the lightning, is regarded by the Dakota as an appeal on our part to the thunder-bird; and statements to the contrary are usually interpreted as white men's lies to deceive the Indians and to guard the power."[55]

Epaulettes were tasseled, woven-wire shoulder decorations that communicated the arcane gradations of rank. In Lewis and Clark's army, corporals wore one red worsted epaulette on the left shoulder, sergeants wore the same on the right shoulder, infantry lieutenants wore one silver epaulette on the left shoulder, captains wore one on the right shoulder, and so on up to generals, who wore two gold epaulettes with stars. These clear-cut symbols of hierarchy were designed to prevent any ambiguity about chains of command; a soldier could instantly tell whom to obey by checking epaulettes. But all rules depend on people's willingness to follow them. If Clark wore an epaulette during the expedition, he was practicing deceptive dressing. As far as the men knew, Clark was a captain equal in rank to Lewis. In secret, army rules had prevented the War Department from issuing Clark the commission that Lewis had promised, leaving him a mere lieutenant. Clothing had to hide the fact that both commanders were complicit in breaking the sacred rules of rank: Lewis by pretending he had the authority to promote Clark, and Clark by pretending that he had been promoted. The situation evidently rankled Clark. One of his first acts on being promoted to brigadier general of militia in 1808 was to buy a new pair of epaulettes that he could wear without misrepresentation.[56]

Perhaps because of the importance Clark gave to insignia of rank, he showed great interest in one he believed he had discovered among the Teton. "Those people have a Description of Men which they Call Soldiars, those men attend to the police of the Band, Correct all vices &. I Saw one to day whip 2 Squars who appeared to have fallen out, when the Soldier approached all appeared [to] give way and flee at night they Keep 4 or 5 men at different distances walking around their Camp Singing the acursenes [occurrences] of the night." Later, when explaining the role of the "policemen" to an interviewer, Clark described their regalia: "They are known generally by having their bodies blacked but their distinguishing mark are several 2 or 3 stuffed raven skins so fixed on the small of the back in such a way that the tails stick horizontally off from the body fixed to the girdle . . . on his forehead a raven skin split in two tied round his head with the beak sticking out from his forehead."[57]

What Clark was observing was an official known as the *akicita*, or camp marshal. It was a civil position, not military. Thomas Tyon, an Oglala Lakota, said of the *akicita*: "He is like a policeman and a judge and a jailer and an executioner. All must do as he says, and he can punish anyone, he may even destroy all the property of anyone, or strike anyone, and he may kill anyone. But if he does anything that is not according to the laws of the Oglalas the other *akicitapi* will punish him, and the council may depose him." The means of appointing the *akicita* varied from camp to camp, but usually the council of headmen or the chief would select one of the men's societies to perform the function for the duration of a camping season. They charged the society, "You shall see that no prairie fires are started; that no one shall scare away the buffalo; that no one shall go away from camp to camp elsewhere; that no one, when on the buffalo chase, goes ahead and shoots the buffalo; and that all offenders be punished." Later in the century, there were six societies that could act as *akicita*, but the ones named most often were the *kangi yuha* (Crow Owners) and *ihoka* (Badgers). At that time, the distinguishing mark of an *akicita* was a stripe of black face paint, not a raven bustle; however, the *kangi yuha*, or Crow Owners society, did use crow skins as part of their regalia. It is possible that Clark saw the Teton camp in a year when the Crow Owners, or a society like them, were acting as *akicita* and that he mistook the society insignia for that of their temporary office. His grasp of Lakota social organization was too rudimentary for him to appreciate the intricate balance of powers in the camp.[58]

Men who go to war together share a bond of brotherhood, and both Plains Indian tribes and Euro-Americans sought ways to formalize such bonds in social organizations. Both agricultural and hunting tribes had elaborate systems of societies, each with its own ceremonies, regalia, and duties. In Mandan and Hidatsa villages, every man who reached a particular age was expected to join his generation in purchasing the appropriate society's rites and songs from the older men above them. In Lakota bands, societies were more independent; the members might choose new men to induct, or a man might earn the right to join through visions or deeds.

One famous Lakota society of the nineteenth century was the *tokala*, or Kit Fox Society. Its members were "Brave young men of good repute." They were named for the kit fox because they emulated that animal in activity and cunning. Symbolic objects (a pipe, lances, whips, and drum) and ceremonial regalia (fox skins, feathers, and a fox jaw on otter skin) were the signs of membership. According to Thomas Tyon and John Blunt Horn, who had been society members in their youth, the Kit Fox initiation rite "taught that one should be brave before friends and foes alike and undergo hardship and punishment with fortitude. . . . That one should search for the poor, weak, or friendless and give such all the aid one could. They inculcated that a Fox should not steal, except from the enemy, should not lie, except to the enemy, and should set an example by complying with the recognized rules of the hunt and camp. That if a fellow Fox were in trouble of any kind he should help him." In short, the principles of the Kit Fox Society were "bravery, generosity, chivalry, morality, and fraternity."[59]

Both Lewis and Clark belonged to a society as well—the Freemasons. This was not specifically a warrior society, but it was widespread among the officer corps of the U.S. Army, and membership was practically a prerequisite for anyone holding public office between 1780 and 1820. Masonry functioned like an Ivy League college degree today—a network among the powerful and prominent. Lewis was the more committed Mason; he joined the Door of Virtue Lodge in Albemarle County in 1797 and received the Royal Arch degree in Staunton, Virginia, two years later. After the expedition, he founded a lodge in

Rattle, c. 1870
Men's military societies such as the Miwatani Society used rattles made from the split dewclaws of buffalo, elk, deer, or antelope as badges of membership. They were used to accompany the songs and ceremonies of the society. The horns on the human face at top indicate a supernatural nature.

Missouri and persuaded Clark to join. Like the Kit Fox, the Freemasons performed rites and rituals using ceremonial regalia such as painted aprons and certificates of initiation. Masonry inculcated spiritual values and high ideals. A Masonic text from the 1770s listed the central tenets as brotherly love, relief of the distressed, and truth. Their cardinal virtues were temperance ("to govern our passions and to check our unruly desires"), fortitude ("to resist temptations and to encounter dangers with spirit and resolution"), prudence ("to regulate our conduct by the dictates of reason"), and justice ("the principles of equity"). Their symbolic objects were the gauge, gavel, plumb, square, compass, level, and trowel. There were many levels of initiation, all of which Lewis achieved. The masculine ideals of Masonry remained important to him until the end. When he died, he was still carrying his Masonic apron, which was found "soiled only by the life-blood of its owner."[60]

Soldiers' minds were not always fixed on lofty ideals. Vanity and fashion also influenced their dress. Hairstyles, in particular, were subject to changing modes. Some Plains Indian hairstyles were dictated by tribal custom or society membership; the Arikara were known for their pompadours, and certain Kit Fox Society officers were obliged to get a "*tokala* haircut"—a "roach," or what is called today a mohawk. All across the northern plains, long flowing hair was greatly admired. Fashionable men who had counted coup were entitled to wear long hair extensions made of buffalo or horse hair, daubed with gum or clay. Long hair was also a mark of fashion in the U.S. Army up to 1801; officers often wore their hair drawn back in a queue, sometimes looped up behind the head and sometimes powdered. But in that year, orders went out: "For the accommodation, comfort & health of the Troops the hair is to be cropped without exception." Queues had come to be associated with the decaying aristocracy of Europe. Even so, many officers—Lewis among them—resisted getting a haircut. As Jefferson's secretary, he continued to wear his luxuriant,

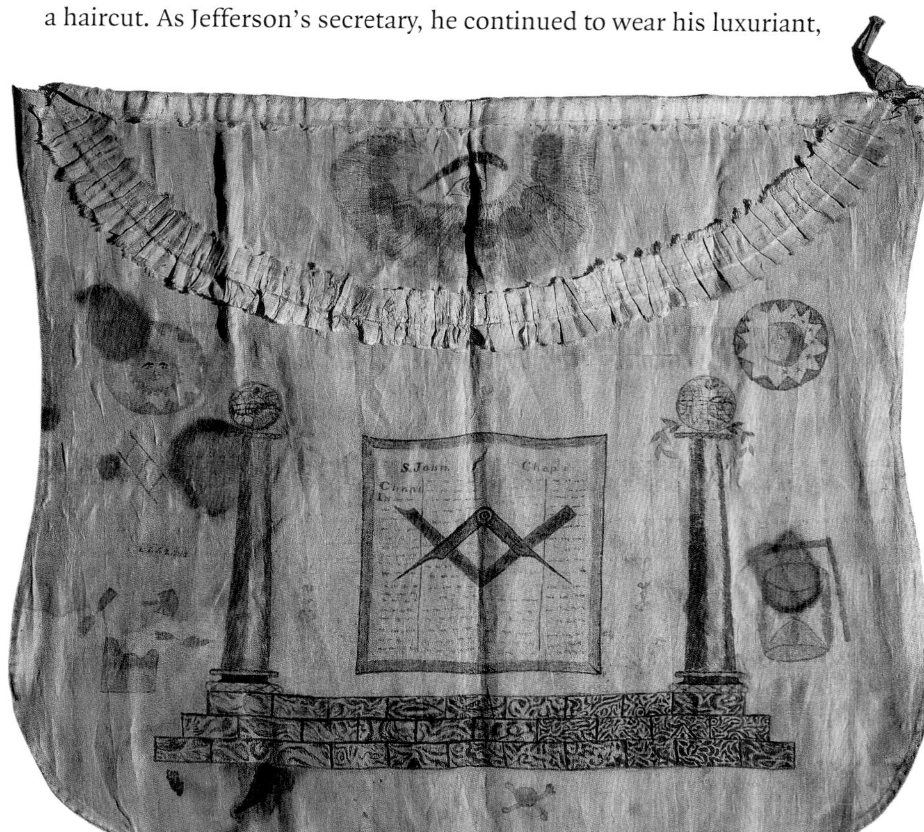

Masonic apron, 1808
According to Lewis family tradition, this apron was in Lewis's pocket when he died. The bloodstains on it tested positive for human and deer blood. This is one of two of Lewis's aprons in existence today. One, at the Missouri Historical Society, was probably presented to him along with the Royal Arch degree at Staunton, Virginia, in 1799. This one was from the St. Louis Lodge No. 111, the first Masonic lodge in Missouri, which he helped found in 1808. He was installed as master for less than a year before he died. Aprons could be presented to distinguished masons on special occasions such as joining or visiting the lodge. The symbols were not consistent or systematic at this date, but the central image shows three steps representing the three degrees (apprentice, fellowcraft, and master) and the three stages of life (youth, maturity, and old age). The pillars are the bronze pillars that stood in front of King Solomon's temple, denoting "Strength" and "To Establish." The Bible is open to John 1:1, "In the beginning was the Word . . ." The crossed square and compasses represent the mason's quest to have his spiritual side (symbolized by the compasses) overcome and control his physical side (the square).

OPPOSITE, BELOW: **Hair extensions, 1800s**
Several tribes of Plains Indians wore their hair in the equivalent of dreadlocks, which this Arikara hairpiece simulates. Long hair was esteemed as a mark of masculine beauty. Hair extensions were popular at least as early as 1819, when they were observed by Stephen H. Long's expedition: "The hair is in great profusion, and is thrown upon the back in long rolls, but upon close inspection the greater portion of it is perceived to be false hair artificially attached to their own." The decorations are made of clay or gum and plated metal disks.

Meriwether Lewis in queue, c. 1802
In 1888 R. L. Dabney wrote: "I first saw it [this portrait] hanging at Locust Hill, in the house of Aunt Marks, and, after, her death, in the house of Cousin Reuben Lewis, the brother of the deceased. I heard either him, or his wife, Aunt Mildred, say that the portrait was taken at the time Cousin Meriwether Lewis was private secretary to Mr. Jefferson." Though on detached duty at the time, Lewis was technically violating army regulations by wearing his hair in a queue, looped up behind his head. The two portraits known to postdate the expedition (by C. W. Peale and Saint-Mémin) show him with cropped and unpowdered hair.

old-fashioned queue until returning to active duty for the expedition. Clark wore a queue even longer, growing his hair out again after the expedition. It was a sign of social class and values, as well as a personal statement.[61]

As the Corps traveled west, they gradually became reclothed in the garb of the land. Their shoes went first, replaced by moccasins. Their cloth shirts gave way to leather ones "of the Indian form." By the time they crossed the mountains, many had no socks left and had wrapped their feet in rags. But the last things to go—the pieces of clothing they treasured until forced to sell the items for food and horses on the way back—were their dress uniforms. The uniforms symbolized rank, discipline, and cultural identity. To take on the clothing of another culture was to surrender part of themselves.

This is a likeness of it; it was 2 feet 8 inches long, and weig

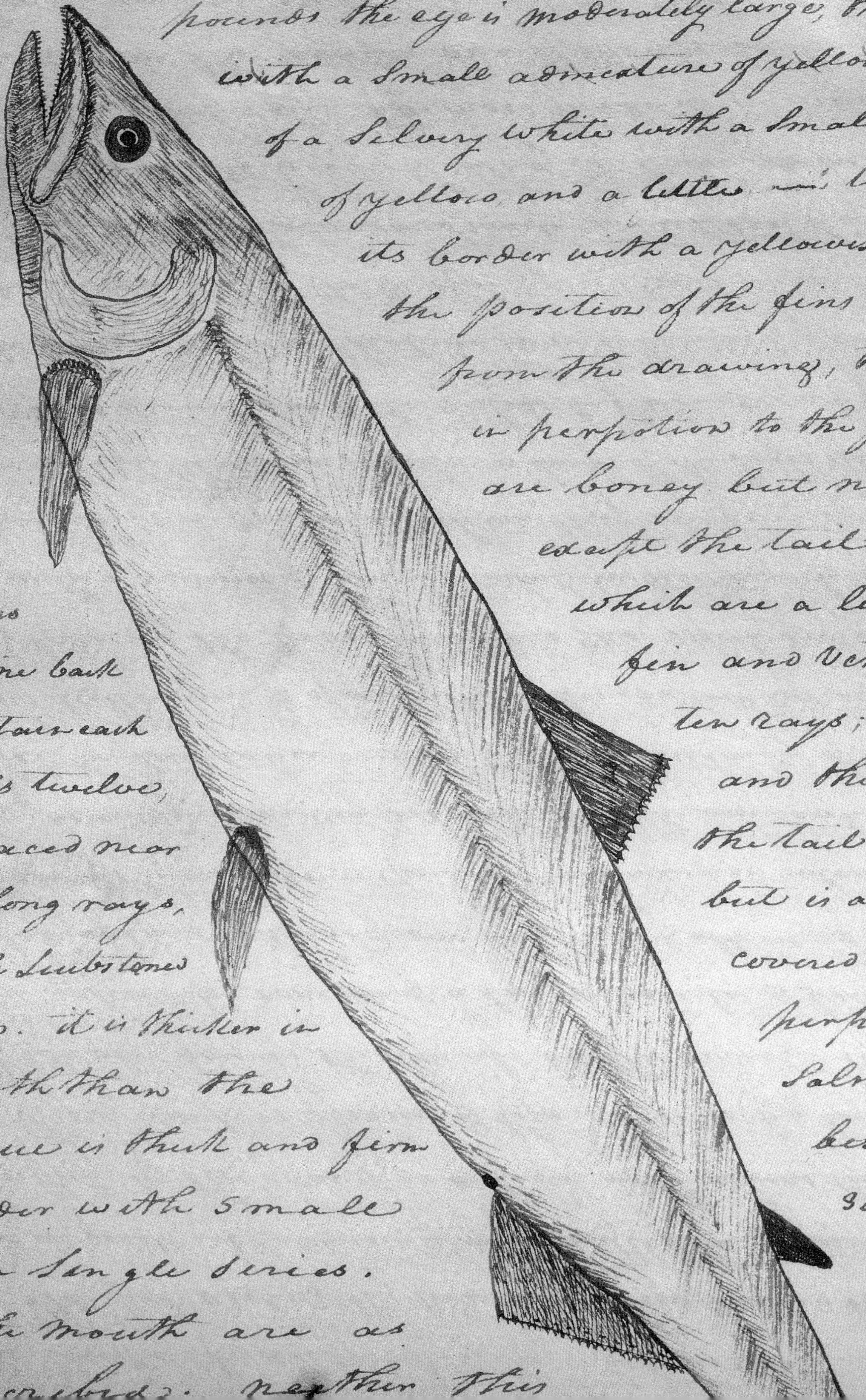

ter

pounds the eye is moderately large, the puple b

with a small admixture of yellow and the

of a Silvery white with a small admixt

of yellow and a little ... turbed nea

its border with a yellowish brow

the position of the fins may be s

from the drawing, they are sm

in perpotion to the fish. the f

are boney but not pointe

except the tail and ba

which are a little so,

fin and Ventral one

ten rays; those of

and the small f

the tail above

but is a tough f

covered with sm

perpotion to

Salmon. th

besit on ea

subulate

the Te

before

fish

fins

treme back

contain each

gills twelve,

placed near

no long rays,

able Substance

skin. it is thicker in

width than the

tongue is thick and firm

border with small

in a Single series.

the mouth are as

described. neather this

SEVEN Trade and Property

In traffic they are keen, acute, and intelligent, and they employ in all their bargains a dexterity and finesse. . . . A handful of roots, will furnish a whole morning's negotiation.

—*HISTORY OF THE EXPEDITION UNDER THE COMMAND OF CAPTAINSLEWIS AND CLARK*[1]

Toiling upstream with the canoes on the morning of August 17, Clark "saw at a distance Several Indians on horseback" coming toward him. He wrote, "The Intertrepeter & Squar who were before me at Some distance danced for the joyful Sight, and She made signs to me that they were her nation, as I aproached nearer them descovered one of Capt Lewis party With them dressed in their Dress."[2]

There followed a series of joyful meetings. "Every thing appeared to asstonish those people," Clark wrote: "the appearance of the men, their arms, the Canoes, the Clothing my black Servent & the Segassity of Capt Lewis's Dog." Lewis added a performance of his own: "I also shot my air-gun which was so perfectly incomprehensible that they immediately denominated it the great medicine." The men of the Corps were no less bemused by Shoshone customs. "They take us round the neck and S[q]weze us in token of friendship . . . in Stead of Shakeing hands," John Ordway noted.[3]

For Sacagawea, the homecoming alternated between "extravagant joy" and tragedy. Scarcely had she come to the Shoshone camp when a childhood friend recognized her, and "they embraced with the most tender affection." An even more emotional reunion followed. When the captains called her in to translate to the chief, Cameahwait, "she recognised her brother. She instantly jumped up, and ran and

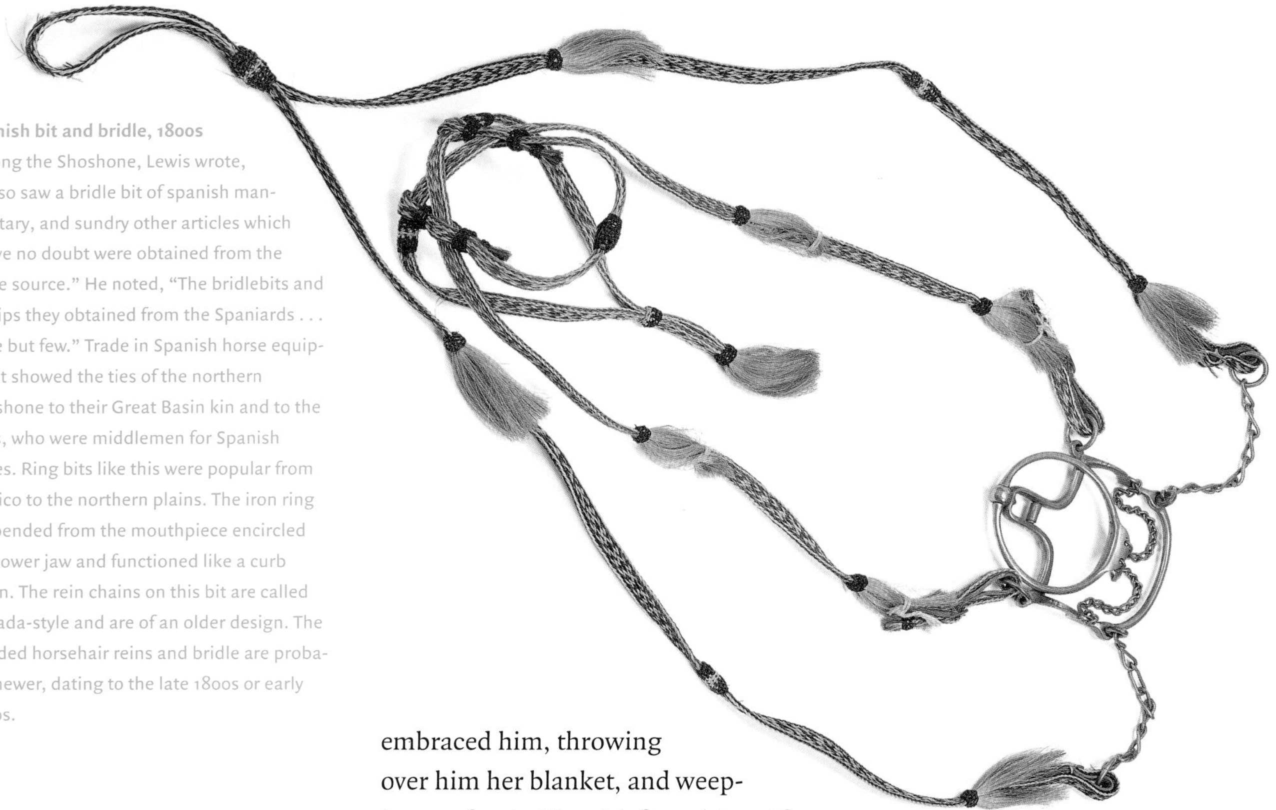

Spanish bit and bridle, 1800s
Among the Shoshone, Lewis wrote, "I also saw a bridle bit of spanish manufactary, and sundry other articles which I have no doubt were obtained from the same source." He noted, "The bridlebits and stirrips they obtained from the Spaniards . . . were but few." Trade in Spanish horse equipment showed the ties of the northern Shoshone to their Great Basin kin and to the Utes, who were middlemen for Spanish wares. Ring bits like this were popular from Mexico to the northern plains. The iron ring suspended from the mouthpiece encircled the lower jaw and functioned like a curb chain. The rein chains on this bit are called Nevada-style and are of an older design. The braided horsehair reins and bridle are probably newer, dating to the late 1800s or early 1900s.

embraced him, throwing over him her blanket, and weeping profusely. The chief was himself moved, though not in the same degree. After some conversation between them she resumed her seat and attempted to interpret for us, but . . . she was frequently interrupted by her tears." Soon after, she learned that all her family members were dead except two brothers and a nephew. The man to whom she had been betrothed as a child "claimed her as his wife but said that as she had had a child by another man . . . he did not want her." She had returned only to find herself an outsider in her own world.[4]

Camp Fortunate, as they called it, was a place of fluid identities, underlined by a series of name changes. No Shoshone person expected to go through life unchanged, and that fact was reflected in their names. "These people have many names in the course of their lives," Lewis wrote, "particularly if they become distinguished characters. for it seems that every important event by which they happen to distinguish themselves intitles them to claim another name." The chief already had at least two names: Cameahwait (translated as "Come and Smoke" by Clark and as "One Who Never Walks" by Lewis); and Too-et´-te-con´-e, his war name, meaning "Black Gun." Soon after meeting Clark, Cameahwait exchanged names as a mark of respect, so that Clark became Cameahwait. Although Sacagawea's original name is not known, a Shoshone tradition states that she was renamed Wadze-wipe, meaning "Lost Woman," after her return. But it was not her only new name. Besides her status as Madame Charbonneau, Sacagawea had been rechristened as "Janey" by Clark, who had also given her baby, Jean-Baptiste, the name "Pompey"—"Pomp" for short. To Clark, the baby's name was a joking reference to the Roman general. But "Pompey" was, coincidentally, also a name in Shoshone, meaning "head" or "leader." A woman who had two Shoshone names, a French name, a Hidatsa name, and an English name, and who had a baby with a French name and a Latin/Shoshone name, embodied the blended selves of those on the frontier.[5]

The name change that altered all their plans was not given to a person but

Page 212: White salmon trout (detail from a journal page), 1806. See page 223.

to a river. Finally able to converse through a translator, the captains plied Cameahwait with questions about their route. The news was, in Clark's word, "alarming." The river beyond the Continental Divide, which Lewis had been calling the Columbia, was in fact what is today called the Lemhi River, a tributary of the Salmon. The Salmon River flowed westward till it was swallowed by "vast mountains of rock eternally covered with snow." No boats could survive on it; "perpendicular and even juting rocks so closely hemned in the river that there was no possibilyte of passing along the shore; . . . the river was beat into perfect foam as far as the eye could reach." Southward lay only "horrors and obstructions"—deserts, hostile tribes, and land devoid of food. To the north was a mountain pass, but "the road was a very bad one. . . . there was no game in that part of the mountains which were broken rockey and so thickly covered with timber that they could scarcely pass." Despite the forbidding report, Clark decided that north was the route they should take. He said, "If the Indians could pass these mountains with their women and Children . . . we could also pass them."[6] In an act that was simultaneously a show of bravado and an admission of defeat, they renamed the Salmon as "Lewis's River." Never again would any of its tributaries be mistaken for the Columbia.

Reconciled to traveling by land, they set about acquiring packhorses. Lewis had had his eye on the elegant Shoshone horses for some time. "Drewyer who had had a good view of their horses estimated them at 400," he wrote. "Most of them are fine horses. indeed many of them would make a figure on the South side of James River or the land of fine horses."[7] They persuaded the puzzled Shoshone to help them carry their baggage and equipment forty miles across the Divide to the Lemhi River—not knowing that a far easier overland route lay straight north from Camp Fortunate. Once across, Lewis set about bargaining in earnest. "The natives do not wish to part with any more of their horses without gitting a higher price for them," Ordway observed. "The most of those he has bought as yet was for about 3 or 4 dollars worth of marchandize. . . . we have now in all 25, but the most of them have Sore backs. three men set at makeing pack Saddles."[8]

They hired a Shoshone guide, to whom they gave an English name: Old Toby. "The Guide apeared to be a very friendly intelligent old man. . . . he was better informed of the country than any of them," Lewis recorded. It was almost September by the time the two groups parted—

Buffalo-hair rope, pre-1846
Lewis described buffalo-hair ropes used by the Shoshone: "The usual caparison of the Shoshone horse is a halter and saddle. the 1st consists either of a round plated or twisted cord of six or seven strands of buffaloe's hair, or a throng of raw hide. . . . these cords of bufaloe's hair are about the size of a man's finger and remarkably strong. this is the kind of halter which is prefered by them. the halter . . . is always of great length and is never taken from the neck of the horse." He also observed Shoshone horsemen using only a line tied around the horse's lower jaw in lieu of reins and a bridle. Hudson's Bay Company fur traders also learned to make ropes using the long hair that grew between the buffaloes' horns. This coil is Nez Perce.

Mule Equipment, c. 1837
"The Indians value their mules very highly," Lewis wrote of the Shoshone. "A good mule can not be obtained for less than three and sometimes four horses. . . . their mules generally are the finest I ever saw." On August 24 he managed to purchase a mule for a price "quite double that given for the horses, the fellow who sold him made a merit of having bestoed me one of his mules. I consider this mule a great acquisition." The Shoshone told him the mules were acquired "from the Spaniards." This sketch by Alfred J. Miller shows the type of pack saddle made by Euro-Americans in the West, using two boards and four cross-pieces. When the men of the Corps set about making them, Lewis wrote, "We find ourselves at a loss for nails and boards." For nails, they substituted rawhide thongs; for boards, they decided "to cut off the blades of our oars and use the plank of some boxes which have heretofore held other articles."

the expedition setting out north down the Lemhi and Salmon Valleys and the Shoshone east to their long-delayed buffalo hunt on the Missouri. Cameahwait's band had barely reached the plains before they were attacked again, this time by a Hidatsa war party.[9]

The route the Corps had chosen was a hard one. Clark wrote, "We were obliged to Cut a road, over rockey hill Sides where our horses were in [per]pitial danger of Slipping to Ther certain distruction & up & Down Steep hills, where Several horses fell, Some turned over, and other Sliped down Steep hill Sides, one horse Crippeled & 2 gave out. with the greatest dificuelty risque &c. we made five miles." As they crossed over Lost Trail Pass, Ordway complained about the weather: "The Snow over our mockasons in places. we had nothing but a little pearched corn to eat. . . . our fingers aked with the cold."[10]

They descended again into the gentle valley of the Bitterroot River, which runs north-south between two mountain ranges on the western edge of present-day Montana. Soon, unknown to them, they were objects of surveillance by the alert inhabitants of the area. The Salish people, misleadingly named "Flatheads" by Lewis and Clark, were originally from the northern plateau region west of the mountains. They shared a lifestyle, but not a language, with their Shoshone neighbors, with whom they lived in peace. In later years, they remembered the expedition well: "One day two scouts came back to report that they had seen some human beings who were very different from any they had known," Pierre Pichette later told the story. "The chief immediately sent his warriors to meet the strange men and to bring them to camp safely. 'Do no harm to them,' he warned his men. 'Do no harm to them at all.'"[11]

Joseph Whitehouse first became aware of the tribe when the Corps "Arrived at a large encampment of the flat head nation of Indians." He wrote: "They had about 40 lodges, & had between four & five hundred horses feeding in the Valley or plain; which lay in our view. These Indians received us as friends, & appeared to be glad to see us. . . . When Captains Lewis & Clark arrived they spread white Robes over their shoulders and smoaked with them."[12]

The Salish language aroused the scientific interest of the visitors. With typically slapdash treatment of his own native tongue, Clark called it "a gugling kind of languaje Spoken much thro the Throught." Whitehouse added: "We could not talk with them as much as we wish, for all that we Say has to go through 6 [5] languages before it gits to them. . . . they appear to us to have an Empeddiment in their Speech or a brogue. . . . We take these Savages to be the Welch Indians if their be any Such from the Language. So Capt. Lewis took down the Names of everry thing in their Language, in order that it may be found out . . . whether they Sprang or origenated first from the welch or not."[13]

The Salish also had horses to spare. After purchasing a number of them,

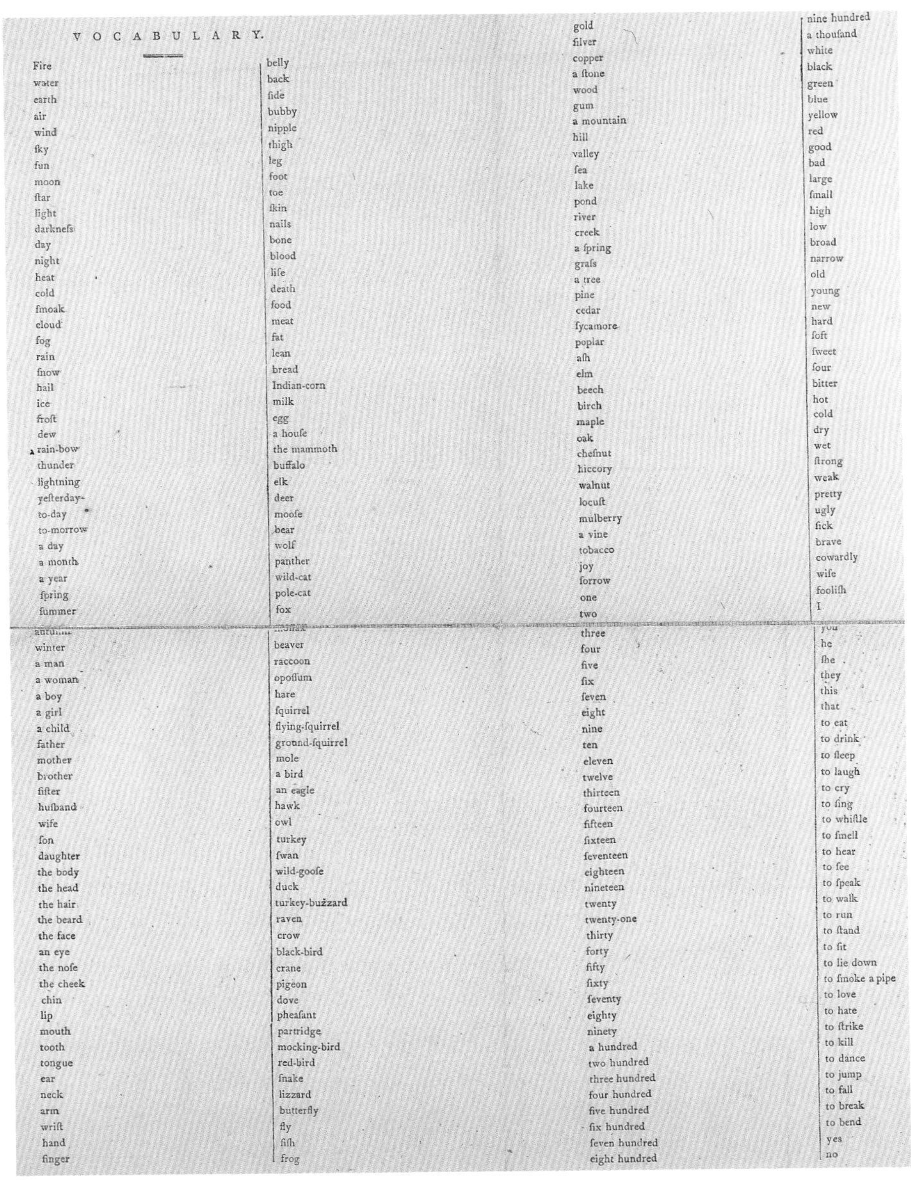

VOCABULARY.

Fire
water
earth
air
wind
ſky
ſun
moon
ſtar
light
darkneſs
day
night
heat
cold
ſmoak
cloud
fog
rain
ſnow
hail
ice
froſt
dew
rain-bow
thunder
lightning
yeſterday
to-day
to-morrow
a day
a month
a year
ſpring
ſummer
[illegible]
winter
a man
a woman
a boy
a girl
a child
father
mother
brother
ſiſter
huſband
wife
ſon
daughter
the body
the head
the hair
the beard
the face
an eye
the noſe
the cheek
chin
lip
mouth
tooth
tongue
ear
neck
arm
wriſt
hand
finger

belly
back
ſide
bubby
nipple
thigh
leg
foot
toe
ſkin
nails
bone
blood
life
death
food
meat
fat
lean
bread
Indian-corn
milk
egg
a houſe
the mammoth
buffalo
elk
deer
mooſe
bear
wolf
panther
wild-cat
pole-cat
fox
[illegible]
beaver
raccoon
opoſſum
hare
ſquirrel
flying-ſquirrel
ground-ſquirrel
mole
a bird
an eagle
hawk
owl
turkey
ſwan
wild-gooſe
duck
turkey-buzzard
raven
crow
black-bird
crane
pigeon
dove
pheaſant
partridge
mocking-bird
red-bird
ſnake
lizzard
butterfly
fly
fiſh
frog

gold
ſilver
copper
a ſtone
wood
gum
a mountain
hill
valley
ſea
lake
pond
river
creek
a ſpring
graſs
a tree
pine
cedar
ſycamore
poplar
aſh
elm
beech
birch
maple
oak
cheſnut
hiccory
walnut
locuſt
mulberry
a vine
tobacco
joy
ſorrow
one
two
three
four
five
ſix
ſeven
eight
nine
ten
eleven
twelve
thirteen
fourteen
fifteen
ſixteen
ſeventeen
eighteen
nineteen
twenty
twenty-one
thirty
forty
fifty
ſixty
ſeventy
eighty
ninety
a hundred
two hundred
three hundred
four hundred
five hundred
ſix hundred
ſeven hundred
eight hundred

nine hundred
a thouſand
white
black
green
blue
yellow
red
good
bad
large
ſmall
high
low
broad
narrow
old
young
new
hard
ſoft
ſweet
ſour
bitter
hot
cold
dry
wet
ſtrong
weak
pretty
ugly
ſick
brave
cowardly
wiſe
fooliſh
I
you
he
ſhe
they
this
that
to eat
to drink
to ſleep
to laugh
to cry
to ſing
to whiſtle
to ſmell
to hear
to ſee
to ſpeak
to walk
to run
to ſtand
to ſit
to lie down
to ſmoke a pipe
to love
to hate
to ſtrike
to kill
to dance
to jump
to fall
to break
to bend
yes
no

Vocabulary form, c. 1790–92
This form was devised by Thomas Jefferson for compiling a comparative vocabulary of Indian languages, in order to shed light on where the tribes originated. Since he considered language to be the portion of speech that could be represented by letters on paper, Jefferson did not include the discursive motions that many Indian tribes used. Lewis collected twenty-three vocabularies, commissioning traders to compile some of the translations and filling in the rest himself. The North West Company trader Charles Mackenzie observed Lewis collecting a vocabulary at the Mandan villages. "The two Frenchmen, who happened to be the medium of information, had warm disputes upon the meaning of every word that was taken down by the expedition. As the Indians could not well comprehend the intention of recording their words, they concluded that the Americans had a wicked design upon their country."

Route map of the Lolo Trail, 1805

Along the difficult route through the Rocky Mountains, Clark named landmarks for the experiences of the Corps. His map shows Killed Colt Creek (bottom), where the party ate one of their horses, and Hungary Creek (top), where they didn't. Both are tributaries of today's Lochsa River. The "Snow Mountains" are the present Bitterroot Range in Idaho.

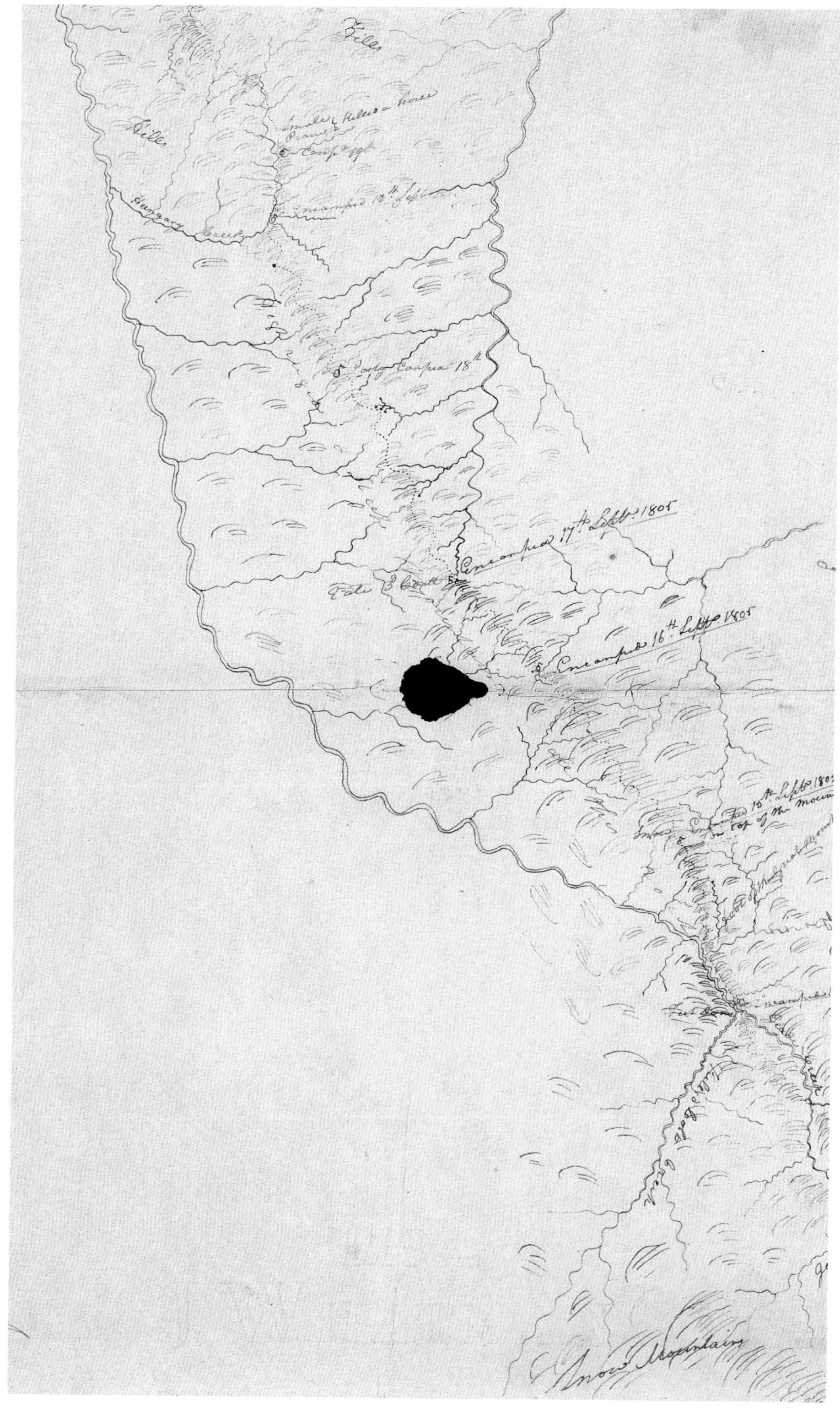

the men of the expedition continued on north to a spot they named "Traveler's Rest," where a creek flowed into the Bitterroot River from the west, its pleasant valley leading up to a pass in the mountains. Today, the path westward up Traveler's Rest Creek is called the Lolo Trail. When the men set out up the trail, they were leaving U.S. territory behind—though neither Lewis nor Clark mentioned that fact.

Nothing in their experience of mountains had prepared them for the Bitterroot Range of the Rockies. Two days up the trail, Clark wrote: "The road through this hilley Countrey is verry bad passing over hills & thro' Steep hollows, over falling timber &c. &c. continued on & passed Some most intolerable

Crossing the Bitter Root Mountains, 1855
The steep and snowy crossing of the Bitterroots by foot and pack train was repeated fifty years later by part of the expedition under Isaac I. Stevens. The artist of this scene, Gustav Sohon, was part of that group. This shows Look Out Pass, north of the Lolo Pass, which Lewis and Clark had taken.

road on the Sides of the Steep Stoney mountains. . . . Party and horses much fatigued." On the third day they paused for respite at "a warm Spring which run from a ledge of rocks and nearly boiled." Ordway recorded: "A little dam was fixed and had been used for a bathing place. we drank a little of the water and washed our faces in it."[14]

"Here the road leaves the river to the left and assends a *mountain* winding in every direction to get up the Steep assents," Clark wrote. "High ruged mountains in every direction as far as I could See." On September 16 the weather turned against them. "When we awoke this morning," Whitehouse said, "to our great Surprise we were covred with Snow which had fallen about 2 Inches the latter part of last night. . . . Some of the men without Socks raped rags on their feet. . . . Set out without any thing to eat." The snow continued falling. That day Patrick Gass wrote: "Proceeded over the most terrible mountains I ever beheld. . . . the snow fell about 10 inches deep." By the time they camped that night, Clark testified to their misery: "I have been wet and as cold in every part as I ever was in my life."[15]

Soon, hunger added to their hardships. "Killed a fiew Pheasents which was not Sufficient for our Supper," Clark said, "which compelled us to kill Something. a coalt being the most useless part of our Stock he fell a Prey to our appetites." By the next day, Lewis was anxiously inventorying their stores. "We dined & suped on a skant proportion of portable soupe, a few canesters of which, a little bears oil and about 20 lbs. of candles form our stock of provision."[16]

To find how far the mountains went on, Clark took a few men and scouted ahead. On the tenth day after leaving Traveler's Rest, they saw a welcome sight: "Decended the mountain to a leavel pine Countrey . . . in which I found maney Indian lodges. . . . I met 3 *Indian* boys . . . gave them Small pieces of ribin & Sent them forward to the village."[17] They had come to the land of the Nez Perce, who called themselves Ni míi puu, or the people.

Tin cup, 1800s
In crossing the Bitterroots, the Corps was forced to rely on portable soup, a dried broth purchased by Lewis in Philadelphia; they probably drank it from tin cups like this, standard issue for army recruits. Lewis started out enthusiastic about the soup, declaring it "one of the most essential articles in this preparation [for the expedition]." He purchased 193 pounds of it, spending $289.50. The men were less enthusiastic. Patrick Gass wrote, "Some of the men did not relish this soup." John Ordway said, "The Soup did not Satisfy." Although the purchase of tin cups is not recorded, the explorers had more than they needed, since they cached some, along with other foods and tools, at the Marias River.

Woman's dress, early to mid-1800s
According to Clark, Nez Perce women dressed "in a Shirt of Ibex [sheep] Skins which reach quite down to their anckles with out a girdle." He added, "Their heads are not ornemented, their Shirts are ornemented with quilled Brass, Small peces of Brass Cut into different forms, Beeds, Shells & curios bones &c." This style of dress, called a "tail dress," is most likely the type he was seeing. A tail dress was made from two deer, elk, or Rocky Mountain sheep skins positioned with the tail at the top and seamed up the sides and across the shoulders. The yoke was formed of the hind part of the skin folded over from the shoulder seams, with the tail fur left on as a triangular decoration at the neck. On this one, the tail is pieced into the yoke. The lack of ornamentation and the style of construction suggest that this is an early piece. The brass bead on the tail and the piece of abalone shell tied to one fringe are both decorations available to the Nez Perce in Lewis and Clark's day.

"DO THEM NO HURT"

Up to this time, the Native peoples on the expedition's path had belonged to the general cultural division of Plains Indians. Though they varied in many respects, all shared common traditions formed around the resources of their land: the buffalo and antelope herds and the cultivation of corn, tobacco, squash, and beans. None of these resources reached beyond the Rockies, and neither did Plains Indian culture. On the plateau—the rolling, arid volcanic plain between the Cascades and the Rockies—the people formed their lives around the seasonal runs of salmon and the harvesting of root crops such as camas and cous. They lived in long, communal lodges built like sheds of woven reed mats, furnished with bags and baskets twined from the hardy grasses of their prairies.

What they did share with Plains tribes were horses, which had arrived from the Spanish settlements in the Southwest over the previous century. But horses had not led to a revolution in lifestyle on the plateau, as they had on the plains, since there were no buffalo herds to follow. Instead, Plateau peoples used horses for wealth and weapons. Their new mobility led to increased trade and war. Prosperity and insecurity resulted.

The hungry explorers stumbled out of the Rocky Mountains at an anxious moment for the Nez Perce band at Weippe Prairie. All the leaders and young men had gone on a war party; the women, children, and old men had taken refuge deep in the mountains. When well-armed strangers descended on them from the least likely direction—the east—they did not know whether to prepare for attack. "A man Came out to meet me with great Caution," Clark wrote. "Great numbers of women geathered around me with much apparent Signs of fear." Yet despite their inability to communicate, the two groups got along. "We were treated kindly in their way and continued with them all night."[18]

The Nez Perce long remembered the incident, but not the same way that Clark did. To them, a critical part was played by a woman named Watkuweis. Years before, she had been captured by the Blackfeet and sold to a Plains Indian tribe, in whose company she met Euro-Americans in Canada. They had treated her kindly, so when similar people appeared from the east, she told her tribe: "These are the people who helped me! Do them no hurt!"[19]

The next day, Clark apparently visited the camp where Watkuweis lived with four other women. "Those people were glad to See us & gave us drid Sammon one had formerly been taken by the Minitarries of the north [Atsina] & Seen white men." Meanwhile, the rest of the travelers, under Lewis, were still struggling out of the mountains. Later that day, when they arrived in sight of the alpine meadow where the now-reassured Nez Perce were camped, Lewis wrote, "The pleasure I now felt in having tryumphed over the rocky Mountains and decending once more to a level and fertile country . . . can be more readily conceived than expressed."[20]

Their arrival was like a festival. "The planes appeared covered with Spectators viewing the White men and the articles which we had," Clark said. "The *Cho-pun-nish* or Pierced nose Indians are Stout likeley men, handsom women, and verry dressey in their way." Whitehouse reinforced the image of crowds and finery: "These natives live well are verry kind and well dressed. . . . they are numerous and talk loud & confused. they live [in] much comfort in their villages."[21]

Woman's hat, pre-1876
Lewis wrote of the Nez Perce, "They also wear a cap or cup on the head formed of beargrass and cedar bark." He or Clark apparently picked some up, since two of the artifacts they donated to Peale's Museum were a "Cap, worn by the women of the Plains of Columbia," and "A Cap worn by the natives of Columbia River, and the Pacific Ocean." This one, made in the traditional style used across the plateau, was purchased from Kow-kow-hi-a-tum on the Nez Perce Reservation as part of Indian Agent John B. Monteith's effort to assemble a Nez Perce display for the 1876 Centennial Exposition.

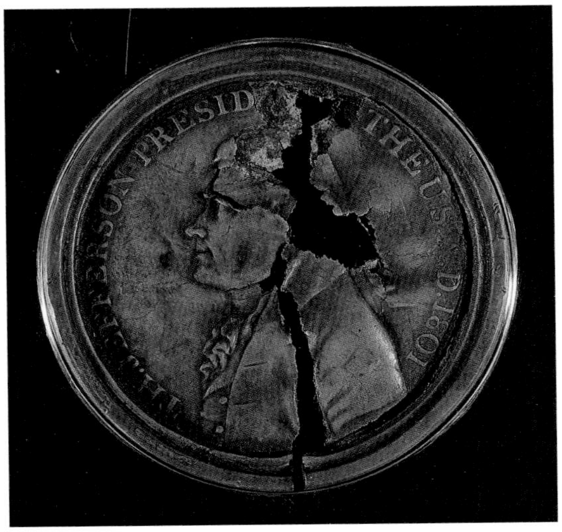

Peace medal, 1801
This is one of the peace medals given out by Lewis and Clark on the Columbia River. According to one story, it was found on an island in the Columbia near the mouth of the Walla Walla River, so it has often been associated with the Wallawalla chief Yellept. However, Lewis and Clark were handing out medals with great abandon on the Columbia as they met chiefs of the many small tribes. On the way downriver, they gave out three at the mouth of the Snake on October 16, another on October 18, Yellept's on October 19, and four at The Dalles on October 24, 25, and 26. On the way back, they gave two medals to the "Pishquitpah" (possibly Yakima) on April 25 and two to secondary chiefs of the Wallawalla on April 29. They implied that they gave Yellept a second, larger, medal as well. This could be any one of the many "small size" medals they passed out. It is the smallest size of Jefferson medal, but the Washington medals were even smaller.

The sudden abundance of strange foods and strange bacteria took a toll on the travelers, however. "8 or 9 men Sick," Clark said. "Capt Lewis Sick all Complain of a *Lax* & heaviness at the Stomack, I gave rushes Pills to Several. . . . Capt. Lewis Scercely able to ride on a jentle horse which was furnished by the Chief, Several men So unwell that they were Compelled to lie on the Side of the road for Some time others obliged to be put on horses."[22]

They did not linger long. Weippe Prairie was on the upper waters of the Clearwater River, which flows westward out of the Bitterroot Range till it joins the Snake River on the boundary of what is now Idaho and Washington. Despite its rocky bed and rapid current, the captains were eager to be once again traveling by water. "Set out early and proceeded on down the river to a bottom opposit the forks," Clark wrote on September 26. "I had the axes distributed and handled and men apotned [apportioned] ready to commence building canoes on tomorrow, our axes are Small & badly Calculated to build Canoes of the large Pine." Nevertheless, with some help from the Indians, they had new canoes ready for launching by October 6. It was time to leave behind their horses, which they did in perfect confidence that the Nez Perce would care for them over the winter and return them the next spring. Whitehouse said: "Got up our horses and cropped their fore mane, and branded them with a Sturrup Iron on the near fore Shoulder, So that we may know them again at our return. a Chief who we Intended leaveing our horses with has engaged to go on with us." Their new guide was "a Cherfull man of about 65" named Walamottinin, which they translated as "Twisted Hair."[23]

The Clearwater was not an easy stream to navigate. "One of the canoes Struck a rock in the middle of the rapid," Ordway wrote soon after setting out, "and cracked hir So that it filled with water. the waves roared over the rocks and

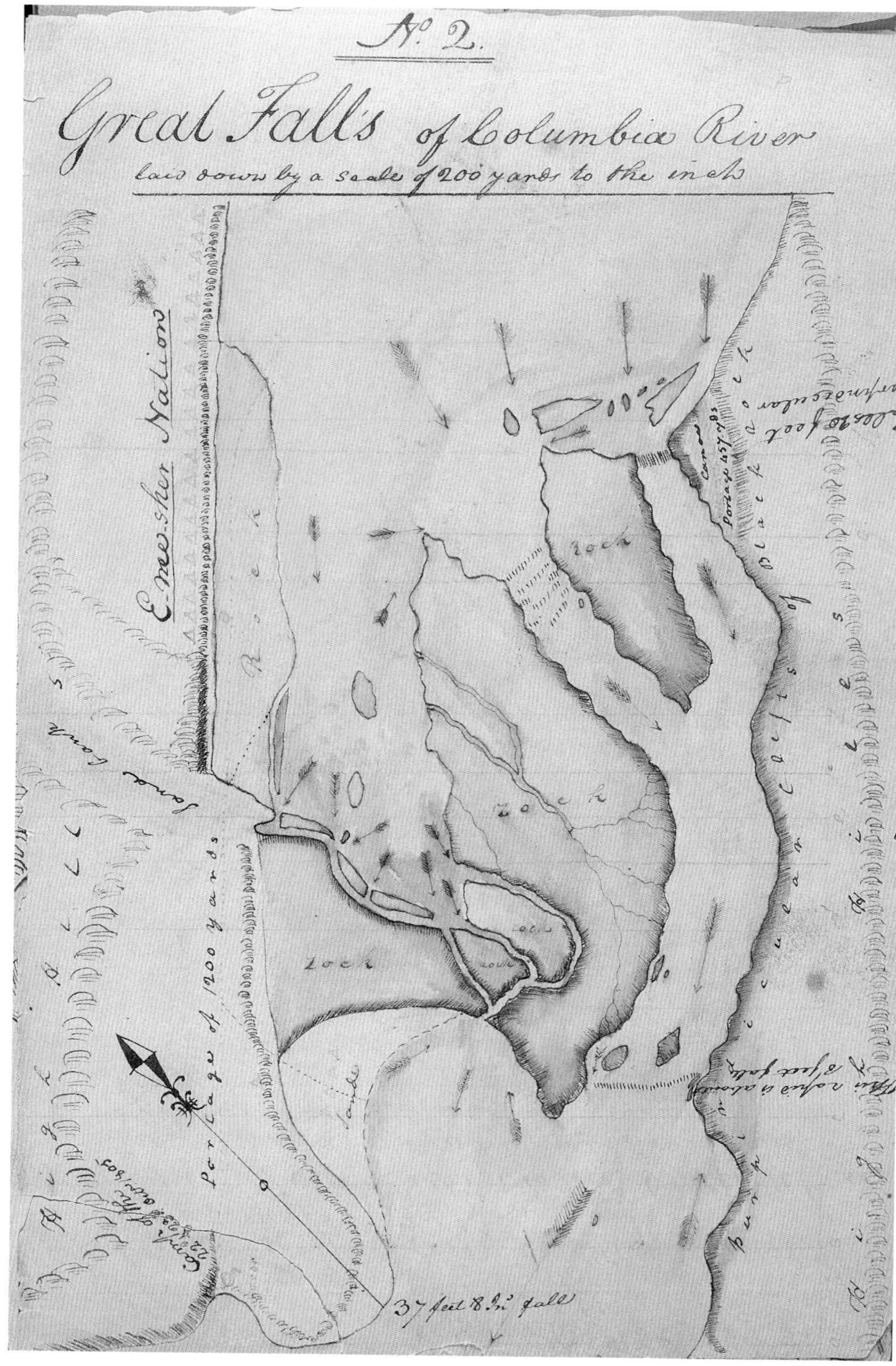

Great Falls of Columbia River, 1805
This map shows Celilo Falls, which were the uppermost falls on the Columbia and are now submerged by The Dalles Dam. This was the most productive salmon fishery on the river, since at this place the salmon (who ate nothing on their upstream migrations) were still fat but the climate was dry enough to preserve the meat without smoking. Each good fishing site on the myriad channels had a name, many of which conveyed information about how it was used, such as *sapawilalatat-pama* ("for netting jumping fish"), *tayxayt-pama* ("for spear fishing"), *qiyakawas* ("gaffing place"), and *swaycas* ("long pole," for long-handled dip nets). The rocks and islands were often named for the families that used them. Clark recorded no names because he thought of the falls mainly as an obstruction to navigation.

OPPOSITE, BOTTOM: ***The Dalles, 1860***
This lithograph shows the entry to the Narrows of The Dalles, just below Celilo Falls, as seen from upriver. Clark described it: "A tremendious black rock Presented itself high and Steep appearing to choke up the river. . . . the Current was drawn with great velocity to the Lar[boar]d Side of this rock at which place I heard a great roreing. . . . the water of this great river is compressed into a Chanel between two rocks not exceeding *forty five* yards wide." Despite the "horrid appear-ance" of the channel below, the travelers shot the rapids. The canoe shown here is the style used on the plateau, and the houses are the mat lodges used in summer.

Some of the men could not Swim. their they Stayed in this doleful Situation untill we unloaded one of the other canoes and went and released them. 2 Indians went in a canoe to their assistance also." Plagued by similar accidents, it took the men several days to reach the mouth of the Clearwater. "Arived at a large Southerly fork which is the one we were on with the *Snake* or *So-So-nee* nation," Clark wrote on October 10. He was only partly right. The river they had followed for a short time in the mountains was a branch of a tributary of the Snake, whose wide, curving valley through southern Idaho would later be a well-traveled portion of the Oregon Trail. Nevertheless, Clark confidently named the Snake "Lewis's River." He noted: "The Countrey about the forks is an open Plain on either Side. . . . The Indians Came down all the Cou[r]ses of this river on each side on horses to view us."[24]

THE GREAT MART OF TRADE

The Corps had passed into the thickly populated plateau region. In the next two months they would meet as many different tribes as they had encountered in the previous two years. Their journals would start registering complaints about their lack of privacy; from September 20 to November 5, they spent not a single night alone. The area offered a glimpse of how most of America had been before the arrival of Europeans and their sicknesses. Disease had passed through the plateau, but it had not taken as bad a toll as elsewhere. The original social organization still survived—a network of interconnected village groups, each considering itself a separate tribe. Depopulation and the need to unite against outsiders had not yet led to political reorganization.[25]

The mid-Columbia Valley was populated by people speaking Sahaptin languages, people from whom the Palouse, Yakima, Wallawalla, Cayuse, and Umatilla nations would form. The members of the expedition were lucky to have their volunteer Nez Perce ambassador, Twisted Hair, who traveled ahead. He "proceeded . . . to inform those bands of our approach and friendly intentions towards all nations." With such an introduction, they were as popular, and as novel, as a traveling circus. Over and over as they passed down the Snake to its mouth, Clark wrote, "Great numbers of Indians Came down in Canoes to view us."[26]

It was October 16 when they finally reached the Columbia, flowing down from the northwest. That evening, "a Chief came . . . at the head of about 200 men Singing and beeting on their drums Stick and keeping time to the musik, they formed a half circle around us and Sung for Some time, we gave them all Smoke, and Spoke to their Chiefs as well as we could by Signs." Visiting one of their villages, Clark had the impression of prosperity and order. "Those people appears to live in a State of comparitive happiness: they take a greater Share [in the] labor of the woman, than is common among Savage tribes, and as I am informd. [are] Content with one wife. . . . Those people respect the aged with veneration." As for their livelihood, he wrote: "The number of dead Salmon on the Shores & floating in the river is incrediable to Say and at this Season they have only to collect the fish Split them open and dry them on their Scaffolds on which they have great numbers."[27]

Near the mouth of the Walla Walla River they met a band that may have

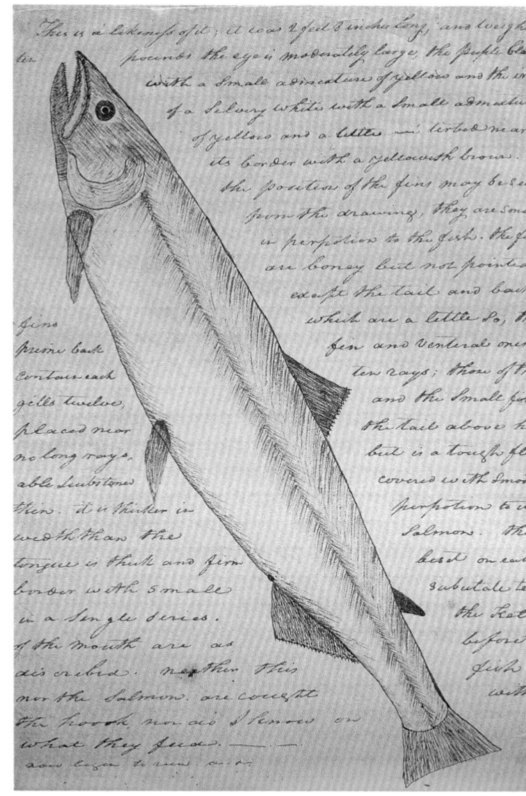

White salmon trout, 1806

What the buffalo were to the Plains tribes, the salmon were to the Columbia River tribes: the basis of their economy and central to their beliefs. Different species of salmon came upriver in pulses throughout the year: Chinook or king salmon, sockeye, coho, dog or chum, and steelhead (a trout often confused with salmon). The first runs were greeted with ceremonies, which varied with each tribe on the river, but were often overseen by men or women with salmon power. Clark observed one ceremony on April 19, 1806, at The Dalles: "There was great joy with the nativs last night in consequence of the arrival of the Salmon; one of those fish was cought, this was the harbenger of good news to them. . . . this fish was dressed and being divided into Small pieces was given to each Child in the village." The salmon shown here arrived at Fort Clatsop on March 16, 1806. The specimen was two feet, eight inches long and weighed ten pounds. Clark did not mention whether he ate it.

Below the Cascades, 1846–48
The cantilevered fishing platform and the dipnet used by this man were typical tools of the Chinookans. Clark described the platform as "a Stand Small Stage or warf consisting of Sticks and projecting about 10 feet into the river and about 3 feet above the water." He added, "On the extremity of this the fisherman stands with his guig or a Skooping Net which differ but little in their form [from] those Commonly used in our Country." Paul Kane, the artist of this sketch, labeled it "Fishing Columbia River."

been the Wallawalla or the closely allied Cayuse. Clark described their "great chief *Yel-lep-pit*" as "a bold handsom Indian, with a dignified countenance about 35 years of age, about 5 feet 8 inches high and well perpotiond." Clark wrote, "He requested us to delay untill the Middle of the day, that his people might Come down and See us, we excused our Selves." Continuing downriver, Clark and his companions soon met evidence that they had entered an area of frequent war raids by the Northern Paiute and Bannock. A village where he stopped seemed deserted till he entered a lodge and "found 32 persons men, women and a few children . . . in the greatest agutation, Some crying and ringing there hands, others hanging their heads." Clark added: "They said we came from the clouds &c. &c. and were not men. . . . as Soon as they Saw the Squar wife of the interperters they . . . appeared to assume new life, the sight of This Indian woman . . . confirmed those people of our friendly intentions, as no woman ever accompanies a war party."[28]

By this time Clark was looking eagerly for an indication that they were close to the Pacific, and he overestimated how far they had come. "The Countrey rises here about 200 feet above The water and is bordered with black rugid rocks. . . . I descovered a high mountain of emence hight covered with Snow, this must be one of the mountains laid down by Vancouver. . . . I take it to be Mt. St. Helens." He was wrong; it was Mount Hood. It was, however, a sign that they were nearing the Cascade range. The river was beginning to cut deep into the basalt rock as it took a final westward turn toward the sea. Around the mouth of the Deschutes River, Whitehouse saw "High clifts on each Side of dark couloured rock, and a high rock Island with rough towers of Solid rough rocks on it a verry rough roaring rapid at the Stard. Side." They had come to the beginning of the series of falls and rapids later called The Dalles.[29]

The Great Falls of the Columbia, like those of the Missouri, were not one but many. Here, the languages, arts, and customs of the Native inhabitants changed again. The expedition had come to the first Chinookan tribes, the Wishram and Wasco. The captains instantly noticed the difference: these vil-

Drying Salmon at The Dalles, Columbia River, 1848

Near Celilo Falls, Gass wrote: "They have six scaffolds of a great size for the purpose of drying their fish on. . . . We purchased from them a quantity of dried pounded fish, which they had prepared in that way for sale." Joseph Whitehouse added that the explorers bought sixteen bags of salmon; according to Clark, each bag weighed ninety to one hundred pounds. The Wishram prepared the salmon by first drying the fish on the hot rocks in the sun, then removing the bones and skins and mashing the flesh by hand; it was then spread four inches deep on mats in the sun and dried for three to four days. The cured fish was then pressed into a basket. It would keep for three years.

lagers lived in plank houses, rode in exquisitely carved canoes with high prows, and produced salmon on an almost industrial scale. "I counted 107 Stacks of dried pounded fish in different places on those rocks which must have contained 10,000 w[eight] of neet fish," Clark wrote.[30]

Not all that fish was for their own use. They were producing it, as Clark instantly recognized, "for market." The Dalles were "the Great Mart of all this Country." Here, tribes from across the western part of the continent gathered to trade products. Since the 1780s, they had even drawn European and American coastal traders into their commercial network. Goods from Alaska, Santa Fe, Boston, and China could be picked up at The Dalles.[31]

Suddenly, the Euro-Americans were no longer a novelty that inspired awe and respect. The Wishram and Wasco were middlemen who had built their wealth by controlling the flow of coastal goods into the interior and of Plateau tribes' goods to the coast. The sight of Europeans coming downriver was not entirely welcome, since they might present a threat to the Chinookan trade monopoly. Though the men of the Corps were unaware of it, they posed exactly the same challenge to Chinookan power as they had to the Sioux—and so tense relations could be expected.

"One of the old Chiefs who had accompanied us from the head of the river, informed us that he herd the Indians Say that the nation below intended to kill us," Clark recorded. "We examined all the arms &c . . . as we are at all times & places on our guard, are under no greater apprehention than is common." He was right not to be too alarmed, since it was to the Nez Perce's advantage to foment suspicion between the Europeans and the Chinookan monopolists; at the same time, ignorant of intertribal rivalries in which Europeans were pawns, he was also right not to be too confident.[32]

The expedition's immediate problem was getting around the obstructions in the river, starting with Celilo Falls. "The grand falls of the Columbia River is . . . in all 37 feet 8 Inches," Whitehouse wrote, "and has a large Rock Island in them and look Shocking. . . . we halled all canoes round the high rocks about a

Mortar, mid-1800s

One method for preparing salmon called for the dried flesh to be pounded in a wooden mortar, like this one, with a stone pestle. Mortars were also used to crush roots and berries. This one, carved from a solid block of hardwood, was traded to a shoe-repair man in The Dalles in about 1915 by its Indian owner. Stylized faces and skeletal figures with ribs showing were common motifs of early Wishram and Wasco carving.

quarter of a mile then put them in the water again. . . . the flees are now verry thick, the ground covd. with them. they troubled us verry much this day."[33]

No sooner were they past the falls than the towering shadow of an ominous black rock wall barred their way, stretching across the river with only a narrow chute to let the water through. Beyond it, the river flowed through a deep chasm between rock cliffs. Against Indian advice, Clark made the decision to shoot the rapids. A crowd gathered to watch them perish, but their luck held. "Notwithstanding the horrid appearance of this agitated gut Swelling, boiling & whorling in every direction . . . we passed Safe to the astonishment of all the Inds . . . who viewed us from the top of the rock," Clark wrote.[34]

All along The Dalles, the shores were dotted with populous villages, built there to take advantage of the salmon fisheries and to control the portages where travelers paid tolls. The people of The Dalles blended cultural traits of their Plateau Indian neighbors—such as twined grass bags and root crops—with the plank houses and elaborate carving traditions of their downstream relations. Clark wrote of one settlement: "The nativs of this village re[ce]ived

Twined bag, pre-1819
This bag matches Clark's description of the ones used for storing dried and pounded salmon at The Dalles. He called them "a speces of basket neetly made of grass and rushes of better than two feet long and one foot Diamiter, which basket is lined with the Skin of Salmon Stretched and dried for the purpose." He continued: "In theis it is pressed down as hard as is possible, when full they Secure the open part with the fish Skins across which they fasten th[r]o' the loops of the basket that part very Securely, and then on a Dry Situation they Set those baskets the Corded part up, their common Custom is to Set 7 as close as they can Stand and 5 on the top of them, and secure them with mats which is raped around them. . . . thus preserved those fish may be kept Sound and Sweet Several years." This bag was collected by the Canadian fur merchant Roderick McKenzie and donated to the American Antiquarian Society in 1819. It is larger than the typical cylinder or "Sally" bag, and the rim has braided loops like a Klickitat basket.

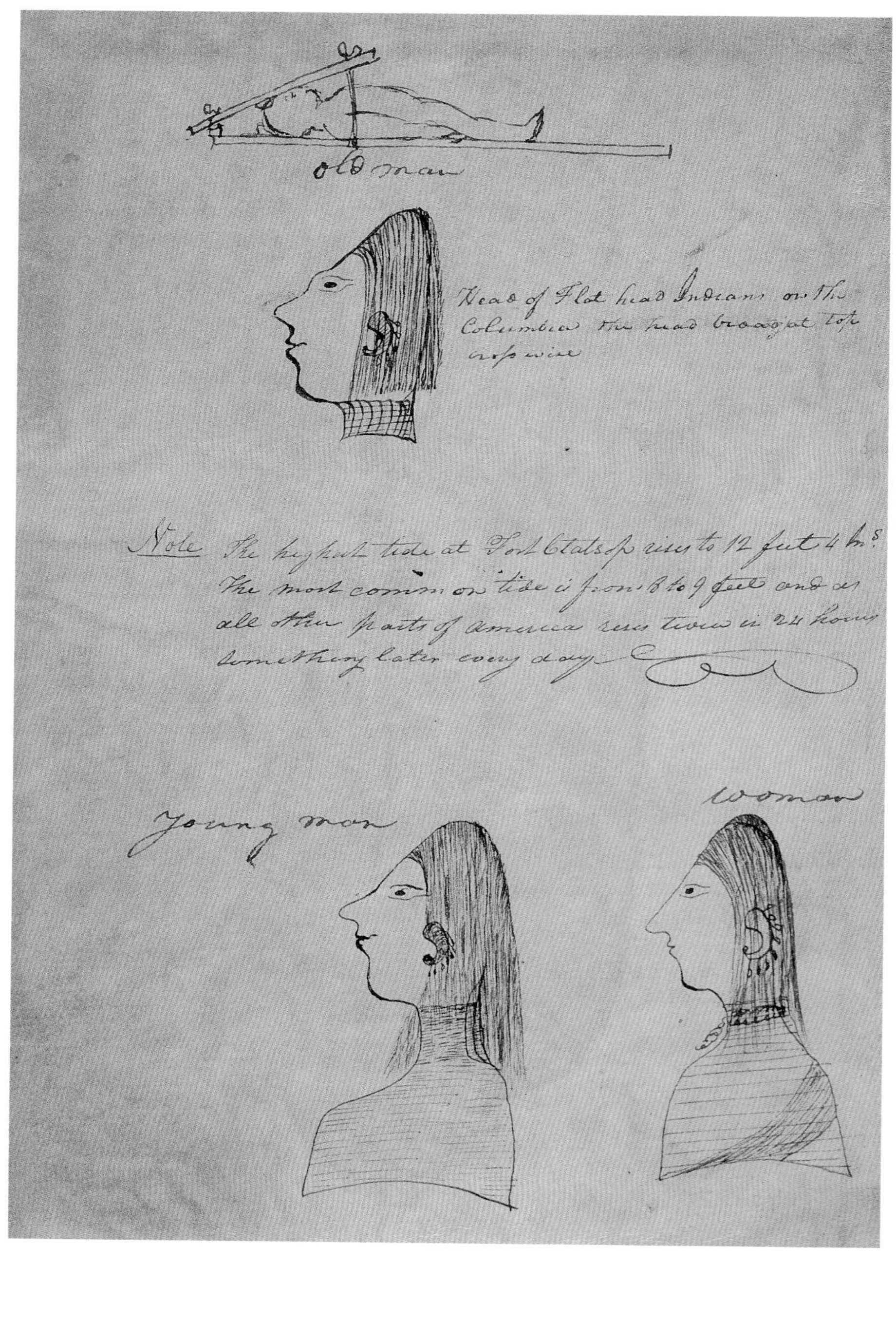

Head of Flathead Indians on the Columbia, 1806
Head flattening was done to give an aristocratic child an elegant profile. Clark here illustrated one of two methods for flattening the heads of infants. Lewis commented, "This is a custom among all the nations we have met with West of the Rocky mountains. I have observed the heads of many infants, after this singular bandage had been dismissed, or about the age of 10 or eleven months, that were not more than two inches thick about the upper edge of the forehead and reather thiner still higher. from the top of the head to the extremity of the nose is one streight line. this is done in order to give a greater width to the forehead, which they much admire."

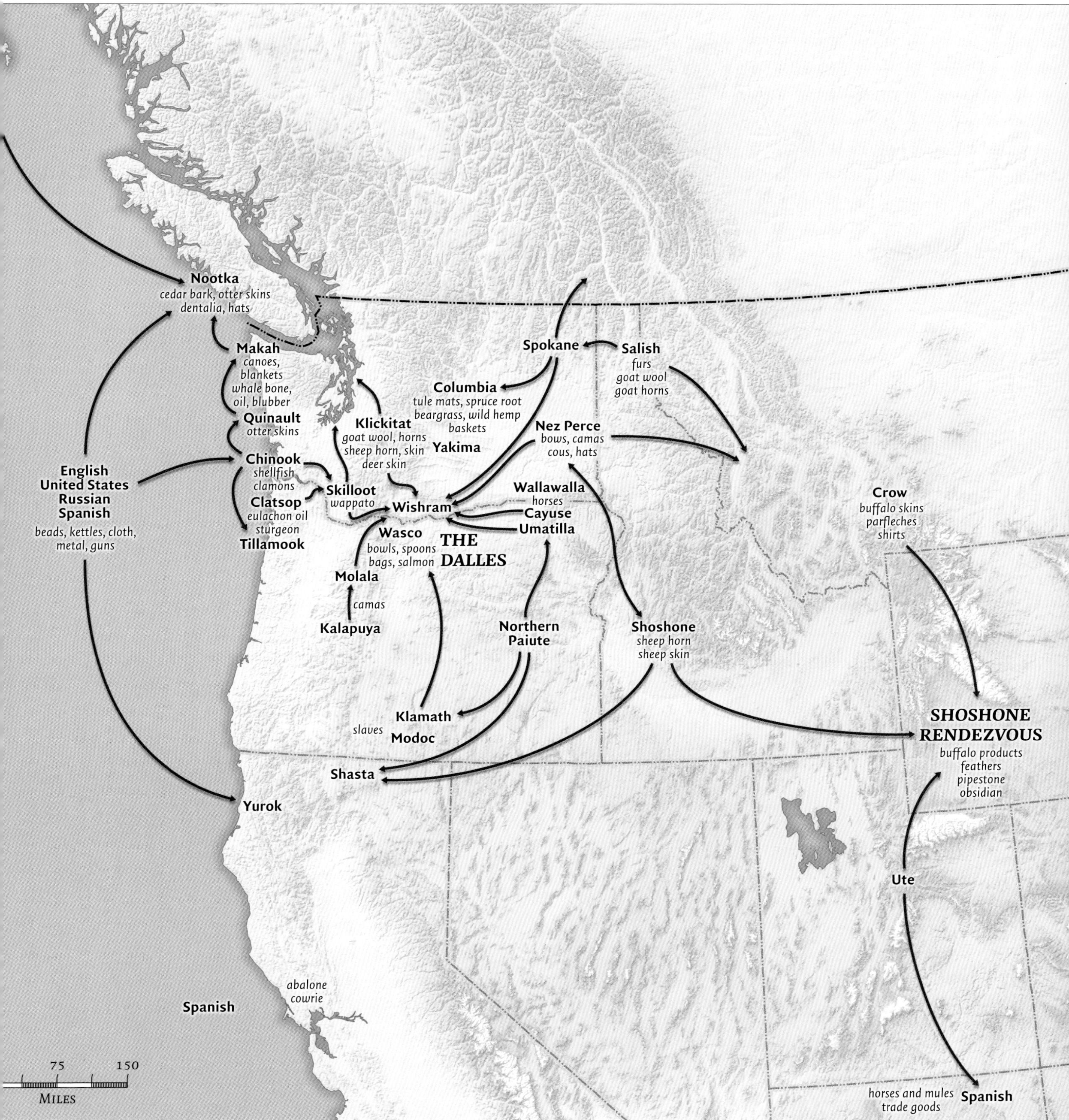

me very kindly, one of whome envited me into his house, which I found to be large and comodious, and the first wooden houses in which Indians have lived Since we left those in the vicinty of the Illinois." Meanwhile, Lewis had his eye on the sleek canoes from farther downriver. Clark said, "I observed on the beach near the Indian Lodges two Canoes butifull . . . wide in the midd[l]e and

Chinook trade network
Tribes traveled hundreds of miles to emporiums like The Dalles to exchange raw materials and finished goods, as well as news, songs, and marriage partners.

Parfleche, pre-1889

The Yakima, who lived on the northern Columbia and Yakima Rivers, used materials from the plains to make objects unlike any made by Plains Indian tribes. They purchased processed buffalo hides from the Nez Perce or Salish to create carrying cases like this one, painted in the classic Columbia Plateau style. When traveling, its owner hung it on a horse, so that its luxurious fringes hung down; at home, she hung it up in the lodge to keep her tools or other odds and ends. Cases like this were widely traded; in 1841 a member of the Wilkes Expedition bought one at Fort Vancouver near the mouth of the Columbia. This one was purchased from a Yakima named White Cloud in 1889.

Parfleche, pre-1900

The Umatilla were equestrians who lived on the grassy hills south of the Walla Walla River. They made long-range expeditions to hunt buffalo and traded with tribes from east of the Rockies for hides. This parfleche, used as a suitcase for storing clothes or other valuables, is the shape of ones used on the plains, but it was painted in a distinctive southern plateau style. It was collected on the Umatilla Reservation in 1900.

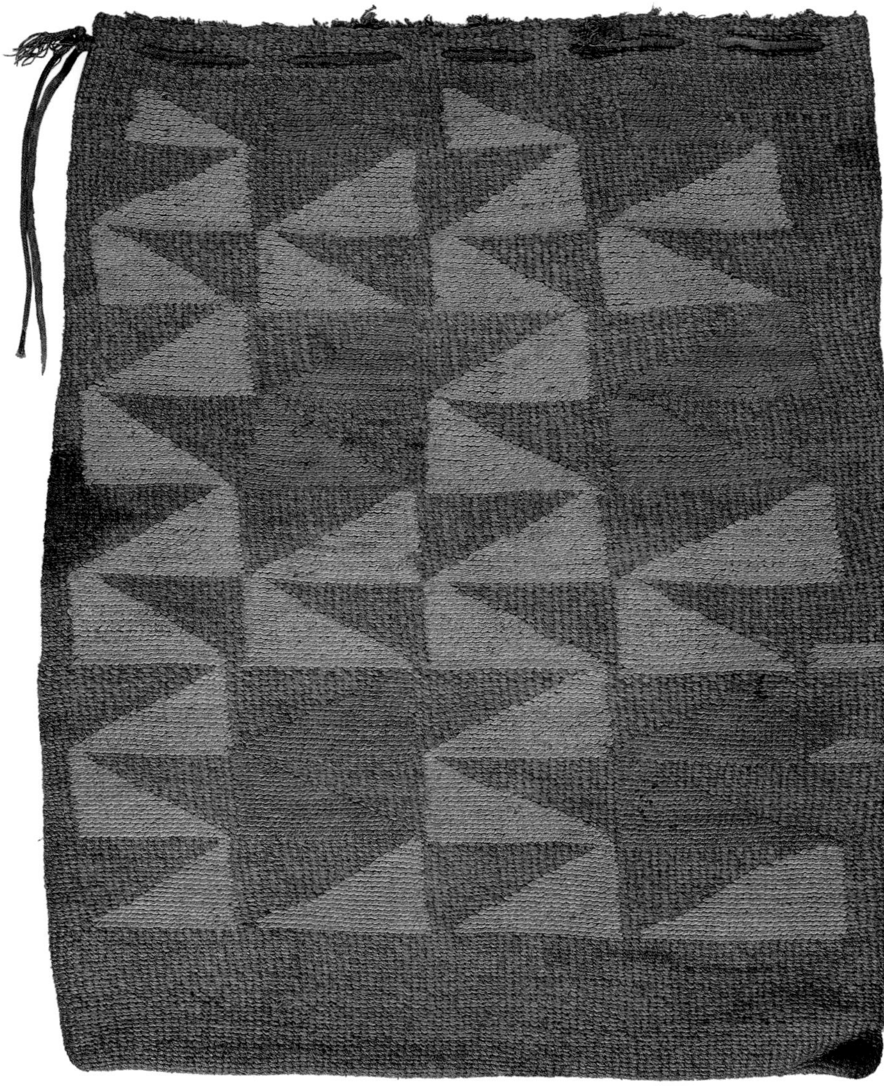

Root bag, 1800s
Nez Perce women brought large flat bags like this to market filled with bushels of camas roots. The bags also served for collecting, storing, and roasting the roots. The earliest ones were twined of wild hemp with simple geometric patterns formed with grasses and rushes; later they were made with corn husk, wool, and other decorative materials. Lewis's first mention of bags like this occurred among the Shoshone, where he saw "a couple of bags wove with the fingers of the bark of the silk-grass containing each about a bushel." Many of these were traded.

Basket, pre-1890s
The Klickitat, who lived between The Dalles and Puget Sound, were renowned for their coiled cedar-root baskets, imbricated with bear grass and made tightly enough to hold water. Baskets made with this technique were called Klickitat baskets even when made by other tribes. The Klickitat traded them at The Dalles for buffalo robes, horses, and other goods. The earliest surviving Klickitat baskets are of this oval shape, used to bathe babies, hold drinking water, and store food, clothes, and other valuables. The design on this one is an ancient way of depicting deer or dogs, with triangular bellies. Lewis appears to refer to Klickitat baskets in a passage about baskets "formed of cedar bark [root?] and beargrass so closely interwoven with the fingers that they are watertight without the aid of gum or rosin; some of these are highly ornamented with strans of beargrass which they dye of several colours and interweave in a great variety of figures. . . . it is for the construction of these baskets that the beargrass become an article of traffic among the natives."

tapering to each end. . . . Capt. Lewis . . . exchanged our Smallest Canoe for one of them. . . . these Canoes are neeter made than any I have ever Seen and Calculated to ride the waves, and carry emence burthens."[35]

"Rocks in every derection for a fiew miles," Clark said. But soon the river widened and became "a butifull jentle Stream." Below The Dalles, they began to notice a change: "The mountains are high on each Side, containing Scattering pine white oake & under groth, hill Sides Steep and rockey."[36] Where the Columbia cuts though the Cascade Mountains, forming the deep Columbia Gorge, the land changes abruptly from arid, grassy plains to rain forest. The expedition soon met new weather: "Cloudy dark and disagreeable with Some rain all day which kept us wet." This refrain would be repeated in their journals all winter.[37]

They descended the valley in eager hopes of finding American or British traders at the coast. The evidence was all around—sailors' hats and jackets, copper teakettles, muskets. Many Indians now spoke the trading patois known as Chinook jargon—a Nootka, Salish, and Chinook mix into which they wove "many words of English, as musquit, powder, shot, [k]nife, file, damned rascal, sun of a bitch &c." Clark speculated, "We are not certain as yet if the whites people . . . are Stationary at the mouth, or visit this quarter at Stated times for the purpose of trafick."[38]

One more obstruction barred their way—the Cascades. "The rapids

Cape Disappointment, 1848
Cape Disappointment, the rocky headland at the northern side of the Columbia's mouth, was where the expedition first saw the sea, but never under weather conditions as good as shown here by the artist Henry Warre. Despite the appropriateness of its name, Cape Disappointment was not named by Lewis and Clark. It was first sighted in 1775 by the Spanish explorer Bruno de Heceta, who noted the presence there of a river estuary. It was named in 1788 by Captain John Meares, a British sea captain, who was looking for Heceta's estuary but concluded that the river did not exist. In 1792 the American captain Robert Gray, in the trading ship *Columbia Rediviva*, entered the estuary and discovered the river, which he named for his ship.

appeared to continue down below as far as I could See," Clark said. "The river is Crouded with rocks of various Sizes between which the water passes with great velociety createing in maney places large Waves." After a long and laborious portage, they were rewarded by a welcome observation: a nine-inch tide. It was proof that they had reached the Columbia estuary, an inland arm of the sea. Two days later Clark wrote: "We had a full view of *Mt. Helien* which is perhaps the highest pinical in America. . . . it rises Something in the form of a Sugar lofe." This time, Clark was looking at the correct mountain, but he greatly exaggerated its height.[39]

They had noticed yet another change in the Native people they met. The lower Chinookans lived in a narrow ribbon along the Columbia, sandwiched between other language groups to the north and south. They were divided into a bewildering variety of tribes—Skilloot, Clackamas, Chilwitz, Kathlamet, Wahkiakum, Chinook, and Clatsop, among others—each consisting of only a village or two occupying a section of the riverbank. Only later, in response to outsiders, would the lower Chinookanss begin to have a sense of political and cultural unity.

Their arts and customs were very different from those of the upper Chinookans, with whom they often warred. They lived in elaborately furnished cedar-plank houses and had adopted some aspects of the fabled Northwest Coast Indian cultures in Canada, including customs such as the potlatch. Theirs was a maritime lifestyle based on fish and on abundant plants with names like wappato, salal, solme, and shannetaque—foods native to their mild, rainy homeland. But above all, they were traders. Trade was the core of their economy and the basis of their great wealth.

Lewis and Clark disliked them almost at once. To begin with, their looks were unfamiliar. "The natives . . . are rether below the Common Size," Clark wrote near the Cascades. "Womin Small and homely, and have Swelled legs and thighs, and their knees remarkably large. . . . They have all flat heads in this quarter both men and women. . . . I observed in maney of the villeages which I have passed, the heads of the female children in the press for the purpose of compressing their heads." A few days later, it was the Indians' manners that caused complaint. "Several Canoes of Indians from the village above came down dressed for the purpose as I Supposed of Paying us a friendly visit, they had Scarlet & blue blankets Salors jackets, overalls, Shirts and Hats. . . . Those fellows we found assumeing and disagreeable. . . . those fellows Stold my pipe Tomahawk. . . . while Serching for the Tomahawk one of those Scoundals Stole a cappo[t]e. . . . we became much displeased."[40]

The Indians kept raising the explorers' hopes of finding a ship or a fort at the end of the trail. "Came to a large Indian village, where they informed us that in two days we should come to two ships with white people in them," Gass wrote. Instead, they met only rain and mist. "The fog So thick we could not See across the river," Clark wrote as they came to the broad inlet at the Columbia's mouth. "We Set out piloted by an Indian dressed in a Salors dress. . . . the river widens into a kind of Bay."[41]

"Great joy in camp," Clark wrote on November 7. "We are in *View* of the *Ocian*, this great Pacific Octean which we been So long anxious to See. and the roreing or noise made by the waves brakeing on the rockey Shores (as I Suppose) may be heard disti[n]ctly." In fact, he was seeing the wide Columbia estuary, but it made little difference. They were at the end of their journey.[42]

Soon, they were nearly at the end of their tether, as well. The steep, wooded north shore of the estuary afforded few good camping spots; for a while, they actually camped on some floating logs jammed against the rocks. "We are all wet and disagreeable," Clark wrote. "We have not leavel land Sufficient for an encampment. . . . our camp entirely under water dureing the hight of the *tide*, every man as wet as water could make them." At the same time, the weather prevented them from moving. With "tremendious waves brakeing with great violence against the Shores, rain falling in torrents," they feared to chance their small canoes on the water. Clark marveled at the casual way the Indians "Crossed the river . . . through the highest waves I ever Saw a Small vestles ride." In their waterlogged misery, the men of the Corps were still

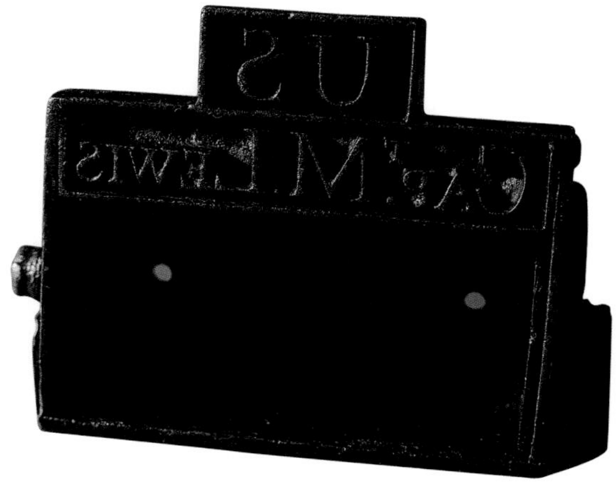

Branding iron, c. 1804
On November 22, 1805, this tool was used to mark the arrival of the expedition at the Pacific, establishing new territorial claims of the United States. "Capt Lewis Branded a tree with his name Date &c," Clark wrote. They had already used it to mark trees around their caches on the Marias River, the farthest north point they had achieved up to then. According to Whitehouse, "The Officers branded several of the trees with the mark of the United States, Captain Lewis's name, the Latitude of the place &ca." The most poignant use of the branding iron had been to make Charles Floyd's grave marker, containing his name and date of death. The hollow box of the iron likely once held interchangeable type. The artifact was found by Lineaus Winans of Hood River, Oregon, among the rocks on the north shore of the Columbia River below Memaloose Island near The Dalles, in the spring of 1892, 1893, or 1894. Contrary to legend, this was not used to brand horses. The men used a stirrup iron for that purpose.

Brass and copper bracelets, early 1800s
"Both males and females wear braslets on their wrists of copper brass or Iron in various forms," Lewis noted. These bracelets, recovered in archaeological digs along the Columbia River, are both trade and Indian-made jewelry. The top one appears to be cast brass; the one on the lower left is hand-worked brass; and the one on the lower right is a hand-made cylinder of copper, probably recycled from a kettle or copper sheet.

Double-bladed knife, pre-1867
and **Sketch of a double-bladed knife, 1806**
When Clark saw the Clatsop using knives like this Tlingit one, or locally made ones based on the same style, he did not think of them as trade goods. "The form of a knife which Seems to be prefured by those people is a double Edged and double pointed dagger the handle being near the middle, the blades of uneaquel length, the longest from 9 to 10 incs. and the Shorter one from 3 to 5 inches. those knives they carry with them habitually and most usially in the hand, Sometimes exposed, when in Company with Strangers under their Robes with this knife they Cut & Clense their fish make their arrows &c." Tlingit metalsmiths made daggers like this of iron from meteors, trade, or salvaged ship-wrecks. They shaped them by forging or cold-working. Traders also learned to make them on shipboard forges.

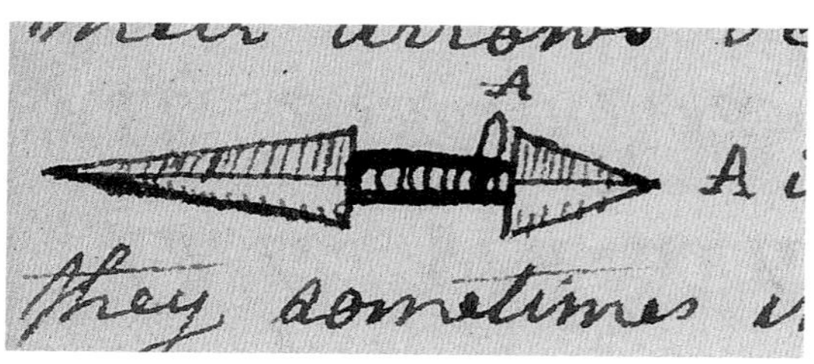

hoping to glimpse lantern light from the window of a snug trader's fort or a ship somewhere around the next headland. "Capt Lewis concluded to proceed on by land & find if possible the white people the Indians Say is below," Clark wrote. But the promised traders were a mirage.[43]

Arriving at their journey's end was sadly anticlimactic. The men took some consolation in performing the ritual acts of European discoverers. "Capt. Lewis Branded a tree with his name Date &c. I marked my name the Day & year on a Alder tree, the party all Cut the first letters of their names on different trees in the bottom," Clark said. Gass and some of the other men found satisfaction in crossing the headland to see the ocean coast. "We could see the waves, like small mountains, rolling out in the ocean. . . . We are now at the end of our voyage . . . the object of which was to discover a passage by the way of the Missouri and Columbia rivers to the Pacific ocean."[44]

Winter lay ahead. The previous winter, the party had survived by trading their goods and services for the abundant food of the Mandan. But already they had gotten off to a bad start with their closest neighbors on the north shore, the Chinook, whose name was later applied to the whole language group. Almost the first thing Clark said to them was that "they Should not Come near us." He warned: "If any one of their nation Stold anything from us, I would have him Shot." Not surprisingly, "they were guarded and resurved." The situation did not bode well for the winter.[45]

To Lewis and Clark, the coastal Indians seemed like the most alien people they had met. But in many ways, the Chinookans and the Americans were too much alike. Both were wealthy, materialistic, class-conscious people, and both had become that way through commerce. Many of the disagreements between the men of the Corps and their neighbors that winter would revolve around attitudes toward property and trade. The exchange of goods and services seems like a simple and universal act; but then as now, it illuminated deeper differences.

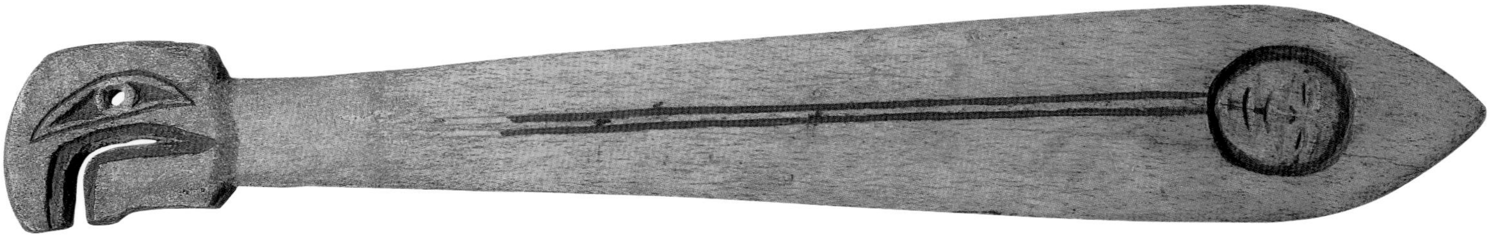

Whalebone club, 1790s
and **Sketch of a bludgeon, 1806**
The Chinookans did not hunt whales but got whalebone artifacts from their northern neighbors, the Makah. The style of this club resembles a sketch Lewis drew of one he saw among the "Kathlapotle" (lower Chinookans). This one was collected by "S. Hills," one of the traders who frequented the Columbia mouth—either Stephen Hills, the third mate on the *Margaret* in 1791–94, or Samuel Hill, the captain of the *Lydia*. The latter (whose name Clark spelled "Haley") was a frequent visitor, described by Clark as "the favourite of the Indians (from the number of Presents he givs)." He arrived just after Lewis and Clark departed in 1806 and was given a letter they left with the Indians. This club was identified as a "weapon used by the natives in killing deer," but it was originally intended as a war club, as Lewis understood. Clubs like it were more than weapons; they were symbols of chiefly status, linked to the whaling traditions of high-ranking Makah and Nootka families, and their imagery evokes the mythical world.

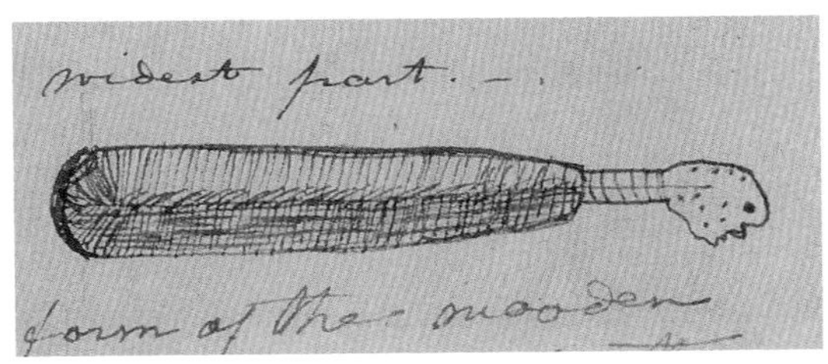

POVERTY AND PROPERTY

> Every man has influence in proportion to his property. . . . Poverty they consider disgraceful. He who has strength and skill enough to obtain property will acquire influence.
>
> —JONATHAN GREEN, ON NORTHWEST COAST INDIANS[46]

All across the continent, Lewis and Clark looked at the Indians and saw poverty. The Missouri River villagers were "Dirty, Kind, pore, & extravegent." The Shoshone lived "in a wretched stait of poverty." The Columbia River Indians were "reches" who were "badly Clad, 3/4 with robes not half large enough to cover them." The coastal Indians "were pore Durty and the house full of flees." The Nez Perce had "very few amusements," for their life was "painful and laborious; all their exertions [were] necessary to earn even their precarious subsistence."[47]

The observations were critical, because to many Europeans, property marked the division line between civilization and savagery. "Property is a matter of progress," wrote the social philosopher Adam Ferguson in 1767. "The industry by which it is gained, or improved . . . is in reality a principal distinction of nations in the advanced state of mechanic and commercial arts." Even the eighteenth-century economist Adam Smith agreed, in *The Wealth of Nations*, that individual property and division of labor were the core differences between affluent, civilized societies and impoverished, savage ones. Given these assumptions, if Lewis and Clark had admitted that the Indians were not poor, they would also have been admitting that the Indians were not savage.[48]

The Chinook would have been shocked to hear themselves described as poor. Their potlatches, held in summer and fall, were festivals that celebrated the affluence of the host. A high-ranking person would send messengers to all the neighboring villages. Each invited village arrived as a group. "They put their canoes side by side and lay planks across. . . . Now they dance, and those who have guardian spirits sing. The people dance on the planks. Their faces are painted red, their hair is strewn with down." The villagers spent five days in the host's house—feasting, dancing, gambling, and gossiping. At the end came the gifts. "They receive presents. One man is asked to stand near the host and to name the people. First he names a chief of one town. . . . After one town is finished, another one receives presents." Massive quantities of goods could change hands, demonstrating the giver's status, generosity, and industry and earning the obligation of the recipients. While the men of the Corps of Discovery eked out a meager existence on rotten elk through the winter of 1805–6, trying to trade empty tin canisters and buttons cut from their clothes, their neighbors held lavish giveaways. The Clatsop Indians would have been amused to know the residents of the fort imagined that the U.S. market economy and manufactured goods would soon bring prosperity to impoverished Indians everywhere.[49]

Spanish dollar, 1791

This coin was money to Europeans but not to the Indians of the Columbia basin. On the Snake River in 1806, Robert Frazer bartered an old razor to a Nez Perce woman for a necklace made from two Spanish dollars, acquired "from about a Snake Indian's neck they had killed some time ago." The dollars had probably traveled along Indian trade routes either from the coast or from Spanish settlements in New Mexico. One of Frazer's dollars may have been donated by Lewis to Peale's Museum. Peale called it a "Spanish Dollar obtained by Captn. M. Lewis, from the Pallotepallers—a nation inhabiting Lewis's River within the Plains of Columbia, who had never previously seen white-men." The "Pallotepallers" are thought to be the Nez Perce or Palouse. This is an eight-real coin, or Spanish peso, called by the Americans a dollar or piece of eight. It is not associated with Lewis or Clark.

Dentalium belt, pre-1841

Queentschich higua? ("How many dentalia?") was the Chinook jargon phrase to ask the value of a commodity. The value of a dentalium shell rose the farther it got from its source on Vancouver Island. Among the Nootka, a slave was sold for five fathoms. But the Chinook could get only one fathom of forty shells for a slave. The Yurok in northern California parted with their slaves for less than half a fathom (27 1/2 inches). Despite its commercial role, dentalium was said by the Chinook to have a supernatural origin. It is likely beads did as well.

By the time Lewis and Clark arrived, Euro-Americans had moved in on the dentalium trade. "They are also fond of a species of wampum which is furnished them by a trader whom they call Swipton," Lewis wrote on March 19, 1806. "This shell is of a conic form somewhat curved, about the size of a raven's quill." This belt was collected on the Wilkes expedition by Titian Ramsay Peale, who identified it as "used as currency by the natives of the North West Coast of America." It was likely acquired at Fort Vancouver on the Columbia.

Why could Lewis and Clark not see the affluence around them? There are several possible answers. Different cultures have different definitions of value. Lewis derided the Indians' sense of value: "Their dispositions invariably lead them to give whatever they are possessed off no matter how usefull or valuable, for a bauble which pleases their fancy, without consulting it's usefullness or value." And yet he and Clark nearly gave away the bulk of their dwindling trade goods in order to get three handsome otter pelts. Theirs was a value system ridiculed by the Indians. As one Hidatsa asked a trader in 1804: "What is the use of beaver? do they make gun-powder of them? Do they preserve them from sickness[?] Do they serve them beyond the grave?" In 1806 another trader wrote of the Hidatsa: "They put little value on any of those skins, and cannot imagine what use we make of such trash, as they call it. They . . . call the whites fools for giving them valuable articles for such useless skins."[50]

Many of the things prized by the Chinookans were symbolic of their strictly stratified class system, an aspect of their culture that Lewis and Clark never even suspected. Chinookan rank was hereditary; children of different classes were kept apart, and intermarriage was forbidden. Wealth was the outward expression of class, and certain styles of dress and appearance were limited to the upper echelons. The custom of head-flattening, which Clark described but never got an explanation for, was in fact a badge of aristocracy. Slaves were forbidden to flatten their children's heads. To the Chinookans, the captains' round heads were a symbol of servility as sure as York's black skin was to Virginians. Another symbol of high status was copper, formerly imported from the Alaskan coast. The shiny brass-and-copper bracelets, thimbles, bells, and wire described by Lewis as "articles of little value" were, to the Chinookans, symbols of wealth: they commanded a premium price for their prestige value, much as platinum watches or elite sportscars do today, regardless of their utility.[51]

Wealth not only was symbolized differently but also was used differently. European men and women achieved status and power by accumulating and keeping wealth. The Chinookans, like other Native Americans, achieved status and power by giving their wealth away. Anyone who aspired to chieftainship was obliged to demonstrate generosity to the point of impoverishing himself, if necessary. European visitors found it strange that chiefs were often so poor in

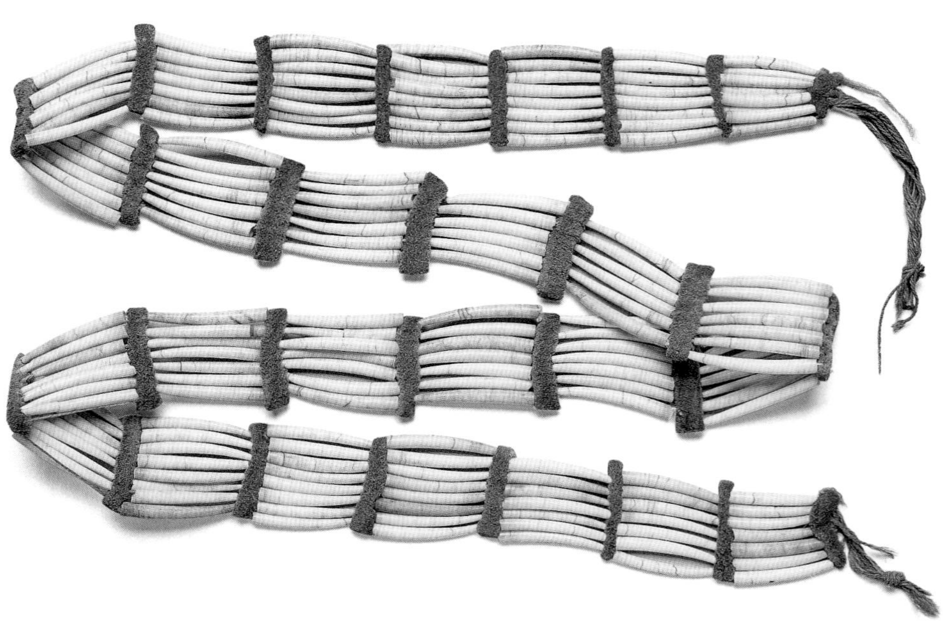

goods. They did not see how rich the chiefs were in community support.[52]

The most abstract symbol of wealth is currency. Money is an object with little intrinsic worth, yet by common consent, it symbolizes the value in other things. There were two currencies in use on the Columbia River in 1805. One was a white, fang-shaped shell called *higua* by the Chinook and *dentalium* by English-speakers. It came in various denominations, with larger shells being worth more than small ones. The problem with this currency, from the Chinook viewpoint, was that the Nootka tribe had a monopoly on its production, since the only harvestable bed of dentalia lay in their territory. So it seems that in 1805, another medium of exchange was being adopted: blue beads. At first, Lewis and Clark were baffled by the Chinookan demand for blue beads. They attributed it to irrationality: "they prefer beeds to any thing and will part with the last mouthfull or articles of clothing they have for a fiew of those beeds," Clark wrote in November. But by the next May, he had realized that the blue beads were used as cash: "This article among all the nations of this Country may be justly compared to gold and Silver among civilized nations." Both dentalia and beads were strung on strands and measured by the fathom, the length between a man's outstretched arms. The Indians' desire for them was no more irrational than the Europeans' desire for little disks of metal stamped with their leaders' images, which the Indians pierced and used as jewelry.[53] By 1811, Euro-American traders' efforts to supply the demand for blue beads had inadvertently caused such inflation that the beads had become useless as currency and were abandoned for other measures.[54]

The Indians' standards of value and media of exchange were not the only things that didn't translate. The Virginians and the Chinookans had even deeper differences: they did not always agree on what constituted property. To Enlightenment gentlemen like Lewis or Clark, "property" was something created by human labor. A salmon in the river was not property. Only after someone had gone to the work of catching the fish did he or she rightfully own it. Land that was not "improved"—surveyed, fenced, plowed—was not property but was worthless "wilderness." Rivers were not property, but locks and canals could be. Human beings were property only after someone had gone to the trouble of subduing them and shipping them from Africa. Man breathed value into things by infusing them with labor.

The Chinookans agreed with the Virginians about some definitions of property, but not others. On human beings, they agreed. Slaves were a commodity traded up and down the Pacific coast, and they constituted a stable unit of value. Virtually all Native American tribes kept some war captives as slaves, but the Chinookans, by trading them, gave them a commercial value they lacked elsewhere. Most slaves were either purchased from the north or captured on raids to what is today southern Oregon and northern California. Twenty years after Lewis and Clark, a fur merchant on the Columbia observed: "Slaves form the principal article of traffick on the whole of this Coast and constitute the greater part of their Riches; they are made to Fish, hunt, draw Wood & Water in short all the drudgery falls on them; they feed in common with the Family of their proprietors and intermarry with their own class, but lead a life of misery. . . . the proprietors exercise the most absolute authority over them even to Life and Death." Another trader wrote, "A Chinooke matron is constantly attended by two, three, or more slaves, who are on all occasions obse-

Beads, early to mid-1800s
Clark said that the Clatsop called blue beads of this type "'*ti-â, co-mo-shack*' which is *Chief beads*," suggesting they were associated with social class. The beads were wearable money; the Chinook displayed them "tightly wound arond their wrists and ankles many times untill they obtain the width of three or more inches. they also wear them in large rolls loosly arond the neck, or pendulous from the cartelage of the nose or rims of the ears." Since blue beads had been in style all along their route, Lewis and Clark had mostly other colors left by the time they reached the Pacific. "I offered red beeds . . . [but] they would give Scercely any thing for Beeds of that Colour . . . not priseing any other Colour than Blue or White." This batch was collected at Cape Prince of Wales, Alaska, in 1905, but they are of a much earlier style.

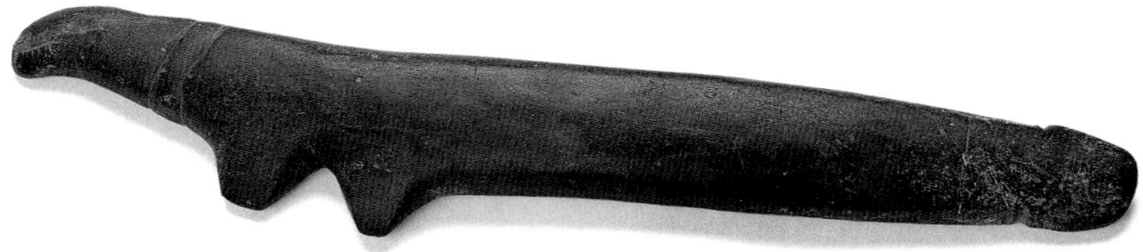

"Slave killer" club, prehistoric
On the northwest coast, clubs known today as "slave killers" are presumed to have been used to kill slaves during certain potlatch ceremonies. Slaves were sacrificed only on rare occasions, after which their owners were compensated with new titles and songs equal in value to the slaves. One purpose of the ceremonial killing of slaves was to demonstrate their owners' disdain for wealth. In addition, slaves were sometimes sacrificed after the death of their owners. The shape of this club is also seen on ceremonial war clubs. This one was recovered in an archaeological dig at one of the upper Chinookan villages on the Columbia River.

I wish to SELL two likely NEGRO MEN for Cash.
WILLIAM CLARK.
St. Louis, Feb. 22. tf.

Advertisement: Slaves for Sale, 1809
Virginians, like Chinookans, counted their wealth in slaves. Both Lewis and Clark were slave-owners. Clark took out this ad in the *Missouri Gazette*, a St. Louis newspaper, to sell two of his slaves, Scippio and Juba. Although he once stated that he thought "perpetual involuntary servitude to be contrary to principles of natural justice," Clark shared the brutal attitudes of most slave-owners of his day. "I have been obliged [to] whip almost all my people," he wrote his brother in 1808. "They are now beginning to think that it is best to do better and not Cry hard when I am compelled to use the whip." His relations with York after the expedition were contentious. "He has got Such a notion about freedom and his emence Services, that I do not expect he will be of much Service to me again," Clark wrote. "I do not think with him, that his Services has been So great." Clark consequently denied York's desire to live near his wife in Louisville. At various times Clark spoke of selling York to New Orleans, of hiring him "to a Severe master," and of beating him. "I gave him a Severe trouncing the other Day," Clark wrote in 1809, because he was "insolent and Sulky." Clark claimed to have freed York sometime after 1816.

quious to her will." A Chinookan slave-owner at The Dalles later rationalized the institution of slavery much the same way Virginians did: "Why should we put away our slaves? They are our *brethren & sisters*—we *love* them. They are not dogs & horses that we should turn them off to take care of themselves." In both Virginia and the Columbia Valley, the reality was much more harsh.[55]

Lewis and Clark never realized that many of the people they were seeing were slaves. One Chinook matron came to see them accompanied by her retinue of slaves, whose sexual services she offered to the men; but rather than seeing her as the equivalent of a plantation mistress (as she undoubtedly saw herself), they compared her with the madam of a brothel, or "baud." It is like-

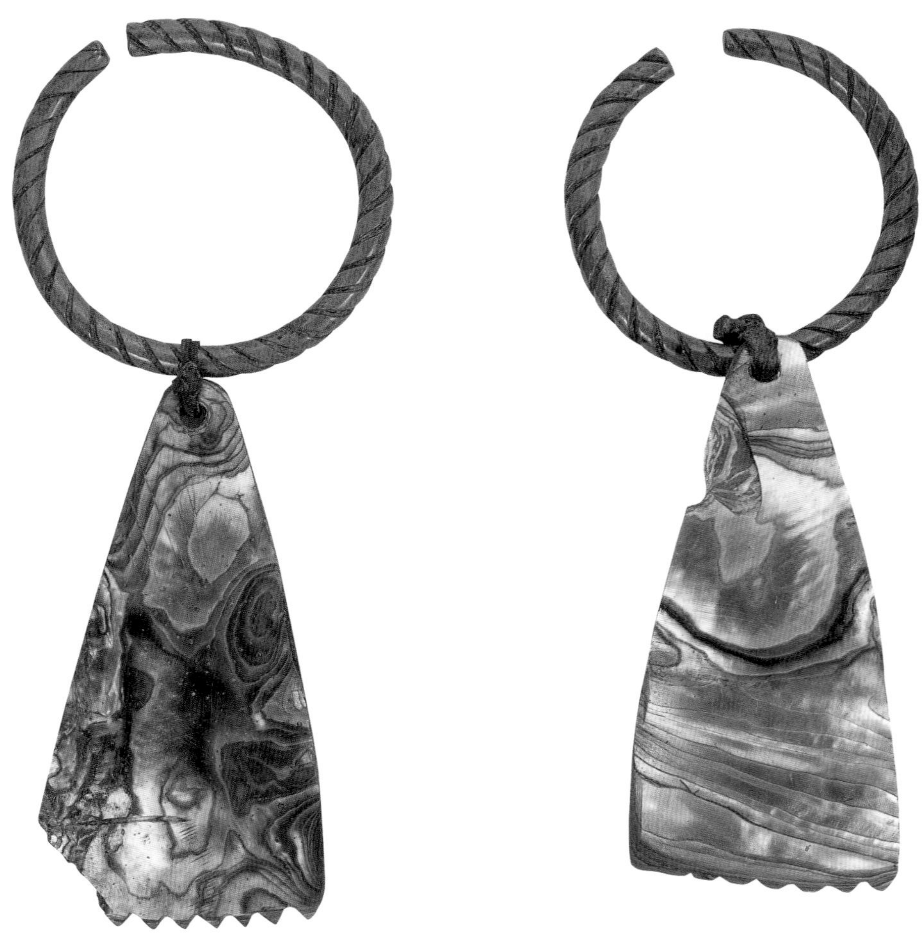

Abalone earrings, late 1800s
The Shoshone, one of whom wore these earrings, were particularly fond of a species of abalone shell found in Monterey Bay. They sometimes acquired the shells on long trading voyages to the Klamath; but as early as 1774, European ships picked up abalone and brought it north, from which it entered the Chinook trade network and could have reached the Shoshone via the Nez Perce. Among the Shoshone, Lewis and Clark saw what was probably abalone ("Shells resembling *perl* which is highly Valued by those people and is prcured from the nations resideing near the *Sea Coast*"), some of which they collected (see Chapter 9).

wise likely the Chinook never realized that York was a slave; the signals of his status were too subtle and culture-specific.[56]

The other principal measure of wealth to Virginians—land—was not a factor in the Chinookan system. Like other Native Americans, the Chinookans did not see land as something that could be owned, bought, or traded. As the Nez Perce Chief Joseph famously stated this principle: "No man owned any part of the earth, and a man could not sell what he did not own." This did not mean that certain families and bands did not own the rights to harvest in certain spots; for example, the fishing rights in the channels of The Dalles were assigned to particular families, a type of ownership that was scrupulously respected. The fruits of the land, such as the salmon, roots, and game, were seen as gifts from sacred powers and came with an obligation to share. Because of their origin, these gifts were not always counted as wealth. Unlike Euro-Americans, Native Americans did not take full credit for having produced their livelihood.[57]

On the other hand, there were things Indians owned that Euro-Americans did not. In most tribes, certain songs, stories, crafts, and rituals belonged strictly to the people who had purchased the rights to them, and no one else dared repeat them for fear of offending the powers who had given the knowledge to humans. In Lewis and Clark's day, after a temporary protection by copyright and patent, published stories and ideas were free community property. Songs were not yet sold. Today, we are drawing closer to the Native American system, but for very different reasons.

Blanket, pre-1841
Blankets like this were manufactured by the Coast Salish in Washington, but the goat wool from which they were made came from the Rocky and Cascade Mountains. The blankets were traded at least as far east as the Nez Perce. Lewis mentioned the Clatsop wearing "a blanket wove with the fingers of the wool of the native sheep." Never having seen a live mountain goat, they erroneously assumed it was a sheep. "We have never met with this anamal ourselves but have seen many of their skins . . . and a[l]so seen the blankets which they manufacture of the wooll of this sheep," Lewis wrote. Clark collected at least one blanket, which he offered to Jefferson in 1808, describing it as "a Blanket made by the Indians of the wool of this species of sheep . . . of the Rocky Mountains." The one pictured here was collected by the Wilkes Expedition in Oregon Territory. Its pattern of horizontal bands with zigzags is an old style. The colors are produced with vegetable dyes.

Sally bag, 1800s

The wild hemp and bear grass used to make bags like this one were brought to The Dalles as raw materials by the tribes "under the rockey mountains," according to Clark. The Wishram, Wasco, and surrounding tribes manufactured hundreds of cylinder bags like this as packaging for food products they sold, distributing them throughout the Columbia River valley. This one, however, was an heirloom passed down in a prominent family of Wasco-Cascade heritage. The designs are in an archaic style and represent condors and four-legged animals, either deer or dogs.

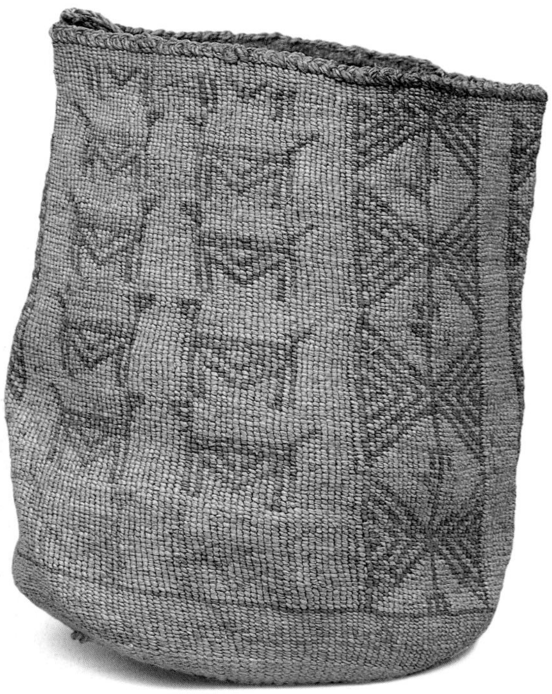

Horn bowl, 1800s

The geometric carvings and rectangular projecting handles of this bowl were a traditional style of the Wasco and Wishram. They made bowls and spoons of material imported from the Rocky Mountains and traded the finished products all up and down the Columbia River. On December 9, 1805, Clark was served a syrup of "Cramberries & Sackacomey berris, in bowls made of horn." Lewis described the bowls of the Chinook and Clatsop as being "extreemly well executed and many of them neatly carved the larger vessels with hand-holes to them." To make a bowl like this, the tip and inner edge of the sheep horn was removed, then the horn was stretched and reshaped by steaming, boiling, or heating. The decorations were carved with woodworking tools.

CHINOOK EMPORIUM

> There is a trade continually carryed on by the natives of the river each trading some article or other with their neighbours above and below them; and thus articles which are vended by the whites at the entrance of this river, find their way to the most distant nations.
>
> —MERIWETHER LEWIS[58]

Long before Lewis and Clark, Native Americans were linked by a web of trade. The Pacific Northwest was a place of particularly sharp variations in environment. Within a few hundred miles lived tribes who specialized in exploiting the products of desert, grassland, mountain, rain forest, and coastal ecologies. By trading, they could all live more prosperously. Even within ecological zones like the plateau, tribes reduced their labor by specializing in certain products and by trading for those they did not produce themselves.[59]

On the eastern edge of the Chinookan trade network, the Nez Perce and the Salish were long-range, mobile traders who crossed the mountains to gather the products of the plains: buffalo skins and horns, obsidian, pipestone, and the finished shirts, parfleches, and headdresses of skilled Plains Indian leather- and feather-workers. The Shoshone, who traded with distant tribes from both the Great Basin and the Great Plains at a rendezvous in present-day western Wyoming, funneled goods from as far as Santa Fe into the Pacific Northwest through their sometime enemies, the Nez Perce. From the Rocky Mountains, the Salish and the Nez Perce brought products like sheep skins and horns, goat wool, and deer and elk hides.

Plateau tribes produced goods of the grassland, the most important being horses, which they sold both to each other and to the Plains Indian tribes. The Nez Perce, Cayuse, Wallawalla, Palouse, and Yakima were all horse breeders. From their meadows also came heaping bags of camas, dried berries, tule mats, bear grass, wild hemp, and finished baskets, bags, and hats. The Klickitat produced trademark baskets of cedar root and bear grass from the Cascade Mountains, and they linked the tribes of Puget Sound to the plateau.

Black-rimmed hat, early 1800s
Both Europeans and Northwest Coast Indians used hats to denote social class. This superbly crafted hat was probably made for a person of elite status, possibly one with elk power. The paintings depict two triangular elk heads with their antlers intertwined around the crown. The hat has eyes on either side. Although it comes from the collection that includes Lewis and Clark's artifacts, there is no evidence linking it to them. It is, however, old enough for them to have seen ones like it. Black-rimmed hats were made by the Nootka and the Makah around the entrance to Puget Sound, as were the knob-top whaler's hats that Lewis and Clark illustrated and collected.

Comb, pre-1841
"The woodwork and sculpture of these people . . . evince an ingenuity by no means common among the Aborigenes of America," Lewis wrote of the lower Chinookans. "They are fond of combs and use them when they can obtain them; and even without the aid of the comb keep their hair in better order than many nations who are in other rispects much more civilized than themselves." Combs were also used in upper Chinookan wedding ceremonies; the mother and the mother-in-law of the bride dressed her hair and inserted combs, which the girl's feminine relatives removed. Others were then inserted and removed again. Combs like this one are sometimes identified as weaving combs, but the Chinook did little weaving and may have used them for grooming and decoration instead.

On the western side of the Chinookan trade network lay the coastal tribes. To the north, the Nootka on Vancouver Island produced some of the classic articles of Northwest Coast Indian culture: high-prowed canoes, basketry hats, woven robes, dentalia, and cedar bark for mats and bags. The Makah at the mouth of Puget Sound were great whalers who went to sea in their oceangoing canoes and produced whalebone, blubber, and oil. The Salishan tribes on the coast of present-day Washington hunted sea otter and wove blankets. At the mouth of the Columbia, the Chinook and Clatsop harvested candlefish, sturgeon, shellfish, and wappato for sale and hunted elk for heavy leather armor called *clamons*, which they sold north to the Haida. The Tillamook returned from their excursions to the area that is now California with abalone shell and slaves.

All of these products were funneled through the Columbia River, where the Chinookan tribes maintained absolute control. The lower Chinookans were distributors, transporting goods in their massive canoes (bought from the Nootka and the Makah) measuring up to fifty feet long and holding ten thousand pounds of cargo. The upper Chinookans were merchants, presiding over annual trade fairs. Everything came together at The Dalles. The name of the main village there, Nixlu´idix, was translated by its inhabitants as "trading place." The fur trader Alexander Ross, who visited in 1811, estimated that over three thousand people gathered there, and he called it "the great emporium or mart of the Columbia, and the general theatre of gambling and roguery." Ross wrote, "All the gamblers, horse-stealers, and other outcasts throughout the country, for hundreds of miles round, make this place their great rendezvous during summer."[60]

The Wishram and the Wasco, "turbulent lords of the falls," made it all possible by stockpiling enormous stores of dried salmon for sale. Passing through in late 1805, after the trading was all over, Clark estimated the stacks of salmon he saw at 10,000 pounds, but he must have forgotten a zero, because even by his own figures (107 stacks of 12 baskets, each weighing 90–100 pounds), he was seeing 115,000 to 128,000 pounds. Lewis estimated that The Dalles Indians produced 30,000 pounds of fish annually for market. The reality was more like 320,000—and this figure does not count the fish produced for their own use.[61]

Often, the raw materials traded at The Dalles were transformed into finished goods by tribes far from their origins—and then were traded again. Goat wool was harvested by tribes in the Rocky and Cascade Mountains but was woven into blankets by the coastal Salish and Nootka. Carved bowls and spoons diagnostic of Wishram and Wasco art were made from Rocky Mountain sheep horn brought to them by the Nez Perce and the Spokane. Styles and ideas were traded as well. Some of the Clatsop weapons illustrated by Lewis and Clark bear a striking resemblance to Athabascan and Tlingit ones.

CLOTH MEN

An event that always stimulated trade on the coast was a whale stranding. The lucky tribe in whose territory the whale chose to beach itself had the right to butcher it and trade the products to neighboring tribes, who gathered from miles around.

A particularly strange stranding was long remembered by the Clatsop

tribe: "An old woman [was] walking along the beach. . . . Now she saw something. She thought it was a whale . . . [with] two spruce trees standing upright on it. . . . Ropes were tied to those spruce trees and it was full of iron. Then a bear came out of it . . . but his face was that of a human being. . . . Now she said all the time, 'Oh . . . the thing about which we heard in tales is on shore.' . . . Then the people ran. They reached the thing that lay there. . . . [They] set fire to the ship. . . . It burnt just like fat. Then the Clatsop gathered the iron, the copper, and the brass. . . . Now the Quenaiult, the Chehalis, the Cascades, the Cowlitz, and the Klickatat learned about it and they all went to Clatsop. . . . Strips of copper two fingers wide and going around the arm were exchanged for one slave each. . . . A nail was sold for a good curried deerskin. Several nails were given for long dentalia. The people bought this and the Clatsop became rich."[62] Thus Europeans entered the Chinookan trade network.

Sandwiched between Russian settlements in present-day Alaska and Spanish ones in what is now California, the Pacific coast had been the destination of European and American ships for almost two decades before Lewis and Clark arrived. Russia, Spain, France, and Britain had all sent scientific expeditions staffed with artists, naturalists, and geographers to the area. Spain had occupied a permanent settlement at Nootka Sound, British Columbia, for six years. But the real boom started after 1784, when Captain James Cook's book reported the fabulous profits that could be made selling sea otter skins in China.[63]

Ships from Boston swarmed to the Pacific coast after 1788. Sailing around Cape Horn, they brought loads of manufactured goods to trade for furs, which they took to China and sold for porcelain, tea, and fabrics. They returned around the southern tip of Africa to Boston, having circled the globe. It was one of these traders, Robert Gray, who discovered the mouth of the Columbia in 1792. Others, like Samuel Hill in the ship *Lydia* and James Magee in the

***View of Majoa's Great Village*, 1791**
José Cardero, an artist on Alejandro Malaspina's scientific expedition to the northwest coast, portrayed two Spanish schooners trading with the Indians at Chief Majoa's village on Vancouver Island. Spanish, Russian, British, and American traders all followed similar customs of exchange, dictated by the Indians. The canoes in which the Indians met the boats are portrayed correctly here, except that they are being paddled stern first.

China platter, c. 1793
Captain Robert Gray, one of the Boston traders, purchased this dish in China with furs from the northwest coast and used it on his ship, the *Columbia Rediviva*. It was Gray who discovered the mouth of the Columbia River in 1792 and named it for his ship. Dishes like this were made at Ching-te-Chen in China, a porcelain center since the seventh century.

Paddle, 1794
Just like Lewis and Clark, the Boston men picked up Indian souvenirs on the northwest coast. This Makah paddle was probably acquired by Stephen Hills, the third mate on the ship *Margaret* under Captain John Magee. Magee (whose name Lewis and Clark recorded as "Mackey") often visited the Chinook and Clatsop, who told Lewis and Clark in January that he would return "in 1 or 2 moons to trade." Clark illustrated paddles of this shape in his journal but did not comment on them. They were used particularly in whale hunting.

Bow, 1795
This sinew-backed bow was given to Captain Charles Bishop of the ship *Ruby* by Comcomly, one of the Chinook chiefs Lewis and Clark also met. In December 1795, Bishop was anchored in Baker Bay at the mouth of the Chinook River. He wrote: "In the Evening, Concomally returned and came along side the Ship. . . . he offered one of his Leathr War Dresses, and Several Bows & Arrows. The latter articles I accepted: and bought from him the Former." Lewis wrote: "The bow and arrow is the most common instrument among them, every man being furnished with them whether he has a gun or not. . . . Their bows are extreamly neat and very elastic, they are . . . formed of the heart of the arbor vita or white cedar, the back of the bow being thickly covered with sinews of the Elk laid on with a gleue which they make from the sturgeon; the string is made of sinues of the Elk also." This bow fits his description.

Margaret, soon made regular visits to the Chinook, casting anchor in Baker Bay on the north shore of the Columbia estuary near where Lewis and Clark first camped on reaching the ocean.[64]

Inexplicably, Lewis and Clark seem to have been unaware of this highly developed commerce. "Whether these traders are from Nootka sound, from some other late establishment on this coast, or immediately from the U' States or Great Brittain, I am at a loss to determine, nor can the Indians inform us," Lewis wrote. The Corps spent quite a lot of time gathering the names and schedules of the traders from the local Indians. A trip to Boston would have been even more informative.[65]

The Chinookans incorporated the sailors into their trading network, calling them "Boston men" or "cloth men" (*pah-shish-e-ooks*). As well as bringing manufactured goods, the mariners soon learned to stop in California for abalone shell, which brought high prices farther north. They purchased clamons from the Chinook to sell to the Haida and the Tlingit, and they brought dentalia south from Nootka Sound. Their presence greatly enhanced the power and wealth of the Chinook and the Clatsop, who jealously guarded, from upriver tribes, their exclusive access to Euro-American trade goods.[66]

Like traders across North America, the Boston men learned to conform to Indian customs. From the outset, trade was a formal and ritualized process. On Vancouver Island, the villagers paddled to one visiting ship "with exceeding great haste, singing the tune, and at the end of every cadence altogether would point their paddles first aft and then forward, first whooping shrill and then hoarse." On the Columbia, welcomes seem to have been less formal. Ships anchored offshore and waited for the Indians to come to them. The Chinook often acknowledged their presence with a gunshot, but the Indians did not come at once. Each village traded as a group, not as individuals. The Indians approached in canoes. Once on board, everyone held back as the captain and the chief exchanged gifts, entertained each other, and set exchange rates. After three to five days, the "trade broke" and all joined in. An exchange of gifts often closed the bargaining, just as a gift exchange had opened it.[67]

"HIGLERS"

> They are great higlers in trade and if they conceive you anxious to purchase will be a whole day bargaining for a handfull of roots; . . . they invariably refuse the price first offered them. . . . I therefore believe this trait in their character proceeds from an avaricious all grasping disposition.
>
> —MERIWETHER LEWIS[68]

For Lewis and Clark, nothing caused more misunderstanding than the trading relationship. The underlying reason was that the role trade occupied in Native society differed from the role it played in their own. To Euro-Americans, trade was an impersonal exchange of goods whose value had nothing to do with either party's character or worth. To Indians, trade was a relationship symbolized by the goods that changed hands. Goods were not just payments but were affirmations of each party's place in the community. Trade, gift-giving, steal-

ing, and gambling were all social acts that used property to carry messages about friendship, power, and respect.

The way a payment was made could be as important as what it was. Goods presented in an offhand or impersonal way were not always valued. Lewis and Clark recorded several instances when their proffered payments were rejected. For example, Old Toby, the Shoshone guide who took them over the Bitterroots, inexplicably left them without receiving his pay. There is no way to know why. But what they saw as wages for services, Toby might have seen as recognition of his status and relationship with them. If they telegraphed the wrong message, it could easily have made the goods offensive and worthless.[69]

On the plateau and the Pacific coast, different rules applied to trade with friends and trade with non-friends. Trade with friends and kin, an activity that merged with gift-giving, was incorporated into almost every milestone of life.

A Sea Otter, 1784
This face launched a thousand ships to the northwest coast of America when it was published in the report of Captain James Cook's last expedition. Cook's men found that the sea otter, quite different from the land otter, was prized by Chinese mandarins for robes. "The Sea Otter is found on the sea coast and in the salt water," Lewis wrote. "This anamal when fully grown is as large as a common mastive dog." He gave a detailed description of it and concluded, "It is the riches[t] and I think the most delicious fur in the world. . . . it is deep thick silkey in the extreem and strong." They brought back several of the skins, having paid dearly for them.

Camphorwood chest, early to mid-1800s
Trade with China was the real goal of the American mariners who visited the northwest coast. They traded their loads of fur in Canton for Chinese goods like this camphorwood chest covered with painted pigskin, a type of item exported to the United States from 1785 on. The chests came in sets nested inside each other, with the innermost one lined in tea paper and containing tea.

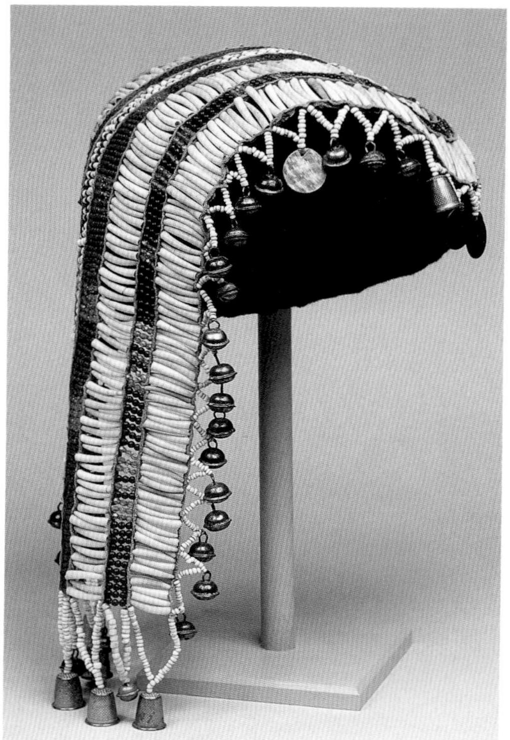

Wedding veil, c. 1890
Exchange of goods was woven into every aspect of life. Marriage was solemnified by gifts between the extended families, without which no union was legitimate. Veils like this, literally made of money, were part of the bride's raiment, ceremoniously removed and given to the groom's family. It is made from dentalium shells, Chinese coins, and European beads—all used as currency. It was worn by Talwasa, a Klickitat woman, for her wedding in 1890, but it reflects much older customs. "If both sides respected their wedding they traded all the time," Delores George, a Yakima woman, said. "This was one way we have of taking care of each other."

Exchanges of goods opened new relationships, expressed honorable intentions, and validated a person's change of status. Occasions for gift exchange included birth, a boy's first hunt, a girl's first root-gathering, a young person's first participation in a public dance or ceremony, ear piercing, name giving, marriage, and death. Of these, marriage was a particularly formal occasion because it was seen—especially in the upper classes—as initiating a kin relationship between whole families, not just the individuals getting married. The upper Chinookan wedding ceremony consisted of a series of formal visits between the two extended families. Each relative would choose a member of the other family as a gift-giving partner, and on each visit they would present goods. At the climax of the ceremony, the bride stood on a robe while her family poured baskets of beads, pouches, and finery over her, goods that the groom's family took. The groom's family then draped the bride in blankets, shawls, and cloth, which the bride's family removed. The relationships did not end with the wedding; family members continued gifting each other years later. "The purpose of the gifts was that people should not gossip later and that the union should be permanent," Mabel Teio, an elderly Wishram, said in 1924–25. In the absence of a church or government, gifts cemented the obligations of each family to the other.[70]

Some trade relationships were like the pseudo-kinship of marriage. On the plateau, some individuals chose a friend from another tribe as a permanent, exclusive trade partner called a "*yah-lipt*." A *yah-lipt* relationship lasted a lifetime and could even be inherited. Sometimes the *yah-lipt* families intermarried. Stwire Waters, born in the early nineteenth century, described the protocol of *yah-lipt* trade: "I come to see you. I bring blankets, furs, beads. . . . These, I give to you. I do not say anything. I leave them without words. You are glad to see me. You take me in and feed me. We are Yah-lipt. I am your Yah-lipt; and you are my Yah-lipt. . . . I stay several days. Then I say: 'Now I go back home.' You say 'All right!' Then you . . . select maybe ten, maybe twenty of best horses and give them to me. We have had a good time, and I go home feeling fine. Yah-lipt is not . . . the way the white people do business. White man goes to another white

Gaming bones, late 1800s
Trade and gifting were not the only ways wealth changed hands. Huge quantities of goods were redistributed through gambling, which accompanied most trade fairs, potlatches, and ceremonies. It was a team sport, with officials and rules, played by one village against another; some professional gamblers were sponsored by village leaders. Gambling luck was granted by one's guardian spirit, and the victor had the honor of giving out the winnings among his or her friends and family. Clark illustrated a gaming bone like these in his journal, saying the contestant "changed it from hand to hand with great dexterity . . . and when he was ready for the opposit party to guess he Separated his hands. . . . if the opposit party guessed the hand of each man the bone was given to them."

King Comcomly's Burial Canoe, 1847
Publicly giving goods to the dead expressed the survivors' grief and upheld the reputation of the family. The tomb of this prominent chief was heaped with kettles and draped with blankets so that he would not be ashamed to enter the spirit world poor. Lewis and Clark met Comcomly on November 20, 1805, and gave him a medal. He was a well-known Chinook leader who later exercised iron control over trade with both the American Astoria expedition and the British Hudson's Bay Company. Lewis and Clark wrote that in the Chinook style of burial a small canoe was placed on crossbars morticed into four upright posts, "in which the body is laid after beaing Carefully roled in a robe of Some dressed Skins; a paddle is also deposited with them." They described offerings of "Brass kittles & frying pans pearced thro their bottoms, baskets, bowls of wood, Sea Shels, Skins, bits of Cloth, Hair, Bags of Trinkets & Small peices of bone &c." From the grave goods, they deduced a Chinook belief in an afterlife, though they added: "We cannot understand them Sufficiently to make any enquiries relitive to their religious opinions."

friend says: 'How long? When you pay back?' . . . That is not Yah-lipt. Indian never says any thing about paying back. . . . That is good, the Indian way."[71] This was a model trade relationship based on generosity and reciprocity.

Nez Perce women also had networks of trading relationships with women from other tribes, relationships that survived into the twentieth century, though they called the exchanges "swaps" or "help-outs" to distinguish them from commercial trades. A person who wanted to trade phrased her request as "asking for help," which could not be refused. Such social trades did not include bargaining but did include visiting, chatting, and eating traditional foods together. The items traded were supposed to be of exactly equal value, such as a blanket for a bag of roots; but sometimes women cheated—a violation never mentioned but often retaliated for in clever ways. The goods received in trades were often used only for other trades, so that they circulated throughout the network, binding women together across the plateau.[72]

Lewis and Clark recorded what seem to have been attempts by Chinookans to initiate cordial trade relationships with them. A Clatsop named Cuscalah visited the fort on Christmas Eve. Clark wrote: "He laid before Capt Lewis and my Self each a mat and a parcel of roots—Some time in the evening two files was demanded for the presents of mats and roots, as we had no files to part with, we each returned the present which we had received, which displeased Cuscalah a little."[73] People who rebuffed overtures of friendly trade fitted into another category—non-friends. With them, trade still went on, but by different rules. The relationship was competitive and adversarial, and the object of the trade was to win. The haggling was intense because it was for prestige as well as profit. It was a form of ritualized conflict, like sports. Even theft was a permissible ploy, expressing disrespect.

Many of Lewis and Clark's complaints about the Chinookans stemmed from the fact that the Corps men had gotten themselves labeled as non-friends. To Clark, the Chinook had a "craveing dispostn." He added, "It is a bad prac-

Woman of Nootka Sound, 1778
Women like this high-ranking individual dressed in chiefly garb were the kind who dealt with Euro-Americans in trade. Captain William Sturgis traded with one woman who "was the keenest and shrewdest among the shrewd. She professed great regard for white people, and often remarked, in a very flattering manner . . . 'All white men are my children.'" Lewis and Clark derisively called the most powerful woman they met "the old baud."

tice to receive a present from those Indians as they are never Satisfied for what they re[ce]ive in return if ten time the value of the articles they gave." The Clatsop were "Close deelers, & Stickle for a verry little, never close a bargin except they think they have the advantage." The Tillamook "would not trade the Smallest piece except they thought they got an advantage of the bargain, their disposition is averitious, & independant in trade." Other Euro-Americans reported similar experiences after they had earned the Indians' contempt as a result of their antisocial acts, such as accepting heaps of gifts to open trade and then sailing away without reciprocating. "When offering objects for sale they are very sulky if their tender is not responded to," wrote Captain Edward Belcher, a perceptive British explorer who visited the mouth of the Columbia in 1839. "I think many of the unprovoked attacks . . . have originated in some transaction of this nature—refusal to trade being deemed almost a declaration of war."[74]

Another aspect of Chinookan trade that startled Lewis and Clark was the role of women. "Their women are permitted to speak freely before them," Lewis wrote, "and sometimes appear to command with a tone of authority; they generally consult them in their traffic and act in conformity to their opinions." In fact, throughout the Pacific Northwest, trading with Euro-Americans was considered women's work. Men justified the division of labor on the grounds that "women could talk with white men *better* than they could, and were willing to talk *more*." Women also had the advantage of being able to offer sex, a transaction no one frowned on as long as it did not result in pregnancy. In addition, they were less threatening to the apprehensive seamen—a reaction they took full advantage of. "We are more or less the dupes of their cunning," Captain John Meares, a trader, wrote. "The women . . . would play us a thousand tricks, and treat the discovery of their finesse with an arch kind of pleasantry that baffled reproach."[75]

Jefferson had specifically enjoined Lewis and Clark to gather information on Indian trade, and they fulfilled their duty by compiling lists of products in demand. They saw trade as utilitarian, something done to meet material needs. But the Chinookans did not need Euro-American goods to survive. They traded for convenience, novelty, prestige, and entertainment. At best, they expected trade to be the start of a long relationship. It took time to sound out a trading partner, learn his character, and build friendship or kinship. The captains were impatient with such time-consuming interaction, thinking the Indians were just holding out for higher prices. Goodwill and a good reputation were not the sorts of capital their commerce hinged on. They never expected to see their Chinookan trade partners again.

Woman's skirt, pre-1840
Lewis professed to being scandalized by the indecency of this style of skirt, worn by Chinookan women. The skirt was, he said, "of sufficient thickness when the female stands erect to conceal those parts usually covered from familiar view, but when she stoops or places herself in many other attitudes, this battery of Venus is not altogether impervious to the inquisitive and penetrating eye of the amorite." Lewis saw skirts like this made of three materials: "white cedar bark, bruised or broken into small shreds"; "little twisted cords of the silk grass knoted at their ends"; and "flags and rushes which are woarn in a similar manner." Most of the skirts in museums today, including this one, are made of cattail. This is from George Catlin's collection. It has been suggested that it was given to him by Clark, who had "two squaw's petticoats" in his museum, but there is no way to prove this.

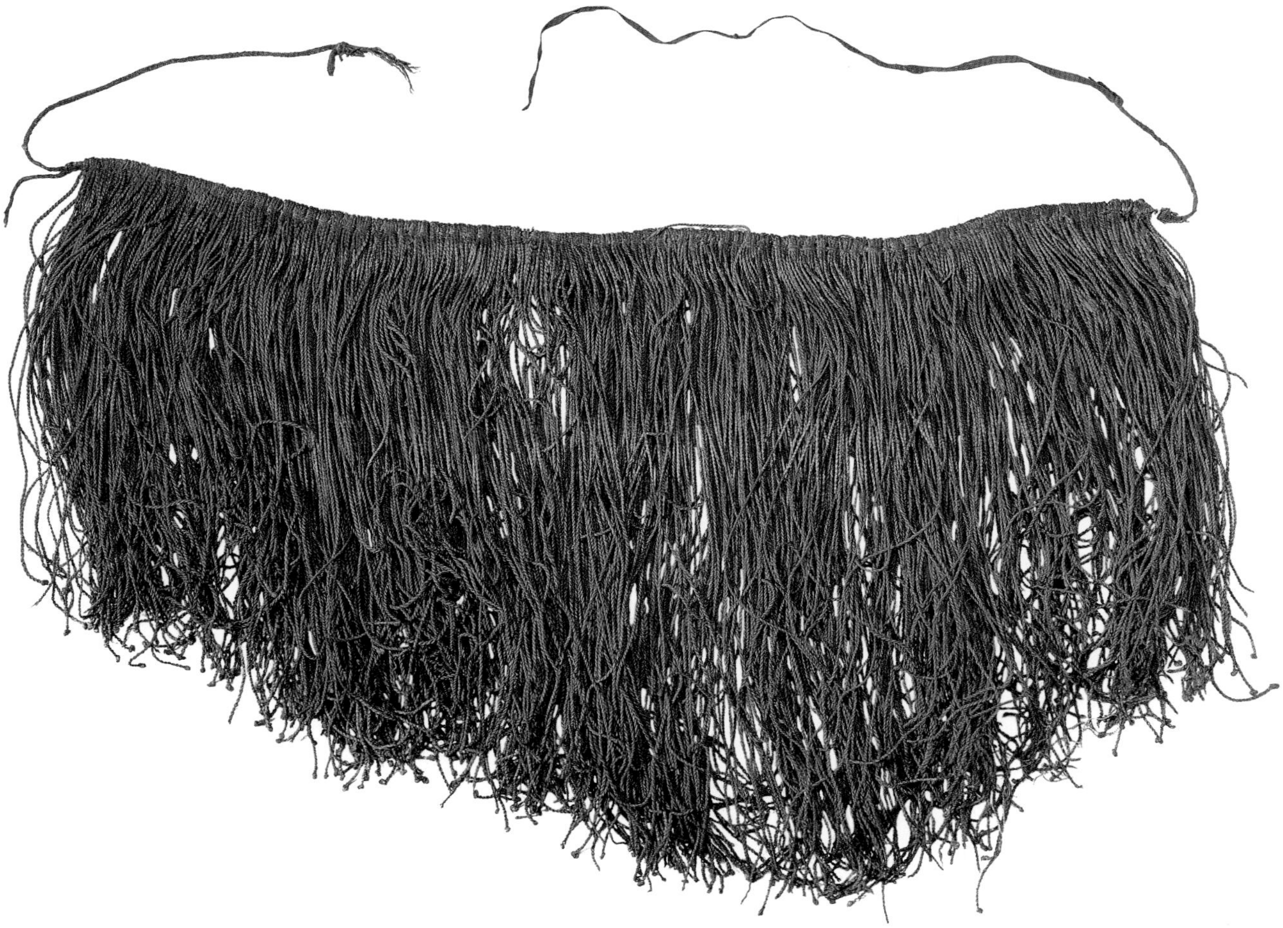

EIGHT Curing and Plants

To know that opening a vein in the arm, or foot, would relieve a pain in the head or side . . . marks an advanced period in the history of medicine.

—BENJAMIN RUSH[1]

O! how horriable is the day," Clark wrote as they huddled in their waterlogged tents on November 22. "Waves brakeing with great violence against the Shore throwing the Water into our Camp &c. all wet and Confind to our Shelters."[2]

The time had come to make a decision about whether to winter on the coast or return partway up the river. As Joseph Whitehouse told it: "In the Evening our Officers had the whole party assembled in order to consult which place would be the best, for us to take up our Winter Quarters at. The greater part of our Men were of opinion; that it would be best, to cross the River, & if we should find game plenty . . . to stay near the Sea shore, on account of making Salt, which we are nearly out of." There was also some lingering hope that a trading ship might arrive to replenish their supplies. "The Solicitations of every individual, except one of our party induced us . . . to fix on a Situation as convenient to the Elk & Sea Coast as we Could find," Clark wrote.[3]

So they crossed the estuary to the south side, where the elk were rumored to be more numerous, and Lewis set out with three men to scout a place to build a fort. The rest of the group waited. The weather did not improve. "24 days Since we arrived in Sight of the Great Western; (for I cannot Say Pacific) Ocian as I have not Seen one

Razor box of Patrick Gass, c. 1805
The descendants of Patrick Gass, the expedition's carpenter, inherited this hand-carved box with the story that it had been given to Gass by Sacagawea. Gass's journal did not record any such gift; but expedition members did exchange gifts at festive times—like Christmas of 1805, when Sacagawea gave Clark two dozen weasel tails. The box cover slides open and can be secured by inserting a pin through a hole in the cover.

pacific day Since my arrival in its vicinity," Clark tried to joke. "Its waters are forming and [per]petially breake with emenc waves on the Sands and rockey Coasts, tempestous and horiable." Sacagawea tried to raise his spirits with a gift. "The Squar gave me a piece of bread made of flour which She had reserved for her child and carefully Kept untill this time, which has unfortunately got wet, and a little Sour—this bread I eate with great Satisfaction."[4]

At last, on December 5, Whitehouse recorded: "Captain Lewis & 3 Men . . . returned to Camp with the Canoe. They informed us, that they had found a tolerable good place, to build our Winter quarters at. The place they said lay up a small river, about 4 Miles on the South side." They would call it Fort Clatsop in honor of the neighboring Indian tribe.[5]

It took most of December to build the fort. "We raised another line of our huts and began the last line of our huts forming three [sides of a] Square and 7 rooms 16 by 18 feet large," Ordway described the project on December 13. "The other [side of the] Square we intend to picket and have gates at the 2 corners." By Christmas, they were all sleeping under roofs again, an improvement that put them in a festive mood. "This morning at day we were Saluted by all our party under our winders, a Shout and a Song," Clark wrote. They "were Chearfull all the morning. . . . all the party Snugly fixed in their huts." He recorded, "I recved a presnt of Capt L. of a fleece hosrie [hosiery,] Shirt Draw[er]s and Socks—, a pr. mockersons of Whitehouse a Small Indian basket of Gutherich, two Dozen white weazils tails of the Indian woman." The men who used tobacco received some as a gift, and the rest got silk handkerchiefs. "We have no ardent Spirits," John Ordway observed, "but are all in good health which we esteem more than all the ardent Spirits in the world. we have nothing to eat but poore Elk meat . . . but Still keep in good Spirits as we expect this to be the last winter that we will have to pass in this way."[6]

The same thought sustained Lewis through a gloomy New Year's Day. "Our repast of this day . . . consisted principally in the anticipation of the 1st day of January 1807, when in the bosom of our friends we hope to . . . enjoy the repast which the hand of civilization has prepared for us. at present we were content with eating our boiled Elk and wappetoe."[7]

That winter, they retreated from the cordiality of their relations with the

Page 248: *Medicine Man, Performing His Mysteries over a Dying Man* (detail), 1832. See page 269.

Indians. On New Year's Day, Lewis wrote up new regulations to govern discipline at Fort Clatsop. He seems to have felt that the men of the Corps were becoming too relaxed and informal, both among themselves and with their Native neighbors, and so he adopted a stricter policy of racial separation: "At sunset on each day, the Sergt . . . will collect and put out of the fort, all Indians. . . . both gates shall be shut, and secured, and the main gate locked and continue so untill sunrise the next morning." The visitors so summarily evicted protested their treatment in vain.[8]

Isolated far from reminders of Euro-American society and social order, Lewis, like many another frontiersman, may have worried that the process of assimilation was in danger of going the wrong way. After their long immersion in Indian culture, the men had become too trusting and sociable, he felt. "So long have our men been accustomed to a friendly intercourse with the natives, that we find it difficult to impress on their minds the necessity of always being

Flathead Indians, 1861
In contrast to Lewis's negative view, other visitors to the Clatsop and Chinook saw "fine-looking, straight-limbed males" and "well Featured" women. George Catlin, the artist of this image, visited them in around 1855 and called them "Flatheads," but he did not paint this picture until 1861. The woman on the left wore the traditional string skirt and carried her baby in a head-flattening cradle.

Head-flattening cradle, pre-1840
This cradle collected by George Catlin was one of two styles of head-flattening cradles. A basketry attachment hinged to the top (right) was gradually tightened to flatten the baby's forehead. "The child is wrapped in rabbits' skins, and placed in this little coffin-like looking cradle, from which it is not, in some instances, taken out for . . . three, five, or eight weeks, until the bones are so formed as to keep their shapes, and preserve this singular appearance through life," Catlin wrote. Since he owned this artifact before he visited the west coast, curators have speculated (probably incorrectly) that Clark gave it to him.

Chinook Lodge (interior), 1844
Clark portrayed life in a Chinook house in terms of domestic harmony: "Several families of those people usially reside together in the Same room; they appear to be the father mother with their Sons and their Sons wives and children; their provisions appears to be in common and the greatest harmoney appears to exist among them." He described the houses much as shown here—as large as thirty by fifty feet, arranged around a large sunken fireplace, carpeted with mats, and furnished with raised beds, "each family haveing a nice painted ladder to assend up to their beads." This sketch of an 1841 scene was published in the report of the Wilkes Expedition.

on their guard. . . . the well known treachery of the natives by no means entitle them to such confidence, and we must check it's growth in our own minds." As the rain fell, he brooded darkly on the return journey of "4000 miles through a country exclusively inhabited by savages."[9]

Lewis had pulled back from the brink of cultural openness that he had been nearing while among the Shoshone. His moment of wavering identity was gone, replaced by a visceral feeling of threat. He expressed an almost physical revulsion to the coastal Indians: "They are low in statu[r]e reather diminutive, and illy shapen; possessing thick broad flat feet, thick ankles, crooked legs wide mouths thick lips, nose moderately large, fleshey, wide at the extremity with large nostrils, black eyes and black coarse hair." At one point he burst out, "I think the most disgusting sight I have ever beheld is these dirty naked wenches."[10]

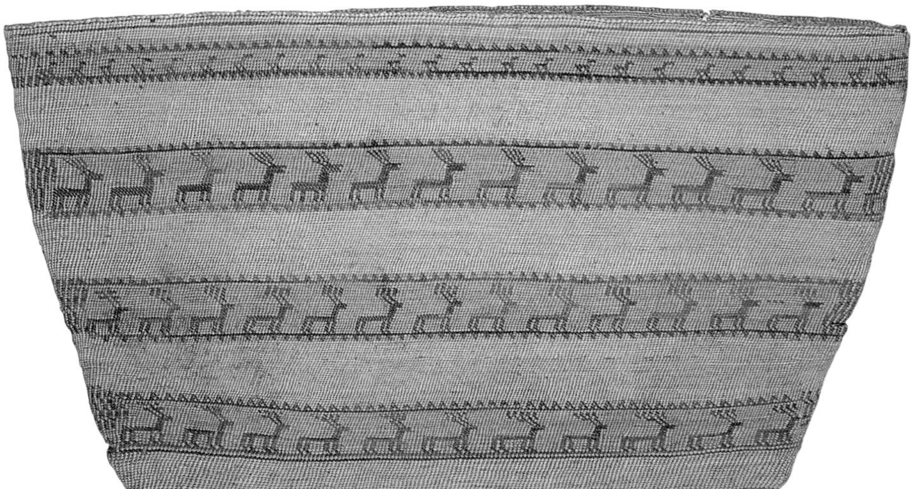

Bag, pre-1841
Among the Clatsop, Clark wrote, "I purchased 3 mats and bags all neetly made of flags and rushes, those bags are nearly Square of different size's open on one Side." Lewis added: "They make a number of bags and baskets not watertight of cedar bark, silk-grass, rushes, flags and common coarse sedge. in these they secure their dryed fish, roots, buries, &c." This one is of sweet grass sedge (*Scirpus americanus*), bear grass, cedar bark, and sea grass. It was collected by the Wilkes Expedition at Neah Bay but is almost certainly Clatsop or Tillamook. On the rim is a common motif known as the hell-diver bird. The animals shown are probably elk.

A Whale Ashore—Klahoquat, 1869
On his visit in about 1855, George Catlin witnessed at Nootka Island much the same scene as Clark might have seen if he had arrived a few days earlier at the Tillamook butchering site. Catlin described the scene: "The monster lying high and dry on the beach, and the group of Indians, like ants around a sugar bowl, moving in all directions about it. . . . The beach, for half a mile, was almost literally covered with something—with reclining groups of women and children—with baskets, and bags, and cribs, and pouches, and every sort of vehicle they possessed, for transporting their respective proportions of the prize." Catlin painted this from memory in 1869.

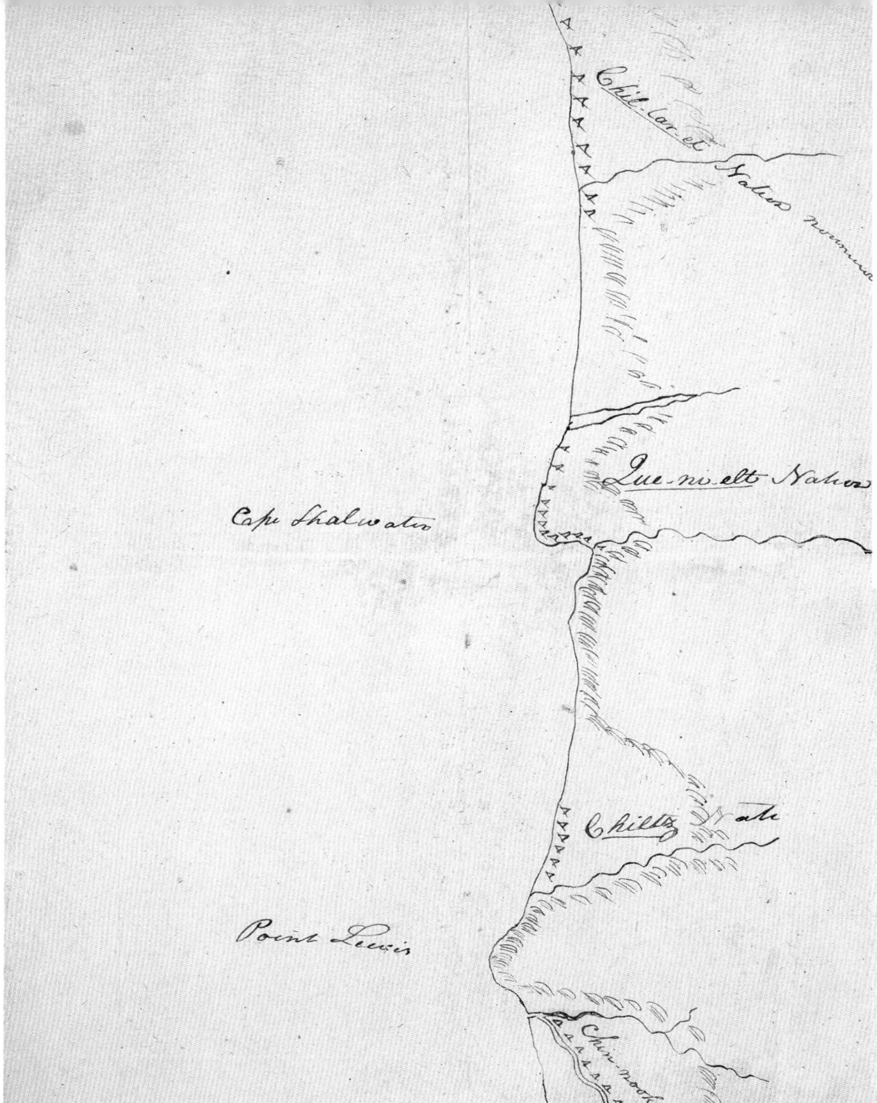

Route maps of the mouth of the Columbia, 1806

Clark made his rough maps of the river and coast to be assembled into a large mosaic. He undoubtedly drew these four segments during the winter at Fort Clatsop.

The Clatsop tribe and its chief, Coboway, never gave the expedition the slightest cause to be concerned for their safety. In calmer moments, Lewis admitted they were a "mild inoffensive people" who were "very friendly" to the Corps. In their frequent visits to the fort, the Clatsop were "loquacious and inquisitive . . . generally cheerfull but never gay." Lewis wrote, "With us their conversation generally turns upon the subjects of trade, smoking, eating or their women." But he went on to express distaste at the ribald tenor of their talk.[11]

"The rain continued as usial all day," Clark wrote, in what became a constant refrain that winter. "The flees are So troublesom that I have Slept but little for 2 nights past. . . . hut Smoke verry bad." To keep the men busy and distracted from their dismal situation, the captains sent several of them to the seacoast to extract salt from the seawater. "Set out eairly to go by land to the Salt works," Ordway wrote. "Crossed the prarie where the land is in ridges like the waves the frozen rain beat in our faces verry hard. we got on the coast crossd. a river where we waided to our middles and was glad to git in an old Indian house where we made a fire and Stayed all night. Sand flew & waves rold." Fortunately, the salt they produced was "excellent, fine, strong, & white." Lewis recorded, "This was a great treat to myself and most of the party." It was not just for seasoning their food; the salt was a preservative without which meat would spoil in a day, greatly increasing the labor of hunting.[12]

Trenchers, 1850s
Lewis and Clark mentioned "troughs" or "trenchers" among the "Culinary articles of the Indians in our neighbourhood." Lewis described troughs "dug out of a solid piece" of wood, as were these. Clark was served a meal of soup "in a neet wooden trencher, with a Cockle Shell to eate it with." The shells decorating the rims of these dishes appear to be cowrie. The artifacts were collected by the early ethnographer George Gibbs at Cape Flattery.

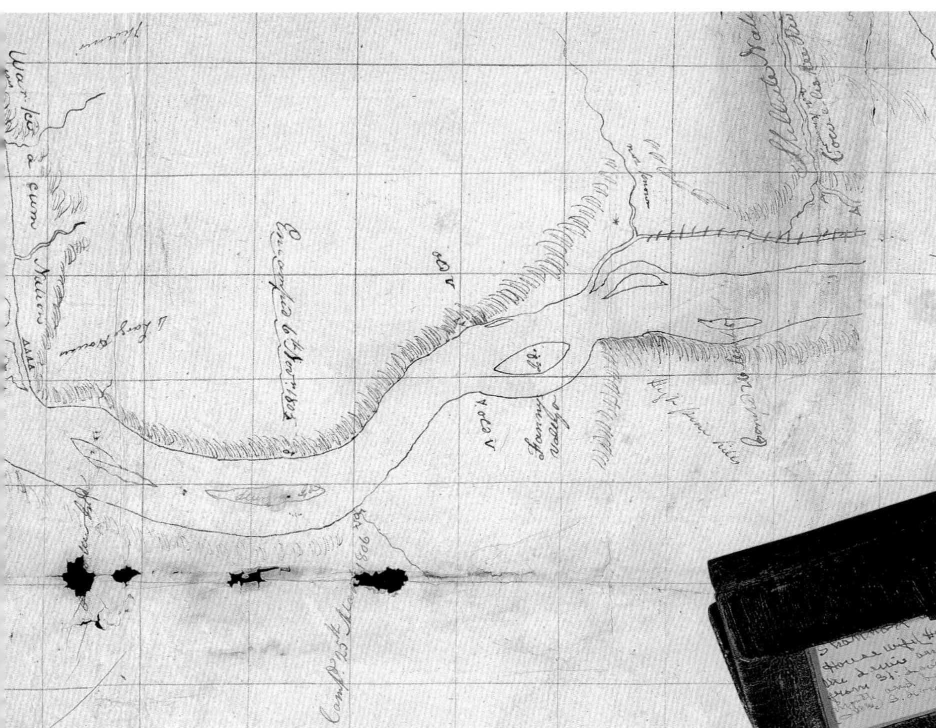

Housewife (sewing kit) of George Shannon, c. 1804
According to George Shannon's descendants, he used this sewing kit to mend his clothes and moccasins during the expedition. It was passed down to Shannon's great-grand-daughter Elizabeth Monroe Story. Shannon, the youngest soldier on the expedition, was in the party returning Shehek-Shote to his home when they were attacked by the Arikara in 1807. He was wounded, and his leg was amputated. Thereafter, with some help from Clark, he attended university and became a lawyer and politician, holding state offices in both Kentucky and Missouri.

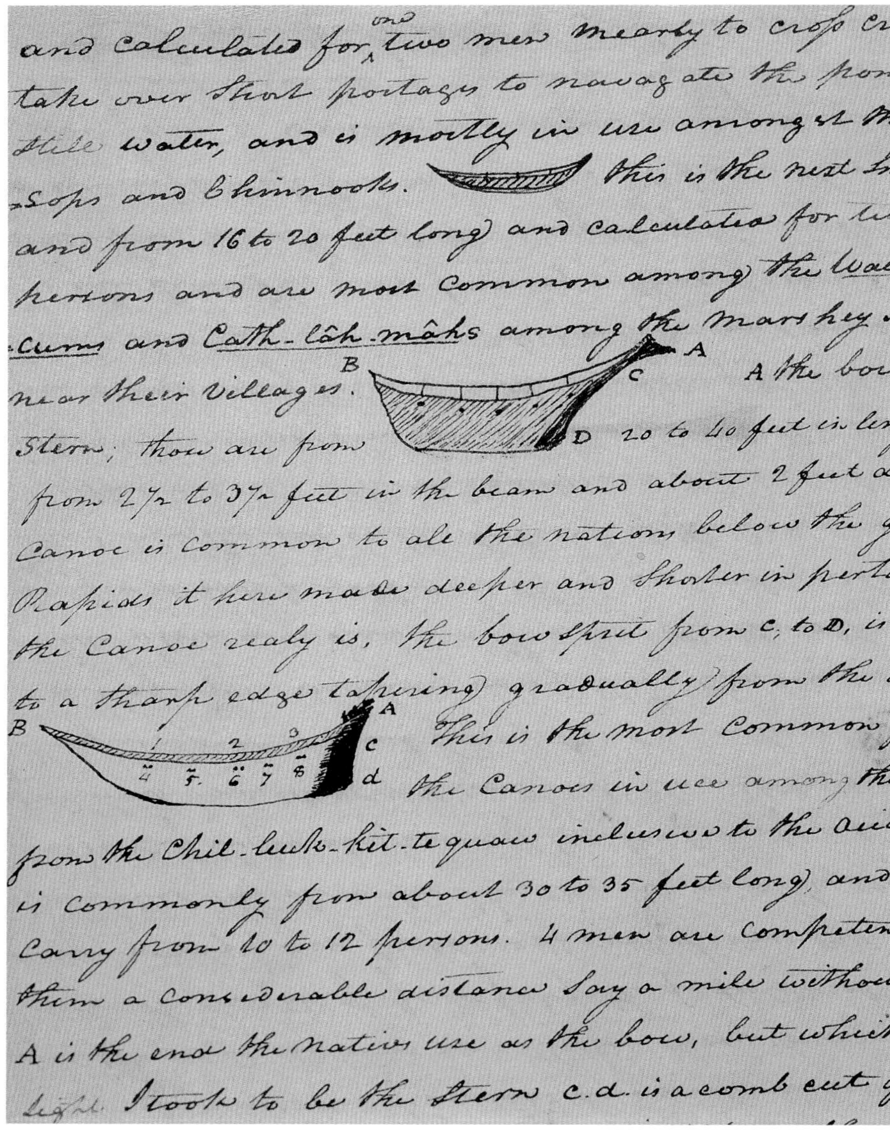
and calculated for one two men nearly to cross Cre
take over short portages to navagate the pon
still water, and is mostly in use among st the
Sops and Chinnooks. this is the next sm
and from 16 to 20 feet long and calculated for tw
persons and are most common among the Wau
-cums and Cath-lâh-mâhs among the marshey I
near their villages. A the bow
Stern; those are from 20 to 40 feet in len
from 2½ to 3½ feet in the beam and about 2 feet d
Canoe is common to all the nations below the g
Rapids it here made deeper and shorter in perpo
the Canoe realy is, the bow sprit from C, to D, is
to a sharp edge tapering gradually from the
this is the most Common
the Canoes in use among the
from the Chil-luck-kit-te quaw inclusive to the ocea
is commonly from about 30 to 35 feet long, and
Carry from 10 to 12 persons. 4 men are competent
them a considerable distance say a mile without
A is the end the nativs use as the bow, but which
light I took to be the Stern c.d. is a comb cut o

Sketch of a condor, 1806
Lewis, the more expert naturalist, spent pages describing animals and plants in his journal during the winter of 1805–6. Here, Clark copied his illustration of the giant California condor (*Gymnogyps californianus*), a species already known to science but never before seen on the Columbia River. Lewis gave a detailed description and added: "Shannon brought me one of the large carrion Crow or Buzzads of the Columbia which they had wounded and taken alive. I bleive this to be the largest bird of North America. . . . between the extremities of the wings it measured 9 feet 2 inches. . . . we did not met with this bird untill we had decended the Columbia below the great falls, and have found them more abundant below tide-water than above."

Another distraction soon arrived. "We were informed . . . that a whale had foundered on the coast to the S.W.," Clark wrote. "I determine to Set out early tomorrow . . . in quest of the whale. . . . [The] Indian woman was very impatient to be permitted to go with me, and was therefore indulged; She observed that She had traveled a long way with us to See the great waters, and that now that monstrous fish was also to be Seen, She thought it verry hard that She Could not be permitted to See either." Her protest gives a rare glimpse of Sacagawea's personality.[13]

The way to the whale took Clark's small party over a steep, rocky headland. "From this point I beheld the grandest and most pleasing prospects which my eyes ever surveyed," Clark said. "In my frount a boundless Ocean . . . rageing with emence wave." He then "proceeded to the place the whale had perished, found only the Skelleton of this monster on the Sand. . . . the Whale was already pillaged of every valuable part by the Kil a mox Inds." Typically, he reacted to the sight by recording in his journal: "This Skeleton measured 105 feet."[14]

The whale was in the territory of the Tillamook. This tribe spoke a language different from that of the Chinook and had less cordial relations with visiting Euro-Americans. Ominously, the American sea captain Robert Gray called the bay on which they lived "Murderer's Harbor" after the Tillamook killed his African servant in 1788. During the night they spent at the Tillamook

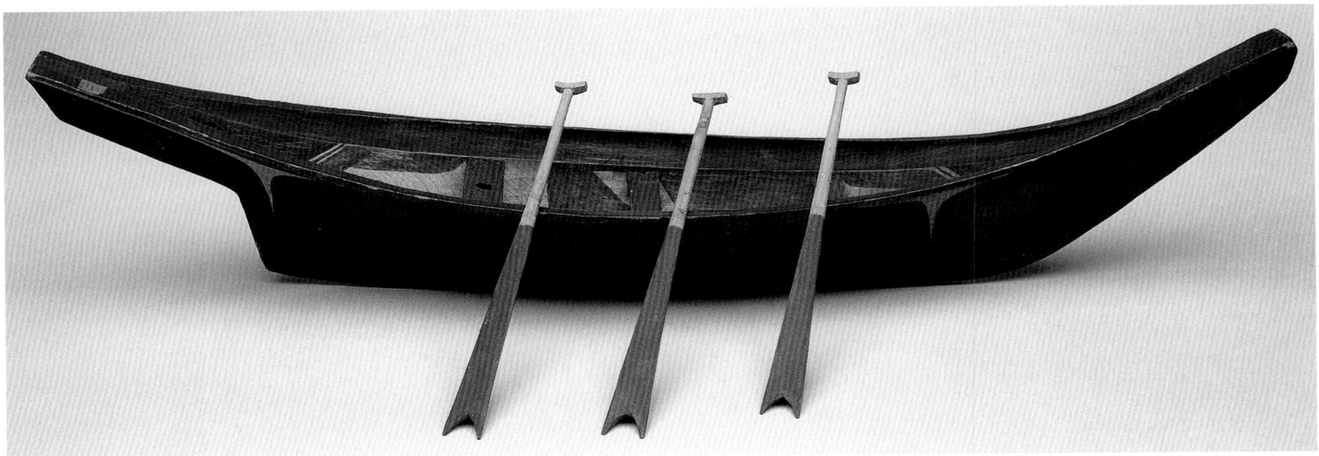

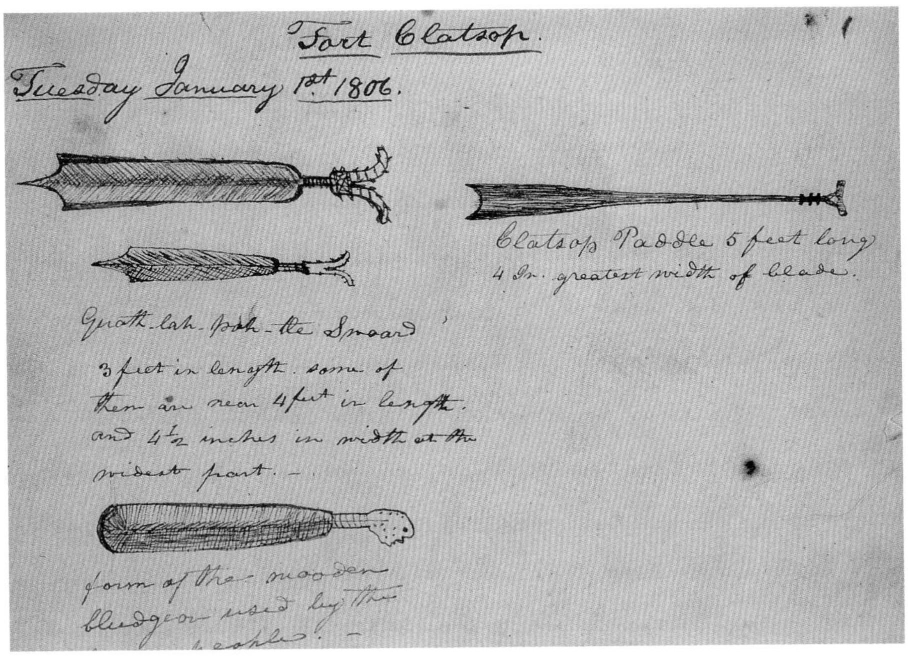

Sketch of Chinookan canoes, 1806 and **Model canoe and paddles, pre-1841** and **Sketch of a Clatsop paddle, 1806**
"The natives inhabiting the lower portion of the Columbia River make their canoes remarkably neat light and well addapted for riding high waves," Lewis wrote. "I have seen the natives near the coast riding waves in these canoes with safety and apparently without concern where I should have thought it impossible for any vessel of the same size to lived a minute. they are built of whitecedar or Arborvita generally, but sometimes of the firr. they are cut out of a solid stick of timber." Lewis described five separate styles of canoe, and Clark described six. The model shown here is either type three ("common to all the nations below the grand rappids . . . from twenty to thirty five feet") or type four ("the most common form of the canoe in uce among the Indians from; the Chil-luck-kit-te-quaw inclusive to the Ocean and is usually about 30 or 35 feet long, and will carry from ten to twelve persons"). One of these is probably the size that the expedition purchased. Clark noted that his sketches were out of proportion; the canoes were much longer in relation to their height.

village, Clark's party had the only near miss of the winter. "Last night about 10 oClock . . . I was alarmed by a loud Srile voice from the Cabins. . . . my guide who Continued with me made Signs that Some one's throat was Cut, by enquiry I found that one man [Hugh] McNeal was absent, I imediately Sent off Sergt. N. Pryor & 4 men in quest of McNeal who' they met comeing across the Creak in great hast." A Tillamook had befriended McNeal, secretly intending "to ass[ass]anate [him] for his Blanket and what fiew articles he had about him." The plot "was found out by a Chin nook woman who allarmed the men . . . in time to prevent the horred act."[15]

The rest of the winter passed in peaceful monotony. "The Men at the fort were employed making of Moccasins & mending their Cloathing . . . repairing the Carpenters Tools . . . dressing Elk & Deer Skins," Whitehouse wrote. Meanwhile, Clark "compleated a *map* of the Countrey" and wrote in his journal: "We now discover that we have found the most practicable and navigable passage across the Continent of North America." While Clark worked on maps, Lewis observed the plants and animals. "There are sveral species . . . in this neighbourhood which I shall discribe as well as my slender botanicall skil will enable me." He then filled page after page with detailed observations of plant and animal life.[16]

By March, they were preparing to set out for home. The occasion did not

Magnet and compass of William Clark, early 1800s
In Philadelphia, Lewis paid one dollar for a magnet to remagnetize the compass needles as necessary. However, Clark also ended up using the magnet to perform "magic" before Indian audiences on the Columbia River. This magnet belonged to Clark, but there is no way of knowing whether it is one he used on the expedition. The bar on the two poles is a "keeper" for maintaining the magnetism. The compass is a piece of jewelry Clark owned later in life; the chain it decorates was probably used to hold his watch.

call forth the heroic rhetoric that the departure from Fort Mandan had inspired. In the absence of the hoped-for traders, their resources had become alarmingly depleted. Lewis analyzed their subsistence and transportation needs and decided to resort to a time-tested expedient: theft. "Two handkercheifs would now contain all the small articles of merchandize which we possess. . . . we yet want another canoe, and as the Clatsops will not sell us one at a price which we can afford to give we will take one from them in lue of the six Elk which they stole from us in the winter." The Clatsop, who followed an ethic of food-sharing, would probably have been surprised at his accusation; they had supplied roots and plant foods in exchange for meat all winter.[17]

In case they perished on the way back home, Lewis planned for their deeds to be remembered: "We gave Delashelwilt . . . a list of our names . . . that through the medium of some civilized person who may see the same, it may be made known to the informed world, that the party consisting of the[se] persons . . . did penetrate . . . the Continent of North America." Delashelwilt, a Chinook chief, conscientiously gave the paper to the next trader who arrived—Samuel Hill, who anchored the *Lydia* in Baker Bay twelve weeks after the departure of the Corps.[18] On March 23, 1806, Clark noted: "We loaded our Canoes & at 1 P.M. left Fort Clatsop on our homeward bound journey. at this place we had . . . lived as well as we had any right to expect . . . not withstanding the repeeted fall of rain."[19]

The first leg of the homeward trip was troubled. Paddling against the spring current, the members of the party laboriously made their way from village to village, buying their meals at each stop. But the river tribes were unfriendly because the expedition was trespassing on their trade route without paying the customary toll. They responded with irritating harrassment, provoking the travelers.

Now Clark showed that some of the spirit of Coyote, the mythic trickster, had rubbed off on him. Rather than adopt the tone of a ruler, as he had on the Missouri, he used his knowledge of Native culture to play tricks on the people he met. At one village, he performed magic with a piece of cannon fuse. "Offered Several articles to the nativs in exchange for Wappato. they were Sulkey and they positively refused to Sell any. I had a Small pece of port fire match in my pocket. . . . I . . . put it into the fire and took out my pocket Compas. . . . the port fire cought and burned vehemently, which changed the Colour of the fire; with the Magnit I turned the Needle of the Compas about very briskly; which astonished and alarmed these nativs and they laid Several parsles of Wappato at my feet, & begged of me to take out the bad fire; to this I consented; at this moment the match being exhausted was of course extinguished."[20]

By contrast, Lewis's reaction was rage. Angered by a theft at the Cascades, he wrote, "This same tribe of villains the Wah-clel-lars, stole my dog this evening. . . . I . . . sent three men in pursuit of the theives with orders if they made the least resistence . . . to fire on them. . . . we . . . informed them by signs that if they . . . insulted our men we should put them to instant death. . . . I am convinced that no other consideration but our number at this moment protects us." Considering his behavior, he may have been right.[21]

At The Dalles, later travelers found the Wishram conducting what amounted to a protection racket: unruly young men would threaten the passing traders; the chiefs would then consent to protect the travelers, for a price. Fur

To-ma-quin, A Cascade Chief, Columbia River, 1847

The Cascade or Watlala Indians, a Chinookan tribe, earned death threats from Lewis by stealing his dog. Their main village was on the north side of the Columbia a mile below Beacon Rock, but they had fishing villages at the Cascades. After Corps member John Colter took a tomahawk from one of their homes, claiming that they had stolen it the year before, they were "very unfriendly." Forty years later Paul Kane, the artist of this portrait, had much the same experience: "They gave us a good deal of trouble and uneasiness." In both cases, their chief earned substantial rewards simply by being cooperative.

traders came to accept the practice as a price of doing business through Wishram territory. The system seems not to have been so organized in Lewis and Clark's day, or perhaps the party's military strength prevented its use; but that did not mean the tribe was cooperative. "Our men seem well disposed to kill a few of them," Lewis wrote. It wasn't just the enlisted men. Lewis himself was on a hair trigger.[22]

The Corps had relied on buying horses at The Dalles to avoid the tedious portage and upstream travel. Accordingly, Clark turned horse trader. "Took my merchindize to a rock . . . at a Short distance from the houses, and divided the articles of merchindize into parsels . . . and thus exposed them to view, informing the Indians that each parcel was intended for a horse. they tanterlised me the greater part of the day. . . . Maney of the natives . . . asked Such things as we had not and double as much of the articles which I had." The next day he resorted to a different stratagem. "I dressed the Sores of the principal Chief. . . . his wife who I found to be a Sulky Bitch . . . was Somewhat efflicted with pains in her back. this I thought a good oppertunity to get her on my Side. . . . I rubed a little Camphere on her temples and back, and applyed worm flannel to her back which She thought had nearly restored her. . . . this I thought a favourable time to trade. . . . I accordingly made him an offer which he excepted and Sold me two horses."[23]

Mt. Hood from Les Dalles, 1848
Clark first noticed Mt. Hood on October 19, 1805: "a conacal mountain S.W. toped with Snow." But it was not until November 3, after they had passed it, that they realized it was the mountain that Lieutenant William R. Broughton of the Vancouver expedition had mapped and named in 1792 for British Admiral Sir Samuel Hood. During their first trip through The Dalles, Clark called it "*Timm* or *falls* Mountain." On their way back, they used the British name.

Meanwhile, other Wishram were seeking entertainment by harassing Lewis and the party as they tried to transport their baggage over the portage. In response, Lewis threatened that if he "caught them attempting to perloin any article" from the party, he "would beat them severely. they went off in reather a bad humour." That day, Clark found that "not a Single horse Could be precured."[24] The enmity continued to escalate until the Corps left The Dalles—with only ten horses, forcing them to put the overflow baggage back in the canoes. They got away just in time to prevent Lewis from burning down the entire village in a rage over a stolen blanket.

"We proceeded on through an open plain country," Lewis wrote. They had left behind the land of the Chinookan merchants and were back on the plateau, among people who ardently desired direct access to Europeans and their goods.[25] The first tribe the Corps met were the friendly Wallawalla, camped opposite the mouth of the river that now bears their name. The autumn before, the captains had put off their statesmanlike chief, Yellept, with a promise that they would spend time at his village on the return voyage. He now made them live up to their promise, despite their eagerness to move on. They enjoyed the tribe's hospitality during a two-day visit that climaxed in an evening dance. "The Wallah wallahs . . . formed a half Circle arround our camp where they waited verry patiently to See our party dance," Clark wrote. "The fiddle was played and the men amused themselves with danceing about an hour. we then requested

Nez Perce Indian, c. 1856

"The Chopunnish are in general Stout well formd active men," Clark said of the Nez Perce. "They have high noses and maney of them on the acqueline order with chearfull and agreeable countinances." Lewis added, "They are generally well cloathed in their stile. their dress consists of a long shirt which reaches to the middle of thye, long legings which reach as high as the waist, mockersons, and robes. these are formed of various skins." This man, first painted by Paul Kane in 1847, appears to be wearing a pierced shirt, a type of war shirt associated with visionary experiences. The perforations signified bullet holes; bullets could pass through the shirts without harming the wearer. The man also has a pierced nose, a custom that gave the tribe its modern name, although it was more commonly practiced by tribes on the Columbia in Lewis and Clark's time. However, Clark did write, "The orniments worn by the Chopunnish are, in their nose a Single Shell of Wampom." By "wampum" he meant dentalium.

the Indians to dance. . . . the whole assemblage of Indians about 350 men women and Children Sung and danced at the Same time."[26]

Under a mistaken impression that the Nez Perce to whom they had entrusted their horses would soon be leaving to cross the mountains, Lewis and Clark "urged the necessity of . . . proceeding on imediately." The Wallawalla obligingly ferried them across the Columbia River and furnished them with enough horses so that they could continue on by land. Guided by a Nez Perce man who was going their way, they cut across country from the Columbia to the Snake, then followed the Snake River east to the Clearwater, the heart of Nez Perce country.[27]

THAT ICY BARRIER

The banks of the Clearwater were dotted with villages, most consisting of one or two unpartitioned longhouses inhabited by many families. It was the end of winter in this high country; the salmon had not yet arrived, and the root foods were still ripening, so food was scarce. When the large band of travelers arrived "extreemly hungary and much fatigued," their demands for food were not always graciously received. For their part, the members of the Corps were still irascible. One day, Clark recorded: "While at dinner an indian fellow very impertinently threw a half Starved puppy nearly into the plate of Capt. Lewis by way of derision for our eating dogs and laughed very heartily." He had chosen the wrong person to joke with. "Capt L.— was So provoked . . . that he cought the puppy and threw it with great violence at him . . . Seazed his tomahawk, and Shewed him by Sign that if he repeeted his insolence that he would tomahawk him, the fellow withdrew apparently much mortified."[28]

It was May 10 when they finally reached the main village of the Nez Perce deep in the mountains near present-day Kamiah, Idaho. "The air keen and Cold the Snow 8 inches deep on the plain," Clark wrote that morning. "We Collected our horses and . . . Set out for the Village of the Chief. . . . at 4 PM we arrived. . . . The Village of the *broken Arm* consists of one house or Lodge only which is 150 feet in length built . . . of Sticks, Mats and dry grass. it contains 24 fires and about double that number of families. . . . the noise of their women pounding the cows roots remind me of a nail factory."[29]

Buttons, late 1700s to early 1800s
Lewis and Clark were neither the first nor the last travelers in Indian country to resort to cutting buttons off their clothing to trade. Buttons were sold across North America; the Indians used them as decorative ornaments, not as fasteners. These brass and copper buttons found in excavations at The Dalles are of styles used in the late eighteenth and early nineteenth centuries. The most recent is the spherical one in the center, a type first manufactured around the War of 1812. There was at least one brass button manufacturer in America in 1802, but Lewis and Clark's buttons more likely came from England.

Broken Arm's first act was to hoist the American flag that the captains had left for him the previous year; his second was to shower them with food. "Those people has Shewn much greater acts of hospitallity than we have witnessed from any nation or tribe Since we have passed the rocky Mountains," Clark testified gratefully. "I directed the men not to croud their Lodge in serch of food the manner hunger has Compelled them to do . . . and which the *Twisted Hair* had informed us was disagreeable to the nativs."[30]

But the news was not all good. "The Spurs of the rocky mountains which were in view from the high plain to day were perfectly Covered with Snow. The Indians inform us that the Snow is yet So deep on the Mountains that we Shall not be able to pass them untill after the next full moon. . . . this [is] unwelcom intiligence."[31]

There was nothing to do but wait. After four days in the Nez Perce village, they moved across the river and "formed a Camp around a very conveniant Spot for defence." Clark wrote, "As we are Compelled to reside a while in this neighbourhood I feel perfectly Satisfied with our position." As they were settling in, Clark noted, with some surprise: "No Indians visit us to day which is a Singular circumstance as we have not been one day without Indians Since we left the long narrows of the Columbia."[32]

Although they were not in U.S. territory, which ended at the Rocky Mountains, the commanders must have felt close enough to switch back into their diplomatic personae. The day after they arrived, they met with the Indians. Clark wrote: "We thought it a favourable time to repeet . . . the views of our government with respect to the inhabitents of this Western part of the Continent . . . the Strength welth and powers of our Nation &c. to this end we drew a map of the Country with a coal on a mat in their way. . . . they appeared highly pleased." But Clark had mistaken politeness for assent; the tribe's official reply did not come until more than two weeks later. Then, "The *Chopunnish* [Nez Perce] held a Council . . . and resolved to pursue our advise. after this Council was over the principal Chief or the *broken arm*, took the flour of the roots of Cows and thickened the Soup in the Kitiles and baskets of all his people . . . enviting all such men as had resolved to abide by the decree of the councill to come and eat. . . . all Swallowed their objections if any they had, very cheerfully with their mush."[33]

A winter's worth of tension drained away as the Corps settled down in the mountain country of the Nez Perce. They spent the next month hunting, trading, and socializing. Part of their time was devoted to preparing for the journey ahead. Clark wrote: "We were obliged to have recourse to every Subterfuge in order to prepare . . . to meet that wretched portion of our journy, the Rocky Mountains. . . . Our traders McNeal and York are furnished with the buttons which Capt L—. and my Self Cut off of our Coats, Some eye water and Basilicon . . . and Some tin boxes which Capt L. had brought from Philadelphia. in the evening they returned with about 3 bushels of roots . . . not much less pleasing to us than the return of a good Cargo to an East India merchant." There was also time for horse races and other sports. On June 8, "in the evening Several foot races were run by the men of our party and the Indians; after which our party divided and played at prisoners base untill night."[34]

All the while, Lewis gazed eastward at "that icy barier" separating him from "friends and Country, from all which makes life esteemable.—patience, patience."[35]

CURING AND HEALTH

> The Indians of North-America are in possession of a number of active and important remedies. . . . What treasures of medicine may not be expected from a people, who although destitute of the lights of science, have discovered the properties of some . . . inestimable medicines?
>
> —BENJAMIN SMITH BARTON[36]

> We have no discoveries in the materia medica to hope for from the Indians . . . . it would be a reproach to our schools of physic if modern physicians were not more successful than the Indians even in the treatment of their own diseases.
>
> —BENJAMIN RUSH[37]

Two of the activities pursued by the captains during their snow-enforced delay showed a renewed spirit of openness and cultural exchange. Clark carried on a brisk business as a healer, and Lewis gathered botanical specimens—at least in part hoping to discover novel medicinal plants to bring back east. Indians and

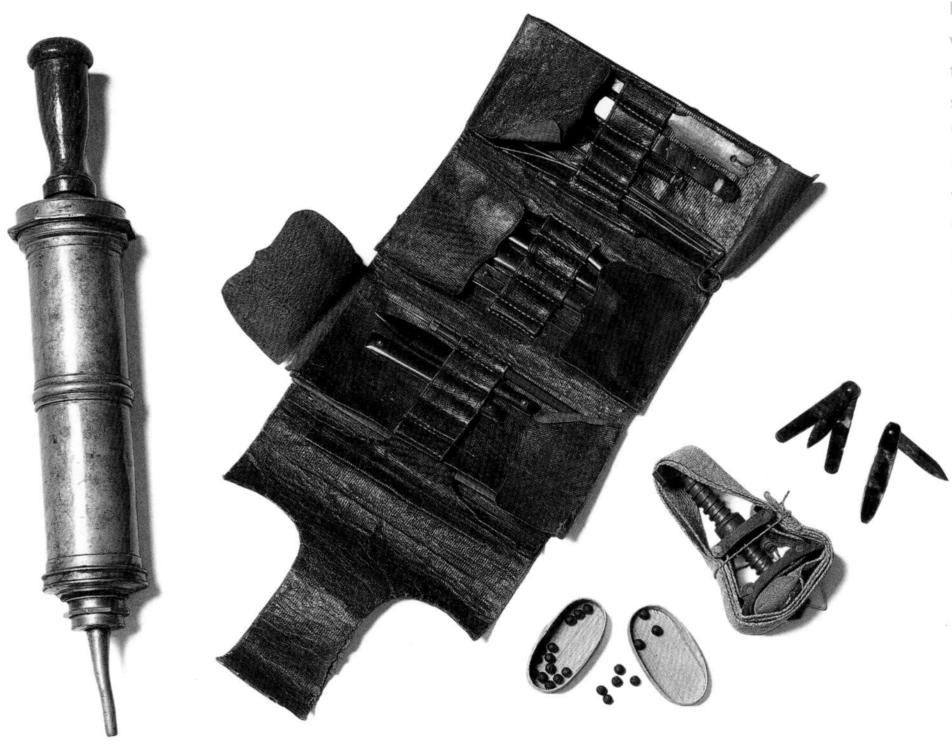

Medical instruments, early 1800s
These instruments correspond to some of the medical tools Lewis purchased for use on the journey (left to right): a clyster syringe (for enemas), surgical instruments, bilious pills (laxatives), a tourniquet, and two lancets (for bloodletting). Lewis originally thought he would need three clysters but settled for one; there are no further mentions of its use. His surgical instruments were described as "Pocket Inst[rument]s. small," so he probably was equipped to extract bullets, to suture wounds, and to lance boils but not to perform amputations or other major surgery. Some of the instruments in this pocket set are a scalpel, needle, forceps, lancet, bistoury, probe, director, and spatula. There is no record of what Dr. Rush's pills looked like, but these may be "Scott's pills," a type that Lewis and Clark also carried; they are labeled "Dr. Patrick Anderson's True Scots Pills." Although he had a tourniquet, Lewis inexplicably did not use it when Potts badly cut a vein in his thigh; instead, he improvised a tourniquet from a bandage and "a little cushon of wood." Lancets, however, he did use frequently, in such dangerous circumstances as heat exhaustion and pelvic inflammation. He resorted to his penknife when the lancets were not handy.

Medicine chest, 1804
Lewis paid the Philadelphia druggists Gillaspy & Strong $90.69 for a supply of medicines and a "Walnut Chest" to hold them. Many of the drugs he purchased correspond to ones in this chest: Peruvian bark (quinine), jalap, rhubarb, ipecac, calomel, tartar emetic, magnesia, and laudanum (tincture of opium and alcohol). Many of these drugs were believed to work by expelling impurities from the body. Medicine chests like this were standard equipment for physicians at the time, but this one is probably more elaborate than Lewis's. Although we know he packed his medicines in glass stoppered bottles and tin boxes, there is no record of what his medicine chest looked like.

Europeans had been benefiting from each other's knowledge about curing and health for three centuries, and yet it was a subject about which they still held very different beliefs.

Clark had gotten into the doctoring practice almost by accident. "As we decended last fall I met with a man, who Could not walk with a tumure on his thye. . . . I . . . left him Some Casteel Soap to wash the Sore which Soon got well. this . . . has raised my reputation and given those nativs an exolted oppinion of my Skill as a ph[ys]ician." His reputation was a lucky break for the Corps members; they had almost no trade goods left to buy provisions for the trip back, and people were willing to pay for cures. "In our present Situation I think it pardonable to continue this deception," Clark wrote.[38] "Great numbers of Indians apply to us for medical aide," he recorded six days later. He treated maladies as alarming as scrofula, ulcers, rheumatism, sore eyes, tumors, paralysis, and depression. He wrote, "All of those pore people thought themselves much benifited by what had been done for them."[39]

Medicine was one of the subjects the explorers had been asked to investigate; they carried a list of questions about such unsoldierlike subjects as the Indians' age at menarche and menopause, weaning of babies, hours of sleep, laxatives used, and tribal pulse rates at different times of day. Not surprisingly, they provided answers to few of these questions. On the plateau, however, they did assemble a lengthy catalog of Native medical complaints. Their interest was

Benjamin Rush, c. 1812
Benjamin Rush, the expedition's medical advisor, was the epitome of the professional physician. Trained in Edinburgh, he became a disciple of the innovative theories of William Cullen, who traced disease to imbalances in nervous energy. Rush developed the unorthodox theory that all disease was caused by one underlying condition: morbid excitement of the nervous system, causing convulsive action of the blood vessels, which produced every symptom from fever to insanity. His invariable treatment: depletion by purging, vomiting, or bloodletting, the last sometimes to the extent of three pints of blood a day.

not simply humanitarian—it was part of their ongoing evaluation of America's suitability for settlement. The best medical theory of the day held that disease could arise from the land, entering the body through impure air (vapors or "miasma") and water. The Indians' state of health was thus an indicator of the habitability of the future nation.[40]

In fact, European and Native American medical practices in 1806 were more similar to each other than either is to medicine today. Neither had any germ theory of disease. European doctors had inherited theories from medieval and classical times, and they varied from these theories only in detail, not substance. Galen's humoral theory, which held that health was due to a balance between the fluids of phlegm, yellow bile, black bile, and blood, was ultimately the rationale behind the most common treatments of the day: bleeding, laxatives, and emetics. Drugs were used not only because of proven efficacy but also because of the medieval Doctrine of Signatures. In this theory, the resemblance of a plant to a body part or symptom was taken as a clue to its effects: thus, yellow plants were thought useful for jaundice, red plants for bleeding, wormroot for worms, and so on.[41]

Primitive as their knowledge was, European doctors had one significant advantage over their Indian counterparts: medical information from around the world, a result of wide travel and trade. The most effective drugs in Lewis's medicine box were the discoveries of indigenous people on other continents—

the malaria remedy quinine, from a Peruvian tree bark; the purgative jalap, from the Mexican morning-glory; the emetic ipecacuanha, from the Brazilian ipecac vine; and the painkiller opium, from Turkish poppies. Using them among the Nez Perce, the Corps acted as a conduit passing herbal knowledge from one Native society to another.[42]

The most potentially beneficial medicine known to Europeans was missing from Lewis's portable dispensary, but not for lack of effort. Smallpox inoculation, discovered by Arabic physicians, had come to Europe in the previous century. Europeans added their own improvements by developing the less risky cowpox vaccine and began the century-long process of eradicating that disease from their population before they understood how the vaccine worked. Thomas Jefferson had instructed Lewis to pack some "matter of the kinepox" for inoculating vulnerable Indian tribes, and Lewis did so; but the material spoiled before he even left Cincinnati.[43]

The Corps' actual medical practices were a combination of two parallel medical traditions that existed in the United States: the professional and the

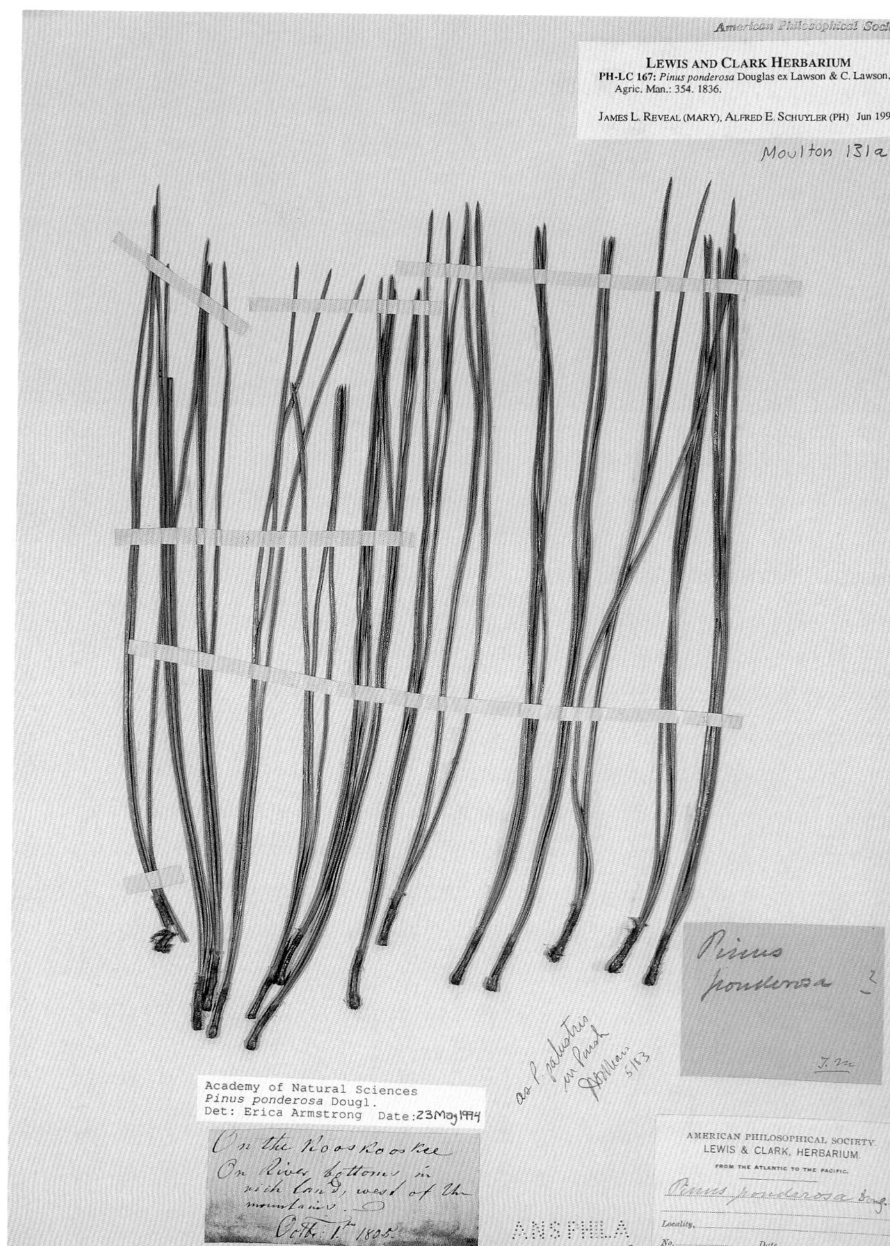

Specimen of *Pinus ponderosa* (ponderosa pine), 1805

Lewis collected this specimen near Canoe Camp, Clearwater River, on October 1, 1805. They called the Ponderosa pine "long leafed pine," and these needles show why. The Salish and Plateau tribes mixed the pitch with tallow to make a salve for boils and abscesses, which may have given Clark the idea to mix "the Rosin of the long leafed pine, Beas wax and Beare oil" to treat Pomp's abscess. Powdered pine was also used like talcum powder to cure diaper rash in babies, and the new shoots were boiled to make a tea to cure flu. Many tribes used the pitch for sealant, torches, and glue. The inside bark of the Ponderosa pine was peeled off and eaten like candy in May and June, when it was tender and sweet. William Gingros, a Kutenai, said: "If any person peeled trees before the bitterroot was ready it was believed it would bring bad luck. The offender was not punished by the people, but the spirits would somehow do that."

Medicine woman's outfit, pre-1891
These curing tools used by a Blackfeet practitioner consisted of (clockwise, from upper left) a hide paint bag, a wood bowl with two deer phalanges in it, a buffalo tail, a brass strainer, a gopher skin, a sage hen wing, a quail head, two eagle bone whistles (right) and two bone tubes (left). The cloth bag used to hold them all lies underneath. Unlike European medicines, these were not for administering to the patient but were for summoning and communicating with the spirit animals who helped effect a cure. The proper objects were usually prescribed to the doctor in a vision. It was not the actual claw, bone, or herb that cured; they were just physical things into which a higher power had been imparted. "A medicine bag is not good for anyone except the one who has dreamed," said Red Cloud. "When the bag is given, the *sicunpi* [spirit-powers] go out of it."

folk. Lewis had the benefit of the best professional advice of the day. In Philadelphia he had consulted with two of the country's most prominent physicians: Benjamin Rush and Benjamin Smith Barton. Rush may have provided suggestions for the extensive pharmacopoeia Lewis purchased. The drugs and tools in his box of cures reflected the European-trained physician's attitude that the body was essentially a mechanical system. Physicians of the day differed over whether it was primarily a hydraulic mechanism or an electrical one; Rush favored the latter explanation, tracing all disease to "morbid excitement" of the nervous system. Regardless, treatment was much the same—purging, vomiting, sweating, blistering, enemas, poultices, diuretics, and bleeding. Such treatments were believed to eliminate "impurities" or "morbific matter" that collected in the blood, making it too sluggish or rapid, and to relieve "congestion of blood in the brains, lungs, liver, spleen, and other internal organs." For the expedition, Rush prescribed fifty dozen of his powerful laxative pills, thought to purge the body of "excessive excitement." He also provided Lewis with a set of medical instructions containing such unwelcome advice as using alcohol to wash their feet instead of for drinking, since alcohol was thought to stimulate the nervous system.[44]

Rattle, c. 1876
Music was essential to healing throughout Native North America. "Everyone who treats the sick should have a drum and rattle," said holy man George Sword. "The drum and the rattles please the *wakan* and they will help. . . . When one has a medicine, he must have a song for it and he must know something to say every time he uses it. If the wrong song or invocation is used, the medicine will do no good." This Nez Perce rattle was probably never used in healing, but ones like it were.

Despite Lewis's consultation with medical professionals, when a physician volunteered to join the expedition, the captain did not think the opportunity significant enough to merit a delay. In this decision he reflected the distrust that most Americans had for professional medicine. Even Jefferson criticized the "presumptious band of medical tyros let loose upon the world," and he relied on prevention and folk cures. Many of those cures—sassafras, seneca snakeroot, sarsaparilla, lobelia, and mayapple root, among others—had been learned from the Indians. "Of the medical knowledge of the Indians the opinion here and there in America is still very high," the physician Johann Schopf wrote in 1787. "The greater number . . . are convinced that the Indians, mysteriously skilled in many excellent remedies, carefully and jealously conceal them from the white Europeans."[45]

The rest of the Corps also reflected the American ambivalence toward

Parfleche medicine case, mid-1800s
This case, which is probably of Nez Perce origin, holds no medicines today, but the painted thunderbirds and dewclaw rattles on it suggest that it may once have been so used. A receptacle used to store plant cures was not the same as the holy "medicine bundle" or "medicine bag" that embodied a person's vision. It had "no more power than a bag to keep corn in," said one authority. However, respect for medicine cases was often indicated by beautiful decoration.

European medicine. When several members became ill among the Nez Perce, it was not always European medicine they turned to. Even as Clark was freely dispensing the contents of the medicine box to the Indians, he treated an abscess on the baby, Pomp, with poultices of wild onion and a plaster of pine rosin, beeswax, and bear oil. To cure John Potts of a dangerous infection, he used poultices of cous root and wild ginger. All were remedies used by the Nez Perce. Nor was it the first time the Corps had resorted to Native cures. In 1805 Lewis had treated indigestion with chokecherry tea, a frontier remedy—or "simple"—that he may have inherited from his mother, the herb doctor.[46]

The most complex cure they undertook was of William Bratton. Bratton had been suffering from crippling back pain all winter, and by May of 1806 he was nearly an invalid—"so weak in the loins," said Lewis, that he was "scarcely able to walk." Lewis wrote: "We have tryed every remidy which our engenuity could devise, or with which our stock of medicines furnished us, without effect." In this situation, Lewis and Clark were willing to try an Indian cure suggested by John Shields: a steam bath.[47] Accordingly, they built a sunken sweat lodge of the style the Nez Perce used, and they treated the patient with steam and horsemint tea, used in lieu of seneca snakeroot. The next day, "Bratton feels himself much better and is walking about today and says he is nearly free from pain." No further mentions of his illness appeared in the journals.

But their openness to borrowing from the Indians had its limits. While adopting the ingredients and techniques of Indian medicine, they dismissed the rationales behind them as "superstition." If Lewis and Clark theorized at all about Bratton's cure, they doubtless resorted to the sort of mechanical explanations that Dr. Rush would have used. Almost certainly, the Nez Perce were doing the same: using Clark's cream of tartar and basilican eye washes but explaining the efficacy of the medicines in ways that fit their own belief systems.

The people of the plateau did not draw lines between spirit and body or between moral, social, and physical ailments: all were treated as one. Doctors did not just seek out mechanical explanations for disease; they also examined the patient's relationship to other beings.

An Indian patient lived in an animate world, surrounded by entities who could make a person ill if offended by some action or inaction. Snakes and lizards could invade the body. Animals that had been killed without respect could visit illness on the hunter. Malicious sorcerers could send disease. "The evil mysteries may impart their potencies to the body and this will cause disease," explained George Sword, a Lakota holy man born in about 1847. "Poisons and snakes and water creatures cause disease in this way. . . . If a magician has made one sick, then medicines will not cure such a one. The magician or a holy man should treat such a person."[48]

The doctor's job was to identify the angry power, then overcome or placate it. The doctor's curing ability came not just from skills and knowledge but also, and more important, from his or her spirit allies. The human being was only an intermediary through whom the spirit-power operated.[49]

The Nez Perce believed that some illnesses were simple, "natural" occurrences; those were treated with herbs. Every adolescent learned about curative plants from his or her parents. A few medicinal plants were widely known, but most were privately owned; each family had its secret recipes. If someone outside the family wanted to use such a medicine, the owner would prepare it for a price, paid in gifts after the cure was achieved. The knowledge was not strictly sacred, but it was private.[50]

If herbs did not work, the illness might be of another type, which called for the intervention of a doctor. This kind of sickness was caused by a moral

Medicine Man, Performing His Mysteries over a Dying Man, 1832
This Blackfeet man, painted by George Catlin, belonged to the Bear Society, a medical fraternity whose healing powers derived from the bear. "Bear medicine men are like a brotherhood," said George Sword, who was one. They "teach each other the songs and ceremonies and the medicines they must use." Bear healers used many plant cures and were famous for their ability to treat wounds.

Flint knife, 1800s
Doctors continued to use flint and obsidian for curing even after metal knives became available. "A Bear medicine man should have something in his medicine bag to cut with," testified George Sword. "He should cut inflamed places and places about wounds that are not healing properly. This should be a sharp flint." When Lewis visited the Shoshone, they were still using flint knives: "With this instrument, [they] skined the animals they killed, dressed their fish and made their arrows. . . . they renew the edge by fleaking off the flint by means of the point of an Elk's or deer's horn. . . . some of this flint . . . flaked of[f] much like glass leaving a very sharp edge." He was correct; obsidian and flint could be brought to a sharper edge than steel, but both were more breakable than metal. This Shoshone knife is from Wind River Reservation, Wyoming.

***Hidatsa Indians Sweat-bathing*, 1851**
Every tribe built steam lodges differently, but usually they had domed tops formed of bent willow poles and were covered with hides or blankets. Clark described a Nez Perce one as "a curious Swet house under ground, with a Small whole at top to pass in or throw in the hot Stones, which those in threw on as much water as to create the temporature of heat they wished." This sketch by Rudolph F. Kurz was made during a cholera epidemic at Like-a-Fishhook Village in North Dakota.

imbalance or a power struggle between animate beings. A person's spirit allies could desert him or her, due to some disrespectful action or the malice of an outside power. In such a case, diagnosis was the most difficult task for Indian doctors. But they did not ask "What disease is it?" They asked, "Who has caused it?" This question could be answered only by a person attuned to the spirit world, since the physical disease was merely a symptom of an underlying spiritual conflict. Nevertheless, the treatment was often physical, since body and spirit were not separate things.[51]

Some diseases on the plateau were caused by object intrusion and spirit possession. In object intrusion, an extraneous item—such as a shell, a feather, a bone, or even a piece of tobacco—became lodged inside the body of the patient. Treatment was public. The doctor sang medicine songs while assistants drummed; then the doctor passed his or her hands over the patient's body to locate the object and finally removed it by kneading, blowing, or sucking. When the object came out, the doctor plunged it forcefully into a bowl of water, then after a time released it into the air, whereupon it disappeared.[52]

Illness could also be caused by a wandering ghost spirit, or *skep* (pronounced "skape" and spelled *ishép*, in Nez Perce). Such disembodied spirits, often depicted as skeletons, made themselves known in dreams or as invisible voices. People possessed by a *skep* might waste away or become insane; they often mutilated themselves with knives. Wild rose was used to repel such spirits.[53]

People became doctors through visions in which powerful guardian spirits granted them medical wisdom. Often, the type of doctor who treated object intrusion could also divine the future and find lost objects. Doctors with sweat lodge power could handle hot stones and drink boiling water and often did so as a prelude to healing. In other tribes, medical societies flourished. Among Plains Indians, bear medicine men formed a powerful fraternity that passed down knowledge to new initiates. Indian doctors had the power to cause disease as well as cure it. Unknown to Clark, doctors who failed to cure were often blamed for the patient's death, and revenge was taken upon them. Luckily, none of Clark's patients died. If they had, he might have faced the same risk as the later missionary Marcus Whitman, who was blamed by Plateau tribes for epidemics he could not cure.[54]

The outward form of curing practices among the Plateau and Northern Plains Indians were often similar to those of Euro-Americans, but their underlying rationale could be different. Purification was a central principle shared by both. Nez Perce men about to set out on a hunting excursion or other important enterprise often undertook a course of internal cleansing by inducing vomiting over a period of several days while fasting. This practice forced out the stomach bile that produced a tired feeling. By doing so, "a man will feel strong, tight, and full of energy. He can easily go through hardships. He can then go to war." Outwardly, it was similar to the purging that Clark several times reported in his journals as a cure for indigestion and fatigue, but it had a spiritual connotation that the Euro-Americans' remedies lacked.[55]

A number of curative plants—including sage, sweetgrass, juniper, and balsam fir—worked mainly when burned like incense, to sanctify a space or purify an object or person. Transforming a substance into smoke freed its spirit or potency, according to George Sword. "The spirit that is in the smoke goes with it into the mouth and body and then it comes out and goes upward. When this spirit is in the body it soothes the spirit of the smoker. When it goes upward, it soothes the God. So the God and the spirit are as friends." It was the doctor who smoked, not the patient, and the doctor did so to honor and invoke the powers that would perform the cure. "If one sings or prays while making the

Turlington's Balsam of Life, early 1800s
Indians and Euro-Americans borrowed medicines from one another on the frontier. This patent medicine manufactured in London was very popular among Indian customers across the northern plains and was often stocked by the Hudson's Bay Company. Lewis listed "4 oz Turlingtons Balsam" on his shopping list for medicines, but he never mentioned whether he purchased it. This bottle was recovered at one of the Knife River Villages visited by Lewis and Clark.

Specimen of *Artemisia longifolia* (long-leafed sage), 1804
Sage was an extremely holy plant to Plains Indians; few ceremonies were conducted without it. This fragrant herb pleased and attracted good influences and drove away the evil ones. It was used as an incense to purify implements, weapons, dwellings, and people. Beds and wreaths of sage played a part in several ceremonies. Purifying baths were scented with sage. It also had medicinal uses when made into a tea or salve or taken like snuff. Perhaps reflecting its importance, Lewis collected eleven specimens of five different varieties of sage. This one was collected in South Dakota on October 3, 1804, and was sent back in the keelboat. Lewis's specimens have all been remounted on new backings and are sometimes combined on the sheet with specimens from other collectors. The only remainder of the original backings are scraps with Lewis's labels, often cut from dark blotting paper, pasted onto the new backings. Here, Lewis's label, at center bottom, compared sage to camomile, another medicinal herb.

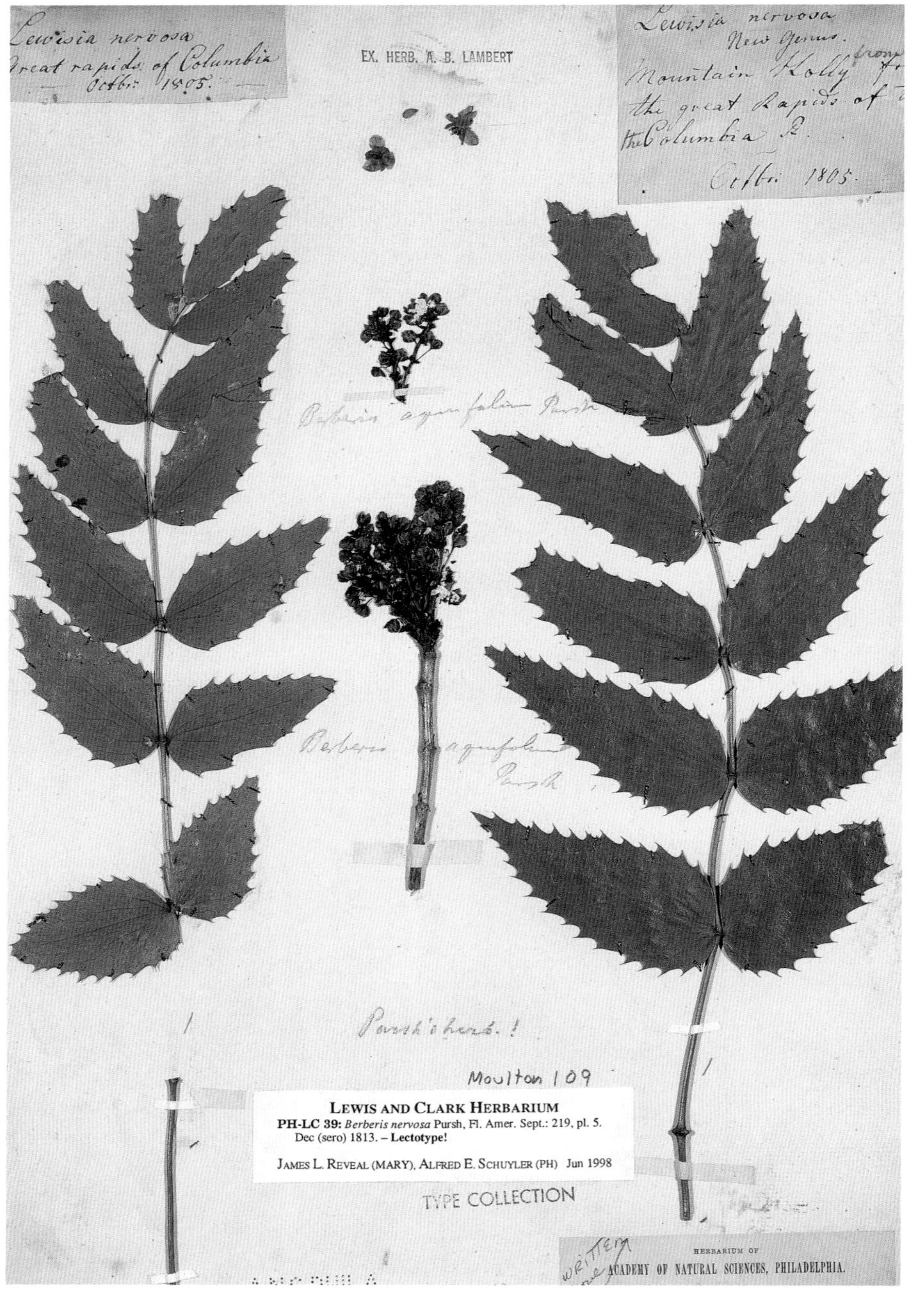

RIGHT: **Specimen of *Berberis nervosa* (dull or low Oregon grape), 1805**
OPPOSITE, TOP: **Sketch of *Berberis nervosa* (dull or low Oregon grape), 1806**
This is a type specimen, meaning that it was used to define and name the species. Lewis collected it at the Cascades of the Columbia in October 1805 but did not get around to describing it in his journal until the next February. He wrote: "There are two species of ever green shrubs [this and *Berberis aquifolium*, high Oregon grape] which I first met with at the grand rappids of the Columbia and which I have since found in this neighbourhood also; they grow in rich dry ground not far usually from some water-course. . . . The Stem . . . is procumbent . . . jointed and unbranched. it's leave are cauline, compound and oppositely pinnated; the rib from 14 to 16 inches long celendric and smooth." This plant was used by the Indians to produce a golden dye. Its root was also made into an infusion for curing paralysis and rheumatism.

smoke, it will be more pleasing to the God." Lewis's box of drugs included several aromatic substances administered by breathing, including a quarter-pound of essence of *Mentha piperita*, an oil extracted from the peppermint plant; however, the peppermint had no sacred implications.[56]

The steam bath the Corps used so effectively on Bratton was a central element of Native American belief and spiritual practice. Virtually every tribe in North America used steam baths but constructed, used, and explained them differently. Euro-Americans theorized that the baths worked by producing sweat, which brought impurities in the blood to the surface and eliminated them. Because non-Indians focused on the sweating, they called the structures "sweat lodges."

The Indian explanation was similar but more complex. George Sword said that a person's life-essence (*ni* in Lakota) can become weak; then "hurtful things get into the body." Breathing steam would "wash the inside of the body," refreshing the patient and eliminating "all that makes him tired, or all that causes disease, or all that causes him to think wrong." Steam bathing was done not only for physical curing but also for moral and emotional curing and for preparing the mind "before undertaking anything of importance."[57]

On the plateau, it was said that the steam bath was first revealed to Coyote in mythic times. To some, its construction was a sacred process filled with symbolism. Martin Louie, a modern-day member of the Colville Confederated Tribes, explained that each set of four willow boughs supporting the domed

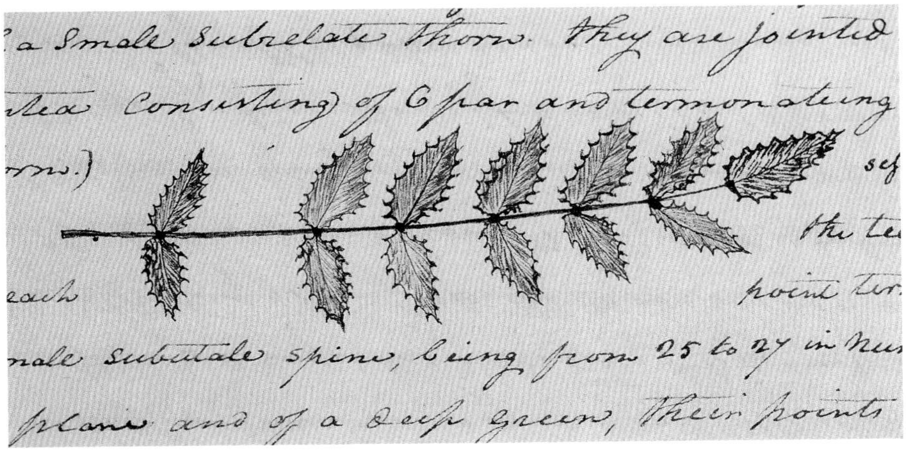

top represented a part of creation: the four directions, the four seasons, the four foods (bitterroot, serviceberry, salmon, and meat), the four colors (yellow, white, black, green), the four winds, and so forth. "When I enter Sweatlodge it's like entering a great cathedral in Europe," he said. "It's quiet, you know—powerful—beautiful. I feel that."[58]

A person's relationship to the steam bath was very personal. The lodge was an animate being, addressed in Sahaptin languages as *pú̂ša* (grandfather). The sweat lodge was also a guardian spirit that gave healing abilities to those

John Miller, *An Illustration of the Sexual System, of Linnaeus*, 1779–89
This was the main reference book Lewis used to identify and describe new plants. Because the classification system of Linnaeus organized plants according to their reproductive parts (a choice that nonspecialists found slightly salacious), plant anatomy assumed a disproportionate importance to nineteenth-century collectors, often overshadowing cultural and ecological information.

Specimen of *Gaultheria shallon* (salal), 1806 and Sketch of *Gaultheria shallon* (salal), 1806
This plant was collected on the coast of the Pacific Ocean near Fort Clatsop on January 20, 1806. Its berries formed one of the foods the party subsisted on through the winter; the explorers called the plant "Shelewele," "Shel-well," and "Shallon." Lewis wrote, "The Shallun or deep purple berry is in form much like the huckkleberry." Later, he added about the shrub: "I have heretofore taken [it] to be a speceis of loral and mentioned as abounding in this neighbourhood and that the Elk fed much on it's leaves." He described the leaf, shown here, as "oval, reather more accute towards its apex than at the point of insertion; it's margin slightly serrate, it's sides colapsing or partially foalding upwards or channelled; it is also thick firm [s]mothe and glossey, the upper surface of a fine deep green, while the under disk is of a pale or whiteish green." The Indians ate the berries fresh or dried. They often pounded and baked the berries in large loaves of ten to fifteen pounds, which kept well for a season. "This bread is broken and stirred in could water until it be sufficiently thick and then eaten."

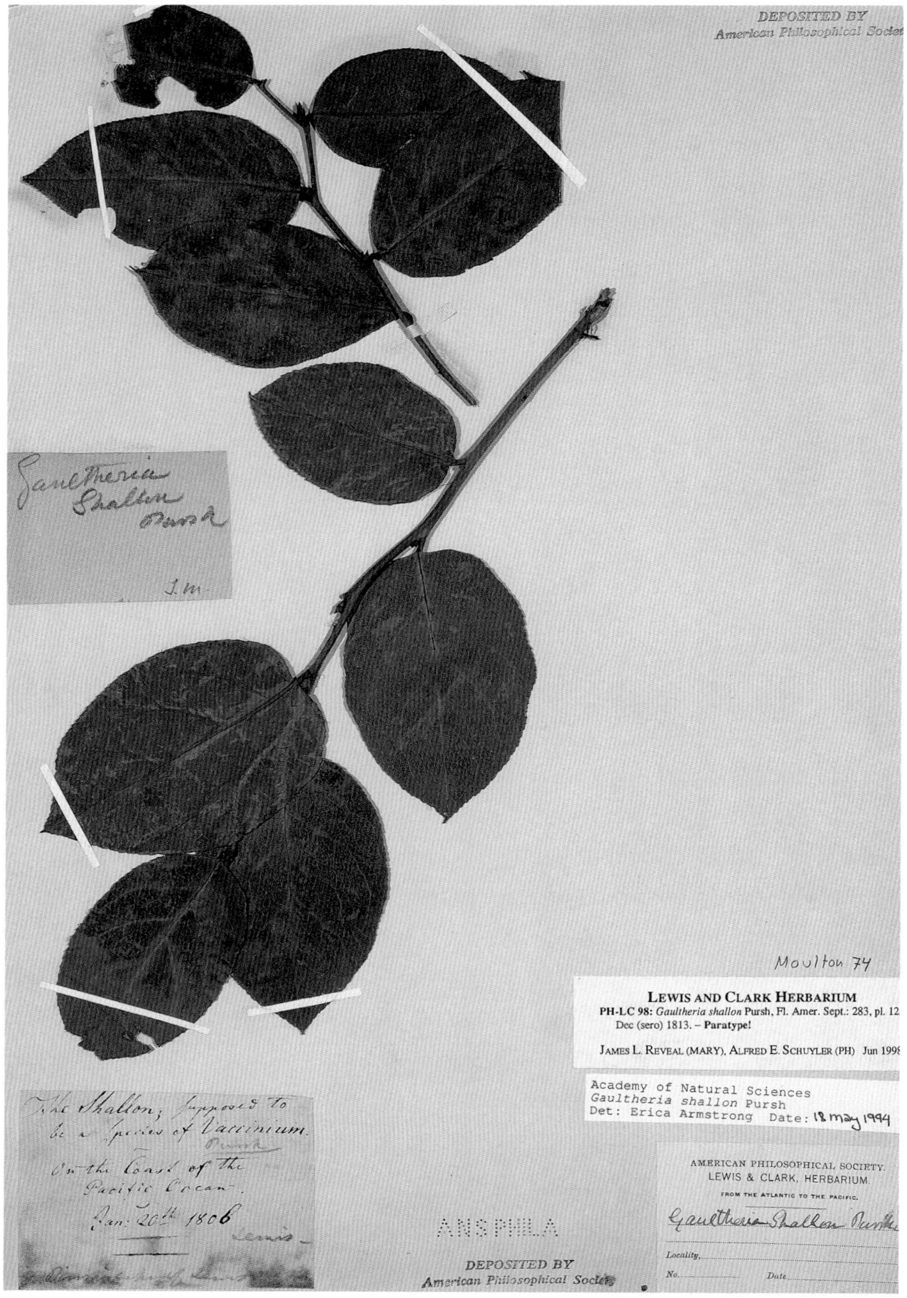

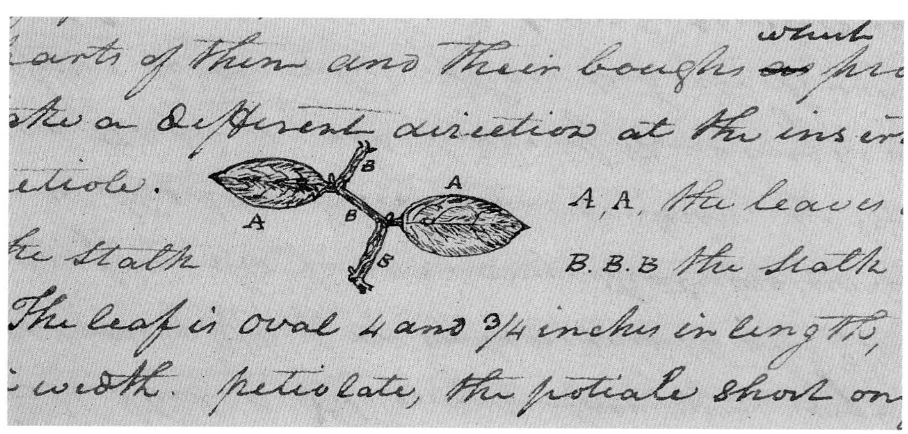

who dreamed of it. Its dark interior, lined with fragrant fir boughs, was a place of prayer and silent contemplation. The voice of the lodge was the quiet whistling of the hot stones as water was sprinkled on them. Bathing was a form of daily worship that evoked the sacredness in ordinary objects.[59]

GATHERING PLANTS

> In a time before humans, there were plant people and animal people.
>
> —MARTIN LOUIE[60]

> Do not needlessly destroy the flowers on the prairies or in the woods. If the flowers be plucked then there will be no flower children (seeds); and if there be no flower children, then in time there will be no people of the flower nation (plant species). And if the flower nations should thus die out of the world, then the earth would be sad.
>
> —UNIDENTIFIED PLAINS INDIAN, QUOTED BY MELVIN GILMORE[61]

The Corps arrived in Nez Perce country at a good time for gathering plants, because many of the spring flowers were in bloom. Lewis embarked on the task of gathering them, as he had done throughout the expedition, with little formal training but with a great deal of practical knowledge. Jefferson had described him as "no regular botanist" but noted that he possessed "a remarkable store of accurate observation on all the subjects of the three kingdoms" and would "therefore readily single out whatever presents itself new."[62]

"New" and "useful" were the criteria that governed Lewis's collecting, requiring him to recognize and reject plants already known to science and to gather only novel ones that had some use. He was not motivated purely by abstract science; lucrative plant cures and crops could be important to commerce. Medicinal and psychoactive plants—particularly tobacco and sassafras—were important to the republic's economy. As the Napoleonic wars in Europe cut into commerce, there were urgent calls to find local replacements for drugs such as quinine and opium, in order to reduce America's dependence on foreign medicine. As a result, Lewis showed a preference for medicinal plants, food plants, showy flowering plants with potential for gardening and landscaping, and those that represented the climate or landscape.[63]

Lewis said little about his collecting methods. He probably had a botanist's specimen book—a bound book of unmarked sheets interspersed with blotting paper. After taking a clipping, he placed it into the book, writing short notes on the date and place of collection and other interesting points, and then pressed it. Though he never mentioned receiving help, he must have had guidance from knowledgeable Native people because so many of the plants he chose were used for food, dyes, basketry, and curing. Like botanists in the tropics today, he probably relied on local knowledge to identify the plants. Chances are good his unnamed informants were women. They must have thought their visitor a very odd sort of man.

Among the Nez Perce, only women harvested plant foods; a man doing so risked derision and contempt. Just as women were prohibited from touching men's weapons and fishing

Digging stick, late 1800s
Clark illustrated a digging stick virtually identical to this one, describing it as "a Strong Stick of three feet and a half long Sharpened at the lower end and its upper inserted into a part of an Elks or buck's horn which Serves as a handle; Standing transvirsely in the Stick. . . . the lower part . . . is a little hooked." To use it, a woman placed it on the right side of the plant, about three inches from the base. She pushed down with both hands, sinking the stick at an angle into the sod, then levering up the root. A woman constructed her own digging stick, which was passed on to close friends or family after her death. Later in the century, blacksmiths manufactured metal digging sticks.

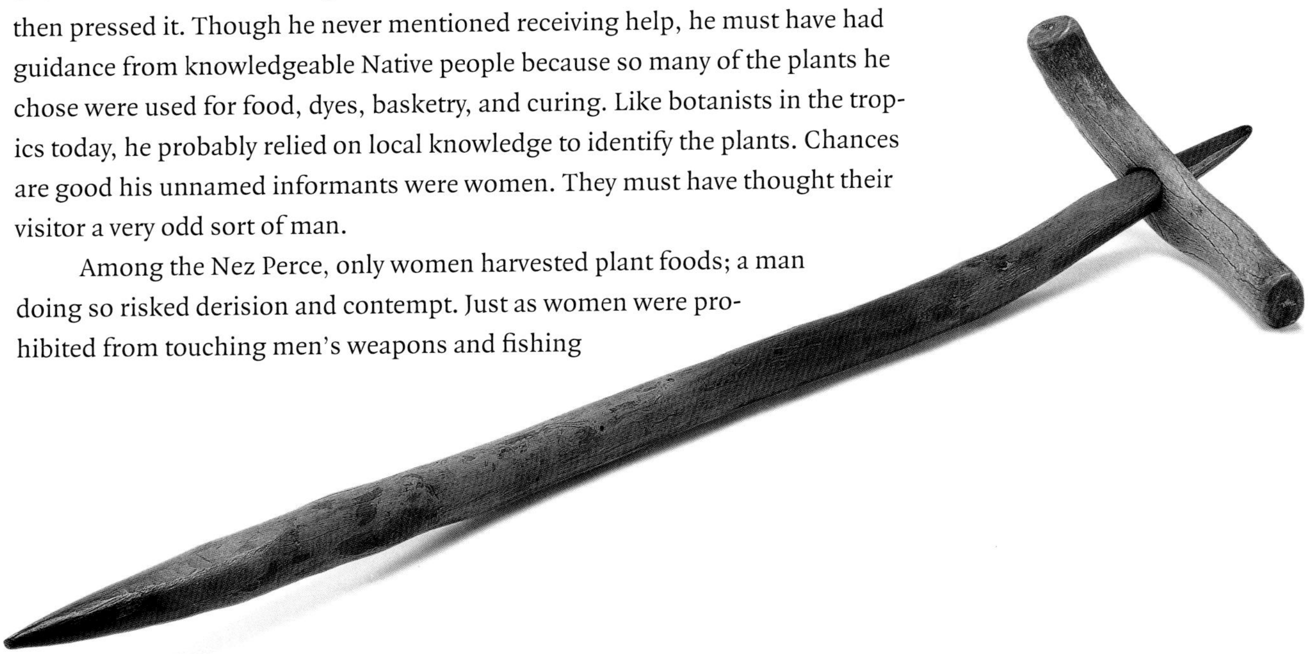

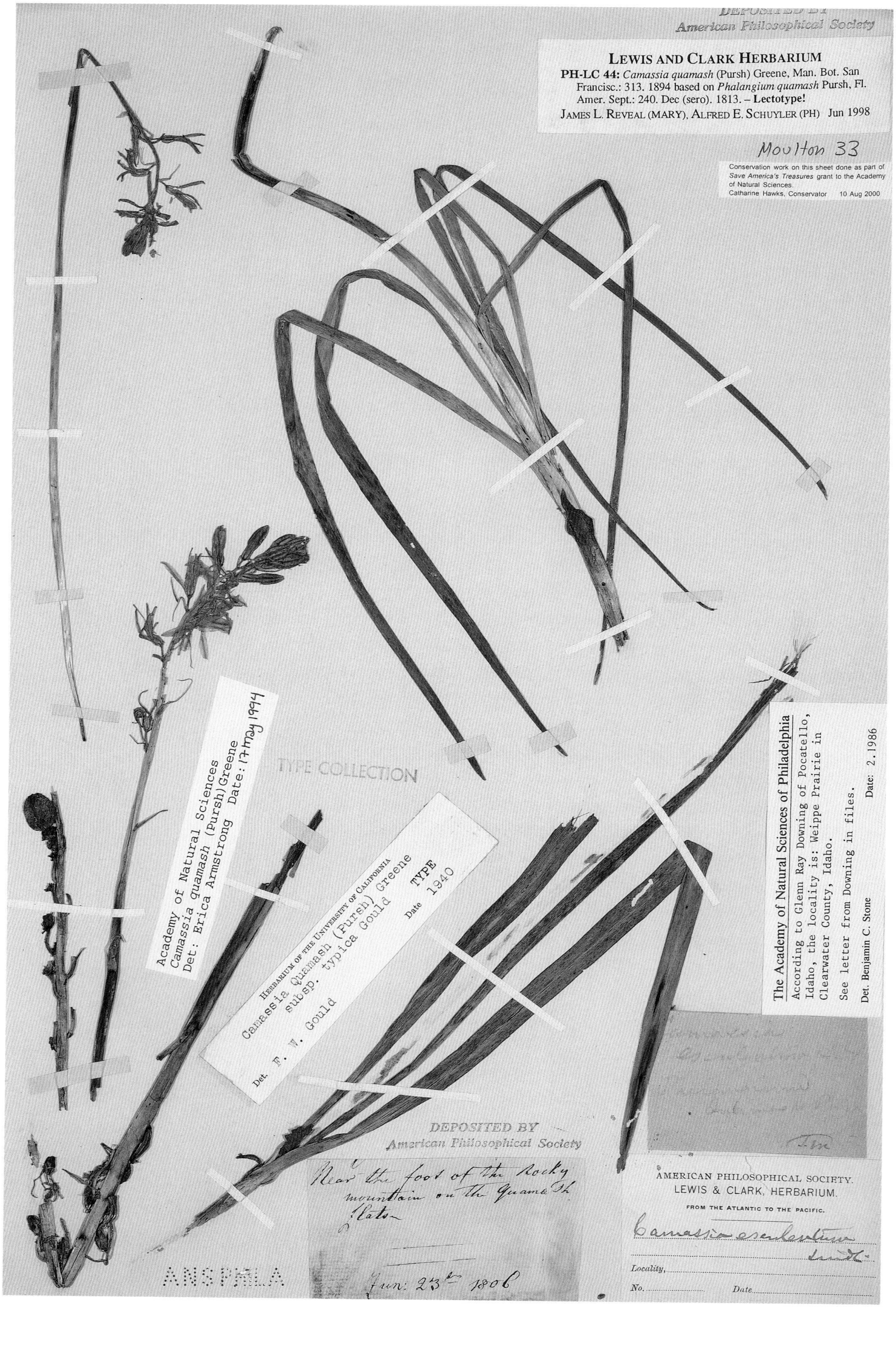
DEPOSITED BY
American Philosophical Society
LEWIS AND CLARK HERBARIUM
PH-LC 44: Camassia quamash (Pursh) Greene, Man. Bot. San Francisc.: 313. 1894 based on Phalangium quamash Pursh, Fl. Amer. Sept.: 240. Dec (sero). 1813. – Lectotype!
JAMES L. REVEAL (MARY), ALFRED E. SCHUYLER (PH) Jun 1998
Moulton 33
Conservation work on this sheet done as part of Save America's Treasures grant to the Academy of Natural Sciences.
Catharine Hawks, Conservator 10 Aug 2000
Academy of Natural Sciences
Camassia quamash (Pursh) Greene
Det: Erica Armstrong Date: 17 May 1994
TYPE COLLECTION
HERBARIUM OF THE UNIVERSITY OF CALIFORNIA
Camassia quamash (Pursh) Greene
subsp. typica Gould
TYPE
Date 1940
Det. F. W. Gould
The Academy of Natural Sciences of Philadelphia
According to Glenn Ray Downing of Pocatello, Idaho, the locality is: Weippe Prairie in Clearwater County, Idaho.
See letter from Downing in files.
Det. Benjamin C. Stone
Date: 2.1986
DEPOSITED BY
American Philosophical Society
Near the foot of the Rocky mountain on the Quamash flats
Jun: 23rd 1806
ANSPHILA
AMERICAN PHILOSOPHICAL SOCIETY.
LEWIS & CLARK. HERBARIUM.
FROM THE ATLANTIC TO THE PACIFIC.
Camassia esculenta
Locality,
No.
Date

Specimen of *Camassia quamash* (camas), 1806
Lewis collected this specimen in the Nez Perce camas fields at Weippe Prairie. Camas was the staple food of the Nez Perce. When Clark first arrived among the tribe, he noted, "They gave us . . . roots in different States, Some round and much like an onion which they call quamash the Bread or Cake is called Pas-she-co Sweet, of this they make bread & Supe." The Nez Perce divided the camas into male and female and preferred to take the female plants. The bulbs were harvested in late July or August. They could not be eaten raw but after being dried, skinned, and pit-baked for three days, they became sweet and nutritious. The removal of the roasted camas from the oven was an occasion of much excitement, and people gathered to eat the freshly roasted bulbs, sometimes dipping them in marrow as a treat. After that the camas bulbs were dried in the sun in bags for a week, then put in a cool place, where they could last up to three years. They were prepared by grinding in a mortar and pestle and then made into porridge or bread. The bread was merely dried in the sun.

Root bag, pre-1876
Camas was gathered, cooked, and stored in bags like this. An industrious woman could dig eighty or ninety pounds in a day, though the average was fifty to sixty. Up to five different plants were used to create a bag like this. The basic structure was twined from a strong, durable cord of wild hemp. Decorations were added with light golden bear grass or rye grass, though the maker of this one used corn husks. Colors could be added with mineral or vegetable dyes. An extract of alder created a reddish-brown or orange, Oregon grape root and wolf moss produced yellow and gold, berries gave red, algae yielded green, and larkspur produced blue. The woman making a bag needed to know not only which plants to gather but also when to harvest, what part to make use of, and how to process it.

tools, boys and men could not touch root-digging implements, baskets, or root ovens. Women setting out to harvest cleansed themselves and abstained from sexual relations beforehand. They said there should be "no man smells on women before digging, or the roots will go away."[64]

A Nez Perce woman's year was structured around plants. Spring began with the appearance of the wild potato. This was followed by cous roots in April or May. Berries began to ripen in June; then in July and August, bands from all over the land gathered at the camas meadows. Every time a new food plant matured, its arrival was welcomed in a first fruits feast (*keʔ ú-yet*). A respected leader with an affinity for the plant presided at the feast and was the first to start the harvest. A modern-day Wenatchee woman expressed the spirit of this thanksgiving ceremony: "Plants and creatures were offering their very lives for the nourishment of the Plateau people. In humble respect, the people acknowledged this gift."[65]

Nez Perce women's relationship to the plants they gathered was personal and intimate. One of the important moments of life passage was a little girl's first berry picking or root digging, marked by a feast at which people gave speeches of praise and encouragement. Older women gave the girl their strength and blessed her work, and her family gave gifts to everyone present. The Nez Perce word for this feast, *talaposa*, was the same as their word for "worship."[66]

The camas harvest was a plant-related event in which everyone participated. It was highly organized. All the villages on the Clearwater went to Weippe Prairie, where Lewis and Clark found Broken Arm's village. Each family camped separately in its own spot and dug in its allotted area. To trespass on another family's spot was considered greedy. "Each group should be in its own place," people said. "The general attitude is one of enjoyment," one eyewitness wrote, "although it is hard, hot work. Everyone is cheerful, takes pride in her work, and enjoys herself. Camas digging is not treated as grim but necessary labor; rather is it hard but pleasant work."[67]

Of course, food plants were not the only ones gathered by the Nez Perce people. They knew plants to repel spirits, to keep away bad dreams, and to fumigate after a death. They knew plants to cure and to make magic with. One ethnobotanist cataloged over seventy-five species used for medicinal purposes on the plateau, including eight remedies for sore eyes, thirteen for colds and sore throats, ten for wounds, bruises, and sores, and eight "hair medicines" for lice. Others were taken for such ailments as sorrow after the death of a loved one. But many of those plants were secret. Gathered without the proper songs and prayers and processed without the proper techniques, their spirits left and they became useless. Lewis attributed the medicinal effect of plants to the way their chemical properties interacted with the body. The Nez Perce attributed curing power to the way plant spirits interacted with the herbalist and with the spirits that caused disease.[68]

Classification, the primary concern of Lewis's science, was not a strange concept to the Nez Perce. They also classified plants, but not according to a hierarchical system like that of Carolus Linnaeus. In Sahaptin languages (which include Nez Perce), plant and animal relationships were more often expressed in terms of "kinship" or "friendship" than hierarchy. Although the Indians named many separate species—including six types of salmon, nine types of coniferous tree, and twenty types of horse—the naming conventions stressed a webwork of comparisons and relationships on a single level rather than a stacked structure in which one being was a subtype of a larger category.

The word for "dog" (*k'usikúsi*) meant, literally, "little horse" (*k'úsi*), but that did not mean a dog was a type of horse.[69]

Both Euro-American and Indian cultures used specialized language to evoke the power of plants—or power over them. Native Americans used songs and prayers to express the nature of plant beings, some of them couched in the words of the plant itself. The song of the twinflower (*pulsatilla hirsutissima*), one of the first flowers to appear on the plains in the spring, was translated rather elaborately:

> I wish to encourage the children
> Of other flower nations now appearing
> All over the face of the earth;
> So while they awaken from sleeping
> And come up from the heart of the earth
> I am standing here old and gray-headed.[70]

Lewis, by contrast, used technical jargon to clarify his analysis of plants. His first encounter with a camas plant produced this description: "The radix is a tunicated bulb. . . . the foliage consists of . . . linear sessile and revolute pointed leaves. . . . the peduncle is soletary. . . . the calix is a partial involucret situated at the base of the footstalk of each flower on the peduncle. . . . the pistillum is only one, of which, the germ is . . . smooth superior, sessile, pedicelled, short in proportion to the corolla. . . . the pericarp is a capsule, triangular, oblong, obtuse, and trilocular with three longitudinal valves." And so forth.[71]

Would a Nez Perce woman have recognized her familiar camas roots in Lewis's description? Possibly not. But she might have recognized the impulse to tame the mystery of herbal power through incantation.

Nez Perce Food, 1891

The Corps stayed with the Nez Perce long enough to witness the harvest of the tribe's main root crops: cous and camas. They collected samples much like those shown here for donation to Peale's Museum. When the Corps first arrived, the cous harvest was in progress. The group of three foods on the right includes a loaf of cous bread (top row, right), cous roots (middle row, second from right), and cous finger cakes (middle row, far right). The bread and cakes were both made from flour created by pounding the roots between two stones. The bread was roasted over a fire on a rack of sticks, which left marks on the loaves. They were pierced with holes to string them together for storage or transport. The finger cakes were made by mixing the flour with water, forming the cakes between the fingers, and then letting them dry. They were eaten without any further preparation or were broken up in water for soup.

By the time Lewis and Clark left the Nez Perce, the camas harvest was beginning. The two samples on the far left are camas bread (top row, left) and cooked camas roots (middle row, far left), both of which Lewis and Clark donated to Peale's Museum. The black color comes from the roasting, a laborious process that could take up to seventy hours. Clark witnessed and described this process in the fall of 1805.

The samples in the center are wild potatoes and cakes made from them (middle row), bitterroot (bottom row, left), and berry cakes (bottom row, right). Wild potato was either *Lomatium canbyi* or *Claytonia lanceolata*; specimens of the latter were brought back by Lewis and Clark. Bitterroot was named for Lewis—*Lewisia rediviva*—because he gathered the first botanical specimen of it on July 1, 1806, noting its use as food. It was one of the principal flavorings used by the Nez Perce, Salish, and neighboring tribes. The berry cakes are probably pounded chokecherry.

NINE Discovering Each Other

White men are curious; they come from afar;
they know much, and wish to learn more.

—LE BORGNE, HIDATSA, QUOTED BY CHARLES MACKENZIE[1]

"Every body seems anxious to be in motion, convinced that we have not now any time to delay if the calculation is to reach the United States this season," Lewis wrote on June 14. So impatient were they that despite Nez Perce warnings that it was too early to cross the mountains, they started off without a guide.[2]

"We Set out with the party each man being well mounted and a light load on a 2d horse," Clark wrote confidently. "We therefore feel ourselves perfectly equiped for the Mountains." At first, the going was idyllic. "The quawmash [camas] is now in blume," Clark said; "at a Short distance it resemhles a lake of fine clear water." But as the elevation increased, they were "invelloped in snow from 8 to 12 feet deep. . . . here was Winter with all it's rigors; the air was Cold my hands and feet were benumed."[3]

Unable to find either the trail or forage for their horses, they were forced to turn back and wait for assistance to find their way. A week later, they tried again, led by Nez Perce guides "over and along the Steep Sides of tremendious Mountains entirely covered with Snow." On June 27 they paused for a smoke in the high mountain silence at the top of the pass. "We were entirely Serounded by those mountains," Clark wrote, "from which to one unacquainted with them it would have Seemed impossible ever to have escaped. . . . this Scene [was] Sufficient to have dampened the Spirits of any except Such hardy travellers as we have become."[4] On July 1 Clark wrote with satisfaction: "Descended the mountain to Travellers rest leaveing those tremendious mountanes behind us—in passing of which we have experiensed Cold and hunger of which I shall ever remember. . . . this is like once more returning to the land of liveing a plenty."[5]

At their camp on the Bitterroot River, they prepared to split up. Their plan, hatched over the winter, was to return in three groups. The first, under Lewis, would go overland to the Great Falls via the short cut they had learned about too late the year before and would then scout the Marias River. The rest, under Clark, would return south to Shoshone country to pick up the canoes and equipment they had cached at the source of the Missouri. Then ten of them, under John Ordway, would take the canoes back down the Missouri to join Lewis at the Marias. The others, under Clark, would cut overland to the Yellowstone River and follow it down to its junction with the Missouri, where they would all reassemble. It would take good timing and good luck.

For Clark, everything started out according to plan. "After brackfast I took My leave of Capt Lewis and . . . we proceeded on through the Vally of Clarks [Bitterroot] river . . . which we found . . . covered with a great variety of Sweet cented plants, flowers & grass." They managed to avoid the steep, snowy route they had followed the previous year, since this time they listened to Sacagawea, who knew the country. Wrote Clark, "The Indian woman . . . pointed to the gap through which she said we must pass."[6]

It took only a week to get back to Camp Fortunate, where they had left the canoes and a cache of supplies. Clark "found every article Safe," including precious tobacco.[7] Before long, he wrote, "I had all the Canoes put into the water and every article which was intended to be Sent down put on board, and the horses collected and packed with what fiew articles I intend takeing with me to the River Rochejhone [Yellowstone]."[8] The two parties, one in canoes and one on horseback, traveled together as far as the Three Forks. The winding Beaverhead and Jefferson Rivers, which had been such obstacles the year before, were easily navigated now that the canoes were going downstream. "Proceded on very well to the enterance of Madicines [Madison] river at our old Encampment," Clark wrote. There, without fanfare, they split up. "After dinner the 6 Canoes and the party of 10 men under the direction of Sergt. Ordway Set out. . . . at 5. P.M I Set out from the head of Missouri at the 3 forks, and proceeded on nearly East."[9]

For the next few weeks, Clark's party followed the general route of present-day Interstates 90 and 94. Following Sacagawea's instructions, they passed through "a low gap in the mountain" where Bozeman, Montana, now lies, and met the Yellowstone just past the point where it emerges from "a high rugid mountain covered with Snow." Southward, beyond that mountain, lay the volcanic region that is now Yellowstone National Park. But at that moment, Clark's attention was fixed on another, more practical, fact: "I can See no timber Sufficient large for a Canoe."[10] They continued on horseback down the river for several days before finding a stand of timber. One morning, as they were camped while constructing canoes, Clark "was informed that Half of [the] horses were absent. Sent out Shannon Bratten, and Shabono to hunt them." But rather than finding the horses, "Sgt. pryor found an Indian Mockerson and a Small piece of a roab." Clark noted, "Those Indian Signs is Conclusive

Page 280: *Packkaab-Sachkoma-Poh, Piegan Blackfeet Man* (detail), 1833. See page 285.

with me that they have taken the 24 horses."[11]

Shortly after, Clark composed a speech to the Crow Indians who inhabited the Yellowstone country. "Children," he chided them, "I have come down the river from the foot of the great snowey mountain to see you. . . . Your Great father will be very sorry to here of the stealing the horses of his Chiefs warrors whome he sent out to do good to his red children." But perhaps showing that he had absorbed some of the Indian idiom of humility, he added: "I am pore necked and nothing to keep of [f] the rain. when I set out from my country I had a plenty but have given it all to my read children . . . and have now nothing."[12]

He would soon have even less. He never got a chance to deliver the speech, because the Crow came back only long enough to steal the rest of the horses. When Clark's party had first set out, they had traveled with fifty horses; when they reached the mouth of the Yellowstone, they had none.

Instead, they traveled by canoe and bullboat. "Had all our baggage put on board of the two Small Canoes which when lashed together is very Study," he wrote. Floating down the Yellowstone proved so pleasant and uneventful that Clark later exaggerated the importance of the river, claiming that boats could navigate it to the Rocky Mountains. "The Country through which it passes . . . is Generaly fertile rich open plains. . . . This delighfull river from indian information has it's extreem sources . . . on the confines of New Mexico. . . . it's westerly sources connected with the Multnomah [Willamette]." His description was an impossible geography of optimism.[13]

They came to the mouth of the Yellowstone on August 3. Lewis's party had not yet arrived, so Clark at first prepared to wait. But they soon found themselves under attack: "The Misquetors was So noumerous that I could not keep them off my gun long enough to take Sight. . . . The torments of those Missquetors and the want of a Sufficety of Buffalow meat . . . induce me to deturmine to proceed on to a more eliagiable Spot on the Missouri below." At a leisurely pace they continued on, waiting for Lewis's party to overtake them.[14]

Exit of the Yellowstone from the Mountains, 1868
Clark's party met the Yellowstone just a mile and a half from where it emerged from a mountain range that hid the volcanic region that is now Yellowstone Park. Clark passed by without discovering it, but one of the men then in Ordway's party, John Colter, would later return to explore the river and bring back the news to the outside world. Clark saw several herds of elk and "great numbers of Antelopes" here, and some were still left in 1867 when the itinerant artist Alfred E. Mathews returned to make this sketch.

Marias River, 1860
"The bluffs of the river are about 200 feet high, steep irregular and formed of earth," Lewis wrote. "Small gravel is every where distributed over the surface of the earth which renders travling extreemly painfull to our bearfoot horses." By the time a U.S. Army expedition led by Isaac I. Stevens retraced portions of Lewis and Clark's route through Montana in 1855, it was standard practice to have an artist along. John Mix Stanley, who drew this sketch, was one of two artists on Stevens's expedition to find the route for a transcontinental railroad and to negotiate land cessions with the Indian tribes.

DEATH ON THE MARIAS

Lewis's journey back started with an admonition of caution from the Nez Perce. "These affectionate people our guides betrayed every emmotion of unfeigned regret at seperating from us," Lewis wrote. "They were confidint that the Pahkees [Blackfeet or Atsina] . . . would cut us off. . . . I gave the Cheif a medal of the small size; he insisted on exchanging names with me according to their custom. . . . I was called Yo-me-kol-lick which interpreted is *the white bearskin foalded*."[15]

Riding overland, Lewis's group reached the Great Falls in only one week. When they got to the Missouri, they found that the "missouri bottoms on both sides of the river were crouded with buffaloe." Lewis wrote: "I sincerely belief that there were not less than 10 thousand buffaloe within a circle of 2 miles. . . . the bulls keep a tremendious roaring. . . . our horses had not been acquainted with the buffaloe they appeared much allarmed."[16]

Returning to their old camp at the head of the portage, they opened the cache and found the contents damaged: "The water had penitrated. all my specimens of plants also lost. the Chart of the Missouri fortunately escaped. opened my trunks and boxes and exposed the articles to dry." After this disappointment, Lewis left most of the men, who proceeded to make the Great Falls portage in reverse, and he went on horseback with just George Drouillard and the two brothers, Joseph and Reubin Field, to the Marias River. His objective was geopolitical: to locate the northernmost boundary of the Louisiana Purchase. He hoped that the Marias, which had seemed like such a major tributary the year before, would reach north beyond the fiftieth parallel, giving his nation claim to the rich fur regions of the Saskatchewan River.[17]

"It being my design to strike Maria's river," Lewis wrote, "I steered my course through the wide and level plains which have somewhat the appearance of an ocean, not a tree nor a shrub to be seen." They soon reached the river and followed it—but not north. To Lewis's frustration, the Marias bent west toward the Rocky Mountains. On July 22 they came to a high plateau: "I could see from hence very distinctly where the river entered the mountains and the bearing of this point being S of West I . . . now have lost all hope of the waters of this river ever extending to N Latitude 50°." He named the spot Camp Disappointment.[18]

The real owners of the land met him on the way back. "I halted and used my spye glass by the help of which I discovered several indians. . . . this was a very unpleasant sight, however I resolved to make the best of our situation and to approach them in a friendly manner. . . . about this time they discovered us and appeared . . . much allarmed."[19] The group he had seen consisted of eight young Piegan Blackfeet men. From the fact that they had many horses with them, it seems likely they were a raiding party returning from a successful foray and at first may have mistaken Lewis's party for pursuing enemies. Wherever

Packkaab-Sachkoma-Poh, *Piegan Blackfeet Man*, 1833
In 1806 the Blackfeet traded with the British, a fact that prejudiced Lewis against them. When Karl Bodmer painted this warrior wrapped in a trade blanket a generation later, Lewis's promise of an American post at the mouth of the Marias had finally been fulfilled, and the Blackfeet had begun to trade there. This young man's French name meant "Wicked Boy."

War shirt, 1843
George Catlin declared, "No tribe . . . dress more comfortably, and more gaudily, than the Blackfeet." This shirt fringed with human hair celebrates the war record of its owner, Le Soulier de Femme (Woman's Moccasin) or Pe-toh-pee-kiss (Eagle Ribs). Catlin met him at Fort Union, an American Fur Company post at the mouth of the Yellowstone, and called him "one of the extraordinary men of the Blackfoot tribe." Catlin added: "[He] boasts of eight scalps, which he says he has taken from the heads of trappers and traders with his own hand. His dress is really superb, almost literally covered with scalp-locks." Ten years after Catlin painted him in a different shirt, Edward Harris visited Fort Union with John James Audubon and was given this shirt by the superintendent, Alexander Culbertson.

Amulet, 1885

The two amulets Lewis took from the shields of the dead Blackfeet formed a grisly display at Peale's Museum, but they no longer exist today. Eighty years later, the Blackfeet were still resisting white encroachment, and their amulets were still being taken by their opponents. This amulet was worn over the heart of a Blackfeet killed while taking part in the Riel Rebellion in Saskatchewan. Made of human hair, it may represent a war honor.

they had been, Lewis wrote, "I beleive they were more allarmed at this accedental interview than we were." But he was not far behind them in suspicion. From their enemies, Lewis had heard what "a vicious lawless and reather an abandoned set of wretches" the Blackfeet were. "I was convinced they would attempt to rob us," he wrote.[20]

He was right to be wary. For the Blackfeet youths, the meeting presented both an opportunity and an obligation to test themselves and achieve an honorable act. What Lewis did not know was that the Blackfeet rated honorable acts differently than did their Plains Indian neighbors. Whereas other tribes valued striking the enemy in battle, the Blackfeet honored more highly the finesse of capturing an enemy's horse or weapon. An anthropologist among the tribe wrote in 1911: "An old man relating his deeds seldom mentions scalps but dwells upon the number of guns, horses, etc. captured; whereas . . . a Dakota boasts of his wounds, enemies slain and coups." What the Blackfeet did not know was that Lewis had resolved to "resist to the last extremity prefering death to that of being deprived of my papers instruments and gun." That resolution—to defend his property even at the expense of life—led inevitably to what followed next.[21]

"We now all assembled and alighted from our horses," Lewis wrote. "The Indians soon asked to smoke with us. . . . I proposed that we should . . . encamp together, I told them that I was glad to see them and had a great deel to say to them." Accordingly, they all adjourned to the river valley and camped. "With the assistance of Drewyer I had much conversation with these people in the course of the evening," Lewis said. "I told these people . . . that I had been to the great waters where the sun sets and had seen a great many nations . . . that I had . . . succeeded in restoring peace among them. . . . I had come . . . to prevail on them to be at peace with their neighbours . . . [and] to come and trade with me when the establishment is made at the entrance of this river." That night, he wrote: "I took the first watch tonight and set up untill half after eleven; the indians by this time were all asleep."[22]

At daybreak he was jarred out of sleep. "Drewyer . . . crying damn you let go my gun awakened me. . . . I saw drewyer in a scuffle with the indian for his gun. I reached to seize my gun but found her gone, I then . . . saw the indian making off with my gun I ran at him with my pistol and bid him lay down my gun which he was in the act of doing when the Fieldses returned and drew up their guns to shoot him which I forbid. . . . as soon as they [the Blackfeet] found us all in possession of our arms they ran and indeavored to drive off all the horses. . . . I called to them . . . that I would shoot them if they did not give me my horse. . . . one of them . . . turned arround and stoped . . . and I shot him through the belly, he fell to his knees and . . . fired at me. . . . I felt the wind of his bullet very distinctly."[23]

Returning to camp, Lewis found that he was not the only one to have killed a man that morning. Reubin Field had also stabbed one of the Blackfeet during a struggle for his gun. "We . . . began to catch the horses and saddle them," Lewis wrote. "I put four sheilds and two bows and quivers of arrows which had been left on the fire"—but not before taking the medicine objects from the men's shields as trophies, in a macabre exchange of amulets. He noted: "I . . . left the medal about the neck of the dead man that they might be informed who we were."[24]

Captain Lewis Shooting an Indian, 1810
The artist who illustrated Patrick Gass's journal portrayed Lewis's fatal encounter with the Blackfeet this way. Gass was not an eyewitness, since he was making the Great Falls portage at the time. Only three men were with Lewis. The man in the capote is probably intended to be George Drouillard.

"My design was to hasten to the entrance of Maria's river . . . having no doubt but that they would pursue us with a large party," Lewis wrote. "No time was therefore to be lost and we pushed our horses as hard as they would bear." They rode until two in the morning.[25] They had good luck and good timing. No sooner had they reached the Missouri than they "had the unspeakable satisfaction" of seeing their canoes coming downstream. "We hurried down from the bluff . . . imbrarking without loss of time with our baggage."[26]

We have only Lewis's version of what happened on the Marias, and he naturally blamed the Indians. But even he never claimed that the Blackfeet did more than try to steal guns and horses—until the Euro-Americans escalated the conflict with deadly force. Lewis made a split-second decision in a confused scuffle. He thought that he was acting in self-defense. But had he just let his horses go, he might have walked back to the Missouri and two lives might have been spared.

The reprisal he expected was to come in later years. The Blackfeet eventually killed Drouillard and two other members of the expedition who ventured back, and they nearly killed John Colter. They would make the upper Missouri so unsafe for Euro-Americans that Lewis's ambition of blazing a commercial route west would be thwarted.[27]

Pistols, 1799–1802
In the struggle with the Blackfeet, Lewis used his pistol to recover his rifle, which he then used to shoot one of the Indians. These Model 1799 regulation .69 caliber U.S. Army pistols may have been the type supplied when Lewis requisitioned "1 p[ai]r. Horsemans Pistols" from the U.S. arsenal in 1803. As opposed to the pair of case pistols, which were probably his private property, he wore the pistol he used to fight the Blackfeet in a holster. He and Clark had already disposed of at least two pistols to buy horses from the Shoshone and Wallawalla.

HOMECOMING

The two halves of the expedition reunited on August 12. "At meridian Capt Lewis hove in Sight with the party," Clark wrote. "I was alarmed on the landing of the Canoes to be informed that Capt. Lewis was wounded by an accident—. I found him lying in the Perogue. . . . I examined the wound and found it a very bad flesh wound the ball had passed through the fleshey part of his left thy . . . and cut the cheek of the right buttock." This was not the noble wound of a hero earned in battle but the result of a humiliating mistake. "Capt L. informed me the accident happened the day before by one of the men Peter Crusat mis-stakeig him in the thick bushes to be an Elk. . . . This Crusat is near Sighted and has the use of but one eye."[28]

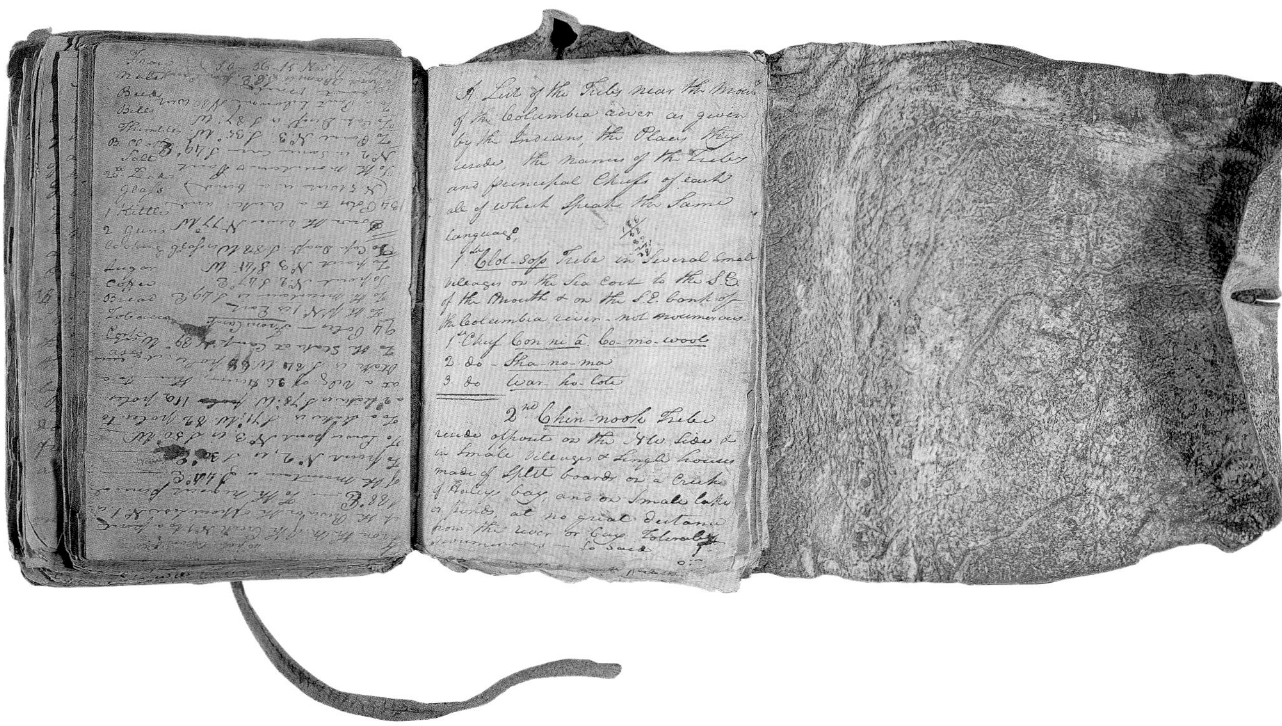

Clark's elkskin journal, 1805
Lewis, who was responsible for writing the book about the expedition, kept a complete eighteen-volume set of the journals but apparently let Clark keep some duplicates and rough notes, including this journal bound in hide. It covers the outward-bound trip from Traveler's Rest over the Bitterroots, down the Columbia River, to the Pacific Ocean. Most of the information it contains was later (probably at Fort Clatsop) copied into the red leather journal books. When Jefferson requested that the journals be archived at the American Philosophical Society, Clark sent Lewis's copies but kept this and four other duplicate volumes. Although it became famous as a "Field-book, bound in a rude piece of elk skin" when Reuben Gold Thwaites first published its contents in 1904, the Missouri Historical Society's 1923 accession records call it "bound in Buffalo hyde."

They were a ragtag crew by this time. "The men with me have not had leasure since we left the West side of the Rocky mountains to dress any skins or make themselves cloaths and most of them are therefore extreemly bare," Lewis wrote. They stopped to dress some leather and make themselves decent before reaching the Mandan villages.[29] They arrived there with a dramatic flourish. "When we were opposit the Minetares Grand Village," Clark wrote, "we derected the Blunderbuses fired Several times. Soon after we Came too at a Croud of the nativs on the bank. . . . those people were extreamly pleased to See us."[30]

Back in the sociable milieu of the villages, Clark caught up on the news. It was not all good; the Missouri Valley was in a state of depressingly familiar upheaval. "This evening Charbono informed me that our back was scercely turned before a war party from the two menetarry [Hidatsa] villages followed on and attacked and killed the Snake [Shoshone] Indians whome we had Seen . . . that they had also . . . killed two Ricaras." The captains' efforts at peacemaking had lasted scarcely as long as the smoke of their pipes. Renewing his diplomatic efforts, Clark repeated his "envitation to the principal Chiefs of all the Villages to accompany us to the U States &c. &c. the Black Cat Chief of the Mandans . . . informed me that as the Sieoux were very troublesom and the

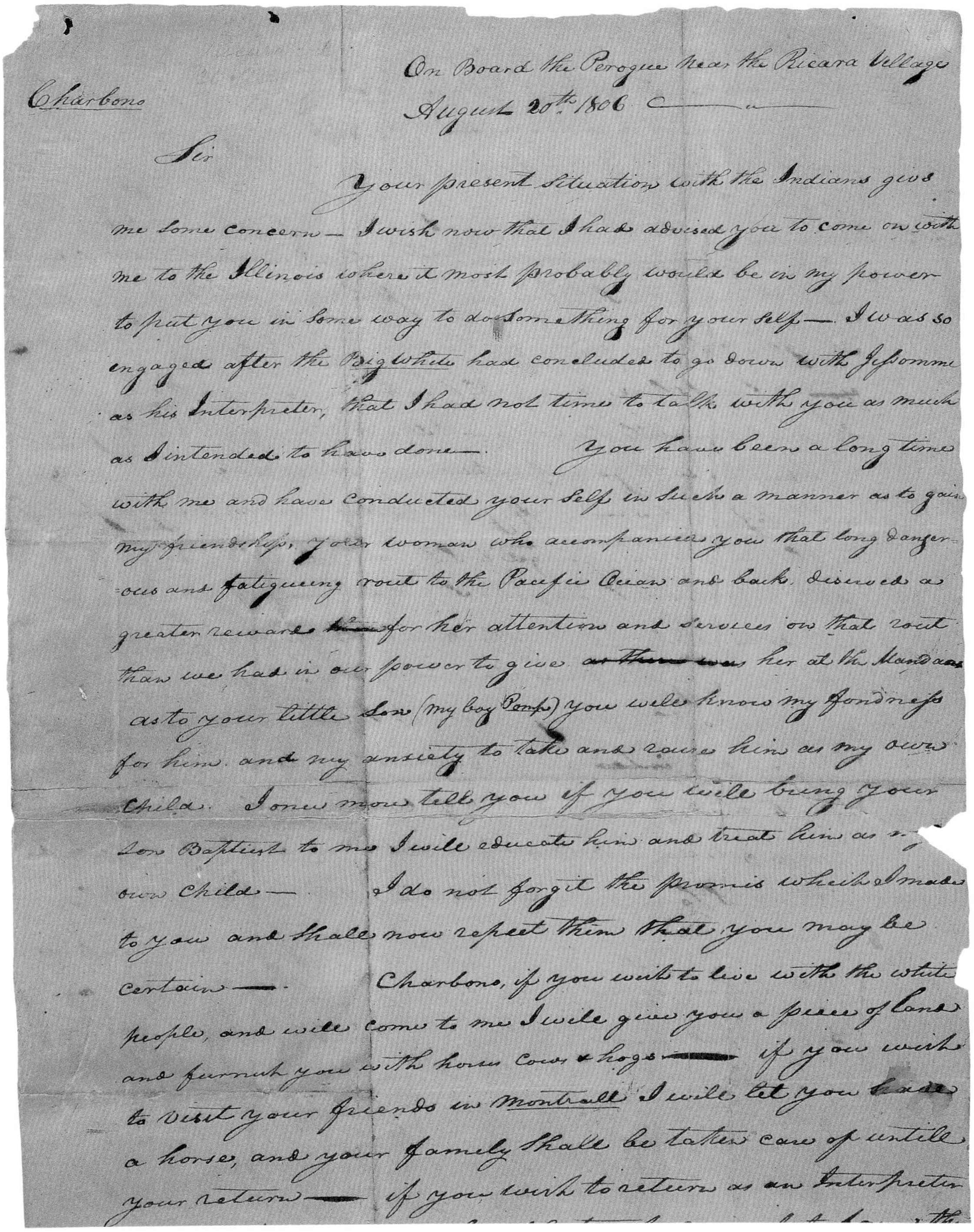

On Board the Perogue Near the Ricara Village
August 20th 1806

Charbono

Sir

Your present Situation with the Indians givs me some concern — I wish now that I had advised you to come on with me to the Illinois where it most probably would be in my power to put you in some way to do something for your self — I was so engaged after the Big White had concluded to go down with Jessomme as his Interpreter, that I had not time to talk with you as much as I intended to have done — You have been a long time with me and have conducted your Self in such a manner as to gain my friendship, your woman who accompanied you that long danger-ous and fatigueing rout to the Pacific Ocian and back diserved a greater reward for her attention and services on that rout than we had in our power to give her at the Mandans as to your little Son (my boy Pomp) you well know my fondness for him and my anxiety to take and raise him as my own Child. I once more tell you if you will bring your Son Baptiest to me I will educate him and treat him as my own Child — I do not forget the promis which I made to you and Shall now repeet them that you may be certain — Charbono, if you wish to live with the white people, and will come to me I will give you a piece of land and furnish you with horses cows & hogs — if you wish to visit your friends in Montreall I will let you have a horse, and your family Shall be taken care of untill your return — if you wish to return as an Interpreter

road to his great father dangerous none of this village would go down with us." After several days of fruitless wheedling, Clark finally heard that "the big white Chief [Shehek-Shote] would go" if they would take the chief's wife and son. This, Clark noted, "We wer obliged to agree to do."[31]

The Corps left behind four members of the company when they resumed their voyage. "At 2 oClock we left our encampment after takeing leave of Colter who . . . Set out up the river in Company with Messrs. Dickson & Handcock," Clark noted. "We also took our leave of T. Chabono, his Snake Indian wife and their Son Child who had accompanied us on our rout to the pacific Ocean. . . . I offered to take his little Son a butifull promising Child who is 19 months old. . . . they observed that in one year the boy would be Sufficiently old to leave his mother & he would then take him to me if I would be so freindly as to raise the Child."[32]

Letter from Clark to Toussaint Charbonneau, 1806
In this letter, written "On Board the Perogue Near the Ricara Village," Clark apologized to Charbonneau for leaving the Mandan villages without talking to him. "Your woman who accompanied you that long dangerous and fatigueing rout to the Pacific Ocian and back diserved a greater reward . . . than we had in our power to give her at the Mandans. As to your little Son (my boy *Pomp*) you well know my fondness for him and my anxiety to take and raise him as my own child." He offered to set the Charbonneaus up in business or farming if Toussaint would bring "Janey" and Pomp to "live with the white people."

They covered as many as seventy-eight miles a day traveling downstream. "I observe a great alteration in the Corrent course and appearance of this pt. of the Missouri," Clark wrote. "In places where there was Sand bars in the fall 1804 at this time the main Current passes, and where the current then passed is now a Sand bar." Passing through Sioux territory, Clark made a point of renewing old animosities. On August 30, "80 or 90 Indian men all armed with fusees & Bows & arrows Came out of a wood on the opposite bank. . . . 3 young men Set out from the opposite Side and Swam next me on the Sand bar. . . . they informed me that they were Tetons. . . . I told those Indians . . . that if any of them come near our camp we Should kill them. . . . 7 of them halted on the top of the hill and blackguarded us . . . of which we took no notice."[33]

Mouth of the Platte River, 900 Miles above St. Louis, 1832
The Corps reached the mouth of the Platte River on September 9, 1806. Thinking in terms of river transportation, the captains paid little attention to the Platte after finding that it "Cannot be navagated with Boats or Perogues." It was, however, the closest thing to a Northwest Passage. The easiest route across the continent, which turned out to be an overland trail, went up the Platte Valley. George Catlin is the artist of this scene.

Soon they began to meet a steady procession of traders passing up the Missouri to do business with the Indians. The first one they met, they plied for news of the outside world. "Our first enquirey was after the President of our country and then . . . the State of the politicks." Clark jotted down the miscellany of answers. "Genl. Wilkinson was the governor of the Louisiana. . . . Two

Letter from Clark to his brother, 1806
This letter was intended as the public announcement of the safe return of the expedition. Although it was addressed to Clark's brother Jonathan, the captains knew it would be published. Lewis, who was the better writer, made this initial rough draft on scraps of paper, probably starting it during a rainy morning layover in St. Charles and completing it in St. Louis. Clark made some corrections, then recopied it. It was first published in the *Frankfort (Ky.) Palladium*, "to gratify, in some measure, the impatient wishes of his countrymen." Within a month it had been reprinted in the *Pittsburgh Gazette*, the *National Intelligencer*, and scores of other papers.

British Ships of the line had fired on an American Ship. . . . 2 Indians had been hung in St. Louis for murder and . . . Mr. Burr & Genl. Hambleton fought a Duel, the latter was killed."[34]

Their own return would soon be the news story of the season, as they began to realize. "We met a Captain McClellin . . . assending in a large boat. this gentleman . . . was Somewhat astonished to See us return and . . . informed us that we had been long Since given out [up] by the people of the U S Generaly and almost forgotton, the President of the U. States had yet hopes of us."[35] "The party being extreemly anxious to get down ply their ores very well," Clark wrote. Soon, signs of Euro-American settlement began to appear. "We Saw Some cows on the bank which was a joyfull Sight to the party and Caused a Shout to be raised for joy."[36]

It was September 23 when they finally arrived back in St. Louis. Ordway described the moment as a mixture of the public and the personal: "About 12 oClock we arived in Site of St. Louis fired three Rounds as we approached the Town and landed oppocit the center of the Town, the people gathred on the Shore and Huzzared three cheers. . . . the party all considerable much rejoiced that we have the Expedition Completed and now . . . we entend to return to our native homes to See our parents once more as we have been So long from them."[37]

THE RESULTS OF THE EXPEDITION

> Never did a similar event excite more joy thro' the United States. The humblest of it's citizens had taken a lively interest in the issue of this journey, and looked forward with impatience for the information it would furnish.
>
> —THOMAS JEFFERSON[38]

Their feet had scarcely touched the St. Louis levee before the United States started to adopt the expedition as its own, constructing new meanings out of the story. Over the next year, as Lewis and Clark were plunged into a brief celebrity, they would try to manage their public images, with mixed success.

Their first move was to write what amounted to press releases, couched as personal letters but intended for publication. Lewis wrote Jefferson a letter full of comments about trade and policy; Clark, writing to his brother Jonathan, concentrated on the trip's route and adventures. Clark's was the first to make it into print, so the public's initial impression was of an expedition full of hardships and geographical discovery—an image that would be slow to fade. Both of the letters claimed a qualified success. Clark wrote: "Such as nature has permited it we have discovered the best rout which does exist across the continent of North America."[39]

The cautious disclaimers were promptly ignored by the enthusiastic citizens of St. Louis, who held a ball as a mark of "respect entertained for those characters who are willing to encounter, fatigue and hunger for the benefit of their fellow citizens." The Frankfort, Kentucky, newspaper reported that by the time of the eighteenth toast, the citizens of St. Louis, evidently feeling exceedingly warm toward their honorees, resolved, "Captains Lewis and Clark—Their perilous services endear them to every American heart."[40] "Perils," "difficulties," "privations," "obstacles"—the words appeared over and over in the subsequent coverage. Discoveries, science, and knowledge played second fiddle. The American public did not want to celebrate a dry achievement of Enlightenment learning, and so they transformed the expedition into an exciting, manly frontier adventure.

Woven bag, c. 1800–50

This could be the bag accessioned by Peale as "A Bag prepared of grass by the Pishquilpahs on the Columbia River," though no direct evidence survives. Clark and Lewis (and Peale, elsewhere) spell the tribal name "Pishquitpah"; this group lived on the north bank of the Columbia across from the Deschutes River and may have been Yakima. Today, this bag is usually identified as Wishram; its stylized human-face design is reminiscent of prehistoric bone and stone sculpture from that tribe. When passing The Dalles, Clark remarked, "They are well Supplied with Straw & bark bags ready to hold their pounded fish." Lewis added, "They use the silk grass in manufacturing their fishing nets and bags." Bags like this, often called "sally bags," were used to store both roots and *ch'lay*, the dried and pulverized salmon that was a major trade item at The Dalles. Among the things Clark shipped home to Louisville at the end of the journey in 1806 were "2 Indian baskets."

***The Evening Fire-Side; or Literary Miscellany*, 1806**

Press coverage of the expedition was uniformly laudatory at first. This magazine, published in Philadelphia, had promoted the news to the front page by November 29. The anonymous author wrote: "The exploration of an overland route to the West, is indeed *a new thing under the sun*, and one of the remarkable occurrences of the present century. . . . a region is at length explored, destined some few half centuries hence, to be inhabited by millions of mankind." The writer then denounced anyone who would "with infinite baseness and cruelty, satiate his avarice by the destruction of the natives."

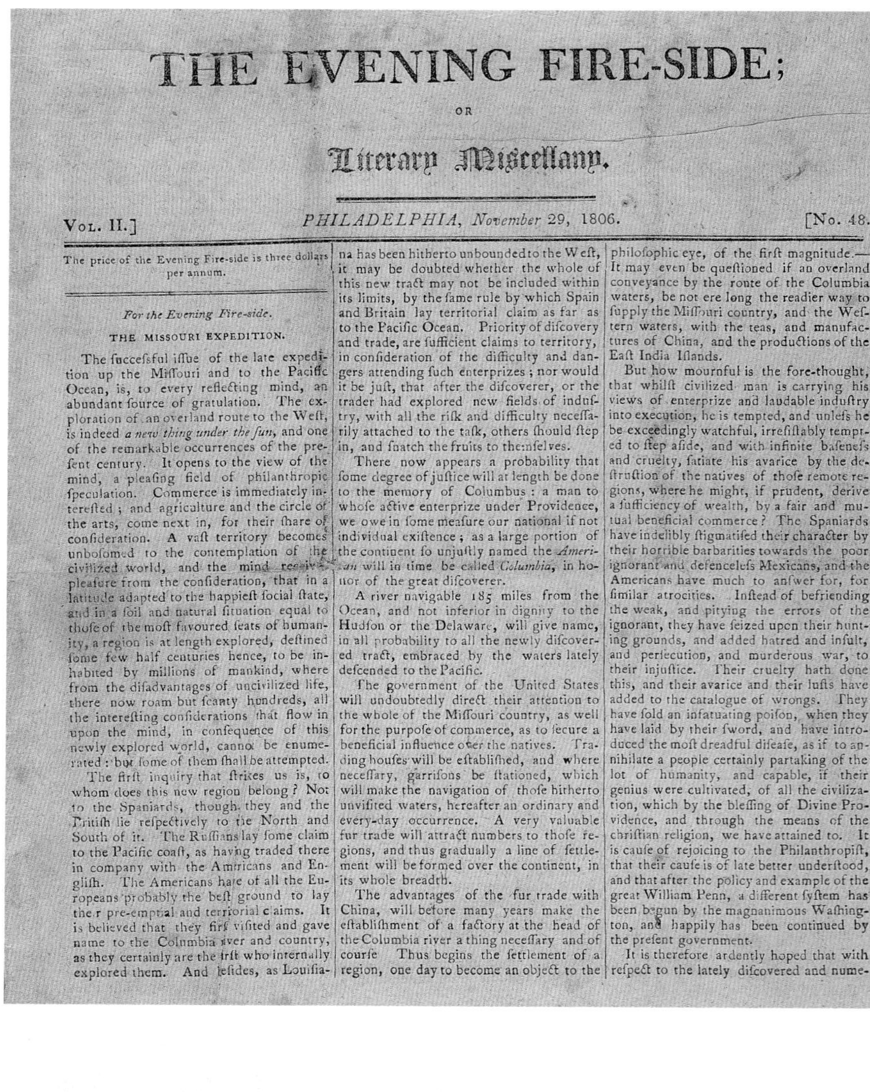

THE EVENING FIRE-SIDE;

OR

Literary Miscellany.

VOL. II.] PHILADELPHIA, *November* 29, 1806. [No. 48.

The price of the Evening Fire-side is three dollars per annum.

For the Evening Fire-side.

THE MISSOURI EXPEDITION.

The ſucceſsful iſſue of the late expedition up the Miſſouri and to the Pacific Ocean, is, to every reflecting mind, an abundant ſource of gratulation. The exploration of an overland route to the Weſt, is indeed *a new thing under the ſun*, and one of the remarkable occurrences of the preſent century. It opens to the view of the mind, a pleaſing field of philanthropic ſpeculation. Commerce is immediately intereſted; and agriculture and the circle of the arts, come next in, for their ſhare of conſideration. A vaſt territory becomes unboſomed to the contemplation of the civilized world, and the mind receives pleaſure from the conſideration, that in a latitude adapted to the happieſt ſocial ſtate, and in a ſoil and natural ſituation equal to thoſe of the moſt favoured ſeats of humanity, a region is at length explored, deſtined ſome few half centuries hence, to be inhabited by millions of mankind, where from the diſadvantages of uncivilized life, there now roam but ſcanty hundreds, all the intereſting conſiderations that flow in upon the mind, in conſequence of this newly explored world, cannot be enumerated: but ſome of them ſhall be attempted.

The firſt inquiry that ſtrikes us is, to whom does this new region belong? Not to the Spaniards, though they and the Britiſh lie reſpectively to the North and South of it. The Ruſſians lay ſome claim to the Pacific coaſt, as having traded there in company with the Americans and Engliſh. The Americans have of all the Europeans probably the beſt ground to lay their pre-emptial and territorial claims. It is believed that they firſt viſited and gave name to the Columbia river and country, as they certainly are the firſt who internally explored them. And beſides, as Louiſiana has been hitherto unbounded to the Weſt, it may be doubted whether the whole of this new tract may not be included within its limits, by the ſame rule by which Spain and Britain lay territorial claim as far as to the Pacific Ocean. Priority of diſcovery and trade, are ſufficient claims to territory, in conſideration of the difficulty and dangers attending ſuch enterprizes; nor would it be juſt, that after the diſcoverer, or the trader had explored new fields of induſtry, with all the riſk and difficulty neceſſarily attached to the taſk, others ſhould ſtep in, and ſnatch the fruits to themſelves.

There now appears a probability that ſome degree of juſtice will at length be done to the memory of Columbus: a man to whoſe active enterprize under Providence, we owe in ſome meaſure our national if not individual exiſtence; as a large portion of the continent ſo unjuſtly named the *American* will in time be called *Columbia*, in honor of the great diſcoverer.

A river navigable 185 miles from the Ocean, and not inferior in dignity to the Hudſon or the Delaware, will give name, in all probability to all the newly diſcovered tract, embraced by the waters lately deſcended to the Pacific.

The government of the United States will undoubtedly direct their attention to the whole of the Miſſouri country, as well for the purpoſe of commerce, as to ſecure a beneficial influence over the natives. Trading houſes will be eſtabliſhed, and where neceſſary, garriſons be ſtationed, which will make the navigation of thoſe hitherto unviſited waters, hereafter an ordinary and every-day occurrence. A very valuable fur trade will attract numbers to thoſe regions, and thus gradually a line of ſettlement will be formed over the continent, in its whole breadth.

The advantages of the fur trade with China, will before many years make the eſtabliſhment of a factory at the head of the Columbia river a thing neceſſary and of courſe Thus begins the ſettlement of a region, one day to become an object to the philoſophic eye, of the firſt magnitude.—It may even be queſtioned if an overland conveyance by the route of the Columbia waters, be not ere long the readier way to ſupply the Miſſouri country, and the Weſtern waters, with the teas, and manufactures of China, and the productions of the Eaſt India Iſlands.

But how mournful is the fore-thought, that whilſt civilized man is carrying his views of enterprize and laudable induſtry into execution, he is tempted, and unleſs he be exceedingly watchful, irreſiſtably tempted to ſtep aſide, and with infinite baſeneſs and cruelty, ſatiate his avarice by the deſtruction of the natives of thoſe remote regions, where he might, if prudent, derive a ſufficiency of wealth, by a fair and mutual beneficial commerce? The Spaniards have indelibly ſtigmatiſed their character by their horrible barbarities towards the poor ignorant and defenceleſs Mexicans, and the Americans have much to anſwer for, for ſimilar atrocities. Inſtead of befriending the weak, and pitying the errors of the ignorant, they have ſeized upon their hunting grounds, and added hatred and inſult, and perſecution, and murderous war, to their injuſtice. Their cruelty hath done this, and their avarice and their luſts have added to the catalogue of wrongs. They have ſold an infatuating poiſon, when they have laid by their ſword, and have introduced the moſt dreadful diſeaſe, as if to annihilate a people certainly partaking of the lot of humanity, and capable, if their genius were cultivated, of all the civilization, which by the bleſſing of Divine Providence, and through the means of the chriſtian religion, we have attained to. It is cauſe of rejoicing to the Philanthropiſt, that their cauſe is of late better underſtood, and that after the policy and example of the great William Penn, a different ſyſtem has been begun by the magnanimous Waſhington, and happily has been continued by the preſent government.

It is therefore ardently hoped that with reſpect to the lately diſcovered and nume-

Jefferson's reaction was "unspeakable joy." He confessed to Lewis: "The length of time without hearing of you had begun to be felt awfully." But his subsequent report to Congress echoed Lewis's cautious wording: "The expedition of Messrs. Lewis & Clarke . . . has had all the success which could have been expected." Rather than making dramatic claims of discovery, he also stressed heroic and patriotic deeds. "Lewis and Clarke, & their brave companions, have, by this arduous service, deserved well of their country."[41]

As Lewis and Clark pursued their separate ways east, each stopping to visit family on the way, they continued to find their story overtaking them. At Fincastle, Virginia, where Clark stopped to negotiate his marriage to young Julia Hancock, the citizens presented him with a resolution honoring his deeds: "You have navigated bold & unknown rivers, traversed Mountains,

Book prospectus, 1807

This is a proof for the prospectus of Lewis's book, sent to him about April 1, 1807, by the publisher, John Conrad. A virtually unchanged final copy is also in Clark's papers. It promised three volumes, each of 400 to 500 pages. Copies of the prospectus went out to at least 148 post offices, where they were displayed to collect signatures of interested buyers. Clark wrote some names on the back of this copy, suggesting that he took it with him on his 1810 trip to Philadelphia to restart work on the book after Lewis's death. A new prospectus was issued at that time, but the final book was not published until 1814.

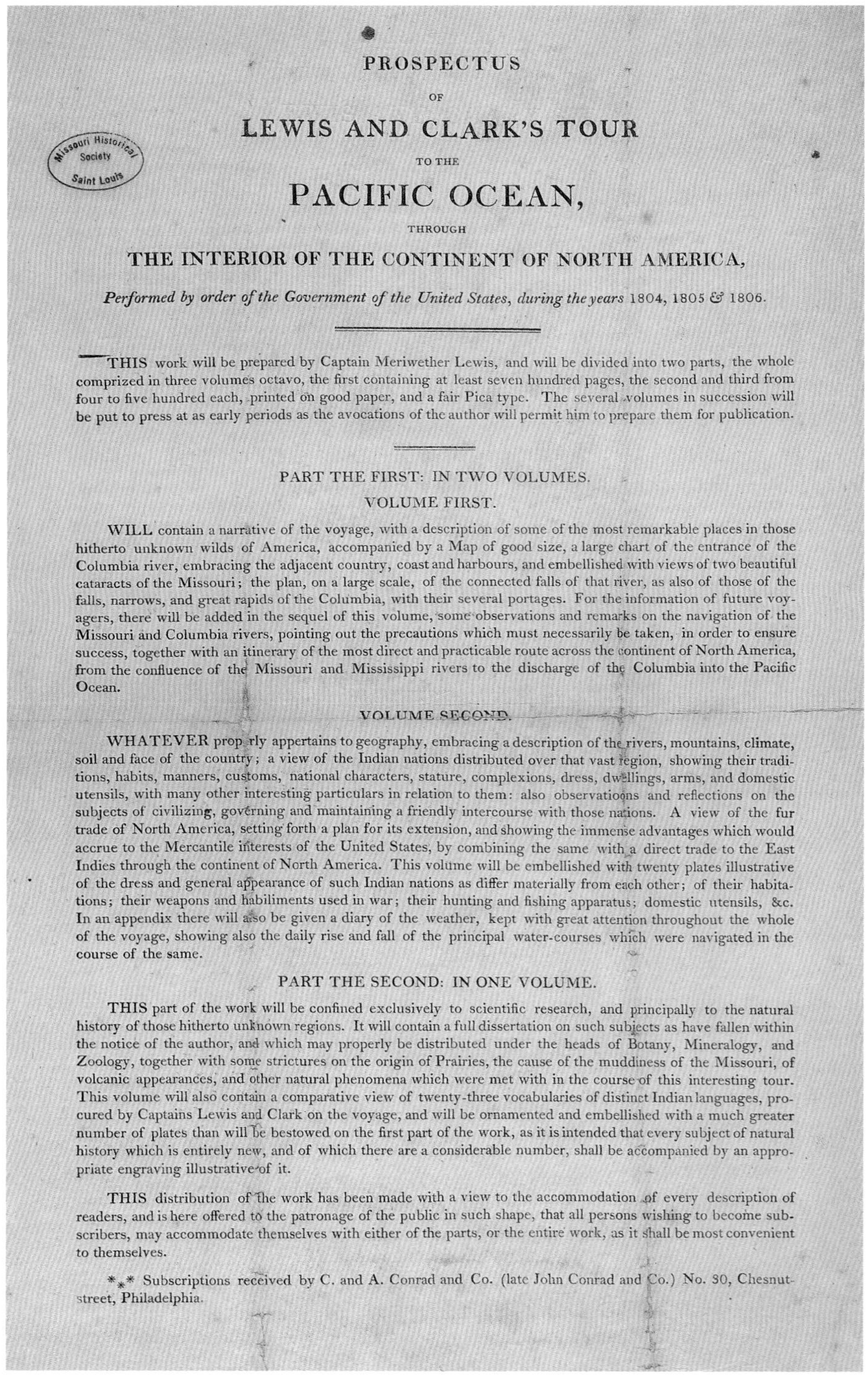

PROSPECTUS

OF

LEWIS AND CLARK'S TOUR

TO THE

PACIFIC OCEAN,

THROUGH

THE INTERIOR OF THE CONTINENT OF NORTH AMERICA,

Performed by order of the Government of the United States, during the years 1804, 1805 & 1806.

THIS work will be prepared by Captain Meriwether Lewis, and will be divided into two parts, the whole comprized in three volumes octavo, the first containing at least seven hundred pages, the second and third from four to five hundred each, printed on good paper, and a fair Pica type. The several volumes in succession will be put to press at as early periods as the avocations of the author will permit him to prepare them for publication.

PART THE FIRST: IN TWO VOLUMES.

VOLUME FIRST.

WILL contain a narrative of the voyage, with a description of some of the most remarkable places in those hitherto unknown wilds of America, accompanied by a Map of good size, a large chart of the entrance of the Columbia river, embracing the adjacent country, coast and harbours, and embellished with views of two beautiful cataracts of the Missouri; the plan, on a large scale, of the connected falls of that river, as also of those of the falls, narrows, and great rapids of the Columbia, with their several portages. For the information of future voyagers, there will be added in the sequel of this volume, some observations and remarks on the navigation of the Missouri and Columbia rivers, pointing out the precautions which must necessarily be taken, in order to ensure success, together with an itinerary of the most direct and practicable route across the continent of North America, from the confluence of the Missouri and Mississippi rivers to the discharge of the Columbia into the Pacific Ocean.

VOLUME SECOND.

WHATEVER prop rly appertains to geography, embracing a description of the rivers, mountains, climate, soil and face of the country; a view of the Indian nations distributed over that vast region, showing their traditions, habits, manners, customs, national characters, stature, complexions, dress, dwellings, arms, and domestic utensils, with many other interesting particulars in relation to them: also observatioons and reflections on the subjects of civilizing, governing and maintaining a friendly intercourse with those nations. A view of the fur trade of North America, setting forth a plan for its extension, and showing the immense advantages which would accrue to the Mercantile interests of the United States, by combining the same with a direct trade to the East Indies through the continent of North America. This volume will be embellished with twenty plates illustrative of the dress and general appearance of such Indian nations as differ materially from each other; of their habitations; their weapons and habiliments used in war; their hunting and fishing apparatus; domestic utensils, &c. In an appendix there will also be given a diary of the weather, kept with great attention throughout the whole of the voyage, showing also the daily rise and fall of the principal water-courses which were navigated in the course of the same.

PART THE SECOND: IN ONE VOLUME.

THIS part of the work will be confined exclusively to scientific research, and principally to the natural history of those hitherto unknown regions. It will contain a full dissertation on such subjects as have fallen within the notice of the author, and which may properly be distributed under the heads of Botany, Mineralogy, and Zoology, together with some strictures on the origin of Prairies, the cause of the muddiness of the Missouri, of volcanic appearances, and other natural phenomena which were met with in the course of this interesting tour. This volume will also contain a comparative view of twenty-three vocabularies of distinct Indian languages, procured by Captains Lewis and Clark on the voyage, and will be ornamented and embellished with a much greater number of plates than will be bestowed on the first part of the work, as it is intended that every subject of natural history which is entirely new, and of which there are a considerable number, shall be accompanied by an appropriate engraving illustrative of it.

THIS distribution of the work has been made with a view to the accommodation of every description of readers, and is here offered to the patronage of the public in such shape, that all persons wishing to become subscribers, may accommodate themselves with either of the parts, or the entire work, as it shall be most convenient to themselves.

*** Subscriptions received by C. and A. Conrad and Co. (late John Conrad and Co.) No. 30, Chesnut-street, Philadelphia.

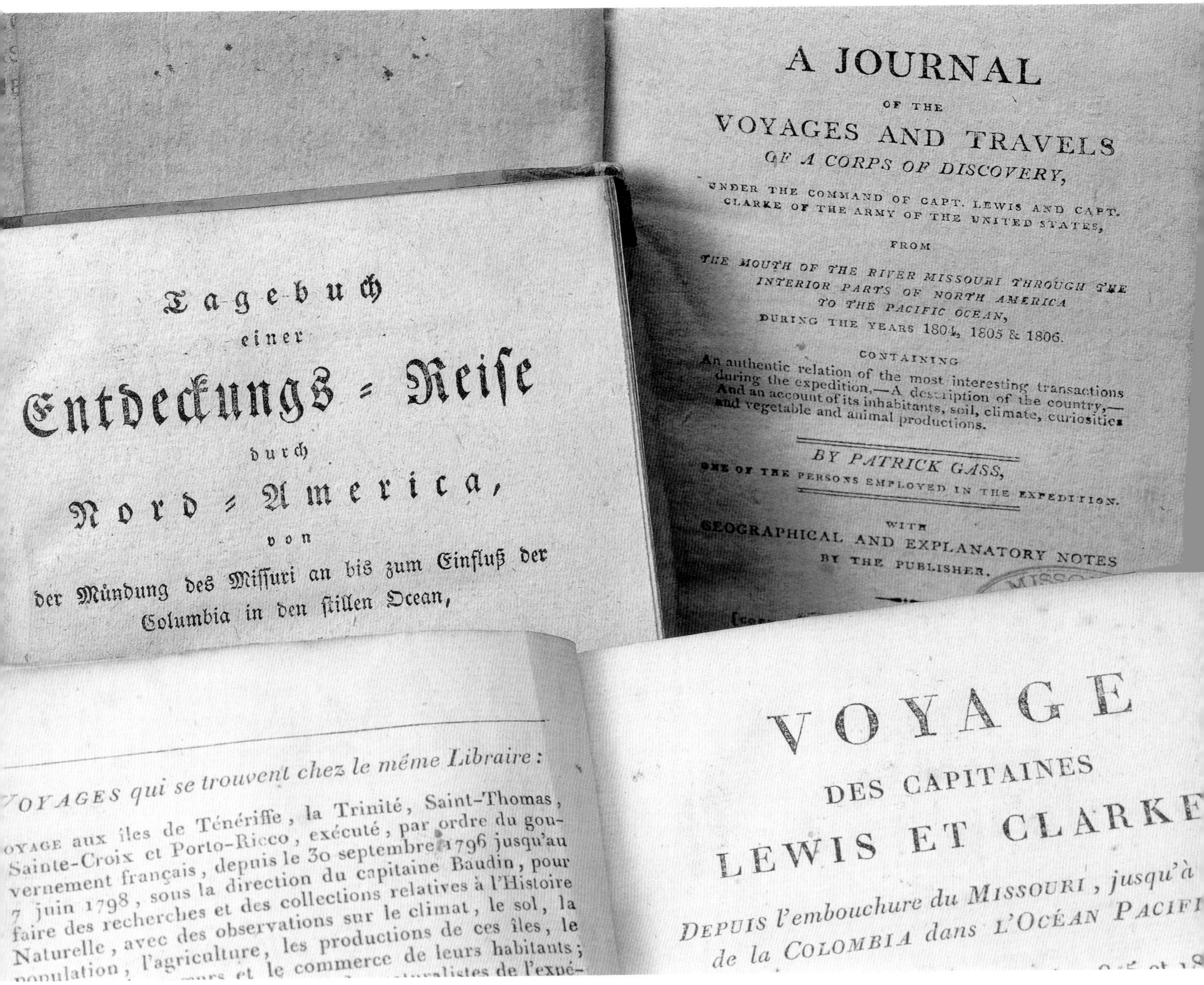

which had never before been impressed with the footsteps of civilized man, and surmounted every obstacle, which climate, Nature, or ferocious Savages could throw in your way." And incidentally, he had "opened to the United States a source of inexhaustible wealth"—all "without the effusion of human blood." Meanwhile, in Washington D.C., Lewis was the guest at an extravagant dinner where, among other florid tributes, he was praised as "Patriotic, enlightened, and brave; who had the spirit to undertake, and the valour to execute an expedition, which reflects honor on his country." When Clark finally arrived in the capital, he found himself "partakeing of the Sumptious far[e] of maney of the members [of Congress]." He noted: "My old western friends . . . appere happy that they have it in their power to pay me much respect which appers to be the general disposition of every member of Congress."[42]

There was bound to be a backlash. The criticism shortly appeared in the form of a satirical poem published anonymously in the March 1807 *Monthly Anthology and Boston Review* but actually composed by none other than John

Patrick Gass, *A Journal of the Voyages and Travels of a Corps of Discovery*, 1807, 1810, 1814
Sergeant Patrick Gass had neither scientific data nor literary panache, but he had timing. His journal, published by the Pittsburgh entrepreneur David McKeehan, was for seven years the only authentic book about the expedition, and it was reprinted widely. The English, French, and German editions are shown here. When Lewis published a warning about "unauthorised and probably some spurious publications" about the journey, McKeehan took umbrage and published a long, intemperate attack on Lewis for "contending with the poor fellows, who for their small pittance were equally exposed with yourself to the toils and dangers attending the expedition." There is no evidence Lewis even knew about the Gass book at the time.

Quincy Adams. Amid catty references to "dusky Sally," Jefferson's reputed mistress, Adams heaped sarcasm on the breathless praise of Lewis:

Good people, listen to my tale,
'Tis nothing but what true is;
I'll tell you of the mighty deeds
Atchiev'd by Captain Lewis—
How starting from the Atlantick shore
By fair and easy motion,
He journied, *all the way by land,*
Until he met the ocean.

Heroick, sure, the toil must be
To travel through the woods, sir;
And never meet a foe, yet save
His person and his goods, sir![43]

If Lewis hoped to be praised for something more productive than going to the coast and returning intact, the publication of their findings was essential. In 1807 he went to Philadelphia to start the process. He parceled out the plant specimens to a botanist for analysis; the bird and animal specimens went to Peale's Museum for reconstruction and study. He arranged for Charles Willson Peale to draw the illustrations, and he had some copper plates made. He then sat down with a publisher to produce an elaborate prospectus for his book, in order to solicit subscriptions. It would be a three-volume work, but only part of the first volume would be devoted to a narrative of the journey; the rest would be scientific reports on geography, ethnology, linguistics, botany, mineralogy, and zoology. The proportions tellingly reveal Lewis's own valuation of his contributions.[44]

He had misjudged the interests of the book-buying public. The expedition's celebrity afforded a brief opportunity, and before Lewis's ambitious book could be published, other authors started rushing to press with spurious editions that bilked unwary buyers with a mishmash of reprints—official reports, newspaper articles, and plagiarized passages from the books of other travel-

Books resulting from Lewis and Clark's discoveries, 1805, 1808–14, and 1828
Some of Lewis and Clark's scientific observations were published, but not by them. Others in the Philadelphia scientific community who had access to their specimens used bits of their information. Benjamin Smith Barton, editor of *The Philadelphia Medical and Physical Journal* (left), started the trend even before the expedition returned, publishing an article on a hare, a marmot, and a stoat that were "observed in the Missouri-country, by Mr. Lewis," and were among the skins sent back to Jefferson. The ornithologist Alexander Wilson used the specimens in Peale's Museum to compile his pioneering *American Ornithology; or, The Natural History of the Birds of the United States* (middle), which illustrated and described four birds collected by the expedition—the Louisiana tanager, Lewis's woodpecker, Clark's nutcracker, and the American magpie. The first illustrated zoology text published in America, John D. Godman's *American Natural History* (right), credited Lewis and Clark as discoverers of several animals, including the grizzly bear, the Rocky Mountain goat, the pronghorn antelope, and the argali or Rocky Mountain sheep. By the time the book was published, however, these animals were already well-known from the descriptions and specimens of other explorers.

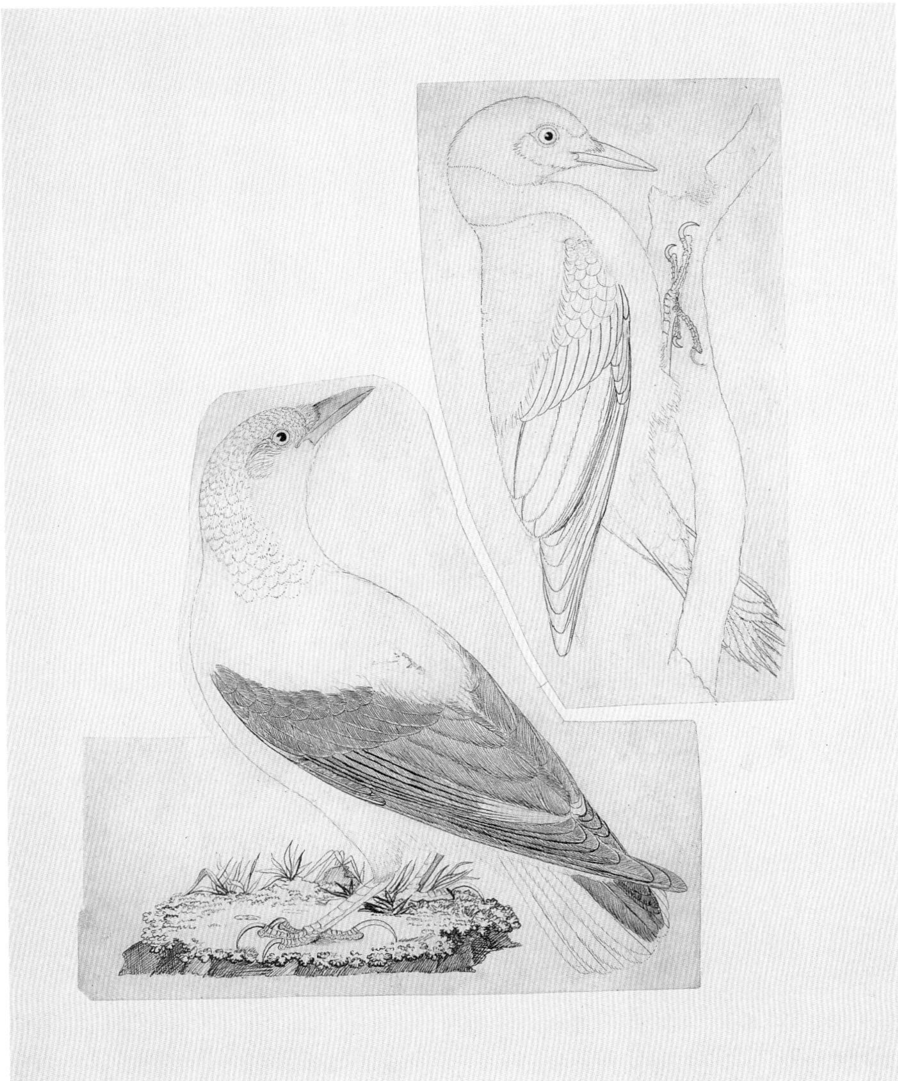

Sketch of Clark's crow and Lewis's woodpecker, 1808
Alexander Wilson drew these preliminary sketches for his *American Ornithology* from the specimens brought back by Lewis and deposited with Peale's Museum. The crow (*Corvus columbianus*) is now called "Clark's nutcracker"; the woodpecker (*Asyndesmus lewis*) still bears the English name Wilson gave it.

ers—all attributed to Lewis and Clark. In 1807 a Pittsburgh publisher printed Patrick Gass's accurate, pedestrian journal of the voyage. It scooped Lewis and became an international success. For years it formed the public's main image of the expedition.

The book Lewis had advertised never came to be. He died in 1809 without producing a single page of manuscript. Clark, who had neither literary nor scientific ambition, embarked on a search for a "proper scientifcul Charrutor" to compile the volumes on botany, zoology, and mineralogy. He gave the journals to a ghost writer, Nicholas Biddle, a Philadelphia scholar, attorney, and financier. Working diligently for over a year, Biddle extracted the narrative portions, leaving the scientific observations for separate publication. When his work, *History of the Expedition under the Command of Captains Lewis and Clark*, finally appeared in 1814, the two-volume paraphrase of the journals was a resounding flop. The public's interests had moved on. The publisher was unable to sell all the copies. "I cannot express to you how much I am disappointed at the unfortunate result of this business," Biddle wrote to Clark.[45]

The projected scientific volume, to be written by Benjamin Smith Barton, never appeared, leading scholars to assume—for ninety years—that Lewis and Clark had made no scientific discoveries. Nevertheless, some of the Corps' information did trickle out in the works of others. The naturalists Alexander Wilson, George Ord, Constantine Rafinesque, and Thomas Say all named and

Sketch of *Fritillaria lanceolata and fritillaria pudica*, c. 1807 and **Frederick Pursh, *Flora Americae Septentrionalis*, 1816**

Although Lewis recorded rich contextual information on the plants he collected—where they grew, when they sprouted and flowered, how they were used—the German botanist who published them did not use that data and reported only anatomical information that affected the plants' classification. Frederick Pursh followed the conventions of botanical illustration when he painted this and several other watercolors for Lewis's planned book on the natural history of the expedition. Pursh showed the plants isolated on the page, with details of their dissected reproductive organs. He left the paintings with Benjamin Smith Barton, in whose papers they were recently found, never having been used. But Pursh took some of the specimens to England and apparently redrew them for his own botany book, first published in London in 1814 (the second edition is shown here). In the meantime, plans for Lewis's book had been abandoned, so Pursh was the first to describe and name many of the expedition's plants.

classified new species based on Lewis and Clark's specimens of birds and mammals. The botanist chosen by Lewis to classify the plant specimens was Frederick Pursh, a young German who was in Philadelphia to study American plants. In the confusion following Lewis's death, no one appeared to notice when Pursh stuck a load of specimens in his luggage and moved to London. There, in 1814, he published *Flora Americae Septentrionalis*, the first scientific work on American botany. In it, he illustrated and classified 130 of Lewis's plants, conscientiously naming a few of them for their collectors: *Lewisia rediviva* (bitterroot) and *Clarkia pulchella* (ragged robin), for example. Under normal circumstances, the explorers would have had reason to be indignant at Pursh for absconding with the evidence; as it turned out, Pursh did them a service.[46]

Other portions of the scientific data were less lucky. The mineral specimens, deposited with the American Philosophical Society, disappeared into the collection of the mineralogist Adam Seybert, and most were never seen again. Ferdinand Hassler, the mathematician enlisted to calculate longitude readings from Lewis's astronomical observations, failed to do the work and excused himself by saying the data were faulty—an inaccurate claim believed for nearly two hundred years. Even more tragic was the fate of the linguistic evidence so laboriously collected by Lewis. En route to Monticello from Washington, D. C., one of Jefferson's trunks containing the word lists was stolen, and its contents were thrown in the river. When he heard of their destruction, Lewis remarked painfully on the irony that they "had passed the continent of America and after their exposure to so many casualties and wrisks [they] should have met such destiny in their passage through a small portion only of the Chesapeak."[47]

One body of scientific information did reach the public: Clark's geographic discoveries, published in his masterful 1814 map. But what the map revealed, and what the American public soon realized, was that Lewis and Clark had not done what they had set out to do—that is, to discover "the most direct & practicable water communication across this continent for the purposes of commerce." The problem was not theirs: they had been sent to find a chimera. There *was* no navigable water route across the continent. The best way west was by land, soon to be called the Oregon Trail. The route that Lewis and Clark followed to the Columbia was so tortuous that even today no major roads follow it and no major cities lie along it. Wheels and rails settled the West, not keelboats.

And what about their objectives regarding the Indians? The Corps did not bring peace and stability to the Missouri Valley. The expedition did not enlist the powerful Sioux as American allies, nor did it make the way safe for commerce. At first glance, it would seem that here as well, Lewis and Clark had returned with disappointing results. But that conclusion would be too simple. With the Indians, as in other ways, Lewis and Clark's true importance was as image-makers.

MAKING SENSE OF INDIANS

> We are all now of one family, born in the same land, & bound to live as brothers. . . . The great Spirit has given you strength, and has given us strength; not that we might hurt one another, but to do each other all the good in our power.
>
> —THOMAS JEFFERSON, TO THE OSAGE[48]

> They gave us things like solid water, which were sometimes brilliant as the sun, and which sometimes showed us our own faces. Nothing could equal our wonder and delight.
>
> —FARO, A SHOSHONE[49]

Later, it was not Lewis or Clark the Shoshone remembered best but rather the looking glasses the two men had brought with them. The memory was the same for the Salish; in the 1890s, an old woman known as Eugenie told how the mirror given to that tribe was kept in the chief's house: "The young

Pipe, c. 1800–50
Many of the artifacts that Lewis and Clark donated to Peale's Museum were diplomatic gifts from Mississippi Valley nations they did not meet during the expedition but dealt with in the years after as government officials for Louisiana Territory. Of the fourteen pipes they donated, one was Winnebago from Prairie du Chien, two were Fox, three or four were Sauk, two were Iowa from the Des Moines River, and one was Sioux from Prairie du Chien. This may be one of those. The beads woven into wool and the quillwork plaited with plant fiber rather than sinew indicate an eastern prairie or western Great Lakes origin for the stem. The effigy bowl of catlinite has an otter on the prow, an animal popular among Great Lakes carvers. Some of the Mississippi Valley pipes Peale accessioned may have been given to Jefferson by a multi-tribe delegation that traveled to Washington, D.C., from St. Louis during the time the expedition was in the West.

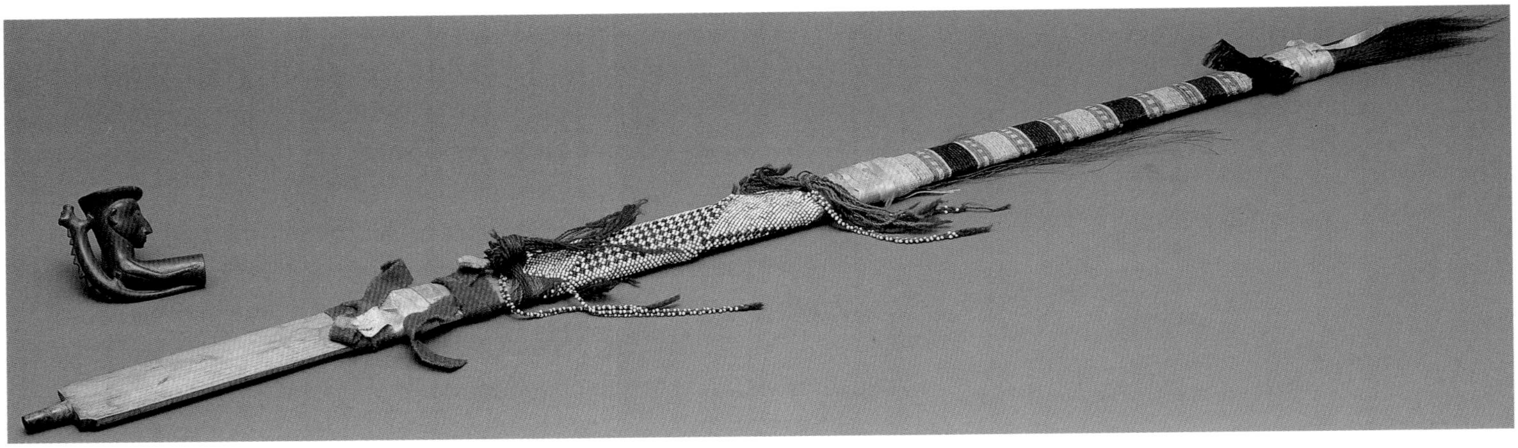

An Indian Chief of Louisiana, 1769
The artist of this engraving followed a long European tradition of portraying Indians in the poses and garb of classical statues to equate their state of nature with an ancient golden age. The noble Indian here treads heedlessly on the corrupting gold of Europe. The illustration appeared in Jean-Bernard Bossu's *Nouveaux Voyages aux Indes Occidentales*, a book that Jefferson and Lewis could have consulted. Bossu, a French soldier who served in the West Indies and Louisiana, said the image showed "the happy innocence in which these people lived before the arrival of the French in their homeland."

girls . . . were admitted, one by one, to look each at her own soul—i.e., her face in the glass, and when thus purified, by prayer and self-contemplation, they . . . prayed aloud, each one crying out the needs of her soul."[50]

People can be mirrors too. When the Corps and the Indians looked at one another, often what they saw was their own faces. But mirrors can give false reflections when distorted or discolored. The flaws in Lewis and Clark's images of the Indians came from the preconceptions they had brought with them and their expectations about the Indians' role in the future of the United States.

For centuries, Europeans had cherished contradictory images of Indians. The "noble savage" stereotype had ancient roots in the European longing for a Golden Age, a state of nature whose simplicity stood in opposition to the artificiality and complexity of European society. Seventeenth-century social critics such as John Locke and Michel Montaigne argued that mankind in a state of

An Indian Warrior Entering His Wigwam with a Scalp, 1789
This engraving, meant to inflame fears and animosity toward the British and their Native allies, portrayed an Africanized Indian wearing the medal of his British sponsors, who look on in the background, indifferent to atrocities. The previous military service of Lewis and Clark had mainly been against the Indians of the Ohio Valley, supposedly portrayed here.

nature was endowed with primitive virtues, which the corrupting flaws of civilization undermined. Jefferson, their intellectual heir, assumed that liberty and independence were natural birthrights of mankind, and so he attributed them to the Indians. In Jefferson's words, the Indians were "endowed with the faculties and the rights of men, breathing an ardent love of liberty and independence, and occupying a country which left them no desire but to be undisturbed."[51]

Lewis found the closest thing to a state of nature among the Shoshone. On the one hand, they were guileless innocents: "notwithstanding their extreem poverty they are not only cheerfull but even gay, fond of gaudy dress and amusements; like most other Indians they are great egotists and frequently boast of heroic acts which they never performed. . . . they are frank, communicative, fair in dealing, generous with the little they possess, extreemly honest,

Seal of the American Philosophical Society, late 1700s
Jefferson's goal "to civilize and instruct" the Indians was illustrated in the seal of the learned society he led for years. Here, an untutored Indian meets the books and philosophical instruments of the Enlightenment, presided over by an imperialistic Athena. The Indian symbolizes America.

and by no means beggarly." Not only that, but the Shoshone lived in a state of republican egalitarianism. "Each individual is his own sovereign master, and acts from the dictates of his own mind; the authority of the Cheif being nothing more than mere admonition. . . . in fact every man is a chief." Here was an image of primitive democracy to warm Jefferson's heart.[52]

There was also a negative stereotype of Indians. Gass's journal expressed his (or his Pittsburgh editor's) expectation of traveling through "a country possessed by numerous, powerful and warlike nations of savages, of gigantic stature, fierce, treacherous and cruel; and particularly hostile to white men." These were the Indians whom Jefferson later addressed when he made a promise about U.S. policy toward them: "If ever we are constrained to lift the hatchet against any tribe, we will never lay it down till that tribe is exterminated, or driven beyond the Mississippi."[53]

Lewis and Clark found those Indians too. In a document compiled at Fort Mandan, Clark sweepingly classified whole nations as good or bad Indians, with no allowances for individuals. The Kansaw, Oto, Missouri, and Ponca were a "fierce pilfering Set." The Omaha and Arikara were "mild Sincere and well disposed toward the whites." The Teton were all "fierce deceitfull unprencipaled robers."[54]

A third stereotype that colored all of Jefferson's thinking, and that came to dominate Clark's as well, was that the Indians were a doomed race. This stereotype ultimately had its roots in the puzzle that Indians posed to the scientific theories of the day. What, Enlightenment savants wondered, could account for the variations in human society being revealed all around the globe? To some, the answer lay in racial characteristics. Carolus Linnaeus's *Systema Naturae* helpfully divided the human race into six subspecies: *Homo sapiens Europaeus, Homo sapiens Asiaticus, Homo sapiens Afer, Homo sapiens Americanus, Homo sapiens Ferus,* and *Homo sapiens Monstrous.* Those inclined to racial explanations could cite inequalities in the abilities and moral traits of these subspecies; some subspecies were just inherently inferior to others. But Jefferson rejected such ideas. Instead, he viewed Indians as part of the universal brotherhood of man, not as fundamentally different from Europeans. He accounted for cultural variations in two ways: first, the Indians were subject to the influence of environment; and second, the Indians were at an earlier stage in a universal process of social development.[55]

The latter explanation, the brainstorm of a group of Scottish theorists known as the Edinburgh school, was the embryo of a theory of social evolution. To Jefferson's circle, it seemed like an optimistic and humanitarian idea. Benjamin Smith Barton wrote: "History informs us, that civilization has been constantly preceded by barbarity and rudeness. . . . The inference from this discovery is . . . that the [Native] Americans are susceptible of improvement." Racial inferiority did not doom them to perpetual savagery; education could uplift them, as Jefferson said, into "that state of society, which to bodily comforts adds the improvement of the mind and morals." This solution became the cornerstone of Jefferson's Indian policy—"to civilize & instruct."[56] But the implication that every society follows the same path to maturity, and that Europeans had traveled farthest on that path, meant that "improvement" equated with becoming more European. In Jefferson's world, Indians had not chosen a different way of life; they were simply behind Europeans in their

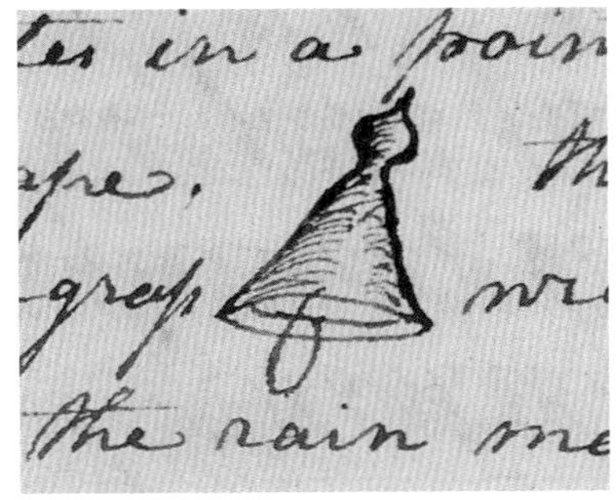

Sketch of a conic hat, 1806 and **Basketry whaler's hat, c. 1790–1830**
Lewis and Clark sketched, described, and collected the basketry hats of the Pacific coast. This could be one they brought back and donated to Peale's Museum. Clark wrote: "Maney of the nativs of the Columbia were hats & most commonly of a conic figure without a brim confined on the head by means of a String which passes under the chin and is attached to the two opposit Sides of a Secondary rim within the hat—the hat at top termonates in a pointed knob of a conic form. . . . these hats are made of the bark of Cedar and beargrass wrought with the fingers So closely that it Casts the rain most effectually. . . . on these hats they work . . . representations of the whales, the Canoes, and the harpooners Strikeing them." Although the captains were convinced that the Clatsop made the hats, modern scholars believe they were made on Vancouver Island or the Olympic Peninsula by the Makah or Nootka and were traded south. This was a whaler's hat, reserved for high-ranking people of lineages with hereditary rights to the whaling traditions. The humpback whales trail harpoon lines with inflated sealskin floats attached. Both the shape of the hat and the designs were symbolic.

social development and needed to be helped along.

Lewis and Clark showed the influence of this idea in their attitudes toward the Missouri Valley tribes. In the scheme of the Edinburgh school, a nomadic way of life was more primitive than agriculture because that was the sequence that Western civilization was believed to have followed. When the explorers discovered that nomadism was a more recently adopted lifestyle on the plains and that agriculture was older, this did not suggest to them that the theory might be wrong; instead, they explained the shift in lifestyle as a "degeneration" of Indian society. Some tribes had inexplicably backtracked on the road to becoming more European.[57]

The other corollary of the evolutionary scheme was, in the words of Adam Ferguson's *Essay on the History of Civil Society*, that "rude nations in general . . . always yield to the superior arts, and the discipline of more civilized nations." It was not just a matter of power relationships. When a primitive society came in contact with a more advanced one, the primitives degenerated from what Clark called "a proud and independent savage" into a state of dependency and cultural decay. Like disease, this was an unfortunate but inevitable consequence of exposure to Euro-Americans. In a process as implacable and morally neutral as celestial mechanics, civilization was destined to spread and savagery to succumb. Thus science removed the burden of responsibility from Euro-American shoulders and replaced it with a humanitarian obligation to ease suffering.[58]

The theory that Indian culture was doomed by its exposure to European

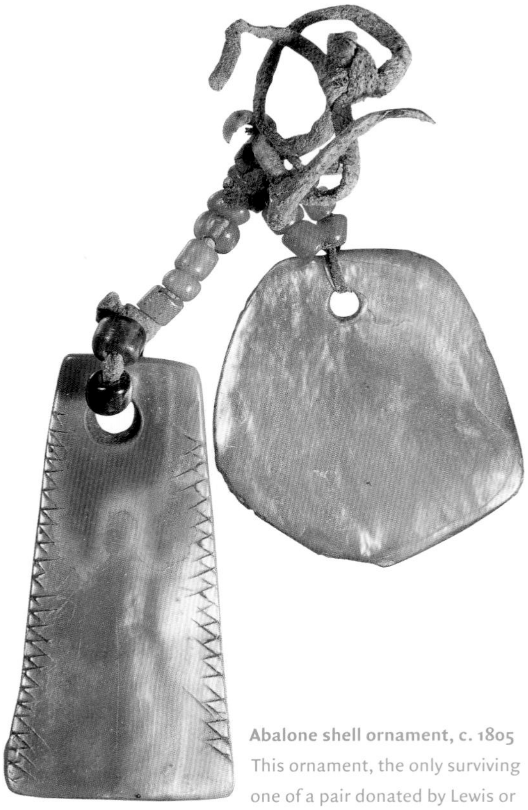

Abalone shell ornament, c. 1805
This ornament, the only surviving one of a pair donated by Lewis or Clark to the American Philosophical Society, may have come from the Shoshone, since that tribe gave the captains abalone jewelry as gifts. Ordway recorded, "The natives gave Capt. Lewis ear bobs to put in ears." Whitehouse added, "They have little things made of mussell shell which they hang in their ears with their beeds." When Clark arrived, Cameahwait welcomed him to a council and, Clark wrote, "imedeately tied to my hair Six Small pieces of Shells resembling *perl* which is highly Valued by those people and is prcured from the nations resideing near the *Sea Coast*." Later, he clarified, "The most Sacred of all the orniments of this nation is the Sea Shells of various Sizes and Shapes and colours, of the bassterd perl kind, which they inform us they get from the Indians to the South." The Indians to the south were probably the Snake River Shoshone, who got the shells from the Klamath or Nez Perce.

civilization had the aesthetic appeal of historical tragedy and gave Jefferson scope for compassionate eloquence. "The aboriginal inhabitants of these countries I have regarded with the commiseration their history inspires. . . . the stream of overflowing population from other regions directed itself on these shores; without power to divert, or habits to contend against, they have been overwhelmed by the current, or driven before it; . . . humanity enjoins us to teach them agriculture and the domestic arts; to encourage them to that industry which alone can enable them to maintain their place in existence."[59] Jefferson was not the only one whose imagination was empowered by the idea of the vanquished warrior bowing to inevitable conquest. In later years, Clark would use the imagery in his impassioned pleas for more federal assistance for the tribes whose dispossession he had overseen. "The tribes nearest our settlements were a formidable and terrible enemy," he wrote in 1826. "Since then, their power has been broken, their warlike spirit subdued, and themselves sunk into objects of pity and commiseration. While strong and hostile, it has been our obvious policy to weaken them; now that they are weak and harmless . . . justice and humanity require us to cherish and befriend them."[60] Of course, neither Jefferson's nor Clark's compassion extended to letting the Indians keep their lands or lifestyles. Theirs was entirely an argument for assimilating the tribes more speedily into Euro-American society.

Unsurprisingly, Lewis and Clark's observations supported the stereotypes underlying Jefferson's Indian policy. They diligently cataloged evidence of the Indians' doom: abandoned villages, starvation, poverty, war, disease, and other "calamities"—while rarely mentioning abundance, prosperity, peace, and health. Their assessments of the tribes grew more positive as their distance from Euro-American influence increased. The Sioux and Blackfeet, corrupted by British traders, were warlike and fierce. The Chinook, exposed to the otter trade, were thieving and treacherous. But the isolated Shoshone and Nez Perce were generous and admirable. The hospitable Mandan were an exception to the rule, but they had the excuse of being farmers.

The research that Lewis and Clark conducted during the journey had the aura of science but the subtext of policy. They set out to employ the same dispassionate methods in studying the people as they used in studying the animals and plants: observation, classification, and collection. They carried along a systematic list of "Inquiries relitive to the *Indians* of Louisiana," organized under ten headings from Medicine to Morals, Agriculture to Amusements. Followed closely, the list would have produced an ethnology comparable to the best of the day. But the captains made oddly little effort to answer most of the questions on their list. A letter from Jefferson's attorney general suggests that ethnology may have been little more than a public relations cover story: "If the enterprise appears to be, an attempt to advance them [the Indians], it will by many people, on that account, be justified, however calamitous the issue."[61]

On the subject of Indians, the major document produced during the expedition's first year was Clark's "Estimate of the Eastern Indians," in which he summarized knowledge about the Plains Indian tribes. This enormous chart was a heroic attempt to force a chaotic subject into the neat, systematic format of an Enlightenment graph. It classified fifty-three tribes according to nineteen categories, with fragmentary information on nineteen more tribes. The information was written into boxes under the proper headings. The "Estimate,"

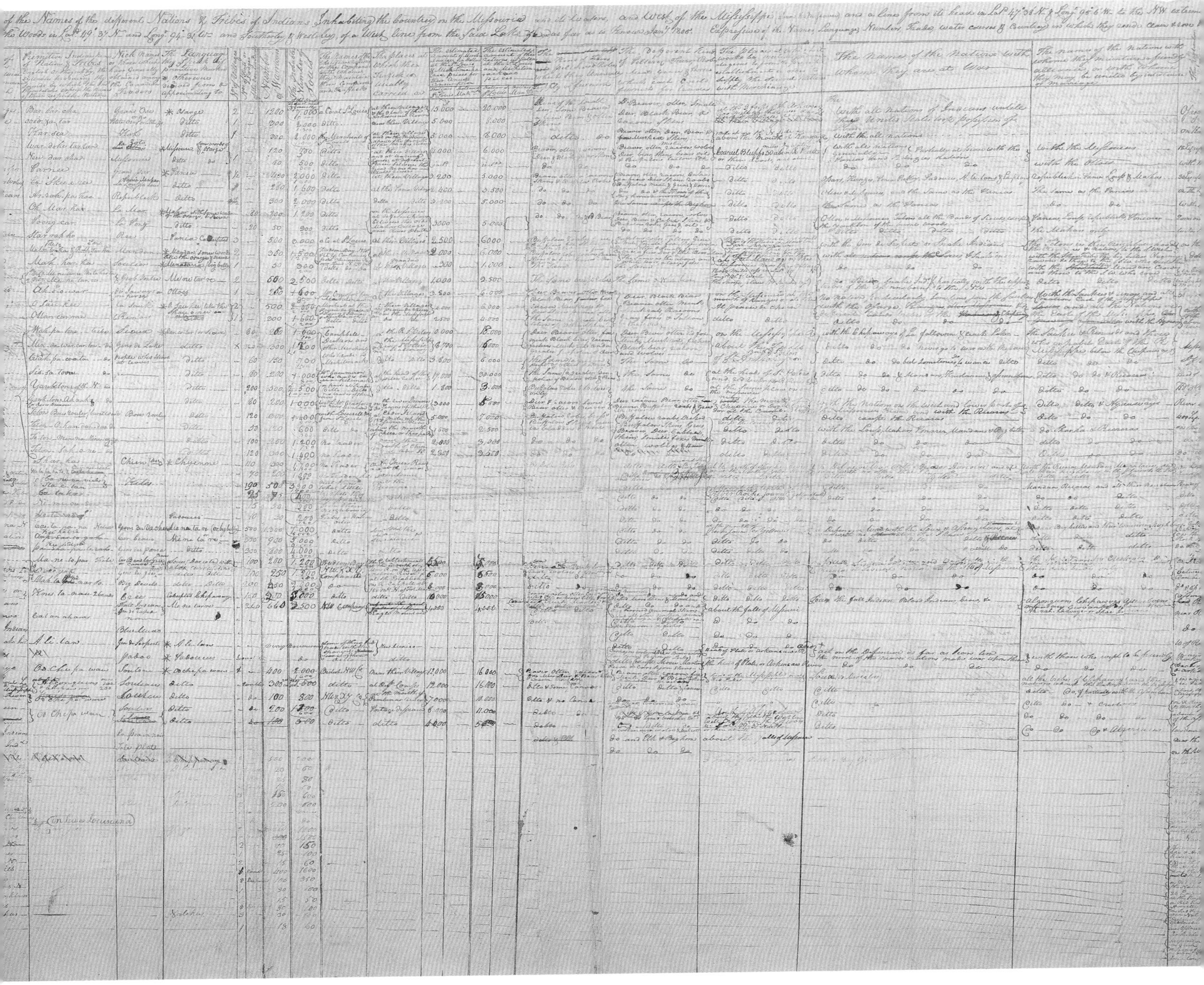

despite its scientific format, was a political document. It was a guide to future government policymakers who might need to know about the tribes' organization, their territorial claims, their alliances and enemies, and their potential power. Unlike the airy ethnological questions that Clark had been asked to study, this was hard-nosed "useful knowledge"—useful, that is, for the ultimate purpose of "extending & strengthening the authority of reason & justice."[62]

But the systematic nature of the "Estimate" was its very downfall. By tabulating the Indians' political organization into boxes and columns, Clark left the impression that the Native Americans, like the European nations, were divided into distinct, unchanging units with well-defined territories and numbers. The reality was much more fluid. The primary political unit was not the tribe at all but was the village or camp, and those were constantly blending, separating, and reforming. Tribal territories overlapped and shifted. Even a person's tribal identity could change during the course of his or her life. But Clark's need to

Estimate of the Eastern Indians, 1805
This massive document, formed from seven sheets pasted together, is divided into twenty-two columns and seventy-two rows. The columns show the tribe's name in English; the name they call themselves; nickname; language they speak; numbers; and information on their trade, political relations, and territory. This chart formed the basis of the "Statistical View of the Indian Nations Inhabiting the Territory of Louisiana," which was published in Jefferson's message to Congress in 1806. Clark sent this copy to his brother Jonathan via the keelboat in 1805. The other copy, sent to the secretary of war, contained at least nine more categories of information; it is now lost.

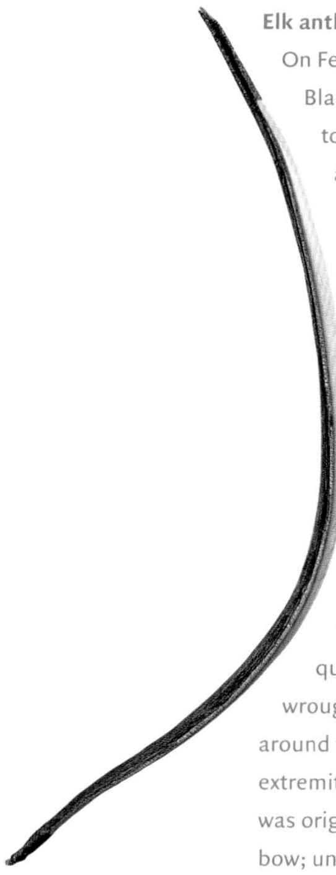

Elk antler bow, c. 1800–40
On February 8, 1805, the Mandan chief Black Cat gave Lewis a bow. Lewis sent it to Jefferson in the spring of 1805, listed as "A Mandan bow with a quiver of arrows." Although Lewis never said it was made of elk horn, this bow has been associated with the one sent to Jefferson. Lewis first described elk-horn bows among the Shoshone: "They sometimes make bows of the Elk's horn and those also of the bighorn. those of the Elk's horn are made of a single peice and covered on the back with glue and sinues like those made of wood, and are frequently ornamented with a stran wrought porcupine quills and sinues raped around them for some distance at both extremities." The dark-brown layer of sinew was originally on the outside curve of this bow; unstrung for over a century, the bow has bent backward.

impose taxonomy on the Indians ultimately had little to do with their reality. The "Estimate" demonstrated to eastern audiences that the United States had mastered the subject of Native Americans' political organization, and for that purpose, its columns and rows were crucial.

Just as Lewis and Clark collected botanical and zoological specimens, they also made an ethnographic collection. But it was nothing like the informed, systematic botany collection. They did not attempt to document Indian technologies or art. If they kept notes on where and when they acquired the artifacts, almost none of those notes survived. Instead, the collection consisted of three categories: gifts of state intended to form alliances between nations; gifts intended to demonstrate the selflessness and wealth of tribal leaders; and things purchased for their usefulness or novelty. So passive were the captains' collecting methods that recent scholars have argued the collection better represents the Indians' selections of appropriate things to give visitors than any choices made by Lewis and Clark. Pipes, clothing, feathers, and tobacco bags figured prominently among the diplomatic gifts that welcomed the expedition into the West. Women's dresses, robes, and moccasins served as ties between friends and family. Some things were souvenirs of the Corps' own experiences, such as a collection of Nez Perce food. But the captains' intentions in assembling this collection were ultimately overshadowed by the effect the artifacts had when the objects were brought to the East.[63]

Lewis and Clark did not try to keep the ethnographic artifacts together. A long list of the objects went to Jefferson, who incorporated them into the Indian Gallery he created in the front hall at Monticello, calling them "tokens of friendship."[64] Clark sent other items to his family. A woman's dress went as a gift to the First Lady, Dolley Madison. Clark apparently kept some materials himself, using them to form the nucleus of the Indian museum he would create in the St. Louis council room where he oversaw the deportation of Indians from

Pot fragments, c. 1805
Only remnants are left of the two Mandan pots given by Lewis or Clark to the American Philosophical Society. They are typical of documented Mandan pots except in having two ridges at the rim, whereas other examples have only one. They were made of pinkish, highly polished clay. The potter decorated the rims by pressing twisted cord into the soft clay and finished the body with a striated paddle. She gave them loop handles only large enough for suspending the pot by a cord. Lewis and Clark barely mentioned Mandan pots, but Alexander Henry, who visited Black Cat's village in 1806, wrote: "They use large earthen pots of their own manufacture of a black clay which is plentiful near their villages. They make them of different sizes, from five gallons to one quart. . . . One or more of the largest kind is constantly boiling prepared corn and beans, and all who come in are welcome to help themselves to as much as they can eat."

Gun case, early to mid-1800s

Clark himself was an avid collector of "Indian curiosities," and he founded the first museum west of the Mississippi River in his St. Louis council room. The visiting scholar Henry R. Schoolcraft wrote in 1821 that Clark evinced "a philosophical taste in the preservation of many subjects of natural history, together with specimens of Indian workmanship, and other objects of curiosity, collected upon the expedition." Whether this object was displayed in Clark's museum is unknown; however, it was passed down in the Clark family, and its beads date to the first half of the nineteenth century.

the Mississippi Valley. But the best-documented portion went to Peale's Museum, where the materials were incorporated into educational displays to teach Philadelphians about Lewis and Clark's encounter with the people of western North America.

In their museum cases, isolated from the cultures that produced them, the artifacts underwent a transformation in meaning. When Peale accessioned a cap, he identified it as "worn by the women of the Plains of Columbia," as if all women wore such a cap, had for all time, and always would. There was no suggestion that it might be one of many fashions, that it might be worn on some occasions but not others, or that it might be the favorite hat design of the woman who made it. The artifact became a type specimen representing all Columbia River hats. The artifacts from 1804–6 were just snapshots of Indian lives that became frozen into timeless archetypes, implying that the artifacts came from a timeless, archetypal culture.[65]

The artifacts were spectacular, novel, and beautiful for those early Philadelphians, as they are for us today. They allowed viewers to have an aesthetic response to exotic Indian cultures, without interference from questions of conflicting values or social justice. They converted a complex and often tragic human story into an afternoon of wonder and nostalgia for lost worlds at the museum. In the end, displays like Peale's would make the conquest of the tribes into a curiously artistic spectacle.

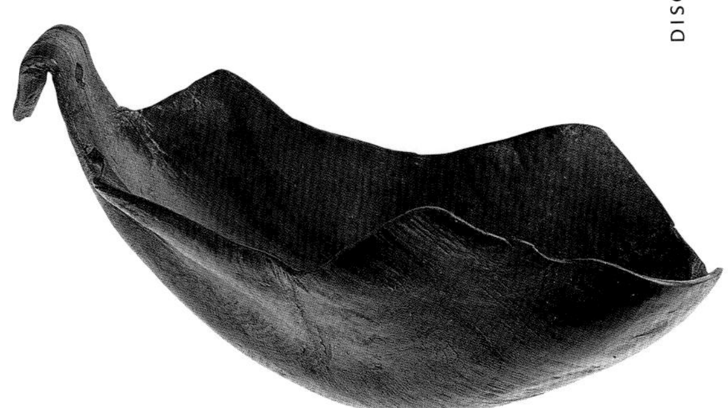

Sheep-horn spoon, early 1800s

This spoon was evidently collected by Clark and passed down in his family. The number or date "1826" is written in pencil inside it. During the expedition the explorers saw sheep-horn spoons among the Sioux and Shoshone and collected a number of the horns; however, only Joseph Fields is recorded as having sent back a spoon. Bodmer illustrated a sheep-horn spoon with a short handle like this one and noted that it was typical of Blackfeet and Mandan ladles.

MAKING SENSE OF WHITES

Discovery is a two-way street, and the Native Americans who met Lewis and Clark were also explorers of strange peoples and their ways. Passing through Indian country, the expedition was a traveling museum of Euro-American culture, and Native people gathered to peer in the windows of the forts just as Philadelphians would later gaze at Indian culture through the windows of Peale's cases.

Lewis and Clark knew they were subjects of investigation, and they recorded many instances when Indians used familiar techniques of learning. One ethnographic interview took place in November 1804 when the Mandan

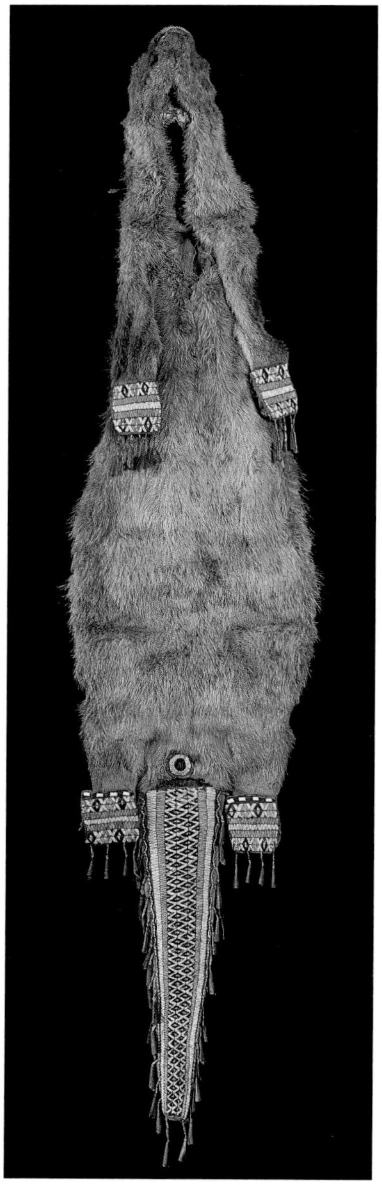

Tobacco pouch, c. 1805
A Peale's Museum label associated with this artifact reads: "Sioux Tobacco Pouch. Sent to Capts. Lewis and Clarke by the Sock nation. Presented by Capts. Lewis and Clarke." The Sioux and "Sock" (Sauk) were different tribes, but their territory overlapped in Iowa. This masterpiece, made from a whole otter skin including the skull, teeth, and claws, employs at least six quillwork techniques including multiple quill plaiting on the paws and tail. Although pouches of this style are often associated with Woodland tribes and the Midéwiwin Society, they were worn on the plains as tobacco containers without religious connotations. Catlin painted and collected a similar pouch belonging to the Mandan chief Four Bears and wrote of it, "His *Tobacco-sack* was made of the skin of an otter, and tastefully garnished with quills of the porcupine; in it was carried his *k'nick-k'neck* (the bark of the red willow, which is smoked as a substitute for tobacco), it contained also his flint and steel, and spunk for lighting."

Chief Black Cat paid a visit to see the soldiers' fort and, as Clark wrote, "made Great inquiries respecting our fashions." The Hidatsa leader Le Borgne employed observation, experimentation, and classification when confronted with the sight of York: "The Borgne was astonished—examined him closely—spit on his hand & rubbed to in order to rub off the paint. The negro pulled off the hand[kerchie]f from his head & shewed his hair—on which The Borgne was convinced that he was of a different species from the whites." Linnaeus had reached the same conclusion based on similar methods.[66]

But Indian observers did not necessarily believe that the truth ended with what they could observe and classify. Their society accepted means of acquiring knowledge that Euro-American science rejected: dreams, visions, intuitions, and analogy to myth, among others. Those were also used to explain the expedition's presence. And even when the Indians used methods like those of Enlightenment ethnographers, they did not reach similar conclusions. Like their European counterparts, Indians fitted new information into their existing preconceptions about the world. Those initial assumptions were vastly different from Lewis and Clark's.

All across North America, Indian tribes told similar stories about their first meeting with Europeans. Often, the first encounter was in a dream. Mary Underwood Lane, a Klickitat whose family heirlooms included two peace medals from Lewis and Clark, later told such a story this way: "A woman on the Columbia River had things revealed to her. She died and came back to life and told all she had seen. She said a people with white hair and skin and eyes were coming. She said they had different materials to work with, different clothing, different food that they would give the Indians. . . . They sang and danced all day and all night. They went crazy. They burned or threw in the river all their things. They destroyed everything because whites were coming to give them everything."[67]

Lewis and Clark actually met a prophet who had foreseen their coming among Yellept's band of Cayuse or Wallawalla. Clark wrote: "[This] Conspicious Charecter in the dance and Songs, we were told was a Medesene man & Could foretell things. that he had told of our Comeing into their Country and was now about to Consult his God the moon if what we Said was the truth."[68]

But dreams could not prepare people for the strangeness of the actual meeting. First-encounter stories told by Indians contrast with the same stories told by whites. Whereas Euro-American tales have an authoritative tone of pretended certainty, Indians' stories stress wonder and misunderstanding. Lizzie Lowery, a Nez Perce, said: "The people of my village ran away when they first saw the white men. They were afraid of their beards, for they had never seen people with hair on their faces. And they had never seen mules before. They thought the mules were some kind of overgrown rabbits." The men's appearance was what caused wonder in Elizabeth Wilson's version of the Nez Perce story. "They have pale faces and eyes like the eyes of a cooked fish. One of the men is black and looks like an evil spirit. . . . They were scared of the black man. 'What had burned him up?' they wondered."[69]

The Salish recounted how they at first thought the visitors were poor because they had no robes, only unseemly trousers. Chief Three Eagles generously gave the white men robes. As Edward Curtis recorded the story: "The

chief said: 'They do not have robes to sit on. Some Indians have stolen them. Bring them some robes.' Buffalo-skins were brought, but instead of sitting on them, the white men threw them about their shoulders." Sophie Moiese, another Salish, said: "When the dried meat was brought to the men, they just looked at it and put it back. It was really good to eat, but they seemed to think it was bark or wood. Also, they didn't know that camas roots are good to eat." There were misunderstandings on the Indian side as well. According to Pierre Pichette: "One of the strange men was black. He had painted himself in charcoal, my people thought. In those days . . . those who had been brave and fearless, the victorious ones in battle, painted themselves in charcoal. . . . So the black man, they thought, had been the bravest of this party." He said about the other men: "All the men had short hair. . . . It was the custom for mourners to cut their hair." Adding up the evidence—the men's poverty, their state of mourning, and York's battle paint—the Salish reached a conclusion: "They have had a narrow escape from their enemies. All their belongings were taken away."[70]

"They were unlike any people we had hitherto seen," a Shoshone named Faro later related, "fairer than ourselves, and clothed with *skins* unknown to us. . . . We thought them the children of the Great Spirit. . . . we soon discovered that they were in possession of the identical thunder and lightning [guns] that had proved in the hands of our foes so fatal to our happiness." But their power was coupled with innocence: "Our eagle-eyed chief discovered from the carelessness of the strangers with regard to their things, that they were unacquainted with theft, which induced him to caution his followers against pilfering any article whatever. His instructions were strictly obeyed." Another Shoshone at first thought their hats were strangely shaped heads: "The head rose high and round, the top flat; it jutted over the eyes in a thin rim; their skin was loose and flowing, and of various colours." He called them "men as pale as ashes."[71]

For most of the tribes, Lewis and Clark were far from the first white men seen, but they were mysterious in other ways. The size of their party; their arms

Effigy pipe bowl, 1820–50

This pipe illustrated a simple cultural difference that caused enormous misunderstanding. In Plains Indian society, staring at another person was considered rude, and keeping one's eyes averted showed respect. Whites had the opposite custom and interpreted Indian body language as evasive and shame-faced, a reaction Lewis and Clark often recorded. George Catlin, who collected a pipe bowl identical to this one in 1832, wrote that Indians resented this perception. The Pawnee sculptor told Catlin the pipe showed "he could sit and look the white man in the face without being ashamed." This became a widespread motif in Plains Indian pipe art, often collected by Euro-Americans who did not understand its connotation as a gesture of defiance.

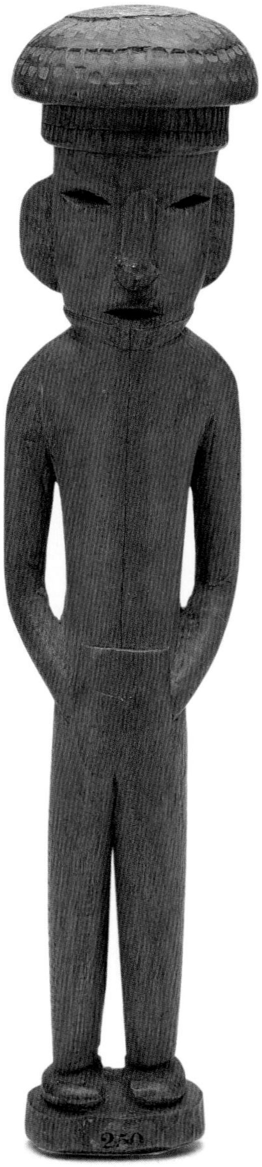

Carving of a sailor, pre-1841
The Chinookan tribes were as fascinated by Euro-American clothing styles as white ethnographers were with theirs, and the Indians collected materials just as avidly. However, their collections were worn rather than placed in museums. "I observed an Indian with round hat Jacket & wore his hair cued," Clark wrote on October 28, 1805, below The Dalles. By the time they got to the mouth of the Columbia, Clark wrote, "Maney men have Salors Clothes." Lewis noted, "They are very fond of the dress of the whites, which they wear in a similar manner when they can obtain them, except the shoe which I have never seen woarn by any of them." This figure, collected by S. B. Elliot when the Wilkes Expedition visited the Oregon coast in 1841, derives from a long tradition of carved sticks depicting supernatural visitors. Called *pat-ash*, sticks depicting guardian spirits were used in Chinookan winter dances and sometimes became so infused with spirit power as to move on their own. Whether this one was so used is not known.

and army discipline; their odd activities like celestial observations, botanical collecting, and language research; their talk of sovereignty; and above all, their novel technology such as the air gun, compass, and telescope—all set them apart. The journals are peppered with accounts of reactions that seemed unusual to the travelers and still seem so to us today. On the Columbia River, fearful villagers said the members of the Corps "came from the clouds &c. &c. and were not men." The Nez Perce attributed to them powers of healing. The Mandan sought them out to enact parts in ceremonies. A Cheyenne chief told Clark that "the white people were all *medecine*," and he was so suspicious of the dangerous powers of a medal that Clark presented to him that he refused to accept the token. A Hidatsa chief gave his medal away to his enemies to be rid of its evil influences.[72]

How are we to interpret these reactions? Traders like Pierre-Antoine Tabeau, who met Lewis and Clark on the Missouri River, interpreted Indian theories about Euro-Americans cynically. On first encounter, a nation "is always disposed in favor of the whites; it worships them, sometimes, up to the point of superstition and especially fears to displease them. A little familiarity destroys the illusion." But this was only a partial truth. The nature of the Indians' "worship" was not what Tabeau implied.[73]

The tribes who reacted with wonder to Lewis and Clark did not draw a sharp line between the natural and the supernatural; the two interpenetrated. In Indian thought, the origins of many things they relied on could be traced to the spirit world. The buffalo herds came to humans through the generosity of the buffalo spirits. The salmon migrated upriver each spring at the behest of the salmon spirit. The ability to hunt, succeed in war, or build an earth lodge came from one's connections in the spirit world. People regularly traveled to and from the spirit world in visions. Everything mysterious and powerful ultimately came from that other world, and there was no reason whites should be an exception to this natural law. So when Native people said explorers "came from the clouds," it was not an extraordinary explanation of their origin; it fit them into a category that many other people and things occupied. Spirit beings were a familiar concept for which there were explanations; imperialist explorers were not.[74]

Spirits were not gods in the European sense. They were beings with whom a person formed an alliance or reciprocal relationship to derive benefits in life. There were well-established forms of address for approaching and communicating with other-than-human beings. The Lakota called one such custom *Hanblecheyapi*, or crying for a vision. A person performed acts of fasting, humility, and lamentation to make a spirit being have pity and come to his or her aid. Other tribes had different customs. But all were experienced in dealing with spirits, and all adapted their customs to deal with the first whites they met.[75]

When an Indian told Clark that "all white flesh" was "medisan," it was not necessarily a compliment. We do not know what word Clark translated as "medicine," but it may have been a Siouan word like *Wakan*. One Lakota speaker defined this word as meaning "anything that was hard to understand." James R. Walker, a doctor and ethnographer who lived on Pine Ridge Reservation and spoke Lakota, added: "Long ago, the Lakotas believed that there were marvelous beings whose existence, powers or doings they could not understand. These beings they called *Wakan Kin* (The *Wakan*). There were many

Basketry sailor's cap, c. 1790–1840
Just as fashions today incorporate designs from Indian art, so Northwest Coast tribes interpreted European clothing in traditional materials and techniques. This Tlingit hat woven from plant fibers mimics the style of a sailor's cap, down to the design of a hat band and buckle woven into the rim. The Tlingit adopted a similar sailor's cap style for their social dancing regalia. This cap is from the Boston Museum collection that included the Lewis and Clark material. Lewis and Clark commented on woven hats in European styles, which they said formed "a small article of traffic with the Clatsops and Chinnooks who dispose of them to the whites." They proved this assertion by buying some. Tlingit basketry was widely traded, and they could easily have seen hats like this.

of the *Wakan*, some good and some bad. . . . Things other than the *Wakan* are called *wakan* by the Lakotas because they amaze as the *Wakan* do. . . . *Wasica wakan* (white citizen of the United States) is called *wakan* because he is able to do marvelous things as the *Wakan* would do them." Note the difference in capitalization.[76]

Another familiar category to Native people was the man-animal. Plains Indian oral literature was full of powerful beings who transformed from human to animal form and back again. This appears to have been the category York fit into. On the Missouri, tribe after tribe found York's black skin and curly hair unaccountable until York, perhaps tired of incessant questions, seems to have hit on an explanation that those around him accepted as logical. "York made Inds. believe that he had been wild like bear & tamed," Clark told Nicholas Biddle. Eventually, upper Missouri tribes would invent a term for African Americans that translated, literally, as "black white man."[77]

Metaphor and myth also provided a context for explaining Lewis and Clark's journey. Tabeau, the trader among the Arikara, recorded: "Kakawita, one of the most intelligent of the Ricaras, told me in all seriousness, after the visit of the Captains . . . (and it is an opinion generally accepted) that these gentlemen, while journeying among many nations, met obstacles perhaps invincible. . . . one obstacle is [a being] without a mouth and is nourished only by breathing the smoke of the meat through the nose. It gains greatly in weight in the springtime and the autumn by its victories over the swans and bustards that obstinately make war upon it in these two seasons. The other is a troop of Amazons who kill all their male children, pulverize their genitals, and conceive again by the injection of the powder obtained."[78]

The stories told in later years were different, but they were no less revealing of the way that everything was reversed in the Indian mirror. In these tales, heroic Indians made journeys in which Lewis and Clark appeared as minor

Effigy pipe, pre-1840
The Haida artist who carved this argillite pipe satirically portrayed a distressed European sailor tangled in the elaborate rigging of his boat, confounded by his own technology. The pipe belonged to Catlin's touring collection of Indian artifacts and was once thought to have been given to him by Clark; if so, Clark acquired it long after the expedition.

characters. The Mandan remembered Shehek-Shote's generosity to strangers and his transformative journey to Washington, D.C.: "On[e] day a white man came up the river with a boat in which were thirty others, part of whom rowed and part of whom pulled the boat by a rope. They were very tired, and those pulling the boat had sore shoulders. No one welcomed them, and so She-he-ke invited them to his tepee, gave them food and cured their sores. When they were all rested they decided to go no further, and the white man asked She-he-ke to go to Washington with him. He consented and took his wife and young son, then about two years old. . . . They stayed away for several years. . . . She-he-ke had been away so long that his son could speak good English. He brought many presents with him from Washington, a medal dated 1797 among the others. . . . His tepee was built four-sided, like the white men's houses, and he had a big American flag flying above it."[79]

The Nez Perce remembered the heroism of Watkuweis: "The girl had been captured and taken away to some place in the east—somewhere on an island. Her baby was born there, a little boy. When he was six or seven months old, able to sit up and crawl around, she decided to come home to her people. She only knew that she should follow the sun. . . . For a long, long time she walked. She used elderberries for food. Old Grizzly Bear went with her and protected her part of the way. . . . When danger came near, Chipmunk made a fog so that nothing could see her. Some white people helped her, too. Somewhere along the way, her baby died and she buried him. She kept on following the sun, and so she came back home to her people. . . . She was in one of our villages when Lewis and Clark came from across the Rising Sun Mountains. She heard the men talking about killing the white men, and she begged them not to because white men had helped her."[80]

These stories so completely reverse the focus that historians have sometimes had trouble recognizing them as evidence of Lewis and Clark's true impact.

But the most revealing testimony was from the Sioux. This tribe set down its history in a pictorial form that supplemented the oral record. Painted on buffalo robes, their chronologies were called "winter counts," or *wan'iyetu wo'wapi.* For each year, the chronicler selected the most memorable event and portrayed it in a symbol. One famous winter count, painted by a Dakota named Lone Dog, started in the year 1800. On it, the years were arranged in a spiral, a shape both linear and cyclical. The types of events portrayed were both unique and recurring: outbreaks of disease, men killed in war, horses stolen, floods and meteors, traders building posts and leaving. The sense of history one gets from reading it is of individuals playing unique parts in a pattern as constant and varying as the weather. The chroniclers chose events that reinforced the pattern, not those that violated it. It was an idealized version of the past used as a guide to future behavior.[81] And where do Lewis and Clark fit in these events? To most Euro-American historians, the meeting with the Corps was the most significant event in Sioux history for 1804, presaging great changes in their story. Not so to the Sioux. The icon for 1804 was a calumet pipe symbolizing the war dance the tribe held before launching an expedition against their enemies, probably the Crow. The symbol for 1806, when the Corps came back downriver, was an Arikara killed.

Euro-American histories often make it seem as if the doings of whites were central to the lives of everyone they touched. Tribal memories tell us otherwise. The Mandan remembered Shehek-Shote; the Nez Perce remembered Watkuweis; the Sioux remembered their conflicts with the Crow and Arikara. Just as Indian preoccupations seemed trivial to Euro-Americans, so the visit of a band of soldiers seemed trivial to the Indians. History depended on who was looking in the mirror.

Woven hat, early 1800s
In later years, many Nez Perce remembered Lewis and Clark through family stories attached to artifacts. This was one such mnemonic object. It belonged to Washkin, born around 1800, who as a child was taken to see Lewis and Clark when they were camped on the Clearwater River. She said she wore the cap on that occasion. Whether it is so old is impossible to say; its true importance is in the way it connected Washkin's family to a historic event that might otherwise have faded from memory. Lewis and Clark unquestionably saw caps like it, and they donated two to Peale's Museum.

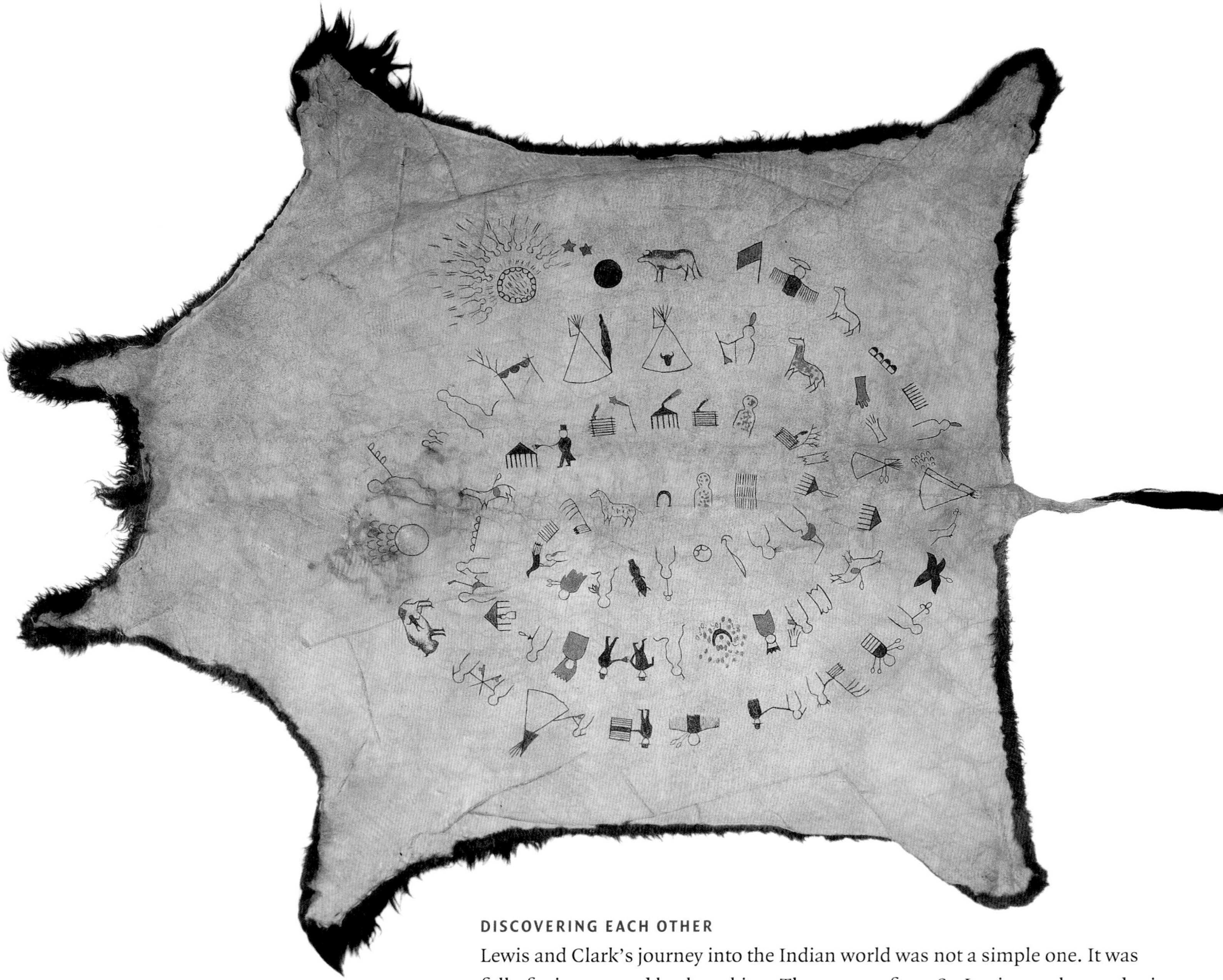

DISCOVERING EACH OTHER

Lewis and Clark's journey into the Indian world was not a simple one. It was full of missteps and backtracking. They set out from St. Louis as rulers and scientists. In their minds, the one role gave them political sovereignty, and the other gave them intellectual superiority. But the next three years of immersion in an Indian world softened the edges of their arrogance.

Their preconceptions became an effort to maintain as they were increasingly surrounded by living evidence of the tribes' military power and social vitality. First, the Sioux administered shock therapy to their assumptions of power. Then the Mandan gently earned their way past the distrustful barriers of the expedition's fort walls. In desperate need and befriended by the Shoshone and Nez Perce, the explorers yielded tentatively to gratitude, learning, and respect. Friendship began to supplant stereotype, and areas of cultural overlap began to appear—so much so that, on the Pacific Coast, Lewis had to reinforce the barriers again, feeling that the "uninterrupted friendly intercou[r]se" had gone too far and had become a threat to their discipline as white men. On the way back, facing renewed friendship and hospitality from the Wallawalla and the Nez Perce, the expedition members felt the acute strain of maintaining suspicion and separation. The mounting contradictions finally resolved themselves in an explosion of violence.

In a way, Lewis and Clark were destined to discover the wrong thing. Sent out to find the Northwest Passage, they instead found the Rocky Mountains. Sent out to study savages both noble and merciless, they instead found a continent full of individuals with their own lives and objectives—some of them irritable and rude, some generous and helpful. Daily interactions undermined the objectivity of science and the authority of empire and revealed the Indians as people with personalities and a past. The Corps' mission of dominion was almost subverted by friendship.

But not quite. With his parting rifle blast to the Blackfeet, Lewis reestablished the order of power. And with their reports and collections of artifacts, the explorers transformed the Indians back into subjects of rule and objects of study. Now, we must remove the distorted mirror they held up to Indian society in order to rediscover all those things it prevents us from seeing.

Lone Dog's winter count, c. 1870
Lewis and Clark did not appear at all in this record of history from the Sioux point of view. The Yanktonai artist, Lone Dog (Shunka-ishnala), was only a child when this chronicle starts, so he must have inherited the symbols from a previous keeper. Since winter counts from other chroniclers duplicated the symbols he used, it was likely a tribal rather than a personal record. On this robe, time starts at the center and grows outward in a spiral. The first symbol, for 1800, shows thirty Dakota killed by the Crow. The next shows that many died of smallpox in 1801. In 1802 a man stole horses with shoes on, and the next year they stole horses with curly hair from the Crow. In 1804 the tribe held a calumet dance before going to war, and in 1805 the Crows killed eight Dakotas. The last symbol here is for 1870, but the Sioux kept making winter counts. For 1876 they did not show the Sioux victory against Custer; instead, the tribal chroniclers chose to depict a seizure of ponies in the same year. They knew about Custer; they just didn't judge the battle appropriate to include.

Clarks River
Buffaloe
Open plains
Smokey hill fork
White River
River La Plat
Arkansaw River
the grass of the bottom is similar to our salt meadow grass from the great quantity of salt

TEN Filling up the Canvas

> We shall delineate with correctness the great arteries of this great country; those who come after us will . . . fill up the canvas we begin.
>
> —THOMAS JEFFERSON[1]

In folktales, the heroes return home to live happily ever after. In history, endings are not always so satisfying.

A grateful country rewarded Lewis and Clark by giving them more responsibilities. Thomas Jefferson appointed Lewis governor of the newly established Louisiana Territory, whose capital was St. Louis. Clark became brigadier general of the territory's militia and superintendent of its Indian affairs.

The appointment of Lewis to a political post was a colossal blunder. He was an introvert accustomed to commanding others rather than beguiling them, and he was unsuited to the deal-making of political life in a town where an entrenched mercantile oligarchy clashed with turbulent new populist factions. St. Louis had always been a colonial community in which fortunes were tied to government contracts and privileges. In this milieu, Lewis was not scrupulous about separating his personal enterprises from the government funds he controlled. Soon, accusations of collusion and conflict of interest were flying through the heated, cliquish atmosphere. In 1809 the rumors apparently reached Washington, D. C., where Jefferson was no longer president. Lewis was called to account for his expenses. Already deeply depressed, alcoholic, and addicted to laudanum, Lewis set out for the capital via the Natchez Trace.

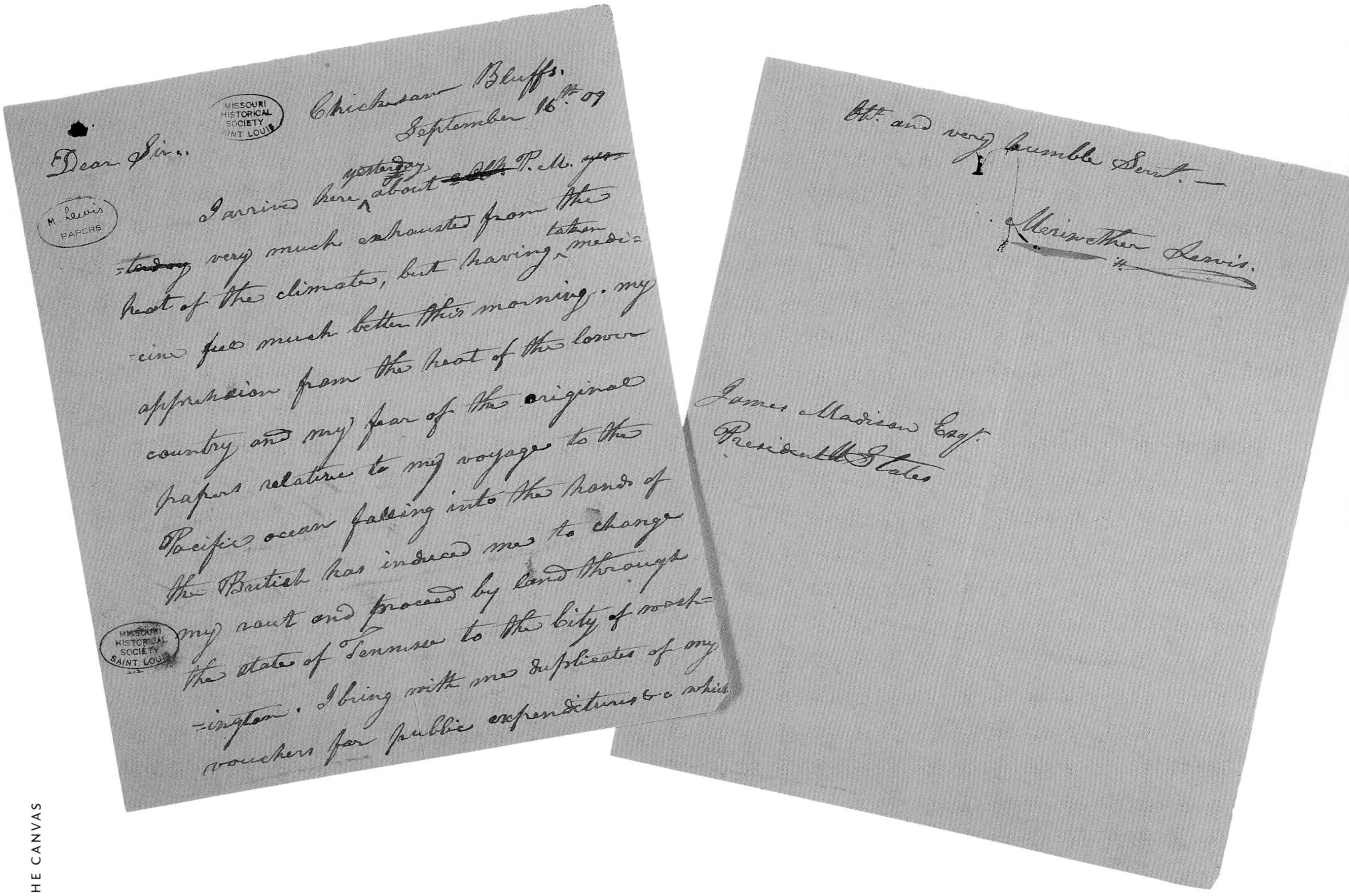
Chickasaw Bluffs, September 16th 09

Dear Sir,

I arrived here yesterday about P.M. very much exhausted from the heat of the climate, but having taken medicine feel much better this morning. my apprehension from the heat of the lower country and my fear of the original papers relative to my voyage to the Pacific ocean falling into the hands of the British has induced me to change my rout and proceed by land through the state of Tennessee to the City of washington. I bring with me duplicates of my vouchers for public expenditures &c which

Obt. and very humble Servt. —

Meriwether Lewis.

James Madison Esqr.
President U States

Letter from Lewis to James Madison, 1809
The chaotic phrasing and shaky penmanship of this letter, written nineteen days before Lewis's death, may indicate his state of mind. He had already twice tried to kill himself when he wrote this and was being detained under a suicide watch at Fort Pickering. The commandant had denied him alcohol but not laudanum, which was probably the "medicine" he mentioned here. The letter informed Madison that Lewis had decided to travel east by way of the Natchez Trace, due to his fear that a nonexistent war with Britain would endanger "the original papers relative to my voyage to the Pacific ocean."

Alone and delusional at an isolated inn in Tennessee, he ended his own life only three years after being hailed as a hero on his return from the expedition.

Those who knew Lewis best never questioned that he had committed suicide. When Clark first heard the rumors he wrote: "I fear this report has too much truth. . . . I fear O! I fear the waight of his mind has over come him, what will be the Consequence?" Jefferson, given the melancholy duty of writing a eulogy for the protégé who should have written his, frankly stated, "He did the deed which plunged his friends into affliction." In later years, assorted conspiracy theorists tried to prove that his death was a murder. They failed to convince most historians.[2]

Clark, on the other hand, proceeded on to a career that was ultimately of far more consequence to American history than was his short stint as an explorer in 1804–6. To the extent that Jefferson's Indian policy was enacted in the Midwest, it was due to Clark's actions. The four cornerstones of the policy to which Clark devoted his life were tight federal control of the Indian trade, treaties to obtain more land, removal of all tribes east of the Mississippi onto the Great Plains, and forced assimilation of Indians into Euro-American culture.[3]

In the years immediately after the expedition, Clark focused his efforts on establishing a chain of federally run trading posts, or "factories," to keep commerce with the Indians under government control. This program, started under George Washington, was an attempt to use trade for purposes of social policy, under the rationale that a free market was exploitive and detrimental to Indian welfare. The policy aroused howls of protest from entrepreneurs chafing to make fortunes on the frontier and was soon abandoned.

Page 316: *A Map of Part of the Continent of North America* (detail), 1807–14. See page 324.

***Meriwether Lewis*, 1807**
Shortly after the return of the Corps of Discovery, Charles Willson Peale incorporated Lewis and Clark into his portrait gallery of the great men of the early republic. The moral message of his gallery was based on a republican idea of fame: these were men who had served the nation and had thus become exemplars to be emulated.

Silhouette of Meriwether Lewis, 1803
Thomas Jefferson, who survived Lewis by seventeen years, is believed to have owned this silhouette. In 1813 Jefferson wrote an account of the "melancholy close of the life of one whom posterity will declare not to have lived in vain."

Clark was more successful at implementing the next two cornerstones: treaties and removal. Over his long career he negotiated a series of treaties with the Indians of the Mississippi Valley, resulting in the cession of most of Missouri and Iowa and portions of Nebraska, Kansas, Arkansas, Illinois, and Wisconsin. As the inevitable consequence of these treaties, he oversaw what amounted to ethnic cleansing—the deportation of thousands of Indian families from their homes in the woodlands and prairies of the Midwest onto the plains. These policies too had a humane rationale. Depriving the Indians of their land and resettling them in the relative isolation of the West were seen as the best ways of protecting them from the hostility of settlers and the exploitations of the unscrupulous, until such time as they might become farmers and blend seamlessly into American society.

But the tribes were never asked whether they wanted such a future—and in the end, they were never really given the chance to become farmers. The lands they were settled on were often ill-suited for agriculture. The schools, blacksmith shops, mills, farmhouses, stock, and seed promised in the treaties were inadequate and slow in coming. In 1826 Clark looked back on his career as a loyal civil servant and penned a damning indictment of his own government. "The condition of many tribes west of the Mississippi is the most pitiable that can be imagined. During several seasons in every year they are distressed by famine, in which many die for want of food, and during which the living child is often buried with the dead mother because no one can spare it as much food as would sustain it. . . . It is vain to talk to people in this condition about learning and religion; they want a regular supply of food."[4] Clark's own complicity in the betrayal of the Indians must have been bitter for him to accept.

Clark became governor of Missouri Territory at the height of the War of 1812 and served for seven years. As governor during the controversy over Missouri's statehood, he advocated the fateful extension of slavery past the Mississippi River, an issue that aroused divisions deep enough to fracture the Union. (His old friend Jefferson, prophetic to the end, wrote that the Missouri controversy, "like a firebell in the night, awakened and filled me with terror.") When Clark died in 1838, his funeral procession was a mile long. The inscription on his tombstone reads: "Behold, the Lord thy God hath set the land before thee: go up and possess it."[5]

The men of the Corps scattered, most returning to the obscurity from which they had come. Several entered the fur trade; others made use of the land warrants given them as a reward for service in the expedition and became farmers. York, after fighting for his freedom for years, finally prevailed over his reluctant master and started a carting business, only to die of disease soon after. Sacagawea's son Pomp, after being raised and educated by Clark, went to Germany in company with Prince Paul of Württemberg. He spent several years there as the prince's professional Indian, then returned to become a guide and interpreter like his father. When Clark drew up a roster of the men in 1828, sixteen of the thirty-three had died, five of them violently. Most of the rest lived in Kentucky, Ohio, Illinois, and Missouri.[6]

The West the men had journeyed through would change with a blinding speed that one no one foresaw in 1803. The captains' assessment of the land had been shaped by Jefferson's dazzling vision of a "vast & fertile country which their sons are destined to fill with arts, with science, with freedom & happiness." But Jefferson's West was not the one that came to be. One year after the Corps' return, Robert Fulton launched the first steam-driven vehicle in America, an event that would have a greater impact on the West than any exploring expedition. Steam power would ultimately make the rivers irrelevant, would help transform the western economy from agrarian to extractive, and would carry an urban frontier forward with undreamed-of speed.[7] The social and natural worlds that Lewis and Clark passed through would be transformed beyond recognition by the end of the century, though the Indian people would remain, defying their predicted doom.

Whereas the explorers thought they were creating a useful guide for those who would come after, instead they created a record of a West that vanished before most Euro-Americans ever encountered it. For years, historians have been fond of claiming that Lewis and Clark "opened the West" or "blazed the trail" for subsequent pioneers. The historian James Ronda, however, has dismissed these claims as "empty praise," writing that "such clichés do the explorers no favors." More recently, a flood of publications praised the sci-

***William Clark*, c. 1808**
Charles Willson Peale painted Clark later than he painted Lewis, but the exact date is unknown. The original publisher of the expedition narrative intended to engrave the pair of portraits for publication in the book. Like many other plans related to the book, this one was never carried out.

entific discoveries of the Corps. James Logan Allen holds a different view, characterizing the expedition damningly as "quite simply . . . an Enlightenment venture which failed to enlighten." Another image of the Corps, as a cross-cultural community that traveled in peace through Indian lands, sprang up in the 1990s, showing remarkable durability in popular culture. Though there is truth to the image, it obscures the fact that the Lewis and Clark expedition resulted in more deaths among the people they were sent to discover than any other U.S. exploring expedition.[8]

So what was the significance of the Lewis and Clark expedition? According to the historian William Goetzmann, the Corps provided a new story for the nation to tell. "They succeeded in making the West itself an object of desire."[9]

Native American societies recognize that storytelling is a powerful act of creation. Among the Hidatsa, stories can be told only at certain times of year, and the listeners have to demonstrate their respect for the seriousness of the act by giving gifts and paying close attention. The Indian historian Robert A. Williams wrote: "For Indians, a storyteller is one who fulfills a most important and vital role in the group. . . . Stories have a capacity to produce material effects." Lewis and Clark's was such a story.[10]

In the years after the return of the Corps of Discovery, everyone agreed that the expedition had been important. Even Jefferson's foes praised it. But at

Camp chest, c. 1789
Clark no longer held a state office in 1825 when the Marquis de Lafayette visited St. Louis on his return tour of America, but as a senior statesman of Missouri, he hosted the visiting celebrity. Lafayette's secretary noted that Clark "presented General Lafayette with a garment bearing a striking resemblance to a Russian riding coat. It is made of buffaloe skin." In return, Lafayette gave Clark this chest full of luxurious camping equipment. It contains items for dining, writing, grooming, and medicine. Not to be outdone, Clark sent Lafayette a live grizzly bear cub, which the Marquis wrote "was the first animal of the kind, living or dead, that had ever made its appearance in Europe." Fortunately dissuaded from keeping it as a pet, Lafayette gave the bear to the Jardin des Plantes, where it developed a "large size and ferocious temper."

A Map of Part of the Continent of North America, 1807–14
This was Clark's master work, the summary of his geographic knowledge of the West. This huge hand-drawn map, measuring over four feet wide, was said to have hung in his office in St. Louis, where he updated it with new information brought in by travelers. It incorporates John Colter's discoveries on the upper Yellowstone and the route Wilson P. Hunt and the Astorians followed to the Columbia in 1811–12.

the same time they groped, as we do, to express why. Ultimately, it was an advertising copywriter who put his finger on it best, in the 1810 prospectus for the history of the expedition. It was the journey that counted, not the results. The Americanness of the expedition was its selling point—"this enterprize, planned by our own government, and achieved through great dangers by our own countrymen." Lewis and Clark had proved that this little country, so new on the world stage, could pull off a project that only Old World powers had attempted previously—and they did so with a New World pluck and ingenuity. To the advertiser, the expedition's appeal was not in its history but in what the

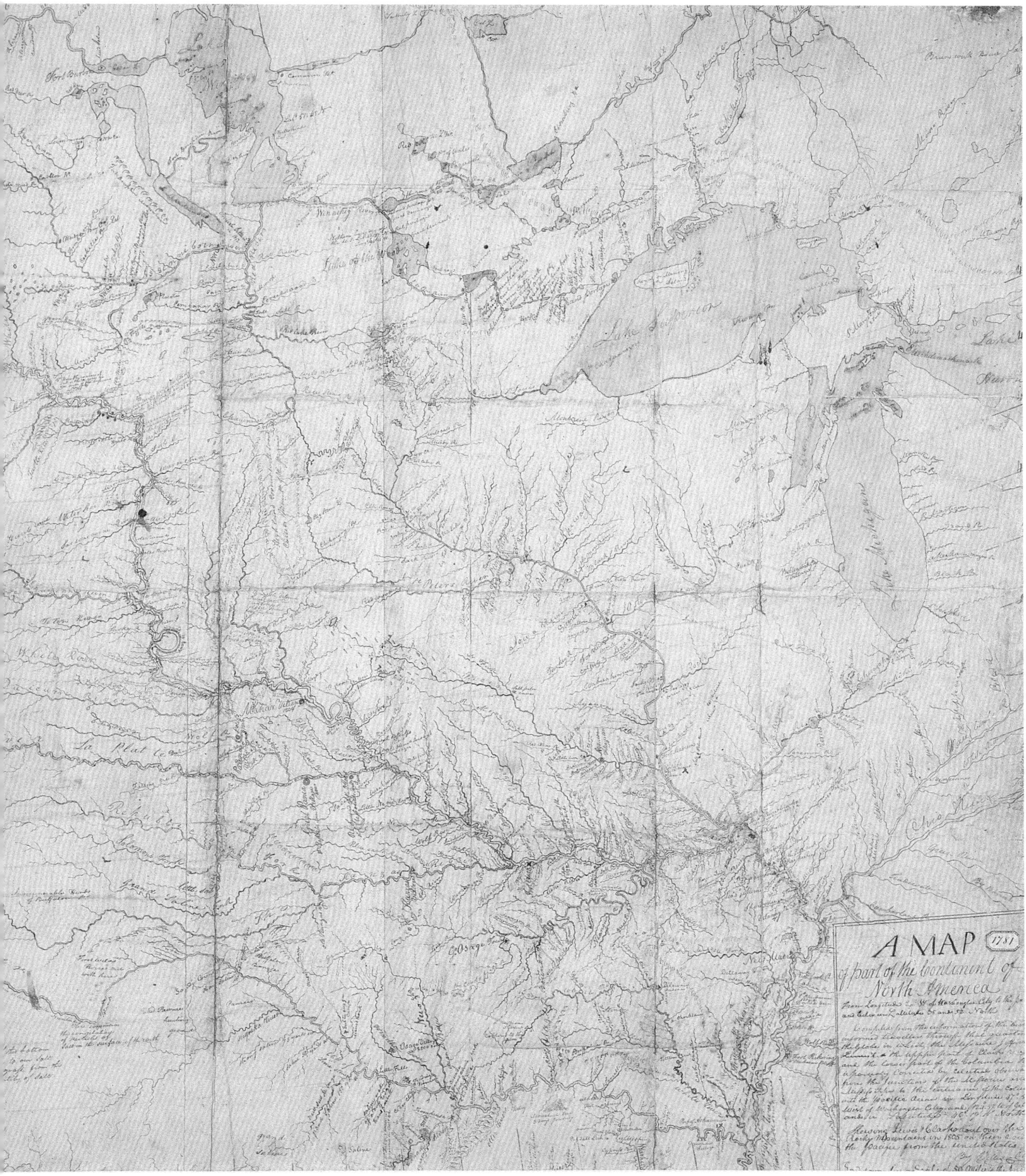

story implied about the future: “Vast regions are now opened, to reward the spirit of commercial adventure, and to receive, hereafter, the overflowing tide of our own population.”[11]

Before the Louisiana Purchase, the perilously disunited United States had lacked the shared history, culture, and institutions that knit a nation together. Without a firm sense of national identity, the United States had looked hesitantly on the risks of westward expansion. By 1814, that was changing. A new national narrative was taking shape, and the West was not the problem but the solution. It was unlike any national identity known to Europe. It was rooted not

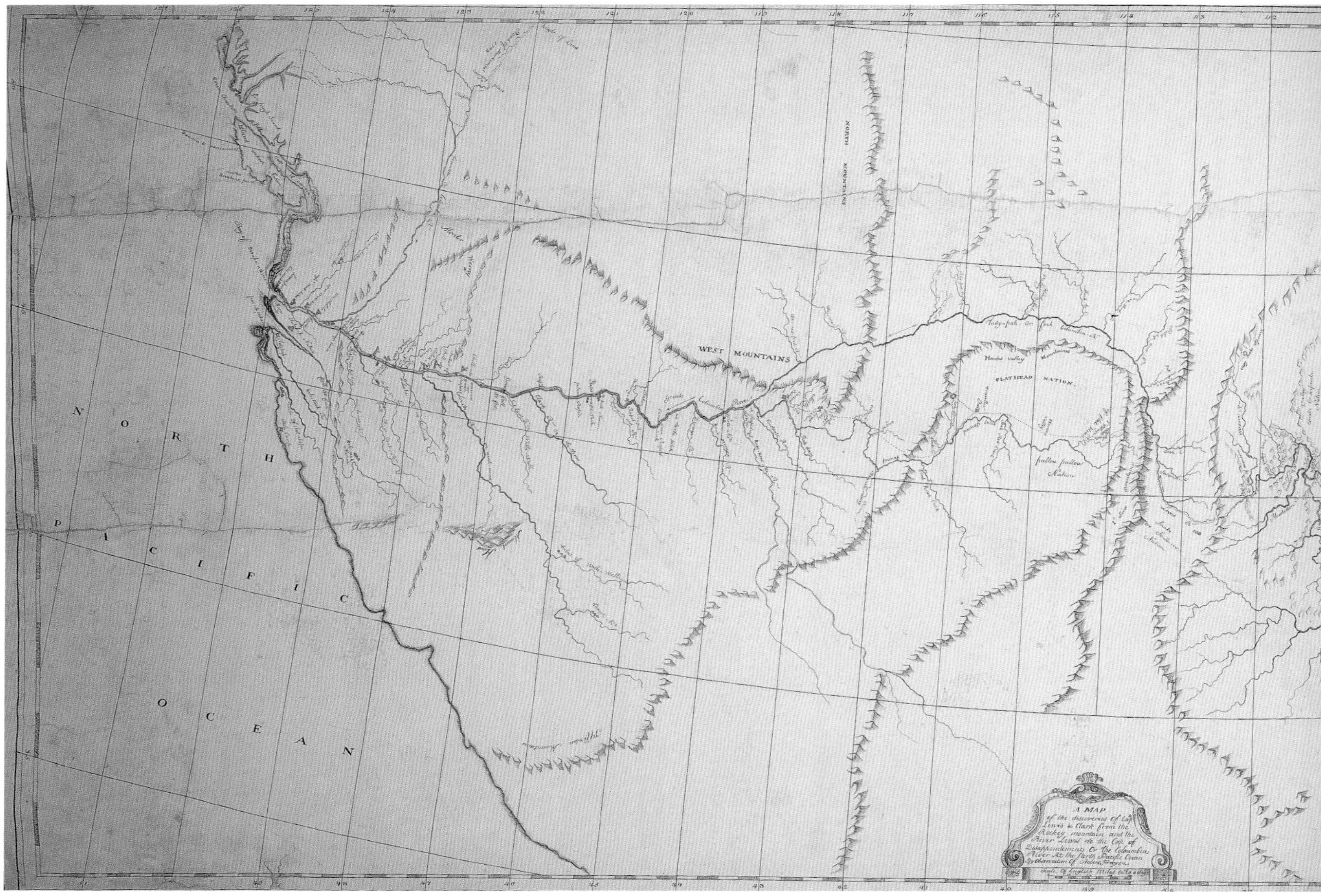

in the past but in the future. America's self-definition was about a destiny, a destination, an identity to be. It was about a people who shared not what they had been but what they were going to become.

Lewis and Clark's journey became an emblem of the national journey: a story about leaving behind the past and setting out in search of new lands and ways of life. In countless retellings, the tale resonated with transformation, regeneration, possibilities, and promise. It is no wonder that Lewis and Clark's story became so firmly knit into the emerging national image: it had, in fact, helped create that image.

In the years after the expedition, unity based on destiny showed its dark side as well: those who did not share the same aspirations were swept aside. The ancient residents of the land belonged to the past, as Euro-Americans saw it, and not to the future. Along with other dissenters, they were classified as obstacles to the historical project of the country, and their perspectives were excluded.

But that can still change. America, like explorers on the divide, is most itself when it is on the verge of becoming something new.

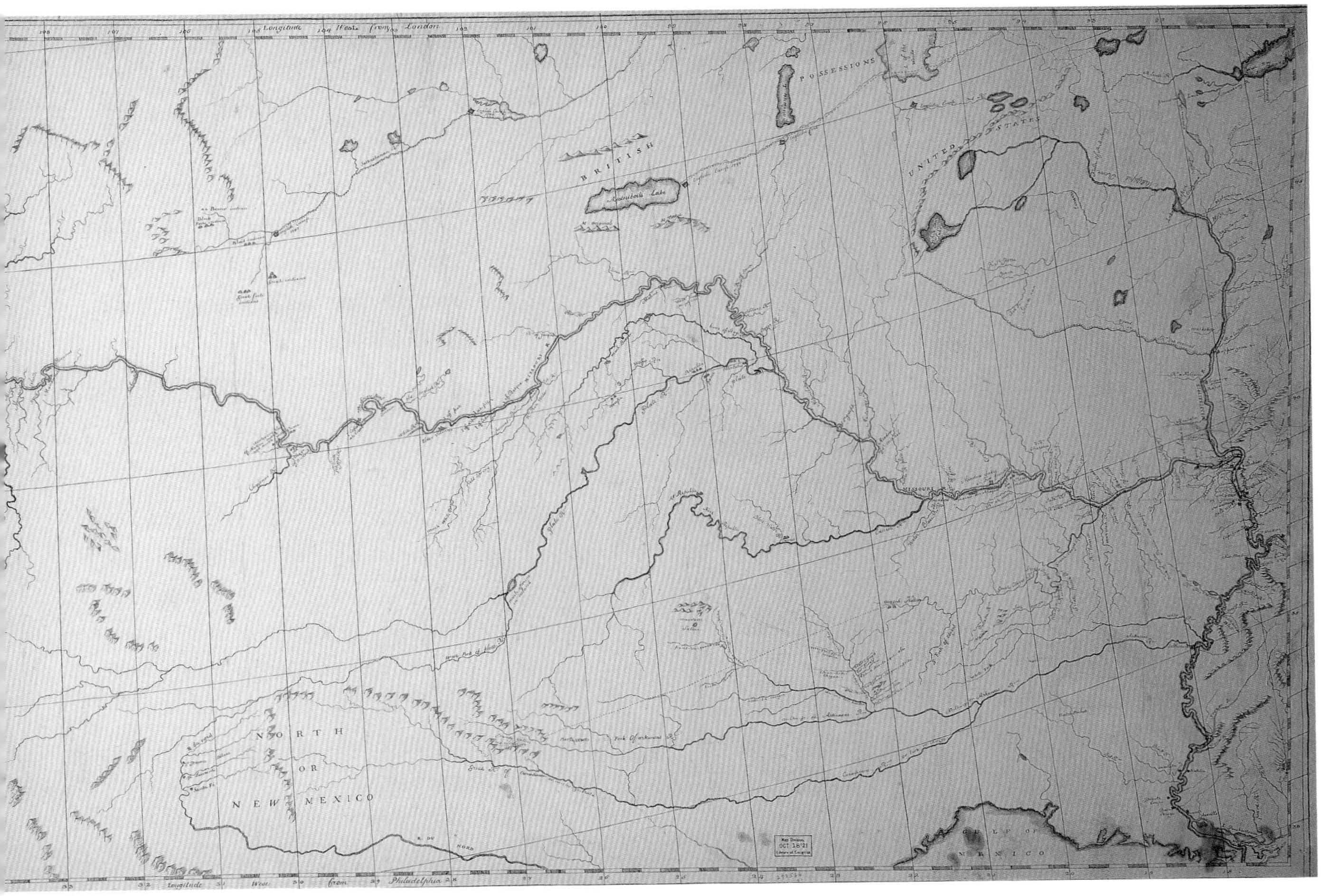

Robert Frazer, ***Map of the Discoveries of Capt. Lewis & Clark*****, c. 1807**

Several of the men tried to profit from their celebrity, but only Patrick Gass succeeded. Frazer was the only member of the expedition to get Lewis's permission to publish his journals. Lewis later regretted his generosity, and he published a notice of warning to book buyers: "Robert Frazier, who was only a private on this expedition, is entirely unacquainted with celestial observations, mineralogy, botany, or zoology, and therefore cannot possibly give any accurate information on those subjects, nor on that of geography." This map bears out his statement. Its fantastically distorted version of western North America was, fortunately, never published. What happened to the Frazer journals is not known. Only this map and a hand-written prospectus for the book survive.

Contemporary Voices

We were happy when the white man first came. We thought he came from the light; but he comes like the dusk of the evening. He comes like a day that has passed, and night enters our future with him.

—CHARLOT, SALISH

HISTORY IS WRITTEN BY THE WINNERS, they say. But it is often the losers who care more about it.

"History is lost on most people," proclaimed the *New York Times.*[1] Indeed, a collective amnesia often seems to grip U.S. schools and media. Mainstream culture is focused on the present and the future, not the past. This is not the case in the Native American community. For Native Americans—as for others, here and abroad, who have seen their very sense of self shaped by the narratives of those who conquered their ancestors—history is still a vital issue, charged with power and worth fighting over.

The descendants of the people who met Lewis and Clark have their own stories, and as in the nineteenth century, these are not the same stories that the majority culture wants to tell or even to hear. No one knows this better than Sally Thompson, who works at the University of Montana. She has spent two years on an expedition into the Indian past. The Lewis and Clark Rediscovery Project of Lifelong Learning Online gave her an opportunity to record interviews with modern members of the tribes who encountered Lewis and Clark so that, as the nation takes stock of itself during the 200-year anniversary of the Corps of Discovery, the Indian viewpoint could be heard. "I suspected that tribes were not happy about the upcoming celebration," she said, "and that most Americans wouldn't really understand why, because we know so little of the story."

The following is taken from Thompson's interviews and research.[2]

UPSIDE DOWN

From Indian America, the view of the past is very different from what the dominant culture sees. "The Chinooks saw the whites (*Suyapee*) as humans with 'upside-down faces,' with hair on their chins and not on their heads," Sally Thompson explains. "The *Suyapee,* in many ways, turned the world of Native Americans upside down." Looking back, even Indians must sometimes crane to see the right-side-up world clearly.

The problems today start, as they did for Lewis and Clark, with translation. Jeff Van Pelt, a Umatilla, says: "The language itself carried a lot of our teaching that can't be translated with the English language. If I was to tell you a story in Indian . . . and then I translated it in English, there would be two different stories with two different meanings."

Transcription creates the next barrier. The Shoshone word for "white people" means "those who write things down." Whereas Euro-American society trusts the written record more than the spoken record, the opposite is true in traditional Indian society: what is spoken is trusted, and what is written is suspected of bias. "The spoken word is revered, and to it are attributed certain qualities," says Anna Lee Walters, a Pawnee-Oto. "One quality is akin to magic or enchantment. . . . The spoken word is believed to be power which can create or destroy."

"We see the world so differently. We really do," says Narcisse Blood, a Kainai of the Blackfeet Confederacy. "It is such a linear-thinking society. . . . How we [Blackfeet] view the world [is that] everything is interconnected. We can't say, 'This is politics, this is economics, and this is spiritual,' when everything is part of the whole. And maybe someday social scientists will come to realize that that's the way the world works."

Native peoples' assessments of Lewis and Clark are shaped by their non-European views. "The thing about Lewis and Clark was that they were insignificant to us in some ways and yet they were so significant subsequent to the initial contact," says Narcisse Blood. To him, it is the distortions that Lewis and Clark first entered into the written record that matter most. "Lewis and Clark wrote a lot of things based on who they were. And whether they were right or wrong is irrelevant to students today who look at their writings and make conclusions based on what they read and will come to us and say, 'Well, we got to set you straight. Lewis and Clark say . . . .' It wouldn't matter that their conclusions were wrong if . . . the matter stopped there. But U.S. Indian policy was based on those erroneous conclusions."

Gerard Baker, a Mandan-Hidatsa who has visited tribes across the country in his role as superintendent of the Lewis and Clark National Historic Trail, reports that it is not the story of Lewis and Clark but rather the events they set in motion that loom largest in Native peoples' memories. "According to many of the Indian people I have visited, what has happened in the last two hundred years or so has been defeat, relocation, and the putting of their culture behind them in order to survive." It is wrong, he argues, to consider Lewis and Clark outside the context of what came after. As *Indian Country Today*, the weekly newspaper of tribal affairs, pointed out, "In most non-Indian accounts, the arrival of Lewis and Clark marks the beginning of history." For Indians, the newspaper added, the arrival was instead "the beginning of the end."[3]

LOOKING BACK THROUGH LOSS

A pervasive and personal sense of loss shapes Indian perceptions of the past. Euro-Americans, accustomed to an optimistic, progressive model of history, cannot hope to understand the Indian experience without imagining the past as a landscape of pain. Sally Thompson found that when Indian people are asked what Lewis and Clark mean to them, the "themes that emerge again and again, are of the fur trade, of missionaries, and policies of the U.S. government, especially loss of language, and traditional places and foods and clean water, and precious cultural objects." She adds that even though much can never be restored, "it is important for Indian people to have these losses recognized."

The losses started with disease, whose impact is still felt in Native communities. "There were all kinds of villages that we'll never know the name[s] of," says Tony Johnson, the son of a Chinook tribal leader. "There are lots of villages that we know the names of, but we don't even know of specific people [who lived] there, because of so much loss through disease."

The introduction of European-manufactured goods with the fur trade created a subtle rift with the natural world—a rift that would become wider as the years passed. Gerard Baker says: "The Indian people had used all natural items, taken from animals they killed or plants they secured. The belief was that these items had been alive and therefore, were to be respected and treated like they were alive because they had a spirit. Iron implements, on the other hand, were looked upon as not being alive." A traditional Chinook canoe maker, says Tony Johnson, feels that he is "transforming something living. If we are asking this log to be a canoe, it's only right to make it a living canoe. Some of these cedar logs want to become canoes. . . . We have to follow all the old rules as to how we take care of it, so that it'll take good care of us out on the water." But with manufactured goods, that tie was broken. As Thompson summarizes what she has been told: "Something dead became the intermediary between a woman and the earth she dug to plant seeds or remove bulbs, something dead provided the container for cooking food, and something dead filled the space between two men fighting, creating an entirely different experience of battle."

The loss of land through treaties is a process that many Native people can recite in precise detail, knowing when every acre was given up. Jeff Van Pelt tells the Umatilla story: "In the treaty of 1855 . . . we ceded 6.5 million acres to the United States government with reserved rights. . . . We specifically mentioned that . . . if you're gonna put us on that little bitty Indian reservation you need to understand that our economic base is very broad. We have many horses. We need to take care of the horses, we need pasturing areas for them horses. We need to have access to our usual and accustomed fishing areas where we always go to gather our fish. We need areas to go hunt. We need areas to go gather different kinds of foods and roots and berries. Those are things that specifically they put into the articles of the treaty. But in reality what we were saying is, we want to continue our way of life as we always have."

The legal maneuvers of U.S. treaty-makers are often recounted by historians, but the desperation and the pain of those who signed the treaties are still most vivid in their descendants' memories. Darrell Kipp, a Piegan Blackfeet, tells the story of an agreement made in 1896. "By that time the Blackfeet had been reduced to living in a refugee camp on Big Badger, and they [the treaty commissioners] came in and said we want to take away the mountains now. The leaders said, 'NO! You've already taken all the rest. We're not going to sign.' After three days of negotiations, the government commissioners took them aside in the evening and told them, 'Well then, we'll stop feeding you.' If you tell this to a group already living in a refugee camp, barely surviving, and you take away their last hope of survival . . . then the whole negotiating process switches and the leaders then are negotiating for their lives. We respect them because they negotiated for survival. They said, 'Go ahead. You take it. You take whatever you want, as long as we survive.' So when we exited this refugee camp, there were only 1,400 of us left. Between then and now, everything on the part of this tribe has been a renegotiating [of] the reality of those years."

"I used to go down and visit an old relative of mine," says Louis Adams, a Salish. "She talked about when our people had to leave the Bitterroot [Valley]. She used to say when they had to leave, everybody was crying . . . even the men, when they crossed the river to leave our home."

The loss of land had a far more profound impact on Indians than it would on Euro-Americans in a comparable situation. To Native Americans, the land was not just property; it was woven into their deepest beliefs. "The natural world is our teacher and teaches us who we are," says Jeff Van Pelt. "All of the knowledge within the creation is within the natural world. And we were brought here on this world as ignorant human beings to learn who the Creator was, and what the creation was and how we fit into that creation. And our teachers were the very natural resources that were around us."

Armand Minthorn, a Cayuse-Nez Perce elder, uses a story to express the origin of his tribe's personal bond to the land: "When the water was created it spoke a promise, 'I am going to take care of the Indian people, I am going to give life to everything.' And then the land was created, and it spoke a promise, 'I am going to take care of the Indian people.' . . . Then it was the man and then the woman. That man and that woman were given a belief to take care of everything that was created before them. And that's what we do today, with our religion we take care of everything that we're dependent on."

Indian religions have had to weather two centuries of missionary efforts and government assimilation policies, and much has been lost in the process. "According to many elders, when Christianity came into Indian country, it caused confusion and doubt," says Gerard Baker. "The early missionaries stated that our religion was one of worshipping false idols and not a 'true God.' They removed medicine bundles, most of the time forcefully, and each group 'fought for the souls of the Indian.'"

Although many Native American people today are Christian, or have found ways to blend ancient beliefs with Christianity, others have bitter memories. Boarding schools, designed under government contract to remove Indian children from the influence of their families in order to break the chain of cultural transmission, receive some of the harshest criticisms. "My grandmother had thirteen children and only four survived," says Kathleen Gordon, a Cayuse-Walla Walla, in a voice charged with emotion. "They spoke the language fluently, until they were forced to go into the parochial schools. . . . My mother's brother Ralph was taken off to Chimawa Indian School which is near Salem [Oregon]. He ran away from there because they were forcing him to stop speaking his language, trying to change his way of life. . . . the third time [he ran away] they took him back and locked him up and only gave him bread and water and he died there. . . . My mother's generation then started speaking English because they feared for our lives and for us being punished for speaking our languages."

The loss of native languages is a source of sorrow for many elders. Kathleen Gordon explains: "The Creator gave us [language] in the beginning of our lives as a gift to us from him. Like he gave every bird a song, their own unique song, and every animal their unique sound, we also had our own unique sounds that were taken away from us." To Allen Pinkham, a Nez Perce, the loss of language was a loss of identity: "When civilization hit us . . . the government said: 'All you people have to have English names now; you've got to be civilized.' So most of us Nez Perce members ended up with English names, not our real names. They tried to take all our identity away from us to mold us into this new kind of citizen."

Edwin Benson, one of the last speakers of the Mandan language, says: "There's nowhere where I could just walk out that door and go any direction in the community and start talking Mandan, and somebody could understand me, and start talking back. There's no one. . . . So I just keep that Mandan language to myself. . . . I do miss my language, that I could speak to someone my native tongue."

COPING WITH MODERNITY

Non-Indians tend to think of the hardships suffered by Indians as historic events, not as something that happens today. But in Indian country, the losses that excite the most passion are within living memory. For tribes along the Lewis and Clark trail, which follows two of the major river systems of America, no other event has had more impact than the damming of the Missouri and Columbia after World War II.

On Fort Berthold Reservation, as Paula Giese explains, the Garrison Dam "flooded the entire sheltered, fertile bottomland and river benches, the villages, roads, schools, hospitals and communities where the Hidatsa, Mandan and Arikara peoples had built and farmed. They were forced to move to the shelterless, windswept, barren prairies, and the arms of the lake now cut off the new communities from each other on the unfriendly expanse of what's left of their destroyed land." In public hearings on the impact of the dam in 1986, another tribal member testified: "The land flooding changed the reservation. . . . The timber resources were all gone, as were many of the coal outcroppings where the people had mined fuel for themselves. The upland proved not only poor for agriculture but difficult for ranching as well."

The losses were far more than economic. Edwin Benson says, "Some days I go back, just to bring back the old memories. . . . There's times as I go along where I see an old wagon trail going down right into that water over where the green trees grew. When I see that then my cry is right here. Even yet today, fifty years later. I live with that, and I guess that's never going to quit either."

On the Columbia River, the hydroelectric dams destroyed age-old salmon fisheries and have come close to destroying the salmon as well. Bobbie Conner, a Cayuse-Nez Perce, says: "Celilo Falls, the richest fishery of the Northwest for thousands of years, [is] now under the backwater of the Dalles Dam. It still lives in the hearts and minds of our people, but in my lifetime it has been changed, altered forever. They had to blast as they were building, so even if the water was drawn down, it would be a different landscape underneath."

Lost along with the falls were hundreds of village sites, burial grounds, and sacred places. But the well-meaning efforts of archaeologists to excavate and preserve evidence from those sites have also caused pain. Tony Johnson explains: "As a highlight of a university class my wife had, a professor proudly brought out a flat-headed skull of a Chinook Indian. . . . There has been long-standing interest for people to go out and rob our graves and take those flattened skulls. Repatriating these skulls is much worse for us than if complete skeletons had been dug up. If we had all of the bones of an individual, we could take care of that person. But with just a head, we don't believe we can ever make that person satisfied. So it's very upsetting to us."

Hunting and fishing rights, often guaranteed to Indian tribes in treaties, are still a source of controversy as access becomes limited by development and legal barriers. Tony Johnson, a younger-generation Chinook, says: "My grandpa and everyone before him, of course, were fishermen, so fishing rights are really important to me. . . . There are plenty of Chinooks who want to make a living fishing. . . . We need that fish—sturgeon, salmon, smelt, and flounder. Those are the foods we must have to be Chinook Indians. . . . Our ability to fish as Indians got taken away in the 1980s. . . . People my age or before me could learn how to gillnet fish and know how to mend a net or run a boat. But young kids, the age of my son, don't have that chance."

Passing on Indian knowledge and values to the younger generation can be a struggle after all that has happened. "We're talking about three generations of Indian people that have been impacted because of the assimilation process," says Jeff Van Pelt. "In our teachings if we don't learn the ways of respect and follow them old laws, we don't go to the next place where our ancestors are. . . . But how am I to come back and to help teach and guide my children? Through polluted water? Through salmon that aren't there? Through eagles that are gone, through wolves that are gone, through bears that are gone? Where is it that I'm supposed to go with my son to teach him?"

"WE SURVIVED DISCOVERY"

Despite the darkness of the two centuries beginning with Lewis and Clark's arrival, emerging from Native American voices today are a determined optimism and a vision for the future.

Allen Pinkham, a Nez Perce, was initially skeptical about the Lewis and Clark bicentennial. "Indian people have never had voices in the interpretation of the expansion of the Northwest simply because we were never considered experts," he said. "We didn't have Ph.d.'s behind our names. . . . They would come and interview us and say, 'Oh, yes, here's a quaint Nez Perce story,' and away that story would go." And yet, when asked to sit on the National Council of the Lewis and Clark Bicentennial, he saw an opportunity. "I recognized that the Bicentennial Council would be a way to educate the general public about who we are and what we are and what we perceived about becoming U.S. citizens. Tribes would have the ability to do this and not have anthropologists talk for us. . . . There are a lot of misconceptions that need to be clarified."

The misconception that Darrell Kipp wants cleared up is that Indians have vanished. "The ultimate demise of Native Americans has been predicted over and over by anthropologists, ethnographers, politicians, and others," he says. "What's amazing is that . . . despite the onslaught, despite the siege that the Lewis and Clark expedition set in motion, today many tribes are still in their original homeland, still in the place where they were encountered by Lewis and Clark, and in many cases, still carrying on the same things in the sense of tribal people."

"We want new words to describe our presence," Kipp continues. "We don't want to be considered the vanishing Americans or the invisible Americans. We are *Americans*. We are part of this country. We don't want to be considered, because we speak our language or know our ways, to be called 'traditionalists,' implying we're remnants of some primordial day. The new word should be 'modernist.' People who speak their tribal language, know their ways, are well versed in society in general, are contributing to American society and are good citizens to their own tribal society—these are modernists. This is what Native American people want to be."

Dr. Richard Littlebear, a Cheyenne, sees an opportunity for fulfilling the promise of core American values. "Personally, despite what has happened to us as indigenous people, I would still rather belong to a minority in this country than anywhere else on this planet. I believe that, among the nations of this world, America has the best chance of realizing its human rights ideals as enumerated in the Declaration of Independence. . . . The bicentennial should celebrate and acknowledge all of our presence here in this country: indigenous and non-indigenous. If this celebration starts to educate people about other people and brings them together, at the very least, it would be the start of a fitting legacy for Sacajawea."

The belief that we are all facing the future together gives many Indian thinkers a sense of urgency, because they feel the values that allowed Indians to survive the last two centuries are essential for the majority society to learn. Armand Minthorn says: "The tribes have foresight, we look generations ahead. . . . You and I are dependent on water, you and I are dependent on how clean this land is. . . . If we don't have any foresight in the future, what will those future generations be dependent on? Are they going to say this is what used to swim in our rivers, and hold a picture of a salmon?"

Bobbie Conner speaks of the need for interconnections between culture and land. "The places had names before Lewis and Clark came, and the names are still there if we keep the language alive. . . . The names of things are actually stories, every place and every person has a story. . . . You take the story and the landscape and the ecosystem, part and parcel, the whole thing together. Our covenant with the Creator, for giving us this place to live and for the animals and the plants here agreeing to sustain us, if we would protect them, transcends all of those modern jurisdictions. Clean air, clean water, clean land, a good place to live, those things are things we should all mutually embrace."

Calvin Grinnell, a Mandan-Hidatsa who grew up on the flooded Fort Berthold Reservation, has a simple piece of advice. "[Those in] the dominant society . . . are realizing that the gift that they got is not infinite, that the resources are not infinite, and now they are wondering, how can we save ourselves? . . . What we need to do for our children two hundred years from now [is] we all need to pray. I have a perception that two hundred years ago one of my ancestors prayed for me, that I might live. I know that's true, because I've heard oral tradition say that. That's our obligation today, is to turn around and say, I hope we leave enough of this good stuff here, enough wilderness and nature, and cut back on our appetites for luxury, that we can have our children and grandchildren enjoy those beautiful sunsets, the beautiful mountains and animals, the legacy that was left to us by our elders."

The Journey of Our Objects

CAROLYN GILMAN

THE NATIONAL Lewis and Clark Bicentennial Exhibition, the project this book represents, was planned to be a reunion of artifacts that had not been seen together in one place since 1806. Almost the instant Lewis and Clark landed their boats on the St. Louis riverfront, the results of their expedition—the equipment, documents, maps, and specimens assembled before and during their voyage to the Pacific—started dispersing. There was no national museum at the time, and the files of the War Department were never considered appropriate for documents whose value was primarily scientific. As a result, the expedition materials became widely scattered in over fifty institutions, from Oregon to London. The task of reassembling a representative sampling for this exhibition turned into a five-year scavenger hunt.

Lewis and Clark left a surprisingly large, but extremely miscellaneous, legacy of material. There is no single museum with a broad-enough collection to mount a major exhibit on Lewis and Clark. Thus for this project, it was necessary to pool the resources of many institutions. The museums and archives with the most significant holdings are the Academy of Natural Sciences of Philadelphia, the American Philosophical Society, the Beinecke Library at Yale, the Library of Congress, the Missouri Historical Society, the National Archives, the Oregon Historical Society, the Peabody Museum at Harvard, and the Smithsonian Institution.

The Lewis and Clark collection is heavily weighted toward documents and scientific specimens—the kinds of material that nineteenth-century Euro-American researchers identified as valuable. So, for example, there were over 220 plant samples but only a handful of personal objects belonging to the men. The surviving collection could never animate the voyage or accurately represent what the expedition members used or saw. Since the objectives of this exhibition were educational rather than antiquarian, we made the decision to supplement original Lewis and Clark objects with articles as close as possible—in design and date—to the ones they used and documented. Fortunately, thanks to the diligent federal accountants who required receipts for the reimbursement of expenses, the paper trail was complete enough that many near-exact matches for expedition equipment could be found. And thanks to the voluminous journals of Lewis and Clark, the material culture of the Native Americans they encountered could be reconstructed as well.

Over the years, layers of mythology have accreted around everything Lewis or Clark touched. From the 1890s through the 1990s, overenthusiastic curators "discovered" dubiously documented Lewis and Clark artifacts in their collections. Art and antique dealers tried to pass off bogus portraits and objects. A few deliberate hoaxes were perpetrated, but many more assertions were simply flights of wishful thinking. Our research revealed that the most diligent previous investigator of Lewis and Clark objects, Paul Cutright, was very often too trusting. With the claims of Charles Willoughby, Thomas Donaldson, and Charles Coleman Sellars, who each leaped to overly optimistic conclusions, the extent of the surviving Lewis and Clark ethnographic collection became greatly exaggerated.

This book does not contain every artifact with a claim to Lewis and Clark associations. The ones not included fall into several categories. Some belong to private owners or public institutions that did not elect to participate in our project. Others are duplicates or are redundant (for example, there are two Masonic aprons belonging to Meriwether Lewis, and only one is included here). Others are too dubious in provenance or date.

The process of tracing and authenticating the artifacts that are included required accounting for their chains of provenance—how they were passed down from owner to owner until they came to their present locations. This process revealed that the objects have gone through nearly as many adventures as the Corps of Discovery itself. Their stories are full of lawsuits, eccentric descendants, scholars absconding with the goods, and tragic museum fires. The charts reproduced here represent the broad outlines of these stories.

The charts should be approached with some caution. They depict the paths the Lewis and Clark artifacts followed, not family genealogies (although the two often overlap). They do not show every path in equal detail; for the sake of clarity, some minor steps and details are skipped. They do not show chronology; some artifacts reached their present locations very early and some very recently; the charts do not attempt to represent this difference in time. Not every artifact is represented—just the major collections whose owners were willing to be identified. Finally, the charts are almost certain to be out of date by the time this book is published, since new artifacts turn up fairly regularly.

ARTIFACTS DISPERSED BY LEWIS, CLARK, AND JEFFERSON

Chart 1 shows artifacts that were disposed of more or less officially, either by Lewis and Clark at the end of the expedition or by Jefferson.

Material collected during the course of the expedition made its way east in at least three batches. Before setting out in 1804, Lewis sent Jefferson a shipment of material from St. Louis, including mineral samples, "curiosities" such as a buffalo hairball and a horned toad, and four maps. The minerals and curiosities have all disappeared, but three of the four maps have been traced. A copy of one has long been known as "Lewis and Clark's Map of 1804," and the other two, both maps of St. Louis, were found during research for this project. All three are in the National Archives, apparently deposited there after Jefferson forwarded them to appropriate government agencies. The horned toad does not survive, but Jefferson apparently sent it to Charles Willson Peale; a sketch of the toad by either Peale or Pietro Ancora is at the American Philosophical Society.[1]

The next batch of artifacts to find its way back to Jefferson was a much larger shipment sent via the keelboat from Fort Mandan in the spring of 1805;

CHART 1

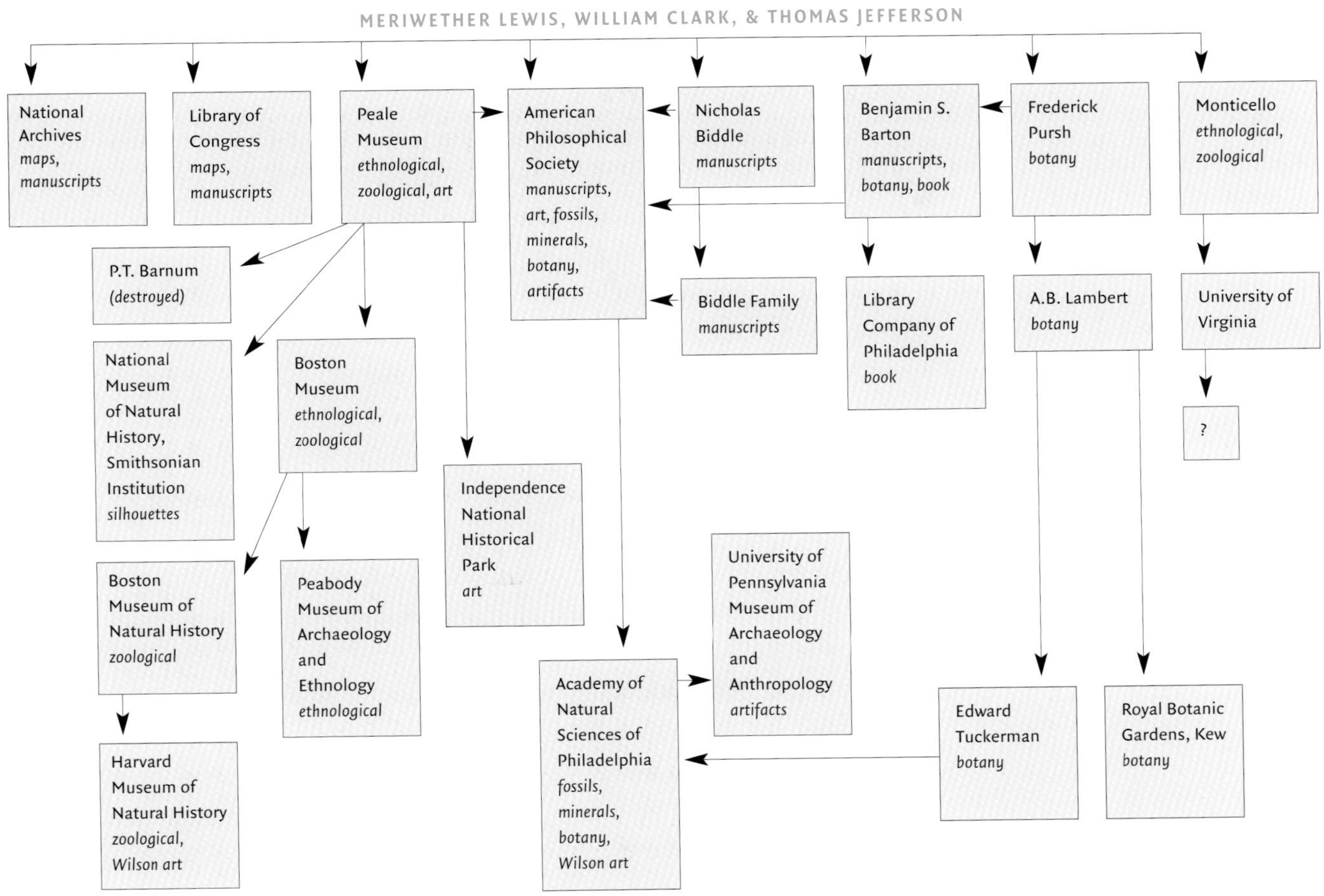

this batch arrived at the White House in August. Lewis wrote a lengthy inventory including natural history specimens, minerals, botanical specimens, seeds, ethnographic artifacts, and five live animals. In disposing of these, Jefferson followed a well-documented procedure. Some of the Indian artifacts and zoological specimens he kept himself, the former "for an Indian Hall" that, he noted, "I am forming at Monticello." The minerals, plants, and seeds went to the American Philosophical Society, and the remainder of the zoological material he forwarded to Peale's Museum. A large proportion of this material has survived, but almost all of it has been transferred to other institutions. Another collection sent via the keelboat, from Clark to his family, will be traced below.[2]

The last batch of material came back with the expedition in 1806. It was probably the most significant but the least documented. The used equipment—"Sundry Rifles, Muskets, powder horns, Shot pouches, Powder, Lead, Kettles, Axes, & other public property"—was auctioned off in St. Louis as army surplus for $408.62 and disappeared forever. As for specimens, Lewis wrote Jefferson that he was bringing skins of a sea otter, a bighorn sheep, a mule deer, and "several other quadrupeds and birds," as well as "a pretty extensive collection of plants, and . . . nine other vocabularies." The only list he wrote included animal skins (this time including prairie dogs, bears, a wolf, and beaver tails), a "Clat sop hat," and several "Boxes Containing Various articles." Clark sent home to Louisville a similar assortment that also included ethnographic artifacts such as four Mandan buffalo robes, a blanket woven of sheep wool, another Clatsop hat, baskets, "Indian wallets," and the maddeningly repeated "sundery articles." No record of the disposition of these objects was made, but we may assume that this batch, like the others, was dispersed among the captains' families, Jefferson, the American Philosophical Society, and Peale's Museum.[3]

The most important public repositories for expedition materials were thus Peale's Museum and the American Philosophical Society. Jefferson's ties to these two Philadelphia institutions—he was president of the latter and was a close personal friend of Peale's—explain why he designated them to keep the records and scientific specimens from the expedition. It is very fortunate that one of them, the American Philosophical Society, still exists. As for the other, the demise of Peale's Museum is the single most tragic event that befell the Lewis and Clark collection.

As mentioned, Lewis and Clark's artifacts arrived at Peale's Museum in several batches. Whereas minerals and plants went to the Philosophical Society, ethnographic material, birds, and animals—alive and dead—went to Peale. Of the natural history material, the only list to survive is Jefferson's of items sent in October 1805, including skins and skeletons of white hares, the "burrowing wolf" (perhaps a coyote), a "Blaireau" (badger), a red fox, an antelope, a prairie dog, and a magpie. But Peale wrote that the collection was supplemented after the expedition by "animals brought from the sea coast, also some parts of the dress &c of the Natives of Columbia River, [and] . . . some animals totally unknown before . . . which we are now mounting to put into the Museum." Peale, an accomplished taxidermist, mounted an antelope, even though it was damaged by insects, and illustrated the animal as well. He also stuffed at least one Rocky Mountain sheep head for Jefferson.[4]

During the heyday of Peale's Museum, scientists used the collection to produce books on American natural history, in the process creating a record of the Lewis and Clark specimens. In the case of the animals, there is no way to be certain that the mounts illustrated in books like John Godman's *American Natural History* were from Lewis's skins. The birds are another matter. Though bird skins rarely figure in Lewis's lists, we know at least four that reached Peale: Lewis's woodpecker, Clark's nutcracker, the Louisiana tanager, and the American magpie. All of these were drawn by either Alexander Wilson or Peale himself.[5]

Peale accessioned most of the ethnographic artifacts in December 1809, after receiving a large shipment of "Indian dresses, pipes, arrows, an Indian pot entire," and more skins sent by Lewis via New Orleans just before his death. But ethnographic material apparently had been accumulating at the museum for some time. Peale's accession record included forty-four entries, many of them for multiple artifacts. The most spectacular must have been the complete Shoshone regalia given to Lewis by Cameahwait. Peale displayed this costume on a wax likeness of Lewis, along with a pacifist label urging racial harmony. Whereas the natural history specimens appear to have been integrated into the taxonomic arrangement of the museum, the Indian artifacts were kept in a special Lewis and Clark display, giving them importance through association with the great explorers.[6]

The last category of Peale's Museum artifacts was created by Peale himself, when he painted the famous portraits of the captains. The two portraits were added to his hall of great men.

By the 1840s the museum world had changed. Public tastes in the age of Andrew Jackson were not what they had been in the age of Jefferson. Cabinets of curiosities gave way to penny arcades of novelties and monstrosities, and Peale's Museum found itself burdened with a significant scientific collection at a time when the public was demanding lowbrow entertainment. The collection was auctioned off in 1849–50. The City of Philadelphia purchased a large batch of Peale's portraits, including Lewis's and Clark's, which are now cared for by the National Park Service at Independence National Historical Park. The rest of the Peale collection was not so lucky. The largest parts went to Moses Kimball's Boston Museum and P. T. Barnum's American Museum in New York. The latter burned, along with all its collections, in 1865. The Boston Museum collection fared only slightly better. Contrary to its name, the Boston Museum was primarily a theater, but to avoid old Puritan laws restricting live entertainment, it decorated the lobby with "educational" displays like "Mad'lle Fanny, the celebrated chimpanzie," an "Enormous Lobster," and "Heathen Idols from different nations." It was quite a comedown for the Lewis and Clark artifacts.[7]

By the 1890s the Boston Museum also fell on hard times and began to dispose of its collection. Natural history items were donated to the Boston Society of Natural History. The birds subsequently survived a sojourn in the barn of the ornithologist Charles J. Maynard, then were transferred back to the Society of Natural History, where they were wrenched from their stands and dissociated from their labels. After that, Peale's surviving natural history specimens were transferred to Harvard's Museum of Comparative Zoology (now the Harvard Museum of Natural History). The only specimen there that has ever been associated with Lewis and Clark is the Lewis's woodpecker, but because of the damage to both the bird and its documentation, the specimen cannot be confidently connected to Lewis.[8]

The ethnographic artifacts remained at the Boston Museum until another fire damaged the building in 1899; then they were offered to the Peabody Museum of Archaeology and Ethnology at Harvard University. Charles C. Willoughby, the curator, accessioned more than fourteen hundred "curiosities" from around the world. That some came from the eclectic ethnographic collection of Peale's Museum was clear, since the original labels were still present, though often attached to the wrong artifacts. Others came from the remainder of the Boston Museum collection. Willoughby rather incautiously cataloged a number of the artifacts as originating with Lewis and Clark, either because they matched things on Peale's accession list, or because a label was found with them, or because Lewis and Clark mentioned something similar. So, for example, he chose the best of several knob-top Nootkan hats and accessioned it as the Lewis and Clark example without (so far as we know) any evidence linking that particular hat to the expedition. Two women's dresses found associated with labels for hunting shirts worn by Lewis and Clark were accessioned as expedition items even though there was no record of any dress donated by Lewis or Clark to Peale. Willoughby wrote that there was "no question" that a buffalo robe he cataloged was the one listed on Lewis's 1805 inventory of articles sent to Jefferson from Fort Mandan, despite a lack of evidence that the listed robe had even made it to Peale. Because few subsequent researchers ever questioned Willoughby's attributions—and many, in fact, continued the practice of attribution without evidence—the number of "Lewis and Clark" artifacts at the Peabody kept growing until a systematic reassessment of the collection, undertaken by the curator Castle McLaughlin and published in 2003, finally put the brakes on the process. In the end, McLaughlin was willing to firmly attribute only six objects (three of them duplicates) to Lewis and Clark, although she identified many others (including several not listed by Willoughby) as potential matches from the right era and tribal traditions.[9]

Art from Peale's Museum can now be found in the Peale Papers at the American Philosophical Society, as well as at Independence National Historical Park. The Smithsonian Institution inherited a collection of Peale's Indian silhouettes; these were made when one of the several delegations that traveled east during 1804–6 visited Philadelphia.[10]

The story of the American Philosophical Society collection is much happier, but only a little less complex. Lewis had a complete set of the journals with him when he died, since he had been intending to begin work on his book manuscript when he reached Philadelphia. The volumes were returned to Clark. When Clark recruited Nicholas Biddle and Benjamin Smith Barton to compile the planned narrative and scientific volumes, both men borrowed the journals to use in their work. After the publication of Biddle's book, Jefferson tried to ensure that all of the manuscripts were safely returned to the American Philosophical Society. The majority made it back in 1817, but Biddle forgot a few. Unknown to Jefferson, Clark also withheld five volumes, which will be described later. After that time, most of the journals rested unused in the library of the American Philosophical Society until Elliott Coues borrowed them to annotate his reprint of the Biddle narrative in the 1890s. Coues arranged them chronologically, assigned them codex letters, pasted labels on the covers, and made notes on the interiors before returning them. Reuben Gold Thwaites was the first person to edit the journals for full publication, in 1904.[11]

The papers that Biddle had forgotten to return included John Ordway's journals (which Lewis had purchased) and the 1803 Eastern Journal documenting the trip from Pittsburgh to Camp Dubois and containing Biddle's invaluable notes on his interviews with Clark. In 1913 Nicholas Biddle's descendants Charles and Edward Biddle discovered these documents among his papers. Though at first the Biddles seem to have considered giving them to the Library of Congress, they instead deposited them at the American Philosophical Society between 1913 and 1915, converting the deposit to a gift in 1949. Other related manuscripts at the American Philosophical Society include Clark's "Estimate of the Eastern Indians" and the only surviving copies of the vocabulary sheets developed by Jefferson. (All of the original twenty-three vocabularies collected on the expedition were lost in transit from Washington, D.C., to Monticello.)[12]

The most significant expedition-related artwork in the American Philosophical Society collection is Charles B. J. F. de Saint-Mémin's portrait of Shehek-Shote (Big White), the Mandan chief who accompanied Lewis to the East at the conclusion of the expedition. The portrait came into the collection at the same time as the Lewis and Clark journals—in 1817. Other artworks include sketches of Lewis's zoological specimens, in the Peale Papers; copper plates of a number of Saint-Mémin's portraits of Indian chiefs, in the Barton Papers; and the copper plates used to print the maps in the Biddle narrative, first located by Thwaites in the hands of Judge Craig Biddle in 1903.[13]

In addition to manuscripts, the American Philosophical Society originally inherited the collection of seventy fossils and minerals that Lewis collected along the Missouri River. These somehow got into the hands of the mineralogist Adam Seybert and became confused with the rest of the materials in his large collection. The Seybert minerals were eventually transferred to the Academy of Natural Sciences of Philadelphia, but by that time all but four of the Lewis and Clark specimens were lost or unlabeled.[14]

The year after the expedition, Clark returned to Big Bone Lick to conduct an excavation of mastodon bones for Jefferson. Jefferson split this large collection between the American Philosophical Society and the National Institute of France. The American Philosophical Society's collection was transferred to the Academy of Natural Sciences.

The American Philosophical Society originally maintained a cabinet of curiosities. When it was deaccessioned, three artifacts from the expedition were transferred, first to the Academy of Natural Sciences and then, in 1937, to the University of Pennsylvania Museum of Archaeology and Anthropology. The artifacts were two Mandan pots and a pair of abalone shell ornaments. The circumstances of their donation have not been found.

The botanical specimens followed a more circuitous route. There were, as mentioned above, two batches of botanical specimens. The first batch of sixty specimens, collected on the Missouri River, was sent back in 1805 from Fort Mandan. Jefferson forwarded this batch to the American Philosophical Society, which passed them on to Benjamin Smith Barton for study. Some time after this, the first thirty of the specimens mysteriously disappeared and have never been found.[15]

When Lewis brought the second batch of botanical specimens back after the expedition, he apparently found Barton unwilling to undertake the botanical studies for the projected publication, so he recruited Frederick Pursh, a young German botanist then living in Philadelphia. Pursh analyzed the specimens and created sketches for the book, but Lewis never returned to pay him or to ask him to continue work on the publication. Needing to move on to new employment, Pursh gave some of the specimens to his sponsor, the horticulturalist Bernard McMahon, and left Philadelphia. Apparently unknown to anyone, nearly fifty other specimens, most of them duplicates, left with him.

By 1811 Pursh was in England, working for A. B. Lambert, a country gentleman with botanical interests. In Lambert's employment, he completed and published *Flora Americae Septentrionalis*, based in part on his collection of Lewis's plants. The specimens he had appropriated remained in Lambert's collection after Pursh's departure. When Lambert died in 1842, his collection was offered for sale at a Sotheby's auction. Edward Tuckerman, an American botanist who happened to be at the auction, purchased most of Pursh's collection of Lewis plants for five pounds, ten shillings. He took the plants back to the United States and in 1856 presented them to the Academy of Natural Sciences of Philadelphia. Another batch of Lambert's plants that were sold at the auction eventually reached Kew Gardens. There, eleven of Lewis's plants were discovered among the collection in the 1950s.[16]

Meanwhile, the specimens that Pursh had given to McMahon were collected by Clark after Lewis's death and were sent to Barton to use in compiling the scientific volume on the expedition. After Barton died, without having set pen to paper for the volume, the plants went back to the American Philosophical Society, where they remained, unknown to almost anyone, until 1896, when they were discovered and transferred to the Academy of Natural Sciences, joining the plants that had traveled to London and back. In all, more than two hundred botanical specimens survive at the Academy of Natural Sciences, and eleven remain at Kew Gardens.

The National Archives is the repository for maps and manuscripts generated by various branches of the federal government. The financial records of the expedition, including Lewis's original receipts for purchases and payroll documents, have mostly been assembled into a central Lewis and Clark file in Record Group 92. The copies of expedition maps made by the War Department are in the Cartographic Records Division, Record Group 77. These include Clark's map of 1804, made before the expedition set out for the West, and Nicholas King's copy of his map of 1805 (made at Fort Mandan) for the War Department.

The Library of Congress inherited two principal collections related to the expedition. The first—the papers of Thomas Jefferson—contains Jefferson's copies of documents such as the expedition instructions, messages to Congress, and correspondence with Lewis and members of the Philadelphia scientific circle. The other major collection is a batch of maps found at the Office of Indian Affairs in about 1916 and associated with the records of Clark's superintendency. Most were maps collected in preparation for the expedition. Among them were a copy of King's 1803 map; a detailed Missouri River map that was made in the 1790s by John Evans and/or James Mackay and on which Clark made notes during the voyage (often called "The Indian Office map"); a western North America map, also based on Evans and Mackay, which shows the Missouri to its source, including the Great Falls; and a copy by Lewis of David Thompson's map of the northernmost bend of the Missouri. These were all transferred to the Library of Congress in 1925. The Library of Congress also collected isolated maps when they became available. In 1921 it purchased Robert Frazer's map of the route of Lewis and Clark, and in 1961 it acquired the State Department's version of King's copy of Clark's 1805 map (the War Department copy of which is in the National Archives).[17]

The fate of the souvenirs that Jefferson retained at Monticello is one of the enduring mysteries of the Lewis and Clark collection. Jefferson kept the cream of the natural history and Native American artifacts sent back by Lewis in 1805, and he added to this collection after the expedition's return. In 1809 he wrote Clark, "Your donations & Governor Lewis's have given to my collection of Indian curiosities an importance much beyond what I had ever counted on." Visitors to Monticello in subsequent years described an impressive array of buffalo robes, arms, clothing, and utensils displayed in the entrance hall. Just before his death, Jefferson wrote Clark that he was giving his whole collection, including the Lewis and Clark material, to the University of Virginia. There, "Mr. Jefferson's collections of curiosities, Indian utensils & dresses & weapons" were admired by a visitor to the lecture halls in 1831. Some of it was still at the university in the twentieth century. Beyond that, the Monticello materials cannot be traced. The only Lewis and Clark piece known to still exist is a set of elk antlers, most likely the ones sent to Jefferson from Fort Mandan in

1805. They are owned by the University of Virginia but are on long-term loan to Monticello. This specimen and a silhouette of Lewis are the only original artifacts related to Lewis and Clark presently at Monticello.[18]

In 1980 Charles Coleman Sellers published a theory that a superb ethnographic collection donated to Peale's Museum in 1828 was, in fact, the nucleus of Jefferson's Monticello collection. Six objects from this collection survive at the Peabody Museum and have several times been published as Lewis and Clark artifacts. This speculation has now been disproven. According to Peale's accession register, the collection had been made on the upper Missouri by Lieutenant George C. Hutter, the son of the donor, Christian J. Hutter. The Hutters crossed paths with both Jefferson's and Clark's families several times. George Hutter served in the Sixth Infantry with Clark's son Meriwether, and in 1830 George married Clark's niece Harriet Risque. In 1840 his brother Edward Hutter married Emma Cobbs, whose family had purchased Jefferson's Poplar Forest plantation in 1828. Sellers's theory that Jefferson's collection was moved to Poplar Forest and somehow came into the possession of the Hutter family twelve years before they had any connection to the house does not hold water. A Hutter family story that the painted buffalo robe in the ethnographic collection was a wedding gift from William Clark is also invalidated by the fact that the wedding took place two years after the robe was donated to Peale's Museum. In sum, there is no provable connection between the Hutter collection and either Jefferson or the Lewis and Clark expedition. This does not detract, however, from the importance of the Hutter collection, which remains one of the earliest documented Plains Indian collections in existence. It was probably assembled by George Hutter himself on the Atkinson-O'Fallon expedition of 1825, which made a series of treaties with the same tribes of Missouri River Indians that Lewis and Clark had met twenty years before.[19]

ARTIFACTS DISPERSED BY WILLIAM CLARK

Chart 2 shows the paths of the artifacts that were retained by William Clark. Clark was an avid collector and museum proprietor in his own right, and he kept a substantial mass of material.

Clark started both collecting and disposing of material during the expedition. In 1805, when the keelboat was preparing to return from Fort Mandan, Clark assembled a shipment of both papers and artifacts to send to his brother Jonathan in Louisville. The papers included his rough field notes from 1804–5, a copy of his Fort Mandan map of 1805, a copy of the "Estimate of the Eastern Indians," a descriptive memorandum of the Missouri River country, and a summary statement of rivers and creeks flowing into the Missouri. Some of these documents he undoubtedly reclaimed at the end of the journey, since papers matching these descriptions can be found in the American Philosophical Society and the Missouri Historical Society. But the field notes passed, by some unknown route, into the family of General John H. Hammond.[20]

In 1953 Lucile Kane, the curator of manuscripts at the Minnesota Historical Society, was called in to clear out some manuscripts in an old desk in the attic of Hammond's descendants in St. Paul, Minnesota. When she got the papers back to her office and looked at them carefully, she immediately recognized them as field notes written by Clark on the first leg of the journey up the Missouri. As soon as this discovery was revealed, it resulted in a well-publicized

CHART 2

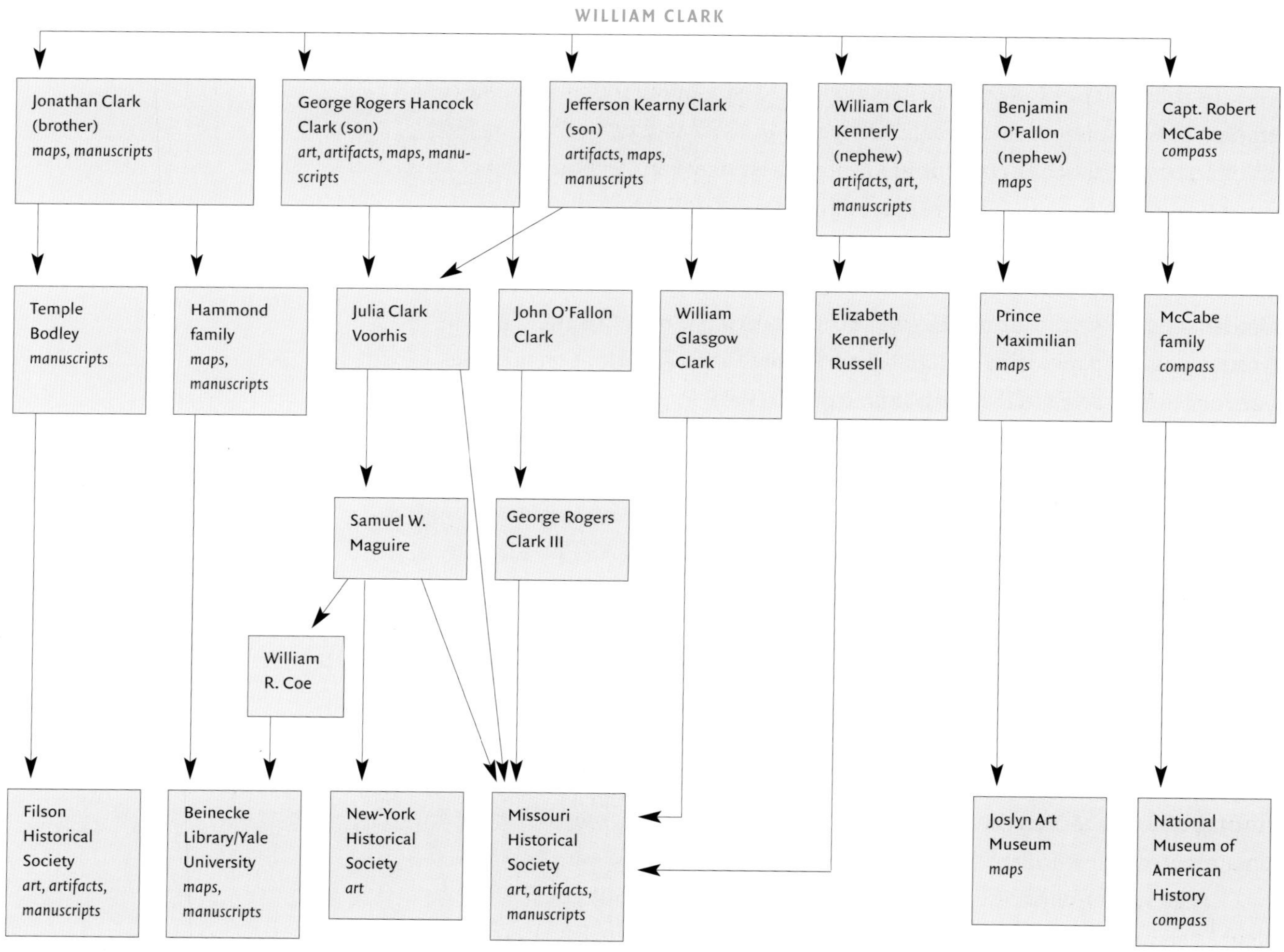

legal battle for the papers. The federal government tried to claim possession because the expedition had been funded by the government. If it had succeeded, every other private institution's collection—not only Lewis and Clark's papers but also those of other government employees—would have been subject to seizure on the same grounds. Major archives organized to resist, particularly the archives at Yale University and the Missouri Historical Society. In the end the government lost, and the collection was sold by the Hammond heirs to Frederick W. Beinecke, who donated them to the Yale library that now bears his name. These papers were first edited by Ernest Osgood and published in 1964. Among the more famous items in this group were Clark's Camp Dubois journal, his rough notes on the trip up the Missouri, and his sketch of the keelboat.[21]

In the early twentieth century Jonathan Clark's great-grandson, a local Louisville historian named Temple Bodley, assembled a collection of family correspondence. Bodley died in 1940, and the letters were discovered in an attic by his grandchildren in 1988. They are now at the Filson Historical Society in Louisville; the letters written between William and Jonathan Clark were edited and published by James Holmberg in 2002. Only a few relate directly to the expedition, but they shed light on Clark's relationship to York and Lewis after the expedition. From other members of the Clark family, the Filson Historical

Society inherited a painting of Clark by Joseph H. Bush and a Rocky Mountain sheep horn.[22]

The fate of a long list of ethnographic and natural history artifacts that Clark sent back to Jonathan via the keelboat in 1805 remains a mystery. The artifacts included such tantalizing items as a woman's antelope-skin dress, several pairs of moccasins, leggings, animal skins and horns, plant samples, a parfleche, a Mandan pot, and several buffalo robes, one with a battle scene. Some items fitting these descriptions later showed up on Peale's accession list, and others were given by Clark to friends and family: for example, he presented his sister Fanny with the sheep horn now at the Filson Historical Society, and he gave Dolley Madison a woman's dress which may or may not be the same one sent to Jonathan. Other items may have formed the nucleus of the museum he later maintained in St. Louis.

What became the most important path for Clark artifacts was via two of his sons: George Rogers Hancock Clark, who was his father's executor, and Jefferson Kearny Clark, his youngest son. Jeff Clark, as he was known, was described as "a courtly gentleman of the old school, and a well known character in St. Louis." He kept a large collection of Indian and western material on display in his suburban estate, Minoma. A photograph, taken in about 1885, of what is probably one of the rooms at Minoma shows the walls decked with guns, bows, paddles, pipes, swords, powder horns, and paintings. Several artifacts seen in the photo are included in this book: a Rocky Mountain sheephorn spoon, a beaded gun case, and a camp chest given to William Clark by Lafayette.[23]

Late in life, the childless Jeff Clark moved in with his niece Julia, the daughter of George Rogers Hancock Clark. Julia, who had married Robert S. Voorhis, had also inherited a collection of family memorabilia, and with Jeff's death in 1900, the two collections apparently were consolidated. Reuben Gold Thwaites discovered the combined collection in Mrs. Voorhis's New York apartment when he was preparing his 1904 edition of the Lewis and Clark journals. Along with artifacts and art, she had a large batch of maps and five volumes of the journals, whose existence no one had suspected up to then: four bound in red morocco leather and one bound in animal hide, the latter of which Thwaites named the elkskin journal. Clark had never turned these volumes over to the American Philosophical Society, probably because they were all duplicates and he preferred to keep them as mementos. All covered the latter part of the journey, from Fort Mandan to the Pacific coast and back. Thwaites negotiated with Julia Voorhis and her daughter Eleanor Glasgow Voorhis (who died before her mother, in 1919) to publish the journals.[24]

When the Thwaites edition came out, the Missouri Historical Society learned of the Voorhis collection. In 1921 Nettie Beauregard, the archivist at the Missouri Historical Society, began a concerted campaign to secure the Voorhis material. In private, she described Julia Voorhis as "the very queerest sort of an old lady that I have ever seen." After a trip to visit Voorhis in New York, she wrote: "She lives quite alone with her servants in two apartments, one is used as a store house for all of these wonderful treasures, no one had been permitted to enter there for eight months, it was her first visit in that time. As you enter her living room, you see letters arranged in great order all around the edge of the room on the floor, her mail is placed there as it arrives, and at her leisure she opens *some* of them; letters which come on Wednesday are never opened, she has some prejudice on this subject." Beauregard enlisted other Clark family members, Voorhis's lawyer, and even the governor of Missouri to lobby for the Missouri Historical Society. She was successful only in getting Voorhis to send the museum a pair of portraits.[25]

In the end, Julia Voorhis's will instructed her executor to dispose of the Clark material to institutions in either New York or St. Louis. Samuel W. Maguire, who administered the estate, obeyed the watchful Beauregard by sending several shipments of Clark family furniture, portraits, personal belongings, and manuscripts to the Missouri Historical Society. The manuscripts included not only the largest collection of William Clark's personal correspondence but also quite a few of Meriwether Lewis's letters, which Clark had come to possess in his position as executor of Lewis's estate. Thus, for example, Jefferson's famous letter of credit had become part of the Clark papers.

Maguire did not, however, send everything to the Missouri Historical Society. Although he originally stated his intention to send a collection of maps, he evidently thought better of the idea. In 1949 his widow put up for sale over fifty of Clark's maps from the Voorhis collection; they were bought by the collector William Robertson Coe, who subsequently donated them to the Beinecke Library at Yale University. When the Missouri Historical Society heard of the Coe donation, it briefly considered legal action to recover this remnant of a collection it considered rightfully its own; but the terms of the Voorhis will proved too vague to uphold such a challenge. The map collection acquired by Coe included expedition route maps, maps by Antoine Soulard and John Evans collected in preparation for the journey, Indian maps collected on the way, and Clark's composite map of western North America. Yale thus brought together two separate Lewis and Clark collections: the maps from the Voorhis collection and the field notes from the Hammond family.[26]

The maps were not the only items that provided revenue for Mrs. Maguire after her husband's death. She also sold, to an art dealer, the famous Saint-Mémin portrait of Meriwether Lewis in Shoshone garb; afterward it passed through the hands of several collectors before being donated to the New-York Historical Society.[27]

On the death of Mrs. Maguire in 1952, the Missouri Historical Society purchased most of the remainder of her holdings, including family miniatures, jewelry, furniture, dishes, books, manuscripts, and photographs. Perhaps the most interesting acquisition from this collection was Julia Hancock Clark's memorandum book, written in one of the leftover red-morocco-leather journal books. Some artifacts not purchased at that time still remain in the hands of Maguire descendants, the most significant being the Missouri Territorial seal.

The artifacts that passed down through other members of the Clark family consisted mainly of personal items such as portraits, guns, furniture, and household items from Clark's later life. Most came to the Missouri Historical Society. However, the locations of some are still unknown. A portrait of a youthful William Clark, a painting that originally belonged to Julia Voorhis, was in the possession of William Clark Adreon, the grandson of Julia Voorhis's brother John O'Fallon Clark, as recently as 1969, if Paul Cutright can be believed. Its current whereabouts are unknown.[28]

The other noteworthy group of documents passed down by Clark consisted of the route maps of the Missouri River. As noted above, most of Clark's route maps made on the expedition passed down to Julia Voorhis and eventually found their way to the Beinecke Library. The twenty-nine maps of the lower Missouri from St. Louis to Fort Mandan were not included in this group. They were originally sent to Jefferson with the shipment from Fort Mandan, but Clark apparently reclaimed them. When Prince Maximilian of Wied-Neuwied arrived in St. Louis on his tour up the Missouri River in 1833, Clark gave all his maps of the Missouri River to his nephew Benjamin O'Fallon for copying. The copies made by O'Fallon or his clerk went to Maximilian, who took them back to Germany. They were later acquired, along with a large collection of Maximilian/Bodmer material, by the Joslyn Art Museum in Omaha, Nebraska. In the meantime, the twenty-nine original maps from the first part of the journey had disappeared. The O'Fallon maps are thus the only surviving copies; however, they cover only the portion of the river from the Platte River to Fort Mandan. The first twelve route maps of the Missouri remain lost.[29]

One isolated but very famous artifact was a pocket compass given by Clark to Captain Robert McCabe, an army man with whom he had dealings in the 1820s. It passed down through the McCabe family to the Smithsonian Institution. It is the only surviving piece of equipment that unquestionably went on the expedition.

ARTIFACTS DISPERSED BY MERIWETHER LEWIS

As seen in Chart 3, the artifacts that passed down through the Lewis family were much fewer and were scattered more widely. A number of the artifacts that remained in the family were from the possessions that Lewis was carrying when he died. Although his official papers were taken by Clark, his personal belongings were returned to his family and seem to have been treasured by them, since so many were passed down through various branches of the family.[30]

Lucy Lewis Marks, Lewis's mother, presided over a blended family. She had two sons (Meriwether and Reuben) and a daughter (Jane) by her first husband and a son (John) and daughter (Mary) by her second husband, John Marks. Artifacts were passed down through both the Lewis and the Marks lines. However, since neither Meriwether nor Reuben had children, all the artifacts on the Lewis side of the family passed down through Jane, whose married name was Anderson.[31]

The main path for Lewis objects was the one that brought the Meriwether Lewis collection to the Missouri Historical Society. In 1934 Dr. Meriwether Lewis Anderson, Jane's great-grandson, stopped in to see the Missouri Historical Society on a visit to St. Louis. Finding the Voorhis collection on display, he decided to will a small but interesting assortment of about thirty-five letters and a number of Lewis artifacts to the Missouri Historical Society. Arriving in 1936, they included Lewis's portrait by Saint-Mémin and his watch, telescope, Masonic apron, and correspondence with his mother.

Other Lewis artifacts are scattered around the country, having passed down through Jane Lewis Anderson's nine children or Mary Marks Moore's eleven. Only a sampling is shown here. Those in private hands include Lewis's commission, a second Saint-Mémin portrait, Lewis's pipe tomahawk, a docu-

CHART 3

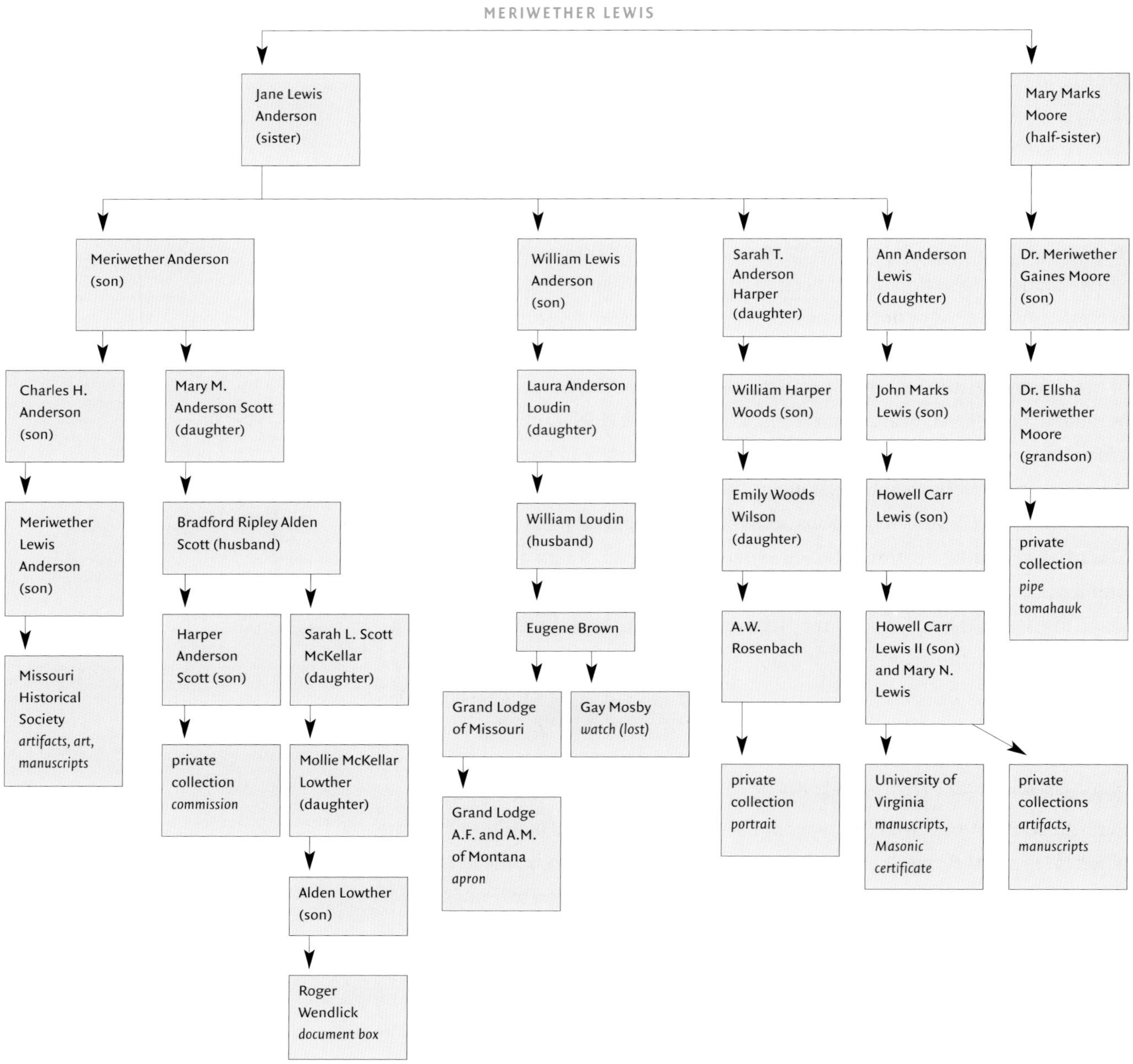

ment box that belonged to Reuben Lewis, and a quilt made by the Lewis-Marks sisters while Meriwether was on the expedition. Isolated artifacts that have come into institutional collections include a second Masonic apron at the Grand Lodge A.F. and A.M. of Helena, Montana, and family letters including a Masonic certificate at the University of Virginia Library.

THE CLARK MUSEUM COLLECTION

One of the enduring mysteries of the Lewis and Clark story is the fate of William Clark's collection of Native American and natural history artifacts.

In 1816 William Clark opened the first museum west of the Mississippi in a building attached to his house on North Main Street in St. Louis. It contained a display of natural history specimens and Indian artifacts and also served as the "Council House" where Clark met with visiting Indian delegations in his capacity as superintendent of Indian affairs for the St. Louis region. An early visitor described the museum as "adorned with a profuse and almost gorgeous display of ornamented and painted buffalo robes, numerous strings of wampum, every variety of work of porcupine quills, skins, horns, claws, and bird skins, numerous and large Calumets, arms of all sorts, saddles, bridles, spears, powder horns, plumes, red blankets and flags." Another visitor praised Clark for his "philosophical taste in the preservation of many subjects of natural history, together with specimens of Indian workmanship, and other objects of curiosity, collected upon the expedition." Over the years Clark added to the collection as his relatives and employees brought back souvenirs, and the museum became an obligatory stop for foreign travelers. From their descriptions, and from an incomplete accession register in which Clark apparently started to keep track of donations, we can get a good sense of this spectacular collection.[32]

The only artifact presently known to survive from Clark's museum is a Mandan calumet that Clark presented to Friedrich Paul Wilhelm, the duke of Württemberg, when they met in the 1820s. It is now at the British Museum.[33] What became of the rest of this collection is a mystery; it seems to have disappeared without a trace. Much speculation has been expended on this question, and Chart 4 shows most of the guesses, some of which are more plausible than others.

In 1838, shortly before Clark's death, a St. Louis newspaper announced that "the scientific portion of [Clark's] well known and valuable collection" was being donated to the Western Academy of Science, an institution that eventually grew into the Academy of Science of St. Louis, whose collections were destroyed in a fire in 1869. Today the St. Louis Science Center, the institutional descendant of the Western Academy of Science, has no Clark material.[34]

In 1837, the ethnographic portion of the collection had been transferred, in whole or part, to the St. Louis Museum, an institution run by the enterprising Albert Koch, a museum impresario and mastodon excavator. The star attraction of Koch's museum was *Missourium theristocaulodon*, the Missouri

CHART 4

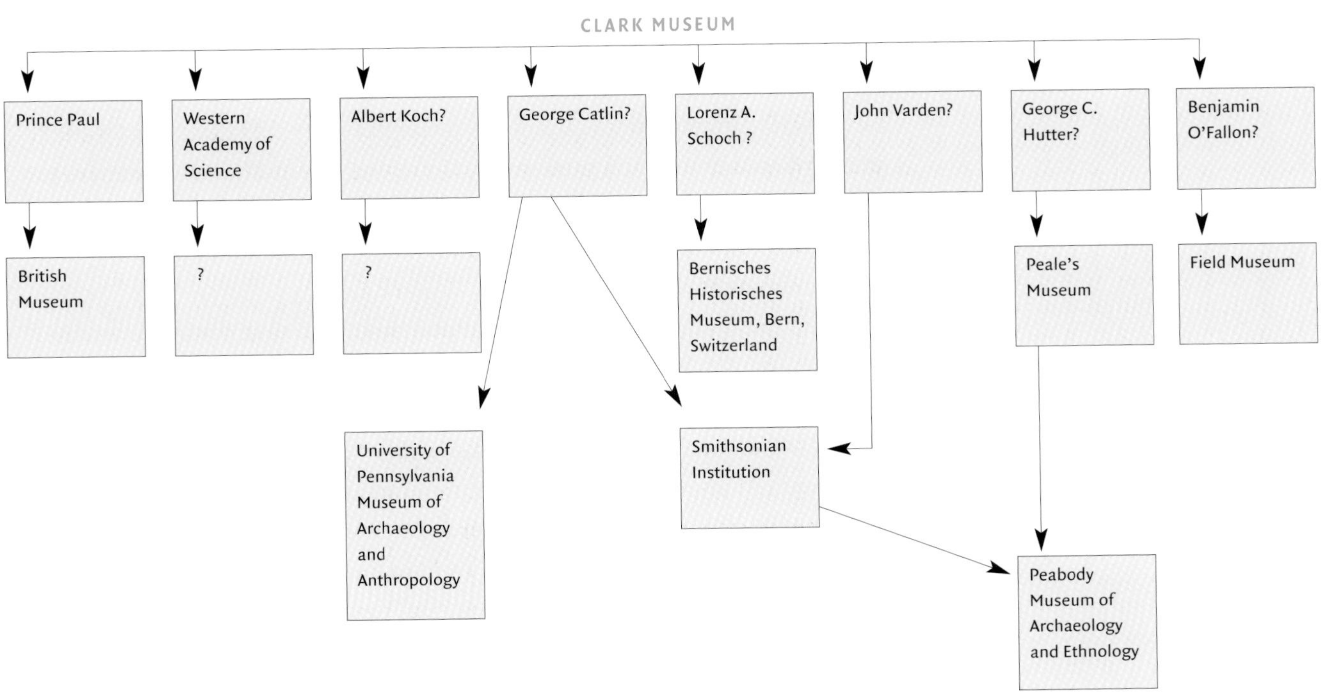

mastodon, a gigantic skeleton excavated and reconstructed (inaccurately, as it turned out) by Koch. It was actually of considerable scientific importance, since it was the first mastodon skeleton found associated with human hunting and butchering tools. But Koch knew his public, and he supplemented this display with attractions such as "Large cosmoramic views of the battle of Austerlitz," wax figures of the Siamese twins and Lord Byron, performances of the "mysterious science of Hindoo Deceology," and live alligators (one of which escaped out a third-floor window in 1838 and fell to its tragic death on Fourth Street). To these attractions he added in 1837 "a large collection of Indian curiosities collected by General Clark," which he received, he explained, "through the liberality and kindness of that gentleman." A Clark family tradition held that Koch subsequently "slipped away from St. Louis, taking the collection with him to England, by the way of New Orleans." This fact, it was noted, "was not discovered in time to recover the articles; but some years later, one of [the] family thought that he identified some of them in London." In fact, Koch's Missouri mastodon skeleton is still on display in the collection of the London Museum of Natural History, but no ethnographic artifacts came with it. Since Koch sold part of his collection to someone named William McPherson before departing St. Louis in 1841, it may be that the Clark family's claim that he had absconded with the artifacts was untrue.[35]

Thomas Donaldson, the late-nineteenth-century collector of Native American artifacts who discovered and rescued the George Catlin collection from near-destruction in a derelict Philadelphia boiler factory, believed that Clark had turned over portions of his collection to Catlin. It was not an implausible idea; Catlin had visited Clark's museum during his St. Louis tenure in 1830–32, had written about it, and may have contributed some paintings to it. He also illustrated some Plains Indian pipe bowls that Clark had given to him (none of which, unfortunately, survive). However, the artifacts that Donaldson focused on were Northwest Coast artifacts—apparently chosen on the assumption that Catlin had not yet been to the Pacific when the collection was made and that Clark had, so the artifacts must have come from Clark. Today we know that Clark was far from the only American to have set foot on the Northwest coast before 1832; there were many other sources Catlin could have tapped for such artifacts. In the absence of any positive evidence that Clark either collected or gave to Catlin many of the things Donaldson ascribed to him, most modern curators discount the theory. However, Donaldson's attributions remain in the catalogs of the University of Pennsylvania Museum, the National Museum of Natural History, and the Peabody Museum and occasionally trap unwary exhibitors into displaying the artifacts as Clark's.[36]

The anthropologist John Ewers added two theories to the hunt for artifacts from the Clark Museum. He was the first to focus suspicion on a breathtaking collection brought to Switzerland in 1842 by an obscure St. Louis shopkeeper named Lorenz Alphons Schoch. Schoch ran a dry-goods store in St. Louis from 1833 to 1842, supplying the American Fur Company, among others. He claimed to have collected his articles from the Shawnee, Delaware, Kansaw, Kickapoo, and Potawatomi he met on a trip to Westport (now in Kansas City) in 1837. This is an implausible story; the artifacts are mostly in the style of upper Missouri tribes: Crow, Blackfeet, Mandan, Hidatsa, Lakota, and Pawnee. Moreover, some of them—including a biographical robe of the famous Mandan leader Mato Tope and a headdress worn by the Pawnee chief La-wee-re-coo-re-shaw-we (The War Chief)—were illustrated by Catlin. One painted shirt bears a striking stylistic resemblance to the buffalo robe, now at the Peabody Museum, attributed to Lewis and Clark or Hutter. The timing of Schoch's acquisition—at exactly the point when Clark's collection was being disassembled—is suspicious, but in the face of Schoch's testimony that he had acquired the artifacts himself, it is impossible to substantiate any connection to Clark.[37]

The other connection proposed by Ewers was to John Varden, the proprietor of the Washington Museum, who on a collecting trip to New Orleans in 1839 acquired two pipe stems "from the old stock of General Clark of St. Louis" and a number of other very early Plains Indian artifacts, several of which are now at the National Museum of Natural History. The fact that these apparently arrived in New Orleans by steamboat, via various hands, implies that the Clark collection was being broken up and scattered.[38]

In the past, speculation has also focused on the George C. Hutter Collection at the Peabody Museum, already discussed above. Hutter's ethnographic collection, assembled in 1825–28, predates both the breakup of the Clark Museum and Hutter's connection by marriage to the Clark family. Although it is possible that Clark may have given the young officer some items from his collection, this theory is impossible to prove.[39]

Several visitors to the Clark Museum mentioned paintings as part of the display there. A number of artists working in St. Louis may have contributed, including George Catlin, Peter Rindisbacher, J. O. Lewis, and Chester Harding. The only intact collection of art that has ever been linked to Clark is a collection of Catlin pieces, now at the Field Museum, which were owned by Clark's nephew Benjamin O'Fallon. If they ever graced the walls of Clark's Museum, it was between 1832, when Catlin painted them, and 1838, when the museum was disassembled.[40]

ARTIFACTS DISPERSED DURING THE EXPEDITION

A particularly fascinating category of artifacts is covered in Chart 5. These are artifacts that were disposed of during the expedition, either given to Indian tribes as diplomatic gifts and trade goods or simply discarded. That some of these items survived is amazing.

The only surviving Indian certificate given out by Lewis and Clark was addressed to a Sioux leader named Warcharpa in 1804. Whether it was sold by him or passed down through many generations of his family is unknown; it eventually came into the collection of Henry E. Huntington and now is at the Huntington Library in San Marino, California.

Five peace medals given out by the expedition have come into institutional collections, but only two can be located today. They are at the Oregon Historical Society and the Nez Perce National Historical Park; the latter one belongs to the Nez Perce Tribe. Another, excavated medal was given to the American Museum of Natural History in New York; it appears in the museum catalog but can no longer be located. The last two were Washington medals passed down in a prominent upper Chinookan family; they were given to the Maryhill Museum but were stolen in 1986. Other peace medals have been reported, but if they exist, they remain in private hands.

Another item is the branding iron with Lewis's name on it. Found on

CHART 5

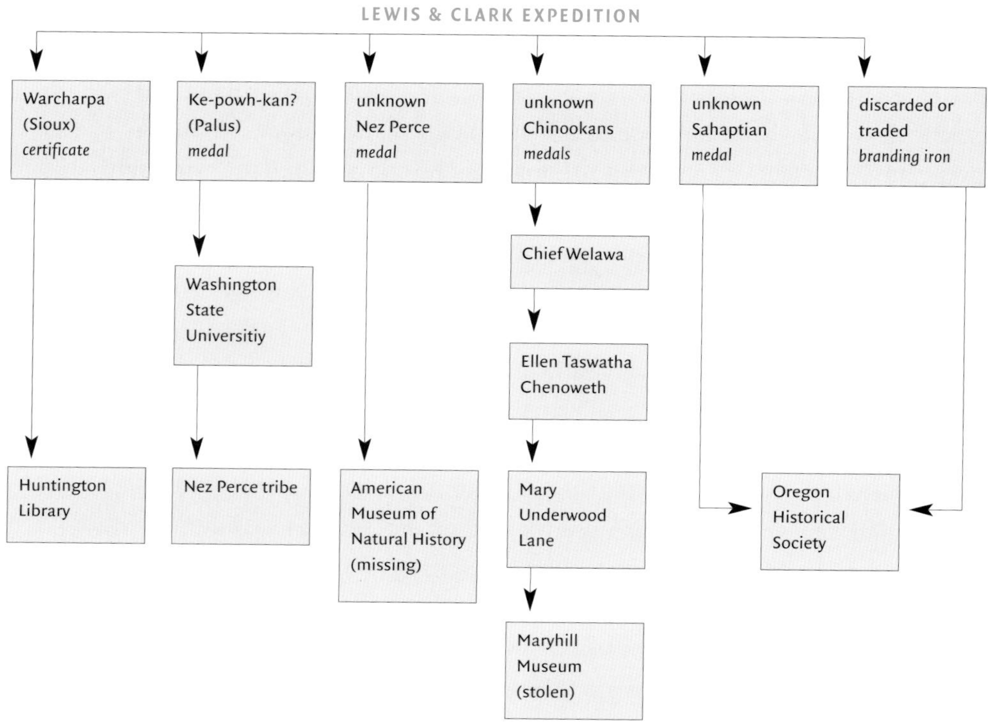

an island in the Columbia River, just above The Dalles, in the early 1890s, it is at the Oregon Historical Society today.

Assorted artifacts and manuscripts related to other expedition members can be found around the country. John Ordway's journal is at the American Philosophical Society; it was purchased by Lewis, given to Nicholas Biddle, and finally sent to the society by Biddle's descendants in 1915. Charles Floyd's journal is at the Wisconsin Historical Society, having been acquired by the nineteenth-century historian and collector Lyman C. Draper, the first secretary of the Wisconsin Historical Society.

Joseph Whitehouse's journal is at the Newberry Library in Chicago. Its story is more circuitous. On his deathbed, Whitehouse gave the journal to an Italian priest, Canon de Vivaldi. In about 1860 Vivaldi deposited it at the New-York Historical Society for safekeeping, before he was transferred to Patagonia. On returning to the United States in 1893, Vivaldi borrowed some money from the husband of a Mrs. Gertrude Haley and gave the Haleys an order on the New-York Historical Society for the journal as collateral. The Haleys collected the journal the next year, and in around 1903 they tried to sell it to the Library of Congress, which balked at their price. However, Reuben Gold Thwaites heard of the journal's existence and persuaded his publisher, Dodd, Mead and Company, to purchase the journal so that he could include it in his edition of the Lewis and Clark journals. After publishing it, Dodd, Mead and Company sold the journal to the manuscript collector Edward Everett Ayer, who gave it to the Newberry Library. Then, in 1966, another copy of the Whitehouse journal, slightly rewritten by someone other than Whitehouse, turned up in a Philadelphia bookstore. Alerted to its existence, the editor Donald Jackson notified the Newberry Library, which purchased the paraphrased copy to add to the original journal already in its collection.[41]

A few artifacts associated with the men have been passed down in their families. A small collection of Patrick Gass's materials, including a hatchet head, razor box, flask, Bible, and account book, is still owned by Gass family members and is on display at the Lewis and Clark Interpretive Center at Fort Canby State Park in Washington. And a sewing kit, or "housewife," owned by George Shannon was given to the Oregon Historical Society by his great-granddaughter.

The histories of other Lewis and Clark artifacts are discussed under the corresponding entries in the following appendix.

Sources for the picture captions are given at the end of the appendix entries. Any information not footnoted is from the records of owning institutions and individuals.

Unless otherwise noted, measurements are given in the form height or length by width by depth, and are in inches.

Numbers and symbols following the credit line indicate an object's unique identification number, as specified by the institution.

INTRODUCTION
The Objects of Our Journey

Yellept's map, 1806

Yellept, William Clark
Ink on paper
7⅝ × 6½
Used by permission, State Historical Society of Missouri, Columbia, Western Historical Manuscript Collection, C1074

This manuscript was purchased in 1928 from a St. Louis rare book dealer, William Clark Breckenridge (no known relation to William Clark). The unclear geographical description that led to the confusion of the Snake and the Willamette is given by Clark on April 29, 1806.
SOURCE: Moulton 1983–2001: 7: 175, 184

Portable desk, pre-1833

American
Mahogany, pine, brass
23 × 36 × 21
General Daniel Bissell House Museum, St. Louis County Parks and Recreation, 1964-125-001a
Gift of the Bissell Family

The date for this artifact is based on Bissell's death. The desk was one of the possessions in the Bissell house at the time the Bissell family donated the property to St. Louis County Parks.
SOURCE: Moulton 1983–2001: 4: 334, 5: 207

Alexander Mackenzie, *Voyages from Montreal, on the River St. Laurence, through the Continent of North America*, 1802

Printed for T. Cadell, Jr., and W. Davies, Strand; Cobbett and Morgan, Pall-Mall; and W. Creech, Edinburgh; by R. Noble, Old-Bailey, London
Ink on paper, bound in brown leather and blue cloth
8 × 5 × 1¼ (each volume, closed)
Photograph courtesy of Lewis & Clark College Library Special Collections, Portland, Oregon
Gift of Roger Wendlick

This is the English octavo edition, which Jefferson tried to get for Lewis from the New York bookseller James Cheetham. He wanted this edition because "The American 8vo edition is defective in it's maps, and the English 4to edition is too large & cumbersome."
SOURCE: Jackson 1978: 56

Books taken on the expedition, 1754–1803

Kelly: Printed for J. Johnson and G. G. and J. Robinson, London; Barton: Printed for the author, Philadelphia; Kirwan: J. Nichols, for P. Elmsly, London; Society of Gentlemen: W. Owen, London; Kelly: ink on paper, bound in cloth; Barton: ink on paper, bound in marbled paper with red leather on spine and corners and gold detailing; Kirwan: ink on paper, bound in leather-covered cardboard with gilding on spine; Society of Gentlemen: ink on paper, bound in marbled cardboard with leather spine
Kelly: 9¾ × 6 × 1¼ (closed); Barton: 10 × 6⅜ × 1⅜ (closed); Kirwan: 8⅜ × 5⅜ × 1¾ (closed); Society of Gentlemen: 9⅛ × 6 × 2⅝ (closed)
Courtesy of the American Philosophical Society, 513.4 K29p, 580 B28h, 549 K63e, 032 N42

The last title is the most speculative; we know only that Lewis and Clark had a four-volume "Deckinsery of arts an ciences" (Clark), which is the title that appears, spelled correctly, on the spine of this book. Ephraim Chambers's *Cyclopedia: or, An Universal Dictionary of Arts and Science* (1786) has also been suggested. The Barton copy shown here was donated to the American Philosophical Society by the author but has been rebound.
SOURCE: Jackson 1959

Le Page du Pratz, *The History of Louisiana*, 1774

Printed for T. Becket, London
Ink on paper, bound in marbled cardboard and leather
8½ × 5½ × 1¼ (closed)
The Library Company of Philadelphia, Am 1774 LeP2478.0

The binding is from the late nineteenth or early twentieth century.
SOURCE: Cutright 1964; Jackson 1978: 695

John Ordway journal, 1804–6

John Ordway
Ink on paper, bound in cardboard with leather spine and corners; volume 3 unbound
Vol. 1: 8½ × 7 (closed); vol. 2: 6⅞ × 4 (closed); vol. 3: 7½ × 4¼ (closed)
Courtesy of the American Philosophical Society, 917.3 Or2 v.1-3
Gift of Edward and Charles Biddle, 1915

Volume 1 opens on the side; the other two hinge at the top. Volume 2 is written in one of the marbled notebooks also used by the captains.
SOURCES: Jackson 1978: 232, 462; Moulton 1983–2001: 2: 513–14

History of the Expedition under the Command of Captains Lewis and Clark, 1814

Bradford and Inskeep, Philadelphia
Ink on paper, bound in leather
8⅞ × 5½ × 1¾ (closed)
Missouri Historical Society, St. Louis, #1 917.8 L58 a3
Gift of Meriwether Lewis Anderson, 1936

SOURCE: Cutright 1976: 53–67

River Bluffs, 1,320 Miles above St. Louis, 1832

George Catlin
Oil on canvas
11¼ × 14½
Smithsonian American Art Museum, 1985.66.399
Gift of Mrs. Joseph Harrison, Jr.

SOURCE: Catlin 1995: 2: 9

Peace medal, 1801

U.S. Mint, Philadelphia
Silver
DIAM 2⅛
Nez Perce Tribal Committee

According to Roderick Sprague, who conducted the excavation in which this medal was found: "It was found in a canoe burial of a young adult male *probably* of the Palus tribe, buried sometime *after* 1890. The site, dating from about 1875 to 1910, is a historic period Palus Indian burial ground located at the confluence of the Palouse and Snake Rivers in eastern Washington." Sprague said that the burial site he excavated was "located at Lyons Ferry," now a state park. He added: "The excavation was conducted by the Department of Anthropology, Washington State University. . . . The excavation was supported by the U.S. Army Corps of Engineers, Walla Walla District."

The ethnographer George Gibbs met Wattai-wattai-how-lis, a Palus chief, wearing a Jefferson medal at the same site in 1854. That medal was said to have been presented to Ke-powh-kan, the father of the owner.

This medal is presently on loan to Nez Perce National Historical Park, Spaulding, Idaho, where it is cataloged as No. 8900.
SOURCES: Sprague to Paul A. Ewald, October 18, 1967, State Historical Society of North Dakota; Gibbs 1855: 403; Cutright 1968: 164–65; Moulton 1983–2001: 5: 226

Pipe, c. 1800–50

Eastern Plains or Western Great Lakes
Stem: wood, dyed and undyed porcupine quills, yarn, dyed horsehair, silk ribbon, sinew, bast fiber cord, warp-faced plain woven wool tape, glass beads; bowl: unidentified stone
Stem: 35¼ × 1⅛; bowl: 3⅜ × 2¾
Photograph from the Peabody Museum of Archaeology and Ethnology, Harvard University, © President and Fellows of Harvard College, photograph by Hillel Burger, cat. 99-12-10/53109.1 (bowl) and .2 (stem), neg. T3864.1
Gift of the Heirs of David Kimball, 1899

The Peale's Museum collection included pipes from many sources, making it impossible to trace this one to a particular donor. Many of the pipes that Lewis and Clark donated to Peale's Museum came from Mississippi Valley tribes such as the Winnebago, Sauk, Iowa, and Fox. Castle McLaughlin suggests that some of the pipes may have been gifts from various Indian delegations to Washington, D.C., including delegations organized by Lewis and Clark.
SOURCES: Catlin 1995: 1: 130–31, 264, 265; Paper 1988: 73; McLaughlin 2003: chapter 8; Jackson 1978: 478

Blunderbuss, 1809–10

Thomas French, Canton, Mass.
Walnut, iron, brass
37 × 11½ (with swivel); BARREL LENGTH 32
Courtesy of the National Museum of American History, Smithsonian Institution, acc. 58284, cat. AF*287117
Gift of Washington Navy Yard, 1915

SOURCES: Moulton 1983–2001: 4: 215, 218, 334, 335, 8: 369, 9: 68; Russell 1967: 45–46

Trade goods, 1800s

British and American
Rings: copper; beads: glass; hair pipes: bone
Rings: DIAM ⅝ to ¾; beads: LENGTH 10 to 19 (strand); hair pipes: LENGTH 2 to 4¾
Courtesy of the Department of Anthropology, National Museum of Natural History, Smithsonian Institution, E#395574, E#1932 and E#1934, E#115695
Gift of Catholic University of America, 1956 (rings); gift of G. K. Warren, 1866 (beads); gift of Mrs. E. A. Smith (hair pipes)

The most common metal for rings was brass, a fact that Clark noted when he saw a Mandan chief wearing "14 ring of Brass on his fingers, this metal the Mandans ar verry fond off." However, Lewis and Clark listed at least some of their own rings as made of silver. These rings were collected by Chaplain E. W. J. Lindesmith or Rev. John M. Cooper at Fort Keogh, Montana, in 1907.

These beads were collected by G. K. Warren when he was mapping the trans-Mississippi West for the Corps of Topographical Engineers from 1854 to 1858.

It is possible that Lewis used "hair pipe" to refer to silver tubes rather than shell or bone ones; he never specified. For an example of bone hair pipes in use in the 1830s, see Karl Bodmer's portrait of Makuie-Poka (Blackfeet).

SOURCES: On rings, see Moulton 1983–2001: 3: 253, 500; Hanson 1982. On the beads, see Woodward 1979: 37; Garraty and Carnes 1999: 22: 715. On hair pipes, see Jackson 1978: 177; Moulton 1983–2001: 3: 500; Ewers 1957; Ewers et al. 1984: 99; Chronister 1999; Goetzmann et al. 1984: 257.

Socks, early 1800s

American
Knitted linen
20 × 8
Courtesy of the National Museum of American History, Smithsonian Institution, acc. 28810, cat. CS*6686A
Gift of John Brenton Copp
SOURCE: Moulton 1983–2001: 11: 318

Carpentry tools, early 1800s

American
Hand saw: sheet iron, wood, brass; felling ax: steel-reinforced iron, wood; shingling hatchet: steel-reinforced iron, wood; cut nails: iron
Hand saw: 30¾ × 7 × 1¼; felling ax: 30¼ × 7¼ × ⅞; shingling hatchet: 10⅛ × 5¼ × 1; cut nails: LENGTH 2 to 3
Collection of the Mercer Museum of the Bucks County Historical Society, 8995, 740, 5039, IN262050-2-04
Gift of Henry C. Mercer
SOURCE: Jackson 1978: 83–84, 101

Fiddle, 1795–1811

James Banks
Spruce, maple, stained beech, ebony
23¼ × 7⅛ × 3½
Colonial Williamsburg Foundation, 1953-950,A

SOURCES: Moulton 1983–2001: 5: 306, 335–36, 7: 127, 9: 107, 11: 114; Hunt 1988: 11–14

A Snow Landscape with Buffalo, 1854

George Catlin
Oil on canvas
19 × 26½
From the Collection of Gilcrease Museum, Tulsa, Oklahoma, 0176.2169 (561)

SOURCES: Moulton 1983–2001: 3: 254, 271; Troccoli 1993: 110

CHAPTER I
Imagining America

Thomas Jefferson (detail), 1805

Rembrandt Peale
Oil on canvas
28 × 23¾
Collection of The New-York Historical Society, cat. 1867.306, neg. 6003
Gift of Thomas J. Bryan

This portrait remained in Peale's Museum until the collection was sold in 1854. Thomas J. Bryan then purchased the portrait and presented it to the New-York Historical Society in 1866. It was the second portrait of Jefferson painted by Rembrandt Peale; the other one was done for his first election in 1800 and is now at the White House in Washington, D.C.

SOURCES: Moulton 1983–2001: 5: 7; Bush 1962: 68–70, fig. 18; Adams 1976: 194, fig. 338

Sculpture of a human figure, prehistoric

Plateau
Basalt
34 × 10 × 4
Maryhill Museum of Art, Goldendale, Washington, LR-09

A very similar stone figure with upraised arms was recovered in archaeological digs by Emory Strong at Celilo Falls.

SOURCE: Strong 1959: 31

Bust of Thomas Jefferson, 1789

Jean-Antoine Houdon
Plaster
29 × 21 × 13
Courtesy of the American Philosophical Society, 58.S.22
Gift of Elizabeth Rittenhouse Sergeant, from the estate of her father, David Rittenhouse, 1811

Rittenhouse died in 1796, so the cast must have been made before that date. It may have been one of those purchased by Jefferson from Houdon in 1789. A marble copy, created from the terra-cotta original, is in the Boston Museum of Fine Arts. Other plasters are at the New-York Historical Society, at the Musée de Blérancourt, and at Monticello.

SOURCES: Stein 1993: 174, 230 (where this copy is incorrectly dated); American Philosophical Society 1961: 52–53

Theodolite of Thomas Jefferson, 1778

Jesse Ramsden, London
Theodolite: brass and copper; tripod: mahogany and brass
Theodolite: 14 × 7¾, DIAM 6¾; tripod: HEIGHT 45½
Monticello/Thomas Jefferson Foundation, Inc., Charlottesville, Virginia,1952-67-1/3
Gift of Mrs. Milton Elliott, 1967

Jefferson is believed to have purchased this theodolite in January 1778 from the mathematician Robert Andrews. He used it for taking astronomical observations and for mapping around Monticello.

SOURCES: Jackson 1978: 21, 48, 49, 69, 75; Stein 1993: 356–57; Adams 1976: 361

George Vancouver, *A Voyage of Discovery to the North Pacific Ocean, and Round the World*, 1798 and Lewis's tracing from Vancouver's map, 1803

Vancouver's book: G. G. and J. Robinson and J. Edwards, London; Lewis's tracing: Meriwether Lewis
Vancouver's book: Ink on paper bound in marbled cardboard with leather spine; Lewis's tracing: Ink on tracing paper
Vancouver's book: 32¾ × 35½ (with Plate 3 unfolded);
Lewis's tracing: 18⅜ × 15
Vancouver's book: Missouri Historical Society, St. Louis, *910.4 V279; Lewis's tracing: Missouri Historical Society, St. Louis, William Clark Papers
Gift of Julia Clark Voorhis in memory of Eleanor Glasgow Voorhis (Lewis's tracing)

Jackson was unable to locate Lewis's tracing. It was discovered in Clark's papers during research for this volume.

SOURCE: Jackson 1978: 12, 53

Aaron Arrowsmith, *A Map Exhibiting all the New Discoveries in the Interior Parts of North America*, 1802

Aaron Arrowsmith, London
Ink and watercolor on paper with linen backing
50 × 58¼
Collection of Roger D. Wendlick

SOURCES: Allen 1975: 79, 82; Jackson 1978: 28, 56; Moulton 1983–2001: 4: 266

Nicholas King, map of western North America, 1803

Ink and wash on paper
20½ × 31
Library of Congress, G4126 .S12 .1803 .K5 VAULT
Transferred from Office of Indian Affairs, Interior Department, 1925

Another source for this map was "the manuscript transcribed from Mr. [Edward] Thornton's map by Cap. Lewis," that is, a sketch of the northernmost bend of the Missouri from the surveys of David Thompson. Lewis's copy from Thompson's map is now at the Library of Congress.

SOURCES: Allen 1975: 97–103; Wheat 1958: 2: map 239; Moulton 1983–2001: 1: 5, map 2; Jackson 1978: 28, 32

Animals, plants, and people of Louisiana, 1758

Artist unknown; published by Chez de Bure, l'Aine; La Veuve Delaguette; et Lambert, Paris
Ink on paper
7 × 4¼
Missouri Historical Society, St. Louis

SOURCES: Du Pratz 1758: 1: opp. p. 107; 2: opp. p. 60, 67; Allen 1975: 96, 114; Prown et al. 1992: 44

Jonathan Carver, *Travels through the Interior Parts of North America in the Years 1766, 1767, and 1768*, 1781

Printed for C. Dilly, H. Payne, and J. Phillips, London
Ink and watercolor on paper, bound in cloth and leather
8¾ × 5½ × 2 (closed)
Library of Congress, F597 .C35

SOURCE: Allen 1975: 15, 26

Lewis's estimate of expenses, 1803

Ink on paper
8⅛ × 7¾
Library of Congress, Thomas Jefferson Papers
SOURCE: Jackson 1978: 8–9, 428, 431n

Patent chamber lamp, early 1800s

British or American
Tinned sheet metal, glass
4¼ × 6
Courtesy of the National Museum of American History, Smithsonian Institution, acc. 136485, cat. DL*376512
Gift of Mrs. Virginia W. Hillyer, 1935

SOURCES: Jackson 1978: 72, 79; Nolan 1991

Set of dental tools, mid-1800s

Horatio G. Kern, Philadelphia
Instruments: steel, tortoise shell, brass, wood; case: leather, silk
Case: 8⅜ × 9⅞ (open)
Courtesy of the National Museum of Dentistry, Baltimore, Maryland, 92.1.7134.001-015
Purchased as part of the Fairleigh Dickinson University School of Dentistry Collection

This is not a matched set; only a few have Kern's mark on them. Kern was a maker of surgical and dental instru-

ments after 1837; however, the designs had not changed markedly from the first decades of the century.
SOURCES: Jackson 1978: 80; Edmondson 1993: 61

Summary of purchases, 1803

Israel Whelen or Thomas Biggs
Ink on paper
12⅝ × 7⅞
National Archives, Washington, D.C., RG 92, Records of the Office of the Quartermaster General, Consolidated Correspondence File, Lewis and Clark (Entry 225)

SOURCE: Jackson 1978: 93–97

Trade kettle, early 1800s

British
Copper, iron
5½ × 8
State Historical Society of North Dakota, 14629-B. Photograph by Sharon Silengo

SOURCES: Jackson 1978: 75, 85, 94, 95; Gilman 1982: 14. The note on Indian goods is misdated as 1803 in Jackson; the watermark on the paper is 1804, meaning that the note was written after the expedition.

Wampum, c. 1800–50

Eastern Woodlands, Western Great Lakes
Marine shell
44⅛
Photograph from the Peabody Museum of Archaeology and Ethnology, Harvard University, © President and Fellows of Harvard College, photograph by Hillel Burger, cat. 99-12-10/53014, neg. T3856.1
Gift of the Heirs of David Kimball, 1899

Peale cataloged Lewis and Clark's donation as "Wampum, of various discriptions, indicating Peace, War, Choice of either, Hostilities commencing, and a disposition for them to ceace &c. From different nations," implying that it was woven in belts. The wampum was one of the last trade goods Lewis and Clark still had on their return journey, probably because it was not much valued. They also used it among the Wallawalla, to whom they "gave Strings of wompom . . . in remembrance of what we Said." This implies the wampum on the expedition was in strands. This is one of several strands in the Boston Museum collection; there is no information on their origin.
SOURCES: Jackson 1978: 72, 477; Moulton 1983–2001: 5: 296, 7: 341; Catlin 1995: 1: 251n; Woodward 1979: 23–31; Trigger 1978: 166, 217, 422–23; McLaughlin 2003: chapter 9

View of Several Public Buildings, in Philadelphia, 1790

James Trenchard, probably after Charles Willson Peale
Engraving on paper
4½ × 8
The Library Company of Philadelphia, 1525.F.39d

The Long Room, Interior of Front Room in Peale's Museum, 1822

Charles Willson Peale and Titian Ramsay Peale
Ink and watercolor on paper
14 × 20¼
Detroit Institute of Arts, 57.261
Founder's Society Purchase from Edward Eberstadt and Sons, New York, Director's Discretionary Fund, 1957

Inscribed on the back is, "Interior of front room/Peale's Museum/State House/Philadelphia/1822/by T.R. Peale." This sketch served as a preliminary background for the famous portrait of Peale in his museum. Edgar Richardson calls it "the best visual document of the contents and arrangement of the museum."
SOURCE: Richardson, Hindle, and Miller 1983: 82, 249

Rifle, c. 1792

Made by George F. Fainot[?]
Maple, iron, brass
57 × 6½,
BARREL LENGTH 41½
Private Collection

The legend that Lewis procured prototypes of the Model 1803 rifles from Harper's Ferry originated with Carl P. Russell. However, on April 20, 1803, Lewis wrote, "My Rifles . . . are preparing at Harper's Ferry, and are already in a state of forwardness." The first letter proposing the manufacture of the Model 1803 (from Henry Dearborn to Joseph Perkins) was written on May 25, 1803. The pattern rifle was not produced until that fall, and it was approved on December 2. George Moller concludes that the expedition's rifles "were previously manufactured rifles on hand." When Harper's Ferry Armory opened in 1801, it had 382 rifles on hand, possibly a mix of Revolutionary War guns and 1792 U.S. contract rifles. Frank Tait argues that Lewis's rifles were from a batch of contract rifles originally allocated to the Virginia militia for use in the Whiskey Rebellion and stored in the arsenal at New London, Virginia, till 1801, when they were transferred to Harper's Ferry.

This rifle matches the specifications for the 1792 contract: caliber ranging from .45 to .49 (this one is .49, or 40 balls to the pound); spring-opened patchbox with button release; maple stock. Some second-issue rifles were stamped with "U.S." The patchbox on this rifle still has conical bullets inside.
SOURCES: Moller 1993: 2: 19–30, 336–37; Tait 1999a, 1999b; Tait, private communication; Jackson 1978: 40; Moulton 1983–2001: 6: 441. See also Flayderman 1990: 428–29; Madaus 1981: 73–74; Brown 1968: 131–32.

Swivel gun, mid- to late 1700s

British
Iron
32½ × 15, DIAM 8½
Collection of the Fort Ticonderoga Museum, 1999.1302

SOURCES: Moulton 1983–2001: 2: 264n, 8: 303–4, 9: 68; Peterson 1968; Russell 1967; Gilkerson 1993: 51–76

Pocket pistols, late 1700s

French
Walnut, iron, steel, silver
10 × 5¼
Courtesy of the National Museum of American History, Smithsonian Institution, acc. 164974, cat. 43545a, b
Gift of Ralph G. Packard, 1943

The notation "P. by L." on the listing for the pocket pistols may mean that Lewis purchased them for himself.
SOURCES: Jackson 1978: 91, 97. For more information on Robert Barnhill, see Kauffman 1960: 179. On pocket pistols, see Miller 1978: 50–63; Wilkinson 1968: 52–54.

Jefferson's instructions, 1803

Ink on paper
9⅝ × 7½ (p. 1), 9¾ × 8⅛ (p. 2)
Library of Congress, Thomas Jefferson Papers

SOURCE: Jackson 1978: 61–66

Letter from Lewis, inviting Clark to join the expedition, 1803

Ink on paper
10 × 8¼ (closed); 10 × 16½ (open)
Missouri Historical Society, St. Louis, William Clark Papers
Gift of Julia Clark Voorhis in memory of Eleanor Glasgow Voorhis

SOURCES: Jackson 1978: 57–60; Duncan and Burns 1997: 119

South East Corner of Third, and Market Streets. Philadelphia, 1799

William and Thomas Birch
Engraving and watercolor on paper
12¾ × 15⅜
The Library Company of Philadelphia, Sn 8/p.2276.14

SOURCES: Jackson 1978: 78–92; Teitelman 1983: pl. 8

Miniature of George Rogers Clark, 1832

George Catlin, after John Wesley Jarvis
Oil on ivory
4⅛ × 3⅞
Missouri Historical Society, St. Louis, 1923 035 0001
Gift of Julia Clark Voorhis in memory of Eleanor Glasgow Voorhis, 1923

A full-size copy, by Matthew Harris Jouett, of the same portrait is now at the Filson Historical Society. This miniature passed down to Meriwether Lewis Clark.
SOURCES: Holmberg 2002: 24, 39; Bakeless 1957: 67–83, 307–10; Lyman Draper interview of Meriwether Lewis Clark, November 25–26, 1868, Draper Papers, Wisconsin Historical Society

Rifle of William Clark, c. 1780–1821

John Small, Vincennes, Indiana
Walnut, iron, silver, silver plate, tooth or bone
53¾ × 8½
Missouri Historical Society, St. Louis, 1923 050 0016
Gift of Julia Clark Voorhis in memory of Eleanor Glasgow Voorhis, 1923

This rifle, which came to the Missouri Historical Society along with the expedition journals and others of Clark's belongings, is probably one of the two undescribed "rifle guns" or the "hunting rifle" on the inventory of Clark's estate at his death. Carl Russell states that it is "obviously of the post-expedition period" but gives no details on why. It bears many stylistic similarities to a John Small gun made around 1800, illustrated in Lindsay 1972. Small lived in Vincennes from about 1780 to his death in 1821 or 1823 and held a number of public posts, including representative to the Indiana Territorial Legislature (1799).

The rifle has a puzzling mix of early and late characteristics, including a hook breech (late) and silver inlays with Revolutionary War iconography on the barrel and the stock (early in style). Its octagonal barrel (37¼″) attaches to the forestock with a pin. It has two sights: the rear one is bone or tooth; the front one is silver, blade-style. The walnut half-stock has curvilinear carving at the end of the forestock and checkering on the wrist. The wooden ramrod runs through three octagonal brass thimbles attached to the underside of the barrel and one attached to the stock. The front end of the half-stock is finished with a brass band that does not extend around the barrel. There is one trigger with a safety catch. Behind the engraved trigger guard, on the bot-

tom side of the buttstock, is a silver inlay with a hole in the center to hold a pick for cleaning the vent.
SOURCES: On Small, see Day 1988: 25; Lindsay 1972: no. 54; Lindert 1968: 147–48; Gill 1974: 101; Sellers 1983: 282. On iconography, see Olson 1991: fig. 50. On Clark's gun, see Moulton 1983–2001: 6: 121, 7: 95. On this rifle, see Russell 1967: 38.

Receipts for purchases, 1803

Clockwise from top left: George Lawton, Beck & Harvey, Thomas Passmore, Matilda Chapman, George Ludlam, François Baillet
Ink on paper
Lawton: 10¼ × 8¼; Beck & Harvey: 6⅝ × 7¾; Passmore: 8¼ × 8; Chapman: 4¼ × 7⅞; Ludlam: 3⅝ × 7¾; Baillet: 6¼ × 7⅞
National Archives, Washington, D.C., RG 92, Records of the Office of the Quartermaster General, Consolidated Correspondence File, Lewis and Clark (Entry 225)

SOURCE: Jackson 1978: 78–92

Meriwether Lewis, c. 1803

Charles Balthazar Julien Févret de Saint-Mémin
Chalk on wove paper, mounted on wooden stretcher
24½ × 18½ (unframed); 26¼ × 20¼ (framed)
Missouri Historical Society, St. Louis, 1936 030 0001
Gift of Meriwether Lewis Anderson, 1936

After Lucy Lewis Marks's death, this portrait went to her daughter Jane, who married Edmund Anderson. Their great-grandson donated it to the Missouri Historical Society. It is not known whether this is the first or second portrait completed by Saint-Mémin. Donald Jackson believed it was painted in either 1802 (Philadelphia) or 1803 (Baltimore). Ellen Miles, of the National Portrait Gallery, argues—on stylistic grounds—that it was done with the Indian portraits (and Clark's) in 1807. Arlen Large votes for 1803 on the basis of Lewis's haircut. I have used 1803 because a tracing of Saint-Mémin's etching from this portrait (now at Monticello) is dated "Juin 1803." Copies of Saint-Mémin's etching are at the National Portrait Gallery, the Corcoran Gallery, Bibliothèque Nationale de France, and the Massachusetts Historical Society. The copper plate was destroyed in a fire at Locust Hill in about 1837. The frame shown here is a reproduction of the original frame.
SOURCES: Jackson 1978: 678; Miles 1994: 140–41, 339; Large 1997. See also Adams 1976: 74, 361; Norfleet 1942: 77, 183; Dexter 1862: no. 420; Valentine Museum 1941: 19 (no. 16), 27 (pl. 7); Fischer and Kelly 1993: 190–91; Wheeler 1904: 1: 31

Telescope of Meriwether Lewis, c. 1800

William Cary, London
Caribbean mahogany, brass, iron, leather, glass
58¼ × 3¼ (extended); 15 × 3¼ (collapsed)
Missouri Historical Society, St. Louis, 1936 030 0004
Gift of Meriwether Lewis Anderson, 1936

This telescope was passed down in the family of Jane Lewis Anderson, Meriwether's sister. In 1904 it belonged to C. H. Anderson of Ivy Depot, Virginia (the grandson of Jane Lewis Anderson and the father of the donor), who told Olin Wheeler that it was used on the expedition. No telescope is listed in purchases for the expedition, but the lists include only government supplies, not Lewis's personal property. At Fort Mandan, when observing a lunar eclipse, Lewis explicitly stated that he had no astronomical telescope and needed to use the telescopic sight on his sextant. This telescope would not have been useful for night observations because the extra lens needed to prevent the image from showing upside down (as in astronomical telescopes) cut down the light-gathering capacity so much.

The first brass section is engraved "Cary London." William Cary (1759–1825) was a pupil of Jesse Ramsden, who had his own business on the Strand in London from 1790 to 1825 and was particularly known for his microscopes. The leather cover on the largest tube is tanned with a vegetable tannin, probably oak or chestnut gall, leaves, or bark, and has very faint incised letters in its surface spelling "ANDERSON." On the tube edge are wear marks and three clumps of solder where something was once attached, possibly a stand clamp or annulus for fastening the instrument to a tripod.
SOURCES: Wheeler 1904: 1: 45; Adams 1976: 78, 362; Moulton 1983–2001: 3: 273, 5: 68, 70, 8: 113, 128. On Cary, see Taylor 1966: 306; *Dictionary of National Biography* 1887: 9: 253. On telescopes, see Warner 1998. See also Gilman 1999.

Watch of Meriwether Lewis, 1796–97

English. Case by Peter Desvignes, London
Silver, enamel watch face, glass, iron, copper alloy, watercolor on laid rag paper
3½ × 2¼ × ¾
Missouri Historical Society, St. Louis, 1936 030 0005
Gift of Meriwether Lewis Anderson, 1936

The date is based on the hallmarks on the case, which belong to Peter Desvignes, a London case-maker listed in 1792 at 221 Piccadilly and in 1796 and 1797 at 13 Denmark St. The date of the assay is 1796–97. Lewis also had work done on Jefferson's watch in Philadelphia, but the cleaning of the "Silver Secont Watch" was charged to the expedition account, suggesting it was his.

Lewis may have had two watches with him when he died. One, described as "One horizontal silver Watch," was received in Washington, D.C., and returned by Isaac A. Coles to Lewis's family in Albemarle County. Apparently another ended up in the possession of James Neelly along with Lewis's rifle, brace of pistols, dirk, and tomahawk. The rifle and pistols were not forwarded to Washington along with the rest of Lewis's effects; possibly the watch remained with them, since a scrap of paper in the Lewis-Marks Papers relating to Lewis's estate says, "Major James Neely former agent of the Chickessaw Nation has M.W. Lewis' gold watch and pistols." A Clark family story related: "Years later, Meriwether's sister and her husband unexpectedly met Pernia [John Pernier, Lewis's servant] on the streets of Mobile, wearing the Governor's watch, which had been presented to him by William Wirt as a testimonial from Congress, and carrying his gun. When accused, he immediately returned these articles to them."

The early date (1796) on this watch argues against the possibility that it is the presentation watch. However, another watch was passed down to Jane Lewis Anderson's son William Lewis Anderson, who gave it to his daughter Laura Lewis Anderson Loudin, whose husband, William Loudin, inherited it in 1905 and then gave it to Eugene Brown of Upshur County, West Virginia, in 1925. It was described as "a double caser open faced silver watch, made by R. T. Raskill, Liverpool, No. 3211, second hand making complete revolution every fifteen seconds. Hours are marked by figures and small circle for second hand marked off into fifteen spaces for seconds. This watch seems to have had a stop watch attachment. The watch has always kept good time. The outer case has a steel spring riveted on to keep case on." Its present location is unknown.

The watch shown here was probably either the horizontal watch (although this term suggests a chronometer) or a third one that Lewis did not have with him at his death, possibly because it had ceased to work. The provenance chain for this one is Jane Lewis Anderson to her son Meriwether Anderson to his son Charles H. Anderson, to his son M. L. Anderson to the Missouri Historical Society. Its hour hand is missing, and the crystal is a replacement.
SOURCES: Jackson 1978: 52, 53n, 91, 468, 471, 488; Moulton 1983–2001: 4: 65, 6: 165; David Blanchfield conservation report, October 9, 1998, at the Missouri Historical Society; affidavit of William Loudin, April 20, 1925, in Grand Lodge A.F. & A.M. of Montana, Helena; Lewis-Marks Collection, Special Collections, University of Virginia Library; Kennerly and Russell 1948: 27. On the touchmarks, see Inglis and Negus 1980: 26.

Newfoundland Dog, 1803

John Scott, engraver; Phillip Reinagle, artist
Engraving on paper
Image: 5¾ × 7¾
Ewell Sale Stewart Library, The Academy of Natural Sciences of Philadelphia

SOURCES: Taplin 1803; Moulton 1983–2001: 2: 79, 5: 112, 8: 110; Byron 1933: 154; Osgood and Jackson 1997; Charbonneau 1989. On the possible fate of Seaman, see Holmberg 2000. On Reinagle and Scott, see Turner 1996: 8: 65, 26: 124.

Commission of Meriwether Lewis, 1802

Printed by U.S. Army, signed by Thomas Jefferson
Ink on paper
18½ × 15½
Private Collection

The commission was passed down in the Lewis family from Jane Lewis Anderson to her son Meriwether Lewis Anderson I to his daughter Mary Miller Anderson and her husband, Bradford Ripley Alden Scott (1851–1925), who was born in Virginia and died in San Antonio, Texas. It was passed on to his son Dr. Harper Anderson Scott (1891–1975) of Austin, Texas, in 1925. His daughter owns it today.

SOURCES: Ambrose 1996: 50, 61; correspondence with Lewis family members

William Clark, c. 1810

Attributed to John Wesley Jarvis
Oil on canvas
29¾ × 25⅛
Missouri Historical Society, St. Louis, 1921 055 0001
Gift of Julia Clark Voorhis in memory of Eleanor Glasgow Voorhis, 1921

This portrait passed from Clark to his son George Rogers Hancock Clark, to his daughter Julia Clark Voorhis, to the Missouri Historical Society. Clark's nephew William Clark Kennerly and his granddaughter Julia Clark Voorhis both believed it was painted by Gilbert Stuart, but Stuart experts consulted are skeptical, partly on stylistic grounds and partly because the canvas is not the twill weave that Stuart preferred. The origin of the Stuart attribution may have been John O'Fallon Clark, William's son, who wrote Lyman Draper in 1867 about a portrait by either John Wesley Jarvis or Stuart who "traveled through Kentucky many years ago." Jarvis was the only one of the two to travel through Kentucky.

A hypothesis that it was painted by Jarvis, who painted both Clark's wife and other members of the Clark family, is supported by the fact that a portrait by Jarvis was listed in the inventory of William Clark's estate. It cannot be confidently identified with this portrait.

In 1905 Reuben Gold Thwaites published what appears to be a copy of this portrait (lacking the drapery in the background) belonging to Julia Clark Voorhis and identified it as the work of Chester Harding, who arrived in St. Louis in 1820. John F. McDermott also attributed to Harding a much less skillful copy now at the Missouri Historical Society, basing his identification on an engraving by J. O. Lewis published with the caption, "His Excellency William Clark . . . Hardin, Pixt." This attribution is doubtful. Harding's best-documented portrait of Clark, now at the Mercantile Library in St. Louis, is a full-length life-size painting showing him as a white-haired elder statesman; the portrait shown here appears to predate that one by a decade or more.

Missouri Historical Society files include photographs of at least two more copies of this portrait. One copy was published in Kennerly and Russell 1948: 75 and remained in the Russell family; the other is unlocated.

Other portraits of Clark include the one by Charles Willson Peale at Independence National Historical Park; one by Joseph Bush at the Filson Historical Society; one by George Catlin at the National Portrait Gallery; an anonymous primitive portrait of an elderly Clark in uniform at the Missouri Historical Society; and the Chester Harding portrait at the Mercantile Library. Charles B. J. F. de Saint-Mémin did a profile portrait of Clark in 1807; copies of the etching are at the National Portrait Gallery, the Corcoran Gallery, and Bibliothèque Nationale de France. Another copy, possibly the chalk original, surfaced briefly in 1936, in the hands of M. Russell, New York City, and has since disappeared. The only portrait of Clark painted before the expedition shows him wearing civilian clothing and holding a cane. Two copies were apparently owned by the Voorhis family, and only photographs of them have been found; one was published in *Century Magazine* in October 1904; the other is in Missouri Historical Society photo files and notes that the portrait (apparently a copy of the *Century Magazine* portrait) was owned by Mrs. William M. Bynie in 1954. She obtained it from the Voorhis estate.

SOURCES: Experts consulted include Ellen Miles, National Portrait Gallery; Dorinda Evans, Emory University; and Marti Radecki, Indianapolis Museum of Art. For the Stuart attribution, see William Glasgow Clark to Nettie Beauregard, October 4, 1921, in Voorhis accession file, Missouri Historical Society Archives; Kennerly and Russell 1948: 75; John O'Fallon Clark to Lyman Draper, November 5, 1867, Draper Papers, Wisconsin Historical Society. For the Jarvis attribution, see Dickson 1949: 347; Weddell 1930: 311–12; Fischer and Kelly 1993: 191; William Clark Probate File, Rare Documents, Missouri State Archives. For the Harding attributions, see Thwaites 1904–5: 4: frontispiece; McDermott 1951a. For the Saint-Mémin, see Miles 1994: 271; Norfleet 1942: 99. See also Katharine Scott to A. Kinnaird, July 9, 1929, Voorhis accession file, Missouri Historical Society Archives. Two sources on Clark portraits contain numerous errors and should be used with caution: Cutright 1969b; McDermott 1951a.

Letter of Clark to Lewis, joining the expedition, 1803

Ink on paper
9 × 7 (closed); 9 × 14 (open)
Missouri Historical Society, St. Louis, William Clark Papers
Gift of Julia Clark Voorhis in memory of Eleanor Glasgow Voorhis

SOURCE: Jackson 1978: 110

Documents signed by men of the Corps, 1804–10

George Drouillard to Frederick Graeter; John Potts and Peter Weiser to Manuel Lisa; Baptiste Le Page to Auguste Chouteau; John Colter to John Comegys
Ink on paper
Drouillard: 7 × 9; Potts and Weiser: 5 × 7 15/16; Le Page: 6¼ × 8; Colter: 6⅝ × 8⅛
Missouri Historical Society, St. Louis, Manuel Lisa Papers, Meriwether Lewis Collection, Chouteau Family Collection

SOURCES: Moulton 1983–2001: 2: 516, 3: 226–27. On Drouillard's later life, see the Fur Trade, Chouteau, and Manuel Lisa Collections, Missouri Historical Society Archives. They contain the paper trail of his troubles for both debt—including the debt on this promissory note—and murder.

Roster of men, 1807

William Clark
Ink on paper
20 × 16
Yale Collection of Western Americana, Beinecke Rare Book and Manuscript Library, WA MSS. 304
Gift of William R. Coe

SOURCE: Jackson 1978: 378

Razor and brush, late 1700s or early 1800s

Razor: Joseph Roberts and Co., Sheffield; brush: American or British
Razor: steel, horn; box: wood, cloth; brush: hair, horn, wood
Razor: 6½ × 1 (closed); box: 9½ × 2 × ¾; brush: 3¾ × ⅞
William H. Guthman Collection

Roberts did business on Garden St., Sheffield, England, in the late 1700s. The "WARRANTED" mark suggests a date between 1740 and 1830. This razor was purchased from Warren Moore, an author on the Revolutionary War.

SOURCES: Razors are mentioned in Moulton 1983–2001: 6: 141, 9: 316, 10: 175, 235, 11: 396. Their use by the Corps is discussed in Moore 2002. On Castile soap, see Jackson 1978: 95. On Roberts, see Levine 1997: 90. On razors, see Ritchie and Stewart 1999.

Finger-woven sash, late 1700s to early 1800s

Western Great Lakes
Dyed wool yarns
126 × 8⅜
Photograph from the Peabody Museum of Archaeology and Ethnology, Harvard University, © President and Fellows of Harvard College, photograph by Hillel Burger, cat. 99-12-10/53002, neg. T2909
Gift of the Heirs of David Kimball, 1899

Peter Rindisbacher illustrates how such belts were worn with frock coats; see, for example, the man third from the left in his War of 1812 painting *Captain W. Andrew Bulger Saying Farewell at Fort McKay*, at the Amon Carter Museum, Fort Worth.

SOURCES: McLaughlin 2003: chapter 9; Penney 1992: 74–75; Jackson 1978: 476–77

Man's shirt, 1785–1800

American
Linen
42 × 27½ (across shoulders); each sleeve, LENGTH 23
Courtesy of the National Museum of American History, Smithsonian Institution, acc. 28810, cat. CS*6658A
Gift of John Brenton Copp

This shirt may have belonged to Samuel Copp (1743–1820) of Stonington, Connecticut.

SOURCES: Jackson 1978: 70, 77, 88; Moulton 1983–2001: 4: 294, 5: 117, 8: 351

Map of the region along the Mississippi River (detail), 1803

Copy by Seth Pease after a map by William Clark
Watercolor and ink on paper
32¼ × 48¾
National Archives, Washington, D.C., Cartographic Records, RG 77, File Mark WUS I.R. 20

Lewis wrote, "This map has but small claims to correctnes, but I hope it will furnish some general ideas of the country which may be servicable." It may have been drawn in January 1804, when Clark noted he was working on a map. His sources may have included the maps of Antoine Soulard, James Mackay and John Evans, Victor Collot, and François Perrin du Lac.

SOURCES: Jackson 1978: 193–94; Moulton 1983–2001: 1: 7, map 6. On the location of Camp Dubois, see Mayer 1968; Plamondon 2000: 4, 25.

The Manual Exercise, 1803

Printed for Daniel and Samuel Whiting, Albany, N.Y.
Engraving and watercolor on paper
10 × 13
© American Antiquarian Society

SOURCES: Von Steuben 1803; Riling 1966

Map of the Mississippi Country, 1804

Antoine Soulard[?]
Ink on paper
8¼ × 13
National Archives, Washington, D.C., Cartographic Records, RG 77, Fortifications Map File, Drawer 139, Sheet 2

Lewis sent "Two plans of the town of St. Louis" to Jefferson on May 18. This map is the smaller of a pair in the National Archives dated 1804. They have never before been identified with the Lewis maps, but his description matches them. He said: "You'l find on examination that they do not perfectly correspond—the small one is that which I believe to be correct—the deviation from which, observable in the large one may properly in my opinion, be attributed to the late unauthorised Sales of land in this quarter. The smallest of these was drawn and presented by Mr. Soulard—the largest was more recently drawn in part by the same Gentleman, and completed by Capt. Clark." The larger one shows an additional row of city blocks added on the west, at the south end of the town.
SOURCES: Jackson 1978: 148–50, 194; Peterson 1993: 92–93

Dinnerware and books from St. Louis, c. 1761–1815

Plate: Strasbourg, France; salt cellar: Solomon Hougham, London; napkin: maker unknown; glassware: La Granja de San Ildefonso of Segovia, Spain; books: printed in Copenhagen, Paris, and Lyon
Plate: tin-glazed earthenware; salt cellar: silver; napkin: linen damask; glassware: gilded glass; books: ink on paper, bound in leather and cardboard
Plate: DIAM 10¼; salt cellar: 1½ × 2¾ × 2¾; napkin: 39 × 25; glassware: 5¼ to 3⅜ × 3½ to 2¾; books: 6⅜ to 8 × 4 to 5¼ × 1¼ to 1⅞
Missouri Historical Society, St. Louis, 1960 041 0006, 1957 074 0003, 1966 050 0001 i, 1960 282 0001 a, b, j, Association Collection (all books)
Gifts of Carl C. Karst, Mrs. Robert S. Corley, Mrs. H. W. Bamford, Mr. Morrison Pettus, and Miss Mary Elise Pettus

The plate, said to have been used by Auguste Chouteau, was passed down in the Chouteau family. The salt cellar was owned and used by Pierre Chouteau, Sr. The napkin is marked "NJ" in the corner for Nicolas Jarrot. The glassware is from a set of ten pieces that belonged to Auguste Chouteau. The book belonging to Charles Delassus is from a set of Baron de Montesquieu, *Oeuvres de M. De Montesquieu* (1759–61). The ones belonging to Saugrain were Jacques Christophe Valmont de Bomare, *Dictionnaire Raisonné Universel D'Histoire Naturelle* (1791) and William Cullen, *Traité de Matiere Médicale* (1789). Saugrain's books were donated by his great-grandchildren.
SOURCES: Pierre Chouteau's home is pictured in Peterson 1993: 123. For mentions of Lewis and Clark's stay there, see Moulton 1983–2001: 2: 240; Holmberg 2002: 77. On Jarrot and Saugrain, see Jackson 1978: 145, 147, 192, 195; Van Ravenswaay 1991: 113. For more on the private libraries of St. Louis, including these books, see McDermott 1938.

Spanish medal and sword, pre-1787 and 1777

Medal: Tomas Francisco Prieto; sword: royal arsenal, Toledo, Spain
Medal: gold-plated silver; sword: steel, brass, wood
Medal: 2¾ × 2¼; sword: 31⅜ × 4⅜ × 4⅜
Missouri Historical Society, St. Louis, 1919 046 0002, 1878 006 0001
Gifts of Mrs. Placide Delassus, James Hardy

SOURCES: Van Ravenswaay 1991: 110. For the medal's maker, see Forrer 1909: 690; Bénétiz 1999: 247. On the sword, see Brinkerhoff and Chamberlain 1972: 21n, 86, figs. 6, 7.

Louisiana Purchase transfer document, 1804

Charles Dehault Delassus, Amos Stoddard
Ink on paper, red sealing wax
12⅛ × 8⅜
Missouri Historical Society, St. Louis, Louisiana Purchase Transfer Collection

The witnesses were Meriwether Lewis, Antoine Soulard, and Charles Gratiot.
SOURCE: Van Ravenswaay 1991: 118–20

Map of the Missouri River (detail), 1797

John Evans and James Mackay
Ink on paper
28¼ × 39½
Library of Congress, G4052 .M5 1796 .M
Transferred from Office of Indian Affairs, Interior Department, 1925

In all, Lewis and Clark had three maps from Mackay and Evans. This map, showing the area from St. Charles to the Mandan villages, was sent to Clark by William Henry Harrison and was found in an Indian Office collection of maps that had belonged to Clark. A six-part route map of the river (a map now at the Beinecke Library) was given to them by Mackay himself. A third Evans-Mackay map was sent to Lewis by Jefferson on January 13, 1804; it could be the watercolor map that is now at the Library of Congress and that came from the same Indian Office collection as this one. The general outline of the western half of the continent on the third map reflects Soulard's map, but the route of the Missouri was from Mackay and Evans's information, since it correctly shows the Yellowstone River, the Great Falls, and the southward bend of the Missouri beyond it. That map is reproduced in Allen 1975: 46–47 and Wheat 1958: 1: 177–78, map 243.

This one was originally called the Indian Office Map and was the source of much confusion. Annie H. Abel thought it was the map sent to Lewis by Jefferson in January 1804, but John Allen and Gary Moulton agree that it was sent by Harrison. Abel and Allen attributed this map to Mackay, but Moulton argues that Evans was the maker. The Library of Congress dates it as 1796, but Moulton gives 1797.
SOURCES: Abel 1916; Allen 1975: 43, 141; Moulton 1983–2001: 1: 6, map 5. For Harrison's cover letter, see Jackson 1978: 135.

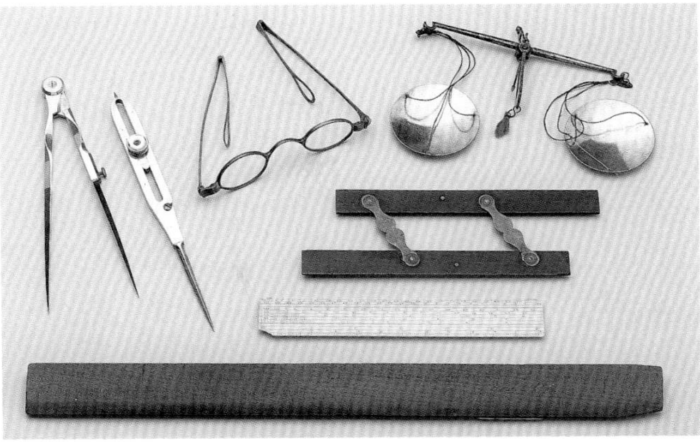

THOMAS JEFFERSON'S DRAFTING INSTRUMENTS

Drafting instruments, scale, and glasses of Thomas Jefferson, c. 1786–1826

Dividers, parallel rule: makers unknown; glasses: attributed to Joseph Willmore, Birmingham; scale: possibly by Young & Son, London; architect's scale: by Watkins & Hill, London; wood rule: attributed to Monticello joinery
Dividers: brass and steel; glasses: silver and glass; scale: steel, brass, string; parallel rule: wood and brass; architect's scale: ivory and brass; wood rule: walnut
Divider: 7; proportional divider: 6⅞; glasses: 1 × 6 × 6⅛ (open); scale: pans DIAM 2, overall 7¼ × 7¾; parallel rule: each straightedge 6, overall 9 7/16 × 2½ (open); architect's scale: 6¼ × 1; wood rule: 13¾ × 1¼
Monticello/Thomas Jefferson Foundation, Inc., Charlottesville, Virginia, 1992-9-2g; 1992-9-2h; 1938-19-1; 1958-99; 1956-32; 1957-17; 1963-19-4
Dividers: purchase from Ruth Horn Crownover, 1992; glasses and architect's scale: gifts of Juliet Graves (Mrs. Henry P.) Meikleham, 1938; scale: gift of Stanley Horn, 1958; parallel rule: gift of John Randolph Burke, 1956

Jefferson used these tools in his own endeavors at architecture, surveying, and science. Clockwise from left, they are a divider, a proportional divider, glasses, a scale, a parallel rule, an architect's scale, and a wood rule. The drafting tools were used in mapping and scale drawings; the scale was used to weigh money, medicines, minerals, and other small samples. The glasses are for reading and other close work. The two dividers may have been purchased in 1786; the glasses date to 1817–18 and the scale to 1812–26. The rest are from the late eighteenth or early nineteenth century. Jefferson purchased most of his drawing instruments from the London mathematical instrument shop of W. and S. Jones; the two dividers shown here are from a set he kept in a mahogany box. The proportional divider is used for reducing drawings; the divider is for comparing or transferring measurements from one place to another on a map or drawing; the parallel rule is for drawing lines that are parallel to existing lines on a map or drawing; the architect's scale is for scale drawings, with various scales engraved on each side; the wood rule is a straightedge with "Thomas Jefferson / Monticello" written in script on one side.
SOURCE: Stein 1993: 370–73

Mastodon jaw, excavated 1807

Excavated by William Clark
Fossilized bone
$9 \times 7\frac{1}{2} \times 5\frac{3}{4}$
Department of Vertebrate Paleontology, The Academy of Natural Sciences of Philadelphia, 13307. Photograph courtesy of Ewell Sale Stewart Library. Transferred from the American Philosophical Society, 1848

"It is not improbable that this voyage of discovery will procure us further information of the Mammoth, & of the Megatherium also," Jefferson wrote to the French scientist Bernard Lacépède. "There are symptoms of it's late and present existence." Jefferson was fascinated by fossil remains as early as 1781, when he asked George Rogers Clark, the brother of William, to send him mammoth bones from Kentucky. The president used philosophical grounds to justify his belief that Lewis might meet living fossils: "Such is the economy of nature, that no instance can be produced, of her having permitted any one race of her animals to become extinct; of her having formed any link in her great work so weak as to be broken."

Lewis's failure to encounter mammoths did not diminish Jefferson's interest. In 1807 he paid for Clark to oversee an excavation at Kentucky's Big Bone Lick. This was one of over three hundred fossils Clark shipped to Jefferson. Other samples from the collection, sent by Jefferson to the National Institute of France, led to the discovery that the mastodon and the mammoth were two distinct species. This is part of a maxillary (upper jaw) bone and dates to the Wisconsonian age, about 17,000 years B.P.

Jefferson divided Clark's fossil bones between the National Institute of France, the American Philosophical Society (APS), and his own collection at Monticello. This is from the APS group.
SOURCES: Jackson 1978: 15–16; Jefferson 1964: 48; Stein 1993: 398–402; Steffen 1977: 48

MASTODON JAW

JAMES COOK, *A VOYAGE TO THE PACIFIC OCEAN*

James Cook, *A Voyage to the Pacific Ocean*, 1784

Printed by W. and A. Strahan, for G. Nicol & T. Cadell, London
Ink on paper, rebound in red cloth
$22\frac{1}{2} \times 16\frac{1}{2}$ (closed)
Library of Congress, *G1036.C69 1784

In 1775 Captain James Cook visited the west coast of North America with a shipload of scientists and an artist, John Webber, who sketched the Native inhabitants. Cook's expedition mapped the coast but missed the mouth of the Columbia River. Jefferson and Lewis modeled many aspirations of their expedition on the sophisticated scientific explorations of Cook, but they could not match his budget or his staff of professionals. This shows a page from the lavish atlas volume.
SOURCE: Cook 1784: 4: pl. 39

ROBERT PATTERSON

Robert Patterson, 1830

Rembrandt Peale
Oil on canvas
$30\frac{1}{8} \times 25\frac{5}{16}$
Courtesy of the American Philosophical Society, 58.P.48
Gift of "A number of members," 1830

Robert Patterson, who trained Lewis in celestial navigation, was a native of northern Ireland. Arriving penniless in America at the age of twenty-five, he established himself as a teacher of navigation and mathematics and became a professor of mathematics at the University of Pennsylvania. This is an 1830 replica by Rembrandt Peale of a portrait he painted in about 1812.
SOURCE: American Philosophical Society 1961: 70–71

Andrew Ellicott, 1809

Jacob Eichholtz
Oil on panel
9×7
Collection of The New-York Historical Society, 1916.3

ANDREW ELLICOTT

Andrew Ellicott was a surveyor and mathematician who instructed Lewis on mapping and celestial navigation. He surveyed the boundaries of Pennsylvania and New York and worked on the western extension of the Mason-Dixon Line. He surveyed the site of the District of Columbia from 1791 to 1793, plotted the border between Florida and the United States from 1796 to 1800, and mapped the lower Mississippi River. He later became a professor of mathematics at West Point.
SOURCE: Garraty and Carnes 1999: 7: 415–16

Benjamin S. Barton, 1789

Samuel Jennings
Oil on canvas
30×25
Courtesy of the American Philosophical Society, L1984.01
Gift of First Pennsylvania Bank, 1984

BENJAMIN S. BARTON

Benjamin Barton's conversations with Lewis may have encompassed his many interests: medicine, botany, natural history, ethnology, and linguistics. A professor of medicine at the University of Pennsylvania, Barton was the author of the first botany text published in the United States and of a 1797 monograph on the origins of the Native Americans. He agreed to author a book based on the natural history discoveries of the Lewis and Clark expedition, but he never completed the project, leaving the scientific accomplishments of the expedition unpublished and unknown for almost a century.
SOURCE: Garraty and Carnes 1999: 2: 287

Astronomy notebook, 1803

Robert Patterson, Meriwether Lewis
Ink on paper, printed cardboard cover
$7\frac{3}{4} \times 6\frac{3}{4} \times \frac{1}{4}$ (closed)
Used by permission, State Historical Society of Missouri, Columbia, Western Historical Manuscript Collection, C1074
Purchased from William Clark Breckenridge, 1928

"I am preparing a set of astronomical formula for Mr. L.," Robert Patterson wrote Jefferson enthusiastically. These are the formulae he promised, written in a school notebook. Lewis

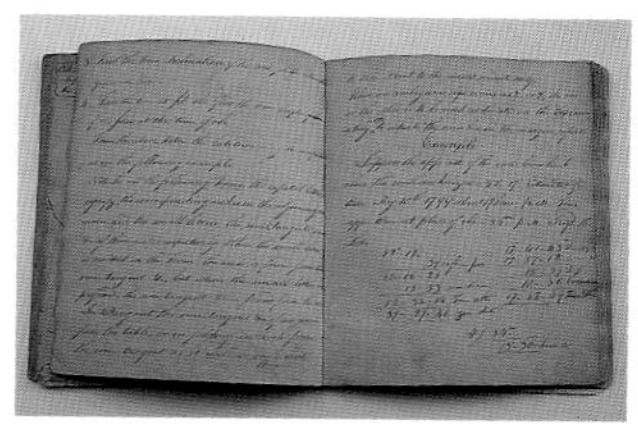

ASTRONOMY NOTEBOOK

took them on the expedition and used some blank pages in the back to jot down latitude readings at the mouth of the Musselshell River in Montana. Patterson believed his system for finding longitude was so simple that it made "the process extremely easy even to boys or common sailors of but moderate capacities." He overestimated his fellow man; the calculations were so tedious

that no one would undertake them, and all Lewis's longitude readings were wasted.
SOURCES: Jackson 1978: 29; Preston 2000

Blanket, 1800–20

American or British
Wool
$87 \times 30\frac{1}{2}$
Courtesy of the National Museum of American History, Smithsonian Institution, cat. AF*316364.003
Gift of Mr. and Mrs. W. Ashbridge, 1975

Lewis did not purchase supplies only from private vendors; he also requisitioned them from the War Department. He got fifteen blankets from military stores at the Philadelphia

BLANKET

arsenal. They may have looked like this one. This design is called a "rose blanket" because of the embroidered roses in the corners; it was used by both civilians and the military in the Revolutionary War and afterward. This one was donated to the Smithsonian, along with a military uniform from the 1790s. Two white rose blankets valued at four dollars were listed on the inventory of Clark's estate at his death.
SOURCES: Jackson 1978: 77; William Clark Probate File, Rare Documents, Missouri State Archives

Receipt of Harvey & Worth, 1803

Harvey & Worth, Meriwether Lewis
Ink on paper
$13 \times 7\frac{3}{4}$
National Archives, Washington, D.C., RG 92, Records of the Office of the Quartermaster General, Consolidated Correspondence File, Lewis and Clark (Entry 225)

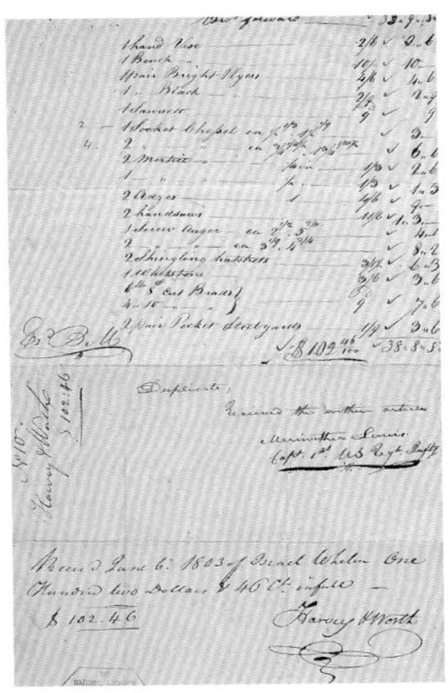

RECEIPT OF HARVEY & WORTH

Harvey & Worth were ironmongers at 62 North Front Street in Philadelphia. Lewis got most of his hardware at their shop, including an extensive set of carpentry tools to build forts, furniture, boats, kegs, crates, and other things. This shows the second page of their receipt.
SOURCE: Jackson 1978: 83–84

Set of carpentry tools, late 1700s to early 1800s

British and American. Pliers: W.C. & Co.; sawtooth file: Simmons; adze head: William Larcham; morticing chisels: John or Hannah Green, Sheffield; socket chisels: James Cam and John Green, Sheffield; drawknife: Cam & Brown, Sheffield; other items: makers unknown
Sawset: iron, brass, wood [boxwood?]; pliers: iron or steel; sawtooth file: steel; rasp: iron; adze head: iron and steel; morticing chisels: iron, steel, beech wood; socket chisels: iron and steel; drawknife: iron, steel, ash wood; bench vise: iron; whetstone: slate
Sawset: $6\frac{3}{4} \times 1\frac{1}{4} \times 1\frac{1}{8}$; pliers: $5\frac{1}{8} \times 1\frac{1}{2}$; sawtooth file: LENGTH $5\frac{1}{8}$; rasp: $10\frac{1}{4} \times 1$; adze head: $10\frac{1}{8} \times 3\frac{7}{8} \times 2\frac{1}{8}$; morticing chisels: $11 \times 1\frac{3}{8} \times 1\frac{1}{8}$ and $12\frac{1}{4} \times 1\frac{3}{4} \times 1\frac{5}{8}$; socket chisels: $7\frac{1}{8} \times 1 \times 1$ and $8\frac{1}{8} \times 1\frac{1}{2} \times 1\frac{1}{8}$; drawknife: $5\frac{1}{4} \times 16 \times 1\frac{1}{4}$; bench vise: $9\frac{1}{2} \times 5\frac{3}{4}$; whetstone: $3\frac{3}{4} \times 1\frac{3}{4} \times \frac{1}{2}$
Colonial Williamsburg Foundation, 1992-114, 1985-189, 1984-199-1, W1936-2280, 1991-146, 1987-754, 1982-244-1, 1982-245, 1988-210, 1990-120, G1966-435, G1986-268-115
Bench vise: gift of Ralph R. Chappell, Richmond; whetstone: gift of Frank M. Smith from the G. W. Cartwright Collection; rasp: bequest of Stephen C. Wolcott; other items: purchased in England and America

SET OF CARPENTRY TOOLS

These tools all match items purchased by Lewis from Harvey & Worth. Clockwise from lower left to center, they are a sawset, or saw wrest, for bending sawtooth blades; pliers; a sawtooth file for sharpening saw blades; a rasp; an adze head used for squaring logs and making planks; morticing chisels for cutting grooves and mortice-and-tenon joints; socket chisels; a drawknife for smoothing

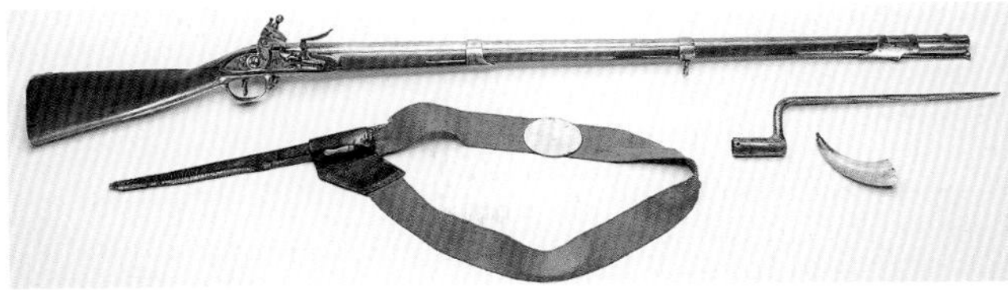

MUSKET AND EQUIPMENT

wood surfaces; a bench vise, probably used for fine work like gun repairs; and a whetstone for sharpening blades. At Fort Clatsop, the tools were so hard to replace that Lewis had to issue regulations for men wanting to use them. "Any individual so borrowing the tools are strictly required to bring the same back the moment he has ceased to use them, and [in] no case shall they be permited to keep them out all night," Lewis wrote.
SOURCES: Jackson 1978: 83–84; Moulton 1983–2001: 6: 158

Knife, early 1800s

British or American
Iron, antler, white metal
$13 \times 1\frac{5}{8}$
Collection of the Mercer Museum of the Bucks County Historical Society, 8351

For Indian presents, Lewis purchased four dozen butcher knives and eleven dozen plain knives. He also included fifteen "Scalping Knives" under the equipment for the soldiers. According to the baling invoices,

KNIFE

three and a half dozen of the knives for Indians (possibly the butcher knives) were "Staghandle," or antler-handled, like this one. The blade of this knife was originally the classic English trade knife shape: a single-edged blade with straight back and pointed tip with no notch. It has been sharpened so many times that the blade has been worn concave. Most knives of Lewis's time came from Sheffield, England.

Although George Catlin said that butcher knives and scalping knives were identical, Charles E. Hanson Jr. describes a difference between the two types. It is doubtful whether Lewis used the terms so specifically. After returning, Lewis noted that the "Knives, with fixed wooden handles stained red, usually called red handled knives & such as are used by the N.W. Co. in their Indian trade" were most in demand by the Indians. The red wood he referred to was barwood, camwood, or rosewood. An example of such a knife is PO. 74.410.26 in the Bernisches Historisches Museum, Bern, Switzerland.
SOURCES: Jackson 1978: 74, 93–94, 98; Moulton 1983–2001: 3: 499, 500; Hanson 1987a, 1987b; Thompson 1977: 185

Musket and equipment, 1795–1800

American. Musket: Springfield Armory; bayonet: Springfield or Harper's Ferry Armory
Musket: walnut, iron; bayonet: iron; scabbard, belt, and belt plate: linen webbing, leather, brass, silver metal; powder charger: horn, wood, tacks
Musket: 57×9, BARREL LENGTH 42; bayonet: $16\frac{1}{2} \times 3\frac{3}{4} \times 1$; scabbard and belt: LENGTH 34; powder charger: $5 \times 2 \times 1\frac{3}{4}$
Courtesy of the National Museum of American History, Smithsonian Institution, acc. 22890, cat. AF*131359; acc. 1980.0399, cat. AF*E-073 ; acc. 1980.0399, cat. AF*E-214; acc. 9304
Musket: gift of J. E. Hargrave and Otis T. Mason, 1890; bayonet and scabbard: gifts of C. B. H. Jackson

Although there is no record of Lewis purchasing muskets to arm the expedition, the men certainly had them, and Lewis purchased musket balls for them. Muskets were large-caliber, smooth-bore guns and were consequently much less accurate than rifles; they were used for massed fire in battle rather than for hunting or sharpshooting. Since the soldiers who joined the expedition came with the arms issued to them at the forts where they had been stationed, they were more likely to have had muskets from the Springfield Armory, which had been in existence for many years, than from Harper's Ferry Armory, which was relatively new. The muskets from both arsenals were of the same design, known as the Model 1795, the first year the design went into production. This is a Model 1795 Springfield musket of an early type. It is shown with a matching bayonet, bayonet scabbard and belt, and powder charger. The bayonet scabbard and belt are probably militia equipment rather than army. The bayonet belts of the Corps were probably white leather rather than the linen webbing shown here.
SOURCES: Jackson 1978: 92; Brown 1968: 132

Powder horn, early 1800s

American
Bison horn, bone
LENGTH 11¼, DIAM 3⅜
Missouri Historical Society, St. Louis, 1923 050 0030
Gift of Julia Clark Voorhis in memory of Eleanor Glasgow Voorhis, 1923

This powder horn was believed to have been owned by William Clark. A number of examples of this ornate style of inlaid powder horn are known from the Ohio, mid-Mississippi, and Missouri Valleys; they may have been by the same

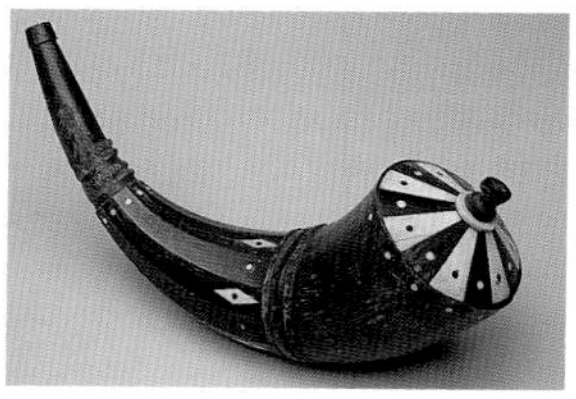

POWDER HORN

maker. The other examples traced are all in private collections except for a second one in the Missouri Historical Society. None have any provenance information.

Powder horn and hunting bag, late 1700s or early 1800s

American
Leather, horn, wood, iron, twine
Horn: 10 × 2¼; bag: 9 × 9
Collection of the Fort Ticonderoga Museum, PH-096.1 and .2

Robert Martin, a Philadelphia saddler, billed the government for fifteen pouches "attached to a like number of Powder Horns and delivered to Capt. M. Lewis." None of those survive; however, this is the classic style of pouch and horn used on the frontier. The bags contained bullets, wads, extra flints, vent picks, gun worms, and other equipment; the horns contained gunpowder.
SOURCES: Jackson 1978: 90, 97; Peterson 1968: 70–72

POWDER HORN AND HUNTING BAG

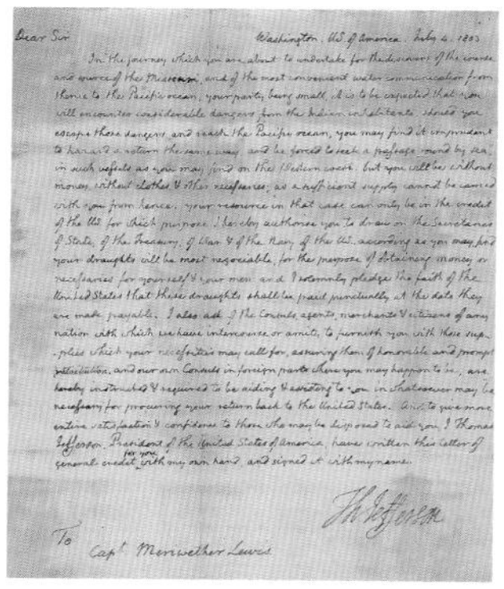

Washington. U.S. of America. July 4. 1803.

Th: Jefferson

To Capt. Meriwether Lewis

LETTER OF CREDIT

Letter of credit, 1803

Thomas Jefferson
Ink on paper
10⅛ × 8¼
Missouri Historical Society, St. Louis, William Clark Papers
Gift of Julia Clark Voorhis in memory of Eleanor Glasgow Voorhis

This was Lewis's "credit card." In this letter, Jefferson authorized Lewis to charge expenses to the federal government, stating no limit. Jefferson intended it to cover the return journey by sea, but that was not how Lewis used it. All through the summer of 1804, a steady stream of bills came in to Washington for sums Lewis had charged "on account of the public Service" before leaving St. Louis. This is the copy Lewis carried on the expedition. It has been folded and was stained by water.
SOURCE: Jackson 1978: 419–28

Louisiana Purchase proclamation, 1803

Par Le Prefet Colonial, New Orleans
Ink on paper
21¼ × 16½
Missouri Historical Society, St. Louis, Louisiana Purchase Transfer Collection

This proclamation, printed in New Orleans by Pierre Clément Laussat, the French prefect for the colony of Louisiana, informed the residents of the transfer. This copy was sent upriver to St. Louis.

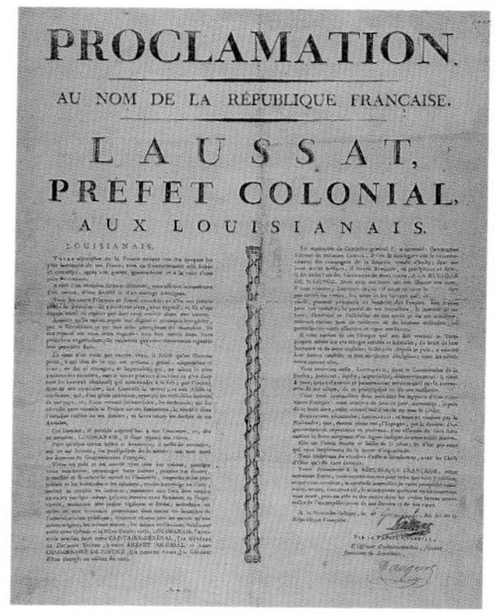

PROCLAMATION.

AU NOM DE LA RÉPUBLIQUE FRANÇAISE.

LAUSSAT,

PREFET COLONIAL,

AUX LOUISIANAIS.

LOUISIANA PURCHASE PROCLAMATION

CHAPTER 2
Learning Diplomacy

Compass, 1803

Thomas Whitney, Philadelphia
Wood case, brass fittings, iron needle with copper wire counter, silver-plated graduated rim, paper card with printed compass rose, glass
1½ × 3⅝ × 7 (open)
Courtesy of the National Museum of American History, Smithsonian Institution, acc. 122864, cat. PL*38366
Gift of Mary E. McCabe

According to the donor, this compass was given by Clark to Captain Robert A. McCabe, who died in 1839. The compass then passed to his brother Richard B. McCabe, then to Richard's son Roche B. McCabe, then to the donor. McCabe was a Pennsylvanian who enlisted as an ensign in the First Infantry on January 3, 1812. After the war he was reinstated as a second lieutenant in the Fifth Infantry and made captain in 1824. McCabe was commandant at Fort Crawford, Wisconsin, in 1825 when Clark went there to negotiate the Treaty of Prairie du Chien and was probably Clark's host during his stay. The captain later assisted with the Potawatomie removals to Missouri. After leaving the army in 1833, he worked as an Indian agent and fort sutler.

The repairs to the compass date to pre-1850 because the screws used were not machine made. An instance on which Lewis mentions his pocket compass was May 26, 1805, when he took a reading on some mountains he erroneously believed to be the Rockies, "the most remarkable of which by my pocket compass I found bore N. 65° W."
SOURCES: On the compass, see Jackson 1978: 82, 96; Moulton 1983–2001: 4: 201. On McCabe, see Hamersly 1881: 611; Merrell 1876: 373, 374, 403–4; Hill 1974: 54, 145, 207; Mahan 1926: 90.

Journals of Lewis and Clark, 1804–6

Meriwether Lewis and William Clark
Ink on paper, bound in red morocco leather with gilt tooling and marbled endpapers; brown suede; and marbled cardboard with leather spine and corners
Morocco: 8¼ × 5⅛ (closed); suede: 8¼ × 5 (closed); marbled: 6⅞ × 4 (closed)
Courtesy of the American Philosophical Society, Codex E, C, A and J (open)

The journals were deposited at the American Philosophical Society by Nicholas Biddle, the ghostwriter of the book on the expedition, at Jefferson's request in 1817. There are eighteen volumes at the society.
SOURCE: Jackson 1978: 62, 231

Sketch of the keelboat, 1804

William Clark
Ink on paper
Image: LENGTH 6⅛
Yale Collection of Western Americana, Beinecke Rare Book and Manuscript Library, WA Mss. s-897 #7
Gift of Frederick W. and Carrie S. Beinecke

SOURCES: Smith and Swick 1997: 52; Jackson 1978: 534; Boss 1993: 68–76; Large 1995: 16–19; Moulton 1983–2001: 2: 162

Snags on the Missouri, 1833

Karl Bodmer
Watercolor and pencil on paper
8⅜ × 10¾
Joslyn Art Museum, Omaha, Nebraska, 1986.49.150
Gift of Enron Art Foundation

SOURCES: Wied 1843: Tableau 6; Moulton 1983–2001: 2: 377; Goetzmann et al. 1984: 150

Keg and canteen, c. 1800 and 1778

Keg: English; canteen: American
Keg: wood staves, iron bands, tar; canteen: white pine sides, maple band and mouthpiece, iron nails
Keg: 11½ × 8½; canteen: 9⅛ × 3
Colonial Williamsburg Foundation, 1947-339 (4302) and 1935-39
Keg purchased from Mrs. W. Webber, Taunton, U.K.; canteen purchased from Stephen Van Rensselaer, Williamsburg, Virginia

Carved on the side of the canteen is: "RC EB A THE8 1778." On the head of the keg is "EB."
SOURCES: Jackson 1978: 88; Moulton 1983–2001: 2: 165, 199–203, 332, 6: 333

Journal of Charles Floyd, 1804

Charles Floyd
Ink on paper, bound in marbled cardboard with leather spine
12⅛ × 7¾ (open)
Wisconsin Historical Society, Draper Collection

SOURCES: Jackson 1978: 232, 370; Moulton 1983–2001: 2: 513, 9: xvii

Floyd's Grave, Where Lewis and Clark Buried Sergeant Floyd in 1804, 1832

George Catlin
Oil on canvas, mounted on aluminum
11⅛ × 14⅜
Smithsonian American Art Museum, 1985.66.376
Gift of Mrs. Joseph Harrison, Jr.

SOURCE: Moulton 1983–2001: 2: 495, 496n

Mineral specimens, collected 1804–5

Patrick Gass, Meriwether Lewis, and William Clark (collectors)
Clockwise from top left: fossilized bone, selenite or gypsum, pumice, coal-bed slag
Fossil: 2 × 4; gypsum: longest 1⅝; pumice: 1¾ × 1¼ × 1; slag: 2½ × 3 × 1
Adam Seybert Collection, Mineralogy, The Academy of Natural Sciences of Philadelphia, 5516, 803, 804, 664, 534, 3916. Photograph courtesy of Ewell Sale Stewart Library

The minerals did in fact go to the American Philosophical Society, but they were subsequently added to the collection of Adam Seybert, a mineralogist whose collection eventually made its way to the Academy of Natural Sciences of Philadelphia. In the process, many of the samples and identifications were lost.

The fossil is the type specimen of the *Xiphactinus*. Gass found it "in a cavern a few miles distance from the Missouri S side of the River" on August 6, 1804, when they were near the mouth of Soldier River. Richard Harlan, the first scientist to describe it, in 1823, named the fish it came from *Saurocephalus lanciformis Harlan*; the species was later renamed. The specimen is a small fragment of the upper jaw; the entire fish could grow as long as eighteen feet.

The selenite or gypsum specimens were probably collected south of Calumet Bluffs on either August 23 or 27, 1804. On the latter date Clark found a "Large Stone resembling lime incrusted with a substance like Glass."

The presence of pumice had been known for some time and was erroneously taken as evidence of volcanism. Clark's experiment to prove an alternative origin took place on March 20, 1805: "I saw an emence quantity of Pumice Stone, and evident marks of the hills being on fire. I collected some Pumice Stone, burnt Stone & hard earth and put them into a furnace, the hard earth melted and . . . became a Pumice-Stone." Lewis sent back two specimens of pumice; one was "found amongst the piles of drift wood on the Missouri, Sometimes found as low down as the mouth of the osage river"; the other was "found in great abundance on the Sides of the Hills in the Neighborhood of Fort Mandan." This is probably the former one, since it was labeled "Found Floating on the river Missouri."

The "lava" is from near Fort Mandan—not, Lewis noted, from a volcano but rather "exposed by the washing of the Hills from the rains & melting Snow."
SOURCES: On the mineral collection, see Jackson 1978: 231, 239–40. On the fish fossil, see Moulton 1983–2001: 3: 474; Harlan 1824: 331–37, pl. 12; Chaky 1998: 24. On the gypsum, see Moulton 1983–2001: 2: 501, 3: 473. On the pumice, see Moulton 1983–2001: 3: 317, 478, 8: 414; Allen 1975: 204. On the lava, see Moulton 1983–2001: 3: 478.

Prairie Dog Village, 1866

George Catlin
Engraving and watercolor on paper
Image: 3⅛ × 4¾
Missouri Historical Society, St. Louis

This is an 1866 print from an 1832 painting.

SOURCES: Catlin 1866: pl. 42; Moulton 1983–2001: 9: 55; Jackson 1978: 256; Cutright 1967

Sketch of the magpie, 1810–11

Alexander Wilson
Watercolor, ink, and pencil on paper
8½ × 7
Ernst Mayr Library of the Museum of Comparative Zoology, Harvard University. Photograph © President and Fellows of Harvard College
Gift of John E. Thayer, 1910

This sketch was later engraved by Alexander Lawson and reproduced in volume four of Alexander Wilson's pioneering work *American Ornithology*, published in 1808–14.
SOURCES: Cutright 1967: 226; Adams 1976: 348, 392; Beckwith 1938: 19–21

Missouri in the Morning below Council Bluffs, 1833

Karl Bodmer
Watercolor on paper
7⅜ × 10¾
Joslyn Art Museum, Omaha, Nebraska, 1986.49.151
Gift of Enron Art Foundation

SOURCES: Moulton 1983–2001: 2: 430, 440, 9: 32; Nichols 1969; Goetzmann et al. 1984: 159

Omaha Man, 1833

Karl Bodmer
Watercolor and pencil on paper
11⅞ × 8½
Joslyn Art Museum, Omaha, Nebraska, 1986.49.236
Gift of Enron Art Foundation

SOURCES: Moulton 1983–2001: 2: 479; Goetzmann et al. 1984: 161

Horse effigy pipe bowl, pre-1839

Plains
Slate
3½ × 3½ × 1
University of Pennsylvania Museum of Archaeology and Anthropology, cat. 38376, neg. T4-2319
Gift of John Wanamaker, from the collection of Thomas Donaldson, 1901

There may originally have been inlay on the horse's mane.
SOURCES: Maurer 1992: 146; Ewers 1986: 64; Catlin 1995: 1: 264, fig. 98

Sioux Encamped on the Upper Missouri, Dressing Buffalo Meat and Robes, 1832

George Catlin
Oil on canvas, mounted on aluminum
11¼ × 14½
Smithsonian American Art Museum, 1985.66.377
Gift of Mrs. Joseph Harrison, Jr.

SOURCES: Moulton 1983–2001: 3: 22; Catlin 1995: 1: 49, fig. 22

The Two Plains

Cartography by Gene Thorp

SOURCES: DeMallie 2001: ix; Ambrose and Abell 1998: 30

Pipe tomahawk of Meriwether Lewis, c. 1809

American
Curly maple stem with silver inlay and mouthpiece, steel head with silver inlay
19 × 8 × 1¾
Private Collection, courtesy of the Alabama Department of Archives and History

This tomahawk, along with other materials, was returned to Lewis's family and was handed down to his half-sister Mary Garland Marks. She married William Harvie Moore and passed the item to her son, Dr. Meriwether Gaines Moore of Wetumpka, Alabama. After his death, the tomahawk went to his grandson, Dr. Elisha Meriwether Moore, then to Elisha Moore's brother John William Moore, then to Elisha Moore's daughter. She has placed it on long-term loan to the Alabama Department of Archives and History in Montgomery.
SOURCES: On pipe tomahawks, see Peterson 1965: 15–17, 33–43; Russell 1967: 278–84. On Lewis's tomahawk, see Jackson 1978: 470; Moulton 1983–2001: 6: 15–16, 11: 250.

Captains Lewis & Clark Holding a Council with the Indians, 1810

Artist unknown
Woodcut on paper
Image: 2¾ × 4¾
Department of Special Collections, Washington University Libraries

SOURCES: Gass 1810: opp. p. 26; Moulton 1983–2001: 3: 111

Gorget, 1783–84

Richard Rugg, London
Silver
4½ × 5¾ × 1⅜
Missouri Historical Society, St. Louis, 1920 053 0005
Gift of Mrs. Pierre Chouteau IV

SOURCES: Woodward 1979: 33–37; Fredrickson 1980: 31

Certificate of loyalty, c. 1803

American
Ink on paper, silk ribbon, sealing wax
8¼ × 12½
Missouri Historical Society, St. Louis, William Clark Papers
Gift of Julia Clark Voorhis in memory of Eleanor Glasgow Voorhis

SOURCES: Jackson 1978: 207; Moulton 1983–2001: 2: 493

Certificate of loyalty, 1796

Spanish, signed by Francisco Luis Hector, Baron de Carondelet
Ink on paper
11 × 19
The Huntington Library, San Marino, California, HM 3989

SOURCE: Jackson 1978: 208

Jefferson peace medals and U.S. dollar, 1801 and 1803

Jefferson medals: U.S. Mint; U.S. dollar coin: U.S. Mint
Silver
Jefferson medals: DIAM 4⅛, 2⅞, and 2⅛; U.S. dollar coin: DIAM 1⅝
The American Numismatic Society, 1923.52.11, 1949.52.1, 0000.999.32994, 1980.109.2376

The Jefferson medals of 1801 were hollow because the U.S. Mint did not have machinery to strike such large medals in solid silver; the obverse and reverse were struck separately and united by a silver band. Later restrikes were made solid and in other metals and were passed out in large quantities.
SOURCES: Prucha 1971: xiii, 16–17, 27, 90–95; Walker 1982: 24

Washington medals, 1798

Bolton and Watt, Birmingham
Silver
DIAM 1¾
The American Numismatic Society, 1915.139.1, 1915.140.1, 1915.141.1

The Washington medals were made of both solid silver and copper, but Lewis and Clark probably carried ones made of only silver.
SOURCE: Prucha 1971: 89–90

Talk of Capt. Lewis to the Oto Nation, 1804

Meriwether Lewis
Ink on paper
Each page: 10 × 8¼
National Archives, Washington, D.C., RG 107, Letters Received, 1805, W-491

Lewis sent this copy of his speech to the Louisiana territorial governor General James Wilkinson, who transmitted it to Washington, D.C.
SOURCES: Jackson 1978: 204–5; Moulton 1983–2001: 2: 440–41

Air gun, c. 1803

Isaiah Lukens, Philadelphia
Brass barrel, walnut stock, iron butt, iron and plate silver fittings
49 × 9½
Virginia Military Institute Museum, 88.031.007
Gift of Henry M. Stewart

The sheet-iron butt of this gun unscrews from the barrel and attaches to an air pump to be filled with compressed air. The trigger mechanism works like a standard flintlock, except instead of a flint, the hammer brings down a pin that strikes a valve, which releases a blast of compressed air to propel the ball. The barrel is rifled.

There is no record of who made Lewis's air gun or where he got it. It has long been speculated that the team of Isaiah Lukens and Jacob Kunz, Philadelphians associated with the Peale circle, were the makers. The weapon was said to be able to fire up to forty rounds between charges, and the only type of air gun with this capacity was made with the air reservoir in the butt. Lukens and Kunz were the primary makers of butt-reservoir guns in America at the time. However, most of their guns were single-shot rather than repeaters, suggesting that Lewis may have acquired an Austrian gun. Girandoni made over fifteen hundred repeating air guns for use in the Austrian army.

Lewis shipped his air gun back to Washington, D.C., in 1806; it apparently came to Lukens, whose estate sale advertised it in 1847 as "*a great curiosity*." After that, it disappeared from record. This gun first came to light in 1956 when Charter Harrison, a collector who owned it, claimed that it was the Lewis and Clark gun. He later retracted his statement, but others repeated his claim, basing their arguments on repairs mentioned in the journals. Although this gun showed no evidence of such repairs, it was impossible to prove they had not taken place because of replacement of the main spring and possibly the hammer in the 1840s. The discovery of Thomas Rodney's description of Lewis's air gun put an end to the speculation.
SOURCES: Smith and Swick 1997: 50; Moulton 1983–2001: 11: 66; Jackson 1978: 735. On the air gun, see Carrick 2003; Stewart 1977; Halsey 1984; Chatters 1977; Beeman and Allen 2002.

Calumet pipe, late 1700s to mid-1800s

Missouri River
Stem: wood, immature bald eagle tail feathers, mallard duck scalp, downy feathers, dyed horse hair, dyed artiodactyl (deer?) hair, unidentified (human?) hair, possible winter weasel fur, dyed and undyed porcupine quills, sinew, bast fiber cord, hide thongs, silk ribbons, pigments; bowl: catlinite
Stem: 22 (with feathers) × 37; bowl: 2¾ × 5½ × 1¾
Photograph from the Peabody Museum of Archaeology and Ethnology, Harvard University, © President and Fellows of Harvard College, photograph by Hillel Burger, cat. 99-12-10/53099.1 (bowl) and cat. 99-12-10/53100.2 (stem), neg. T3866.1
Gift of the Heirs of David Kimball, 1899

The classic calumet form had a round stem wrapped with ornaments and a "fan" of feathers hanging from it. Catlin wrote that a blue stem was sometimes used to symbolize peace, whereas a red one was thought to stand for war. Lewis and Clark brought back enough gift pipes to donate fourteen of them to Peale's Museum. About seventeen pipes associated with the Peale collection survive, but there is no record of which, if any, came from Lewis and Clark. This one was selected for the antiquity of its style. The bowls and stems of the Peabody pipes were arbitrarily matched when they were accessioned. This bowl and stem have been paired on the basis of their close resemblance to Jonathan Carver's illustration of a Dakota calumet observed in 1766.
SOURCES: Jackson 1978: 517; McLaughlin 2003: chapter 8; Paper 1988: 19, 56; Ewers 1979: 32; Carver 1956: pl. 4

Sioux Dog Feast, 1832–37

George Catlin
Oil on canvas mounted on aluminum
24 × 29
Smithsonian American Art Museum, 1985.66.494
Gift of Mrs. Joseph Harrison, Jr.

SOURCE: Catlin 1995: 1: 257, 259

Feast bowl, pre-1865

Lakota[?]
Wood, brass tacks, lead inlay
7 × 13 × 15½
Photograph from the Peabody Museum of Archaeology and Ethnology, Harvard University, © President and Fellows of Harvard College, photograph by Hillel Burger, cat. 28-16-10/98291, neg. T2719.4
Exchange with the Worcester Historical Society, 1928

This bowl was thought, by its donor, to have been collected from the Blackfeet in 1865 by a "Colonel Sibley," possibly a reference to General Henry H. Sibley, who led an expedition against the Sioux in Dakota Territory in 1863 and returned to the Missouri River in 1865 to negotiate treaties. It is typical of Lakota carving styles.
SOURCES: Maurer 1992: 116; Ewers 1986: 166–67, 171, pl. 25

Belt, early 1800s

Western Great Lakes or Eastern Plains
Mammal hide, dyed and undyed porcupine quills, metal cones, unidentified mammal hair, sinew
46½ × 4
Photograph from the Peabody Museum of Archaeology and Ethnology, Harvard University, © President and Fellows of Harvard College, photograph by Hillel Burger, cat. 99-12-10/53062, neg. T2933.1
Gift of the Heirs of David Kimball, 1899

Peale identified the belts donated by Lewis and Clark as Winnebago and "Saux" (presumably Sioux). This one is made in a style usually associated with western Woodlands tribes such as the Santee Sioux, Winnebago, and Sauk; but the earliest Missouri Valley collections also contain items, including belts (see National Museum of Natural History, Smithsonian Institution, cat. 5429), with this orange-white-yellow-purple color combination and elegant style of quillwork. A very similar belt in the Ethnological Museum, Berlin, has a raven skin bustle attached, and it is possible that the belt pictured here originally went with one of the bustles collected from among the Sioux by Lewis and Clark.
SOURCES: Jackson 1978: 476–77, 516–17; McLaughlin 2003: chapter 9; Bolz and Sanner 1999: 83

Saber of William Clark, c. 1808

English
Blued steel blade, ivory grip, brass and gilded brass hilt
39 × 4½ × 1¼
Missouri Historical Society, St. Louis, 1923 050 0022
Gift of Julia Clark Voorhis in memory of Eleanor Glasgow Voorhis

The blade is marked "Warranted," which suggests an English origin.
SOURCES: Moulton 1983–2001: 3: 112, 11: 89; Catlin 1995: 1: 211; Walker 1982: 34. On swords, see Peterson 1977.

Scalp Dance, Sioux, 1832

George Catlin
Oil on canvas mounted on aluminum
26¼ × 32⅝
Smithsonian American Art Museum, 1985.66.438B
Gift of Mrs. Joseph Harrison, Jr.

This painting is undated, but it shows an 1832 event.
SOURCE: Moulton 1983–2001: 9: 69

Gun stock war club, pre-1841

Missouri Valley
Wood handle decorated with brass tacks, cured hide, red and black pigments; iron blade
15¼ × 27½
Courtesy of the Department of Anthropology, National Museum of Natural History, Smithsonian Institution, E*2647
Collection of the U.S. War Department

SOURCES: Moulton 1983–2001: 3: 28; Catlin 1995: 1: fig. 99; Goetzmann et al. 1984: 316, 338

Knife and sheath, c. 1820–40

Dakota[?]
Knife: iron blade, wood handle; sheath: cured hide, dyed bird quills
14¼ × 3½
Courtesy of the Department of Anthropology, National Museum of Natural History, Smithsonian Institution, E*5417
Collection of John Varden

John Varden got this knife from someone named J. Scott. Prince Paul of Württemberg collected another sheath like it on the Missouri in the 1820s. The knife is hand-forged, in a style reminiscent of "Tecumseh's dagger," a British presentation knife at Le Musée du Château de Ramezay, Montreal.
SOURCES: Feder 1987; Bolz and Sanner 1999: 61; Thompson 1977: 185; Ewers 1967: 68–69; Russell 1967: 178–79

Quiver, pre-1839

Dakota[?]
Cured hide, dyed quills, tin cones, printed cotton, glass beads
28½ × 9
Courtesy of the Department of Anthropology, National Museum of Natural History, Smithsonian Institution, E*386539
Gift of Sarah (Mrs. Joseph) Harrison, 1881

SOURCES: Moulton 1983–2001: 3: 23; Catlin 1995: 1: fig. 101

Buffalo robe, c. 1780–1825

Upper Missouri River, Mandan or Yankton[?]
Bison hide with hair, deerskin fringe, native and trade pigments, dyed and undyed porcupine quills, dyed bird quills, unidentified plant fiber, sinew
94⅛ × 102
Photograph from the Peabody Museum of Archaeology and Ethnology, Harvard University, © President and Fellows of Harvard College, photograph by Hillel Burger, cat. 99-12-10/53121, neg. T1908aVIII
Gift of the Heirs of David Kimball, 1899

The theory that this was the battle robe sent to Jefferson from Fort Mandan in 1805, described as "1 Buffalow robe painted by a Mandan man representing a battle which was faught 8 years since, by the Sioux & Ricaras, against the Mandans, Minitarras & Ahwahharways," started with Charles Willoughby, the Peabody Museum curator who accessioned the Boston Museum collection in 1899. The only evidence he cited was Coues 1893. The supposition was never questioned by subsequent researchers, including John Ewers, who described it as a "type specimen" of pre-contact Plains Indian art.

There were seven robes in the shipment from Fort Mandan to Jefferson; Henry Dearborn described them as "good skins, well dressed, and highly embellished with Indian finery." Two of them were identified as Mandan, one was attributed to the Minetarre (Hidatsa), and the other four were unidentified. There is no evidence that Jefferson ever sent the Mandan battle robe to Peale; if he did, Peale never accessioned it as such. Augustus John Foster later saw a battle robe in Jefferson's library that he identified as having been painted by "one of the Bigbellied Tribe" (Hidatsa). Baron de Montlezun also described a battle robe still at Monticello in 1816—a description that does not match this one. (However, Jefferson also owned a robe showing a battle between the Pawnee and the Osage, and that robe may have been the one described.) If the Mandan robe remained at Monticello, it was later lost along with the rest of Jefferson's Indian artifact collection—which, despite rumors, has never been located.

Peale accessioned only one Lewis and Clark robe, "A Large Mantle, made of the Buffalow skin, worn by the Scioux, or Soue, Darcota Nation," plus a Crow or Hidatsa "Mantle of very fine wool," which could have been a skin or a woven blanket. This robe is not necessarily one of those two, since Peale also received two robes collected by George C. Hutter on the Atkinson-O'Fallon expedition up the Missouri in 1825; these were described as "A buffaloe robe on which is painted, a battle between the Sioux and Arrickara Indians; by a Sioux" and as a "Mandan chiefs Buffaloe robe." Since Hutter married Clark's niece two years after donating his collection to Peale, it has been suggested that he acquired his robes from Clark.

This robe could also conceivably be one of "five Buffalow robes of Different figures" that Clark sent to his brother Jonathan in Louisville in the 1805 shipment from Fort Mandan. He wrote: "One represents three actions between the Sioux & Mandans near this place, the Mandans on horsback and sucksessfull. The scalps represented [two drawn shapes resembling c and o] on the Sioux of the robe. One other robe of the Chyenne figures which I send you." Or it could be one of the additional "4 Mandan Robes of Buffalow" that Clark shipped to Louisville at the end of the expedition. If so, Clark must have donated it to Peale some time before 1809.

The way the bison cow was skinned and the way the bird (probably gull) quills were incorporated into the center strip suggests that this robe was made by a Mandan or Hidatsa woman. The quillwork also includes strands of what appears to be hairy grama grass, which the Hidatsa called *amauxihica*, or "antelope grass," and incorporated into their early quillwork. The pigments are iron oxide (hematite or red ochre) for brown and yellow, copper salts for green, and vermilion—a trade object—for red.

Maurer calls this robe the earliest example of Plains Indian biographical art and interprets it as showing a sequence of individual events, not a single battle scene. Both Evan Maurer and Castle McLaughlin believe the robe was painted by more than one hand, "probably comrades-in-arms who had participated in the great battle."
SOURCES: Moulton 1983–2001: 3: 117, 217, 219. On the Fort Mandan shipment, see Jackson 1978: 235–36, 254. On Jefferson's collection, see Jackson 1978: 733–34; Elizabeth Chew, internal research report, Thomas Jefferson Foundation. On the Peale collection, see Jackson 1978: 476; Peale 1809–28: entry for June 18, 1828; McLaughlin 2003: chapter 4. On other Clark robes, see Holmberg 2002: 86; Moulton 1983–2001: 8: 418–19. On this robe, McLaughlin 2003: chapter 7; Maurer 1992: 188–89.

Arrows (detail), early to mid-1800s

Plains
Wood shafts with red and black pigment, raptor and turkey feather fletching, sinew wrapping, tips of bone, chalcedony, quartz, and iron
LENGTH 25¼ to 26½
Photograph from the Peabody Museum of Archaeology and Ethnology, Harvard University, © President and Fellows of Harvard College, photograph by Hillel Burger, cat. 99-12-10/52959, cat. 99-12-10/52961, cat. 99-12-10/52964 , cat. 99-12-10/52967, cat. 99-12-10/52968, and cat. 99-12-10/52971, neg. T3851.1
Gift of the Heirs of David Kimball, 1899

SOURCES: Jackson 1978: 477; Moulton 1983–2001: 3: 112, 288; McLaughlin 2003: chapter 9

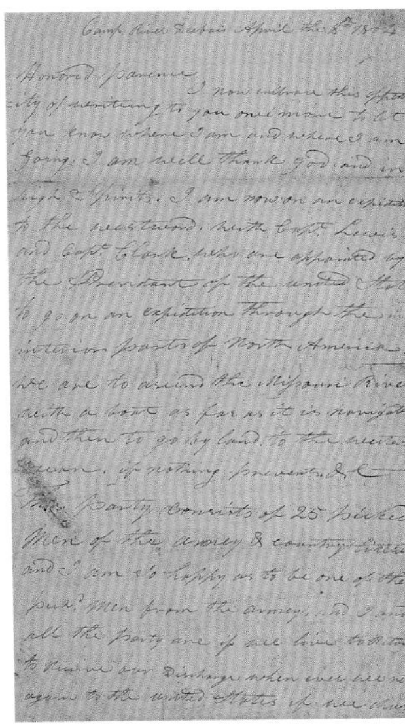
Camp River Dubois April the 8th 18
Honored Parence
I now embrace this opportun-
-ity of writing to you once more to let
you know where I am and where I am
going. I am well thank God and in
high spirits. I am now on an expedition
to the westward with Capt. Lewis
and Capt. Clark who are appointed by
the President of the united States
to go on an expedition through the in
interior parts of North America.
We are to ascend the Missouri River
with a boat as far as it is navigable
and then to go by land to the western
ocean, if nothing prevents. &c
This party consists of 25 picked
Men of the army & country likewise
and I am so happy as to be one of them
pick'd Men from the army, and I and
all the party are if we live to return
to receive our discharge when ever we return
again to the united States if we chuse

LETTER OF JOHN ORDWAY

Letter of John Ordway to his "Honored Parence"

John Ordway
Ink on paper, wax
12⅜ × 7⅛
Oregon Collection, Rosenbach Museum & Library, Philadelphia, Pennsylvania, 231/23

Young Sergeant Ordway wrote this letter to his family in Hebron, New Hampshire, before setting out. Long known only from a transcript, the original letter recently turned up.
SOURCE: Jackson 1978: 176–77

A "Surround" of Buffaloes by Indians, 1859

Alfred Jacob Miller
Watercolor on paper
9⅝ × 17⅝
The Walters Art Museum, Baltimore, Maryland, 37.1940.200
Acquired by William T. Walters from the artist

A "SURROUND" OF BUFFALOES BY INDIANS

In the fifty years preceding Lewis and Clark's expedition, the horse had created a transportation revolution for Native peoples. Mounted hunting of buffalo provided a new source of livelihood. The upshot was a transformation in power relationships between tribes. Alfred J. Miller, who traveled west with the Scottish sportsman William Drummond Stewart in 1837, painted this buffalo hunt. This painting is an 1859 copy of the 1837 original.
SOURCE: Ross 1951: fig. 200

Certificate of Warcharpa, 1804

American / Lakota
Ink on paper, silk ribbon, sealing wax
7¾ × 12⅝
The Huntington Library, San Marino, California, HM 13444

This is the only surviving certificate known to have been given out by Lewis and Clark. Either the date is an error or there were two men with similar names. Warcharpa (The Sticker) could have been one of the two anonymous "Men of War, attendants on the Chief," to whom Clark

THOMAS JEFFERSON,
PRESIDENT
OF THE UNITED STATES OF AMERICA.

CERTIFICATE OF WARCHARPA

gave certificates on August 31, the date written on this form. If so, he was Yankton. However, on September 27, 1804, they also met a Teton named Warchapa (On His Guard), and Clark implied that this Teton also received a certificate. The history of the certificate after that time is unknown. It was probably collected by Henry M. Huntington.
SOURCE: Moulton 1983–2001: 3: 31, 121–23

Trade goods, late 1700s and early 1800s

British and American
Ax: iron and steel; burning glass: glass and copper wire with case of embossed paper and wood; brooch: silver; fire steel: steel with pouch of hide and twine
Ax: 2¾ × 5 × 1⅝; burning glass: 2 × 3¼; brooch: DIAM 1⅝; fire steel: 2½ × 1¾
Ax and brooch: personal collection of Dr. J. Frederick Fausz; burning glass and fire steel: William H. Guthman Collection

Although Lewis and Clark's gifts were intended as samples of U.S. wares, American traders imported most of their goods from England. This trade ax is typical of the type made in foundries around Birmingham, the burning glass is almost certainly English, and trade silver brooches were a specialty of silversmiths in British Montreal. The Chouteaus of St. Louis often ordered oval fire steels from Sheffield, but this hand-forged example, which

TRADE GOODS

came from Pennsylvania, could have been made in the United States. Lewis and Clark's inventory of trade goods included twenty-four "Tomy hawks," twenty-four "Squaw Axes" (this one could be either), seven and three-fourths dozen burning glasses, fifteen hundred brooches, and twelve dozen fire steels. Both the burning glass and the fire steel were used to start fires; the Indians called the former "sun glasses."

The trade ax comes from an Osage site in northeastern Oklahoma. The burning glass is a cheap style used by both Euro-Americans and Indians in the eighteenth century. Lewis and Clark mention giving burning glasses to Oto, Chinookan, and Wallawalla Indians. The trade silver brooch is from Minnesota and has no maker's mark but is typical of ones mass-produced in Canada.
SOURCES: Moulton 1983–2001: 3:500–1. On axes, see Peterson 1965: 90, nos. 42–45. On silver, see Fredrickson and Gibbs 1980: 129; Quimby 1966: 91–101. On burning glasses, see The Engages 1979; Moulton 1983–2001: 2: 490, 7: 54, 9: 301. On fire steels, see Russell 1967: 352.

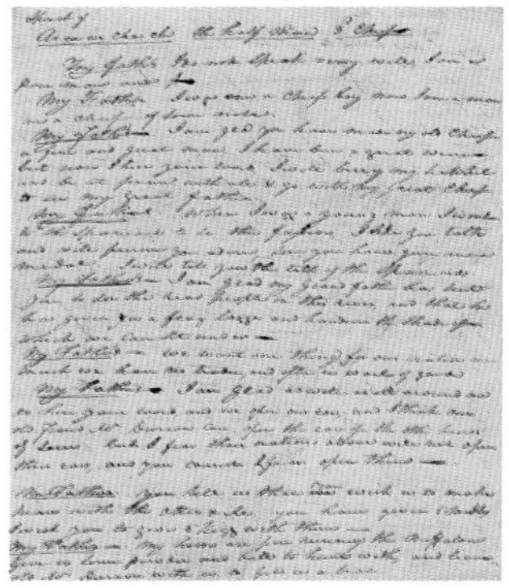

SPEECHES

Speeches of Yankton Sioux chiefs, 1804

William Clark, transcribed from Shake Hand, Mar-to-ree (White Crane), Par-nar-ne-Ar-par-be (Struck by the Pawnee), Tarromonee, and Ar-ca-we-char-chi (The Half Man)
Ink on paper
10 × 16⅜
Yale Collection of Western Americana, Beinecke Rare Book and Manuscript Library, WA Mss. s-897 #44

Clark did not record any speeches during the Teton encounter, possibly due to translation problems, but he did write down the replies of Oto, Omaha, Yankton, Arikara, and Mandan orators to Lewis's speech. These transcripts preserve the Indian rhetorical conventions that Euro-Americans often misunderstood. In these speeches, "Take pity on us this day" is repeated as a formulaic refrain.
SOURCE: Moulton 1983–2001: 3: 28–31

SHEEP HORN LADLE

Sheep horn ladle, 1800s

Lakota
Rocky Mountain sheep horn
20½ × 6 × 4
Courtesy of the Department of Anthropology, National Museum of Natural History, Smithsonian Institution, E*153937
Gift of Mildred McLean Hazen

Among the Teton, Clark noted "a Spoon made of a horn of an animile of the sheep kind the spoon will hold 2 quarts." Since the expedition had not yet seen Rocky Mountain bighorn sheep, this was their first intimation of the animal's existence. The Lakota used such spoons to dish up food at feasts.
SOURCE: Moulton 1983–2001: 3: 119

RATTLE

Rattle, 1850s

Lakota
Wood stick covered with cured hide, beads, dewclaws, quills, tin cones, wool
LENGTH 14
Courtesy of the Department of Anthropology, National Museum of Natural History, Smithsonian Institution, E*1925
Gift of Lieutenant G. K. Warren

The Teton musicians used "long sticks with Deer & Goats [antelope] Hoofs tied So as to make a gingling noise," according to Clark. This is the style of rattle he was describing. It was collected by a U.S. Army officer in the 1850s, but is an old type. Karl Bodmer illustrated similar rattles in the 1830s as part of the Mandan Dog Society regalia.
SOURCES: Moulton 1983–2001: 3: 119; Goetzmann et al. 1984: 319

CHAPTER 3
A World of Women

Arikara Village, 1866

George Catlin
Engraving and watercolor on paper
5⅞ × 9½
Missouri Historical Society, St. Louis

This is from an 1866 reprint of Catlin's 1841 book and shows an 1832 scene.
SOURCES: Catlin 1866: pl. 80; Moulton 1983–2001: 3: 152, 10: 53; Gilman and Schneider 1987: 116

Fort Clark on the Missouri, c. 1834

Karl Bodmer
Aquatint on paper
Image: 11⅞ × 17⅜
Joslyn Art Museum, Omaha, Nebraska
Gift of Enron Art Foundation

SOURCES: Wied 1843: Tableau 15; Moulton 1983–2001: 3: 211; Meyer 1977: 37

Shehek-Shote's village, 1900

Sitting Rabbit
Colored pencil and ink on canvas
Image: 39½ × 63⅞; overall: 39½ × 141½
State Historical Society of North Dakota, 800. Photograph by Sharon Silengo

SOURCES: For Mandan towns, see Bowers 1950: 111–13. For Sitting Rabbit's art, see Libby 1906: 433–36; Thiessen, Wood, and Jones 1979.

Eh-toh'k-pah-she-pée-shah, Black Moccasin, Aged Chief, 1832

George Catlin
Oil on canvas
29 × 24
Smithsonian American Art Museum, 1985.66.171
Gift of Mrs. Joseph Harrison, Jr.

SOURCES: Coues 1965: 350; Catlin 1995: 1: 211

Captain Clark & His Men Building a Line of Huts, 1810

Artist unknown
Woodcut on paper
Image: 2¾ × 4¾
Department of Special Collections, Washington University Libraries

SOURCES: Gass 1810: opp. p. 60; Masson 1889: 307–8; Coues 1893: 196; Moulton 1983–2001: 10: 64

Trade goods from Shehek-Shote's village, late 1700s and early 1800s

British and American
Beads: glass; fishhooks: iron; buttons: brass and iron; hammer: iron; shot: lead; flint; gun parts: iron and brass; arrowheads: iron
Beads: LENGTH up to 1½; fishhooks: up to 2 × 1; buttons: DIAM ¾ to 1; hammer: 3⅛ × 1¼; shot: DIAM up to ½; flints: up to 1 × 1¼; lock plate: 1¼ × 5; worm: LENGTH 1; side plate: LENGTH 3; arrowheads: up to 2⅞ × 1
Ralph Thompson Collection of the North Dakota Lewis & Clark Bicentennial Foundation, 32ME5-2000.1.21, 32ME5-2000.1.22, 32ME5-2000.1.87, 32ME5-2000.1.285, 32ME5-2000.1.286

Clark's list of trade goods in demand among the Mandan and Hidatsa included war axes, "Blue beeds, pipes, paint, The tale & [top?] feathers of the Calumet Eagle, Knives, Guns, Powder & Ball, White Buffalow Skin, & Horses &. &. arrow points."
SOURCES: Lehmer 1971: 172–79; Lehmer, Wood, and Dill 1978: 180; Wood 1986: 20; Moulton 1983–2001: 3: 484

Side-fold dress, late 1700s to early 1800s

Central or Northern Plains
Mammal hide, pigments, glass beads, dyed porcupine quills, unidentified plant fibers, sinew
47¾ × 26
Photograph from the Peabody Museum of Archaeology and Ethnology, Harvard University, © President and Fellows of Harvard College, photograph by Hillel Burger, cat. 99-12-10/53046, neg. T2925
Gift of the Heirs of David Kimball, 1899

Clark sent a woman's dress ("1 Shirt worn by the mandan Indian women of this countrey made of the Skins of the Antilope or goat") to his brother from Fort Mandan in 1805 and presented First Lady Dolley Madison with "part of an Indian dress, such as the Soes woman ware in their dances" in 1809. But the only mention of a Plains Indian woman's dress in Peale's accession records is a "Sioux squaws dress" from George C. Hutter. The one shown here was accessioned by the Peabody curator Charles Willoughby in 1899 as "Formerly owned by Capt. Lewis and presented by Lewis & Clark to Peal's," probably a misconception based on the fact that a Peale label for an Indian hunting shirt was found mistakenly associated with it. Willoughby identified it as Knisteneaux (Cree) on the basis of Alexander Mackenzie's *Voyages*; Norman Feder and John Ewers both rejected this attribution, though they did not suggest another. Rudolph F. Kurz and Karl Bodmer both illustrate what appear to be side-fold dresses, which seem to have been worn by Sioux, Cree, and possibly Cheyenne and Assiniboine women. Another side-fold dress accessioned with this one can be dated to the first quarter of the nineteenth century on the basis of buttons attached to it.

Clark's description of Sioux women's dress better fits the more common strap or tail dresses: "A loose shift of skins without sleeves fastened over the shoulders by a string falls to nearly the ancles. Some ends of the skin fall from their armpits down the arm a little way."
SOURCES: Moulton 1983–2001: 3: 488; Jackson 1978: 517; Feder 1984; McLaughlin 2003: chapter 7; Peale 1809–28: entry for June 18, 1828. For other dresses collected by Clark, see Holmberg 2002: 84; Clark to Madison, December 3, 1809, in Mary E. Cutts scrapbook, Cutts-Madison Papers, Massachusetts Historical Society. For side-fold dresses, see Jarrell and Hewitt 1937: pl. 31; Goetzmann et al. 1984: 190; Mackenzie 1802: 1: 116–17; Harrison et al. 1987: 109–10, fig. 100.

Beaded baby carrier, c. 1800–25

Crow[?]
Wood, mammal hide, glass beads, sinew, wool cloth, red ochre pigment
26 × 10 × 4½
Photograph from the Peabody Museum of Archaeology and Ethnology, Harvard University, © President and Fellows of Harvard College, photograph by Hillel Burger, cat. 99-12-10/53016, neg. T2914
Gift of the Heirs of David Kimball, 1899

This cradle has always been identified with Hutter's, which came into Peale's Museum in 1828 and was cataloged as "a Cradle—Crow Indian."

There is much debate about whether Sacagawea carried her baby in a cradleboard or a blanket. The only reference in the journals was when, in a flash flood near the Great Falls, "the bier in which the woman carrys her child and all it's cloaths wer swept away as they lay at her feet she having time only to grasp her child." What Lewis meant by "bier" (which Clark spelled "bear") is a source of disagreement; Joseph Mussulman argues that it was a mosquito bar or folded cloth.

This cradleboard is an early example of U-shaped cradles used in the Rocky Mountains and the plateau. It shows stylistic similarities (wooden backboard with pointed bottom and square top, inward-hanging fringe at top, baby pouch fastened with laces in front) to a model baby carrier at the National Museum of Natural History, Smithsonian Institution (cat. 2575), collected by the Wilkes Expedition and said to be "Made by the natives of Oregon after the fashion of the natives living east of the Rocky Mountains."
SOURCES: McLaughlin 2003: chapter 6; Mussulman 2001: 39–40; Moulton 1983–2001: 4: 341 (Lewis), 4: 343 (Clark)

Box and border robe, early 1800s

Central Plains
Bison calf skin, glue sizing, pigments
46 × 38
Photograph from the Peabody Museum of Archaeology and Ethnology, Harvard University, © President and Fellows of Harvard College, photograph by Hillel Burger, cat. 99-12-10/53124, neg. T2980.1
Gift of the Heirs of David Kimball, 1899

Several design elements of this robe are Sioux. The pigments are hematite, iron oxide, and vermilion mixed with a protein sizing. A robe with thin parallel lines was used in the Buffalo Ceremony that prepared a girl for womanhood.
SOURCES: McLaughlin 2003: chapter 9; Maurer 1992: 289; Lowie 1982: 131–32, 149; Brown 1992: 14, 75, 92–94; Goetzmann et al. 1984: 190, 304; Ewers 1939: 9–10, pls. 5-A, 7

Rattlesnake tails and necklace, 1800s

Tribe unknown
Rattlesnake tails, cured hide, seed pods
Rattles: APPROX. LENGTH 1¼; necklace: 10⅝ × 5⅞
Missouri Historical Society, St. Louis, 1953 129 0033
Gift of Mrs. Philo Stephenson

SOURCES: Moulton 1983–2001:3:291, 5:171; Vogel 1970:92

Spellings of Sacagawea's name, 1804–6

Meriwether Lewis and William Clark
Ink on paper
Up to ¼ × 1½
First two: American Philosophical Society, Codex F; last three: Missouri Historical Society, St. Louis, William Clark Papers, Voorhis #1 and Elkskin journal
Last three: Gift of Julia Clark Voorhis in memory of Eleanor Glasgow Voorhis

SOURCES: The dates on which these spellings appear are July 28, 1805, and August 19, 1805 (Codex F); June 10 and 22, 1805 (Voorhis #1); and November 24, 1805 (Elkskin journal). For spellings of Sacagawea, see Moulton 1983–2001: 4: 277, 326, 5: 9, 120, 6: 84. For other references to her, see Moulton 1983–2001: 4: 15, 171, 281, 5: 59; Anderson and Schroer 1999.

The Travellers Meeting with Minatarre Indians near Fort Clark, c. 1833

Karl Bodmer
Aquatint on paper
7¾ × 11¼
Joslyn Art Museum, Omaha, Nebraska
Gift of Enron Art Foundation

SOURCES: Wied 1843: Vignette XXVI, 315-17; Moulton 1983–2001: 3: 228, 5: 93 (wife beating); Jackson 1978: 369

Umbilical bag, mid-1800s

Probably Hidatsa
Cured hide, quills, seed beads, sinew
4¼ × 2½ × 1¼
State Historical Society of North Dakota, 9960. Photograph by Sharon Silengo
Gift of Emily Latimer, 1945

Daniel W. Longfellow, the collector of this artifact, was the manager of the agency store at Like-a-Fishhook Village, the main Mandan-Hidatsa town in the late 1870s.
SOURCES: Torrence 1994: 246–47; Lowie 1982: 147–48; Brown 1992: 30 (quotation); Wissler 1904: 241–42, 257; Beckwith 1938: 119. For Longfellow, see Gilman and Schneider 1987: 134.

Hideworking tools, late 1700s to late 1800s

Mandan / Hidatsa
Flesher: bison metatarsus; scraper: elk antler, sheet iron, brain-tanned hide cord, sinew; awls: marrow bone and bird bone; quill flattener: bone; quill case: dried bison bladder, dyed porcupine quills
Flesher: 10⅜ × 2 × 2⅛; scraper: 12 × 7 × 1¾; awls: 6¼ to 3½; quill flattener: 5¾ × ¾; quill case: 1¼ × 9 × 4
State Historical Society of North Dakota, 32ME5–2001.4.480 (flesher), 183 (scraper), 32ME5–2001.4.271, 2001.4.275 (awls), 32ME5–8194 (quill flattener), 1454 (quill case). Photograph by Sharon Silengo
Gift of Ralph Thompson (flesher, awls); field work by Thad Hecker for State Historical Society of North Dakota (quill flattener)

The flesher, awls, and quill flattener come from the site of Shehek-Shote's village; the awls were found in 1965 as power equipment was stripping earth from the site for use by United Power Electric, which built a power plant there. The scraper and the quill case were collected in the 1880s and 1890s but represent an older style.
SOURCES: Gilman and Schneider 1987: 43–47; Brown 1992: 92. On the artifacts, see Lehmer 1971: 86, 88–89.

Jeune Indienne, 1807

Charles Balthazar Julien Févret de Saint-Mémin
Black and white chalk on paper
23 × 17
Collection of The New-York Historical Society, 1860.96

Contradictory identifications written on Saint-Mémin's portraits are the origin of the doubt about the identity of this portrait-sitter. There are two copies of this portrait: a life-size chalk sketch at the New-York Historical Society and a watercolor at the Gilcrease Museum. Saint-Mémin identified the first as "Jeune Indienne des Iowas du Missoury," and another person (possibly Augustus John Foster) identified the second as "Mandan Queen," a description that could refer only to Yellow Corn. However, this portrait has never been paired with the portrait of Shehek-Shote, but with a portrait of a much younger man identified variously as "Jeune Indien des Iowas du Missoury" and "Mandan King." Saint-Mémin's identifications are often confused; the portrait of Shehek-Shote is also identified two ways: as "Indien Delaware" and as "Mandan nomme Le Grand blanc." (See entry for his portrait.)
SOURCES: Miles 1994: 145–48, 157, 435–36; Brackenridge 1904: 137

Pot, 1700s

Mandan
Clay tempered with grit (crushed, fire-cracked rock)
12 × 9¾
State Historical Society of North Dakota, 32MO26–83.442.006.3. Photograph by Sharon Silengo

SOURCES: Gilman and Schneider 1987: 116, 118; Coues 1965: 328; Catlin 1995: 1: 132. For the pots collected by Lewis and Clark, see chapter 9.

Agricultural tools, c. 1914

Hidatsa, made by Wolf Chief, Goodbird, and Buffalo Bird Woman
Rake: deer antler, ash wood, rawhide; hoe: buffalo scapula, ash wood, sinew or rawhide, plant fiber; digging stick: pine; basket: willow frame, willow and box elder bark sides, rawhide tumpline
Rake: LENGTH 50½; hoe: 30¼ × 12¾; digging stick: LENGTH 37½; basket: 18½ × 17¾
Museum Collections, Minnesota Historical Society, 7059.43a, 7059.39, 7059.41, 7059.61

These were collected by Gilbert L. Wilson.
SOURCES: Gilman and Schneider 1987: 16, 32, 35, 37; Moulton 1983–2001: 4: 15

Food samples and replicas, early 1900s

Mandan, Hidatsa, and Arikara
Dried plant material, plaster shell with painted wax surface
Corn: LENGTH up to 7; tipsin: LENGTH 28¼; squashes: up to 11¼ × 5½; beans: LENGTH up to ¼
State Historical Society of North Dakota, 66, 68, 2001.46.5, 2001.46.9 (corn); 135 (tipsin); 34, 32, 27 (squashes); 81, 83 (beans). Photograph by Sharon Silengo

These were collected or grown by George F. Will, Herbert C. Fish, and Melvin Gilmore, all researchers into traditional Mandan/Hidatsa varieties in the early twentieth century. The pumpkins and squashes are replicas created by the American Museum of Natural History, New York.
SOURCES: Moulton 1983–2001: 2: 436, 3: 261; Gilmore 1977: 15, 40, 44–45, 65–67

Mortar and pestle, pre-1913

Mandan or Hidatsa
Ash pestle, hollow tree trunk
Pestle: 42 × 5½; mortar: 19 × 8¼
Museum Collections, Minnesota Historical Society, 7059.50a, b

These were collected by Gilbert L. Wilson.
SOURCE: Gilman and Schneider 1987: 16, 63

Corn mill, late 1700s

English
Sheet iron, steel burr, wood block
HEIGHT 14¾
Colonial Williamsburg Foundation, 1950-180

Lewis purchased his three mills from E. Shoemaker & Co., Philadelphia: one for nine dollars for the use of the Corps (later cached at the mouth of the Marias), and two more for ten dollars each as Indian gifts. On October 11, 1804 (according to Ordway), they presented one to the Arikara, and on October 29 they presented the other one to the Mandan. The journals mention, several times, the admiration and delight of both tribes for the device: "they appeared delighted with the Steel Mill"; "Those people ap[peare]d much pleased with the Corn Mill"; the mill was "very pleasing to them"; it was "very Thankfully recived." However, a year later, when the North West Company trader Alexander Henry visited the Mandan village, he noted, "I saw the remains of an excellent large corn mill, which the foolish fellows had demolished to barb their arrows; the largest piece of it, which they could not break or work up into any weapon, was fixed to a wooden handle, and used to pound marrow-bones to make grease."

From the fragmentary references to them, the corn mills were apparently "hand mills"; at least one component (presumably the burr) was steel; at the Arikara village, a mill was "erected" on shore; later another one was "was fixed in the boat." A large portion of the device must have been sheet iron suitable for making arrows. This mill, composed largely of sheet iron and unusable unless "fixed" to a post or stand that had to be "erected," seems to fit most of these criteria. The piece that could not be demolished would be the burr inside the drum. Although of English design and manufacture, like much of Lewis's equipment, this type of mill was used in America, since one like it was excavated at a site in Newport News, Virginia. A similar potential design for the corn mill is illustrated in Denis Diderot's *Encyclopedie*.
SOURCES: Diderot 1762-72: 1: pl. 9; Hornung 1972: 492, fig. 1788. For the Lewis and Clark corn mills, see Jackson 1978: 44, 84, 94, 95; Moulton 1983–2001: 3: 199, 200, 209, 210 (Indians pleased), 221 (mill "erected"), 9: 82, 92 (Ordway on mills given away), 11: 193–94 ("hand mill" cached); Coues 1965: 329.

Dance of the Mandan Women, c. 1833

Karl Bodmer
Aquatint on paper
Image: 6½ × 9½
Joslyn Art Museum, Omaha, Nebraska
Gift of Enron Art Foundation

SOURCES: Wied 1843: Vignette XXVIII; Bowers 1965: 204–7; Peters 1995: 58

Courting flute, late 1800s

Dakota
Wood, sinew, feather, pigment, cured hide
29½ × 2¾ × 1½
Courtesy of the National Museum of the American Indian, Smithsonian Institution, 023174
Gift of E. W. Lenders

SOURCES: Coues 1965: 327; Beckwith 1938: 81; Maurer 1992: 118; Ewers 1986: 160–61

Child's dress with elk design, pre-1903

Lakota
Cured hide, quills, thread, ribbon
23 × 21
Missouri Historical Society, St. Louis, 1977 147 0018
Gift of Henry Hamilton, 1977

This was collected by Remington Schuyler, an artist who lived on the Rosebud Reservation in 1903–4. It then passed on to the donor, who wrote the book *The Sioux of the Rosebud: A History in Pictures* (1971). The motif is variously interpreted as an Elk Dreamer Society or Blacktail Deer Society symbol, both masculine symbols having to do with courtship.
SOURCES: Maurer 1992: 132; Coe 1977: 181

Cradle cover with Double Woman design, late 1800s

Lakota
Cured hide, porcupine quills, glass beads, down feathers, brass bells
26 × 25⅛
Courtesy of the National Museum of the American Indian, Smithsonian Institution, 009048
Gift of Joseph Keppler

SOURCES: Maurer 1992: 159; Wissler 1907: 48–50; Brown 1992: 43; Walker 1980: 165–66

Cradle cover, late 1800s

Probably Sioux
Cured hide, quills, sinew
25½ × 27½
Courtesy of the National Museum of the American Indian, Smithsonian Institution, 029635
SOURCES: For spiders and lizards, see Horse Capture and Horse Capture 2001: 101; Brown 1992: 41–43.

Calomel bottle and urethral syringe, late 1700s to early 1800s

American
Bottle: glass, ink on paper label, cotton string, white powder [mercurous chloride?]; syringe: pewter, wood
Bottle: 3 × ⅞; syringe: 8⅝ × 1½ (plunger in)
Mütter Museum, The College of Physicians of Philadelphia, 17837.86, 17090.52
Bottle: Gift of Mr. Edward Shippen Morris, 1952

This bottle is from the medicine chest of Dr. William Shippen (1736–1808), a prominent Philadelphia physician who conducted the first anatomical lectures and dissections in America. The syringe is undocumented.
SOURCES: Jackson 1978: 74, 80; Seaman 1797; Lentz 2000: 12–13; Moulton 1983–2001: 6: 239; Chuinard 1980: 133–34, 264–65, 346, 379–80

Lucy Marks, c. 1830

John Toole
Oil on canvas
22 × 17
Missouri Historical Society, St. Louis, 1936 030 0002
Gift of Meriwether Lewis Anderson

According to the donor, this is the original portrait made during Lucy's life. In 1842 Reuben Lewis (Meriwether's brother) paid John Toole thirty dollars to paint two copies of it. The copies are now at the Virginia State Library, Richmond, and the University of Virginia Art Museum, Charlottesville.
SOURCES: Bakeless 1947: 15–18; Toole to Lewis, July 4, 1842, in Lewis-Marks Papers, University of Virginia Library, Special Collections

Spectacles of Lucy Marks, c. 1830

Edmund Hughes, Middletown or Hampton, Connecticut
Silver-plated copper, glass
1 × 4½ × 4⅜ (unfolded, but not fully extended)
Missouri Historical Society, St. Louis, 1937 026 0001
Gift of Sarah Lewis Scott McKellar

The donor was Lucy's great-great-granddaughter.

Letter of Meriwether Lewis to Lucy Marks, 1805

Meriwether Lewis
Ink on paper
15 × 9⅜
Missouri Historical Society, St. Louis, Meriwether Lewis Collection
Gift of Meriwether Lewis Anderson

The watermark on the paper is "Hayes & Wise 1799."
SOURCE: Jackson 1978: 222–25

Julia Hancock Clark, c. 1810

John Wesley Jarvis
Oil on canvas
30 × 25
Missouri Historical Society, St. Louis, 1921 055 0002
Gift of Julia Clark Voorhis in memory of Eleanor Glasgow Voorhis

The date of this portrait is a puzzle. An inscription written in ink on the back, photographed before it was obliterated by relining, said, "Mrs. Julia Hancock Clark / To G.R.H. Clark from his uncle Geo. Hancock / Jarvis pinx." "G.R.H. Clark" was Julia's youngest son, George Rogers Hancock Clark. His uncle George was Julia's brother. The fact that the painting stayed in the Hancock family before being given to Julia's son implies that it was made before or at her marriage in 1808. Julia's gown is consistent with brides' clothing of the period. Jarvis (1780–1840) worked in Philadelphia from 1796 to 1801 and in New York after that, though he made frequent trips to New Orleans in the winter. In late 1820 he came to Louisville and painted William and Lucy Croghan, William Clark's sister and brother-in-law, and either painted or gathered material for his posthumous portrait of George Rogers Clark. Julia had recently died in Virginia, on June 27, 1820. James Holmberg, of the Filson Historical Society, hypothesizes that this portrait could have been commissioned posthumously from Jarvis in 1820, either by William Clark or by George Hancock, her brother, who was at that time living in Jefferson County, Kentucky. A copy of this portrait was painted by Sarkis Erganian and was owned by Elizabeth (Mrs. Daniel R.) Russell, the daughter of William Clark Kennerly, in 1948, but it has not been located. The portrait shown here was listed in the inventory of Clark's estate at his death. When it came to the Missouri Historical Society in 1921, this and the portrait of William Clark were framed in matching Victorian rococo frames, giving rise to a legend that they were a matched set.
SOURCES: Holmberg 2002: 189; Bakeless Papers, Microfilm 2580, University of Virginia Library. For this painting, see Dickson 1949; personal correspondence of Holmberg to Gilman, March 8, 2001; Kennerly and Russell 1948: facing p. 60; William Clark Probate File, Rare Documents, Missouri State Archives.

Notebook of Julia H. Clark, 1808–20 and Locket with hair of Julia and Mary Clark, c. 1820

Notebook: Julia H. Clark; locket: maker unknown
Notebook: ink on paper bound in red morocco leather with copper alloy clasp; locket: copper alloy, gold, black enamel, glass, hair
Notebook: 16½ × 5⅛ (open); 8¼ × 5⅛ × ⅜ (closed); locket: 2 × 1½ × ½
Missouri Historical Society, St. Louis, William Clark Papers (notebook), 1952 095 0003 (locket)
Purchase from Mrs. Samuel Maguire

The locket was purchased from the widow of Julia Clark Voorhis's attorney and executor.

SOURCE: Kennerly and Russell 1948: 52–55

Letter from Mary Margaret Clark to Papa, 1821 and Miniature of Mary M. Clark, pre-1821

Letter: Mary Margaret Clark; miniature: artist unknown
Letter: ink on paper; miniature: watercolor on ivory
Letter: 10⅛ × 8 (folded); miniature: 2¼ × 1¾
Missouri Historical Society, St. Louis, William Clark Papers (letter), 1961 132 0006 (miniature)
Gift of Claire (Mrs. Harry) Seeley

SOURCE: Kennerly and Russell 1948: 55

Capote, late 1800s

Canadian / Ojibway
Blanket wool, trade wool, brass beads
48½ × 25 (at shoulder)
State Historical Society of North Dakota, 856. Photograph by Sharon Silengo
Gift of Mrs. A. M. Perdriaux, 1928

The favored style among French and métis (mixed-blood) fur traders of the Northern Plains was a capote, a hooded coat made from a trade blanket. Capotes had been part of traditional French-Canadian dress since the 1600s and were often traded to and worn by Indians. At Fort Mandan, John Ordway wrote, "Blanket cappoes provided for each man who Stood in need of them." They were worn with a belt or sash. This one came from near Turtle Mountain Reservation in northern North Dakota, where capotes were used virtually unchanged into the early twentieth century. It was collected by W. L. Harris, the brother of the donor, whose husband ran the drugstore in Towner, North Dakota, in 1916.
SOURCES: Moulton 1983–2001: 4: 257, 5: 18, 7: 310, 9: 102 (quotation); Back 1991

CAPOTE

Headdress of the White Buffalo Cow Society, c. 1900

Mandan / Hidatsa
White bison hide, magpie and owl feathers, dyed eagle plume
16½ × 10
State Historical Society of North Dakota, 585. Photograph by Sharon Silengo
Gift of Mrs. C. W. Hoffman, 1907

There were still living members of the White Buffalo Cow Society in 1900, when this headband was collected by the Indian agent for the Mandan and Hidatsa. When the women held their ceremony, the headbands were smoked in the fumes from wild peppermint stems.
SOURCE: Bowers 1965: 207

HEADDRESS

Quilt, c. 1805

Jane Lewis Anderson and Mary Garland Marks
Cotton
84½ × 81½
Collection of Mary Johnston Evans

According to family tradition, Lewis's sisters made this quilt for him while he was away on the expedition. He had one full sister, Jane Lewis, and one half sister, Mary Marks. This quilt was passed down in the family of one of Jane's daughters.

QUILT

Infant cap of Meriwether Lewis Clark, 1809

Maker unknown
Cotton batiste
6¼ × 3¾ × 5½
Missouri Historical Society, St. Louis, 1961 132 0002
Gift of Claire (Mrs. Harry) Seeley

Much of Julia's life, and influence, revolved around her children. Her first son, born in January 1809, was named Meriwether Lewis Clark. Julia dressed the baby in this cap. When he was five, Julia wrote, "Lewis . . . has the greatest taste for drawing I ever saw, he is constantly at it." Eventually he joined the army and became an engineer. He fought for the Confederacy in the Civil War.
SOURCES: Julia Clark to her brother George Hancock, February 27, 1814, William Clark Papers, Missouri Historical Society Archives; Christensen et al. 1999: 188–89

INFANT CAP

CHAPTER 4
Depictions of the Land

Winter Village of the Minatarres, c. 1833

Karl Bodmer
Aquatint on paper
Image: 10¼ × 13
Joslyn Art Museum, Omaha, Nebraska
Gift of Enron Art Foundation

SOURCES: Wied 1843: Tableau 26; Goetzmann et al. 1984: 284, 310

Tin horn, 1800s

American
Tinned sheet iron, brass
13½ × 2⅜
Courtesy of the National Museum of American History, Smithsonian Institution, cat. DL*257491.101
Gift of Kenneth E. Jewett, 1964

This horn is from a collector of tinware in Peterborough, New Hampshire, who concentrated on "representative examples of the tinsmith's art" and "early American tinware," mainly from New England.
SOURCES: Jackson 1978: 71, 79, 175; Moulton 1983–2001: 2: 72, 103, 9: 83, 107, 115. For more on this artifact, see Gould 1958: 124, pl. 250; Dover Stamping Co. 1971: 45.

The Interior of the Hut of a Mandan Chief, c. 1833

Karl Bodmer
Aquatint on paper
Image: 11 × 16⅜
Joslyn Art Museum, Omaha, Nebraska
Gift of Enron Art Foundation

SOURCES: Wied 1843: Tableau 19; Moulton 1983–2001: 3: 489; Catlin 1995: 1: 130; Goetzmann et al. 1984: 291

Sketch of a Mandan battle ax, 1805

William Clark
Ink on paper
Image: ¼ × ¾
Courtesy of the American Philosophical Society, Codex C, p. 158

SOURCE: Moulton 1983–2001: 3: 280 (sketch), 286–87 (description), 288 (last quotation)

Missouri war ax, pre-1870

Osage
Iron, wood, cured hide, beads, twine, cotton cloth, brass tacks
30 × 8½ × 1¼
Courtesy of the National Museum of the American Indian, Smithsonian Institution, 007080

This was collected in 1870 from the Osage but may be considerably older. Bodmer illustrated Mato-Tope (Mandan) and Addih-Hiddisch (Hidatsa) holding Missouri war axes in 1833–34.
SOURCES: Peterson 1965: 22–23, 91 (no. 46); Goetzmann et al. 1984: 309, 315

Anvil, c. 1809

American
Iron
6½ × 12⅝ × 6
Courtesy of Headwaters Heritage Museum
Gift of Margaret Hutchinson

James Aplin gave this anvil to Carl Hopping, who used it in the Copper City mines. After his death, Mrs. Hopping moved in with Asa Hutchinson and his sister Margaret. Margaret Hutchinson presented it to the Gallatin County Historical Society, and it was transferred from there to Headwaters Heritage Museum in the 1980s. There is no inventory of the auction of equipment from the expedition, so the hypothetical connection for this anvil cannot be proved. It is identifiable as a U.S. Army anvil from the design of an eagle holding arrows cast in relief on the side; this design was used on buttons and other uniform components in the pre-1812 era. The small size of the anvil shows it was meant to be portable. In addition to Lewis's auction, Clark also auctioned off "A large quantity of other property belonging to the U States," possibly including expedition equipment, in July 1809.
SOURCES: Chittenden 1954: 137–45; Williams 1976: 5–6; Colter-Frick 1997: 474–76; Jackson 1978: 424; "Sales at Auction," *Missouri Gazette*, July 19, 1809

Shehek-Shote, 1807

Charles Balthazar Julien Févret de Saint-Mémin
Black and white chalk on paper, with gilded wood frame and glass with black paint and gold leaf
24⅞ × 18⅞ × 1¾ (framed)
Courtesy of the American Philosophical Society, FAP 144

Shehek-Shote never benefited much from his association with Lewis and Clark. According to a member of the escort party that returned him to his home in 1809: "The Indians saw their chief, Shehaka, on our boats, and were almost frantic with joy and eagerness to speak with him. . . . The natives made a jubilee and celebration for the return of Shehaka and neglected everything and everybody else." But by 1811, when he received visits from John Bradbury and Henry M. Brackenridge, his status had changed. Bradbury wrote, "He met us at the door, and after shaking hands with us, to my great surprise he said in English, 'come in house.'" Later, he "came dressed in a suit of clothes brought with him from the United States." Bradbury added, "He informed us that he had a great wish to go live with the whites, and that several of his people, induced by the representations he had made of the white people's mode of living, had the same intentions." Brackenridge described him with "complexion fair, very little different from that of a white man much exposed to the sun." He noted: "They [he and his wife] had returned home loaded with presents, but have since fallen into disrepute from the extravagant tales which they related as to what they had witnessed. . . . He . . . spoke sensibly of the insecurity, the ferocity of manners, and the ignorance, of the state of society in which he was placed." The Hidatsa chief Le Borgne called him a "bag of lies" in Brackenridge's presence. Shehek-Shote paid a second visit to St. Louis in 1812 and was apparently killed by a party of Gros Ventres (either Hidatsa or Atsina) while returning from that journey.

From 1818 to 1994, the man in this portrait was identified as Shehek-Shote. The portrait, along with the Lewis and Clark papers, was acquired by the American Philosophical Society in 1817. Written on the reverse is: "Mandan/ nomme Le Grand Blanc/venu Philada 1807/accompagne Par [M. Cheste?] Lewis and Clark." ("M. Cheste?" is inserted and may refer to René Jusseaume, the interpreter who accompanied Shehek-Shote to the East.) The inscription was written either by the artist or by John Vaughan, the librarian of the American Philosophical Society who accessioned the Lewis and Clark material. When the portrait was exhibited at the Pennsylvania Academy of the Fine Arts in 1818, it was titled "portrait of Mandan, surnamed the Great White, an Indian Chief, who accompanied Messrs. Lewis and Clark to Philadelphia in 1807." It was lithographed as "Sha-ha-ka, a Mandan chief," for McKenney and Hall in 1838.

However, in 1994 Ellen Miles, of the National Portrait Gallery, disputed this long-standing identification because a second version of the portrait (at the New-York Historical Society) was labeled "Indien Delaware" by the artist. Miles speculated that the portrait shows Montgomery Montour, a chief of the Delaware, partly because it shows the Delaware custom of cutting the rim of the ear from top to bottom. (This is not, however, a custom confined to the Delaware; Victor Collot's print *Indian of the Mandanes*, published in 1826 but drawn in 1796, apparently shows a Mandan with a similar ear treatment, and Alfred J. Miller described and portrayed the custom on a Nez Perce man in 1837.) There are portraits of a much younger man and woman, whom Miles believes to be Shehek-Shote and wife, at the New-York Historical Society and the Gilcrease Museum; however, the versions at New York are labeled by Saint-Mémin as "Jeune Indien [*and* Indienne] des iowas du missoury," making their identification unsure.

In 1807 Shehek-Shote was about forty years old and known for his obesity, which strongly suggests this portrait rather than the others. In addition, the early identification of this portrait by Vaughan, who probably met Shehek-Shote, is persuasive. A copper plate engraving of this portrait in the Benjamin Smith Barton Papers at the American Philosophical Society may be linked to Lewis's early efforts to illustrate his book.

SOURCES: Coues 1965: 331, 333, 373; Jackson 1978: 325, 432–38; Brackenridge 1904: 137. On Shehek-Shote's return and later life, see James 1966: 26; Bradbury 1817: 138, 142–43, 151–52; Brackenridge 1904: 137; Brackenridge 1962: 261. On his death, see James 1966: 6; Holmberg 2002: 117–18, 258. Kennerly and Russell 1948: 18 add the information that he stood six feet, ten inches tall. For the identification of this portrait, see Miles 1994: 144–48, 156–57, 287, 389; McKenney and Hall 1838–44: 1: 201; Collot 1826: atlas, pl. 24; Bell 1973: 92; Moulton 1983–2001: 3: 213n, 8: 308. Lewis's purchase of copper plates (although not the one of Shehek-Shote) is documented in Jackson 1978: 462–63.

Shehek-Shote's map, 1805

William Clark and Shehek-Shote
Ink on paper
8½ × 12
Yale Collection of Western Americana, Beinecke Rare Book and Manuscript Library, WA Mss. 303 #12
Gift of William R. Coe

An incomplete draft is on one side of the paper, with the final map on the reverse. This photograph shows the final map. The draft shows the war path leading to a camp with a pictograph, just past the mouth of the Big Horn River, possibly the camp raided in the war party.

SOURCES: Withington 1952: 170; Moulton 1983–2001: 1: maps 31a, 31b, 3: 269

Map of "Lewis's River" and "Clark's River," 1806

William Clark and "Sundery Indians of the Chopunnish [Nez Perce] Nation together"
Ink on paper
13¾ × 9⅞
Missouri Historical Society, St. Louis, William Clark Papers
Gift of Julia Clark Voorhis in memory of Eleanor Glasgow Voorhis

This was made at Camp Chopunnish, on the Clearwater. It shows mostly names of tribes and a schematic diagram of rivers and routes.

SOURCE: Moulton 1983–2001: 1: 11, 23, map 102. This map is the rough source for Moulton's map 101 ("Chopunnish map," below).

Shirt and leggings, 1830s[?]

Mandan
Shirt: cured hide, dyed quills, horsehair, beads, pigment; leggings: same, with human hair
Shirt: 29 × 64 (with arms out); leggings: LENGTH 40
University of Pennsylvania Museum of Archaeology and Anthropology, cat. nos. 38251a, 38251b, neg. nos. T4-2330, T4-2329
Gift of John Wanamaker

The collector and Catlin scholar Thomas Donaldson bought this suit from the sale of John H. McIlvain's collection in Philadelphia in 1885 and transferred it to the University of Pennsylvania Museum in 1901. McIlvain is known to have acquired some of the Catlin collection.

SOURCES: Bodmer's aquatint of Pehriska-Ruhpa is reproduced in Ewers et al. 1984: 71. See also Ewers et al. 1984: 22–23; Haseltine 1885.

Cut Nose's map, 1806

Cut Nose and the brother of Twisted Hair, Nez Perce
Ink on paper
13½ × 9⅝
Yale Collection of Western Americana, Beinecke Rare Book and Manuscript Library, WA Mss. 303 #41
Gift of William R. Coe

The caption, in Clark's hand, reads, "Sketch given us May 8th 1806 by the *Cut nose*, and the brother of the *twisted hair*."

SOURCE: Moulton 1983–2001: 1: map 98

Chopunnish map, 1806

"Sundery Indians of the Chopunnish [Nez Perce] Nation"
Ink on paper
13½ × 9⅝
Yale Collection of Western Americana, Beinecke Rare Book and Manuscript Library, WA Mss. 303 #43
Gift of William R. Coe

Reuben Gold Thwaites, looking for a continuous waterway he could identify with "Clark's River," concluded it was the route running from the Columbia via the Pend Oreille River to Clark's Fork and the Bitterroot. Moulton followed him. However, Clark's map of the lower "Clark's River" much more closely resembles the Spokane, including a major waterfall corresponding to Spokane Falls at present Spokane, Washington. Because a well-known Indian route went up the Spokane and thence overland to Lake Pend Oreille, my hypothesis is that both Clark and Thwaites were misled by Indian mapping conventions into thinking this route had to be a continuous waterway. The caption to this map, in Clark's hand, reads, "This Sketch was given by Sundery Indians of the Chopunnish Nation together on the 29th 30th and 31st of May 1806 at Our Camp on the Flat Head [Clearwater] river."

SOURCE: Moulton 1983–2001: 1: map 101

Skaddot map, 1806

"A Skaddot [Klickitat] Chief a Chopunnish [Nez Perce] and a Skillute [Clackamas]"
Ink on paper
13⅝ × 9¾
Yale Collection of Western Americana, Beinecke Rare Book and Manuscript Library, WA Mss. 303 #40
Gift of William R. Coe

The caption, in Clark's hand, reads, "This Sketch was given by a Skaddot Chief a Chopunnish and a Skillute Several other Indians at the Great Narrows of Columbia on the 18th April 1806."

SOURCE: Moulton 1983–2001: 1: map 96

Subway map of Washington, D.C.

© Washington, D.C. Metropolitan Area Transit Authority

Clatsop map, 1806

"A Clott Sopp Indn."
Ink on paper
7⅛ × 9
Yale Collection of Western Americana, Beinecke Rare Book and Manuscript Library, WA Mss. 303 #39
Gift of William R. Coe

SOURCE: Moulton 1983–2001: 1: map 94

Map of the Columbia, Snake, and "Clark's River"

Cartography by Gene Thorp

Octant, c. 1800

Spencer, Browning, and Rust, London
Ebony frame, ivory scales, brass index arm and fittings, glass lenses and filters
15¾ × 13 × 3
Courtesy of the National Museum of American History, Smithsonian Institution, acc. 257245, cat. PH*326111
Gift of Mount St. Mary's College, Emmitsburg, Maryland, 1965

SOURCES: Jackson 1978: 82, 96; Moulton 1983–2001: 2: 411, 9: 121. For how to use the instrument, see Hawkes 1981: 36; Benson, Irwin, and Moore 1995: 75–76. See also Bedini 1984; Bedini 1990: 339–72.

Sextant, late 1700s or early 1800s

W. & S. Jones, London
Brass body, German silver scales, wood handle, glass lenses; mahogany case
11 × 12 × 4
Courtesy of the National Museum of American History, Smithsonian Institution, cat. PH*81.745.6
Gift of Haverford College Observatory

W. and S. Jones operated from 1788 to 1860 in Holborn, London.
SOURCES: Jackson 1978: 82, 96; Moulton 1983–2001: 2: 410–11; Stein 1993: 351, 358, 359, 371, 372

Latitude reading, 1805

William Clark
Ink on paper
Image: 2⅛ × 4⅞
Missouri Historical Society, St. Louis, William Clark Papers, Voorhis #1
Gift of Julia Clark Voorhis in memory of Eleanor Glasgow Voorhis

SOURCES: Moulton 1983–2001: 4: 321; Starr 2001: 17

Pocket chronometer, 1807–8

Joseph Romer, London
Gold, glass, enamel, silver
3⅛ × 2⅛ × ⅞
Courtesy of the National Museum of American History, Smithsonian Institution, acc. 57657, cat. ME*285465
Gift of U.S. Coast and Geodetic Survey, 1914

Lewis never specified the maker of his chronometer. Andrew Ellicott recommended "One of Arnolds chronometers, (if it could be had,)" but this refers to a design rather than a maker. Lewis implied, but did not state, that he did purchase the type designed by the British instrument-maker John Arnold. With his penchant for endowing his instruments with gender, he wrote: "Her ballance-wheel and [e]scapement were on the most improved construction. she rested on her back, in a small case prepared for her, suspended by an universal joint. she was carefully wound up every day at twelve oclock." On another occasion he added: "The in[n]er cases of the Chronometer are confined by a screw. She is wound up and the works are stoped by inscerting a hog's bristle." The chronometer did not come mounted in a box, and so Lewis had to have one custom-made, along with the "universal joint" or gimbals to keep it level. However, later he removed the instrument from the box and "placed [it] in my fob as I conceived for greater security." These scattered references point to a pocket chronometer (a fob pocket being too small for anything else) with a spring-detent escapement ("the most improved construction"). The fact that it was not originally boxed supports this assumption, since deck watches and nautical chronometers tended to come already boxed.

This pocket chronometer has a spring-detent escapement and a blued, oversprung, helical balance spring. Its crystal has been replaced; the original crystal was probably a thick, high-domed glass, possibly with a bull's eye center. It was replaced with the present shallow, bevelled crystal by the addition of a silver spacing ring, forming a rim around the crystal. The watch is in an eighteen-carat gold pair case, of which the outer case is missing. Marked on the movement is: "Jos[h] Romer Rosomon Street London No 206." Nothing is known of Romer. The case has a London mark, "M," for 1807–8. The case-maker was most likely William Mansell, who was working on Rosomon Street, Clerkenwell, in 1800 and was in business for many years.
SOURCES: Jackson 1978: 23, 48, 51, 88, 91; Moulton 1983–2001: 2: 382 (stopped), 412 (description), 7: 266 (wet, oiled), 8: 83, 85 (fob pocket); e-mail to Carolyn Gilman from W. David Todd, National Museum of American History, July 17, 2000. See also Betts 1996.

Chart from *The Nautical Almanac and Astronomical Ephemeris*, 1804

Printed for the Commissioners of Longitude by C. Buckton and sold by P. Elmsly, London
Ink on paper, bound in modern marbled cardboard with cloth spine
9 × 12¾ × 1½ (open); 9 × 6 (closed)
Courtesy of the American Philosophical Society, 528.2 N22

The 1804 volume, shown here, was printed in 1796.
SOURCE: Preston 2000

Boat compass, early 1800s

Edmund M. Blunt, New York
Wood box, copper bowl, iron and brass gimbals, lead weight, paper compass rose, glass cover, paint
6⅛ × 10⅛ × 10¼
Courtesy of the National Museum of American History, Smithsonian Institution, cat. PH*81.20.1
Gift of Robert C. Bichan, 1981

Edmund M. Blunt, Chartseller, did business at 202 Water St., New York. He was making and selling surveying instruments during the War of 1812 and had been in business for several years before the war. In 1849 his two sons, Edward and George W., succeeded to the business established by their father.
SOURCES: Jackson 1978: 82, 96; Smart 1962: 13

List of courses and distances, 1805

William Clark
Ink on paper
2⅞ × 4⅞
Missouri Historical Society, St. Louis, William Clark Papers, Voorhis #1
Gift of Julia Clark Voorhis in memory of Eleanor Glasgow Voorhis

SOURCE: Moulton 1983–2001: 4: 17–18

Route map, 1805

William Clark
Ink on paper
8⅛ × 12
Yale Collection of Western Americana, Beinecke Rare Book and Manuscript Library, WA Mss. 303 #14-1
Gift of William R. Coe

SOURCE: Moulton 1983–2001: 1: map 46

Surveyor's compass, c. 1817

Thomas Whitney, Philadelphia
Instrument: brass, silvered brass, iron, glass; case: wood, paper
Instrument: 9 × 15¼ × 6½; case: 16½
Collection of Historical Scientific Instruments, Harvard University, Cambridge, Mass., 5207
Purchased from Margaret Zervas, 1969

SOURCES: Jackson 1978: 48, 96; Moulton 1983–2001: 2: 413, 4: 341–43, 345, 9: 177; Smart 1962: 1: 166–67

Map of Columbia River near the mouth, 1805

William Clark
Ink and watercolor on paper
8 × 5
Courtesy of the American Philosophical Society, Codex I, p. 152

SOURCE: Moulton 1983–2001: 6: 49–50, 52, 65–67

Sitting Rabbit's map of the Missouri River (detail), 1906–7

Mandan
Colored pencil and ink on canvas
Image: 18 × 100; overall: 18 × 279
State Historical Society of North Dakota, 679. Photograph by Sharon Silengo

SOURCES: Thiessen, Wood, and Jones 1979; Warhus 1997: 43–52

Clark's route maps of the Missouri River, 1833

Benjamin O'Fallon, after William Clark
Ink, pencil, and watercolor on paper, bound in leather covered with blue paper
15¾ × 10¼ (each page)
Joslyn Art Museum, Omaha, Nebraska, NNG 513
Gift of Enron Art Foundation

Shown here are sheets 16, 17, and 18. The maps appear to be in the hand of O'Fallon and another person (probably a clerk). They were purchased by Northern Natural Gas Co. (later InterNorth, which was purchased by Enron) in 1962. The company returned them to the United States from Germany and deposited them at the Joslyn Art Museum. They consist of seventeen maps showing the Missouri from near Omaha to the Knife River. The first sheet is numbered "No. 13," implying that twelve other maps, from Camp Dubois to Omaha, originally existed; these are now lost. In July 1805 Jefferson received, along with the shipment from Fort Mandan, "29. half sheets" showing the "survey of the river & no more." These were probably the twelve sheets now missing plus the seventeen from Omaha to the Knife River.
SOURCES: Wood and Moulton 1981; Moulton 1983–2001: 1: 7–8, maps 27–29

Map of the Missouri River

Cartography by Gene Thorp

Rocky Landscape with a Hunter and Soldiers, late 1600s

Salvator Rosa
Oil on canvas
56 × 75⅝
Musée du Louvre, Paris. Photograph © Réunion des Musées Nationaux/Art Resources, NY, 99DE10528/INV 586

SOURCES: Scott 1995: 209, pl. 221; private communication to Carolyn Gilman from Elizabeth Chew, Monticello

Parfleche with landscape design, c. 1900

Arapaho
Rawhide, pigment
27¼ × 15⅜ × 1¾
American Museum of Natural History Library, 50/956
Gift of Mrs. Morris K. Jessup

This was collected by Alfred L. Kroeber.
SOURCE: Kroeber 1983: 105–6

Landscape with the Marriage of Isaac and Rebekah ("The Mill"), 1648

Claude Lorrain
Oil on canvas
58¾ × 77⅝
© National Gallery, London, NG 12

SOURCES: Langdon 1989: 6–7, pl. 1. For Claude Lorrain glass, see Tesseract 1998: no. 35 and Tesseract 1999: no. 40.

A Map of Part of the Continent of North America, 1805

Nicholas King, after William Clark
Ink and wash on paper
30¾ × 44⅛
Library of Congress, G3300.1805.C5 vault
Transferred from the State Department, 1961

Lewis sent the original from which this copy was made to Henry Dearborn, the secretary of war, and wrote Jefferson that it would give "the idea we entertain of the connection of these rivers, which has been formed from the corresponding testimony of a number of Indians who have visited the country, and who have been seperately and carefully examined on that subject, and we therefore think it entitled to some degree of confidence." The copy in the Library of Congress is known as the State Department copy, and the one in the National Archives is the U.S. War Department copy, as its cartouche states. The extended titles of both are: "A Map of part of the Continent of North America, Between the 35th and 51st degrees of North Latitude, and extending from 89° Degrees of West Longitude to the Pacific Ocean." The State Department copy adds, "Copied by Nicholas King 1805." A third copy by King, now lost, was printed in the magazine *Science* in 1887.
SOURCES: Wheat 1958: 2: map 270; Moulton 1983–2001: 1: 9, 22, maps 32a, 32b; Jackson 1978: 230, 233

A Map of Part of the Continent of North America, 1806

Nicholas King, after William Clark
Black, blue, and red ink on paper
28 × 38¾
Boston Athenaeum, Rare $ Δ 8 .G5 .1
Purchased from Leonard and Co.

The creation and the subsequent history of this map are unknown until its purchase by the Boston Athenaeum from a map dealer in 1866. Its full title is "A Map of part of the Continent of North America, Whereon is laid down the Missouri, Jeffersons, Lewis's, Clarks, and the Columbia, Rivers; from the Mississippi to the Pacific Ocean, as corrected by the Celestial observations of Messrs Lewis & Clark, during their tour of discovery in 1805. Copied from Lewis & Clarks Map By N. King, for the War Departmt. of U.S."
SOURCES: Moulton 1983: 21–22; Moulton 1983–2001: 1: 12, map 123; Wheat 1958: 43–44, opp. p. 50; Jackson 1978: 323

A Map of Lewis and Clark's Track, 1814

Samuel Lewis, copyist; Samuel Harrison, engraver; after original by William Clark
Ink on paper
11⅞ × 27½
Library of Congress, G4126 .S12 .1814 .L4 vault COPY 1
Force Map Collection No. 409

This is the version of the map printed with the Philadelphia edition of Lewis and Clark's book. The map was reengraved with a more elaborate cartouche and printed on better paper for the London edition.
SOURCE: Moulton 1983–2001: 1: 13, map 126

Ice glider tip, early 1800s

Mandan
Incised rib bone
4¼ × 1
State Historical Society of North Dakota, 32ME5–8194
Field work by Thad Hecker for the State Historical Society of North Dakota

This rib-bone tip was fixed to a shaft for sliding along the snow. John Ordway saw the Mandan playing the game: "Although the day was cold & Stormy we Saw Several of the chiefs and warries were out at play. . . . they had flattish rings made out of clay Stone & two men had sticks abt. 4 feet long with 2 Short peaces across the fore end of it . . . in such a manner that they would Slide Some distance they had a place fixed across their green from the head chiefs house . . . which was Smothe as a house flour. . . . two men would run at a time with Each a Stick & one carried a ring. they run abt. half way and then Slide their sticks after the ring. they had marks made for the Game but I do not understand how they count the game." This tip was collected at Deapolis, probably the site where Ordway saw the game, in the late 1950s or early 1960s.
SOURCES: Moulton 1983–2001: 9: 104. For more on ice glider tips, which abound at Mandan archaeological sites, see Lehmer 1971: 119, 156, 157; Wood 1986: 104–10.

ICE GLIDER TIP

Sketch of a spontoon ax, 1805

Meriwether Lewis
Ink on paper
Image: ¾ × ¾
Courtesy of the American Philosophical Society, Codex C, p. 165

Lewis illustrated this style of blade, calling it "the oalder fassion," and criticizing it as "inconvenient." He wrote: "It is somewhat in the form of the blade of an Espantoon but is attatchd to a helve of the dementions

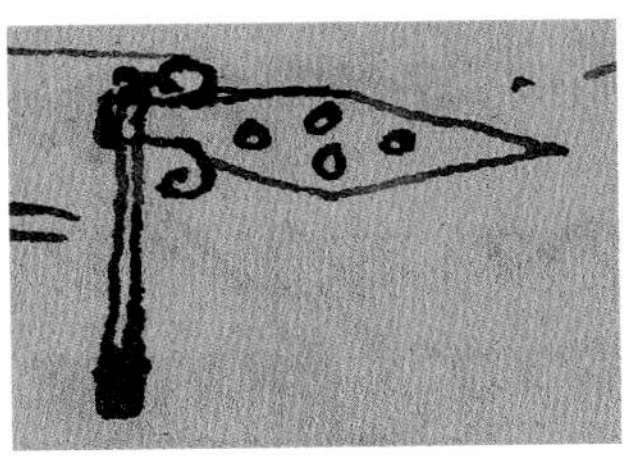

SKETCH OF A SPONTOON AX

before described [14 inches long]. the blade is sometimes by way of ornament purforated with two three or more small circular holes. . . . it is from 12 to 15 inches in length." In 1804 the spontoon ax was out of fashion and the Missouri war ax was popular. Spontoon tomahawks received their name from the military espontoon, a polearm carried by commissioned officers who fought on foot. The evidence points to an eighteenth-century French origin for the tomahawk design, but they were traded by the North West and Hudson's Bay Companies well into the mid-nineteenth century.
SOURCE: Moulton 1983–2001: 3: 287

SPONTOON AX

Spontoon ax, 1830–50

Northern Woodlands
Iron, wood, fur, string
23¼ × 11½ × 2½
Courtesy of the Department of Anthropology, National Museum of Natural History, Smithsonian Institution, E*359628
Gift of Victor J. Evans, 1931

Spontoon ax heads are relatively common on the Upper Missouri; there is one at the Four Bears Museum in New Town, North Dakota, and another at the Montana Historical Society. A datable specimen with a Sheffield maker's mark (cross and L) was recently found near the confluence of the Yellowstone and Missouri Rivers and is in a private collection. The cross and L was used by a series of Sheffield cutlers after 1821.
SOURCES: Peterson 1965: 24–26, 92; Moulton 1983–2001: 3: 287; Lassey 2000

Log reel and sandglass, 1800s

American[?]
Reel: wood; sandglass: glass, wood, cord, sand
Reel: 26 × 6⅞; sandglass: 4 × 2⅞
Courtesy of the National Museum of American History, Smithsonian Institution, cat. nos. 1980.0229.01 and .02

Navigators used a device called a log to measure distance traveled on water. A log consisted of a line, a reel, and a log chip. The line was tied with knots at measured intervals and wrapped around the reel; at its end was the log chip, a triangular, weighted piece of wood. To measure a boat's speed, the navigator threw

LOG REEL

SANDGLASS

the log chip into the water and let the line run out for thirty seconds, measured by the sandglass. When the time was up, he counted how many knots had paid out, giving the boat's speed in knots. On a river, it was necessary to subtract the speed of the current. Lewis purchased a "Log line reel & log ship [chip]" for $1.95 from Thomas Whitney in Philadelphia. In his list of requirements, he specified that he wanted a "patent log." The men would have used it mainly when the boat was under sail or when they measured the river current.
SOURCES: Jackson 1978: 69, 82; Knight 1874–76: 1348–49

Surveyor's chain, 1800s

American
Iron links, brass markers
Overall: 396 (33 ft.); links: 7½
Missouri Historical Society, St. Louis, X14779

Though Lewis tried to get a tape measure custom made, he ended up taking a chain, the usual tool that surveyors used to measure land. The men stretched the chain taut between

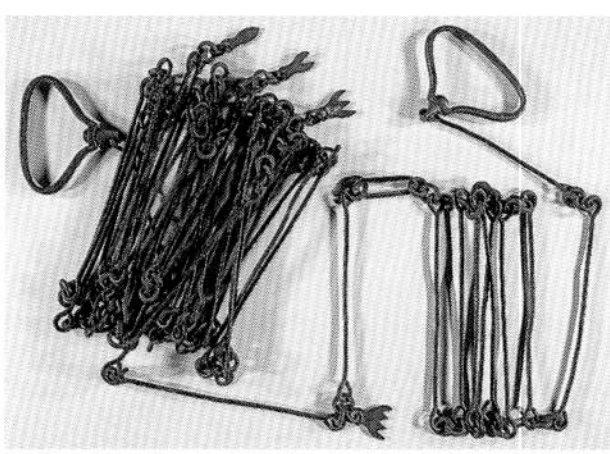

SURVEYOR'S CHAIN

two poles or rods through the rings at the ends. The links averaged 7.92 inches, so one hundred links equaled 66 feet or four poles (also called rods). Every ten links were marked with a metal tab. Often the distances so measured were used in trigonometric calculations, for instance to find the width of a river. Like this one, Lewis's was a two-pole chain. He purchased his from Thomas Whitney for two dollars; it no longer exists.
SOURCES: Jackson 1978: 96; Moulton 1983–2001: 2: 92–93n

Drafting instruments, late 1700s or early 1800s

Maker unknown
Case: wood, shagreen; instruments: ebony, brass, ivory, steel
Case: 6¾ × 2⅝ × 1¼
Courtesy of the National Museum of American History, Smithsonian Institution, acc. 236805, cat. PH*319341
Gift of Preston R. Bassett, 1961

Lewis purchased a "Case of plotting Instruments" from Thomas Whitney

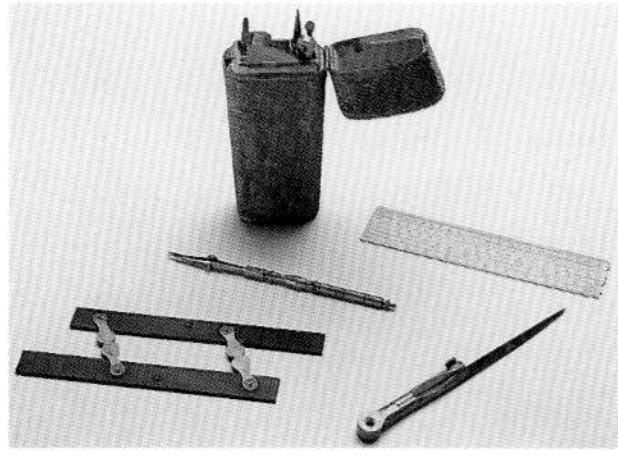

DRAFTING INSTRUMENTS

for fourteen dollars. Clark used them to create his route maps and maps of the continent. They were probably much like these. This set shows: a parallel rule, a drawing pen/pencil, an ivory scale, and a compass. The case contains a brass protractor, a set of dividers, a pencil point, pen point, and compass point.
SOURCE: Jackson 1978: 82

CHAPTER 5
Animal Encounters

Rocky Mountain sheep horn, 1805

Collected by William Clark
Horn
13 × 15 × 10¼
The Filson Historical Society, Louisville, Kentucky
Gift of Rogers Clark Ballard Thruston

Clark described the sheep horns he sent home in 1805 as "3 horns of the mountain Ram all Small one a faun those Animals inhabit *Coat noir* & Rockey mountains in great numbers, and much prized by the Indians (one for Govr. Harrison)." He may have acquired at least two of them on December 22, 1804. The ones Clark sent to Louisville from St. Louis in 1806 were "4 large Horns of the Bighorn animal." They may have been from the three sheep killed on May 25, 1805, one each by Clark, George Drouillard, and William Bratton. The party subsequently cached some "horns of the bighorned anamal" along with other "superfluous baggage" at the mouth of the Marias River. Or the horns may have been from the sheep Clark killed on July 25, 1806, near Pompey's Pillar; he described those as "a large doe and the other a yearlin Buck."

This horn was given to Clark's sister Fanny (Frances). Fanny first married Dr. James O'Fallon and then Captain C. M. Thruston. The horn was passed down through her family to R. C. B. Thruston, who donated it to the Filson Historical Society in 1929.
SOURCES: Holmberg 2002: 85; Moulton 1983–2001: 3: 260 (bought two), 4: 193 (killed three), 194 (picture caption quotation), 275 (cached), 8: 226 (killed two), 418 (shipped home)

Letter to Jefferson from Lewis at Fort Mandan, 1805

Meriwether Lewis
Ink on paper
9⅝ × 7½
Library of Congress, Thomas Jefferson Papers

SOURCES: Jackson 1978: 231-34; Jefferson 1806

Junction of the Yellowstone and the Missouri, c. 1833

Karl Bodmer
Watercolor on paper
10⅜ × 16¾
Joslyn Art Museum, Omaha, Nebraska, 1986.49.376
Gift of Enron Art Foundation

SOURCES: Goetzmann et al. 1984: 193; Wied 1843: Tableau 29

"Perogue of 8 Tuns," 1804

William Clark
Ink on paper
Image: LENGTH 3⅝
Yale Collection of Western Americana, Beinecke Rare Book and Manuscript Library, WA Mss. S-897 #10
Gift of Frederick W. and Carrie S. Beinecke

One pirogue was purchased on the Ohio, the other at Kaskaskia. The Corps left the red one at the Marias River and the white one at the Great Falls. It is not known which one this sketch shows or what the divisions mean—although some pirogues had partial decks at fore and aft, which may be indicated.

There is much disagreement on the design of the pirogues. Boss 1993, an otherwise reliable source, lacked research on traditional Mississippi River craft and dismissed the idea that the pirogues were dugouts, claiming instead that they were plank boats called batteaus. However, Lewis used the words *canoe* and *pirogue* interchangeably (Moulton 1983–2001: 2: 71n), and Clark distinguished between a *pirogue* and a *batteau*, describing the latter as a novelty when they met one headed upriver in 1806 (8: 278, 367). Whitehouse used the term "pettyauger" (11: 193), which can indicate a specific type of pirogue made from two logs, each formed to serve as a side, with planks inserted between to form the flat bottom. Creole dugouts were elegantly crafted boats that could reach great sizes; Du Pratz described ones forty feet long and three feet wide with a sloping bow "as broad as the body of the pirogue" (as in Clark's sketch), which could carry twelve people. Perrin du Lac in 1802 embarked on the Ohio River in a pirogue ("a sort of boat made of a hollow tree") that was thirty feet long and three feet wide.
SOURCES: Large 1995; Swanton 1911: 66–67; Perrin du Lac 1807: 40. On the creation of French pirogues (although smaller than historic ones), see Glassie 1968: 119–24 and Yoder 1976: 105–49. The American technique of making dugouts, likely used for the canoes created by the Corps, is described in Newhouse 1867. His illustration shows an outline with pointed prow and highly finished sides.

View of the Stone Walls, 1833

Karl Bodmer
Watercolor on paper
9⅞ × 16⅞
Joslyn Art Museum, Omaha, Nebraska, 1986.49.392
Gift of Enron Art Foundation

SOURCES: Moulton 1983–2001: 10: 96; Goetzmann et al. 1984: 233; Wied 1843: Tableau 34

Route map of the Marias River, 1805

William Clark
Ink on paper
8⅛ × 12 (aligned with north at top)
Yale Collection of Western Americana, Beinecke Rare Book and Manuscript Library, WA Mss. 303 #14-8
Gift of William R. Coe

SOURCE: Moulton 1983–2001: 1: 53, 4: 266

Falls of the Missouri, 1868

Alfred Edward Mathews
Lithograph on paper
Image: 5¾ × 9¼
Montana Historical Society
Gift of Mrs. Langford Smith

Mathews was an itinerant artist who published sketches of Colorado and Montana.
SOURCES: Mathews 1868: pl. 23; Moulton 1983–2001: 4: 290. For Mathews, see Taft 1949.

Draught of the Falls and Portage of the Missouri, 1805

William Clark
Ink and watercolor on paper
Image: 12⅜ × 4⅞
Missouri Historical Society, St. Louis, William Clark Papers, Voorhis #1
Gift of Julia Clark Voorhis in memory of Eleanor Glasgow Voorhis

SOURCE: Moulton 1983–2001: 4: 362

Engraving of a modular boat, 1799

Possibly engraved by Benjamin Jones
Engraving on paper
Image: 5½ × 5½
Courtesy of the American Philosophical Society, 506.73 AM4T

SOURCES: King 1799: 298–302, opp. p. 354; Moulton 1983–2001: 4: 330 (dimensions), 344 (skins), 363 (cargo), 11: 207 (yawl). For Jones, see Croce and Wallace 1957: 357.

Buffalo and Elk on the Upper Missouri, 1833

Karl Bodmer
Watercolor on paper
9¾ × 12¼
Joslyn Art Museum, Omaha, Nebraska, 1986.49.214
Gift of Enron Art Foundation

SOURCES: Moulton 1983–2001: 4: 283; Wied 1843: Tableau 47

Specimen of Lewis's woodpecker, 1806[?]

Possibly collected by Meriwether Lewis
Preserved body and feathers
HEIGHT 9
Museum of Comparative Zoology, Harvard University, © President and Fellows of Harvard College, photograph by Mark Sloan, 67854
Gift of Boston Society of Natural History

Though Charles Willson Peale never recorded any donation of a woodpecker from Lewis, both he and Alexander Wilson sketched one that looks not unlike this specimen. However, Titian Ramsay Peale also collected a Lewis's woodpecker on the Stephen H. Long Expedition, and there is no way to prove this is not that one. Both sketches show the woodpecker Lewis collected mounted to a vertical tree branch; although this one is not mounted, all the Peale specimens were taken from their mounts before arriving at Harvard. Wilson named it *Picus torquatus* when he published it in *American Ornithology* in 1811; his original sketch is at the Academy of Natural Sciences, Philadelphia. The bird later bore a variety of names, including *Picus lewis* (Gray 1849), *Asyndesmus lewis* (Coues 1866), and *Melanerpes lewis* (A.O.U. 1983). After the demise of Peale's Museum, this specimen went to Moses Kimball's Boston Museum. In 1900 it was acquired by the ornithologist Charles J. Maynard. It then went to the Boston Society of Natural History, then to the Museum of Comparative Zoology in 1914.
SOURCES: Moulton 1983–2001: 4: 407, 7: 293; Wilson 1808–14: 3: pl. 20, fig. 3; Cutright 1969a: 384–86, 390–92; Faxon 1915: 136. On the Lakota, see Brown 1992: 37, quoting Wissler 1907.

Sketch of mountain quail and Lewis's woodpecker, 1806

Charles Willson Peale
Graphite and watercolor on wove paper
8¼ × 7¼
Courtesy of the American Philosophical Society, BP31.15a #1

On the front is written in pencil: "Drawn for Capt. M. Lewis/(1806?)/ by CWPeale." The sketch is signed "CWP del."
SOURCES: Richardson, Hindle, and Miller 1983: 257; Cutright 1967: 227; Ewers 1965: 20; Moulton 1983–2001: 4: 407, 7: 90 (quail), 293

Elk antlers, 1805

Collected by Meriwether Lewis and William Clark
Antler and bone mounted to painted wood plaque
45 × 39⅝ × 40
University of Virginia, Charlottesville, Virginia

After Jefferson's death in 1826, the antlers were given to the University of Virginia. When they were loaned back to Monticello in 1949, the plaque identifying them as a Lewis and Clark specimen seems not to have existed, since Fiske Kimball, the first curator of Monticello, wrote to Ivey F. Lewis, "We shall have printed labels prepared to bring out the history and ownership of these pieces." A pair of moose horns was also given a plaque connecting them to Lewis and Clark; but since there is no record that the expedition killed or collected any moose, much less sent one to Jefferson, that plaque has been removed. The antlers are still on long-term loan to Monticello.
SOURCES: Jackson 1978: 236; Stein 1993: 397; Kimball to Lewis, April 14, 1949, in accession files at Monticello

Bighorn sheep, 1819–20

Titian Ramsay Peale
Watercolor and ink on paper
7½ × 9¾
Courtesy of the American Philosophical Society, BP31.15d #162

This sketch was later engraved for use in John D. Godman's *American Natural History*.

SOURCE: Moulton 1983–2001: 4: 193–95, 397 (quotation)

American antelope, 1819

Titian Ramsay Peale
Watercolor on paper
11 × 12
Courtesy of the American Philosophical Society, BP31.15d #101

The antelope on the right in this sketch may have been used (reversed) as the model for the illustration in John D. Godman's *American Natural History*.
SOURCE: Moulton 1983–2001: 3: 70, 81–82 (Lewis quotation), 94 (Clark quotation), 9: 59

Coyote, 1819

Titian Ramsay Peale
Ink and pencil on paper
5 × 8
Courtesy of the American Philosophical Society, BP31.15d #49

SOURCE: Moulton 1983–2001: 3: 87

Apron with spirit birds, early 1800s

Missouri Valley
Cured hide, pigment
21½ × 36 (approximate)
Courtesy of the Department of Anthropology, National Museum of Natural History, Smithsonian Institution, E*5435
Gift of John Varden

SOURCES: Brown 1992: 87. For a robe at the Musée de l'Homme, Paris, with a similar art style, see Horse Capture et al. 1993: 131.

Bird war club, pre-1840

Lakota
Antler, hide, brass buttons
19½ × 9 × 1¾
Courtesy of the Department of Anthropology, National Museum of Natural History, Smithsonian Institution, E*73278
Gift of Sarah (Mrs. Joseph) Harrison, 1881

Bodmer originally identified an elk antler bird war club he illustrated as Monitarri (Hidatsa), then corrected the attribution to Assiniboine. That club, in the Linden-Museum, Stuttgart, is now identified as Atsina, following Maximilian's notes.

SOURCES: Brown 1992: 32; Goetzmann et al. 1984: 334. See also Ewers 1986: 134.

Buffalo headdress, 1800s

Lakota
Bison hide, horns, wool fabric, beads, feathers, ribbon
28 × 14¼ × 12¾
Courtesy of the Department of Anthropology, National Museum of Natural History, Smithsonian Institution, E*129473
Gift of William T. Van Doren

SOURCES: Brown 1992: 65; Densmore 1918: 284–85. Catlin also described buffalo headdresses worn in a Mandan buffalo-calling ceremony: Catlin 1995: 1: 143–45. See also Wissler 1912 for buffalo headdresses associated with societies.

Buffalo effigy pipe, pre-1872

Lakota
Catlinite
2⅜ × 4¼ × 1
Missouri Historical Society, St. Louis, 1953 131 0005
Gift of Dr. Robert Terry

SOURCE: Ewers 1986: 41–42, 59, 123

Bag with buffalo design, late 1800s

Lakota
Cured hide, quills, sinew
9½ × 7¾
Courtesy of the National Museum of the American Indian, Smithsonian Institution, 002196
Gift of J. W. Benham

SOURCES: Walker 1980: 68. For a similar representation, see the dance shield illustrated in Maurer 1992: 126 and Densmore 1918: 285, pl. 43.

Elk courting flute, pre-1889

Oglala[?]
Ash wood, sinew, reed, pigment
27¾ × 2¼ × 2
University of Pennsylvania Museum of Archaeology and Anthropology, cat. 45-15-1207, neg. T4-2315
Collected by Charles H. Stephens, gift of Mrs. Owen Stephens

The collector of this piece was an illustrator who used Indian artifacts as props and models. He bought this in 1889 from the dealers Elliott and Shaw, and he believed it was used in the Grass Dance or Omaha Dance. Courting flutes often were carried by young men in that dance, which diffused across the Great Plains in the 1860s, but the instruments predate that dance. A very similar one, possibly by the same artist, is at the National Museum of Natural History, Smithsonian Institution (cat. 200588). That one is identified as Sioux and is made of cedar.
SOURCES: Maurer 1992: 130; Ewers 1986: 29, 160, 162; Harrison et al. 1987: 125, fig. 114

Beaded garter with birds, early 1800s

Western Great Lakes / Eastern Plains; Sauk[?]
Glass beads, wool and cotton yarns, unidentified plant fiber
11¼ × 2⅜; with fringe: 22¼
Photograph from the Peabody Museum of Archaeology and Ethnology, Harvard University, © President and Fellows of Harvard College, photograph by Hillel Burger, cat. 99-12-10/53005, neg. T2910
Gift of the Heirs of David Kimball, 1899

The accession register gives Sioux, Osage, and Algonquian for the tribal origin of this piece. Prince Maximilian collected a similar garter identified as Sauk.
SOURCES: Jackson 1978: 477; McLaughlin 2003: chapter 9

Grizzly bear headdress, pre-1881

Western Sioux
Bear head, brass tacks, cotton cloth, hawk feather, wool cloth
35 × 28 × 16
Courtesy of the Department of Anthropology, National Museum of Natural History, Smithsonian Institution, E*384,121
Gift of Mrs. T. T. Brown

SOURCES: Ewers 1982b: 36, 39; Catlin 1995: 1: 46, 275–76; Walker 1980: 91

Bear effigy pipe bowl, pre-1830s

Pawnee[?]
Catlinite
3⅛ × 7 × 2⅛
Missouri Historical Society, St. Louis, 1926 006 0001
Gift of Mrs. W. B. (Mary Kearny) Coombe and Mrs. Henry S. Kearny

Ewers identifies all the pipes of this design as Pawnee, based on the man's hair style and the correspondence of the design to a well-known Pawnee myth. Catlin wrote, "The Pawnees and Sioux manufacture more pipes of the red pipe stone than any of the other tribes & the Pawnees may be said to be the most ingenious of the two, for design." The Catlin pipe, which was Pawnee, no longer exists; it is illustrated in Catlin 1995: 1: fig. 98. The Duke Paul pipe, identified as Sioux, is in the Linden-Museum, Stuttgart; it is so similar to this one that it is difficult to believe the two are not by the same artist. This pipe was identified as both Sioux and Osage. General Stephen Watts Kearny, who collected it no later than 1842, married Clark's stepdaughter, Mary Radford, in 1830. An entry in his journal on June 25, 1825, mentions a gift of pipes from the Sioux.
SOURCES: Brown 1992: 22; Ewers 1986: 52–54; Ewers 1979: 34, 36; Ewers 1982b: 44. On Kearny, see Christensen et al. 1999: 447.

Grizzly bear claws, c. 1780–1825

Plains
Grizzly bear foreclaws, glass beads
Largest claw: 5 × ⅞
Photograph from the Peabody Museum of Archaeology and Ethnology, Harvard University, © President and Fellows of Harvard College, photograph by Hillel Burger, cat. 99-12-10/53007, neg. T2582.1
Gift of the Heirs of David Kimball, 1899

The Peabody has two original paper labels from Peale's Museum saying, "Claws of the Grizly Bear" (printed) and "Indian Necklace made of the claws of the Grizly Bear Presented by Capt. Lewis and Clark. 13" (handwritten). However, a notation suggesting that the necklace was not received by the Peabody makes the attribution of these ornaments to the Lewis and Clark expedition uncertain. The accession register simply states: "Ornaments made from the claws of Grizzly Bear. American Indian."

Catlin showed mainly lower Missouri tribes, such as the Iowa and Missouri, wearing bear claw necklaces; Bodmer drew Mandeh-Pahchu, a Mandan, wearing one.
SOURCES: Moulton 1983–2001: 5: 135; McLaughlin 2003: chapter 9; Richardson, Hindle, and Miller 1983: 137. For paintings, see Catlin 1995: 2: 26, 31; Thomas and Ronnefeldt 1976: 237.

Bear shield cover, c. 1820

Upper Missouri
Cured hide, pigment
DIAM 23½
Courtesy of the Department of Anthropology, National Museum of Natural History, Smithsonian Institution, E*2671
Collection of the U.S. War Department

SOURCES: Densmore 1918: 348; Maurer 1992: 121

Captain Clark and His Men Shooting Bears, 1810

Artist unknown
Woodcut on paper
Image: 2¾ × 4¾
Department of Special Collections, Washington University Libraries

SOURCE: Gass 1810: opp. p. 95

The Bear Pursueing His Assailant, 1813

Artist unknown
Woodcut on paper
Image: 3⅛ × 6
Missouri Historical Society, St. Louis
SOURCE: Fisher 1813: opp. p. 35

CHAPTER 6
Crossing the Divide

Gates of the Mountains, 1868

Alfred Edward Mathews
Lithograph on paper
Image: 5⅞ × 9¼
Montana Historical Society
Gift of Mrs. Langford Smith

SOURCES: Moulton 1983–2001: 4: 402–3; Mathews 1868: pl. XVII. For Mathews, see Taft 1949.

The Three Forks, 1868

Alfred Edward Mathews
Lithograph on paper
Image: 10 × 18¾
Montana Historical Society
Gift of Mrs. Langford Smith

SOURCES: Moulton 1983–2001: 4: 437, 9: 190; Mathews 1868: pl. XI. For Mathews, see Taft 1949.

Route map of Jefferson River, 1805

William Clark
Ink on paper
16½ × 10
Yale Collection of Western Americana, Beinecke Rare Book and Manuscript Library, WA Mss. 303 #29-1
Gift of William R. Coe

SOURCE: Moulton 1983–2001: 1: map 66, 9: 195

Telescope of Meriwether Lewis, c. 1790

Charles Lincoln, London
Mahogany, brass, glass
13¾ × 1¾ (collapsed);
LENGTH 23½ (extended)
The Athenaeum of Philadelphia, 76.16
Gift of Milton Hammer

Dale Sundale stated of this telescope: "[It] was given to me as a gift in 1975 by my maternal Grandfather, Lawrence Lewis Sr., 'A direct descendant of Meriwether Lewis and member of a pioneer San Jose (California) family.' . . . He told me the telescope was used on the famous Lewis and Clark Expedition and had been passed down in the family to him. In 1972 [*sic*] I sold the Meriwether Lewis telescope to Milton Hammer, a rare book dealer in Santa Barbara, California." A Lawrence Lewis was the great-great grandson of Nicholas Lewis, Meriwether's uncle and his guardian after the death of his father. Hammer gave the artifact to the Athenaeum in 1976. The maker's mark on the lens cover is: "Lincoln/London." Charles Lincoln (c. 1744–1807) did business at 11 Cornhill near the Poultry and 62 Leadenhall Street. He made telescopes, microscopes, nautical and mathematical instruments, and globes.

SOURCES: Moulton 1983–2001: 5: 68, 70; Sorley 1991: 601, 618, 642, 691, 698–99; Taylor 1966: 266

Shoshonee, Wind River, 1837

Alfred Jacob Miller
Watercolor on paper
4⅜ × 4¾
Yale Collection of Western Americana, Beinecke Rare Book and Manuscript Library, WA Mss. 341 #7
Gift of William R. Coe

This is probably one of Miller's field sketches. It was passed down in the Miller family until the 1940s.
SOURCES: Moulton 1983–2001: 5: 68; Tyler 1982: 55, 306; Lowie 1909: 183

Omaha man demonstrating robe language, c. 1905

Taken by Alice C. Fletcher and Francis La Flesche
Photographs
National Anthropological Archives, Smithsonian Institution, neg. nos. 2000-4461, 2000-4462, 2000-4460.

SOURCES: Fletcher and La Flesche 1911: 360–62; Kapoun and Lohrmann 1997: vii–ix, 3, 5

Group of gifts, 1800s

Shoshone, Mandan
Mirror: silvered glass and wood; beads: glass; paint bag: cured hide and vermillion
Mirror: DIAM 4; beads: DIAM ⅛; paint bag: 5¼ × 3
University of Pennsylvania Museum of Archaeology and Anthropology, cat. nos. 37108, 38189a, neg. nos. T4-2317, T4-2313 (mirror and paint bag); Ralph Thompson Collection of the North Dakota Lewis & Clark Bicentennial Foundation, 32ME5–2000.1.87 (beads)
Gift of John Wanamaker (mirror and paint bag)

The mirror was collected by Stuart Culin, who headed several collecting expeditions to the Shoshone and other Great Basin tribes. It came from White Rocks, Utah. The beads were acquired at the Deapolis site in North Dakota in the late 1950s. The paint bag was from the collection of Thomas Donaldson.
SOURCES: Moulton 1983–2001: 5: 69; Hanson 1986; Gilman 1982: 33; Wood 1986: 20

Flag, c. 1808

American, possibly by Christopher Gullergey
Wool, paint
58 × 150
Chicago Historical Society, 1920.744
Gift of Charles Gunther, 1920

The only direct evidence on the expedition flags is Clark's sketch of a triangular pennant flying from the keel boat mast; the Indian presentation flags were probably rectangular. This flag was collected in the 1880s or 1890s by J. E. Wendell (or possibly his brother, G. T. Wendell) of Milwaukee, former residents of Mackinac, Michigan, from Native Americans on Manitoulin Island in Lake Huron. The flag was said to have been captured by the Ojibway from American forces at Drummond Island, near Sault Ste. Marie, in 1812. Garrison flags were much larger and would not have had painted designs, which did not withstand the elements. This design resembles a flag painted by Gullergey for the First Troop of Philadelphia Light Horse in 1798.
SOURCES: Madaus 1988: 70–73; Saindon 1981; Jackson 1978: 177; Moulton 1983–2001: 3: 496; communication to Jeff Meyer, Missouri Historical Society, from Howard Michael Madaus, National Civil War Museum, Harrisburg, Pennsylvania. For a history of U.S. flags, see Quaife, Weig, and Appleman 1961.

Sketch of a Shoshone pipe, 1805

Meriwether Lewis
Ink on paper
Image: ½ × 3½
Courtesy of the American Philosophical Society, Codex F, p. 99
SOURCE: Moulton 1983–2001: 5: 80–81

Moccasins, pre-1860

Upper Missouri / Sioux[?]
Cured hide, quills, wool, beads
3¾ × 10 × 3½ (each)
Courtesy of the Department of Anthropology, National Museum of Natural History, Smithsonian Institution, E*1897
Gift of G. K. Warren, 1866

Lewis and Clark collected moccasins, but none survive; Clark sent his brother "2 pr. of Summer & 1 pr. of winter mockersons comr [comprised?] all of Buffalow Skin" from Fort Mandan. This pattern of quillwork was illustrated by Karl Bodmer among the Mandan.
SOURCES: Moulton 1983–2001: 5: 133–34; Holmberg 2002: 84; Goetzmann et al. 1984: 300, 307

Sign language gestures, 1881

Artist unknown
Engravings on paper
Up to 2½ × 2¼
Missouri Historical Society, St. Louis

SOURCES: Mallery 1881: 486–90; Coues 1965: 335

Snake Indians Migrating, c. 1837

Alfred Jacob Miller
Pen and ink, wash, and gouache on paper
9⅛ × 12⅛
Joslyn Art Museum, Omaha, Nebraska, 1988.10.22

SOURCE: Tyler 1982: no. 481

Parfleche, 1800s

Shoshone
Hide, pigment, wool, beads
12 × 11; fringe: 26 (each side)
University of Pennsylvania Museum of Archaeology and Anthropology, cat. 36801, neg. T4-2310
Gift of John Wanamaker, 1900

This was collected by Stuart Culin at Wind River Reservation, Wyoming.
SOURCES: Moulton 1983–2001: 5: 142–43; Torrence 1994: 49–51, 212; Lowie 1909: 203–5

Elk teeth, 1800s

Shoshone or Sioux
Ivory, pigment
1⅛ × ¾
University of Pennsylvania Museum of Archaeology and Anthropology, cat. nos. 45-15-686, 45-15-687, neg. T4-2324
Collection of Charles H. Stephens, gift of Mrs. Owen Stephens, 1945

These may have been collected by Peter Moran from the Shoshone of Wyoming. They are also identified as Sioux.
SOURCES: Moulton 1983–2001: 5: 135, 146; Densmore 1918: 176

Îhkas-Kínne, Siksika Blackfeet Chief, 1833

Karl Bodmer
Watercolor and pencil on paper
17 × 11⅞
Joslyn Art Museum, Omaha, Nebraska, 1986.49.285
Gift of Enron Art Foundation

SOURCES: Moulton 1983–2001: 5: 127–28; Goetzmann et al. 1984: 260; David Thompson in Tyrrell 1916: 336

Captain Meriwether Lewis in Shoshone regalia, 1807

Charles Balthazar Julien Févret de Saint-Mémin
Watercolor over graphite on paper
6¼ × 3¾
Collection of The New-York Historical Society, 1971.125
Gift of the Heirs of Hall Park McCullough

In 1816, when it was engraved by William Strickland for the *Analectic Magazine and Naval Chronicle* (volume 7, facing p. 329), the original painting was owned by William Clark. It passed down to his son Jefferson Kearny Clark, whose family artifacts went to Julia Clark Voorhis. On her death the painting became part of the collection that her executor, Samuel Maguire, kept for himself. Mrs. Maguire eventually sold it to an art dealer. It went through the hands of several collectors before coming to the New-York Historical Society. The Strickland engraving of it was reissued by P. Price, Jr., Philadelphia. Another reproduction was printed in the late nineteenth century when it was in Mrs. Voorhis's hands.
SOURCES: Miles 1994: 140, 339; Jackson 1978: 439–40; Norfleet 1942: 184; Sellers 1980: 187, 191; Richardson, Hindle, and Miller 1983: 256–57

Payouska, Chief of the Great Osages, 1804

Charles Balthazar Julien Févret de Saint-Mémin
Black and white chalk on paper
23 × 17
Collection of The New-York Historical Society, cat. 1860.92, neg. 1111

SOURCE: Miles 1994: 142–43, 368

War shirt, pre-1819

Upper Missouri
Tanned hide, quills, human hair, red and black pigment
55 × 30
Photograph from the Peabody Museum of Archaeology and Ethnology, Harvard University, © President and Fellows of Harvard College, photograph by Hillel Burger, cat. 90-17-10/49309, neg. T1481
Gift of the American Antiquarian Society, 1890

Roderick McKenzie donated a collection containing mostly Northwest Coast material to the American Antiquarian Society in 1819. He had been active in the fur trade since 1785. The accession record at the American Antiquarian Society read, "An Indian War dress ornamented with Human Hair from the Northwest."
SOURCES: Walker 1982: 36; Moulton 1983–2001: 5: 126; Maurer 1992: 184–85; "Articles from the North West, Pacific Ocean &c. for the American Antiquarian Society," American Antiquarian Society correspondence file, February 4, 1818, Peabody Museum. Also pictured in Walker Art Center 1972: 107. On McKenzie, see Coues 1965: 223n.

Leggings, mid-1800s

Upper Missouri
Cured hide, quills, hair
Largest: 45 × 16
Courtesy of the Department of Anthropology, National Museum of Natural History, Smithsonian Institution, E*403344b
Gift of Robert L. Dwight, 1964

SOURCES: Jackson 1978: 476, 516; Moulton 1983–2001: 5: 127

1804 Infantry captain's uniform, reproduced 2002

Timothy Pickles, New Orleans
Coat, waistcoat, and pantaloons: wool face cloth (coat with silver lace); shirt: linen; neck stock: leather; gorget: silver-plated copper with silk ribbon; sword belt and belt plate: leather, silver-plated brass; sword and scabbard: steel, leather grip, paint; sash: cotton; boots: leather; buttons: silver-plated zinc alloy
HEIGHT 66 (overall); coat: 45½ × 11½ (at shoulders), LENGTH 29½ (sleeve); pantaloons: 41 × 34 (at waist); boots: 17½ × 12
Missouri Historical Society, St. Louis

SOURCES: Moulton 1983–2001: 5: 117. Bob Moore, Historian at the Jefferson National Expansion Memorial, provided invaluable research for the uniform reconstruction. Other sources included Hamtramck 1802; Moore 1994 and 1998; Zlatich 1992b. A painting of Captain Daniel Bissell at the Bissell House Museum, St. Louis County Parks and Recreation, shows the 1804 captain's uniform.

Eagle bone whistle, early 1800s

Mandan / Hidatsa
Bald eagle ulna, deer skin, porcupine quill, dyed bird quill, mammal hide thongs, glass beads, sinew, pigment, resinous material
13½ (with tassel) × ¾
Photograph from the Peabody Museum of Archaeology and Ethnology, Harvard University, © President and Fellows of Harvard College, photograph by Hillel Burger, cat. 99-12-10/53010, neg. T3073
Gift of the Heirs of David Kimball, 1899

Bodmer painted at least two Mandan whistles resembling this one. The Mandan Pehriska-Ruhpa also wore one as part of his Dog Society regalia. Ones collected by Maximilian are now in the Linden-Museum, Stuttgart, and Ethnologisches Museum, Staatliche Museen, Berlin.
SOURCES: Catlin 1995: 1: 273; Wissler 1912: 48; Goetzmann et al. 1984: 317, 319, 339; McLaughlin 2003: chapter 6

Chapeau de bras, 1795–1815

American
Beaver felt, silk ribbon, white metal button, leather
9½ × 16⅞
William H. Guthman Collection

SOURCES: Howell and Kloster 1969; Moore 2001; Lewis 1960. For the men's hats, see Zlatich 1992a.

Espontoon, 1775–80

American
Iron, wood
LENGTH 93 (overall)
Valley Forge National Historical Park, 627
The George C. Neumann Collection, a gift of the Sun Company to Valley Forge National Historical Park, 1978

SOURCES: Moulton 1983–2001: 4: 145, 201–2, 217, 262, 292–94; Hunt 1990; Peterson 1968; Neumann and Kravic 1975: 218

Split-horn bonnet, c. 1875–85

Mandan / Hidatsa
Tanned hide, ermine skin, feathers, horn, quills, horsehair, wool, beads
32 × 27 × 12
State Historical Society of North Dakota, 973. Photograph by Sharon Silengo
Gift of Mrs. C. W. Hoffman, 1907

This headdress was used in the Foolish Dog Society, a warrior association. The collector of this item was an early agent at Fort Berthold Reservation.
SOURCE: Catlin 1995: 1: 39, 115, 117–18

Bear claw necklace, mid-1800s

Upper Missouri
Bear claws, wool, glass beads, leather, unidentified resin
DIAM 14½; claws: approx. LENGTH 4
Courtesy of the Department of Anthropology, National Museum of Natural History, Smithsonian Institution, E*403347
Gift of Robert L. Dwight, 1964

SOURCE: Moulton 1983–2001: 5: 135

War robe of Chief Washakie, pre-1897

Shoshone
Deer hide, pigment
24 × 56
Courtesy of the National Museum of the American Indian, Smithsonian Institution, 164845

This robe was collected by Colonel R. H. Wilson in 1897, but it may predate that year. The collector believed it showed battles with the Ute Indians, but the exploit in the lower middle was a battle against the Lakota when Washakie's horse was wounded and he counted coup, shown on other war robes.
SOURCES: Moulton 1983–2001: 5: 126; Maurer 1992: 218–19

The Death of General Wolfe, 1770

Benjamin West
Oil on canvas
60 × 84½
National Gallery of Canada, cat. 8007
Transfer from the Canadian War Memorials, 1921 (Gift of the 2nd Duke of Westminster, Eaton Hall, Cheshire, 1918)

SOURCE: Schama 1991

Feather war insignium, mid-1800s

Northern Plains
Bald eagle feather, steel, cured hide
13¾ × 2½
Photograph from the Peabody Museum of Archaeology and Ethnology, Harvard University, © President and Fellows of Harvard College, photograph by Hillel Burger, cat. 99-12-10/53034, neg. T3862.1
Gift of the Heirs of David Kimball, 1899

SOURCES: Jackson 1978: 476–77; Moulton 1983–2001: 3: 117; Walker 1980: 271–72

Cockade and eagle, early 1800s

American
Satin, silver
Cockade: DIAM 3¾; eagle: ⅞ × ⅞
William H. Guthman Collection

SOURCES: Hamtramck 1802; Emerson 1983; Emerson 1996: 25–30, 119–21

Epaulettes of William Clark, 1808

American
Metal fabric and bullion of gold-washed silver, sequins, wire, wool, silk thread
Strap: 5⅝ × 3; bullion: 2¾
Missouri Historical Society, St. Louis, 1924 004 0006 a-c
Gift of Julia Clark Voorhis in memory of Eleanor Glasgow Voorhis

An anonymous, primitive painting of Clark in uniform at the Missouri Historical Society shows him wearing epaulettes, presumably these. They are probably the "pair Gold Epaulettes" valued at $1.50 on the inventory of Clark's estate at his death. The gold wash has now worn off.
SOURCE: William Clark Probate File, Rare Documents, Missouri State Archives

Epaulette, c. 1804–8

American
Gold lace and bullion, wire, silk, sequins, wool cloth and batting
Strap: 6 × 3; bullion: 3
William H. Guthman Collection

SOURCES: Peterson 1950; Jackson 1978: 428

Dance shield, pre-1885

Lakota[?]
Cloth, wood, pigment, feather, hide
DIAM 12¾
University of Pennsylvania Museum of Archaeology and Anthropology, cat. 38369, neg. T4-2321
Gift of John Wanamaker, 1901

This item was acquired in about 1885 by Thomas Donaldson.
SOURCES: Moulton 1983–2001: 5: 150; Wissler 1907: 26, 48–50

Raven bustle, c. 1780–1806

Plains / Prairie
Raven body with feathers, dyed and undyed porcupine quills, rawhide, wood, dyed and undyed horsehair, sinew, winter weasel fur, dyed bird quills
30¾ × 6
Photograph from the Peabody Museum of Archaeology and Ethnology, Harvard University, © President and Fellows of Harvard College, photograph by Hillel Burger, cat. 99-12-10/53050, neg. T2928
Gift of the Heirs of David Kimball, 1899

This is one of three raven bustles from the Peale Collection at the Peabody Museum. An original Peale label associated with one of the three states: "Ornament. Worn upon the elbow [*sic*] by the Tioux [*sic*] Indians. Presented by Captains Lewis and Clarke." For how the bustle was actually worn, see George Catlin's *Beggar's Dance, Mouth of the Teton River* in the Smithsonian American Art Museum.
SOURCES: Jefferson inventory, [1807], in Thomas Jefferson Papers, Massachusetts Historical Society; Jackson 1978: 478; Catlin 1995: 1: pl. 103; McLaughlin 2003: chapter 5

Rattle, c. 1870

Plains [Lakota?]
Wood, leather, dewclaws, bird talons, brass bells, red pigment
19¾ × 2½ × 2
University of Pennsylvania Museum of Archaeology and Anthropology, cat. 52-6-10, neg. T4-2316
Gift of Church Training School, Philadelphia, 1952

SOURCES: Maurer 1992: 156; Wissler 1912: 48

Masonic apron, 1808

American
Silk front, linen back, paint, blood
14½ × 16½
Library-Museum, Grand Lodge A.F. and A.M. of Montana, Helena
Gift of Joseph Hopper (purchased from Grand Lodge of Missouri)

The apron was passed from Jane Lewis Anderson (Meriwether's sister) to her son William Lewis Anderson, to his daughter Laura Lewis Anderson Loudin (in 1875), to her husband William Loudin (in 1905), to his near relation Eugene Brown, to Brown's widow (in 1924), to the Grand Lodge of Missouri, to the Grand Lodge of Montana at Helena (in 1960). A 1925 affidavit by William Loudin says that the apron was in his father-in-law William Anderson's possession when Anderson moved into their house in 1856. The apron, along with a watch (now missing), were said to have been retrieved from the site of Lewis's death in Tennessee by "one of Meriwether Lewis' brothers." The bloodstains were tested in about 1989 by the Hematology-Criminal Division of the University of Oregon Medical School. The five stains soak through onto the back, but none seem to match up when folded, as if the apron were unfolded when stained.

The petition to form the St. Louis Lodge was addressed to the Grand Lodge of Pennsylvania on August 2, 1808, and Lewis was recommended as a "Past Master to be the first Master." The lodge was constituted on November 8, 1808.

The other Lewis Masonic artifacts in existence are his Royal Arch apron at the Missouri Historical Society (cat. 1936 030 003) and a certificate dated October 31, 1799, from the Staunton Lodge at the University of Virginia Library, which goes with the Royal Arch apron. Clark's Masonic certificate, dated September 18, 1809, from the St. Louis Lodge, is at the Missouri Historical Society, and his apron is at the Masonic lodge of St. Charles, Missouri.

SOURCES: Affidavit of William Loudin, April 20, 1925, in files of Grand Lodge of Montana, Helena; Denslow 1959: 3: 83–84; Denslow 1941: 4–12; Baumler 1997; Chuinard 1989. The interpretations of the symbols were supplied by Mark Tabbert, Museum of Our National Heritage.

Meriwether Lewis in queue, c. 1802

Charles Balthazar Julien Févret de Saint-Mémin
Black and white chalk on paper
24½ × 17¾
Private Collection, photograph courtesy of the Valentine Richmond History Center

According to Norfleet, this portrait was "left by Mrs. Jane [Lewis] Anderson, only sister of Meriwether Lewis to her daughter Mrs. Sarah [Thornton Anderson] Harper," who in turn left it to "her grandson, Hon. Wm [Harper] Woods, Charlotte Co., Va." In about 1890, Woods tried but failed to sell it to the U.S. government. It went to Emily Gwathmey Smith Woods, his widow, then was kept at the home of Emily Gwathmey Woods Wilson, her daughter, then sold by William C. Scott, Mrs. Woods's son-in-law, to Dr. A. W. Rosenbach, Philadelphia. In 2002 it was found by the Rosenbach heirs and auctioned at Sotheby's. Copies of the engraving made from this painting are in the Valentine Richmond History Center and Corcoran Gallery of Art. The outline is very similar (although reversed) to the silhouette of Lewis by Uri Hill, a work once owned by Dolley Madison and now in the National Portrait Gallery. On the basis of style, Ellen Miles argues that this is the earliest Saint-Mémin portrait of Lewis, although he appears older than in the Missouri Historical Society portrait. She argues that it may have been executed in May 1802, when Lewis, on a visit to Philadelphia, was socializing with Mahlon Dickerson, who had his portrait done.

SOURCES: Woods 1890[?]; Norfleet 1942: 184; Miles 1994: 338–39; Stein 1993: 201

Hair extensions, 1800s

Arikara
Human hair, clay or gum, plated sheet iron, leather, silk ribbon
33 × 7
Courtesy of the National Museum of the American Indian, Smithsonian Institution, 155622
Gift of Melvin R. Gilmore, 1915

This hairpiece was collected at Fort Berthold Reservation. A similar Shoshone one is at the American Museum of Natural History, New York (cat. 50-2344). An earlier, unidentified one is at the National Museum of Natural History, Smithsonian Institution (cat. 167145).

SOURCES: Catlin 1995: 1: 57, 63, 107; Bushnell 1909: 414–19

CHAPTER 7
Trade and Property

Spanish bit and bridle, 1800s

Plains
Iron, horsehair, leather, string
Bit: 6¾ × 5½; bridle: 19½ × 5½;
reins: LENGTH 41½
Missouri Historical Society, St. Louis, 1932 027 0228
Gift of William R. Faribault

The collector of this item also acquired several pieces of northern Rocky Mountain horse equipment from Crow, Nez Perce, and possibly Shoshone sources. The Nevada style of rein chain had eight to ten links and a swivel mounted on the end rather than the middle of the chain.

SOURCES: Moulton 1983–2001: 5: 92, 124, 149; Martin and Martin 1997: 22, 30–31

Buffalo-hair rope, pre-1846

Nez Perce
Bison hair
48½ × ½
Nez Perce Tribal Committee

This rope was collected between 1840 and 1846 by Rev. Henry H. Spaulding, a missionary to the Nez Perce, and was sent to Dr. Dudley Allen in Kinsman, Ohio, in 1846. The rope is now on loan to Nez Perce National Historical Park, Spaulding, Idaho, where it is cataloged as No. 8742 in the Spaulding-Allen Collection.

SOURCES: Moulton 1983–2001: 5: 68, 160; Coues 1965: 299

Mule Equipment, c. 1837

Alfred Jacob Miller
Watercolor on paper
6½ × 7⅝
Joslyn Art Museum, Omaha, Nebraska, 1988.10.31

This copy is undated, but it portrays a scene from 1837.

SOURCE: Moulton 1983–2001: 5: 92, 123, 125, 158

Vocabulary form, c. 1790–92

Thomas Jefferson
Ink on paper
18⅞ × 15⅜
Courtesy of the American Philosophical Society, 497 v85 #18 (os)

Jefferson explained his vocabulary project: "Were vocabularies formed of all the languages spoken in North and South America . . . deposited in all the public libraries, it would furnish opportunities to those skilled in the languages of the old world . . . to construct the best evidence of the derivation of this part of the human race."

Jefferson gave two accounts of what happened to Lewis's vocabularies. In 1809 he told Benjamin Smith Barton that they had all been destroyed, along with the rest of his collection of vocabularies, when a trunk of his papers was stolen and ransacked on its way up the James River from Washington, D.C., to Monticello. However, in 1816 he stated that Lewis had taken copies for publication, and he speculated they might be in Barton's papers. This would seem like an error except that a bundle of vocabularies was found among Lewis's papers after his death in 1809 and delivered to Clark, and in 1818 Nicholas Biddle reported having received from Clark and passed on to Barton, in 1810, some "Indian vocabularies, collected during the journey." However, they were not among the Barton papers that came to the American Philosophical Society in 1818.

SOURCES: Jackson 1978: 212–23, 323, 396, 465, 471, 611, 636; Jefferson 1964: 97; Saindon 1977: 4–6

Route map of the Lolo Trail, 1805

William Clark
Ink on paper
16⅜ × 10
Yale Collection of Western Americana, Beinecke Rare Book and Manuscript Library, WA Mss. 303 #30-4
Gift of William R. Coe

SOURCES: Withington 1952: 170; Moulton 1983–2001: 1: map 70

Crossing the Bitter Root Mountains, 1855

Gustav Sohon
Pencil and watercolor on paper
5 × 6
Washington State Historical Society, 1918.114.9.33
Gift of the Estate of Hazard Stevens

There is another version of this drawing at the National Anthropological Archives, Smithsonian Institution, Ms. 385679.

SOURCES: Ewers 1965: 172; Nicandri 1986

Tin cup, 1800s

American
Tinned sheet iron
3¼ × 4⅞ (with handle)
Courtesy of Valley Forge National Historical Park, 3706

SOURCES: Meriwether Lewis to General William Irvine, April 15, 1803, Grace Lewis Papers, Jefferson National Expansion Memorial, St. Louis, National Park Service; Jackson 1978: 81; Moulton 1983–2001: 4: 275, 9: 223, 10: 142. On portable soup, see Holland 2001. A 1753 recipe for the soup is printed in *We Proceeded On*, October 1983, p. 11.

Woman's dress, early to mid-1800s

Plateau
Deer or antelope hide, brass bead, abalone shell
54 × 52 (with sleeves extended)
Maryhill Museum of Art, Goldendale, Washington, 1952.09.003

SOURCES: Moulton 1983–2001: 5: 259; Harless 1998: 50–51. A Cree woman wearing a tail dress is pictured by Karl Bodmer in Goetzmann et al. 1984: 265.

Woman's hat, pre-1876

Nez Perce
Indian hemp, bear grass
5½ × 7½
Courtesy of the Department of Anthropology, National Museum of Natural History, Smithsonian Institution, E*23857
Gift of John B. Monteith

Caps similar to this are found in the Spaulding-Allen Collection at the Nez Perce National Historical Park. Henry H. Spaulding, who made the collection between 1840 and 1846, noted that they were also used as water cups.
SOURCES: Moulton 1983–2001: 7: 254; Jackson 1978: 476, 478; Grafe 1999: 62. See also Conn and Schlick 1998.

Peace medal, 1801

U.S. Mint, Philadelphia
Silver
DIAM 2¼
Oregon Historical Society, cat. 84-84, neg. OrHi98961
Gift of W. B. Ayer

There are two versions of the recovery of this artifact. The first version, given by George Himes, holds that in the "latter eighties," some engineers of the Oregon Railway and Navigation Co. were visiting an island in the Columbia River near Wallula, Washington, one Sunday to search for Indian relics. They found the medal by stirring the surface sand with their canes. It was later presented to W. B. Ayer, who gave it to the Oregon Historical Society in 1899. In the second version, given in the *Oregon Historical Society Proceedings* for 1900, the medal was found on the Nez Perce Reservation, Idaho, and given to Major E. McNeill, a manager of the Oregon Railway and Navigation Co., who gave it to W. B. Ayer. Supporting the first version, Elliott Coues in 1893 mentioned that Yellept's medal was "found last year on an island about mouth of Walla-walla river (James Wickesham, in lit.)."

This is one of five authenticated Lewis and Clark medals found, of which only two survive today. Two George Washington medals were passed down in the family of Mary Underwood Lane, the descendant of a prominent upper Chinookan family. She claimed the medals had been given to her maternal grandfather Welawa (Wasco) and grandmother Mumshumsie (Cascade), but they were born too late and must have inherited them. The medals went to the Maryhill Museum of Art but were stolen in 1986; their current whereabouts are unknown.

Another Jefferson medal was found by Lester S. Handsaker on March 1, 1899. It was wrapped in many folds of buffalo hide, in an Indian grave that was opened by the excavation made in the construction of the Northern Pacific Railroad, around the bluff on the east side of the Potlatch River at its junction with the Clearwater River, on the Nez Perce Reservation, Idaho. This medal was donated to the American Museum of Natural History, New York (not the American Numismatic Society, as Moulton states), but it has since disappeared. Neeshneparkkeook had his village at the mouth of the Potlatch, and Tunnachemootoolt also received a Jefferson medal in this vicinity.

The fifth authentic Lewis and Clark medal is the Jefferson medal at Nez Perce National Historical Park, which is shown in the Introduction, above.

Other medals have been reported at various times but never verified. John Bakeless said that the medal given to Shehek-Shote was in the possession of Burr Crows Breast in 1947; Paul Cutright later claimed to have found it in the hands of a local collector, but he had been fooled by a reproduction. He published what appears to be a completely fictional provenance chain; the owner of the reproduction wrote, "I was absolutely surprised to see all the family history some one, but not me, put with it in an attempt to authenticate it." The authentic medal may still be in the possession of the Crows Breast family, but it has not been located. The only known original medal from this period presently at Fort Berthold Reservation is a Madison medal in private hands.

Another Jefferson medal, found by a sheepherder on the Milk River, was owned by R. C. Sinclair of Kendrick, Idaho, in 1905; it was displayed at the Portland World's Fair but has since disappeared. In 1834, the naturalist J. K. Townsend wrote that some local residents near Fort Clatsop found a Jefferson medal, but it has also disappeared.

SOURCES: Moulton 1983–2001: 5: 278, 291, 301, 335, 337, 341, 7: 165, 173, 183. On this artifact, see Himes n.d.; *Oregon Historical Society Proceedings*, 1900, p. 69; Cutright 1968: 164; Cutright 1969a: 454; Coues 1893: 970n. On the Maryhill medals, see Maryhill Museum files. On the American Museum of Natural History medal, see Wheeler 1900: 48–50; Edward D. Adams to F. W. Putnam, November 26, 1901, American Museum of Natural History files; Moulton 1983–2001: 7: 211, 215. On the supposed Shehek-Shote medal, see Bakeless 1947: 407; Cutright 1968: 165–66; Leonard 1995. On the Sinclair medal, see *Portland Evening Telegram*, July 7, 1905. On the Fort Clatsop medal, see Coues 1893: 905n.

Great Falls of Columbia River, 1805

William Clark
Ink and watercolor on paper
7⅞ × 4⅞
Missouri Historical Society, St. Louis, William Clark Papers, Voorhis #4
Gift of Julia Clark Voorhis in memory of Eleanor Glasgow Voorhis

Another copy of this map is in Codex H at the American Philosophical Society.
SOURCES: Wood 1972: 156; Hunn in Wright 1991: 173; Moulton 1983–2001: 5: 323, 324, 327

White salmon trout, 1806

William Clark
Ink on paper
Image: 7¾ × 2⅛
Missouri Historical Society, St. Louis, William Clark Papers, Voorhis #2
Gift of Julia Clark Voorhis in memory of Eleanor Glasgow Voorhis

Gary E. Moulton identified this as coho salmon. Another sketch is in Codex J at the American Philosophical Society.
SOURCES: Ruby and Brown 1981: 21; Moulton 1983–2001: 6: 421–23, 424–25, 7: 144

The Dalles, 1860

John Mix Stanley
Lithograph on paper
Image: 5¾ × 9
Missouri Historical Society, St. Louis

SOURCES: Stevens 1860: pl. XLIII (opp. p. 154); Moulton 1983–2001: 5: 331

Below the Cascades, 1846–48

Paul Kane
Watercolor on paper
5½ × 9½
Stark Museum of Art, Orange, Texas, 31.78/91, WWC92

SOURCES: Moulton 1983–2001: 7: 245; Harper 1971: fig. 146

Drying Salmon at The Dalles, Columbia River, 1848

Paul Kane
Watercolor on paper
5½ × 9¼
Stark Museum of Art, Orange, Texas, 31.78/50, WWC50

SOURCES: Moulton 1983–2001: 5: 324–25, 10: 162, 11: 370; Griswold 1970: 21; Harper 1971: pl. XXXI

Mortar, mid-1800s

Wishram / Wasco
Hardwood
8½ × 10
Oregon Historical Society, cat. 65-530, neg. OrHi104219
Gift of Donald F. and Leah Menefee

Twined bag, pre-1819

Columbia River
Cedar bark, grasses
15¼ × 10⅝
Photograph from the Peabody Museum of Archaeology and Ethnology, Harvard University, © President and Fellows of Harvard College, photograph by Hillel Burger, cat. 90-17-10/48407, neg. T3858.1
Gift of the American Antiquarian Society, 1890

The museum catalog originally identified this as a bag for carrying water. Clark also made frequent mention of "Basquets of which they make great use to hold water boil their meet &c. &c." Among the things in Clark's museum was a waterproof cooking basket from the Columbia River.
SOURCES: "Articles from the North West, Pacific Ocean &c. for the American Antiquarian Society," February 4, 1818, American Antiquarian Society correspondence file, Peabody Museum; Moulton 1983–2001: 5: 323, 325, 347; Schlick 1994: 55; Ewers 1967: 58

Head of Flathead Indians on the Columbia, 1806

William Clark
Ink on paper
7¾ × 4⅞
Missouri Historical Society, St. Louis, William Clark Papers, Voorhis #2
Gift of Julia Clark Voorhis in memory of Eleanor Glasgow Voorhis

SOURCE: Moulton 1983–2001: 6: 252, 433

Chinook trade network

Cartography by Gene Thorp

Parfleche, pre-1889

Yakima
Cured hide, pigment
10½ × 14¾; fringe: 26 (each side)
University of Pennsylvania Museum of Archaeology and Anthropology, cat. 45-15-832, neg. T4-2309
Gift of Mrs. Owen Stephens, 1945

This artifact was collected by Charles H. Stephens. Ones like it are at the National Museum of Natural History: cat. 2618, collected by Lieutenant R. R. Waldron and J. L. Fox of the Wilkes Expedition at Fort Vancouver in 1841, and cat. 672, collected by George Gibbs at Fort Colville in the 1850s.
SOURCES: Wright 1991: 36, 62; Torrence 1994: 36, 60, 241

Parfleche, pre-1900

Umatilla
Cured hide, pigment
14½ × 26 × 2¾
University of Pennsylvania Museum of Archaeology and Anthropology, cat. 37534, neg. T4-2312
Gift of John Wanamaker, 1900

The collector of this artifact was Stuart Culin, who made several collecting trips for the museum around 1900.

Root bag, 1800s

Nez Perce
Wild hemp, grasses, corn husk
21⅝ × 15⅜ × ⅜
Photograph from the Peabody Museum of Archaeology and Ethnology, Harvard University, © President and Fellows of Harvard College, photograph by Hillel Burger, cat. 05-34-10/65411, neg. T3859
Museum Purchase (Huntington Frothingham Wolcott Fund), 1905

The style and the coloring of this bag are early. The collector stated it was decorated with corn husk, a material not used in Lewis and Clark's time but introduced at least as early as the 1870s (see National Museum of Natural History, cat. 23864, a corn-husk bag collected in 1876).
SOURCES: Turnbaugh and Turnbaugh 1986: 171; Wright 1991: 55–56; Moulton 1983–2001: 5: 142

Basket, pre-1890s

Klickitat
Cedar root, bear grass, cured hide
5 × 11¼ × 5
Maryhill Museum of Art, Goldendale, Washington, 1951.01.088
Gift of Winterton C. Curtis

This basket was collected by Rev. William C. Curtis during his tenure as pastor of the First Congregational Church in The Dalles, Oregon, from 1888 to 1898, but chances are it predates that. Its shape matches one at the British Museum collected by Captain Edward Belcher, who visited Fort Vancouver on the lower Columbia in 1839. Lewis's reference to the watertight baskets serving "the double perpose of holding their water or wearing on their heads" makes it unclear which baskets he was referring to, since headgear was made of flexible wild hemp, not the stiff cedar root.
SOURCES: Moulton 1983–2001: 6: 215; Wright 1991: 35, 76; Schlick 1994: 77–83, 91–92

Cape Disappointment, 1848

Henry Warre
Lithograph on paper
7½ × 11⅝
Yale Collection of Western Americana, Beinecke Rare Book and Manuscript Library

SOURCES: Warre 1848; Moulton 1983–2001: 6: 36n

Branding iron, c. 1804

American
Iron
4⅛ × 5½ × 1⅝
Oregon Historical Society, cat. 3670.1, neg. OrHi100061
Gift of Philip L. Jackson, 1941

SOURCES: Wheeler 1900: 50; Moulton 1983–2001: 4: 275–77, 6: 81, 9: 41 (Floyd's grave), 11: 193, 338 (horses); Hunt 1995: 8n–9n (horses, use, and manufacture)

Brass and copper bracelets, early 1800s

European / Upper Chinookan
Brass, copper
Top: 2¾ × 1⅝; lower left: 1½ × 1; lower right: 2½ × 2
From the collections of the Columbia Gorge Interpretive Center, Stevenson, Washington, ES10:18.23, ES10:18.12, ES10:18.7
Emory Strong Collection

SOURCE: Moulton 1983–2001: 6: 436

Double-bladed knife, pre-1867

Tlingit[?]
Iron, hide, sinew, wood
24⅛ × 3⅜
Photograph from the Peabody Museum of Archaeology and Ethnology, Harvard University, © President and Fellows of Harvard College, photograph by Hillel Burger, cat. 69-30-10/2179, neg. T3852.1
Collected by Edward G. Fast, 1867

The Nootka had John Jewitt make a dagger like this from recycled bayonets during his captivity at Nootka Sound in 1803–5.
SOURCES: Moulton 1983–2001: 6: 246–48, 250; Vaughan and Holm 1990: 70; Brown 2000: 181; Malloy 2000: 85

Sketch of a double-bladed knife, 1806

Meriwether Lewis or William Clark
Ink on paper
Image: ⅜ × 1⅛
Courtesy of the American Philosophical Society, Codex J, p. 48

SOURCE: Moulton 1983–2001: 6: 247, 250

Whalebone club, 1790s

Nootka
Whalebone, pigment
20 × 3 × ½
Photograph from the Peabody Museum of Archaeology and Ethnology, Harvard University, © President and Fellows of Harvard College, photograph by Hillel Burger, cat. 67-10-10/256, neg. T3857.1
Gift of the Massachusetts Historical Society, 1867

Clubs of this style have great antiquity, having been excavated at the prehistoric Ozette archaeological site on the Washington coast. Captain James Cook collected three of them in 1778.
SOURCES: Moulton 1983–2001: 6: 152, 155, 432n; Malloy 2000: 95; Brown 2000: 90–91

Sketch of a bludgeon, 1806

Meriwether Lewis
Ink on paper
Image: ¼ × 1¾
Courtesy of the American Philosophical Society, Codex J, p. 1

SOURCE: Moulton 1983–2001: 6: 152

Spanish dollar, 1791

Minted in Lima, Peru
Silver
DIAM 1⅝
Missouri Historical Society, St. Louis, X3481

SOURCES: Moulton 1983–2001: 10: 235; Ronda 1981; Jackson 1978: 478. On Pallotepallers, see Moulton 1983–2001: 7: 348n. On the coin, see Craig 1971: 370–71. On pieces of eight, see Rulau 1997: 14.

Dentalium belt, pre-1841

Columbia River
Dentalium shells, cured hide
44 × 1½
Courtesy of the Department of Anthropology, National Museum of Natural History, Smithsonian Institution, E*2706
Gift of Lt. Charles Wilkes, 1858

SOURCES: Griswold 1970: 13, 33, 34; Moulton 1983–2001: 6: 435–36

Beads, early to mid-1800s

Alaska
Glass, plant fiber cord
LENGTH 24 (approx.)
University of Pennsylvania Museum of Archaeology and Anthropology, cat. NA 374, neg. T4-2322
Collected by G. B. Gordon, 1905

SOURCE: Moulton 1983–2001: 6: 81, 120, 121, 435

"Slave killer" club, prehistoric

Upper Chinookan
Basalt
10¾ × 2 × ¾
From the collections of the Columbia Gorge Interpretive Center, Stevenson, Washington
Emory Strong Collection

This artifact was recovered by Emory Strong, an archaeologist who excavated several village sites before the flooding of the Columbia Valley. Another, very similar one was recovered by Strong in a cremation pit at the Leachman Site, near the Wishram village of Nixluidix. He noted that the clubs were rare on the Columbia and that most were double-bladed, as is this one.
SOURCES: Brown 2000: 174–75; Strong 1959: 30, 32; Strong 1960: 141–45

Advertisement: Slaves for Sale, 1809

American
Ink on paper
¾ × 2⅝
Missouri Historical Society, St. Louis

SOURCES: *Missouri Gazette*, April 26, 1809; Holmberg 2002: 98–99, 100, 144, 160, 183–84, 199, 201

Abalone earrings, late 1800s

Shoshone
Abalone shell, brass
3¼ × 1 (each)
University of Pennsylvania Museum of Archaeology and Anthropology, cat. nos. L-84-2022a,b, neg. T4-2318
Transfer from the Academy of Natural Sciences, 1936

These earrings were collected by Amos H. Gottschall at Weber River, Utah. Gottschall's collection was amassed from 1871 to 1905, when he traveled in the West making a living as a peddler of patent medicines. He became a connoisseur of Indian artifacts and tried to start a business selling them.
SOURCES: Griswold 1970: 14–15, 36–38; Moulton 1983–2001: 5: 114, 140

Blanket, pre-1841

Coast Salish
Goat wool
57⅞ × 76¼ (including fringe)
Courtesy of the Department of Anthropology, National Museum of Natural History, Smithsonian Institution, E*2124
Gift of Lt. Charles Wilkes, 1858

This blanket was collected by Lieutenant R. P. Robinson and was supposedly made of goat wool and dog hair; however, the dog hair (a common myth) is dubious. Philip Drucker called it a "nobility blanket." The central panel was woven separately and pieced in. The trade in blankets like this led to reports that "the Nez Perces and other tribes in the Fraser-Columbia area were extremely skillful in producing heavy and tastefully decorated blankets in twined weaving from mountain goat's hair with warp of vegetal fiber." Their blankets probably came from the coast. The design of this blanket resembles one in the George Catlin collection, fragments of which are at the National Museum of Natural History (cat. 177710); it was originally identified as Nez Perce and was once thought to have been from William Clark. One of the artifacts donated to Peale's Museum by Lewis and Clark was "A small Mantle of very fine wool, worn by the Crow's nation Menetarre." If this refers to a woven blanket, it may indicate a trade in woven blankets as far as the plains. The blanket that Clark offered to Jefferson was acknowledged on September 10, 1809.

SOURCES: Moulton 1983–2001: 6: 336, 434; Clark to Jefferson, June 2, 1808, Thomas Jefferson Papers, Massachusetts Historical Society; Jefferson to Clark, September 10, 1809, William Clark Papers, Missouri Historical Society. On this and other blankets, see Wright 1991: 44; Drucker 1955: 84; Kapoun and Lohrmann 1997: 8 (quotation on Nez Perce, from G. O. Shields); Jackson 1978: 476. On the Catlin blanket, see Krieger 1929: 640, pl. 9-A.

Sally bag, 1800s

Upper Chinookan
Corn husk, hemp, cotton
9½ × 6
Maryhill Museum of Art, Goldendale, Washington, 1940.01.004
Gift of Mary Underwood Lane

The donor was the granddaughter of the Wasco Chief Welawa (also known as Chenoweth) and Mumshumsie, the daughter of a prominent Cascade family.

SOURCES: Moulton 1983–2001: 5: 373; Schlick 1994: 74

Horn bowl, 1800s

Wishram / Wasco
Rocky Mountain sheep horn
5 × 3½
Maryhill Museum of Art, Goldendale, Washington, 1958.01.018
Gift of Mary Underwood Lane

The style of this bowl is similar to that of two bowls collected by George Gibbs on the Columbia in the 1850s; see National Museum of Natural History (cat. nos. 691 and 10079).

SOURCES: Moulton 1983–2001: 6: 118, 119, 215; Vaughan and Holm 1990: 58; Wright 1991: 93

Black-rimmed hat, early 1800s

Nootka or Makah
Spruce root, cedar bark, pigment
4¾ × 15
Photograph from the Peabody Museum of Archaeology and Ethnology, Harvard University, © President and Fellows of Harvard College, photograph by Hillel Burger, cat. 99-12-10/53081, neg. T2514aii
Gift of the Heirs of David Kimball, 1899

Robin Wright calls this the earliest known example of a black-rimmed hat from the northwest coast.

SOURCES: McLaughlin 2003: chapter 5; Wright 1991: 84, 86; Vaughan and Holm 1990: 34–35

Comb, pre-1841

Chinook[?]
Wood, pigment
7½ × 2¼ × ¾
Courtesy of the Department of Anthropology, National Museum of Natural History, Smithsonian Institution, E*2701
Gift of Lt. Charles Wilkes, 1858

Similar combs from farther north were collected on Captain James Cook's expedition in 1778.

SOURCES: Moulton 1983–2001: 6: 336, 433; Spier and Sapir 1930: 219; Brown 2000: 94

View of Majoa's Great Village, 1791

José Cardero
Watercolor on paper
10 × 17⅛
Museo de América, Madrid, 2280

The title beneath this watercolor reads: *Vista de la Gran Rancheria de Maguaa.*

SOURCE: Brown 2000: 76, pl. 30

China platter, c. 1793

Chinese
Porcelain
11¼ × 8⅛ × 1
Oregon Historical Society, cat. 3669.36, neg. ORHi104217
Gift of Miss Amelia Peabody

SOURCE: Vaughan and Holm 1990: 13

Paddle, 1794

Makah
Spruce wood, resin
70¾ × 7½
Photograph from the Peabody Museum of Archaeology and Ethnology, Harvard University, © President and Fellows of Harvard College, photograph by Hillel Burger, cat. 67-10-10/337, neg. T3853.1
Gift of the Massachusetts Historical Society, 1867

The Peabody accession register gave the collector's name as "Thomas Hills," probably a mistake.

SOURCES: Malloy 2000: 95; Moulton 1983–2001: 6: 155, 268

Bow, 1795

Chinook
Wood, sinew, deerskin, plant fiber, glue
30½ × 5 × 1½
Photograph from the Peabody Museum of Archaeology and Ethnology, Harvard University, © President and Fellows of Harvard College, photograph by Hillel Burger, cat. 99-12-10/52951, neg. T3850.1
Gift of the Heirs of David Kimball, 1899

SOURCES: Malloy 2000: 133; Moulton 1983–2001: 6: 206–7

A Sea Otter, 1784

John Webber
Engraving on paper
Image: 6 × 9½
Library of Congress

SOURCES: Moulton 1983–2001: 6: 339; Jackson 1978: 323; Cook 1784: 4 [atlas]: pl.43

Camphorwood chest, early to mid-1800s

Chinese
Camphorwood, pigskin, brass, paint
12 × 29⅝ × 15⅜
Oregon Historical Society, cat. 74-58.1, neg. ORHi104218
Gift of Lucille Cummins

SOURCE: Vaughan and Holm 1990: 20

Wedding veil, c. 1890

Klickitat
Beads, dentalia, brass bells, thimbles, Chinese coins, hide, conch shell
22 × 10
Maryhill Museum of Art, Goldendale, Washington, 1989.13.001

SOURCE: Wright 1991: 91

Gaming bones, late 1800s

Nez Perce
Incised bone
Up to 2½ × 1
Nez Perce National Historical Park, 81, 82, 83, 84, 2156

These are probably from two different sets of gaming bones.

SOURCES: Anastasio 1975: 171–72; Moulton 1983–2001: 7: 137–38. For a description of the game among the Tillamook, see Sauter and Johnson 1974: 129–30.

King Comcomly's Burial Canoe, 1847

Paul Kane
Watercolor on paper
5⅜ × 9¼
Stark Museum of Art, Orange, Texas, 31.78/85, WWC86

Kane identified this as "the grave of Com-comly at Astoria, Chief of the Chinooks."

SOURCES: Harper 1971: 302, fig. 167; Moulton 1983–2001: 5: 361, 6: 97–98, 182, 186, 285

Woman of Nootka Sound, 1778

John Webber
Ink and graphite on paper
15¾ × 12⅝
Photograph from the Peabody Museum of Archaeology and Ethnology, Harvard University, Bushnell Collection, photograph by Hillel Burger, cat. 41-72-10/498, neg. T2359
Gift of the Estate of Belle J. Bushnell, 1941

This is the watercolor from which Plate 39 in James Cook's *A Voyage to the Pacific Ocean* was engraved.

SOURCES: Malloy 2000: 9; Moulton 1983–2001: 6: 416; Cook 1784

Woman's skirt, pre-1840

Chinook
Cattail, hide, pigment
20½ × 32½
Courtesy of the Department of Anthropology, National Museum of Natural History, Smithsonian Institution, E*73291
Gift of Sarah (Mrs. Joseph) Harrison, 1881

There is a similar skirt at the Peabody Museum (cat. 99-12-10/52990), but there is as much evidence for linking this one with Lewis and Clark as there is for that one.

SOURCES: Wright 1991: 34; Moulton 1983–2001: 6: 75, 435; McLaughlin 2003: chapter 9

CHAPTER 8

Curing and Plants

Razor box of Patrick Gass, c. 1805

Attributed to Sacagawea
Cottonwood
7⅞ × 2⅜ × 1¼ (closed)
On loan to Fort Canby State Park by the family of Owen Buxton, the great-grandson of Patrick Gass

This is one of several Gass artifacts that were passed down to Gass's daughter, Rachel Gass Brierley, after his death in 1870 at the age of ninety-nine. After her death in 1926, the artifacts passed to her grandson, Owen Buxton; the present owners are Buxton's widow and daughter. The artifacts are on long-term loan to the Lewis and Clark Interpretive Center at Fort Canby State Park, Ilwaco, Washington. They consist of this box; a shingling hatchet head said to have been carried on the expedition; a liquor flask; an account book for 1826–37 and 1847–48; and a family Bible. There are examples of Indian-made wooden boxes with sliding covers like this; one collected in 1832 and identified as Ojibway is shown in Thompson 1977: 189.

SOURCES: Forrest 1950; MacGregor 1997

Flathead Indians, 1861

George Catlin
Oil on card mounted on paperboard
18 × 23⅞
Paul Mellon Collection, National Gallery of Art, Washington, D.C.
Photograph © 2002 Board of Trustees, 1965.16.149.(2107)/PA

SOURCE: Ruby and Brown 1976: 46, 69

Head-flattening cradle, pre-1840

Chinook
Western red cedar wood, deer skin, plant fiber
30¼ × 9 × 5½
Photograph from the Peabody Museum of Archaeology and Ethnology, Harvard University, © President and Fellows of Harvard College, photograph by Hillel Burger, cat. 88-51-10/50696, neg.T1260
Exchange with the Smithsonian Institution, 1888

This was originally part of the Catlin collection donated to the Smithsonian Institution by Sarah (Mrs. Joseph) Harrison in 1881. Since Catlin took it to London in 1839–40, it must predate that time. The chapter of Catlin's book in which he describes the Chinook was written in St. Louis, and some of his information may have come from Clark.

SOURCES: Catlin 1995: 2: 126, pl. 210½; Goetzmann 1988: 66

Chinook Lodge (Interior), 1844

A. T. Agate
Engraving on paper
Image: 4⅝ × 7
Yale Collection of Western Americana, Beinecke Rare Book and Manuscript Library

SOURCES: Wilkes 1844: 4: 365; Moulton 1983–2001: 5: 371, 6: 223

Bag, pre-1841

Clatsop or Tillamook
Plant fiber
12½ × 20½
Courtesy of the Department of Anthropology, National Museum of Natural History, Smithsonian Institution, E*251626
Gift of Miss S. P. Casey, 1908

The tribal attribution is based on the bag's similarity to two other Clatsop/Tillamook bags: cat. T-17569 from the Wilkes Collection at the National Museum of Natural History, and one in the Edwin C. Cross Collection at the Hallie Ford Museum of Art, Willamette University.

SOURCES: Moulton 1983–2001: 6: 135, 216; Marr 1984: 50, 51; Dobkins 2000: 49

A Whale Ashore—Klahoquat, 1869

George Catlin
Oil on card mounted on paperboard
18⅞ × 25¼
Paul Mellon Collection, National Gallery of Art, Washington, D.C. Photograph © 2002 Board of Trustees, 1965.16.214.(2172)/PA

SOURCE: Catlin 1868: 106, 110

Route maps of the mouth of the Columbia, 1806

William Clark
Pencil and ink on paper
8⅛ × 10⅜ (#32-7); 11⅞ × 10⅜ (#32-8); 11⅞ × 8⅜ (#32-9); 5¾ × 10⅝ (#32-10)
Yale Collection of Western Americana, Beinecke Rare Book and Manuscript Library, WA Mss. 303 # 32-7 to 32-10
Gift of William R. Coe

SOURCE: Moulton 1983–2001: 1: maps 81–84

Trenchers, 1850s

Makah
Wood, shell
Right (693): 6¼ × 5⅛ × 1⅞;
left (694): 7 × 6⅛ × 2⅛
Courtesy of the Department of Anthropology, National Museum of Natural History, Smithsonian Institution, E*693, E*694
Gift of George Gibbs, 1862

SOURCE: Moulton 1983–2001: 6: 118, 215

Housewife (sewing kit) of George Shannon, c. 1804

American
Red morocco leather, metal clasp, green leather interior, white silk lining, needle and thread
7⅝ × 15¼ (partially unfolded)
Oregon Historical Society, cat. 4014, neg. OrHi100138
Gift of Elizabeth Monroe Story

Several similar red morocco leather folders belonging to Clark are at the Missouri Historical Society (cat. 1924 004 0008 through 0011).

SOURCES: Wheeler 1904: 1: 119; Holmberg 2002: 152–53

Sketch of a condor, 1806

William Clark
Ink on paper
Image: 1½ × 2
Missouri Historical Society, St. Louis, William Clark Papers, Voorhis #2
Gift of Julia Clark Voorhis in memory of Eleanor Glasgow Voorhis

SOURCE: Moulton 1983–2001: 5: 357n, 6: 322–23

Sketch of Chinookan canoes, 1806

William Clark
Ink on paper
Images: ¼ to ½ × 1 to 1⅝
Missouri Historical Society, St. Louis, William Clark Papers, Voorhis #2
Gift of Julia Clark Voorhis in memory of Eleanor Glasgow Voorhis

SOURCE: Moulton 1983–2001: 6: 264, 268, 269

Model canoe and paddles, pre-1841

Columbia River
Wood, pigment
26¼ × 5½ × 5⅝
Courtesy of the Department of Anthropology, National Museum of Natural History, Smithsonian Institution, E*2583
Gift of Lt. Charles Wilkes, 1858

SOURCE: Moulton 1983–2001: 6: 262–65

Sketch of a Clatsop paddle, 1806

Meriwether Lewis
Ink on paper
Image: ¼ × 2
Courtesy of the American Philosophical Society, Codex J, p. 1

SOURCE: Moulton 1983–2001: 6: 152

Magnet and compass of William Clark, early 1800s

American
Magnet: iron alloy, paint; compass: gold-clad copper alloy, jasper, glass, paint
Magnet: 1⅜ × ⅜; compass: 1 × 1; chain: LENGTH 14
Missouri Historical Society, St. Louis, 1924 004 0014, 1924 004 0017
Gifts of Julia Clark Voorhis in memory of Eleanor Glasgow Voorhis

SOURCE: Jackson 1978: 82

To-ma-quin, A Cascade Chief, Columbia River, 1847

Paul Kane
Watercolor on paper
7 × 5
With permission of the Royal Ontario Museum © ROM, 946.15.195

SOURCES: Moulton 1983–2001: 7: 97; Harper 1971: 111–12, 297

Mt. Hood from Les Dalles, 1848

Henry Warre
Color lithograph on paper
Image: 10½ × 15¾
Yale Collection of Western Americana, Beinecke Rare Book and Manuscript Library

SOURCES: Warre 1848; Moulton 1983–2001: 5: 304, 342, 6: 12–13, 9: 249n

Nez Perce Indian, c. 1856

Paul Kane
Oil on canvas
25 × 20
With permission of the Royal Ontario Museum © ROM, 912.1.72

A sketch on which this painting is based is in the Bushnell Collection at the Peabody Museum (41-72/394). This oil version was completed around 1856.

SOURCES: Moulton 1983–2001: 7: 224, 253, 254; Horse Capture and Horse Capture 2001: 38; Harper 1971: 232, 296

Buttons, late 1700s to early 1800s

Columbia River
Copper and brass
DIAM ½ to 1
From the collections of the Columbia Gorge Interpretive Center, Stevenson, Washington
Emory Strong Collection

Emory Strong, the archaeologist who excavated these buttons, identified the patterned ones as "Colonial" style, large handmade buttons of the eighteenth century, from both America and Europe. The first American brass button manufacturer was Abel Parter & Co., which later became the Scovill Manufacturing Co., well represented on the Columbia.

SOURCES: Woodward 1989: 24–27, 31–33; Strong 1960: 212, 220

Medical instruments, early 1800s

American, German, English
Clyster: pewter, wood; instruments and case: leather, tortoise shell, steel, ebony; pill box: wood; pills: unidentified substance; tourniquet: brass, steel, wood, kid leather, linen, cotton; lancets: tortoise shell, steel

Clyster: 15 × 2½ (plunger in); instrument case: 17 × 11 (fully open); pill box: 2⅜ × 1⅛; tourniquet: 4¼ × 2⅝; lancets: 2¼ × ⅜
Mütter Museum, The College of Physicians of Philadelphia, 17090.90, 1797 misc., 17837.86, 17157, 17833.03, 17824.48
Gift of Mrs. Hazel Koch, 1976 (instruments); gift of Mr. Edward Shippen Morris, 1952 (pills); Gift of Dr. John B. Roberts (lancets); others unknown

The surgical instruments belonged to "Dr. Funcke," the great-great-grandfather of the donor; the doctor practiced in or near Westphalia or Cologne. The instruments were brought to the United States by the donor's grandfather. The pills are from the medicine chest of the Philadelphia doctor William Shippen, Sr. (1712–1801), and were made by Mrs. Isabella Inglish, England. Patrick Anderson's Scots pills were a popular English patent remedy of the seventeenth and eighteenth centuries; they were first made in the 1630s, when Anderson claimed to be the physician to Charles I. The formula varied with each maker. This style of tourniquet, invented in 1718, was called the Petit type. One of the lancets was made by Charrière, Paris (established pre-1836), the other by Schively, Philadelphia (established 1783).
SOURCES: Jackson 1978: 74 (clysters), 80; Moulton 1983–2001: 4: 334 (penknife), 6: 329 (Scott's pills), 7: 35 (tourniquet); Edmondson 1993: 16, 17, 19, 89, 263

Medicine chest, 1804

Paytherus, Savory & Co., London
Mahogany, glass, brass, fabric, plant and mineral products
10½ × 10⅛ × 9⅛ (closed)
Courtesy of the National Museum of American History, Smithsonian Institution, acc. 118923, cat. MG*M-03233
Gift of William C. Baur, 1932

This box was owned successively by the following: Jan Abraham Willink, Amsterdam; Cornelia A. Ludlow; Elizabeth Ludlow; M. P. James; John P. Treadwell; and the donor.
SOURCES: Jackson 1978: 80–81; Lentz 2000; Loge 1997

Benjamin Rush, c. 1812

Thomas Sully
Oil on canvas
48⅛ × 38⅛
Courtesy of the American Philosophical Society, 58.P.51 FAP 087

The date of this painting is uncertain. Sully recorded painting a three-quarter-length portrait of Rush in 1812 and a replica of it in 1815, after Rush's death. However, this one is apparently unfinished and was "found amongst old papers &c. in the Library" of the American Philosophical Society in 1899. Found folded, it was restored and framed at that time.
SOURCES: Vogel 1970: 63; Garraty and Carnes 1999: 19: 72–75; American Philosophical Society 1961: 86–87

Specimen of *Pinus ponderosa* (ponderosa pine), 1805

Collected by Meriwether Lewis
Dried pine needles and ink on paper
Sheet: 16¾ × 11½
Department of Botany, The Academy of Natural Sciences of Philadelphia, PH-LC 167. Photograph courtesy of Ewell Sale Stewart Library
On loan from the American Philosophical Society

SOURCES: Moulton 1983–2001: 7: 336, 12: no. 131a; Harbinger 1964: 18–19; Hart and Moore 1976: 50–51; Hunn 1990: 185, 356

Medicine woman's outfit, pre-1891

Blackfeet
Wood, cloth, brass, bone, hair, feather, hide, beads
Bowl: 9½ × 8½ × 4; cloth bag: 14¼ × 10¾
University of Pennsylvania Museum of Archaeology and Anthropology, cat. nos. 45-15-1231 to 1243, neg. T4-2314
Charles H. Stephens collection, gift of Mrs. Owen Stephens, 1947

This was collected in 1891.
SOURCE: Walker 1980: 96, 117

Rattle, c. 1876

Nez Perce
Wood, cured hide, dewclaws
18¼ × 2¾ × 1½
Courtesy of the Department of Anthropology, National Museum of Natural History, Smithsonian Institution, E*23859
Gift of John P. Monteith

This was collected by the agent on the Nez Perce Reservation for the 1876 Centennial Exposition.
SOURCE: Walker 1980: 91

Medicine case, mid-1800s

Nez Perce[?]
Hide, dewclaws, pigment
Case: 8½ × 15½ × 3; thong: LENGTH 19
University of Pennsylvania Museum of Archaeology and Anthropology, cat. 38-8-25, neg. T4-2311
Gift of Rodman Wanamaker, 1938

This may have been collected by Edward Curtis in around 1910. Rudolph F. Kurz, an artist who lived on the Missouri River in 1846–52, drew one very like it, including a U-shaped top, painted stripes, and thunderbird. He labeled it "Medicine Sac. Queue Rouge." Queue Rouge was a man Kurz had painted, possibly at Fort Union.
SOURCES: Walker 1980: 80; Jarrell and Hewitt 1937: pl. 14

Medicine Man, Performing His Mysteries over a Dying Man, 1832

George Catlin
Oil on canvas
29 × 24
Smithsonian American Art Museum, 1985.66.161
Gift of Mrs. Joseph Harrison, Jr.

SOURCES: Walker 1980: 91–92,104; Catlin 1995: 1: 45–47

Flint knife, 1800s

Shoshone
Wood, flint, hide
7½ × 1¼
Courtesy of the National Museum of the American Indian, Smithsonian Institution, 122046
Gift of W. Wildschut

SOURCES: Walker 1980: 91–92; Moulton 1983–2001: 5: 143, 149

Hidatsa Indians Sweat-bathing, 1851

Rudolph Friederich Kurz
Ink on paper
5⅛ × 3⅛
© Ethnographic Collection, Bernisches Historisches Museum. Photo by Stefan Rebsamen, 1894.404.57.1:145.

SOURCES: Moulton 1983–2001: 5: 262. On sweat lodges, see Wright 1991: 164–65; Walker 1980: 78. On this sketch, see Jarrell and Hewitt 1937: pl. 2; Ewers 1965: 141.

Turlington's Balsam of Life, early 1800s

Robert Turlington, London
Bottle: glass
2½ × 1½ × 1
State Historical Society of North Dakota, 13766.1. Photograph by Sharon Silengo
Collected by Norman Paulson and Isadore Smith for the State Historical Society of North Dakota, 1958

An American patent medicine under the same name continued in use for many years, and in the early 1900s the Illinois Glass Company manufactured facsimiles of the eighteenth-century Turlington's bottle. The inscription on this one is "By the King's Royall Patent Granted to / Rob. Turlington For his Invented Balsam of Life / London / Jany 26 1754."
SOURCES: Woodward 1989: 27; Jackson 1978: 74; Museum of the Fur Trade 1967; Wedel and Griffenhagen 1954

Specimen of *Artemisia longifolia* (long-leafed sage), 1804

Collected by Meriwether Lewis
Dried plant on paper
Sheet: 16⅝ × 11⅝
Department of Botany, The Academy of Natural Sciences of Philadelphia, PH-LC 27. Photograph courtesy of Ewell Sale Stewart Library
On loan from the American Philosophical Society

Lewis's label reads, "No. 53 October 3rd flavor like the camomile radix perennial growth of the high bluffs."
SOURCES: Moulton 1983–2001: 12: no. 20; Gilmore 1977: 83; Hart and Moore 1976: 44–45

Specimen of *Berberis nervosa* (dull or low Oregon grape), 1805

Collected by Meriwether Lewis
Dried plant and ink on paper
Sheet: 16 × 10
Department of Botany, The Academy of Natural Sciences of Philadelphia, PH-LC 39. Photograph courtesy of Ewell Sale Stewart Library
Gift of Edward Tuckerman

This was one of the specimens taken to London by Frederick Pursh and published there. The two labels at left and right top are by Pursh.
SOURCES: Moulton 1983–2001: 6: 299–302, 12: no. 109; Pursh 1816: 1: 219; Cutright 1969a: 404; Hunn and Selam 1990: 352

Sketch of *Berberis nervosa* (dull or low Oregon grape), 1806

William Clark
Ink on paper
Image: ¾ × 3¼
Missouri Historical Society, St. Louis, William Clark Papers, Voorhis #2
Gift of Julia Clark Voorhis in memory of Eleanor Glasgow Voorhis

SOURCE: Moulton 1983–2001: 6: 301

John Miller, *An Illustration of the Sexual System, of Linnaeus*, 1779–89

Published by the author, London
Ink and watercolor on paper, bound in cloth with leather spine and corners
9¼ × 6 × 1½ (closed)
Library of Congress, QK 92 .M6

The title above is for the first volume, published 1779. The second volume, published in 1789, is titled *An Illustration of the Termini Botanici of Linnaeus*.
SOURCE: Jackson 1959

Specimen of *Gaultheria shallon* (salal), 1806

Collected by Meriwether Lewis
Dried plant and ink on paper
Sheet: 16¾ × 11½
Department of Botany, The Academy of Natural Sciences of Philadelphia, PH-LC 98. Photograph courtesy of Ewell Sale Stewart Library

On loan from the American Philosophical Society

Pursh's copy of Lewis's label reads, "The Shallon; Supposed to be a Species of Vaccinium. On the Coast of the Pacific Ocean. Jan: 20th 1806."
SOURCE: Moulton 1983–2001: 6: 237–38, 287, 289, 12: no. 74

Sketch of *Gaultheria shallon* (salal), 1806

William Clark
Ink on paper
Image: $\frac{5}{8} \times 1\frac{1}{8}$
Missouri Historical Society, St. Louis, William Clark Papers, Voorhis #2
Gift of Julia Clark Voorhis in memory of Eleanor Glasgow Voorhis

SOURCE: Moulton 1983–2001: 6: 289

Digging stick, late 1800s

Nez Perce
Fire-hardened wood, elk antler
Stick: LENGTH $29\frac{1}{2}$; handle: LENGTH 8
Nez Perce National Historical Park, 159 and 8715
On loan from Nez Perce Tribe (stick); gift of Mrs. Doris Chapman Babcock, 1970 (handle)

The handle is thought to have been found by the donor at a traditional camping ground on the Snake River below Lime Point.
SOURCES: Moulton 1983–2001: 6: 231–32; Spinden 1908: 200; Harbinger 1964: 27

Specimen of *Camassia quamash* (camas), 1806

Collected by Meriwether Lewis
Dried plant and ink on paper
Sheet: $16\frac{3}{4} \times 11\frac{1}{2}$
Department of Botany, The Academy of Natural Sciences of Philadelphia, PH-LC 44. Photograph courtesy of Ewell Sale Stewart Library
On loan from the American Philosophical Society

SOURCES: Moulton 1983–2001: 5: 222, 12: no. 33; Harbinger 1964: 11–13, 58, 77; see also Hart and Moore 1976: 14–18

Root bag, pre-1876

Nez Perce
Plant fibers, including wild hemp (*Apocynum cannabinum*), corn husk
$29\frac{1}{2} \times 24$
Courtesy of the Department of Anthropology, National Museum of Natural History, Smithsonian Institution, E*23864
Gift of John B. Monteith

Indian agent John B. Monteith purchased this bag from Pen-me-kin-me-wat for $2.50, for a Nez Perce display at the 1876 Centennial Exposition.
SOURCES: Linn 1994: 8; Grafe 1999: 62

Nez Perce food, 1891

Nez Perce
Dried plant material
Camas bread: $5\frac{1}{8} \times 10\frac{5}{8} \times 2$; cous loaf: $6\frac{5}{8} \times 12\frac{5}{8} \times 1\frac{1}{4}$; berry cakes: DIAM $2\frac{3}{8}$; others: LENGTH 1 or less
Photograph from the Peabody Museum of Archaeology and Ethnology, Harvard University, © President and Fellows of Harvard College, photograph by Hillel Burger, cat. 92-1-10/47777 (cooked camas root), cat. 92-1-10/47778 (dried cous), cat. 92-1-10/47779 (wild potato), cat. 92-1-10/47780 (bitterroot), cat. 92-1-10/47783 (cous loaf), cat. 92-1-10/47784 (cous cakes), cat. 92-1-10/47785 (camas bread), cat. 92-1-10/47786 (mashed potato cakes), cat. 92-1-10/47787.4 (berry cakes); neg. T3851.1
Gift of Alice C. Fletcher, 1892

These foods were collected by James Stuart, a Nez Perce Indian, in 1891. The samples of cous that Lewis and Clark gave to Peale's Museum were described as "The Roots of Cows. So called by the Pallatepallers with whom it forms a principal article of food." Also: "Bread . . . called by them cows—it is pripared from the bulb of an umbellaferous plant to which they give the same name. these bulbs are pounded between two stones while in a succulent state and then exposed to the sun untill dry when they assume the appearance and consistance of this specimen. This article for many weeks constituted the principal part of the food of Lewis and party, while in that country." The camas roots were: "Bulbus Roots. These bulbs form the food of many Indian Nations residing within and west of the Rocky Mountain. They are called by the Pallotepallers Quaw-mash." Also: "Bread. This is called Passhequo-quaw-mash being only a varied preparation of the quaw-mas bulb." Lewis and Clark also collected some unnamed roots, given them by the Nez Perce chief Neeshneparkeooh (Cut Nose) and some shappellel bread. Moulton identifies "shappellel" as the Chinookan word for cous, but Peale and the journals differentiate the two. It may have been an alternative preparation.
SOURCES: Jackson 1978: 477. On cous, see Hart and Moore 1976: 26. On camas, see Moulton 1983–2001: 5: 222; Hart and Moore 1976: 17; Meehan 1898: 43. On wild potatoes, see Moulton 1983–2001: 7: 207; Hart and Moore 1976: 29; Harbinger 1964: 14–15; Hunn and Selam 1990: 172. On bitterroot, see Meehan 1898: 19.

Carved house posts, early 1800s

Cascade[?]
Cedar
24 to 30 × 6 to 10 × 4 (approx.)
From the collections of the Columbia Gorge Interpretive Center, Stevenson, Washington, 1986.48.1-6
Gift of the Biddle Family

Chinookan houses were often adorned and protected by lavishly carved and painted images that depicted the spirit guardians of the owners. Just past Beacon Rock, where these posts were found in 1904, Clark "Saw in those houses Several wooden *Images* all cut in imitation of men, but differently fasioned and placed in the most conspicious parts of the houses." He later added, "I cannot Say certainly that those nativs worship those wooden idols as I have every reason to believe they do not; as they are . . . treated more like orniments than objects of aderation."

CARVED HOUSE POSTS

These posts were originally painted red and black. Henry J. Biddle, who purchased Beacon Rock in 1915, may have discovered them and came to own them. Like any other household property, such images were sometimes transferred to graves on the death of the owner, but they were not made specifically for burial purposes.
SOURCES: Moulton 1983–2001: 5: 361, 371; Biddle 1978; Boyd 1996: 122–23

Sketch of a fishhook, 1806

Meriwether Lewis
Ink on paper
Image: $\frac{1}{4} \times 2$
Courtesy of the American Philosophical Society, Codex I, p. 122

Lewis and Clark spent part of the monotonous winter months studying the Indians around them. Lacking a translator, they were limited to what they could observe directly, so they wrote about dress, tools, and other external things. "The gig and hook are employed indiscriminately at all seasons in taking such fish as they can procure," Lewis wrote. "Their hooks are generally of European manufactary, tho' before the whites visited them they made hooks of bone and other substances . . . firmly attached together with sinues and covered with rosin."
SOURCE: Moulton 1983–2001: 6: 211, 212–13

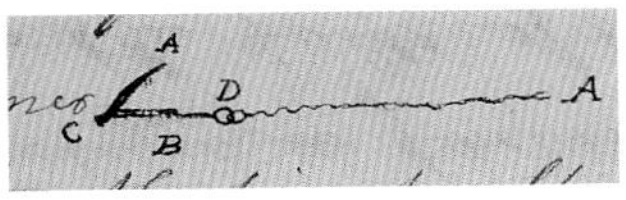

SKETCH OF A FISHHOOK

Fishhooks, 1841

Northwest Coast
Hemlock, spruce root, bone, sinew, baleen, gut
Codfish hooks: $12\frac{3}{4}$ to $13\frac{3}{4} \times 1\frac{1}{2}$; halibut hook: $7 \times 4\frac{5}{8}$
Courtesy of the Department of Anthropology, National Museum of Natural History, Smithsonian Institution, E*2629
Gift of Lt. Charles Wilkes, 1858

These fishhooks with bone barbs were collected by the Wilkes Expedition thirty-five years after Lewis and Clark were on the northwest coast. The smaller ones were for catching cod, and the U-shaped one was for halibut.
SOURCE: Swan 1870: 23, 41

FISHHOOKS

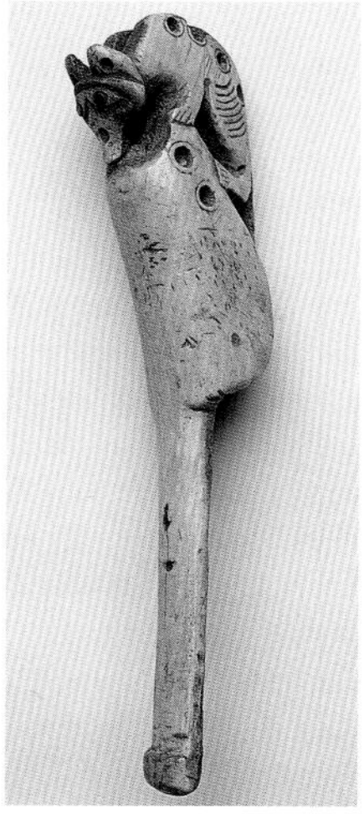

ADZE HANDLE

Adze handle, pre-1850

Chinookan
Animal leg bone
8¾ × 2 × 1½
Courtesy of the Department of Anthropology, National Museum of Natural History, Smithsonian Institution, E*708
Gift of George Gibbs, 1862

Even the tools used to make canoes were elaborately carved. This bone adze handle was designed for use with a steel blade; the carver would lash an ax head, chisel, or sharpened file to the flat part at the bottom so that the blade projected beyond the end of the bone. Clark wrote: "The only tool usially employd in forming the Canoe, carveing &c is a chissel formed of an old file. . . . this chissel has Sometimes a large block of wood for a handle; they grasp the chissel just below the block with the right hand holding the top of the block, and Strikes backwards against the wood with the edge of the Chissel." Lewis added, "A person would suppose that the forming of a large canoe with an instrument like this was the work of several years; but these people make them in a few weeks."

This handle was collected at the mouth of the Columbia River. Straight adzes like it were used only in the southern region of the northwest coast, from Puget Sound to the Columbia River. North of that, tribes hafted their adzes differently.

SOURCES: Moulton 1983–2001: 6: 265, 271; Wright 1991: 103

Claw necklace, 1800s

Nez Perce
Hide, bear claws, pigment
21 × 12
Photograph from the Peabody Museum of Archaeology and Ethnology, Harvard University, © President and Fellows of Harvard College, photograph by Hillel Burger, cat.07-5-10/72413, neg. T3855.1
Museum Purchase (Huntington Frothingham Wolcott Fund), 1907

This powerful necklace is said to have been worn by a Nez Perce shaman. The rattles are bear claws, carved to look serrated. They would have made a clacking, rustling sound when the wearer moved, enhancing the mood of the performance. This artifact was collected by Herbert J. Spinden, who did research among the Nez Perce in 1907. A similar necklace is in the University of Pennsylvania Museum (cat. NA 5443). It is more elaborate, and probably Sioux.

SOURCE: Spinden 1908

CLAW NECKLACE

Bath switch, 1800s

Blackfeet
Wood, bison hide with hair
14½ × 2¼
University of Pennsylvania Museum of Archaeology and Anthropology, cat. 45-15-1252, neg. T4-2323
Charles H. Stephens collection, gift of Mrs. Owen Stephens, 1947

Switches like this were used in steam baths for sprinkling water on the stones and for striking the body to stimulate the skin.

BATH SWITCH

Specimen of *Sphaeralcea coccinea* (red false mallow), 1806

Collected by Meriwether Lewis
Dried plant and ink on paper
Sheet: 16¾ × 11½
Department of Botany, The Academy of Natural Sciences of Philadelphia, PH-LC 207. Photograph courtesy of Ewell Sale Stewart Library
On loan from the American Philosophical Society

The Dakota called this plant *Heyoke ta pezhuta*, which means "medicine [pezhuta] of the heyoka [a vision society]." The heyoka were sometimes spoken of as clowns, or lunatics, because they did things contrary to nature. Their most famous act was plunging their arms into boiling water and splashing it over each other, complaining that it was cold, to the mystification of beholders. This plant was the secret to the performance. They would chew it into a paste or mucilage which was rubbed over the hands and arms, thus making them immune to the effect of scalding water. The plant was also chewed and applied to inflamed sores and wounds as a cooling and healing salve. Lewis collected this specimen on July 20, 1806, on the Marias River in present-day Montana.

SOURCES: Moulton 1983–2001: 12: no. 163; Gilmore 1977: 51; Wissler 1912: 82

SPECIMEN OF *SPHAERALCEA COCCINEA*

CHAPTER 9
Discovering Each Other

***Exit of the Yellowstone from the Mountains*, 1868**

Alfred Edward Mathews
Lithograph on paper
Image: 5⅝ × 9⅛
Montana Historical Society
Gift of Mrs. Langford Smith

SOURCES: Mathews 1868: pl. VII; Moulton 1983–2001: 8: 186, 187. For more on Mathews, see Taft 1949.

***Marias River*, 1860**

John Mix Stanley
Engraving with watercolor on paper
Image: 6¼ × 9¼
Missouri Historical Society, St. Louis

SOURCES: Stevens 1860: pl. XXVI; Moulton 1983–2001: 8: 118; Nicandri 1986

***Packkaab-Sachkoma-Poh, Piegan Blackfeet Man*, 1833**

Karl Bodmer
Watercolor on paper
12½ × 10
Joslyn Art Museum, Omaha, Nebraska, 1986.49.287
Gift of Enron Art Foundation

SOURCE: Goetzmann et al. 1984: 253

War shirt, 1843

Pe-toh-pee-kiss, Blackfeet
Cured antelope hide, quills, hair, wool, sinew, shell
55 × 63 (with sleeves extended)
Courtesy of the Alabama Department of Archives and History, Montgomery, Alabama, 86.3147.23
Gift of William Ustick Harris, 1941

Edward Harris and John James Audubon spent two months at Fort Union while on a research and collecting expedition in 1843. Alexander Culbertson called the shirt's owner Le Soulier de Femme (Woman's Moccasin), but substantial documentation indicates this was the same person as Pe-toh-pee-kiss (Eagle Ribs). Culbertson added that he "killed a Mr. Vandenburgh of the [American Fur] Company's service, some ten years ago." Harris's collection passed down to his grandson William Ustick Harris, a resident of Jackson, Alabama, who was the donor.

SOURCES: Catlin 1995: 1: 34, 39; Peterson and Peers 1993: 71; McDermott 1951b: 134

Amulet, 1885

Blackfeet
Human hair, cured hide, beads, pigment
8 × 2
University of Pennsylvania Museum of Archaeology and Anthropology, cat. 45-15-750, neg. T4-2325
Collection of Charles H. Stephens, gift of Mrs. Owen Stephens, 1947

Stephens bought this in 1898 from the dealer C. E. Osborn.
SOURCE: Jackson 1978: 477

Captain Lewis Shooting an Indian, 1810

Artist unknown
Woodcut on paper
Image: 2¾ × 4¾
Department of Special Collections, Washington University Libraries

SOURCE: Gass 1810: opp. p. 245

Pistols, 1799–1802

Simeon North and Elisha Cheney, Berlin, Conn.
Walnut, cherry, brass, iron, steel
14 × 5½ to 6; barrel: LENGTH 8½
Courtesy of the National Museum of American History, Smithsonian Institution, acc. nos. 1988.0518.02 and .03

This was the first model of pistol adopted by the U.S. Army. Only fifteen hundred North and Cheney pistols were made, of which these are serial numbers 311 and 138. They are not a matched pair; the top one is the first model, made with a cherry wood grip; the bottom one is the second model, made with a slightly longer, walnut grip. The signature is "S. North" and "E. Cheney" on the first model; only the last names were used on the second.
SOURCES: Jackson 1978: 97, 98; Moulton 1983–2001: 5: 178, 7: 183, 186n, 8: 134, 135; Russell 1967: 43; Flayderman 1990: 286

Clark's elkskin journal, 1805

William Clark
Ink on paper, bound in cured hide
6¾ × 16½ × ¾ (open); 6¾ × 5½ × ⅞ (closed)
Missouri Historical Society, St. Louis, William Clark Papers
Gift of Julia Clark Voorhis in memory of Eleanor Glasgow Voorhis

Reuben Gold Thwaites published this journal while it was still in the possession of Julia Clark Voorhis, who had inherited it from her father, George Rogers Hancock Clark (1816–58), who was his father's executor.
SOURCES: Moulton 1983–2001: 2: 557; Thwaites 1904-5: 1: li; "Gifts and Loans to April 1, 1923," Minutes of the Missouri Historical Society Advisory Board, April 4, 1923, Missouri Historical Society Archives

Letter from Clark to Toussaint Charbonneau, 1806

William Clark
Ink on paper
15⅛ × 9¼
Missouri Historical Society, St. Louis, William Clark Papers
Gift of Julia Clark Voorhis in memory of Eleanor Glasgow Voorhis

SOURCE: Jackson 1978: 315–16

Mouth of the Platte River, 900 Miles above St. Louis, 1832

George Catlin
Oil on canvas mounted on aluminum
11¼ × 14½
Smithsonian American Art Museum, 1985.66.369
Gift of Mrs. Joseph Harrison, Jr.

SOURCE: Moulton 1983–2001: 2: 402, 403

Letter from Clark to his brother, 1806

Meriwether Lewis and William Clark
Ink on paper
First three sheets: 7⅝ × 4⅞; last three sheets: 7⅝ × 6¼
Missouri Historical Society, St. Louis, William Clark Papers
Gift of Julia Clark Voorhis in memory of Eleanor Glasgow Voorhis

The final copy of this letter is in Jonathan Clark's papers at the Filson Historical Society. It was formerly thought to have been addressed to George Rogers Clark, an assumption now disproved.
SOURCES: Jackson 1978: 330n–35; Holmberg 2002: 101–6; *Frankfort Palladium*, October 9, 1806

The Evening Fire-Side; or Literary Miscellany, 1806

Published by Joseph Rakestraw, Philadelphia
Ink on paper
10⅜ × 8½
Missouri Historical Society, St. Louis, #1 917.8 L58

SOURCE: *Evening Fire-Side* 1806

Woven bag, c. 1800–50

Wishram or Wasco
Indian hemp, rushes
12 × 6
Photograph from the Peabody Museum of Archaeology and Ethnology, Harvard University, © President and Fellows of Harvard College, photograph by Hillel Burger, cat. 99-12-10/53160, neg. T2512.b
Gift of the Heirs of David Kimball, 1899

SOURCES: Jackson 1978: 478; Moulton 1983–2001: 7: 146, 147, 153, 166–68, 8: 419; Schlick 1994: 55–56, 63, opp. p. 96; Wright 1991: 75; McLaughlin 2003: chapter 9

Book prospectus, 1807

John Conrad, Philadelphia
Ink on paper
17⅝ × 11½
Missouri Historical Society, St. Louis, William Clark Papers
Gift of Julia Clark Voorhis in memory of Eleanor Glasgow Voorhis

SOURCE: Jackson 1978: 393–97, 417, 546

Patrick Gass, *A Journal of the Voyages and Travels of a Corps of Discovery*, 1807, 1810, 1814

Pittsburgh: Printed by Zadok Cramer for David M'Keehan; Paris: Chez Arthus-Bertrand; Weimar: Verlag des H.S. privil. Landes-Industrie-Comptoire
Ink on paper, bound in marbled cardboard, leather, and gilt
Pittsburgh: 7⅛ × 4½ × 1; Paris: 8¼ × 5½ × 1¼; Weimar: 8 × 4¾ × 1
Missouri Historical Society, St. Louis, *1 917.8 L58g, *1 917.8 L58g, 917.8 L58w

The copy of McKeehan's 1807 edition shown here belonged to Benjamin O'Fallon, Clark's nephew. The famous woodcut illustrations first appeared in the 1810 American edition, which is not shown.
SOURCE: Jackson 1978: 385, 402

Books resulting from Lewis and Clark's discoveries, 1805, 1808–14, and 1828

Barton: J. Conrad & Co.; Wilson: Bradford and Inskeep; Godman: H. C. Carey and I. Lea; all Philadelphia
Ink and watercolor on paper, bound in cardboard, leather, and marbled paper
Barton: 9½ × 6; Wilson: 14¼ × 11 × ⅞; Godman: 8¾ × 5½ × 1¼ (all closed)
Wilson: The McLean Library, Pennsylvania Horticultural Society, Philadelphia, QL681 W35; Barton and Godman: Courtesy of the American Philosophical Society, 610.5 P53 and 591.97 G54

SOURCES: Cutright 1969a: 383–84, 388–89; Wilson 1808–14: 3: 27, 29, 31, pl. 20, 4: 75, pl. 35

Sketch of Clark's crow and Lewis's woodpecker, 1808

Alexander Wilson
Pencil, ink, and wash on paper
Crow: 9⅛ × 8⅞; woodpecker: 9⅛ × 5⅛
Ewell Sale Stewart Library, The Academy of Natural Sciences of Philadelphia, Alexander Lawson Papers (Coll. 79, v. 2)

This sketch was owned by Alexander Lawson, the engraver for Wilson's volume, who died in 1846. It passed to his daughters, Malvina Lawson and Mary Lawson Birckhead, and from them to the Academy of Natural Sciences.
SOURCES: Cutright 1969a: 384-86; Richardson, Hindle, and Miller 1983: 253

Sketch of *Fritillaria lanceolata* and *Fritillaria pudica*, c. 1807

Frederick Pursh
Graphite and watercolor on wove paper
21⅝ × 14⅞
Courtesy of the American Philosophical Society, B B284d
Gift of Violetta Delafield

The watermark on the paper is "J Ruse 1805."
SOURCE: Moulton 1983–2001: 12: 3, 4, Appendix C

Frederick Pursh, *Flora Americae Septentrionalis*, 1816

James Black & Son, London
Ink and watercolor on paper, bound in marbled cardboard and green leather
8⅝ × 5½ × 1½ (closed); 8⅝ × 11 × 2½ to 3 (open)
Courtesy of the American Philosophical Society, 581.97 P971

Pipe, c. 1800–50

Eastern Plains or Western Great Lakes
Bowl: catlinite; stem: ash[?] wood, dyed and undyed porcupine quills, silk ribbons, wool, glass beads, plant fiber, pigment, bast fiber cord, dyed horse hair
Bowl: 3⅛ × 3⅝; stem: 46⅞ × 2 × 2
Photograph from the Peabody Museum of Archaeology and Ethnology, Harvard University, © President and Fellows of Harvard College, photograph by Hillel Burger, cat. 99-12-10/53106.1 (bowl) and .2 (stem), neg. T3865.1
Gift of the Heirs of David Kimball, 1899

SOURCE: McLaughlin 2003: chapter 8

An Indian Chief of Louisiana, 1769

Artist unknown
Engraving on paper
Image: 4¾ × 3
Missouri Historical Society, St. Louis

SOURCE: Bossu 1769: frontis., XVI

An Indian Warrior Entering His Wigwam with a Scalp, 1789

Barlow
Engraving on paper
Image: 5⅝ × 3⅝
Library of Congress

SOURCE: Anburey 1789: 1: opp. p. 291

Seal of the American Philosophical Society, late 1700s

James Poupard
Ink on paper
DIAM approx. 2¼
Courtesy of the American Philosophical Society

This version of the seal has revisions that date to the early twentieth century.

SOURCE: On Poupard, see Fielding 1945: 288.

Sketch of a conic hat, 1806

Meriwether Lewis or William Clark
Ink on paper
Image: ¾ × ¼
Courtesy of the American Philosophical Society, Codex J, p. 48

SOURCE: Moulton 1983–2001: 6: 250

Basketry whaler's hat, c. 1790–1830

Makah or Nootka
Cedar bark, surf grass, spruce root, unidentified fur, unidentified mammal hide
8⅞ × 10⅝
Photograph from the Peabody Museum of Archaeology and Ethnology, Harvard University, © President and Fellows of Harvard College, photograph by Hillel Burger, cat. 99-12-10/53080, neg. T2268
Gift of the Heirs of David Kimball, 1899

At the end of the journey in 1806, Clark sent home to Louisville "1 Hat made by the Clatsops Indians," and Lewis sent to Washington "1 Clat sop hat." In 1809 Peale accessioned from them "A hat manufactured by a Catsop woman near the Pacific Ocian." It has always been assumed these were whalers' hats; however, Lewis and Clark also purchased some European-style hats made by the Clatsop, and such a style of basketry hat also exists in the Peabody's Boston Museum collection (99-12-10/53176), often identified as Tlingit or Haida. Lewis wrote that the European-style hats "form a small article of traffic with the Clatsops and Chinnooks who dispose of them to the whites. the form of the hat is that which was in vogue in the Ued States and great Britain in the years 1800 & 1801 with a high crown reather larger at the top than where it joins the brim; the brim narrow or about 2 or 2-1/2 inches." Clark bought one of these top hats on November 21, 1805, and on February 22 the captains purchased a parcel of hats, including European-style ones made to fit the captains. Lewis wrote, "Capt Clark and myself had given one of the women [measurements] some time since with a request to make each of us a hat; they fit us very well, and are in the form we desired them. we purchased all their hats and distributed them among the party."

The hat shown here is made of black-dyed cedar bark with an overlay of white surf grass, on a warp of split spruce root. The weaving is overlay twining. Several artists of the 1780s and 1790s— including John Webber, José Cardero, and Tomas Suria—portrayed the elites of Nootka Sound wearing these hats.

SOURCES: Moulton 1983–2001: 6: 76, 221, 246, 335-36, 8: 418–19; Jackson 1978: 476; Vaughan and Holm 1990: 39; Wright 1991: 84, fig. 1; McLaughlin 2003: chapter 5; Brown 2000: 27, 72, 76; Feder 1995: fig. 186; Malloy 2000: 134

Abalone shell ornament, c. 1805

Shoshone[?]
Abalone shell, blue glass beads, hide
3½ × 1
University of Pennsylvania Museum of Archaeology and Anthropology, cat. L-83-4 a, b, neg. T4-2320
Transfer from the American Philosophical Society, 1937

This artifact, or its lost pair, once included a dentalium shell. It was transferred from the American Philosophical Society to the Academy of Natural Sciences and from there to the University of Pennsylvania Museum. Karl Bodmer illustrated western Plains Indians wearing ornaments like this on the ears; see, for example, his portraits of Mexkemauastan (Atsina) and an unidentified Piegan Blackfeet man.

SOURCES: Moulton 1983–2001: 5: 114, 140, 6: 435–36, 9: 206, 11: 276. For Bodmer, see Goetzmann et al. 1984: 239, 251, 301.

Estimate of the Eastern Indians, 1805

William Clark
Ink on paper
35 × 28
Courtesy of the American Philosophical Society, 917.3 L58 v. 7 double oversize
Gift of Nicholas Biddle, 1818

Clark's title is, "A List of the Names of the different Nations & Tribes of Indians Inhabiting the Countrey on the Missourie and its Waters." Thwaites and Moulton gave it its common name.

SOURCES: Ronda 1984a: 124; Moulton 1983–2001: 3: 386–450

Elk antler bow, c. 1800–40

Upper Missouri River
Elk antler, sinew, mica particles, hide glue
30¾ × 1 × ¾
Photograph from the Peabody Museum of Archaeology and Ethnology, Harvard University, © President and Fellows of Harvard College, photograph by Hillel Burger, cat. 99-12-10/52946, neg. T2696.1
Gift of the Heirs of David Kimball, 1899

Peale accessioned only one bow from Lewis and Clark, listed as "A great number of arrows from different Tribes of Saux. And a Bow." There is no way to know whether it was the same bow sent to Jefferson in 1805, but it seems unlikely. Clark also had elk-horn bows in his museum. George Catlin observed the use of horn and antler bows and noted their value; Bodmer portrayed Pehriska-Ruhpa holding one. The Mandan/Hidatsa Wolf Chief described the making and use of elk-horn bows for the anthropologist Gilbert Wilson. He said they were ornamental, not useful.

SOURCES: Moulton 1983–2001: 3: 289–90, 5: 150; Jackson 1978: 235, 477; McDermott 1948: 131; Catlin 1995: 1: 165; Goetzmann et al. 1984: 319; McLaughlin 2003: chapter 9. For sheep-horn bows, see Moulton 1983–2001: 4: 194.

Pot fragments, c. 1805

Mandan
Granite-tempered earthenware
Largest piece: 4 × 6; original DIAM at mouth: 4¾ and 4⅜
University of Pennsylvania Museum of Archaeology and Anthropology, cat. nos. L-83-5a, b, neg. nos. T4-2326, T4-2328
Transfer from the American Philosophical Society, 1937

These were transferred from the American Philosophical Society to the Academy of Natural Sciences and from there to the University of Pennsylvania. At what point they were given to the American Philosophical Society is not clear; the only donation that appears in the *Transactions* is "Specimens of plants, earth, seeds, and minerals." The captains did collect at least two pots, though; via the keelboat in April 1805, Clark sent his brother Jonathan in Louisville "1 Small pot in the Mandan fashion," and Lewis sent Jefferson "1 earthen pot, such as the Mandans manufacture, and use for culinary purposes." Many other travelers provided better information on Mandan pottery than Lewis and Clark, including Pierre Antoine Tabeau, John Bradbury, George Catlin, and Prince Maximilian.

SOURCES: Holmberg 2002: 86; Jackson 1978: 235; Wedel 1957: 93–95 (Henry quotation); American Philosophical Society 1809: xlii; Moulton 1983–2001: 3: 199, 330

Gun case, early to mid-1800s

Northern Plains
Cured and smoked bison hide, sinew, glass beads, glass button
34⅛ (with fringe) × 45¾ × 1
Missouri Historical Society, St. Louis, 1923 050 0041
Gift of Julia Clark Voorhis in memory of Eleanor Glasgow Voorhis

SOURCE: McDermott 1948: 130

Sheep-horn spoon, early 1800s

Northern Plains
Rocky Mountain sheep horn
6 × 12¾ × 7⅜
Missouri Historical Society, St. Louis, 1923 050 0043
Gift of Julia Clark Voorhis in memory of Eleanor Glasgow Voorhis

SOURCES: Moulton 1983–2001: 3: 119, 5: 150, 8: 418; Jackson 1978: 235; Holmberg 2002: 86; Goetzmann et al. 1984: 335

Tobacco pouch, c. 1805

Eastern Plains
Otter skin, deer hide, porcupine quill, bird quill, plant fiber, sinew, glass, dye colors, tin-plated steel, wool
43¼ × 9 × 2⅜
Photograph from the Peabody Museum of Archaeology and Ethnology, Harvard University, © President and Fellows of Harvard College, photograph by Hillel Burger, cat. 99-12-10/53052, neg. T940
Gift of the Heirs of David Kimball, 1899

Peale accessioned five tobacco pouches from Lewis and Clark, attributed to the "Saux" (which elsewhere means Sioux), Iowa, Fox, and "Sacks" (or Sauk). This one fits the description of "Two very handsomely ornamented Tobacco pouches, ornamented with Porcupine Quills, and Tin, &c. Of the Saux Tribe." Only the Sauk bag was described as "not ornimented," which would seem to rule out this one, even though the Peabody originally cataloged it as Sauk. George C. Hutter also donated an Omaha otter-skin pouch, and Jefferson sent four others, but the associated label supports the attribution of this one to Lewis and Clark. The otter skin has been gutted through the bottom, then sewn together again. The bag opening is in the throat. All the quillwork is on separate deer hide panels.

SOURCES: Catlin 1995: 1: 130, 165; Jackson 1978: 476; Peale 1809–28; McLaughlin 2003: chapter 5. For similar Plains Indian pouches used to carry tobacco, see Catlin in Ewers 1979: 46; Goetzmann et al. 1984: 337.

Effigy pipe bowl, 1820–50

Oto
Catlinite
3 × 6¼
Courtesy of the National Museum of the American Indian, Smithsonian Institution, 120889
Collected by M. R. Harrington

Although this pipe was collected among the Oto, it was probably made by the same Pawnee sculptor who made Catlin's pipe.
SOURCE: Ewers 1986: 92–93

Carving of a sailor, pre-1841

Oregon
Wood
8 × 1⅝
Courtesy of the Department of Anthropology, National Museum of Natural History, Smithsonian Institution, E*2697
Gift of Lt. Charles Wilkes, 1858

SOURCES: Moulton 1983–2001: 5: 347, 6: 74, 434; Boyd 1996: 122

Basketry sailor's cap, c. 1790–1840

Tlingit
Spruce root, maidenhair fern, cedar bark, unidentified grass
5⅝ × 11
Photograph from the Peabody Museum of Archaeology and Ethnology, Harvard University, © President and Fellows of Harvard College, photograph by Hillel Burger, cat. 99-12-10/53083, neg. T2953.1
Gift of the Heirs of David Kimball, 1899

SOURCES: Vaughan and Holm 1990: 40; Moulton 1983–2001: 6: 221

Effigy pipe, pre-1840

Haida
Argillite
2½ × 14 × 1
Courtesy of the National Museum of the American Indian, Smithsonian Institution, 019271
Exchange from Free Museum of Science and Art, Philadelphia

Catlin portrayed this pipe in *Letters and Notes on the Manners, Customs and Condition of the North American Indians* at a time (1841) before he had toured the west coast himself. It was part of the collection he had to sell to pay off his creditors in 1852. Thomas Donaldson, who discovered the collection and had most of it transferred to the Smithsonian Institution in 1881, is the source of the story that Clark gave him this pipe. Catlin made no such claim, and Ewers doubts it.
SOURCES: Catlin 1995: 2: 129, pl. 210½; Ewers 1979: 13, 42

Woven hat, early 1800s

Nez Perce
Indian hemp, beargrass, cured hide, dentalium shells, sinew
9 × 5½ × 6¼
Nez Perce County Historical Society, Inc., Lewiston, Idaho — Courtesy of Denise Stranahan Lowe

The hat was collected by the Indian agent Clinton Terry Stranahan in around 1900 and is still owned by his family. It was examined in 1985 by Marcia Lehman-Kessler, who did fiber analysis and said the warp is Indian hemp (a bast fiber also called Kamiah hemp or kamo; *Apocynum cannabinum*). The weft is in three strands: two of Indian hemp and a third of beargrass (*Xerophylum tenax*). In some places the beargrass is left its natural (cream) color, and in other places it is dyed golden with Oregon grape bark. There is also an unidentified, dark-brown vegetable fiber. The leather tassels are tied on with sinew and decorated with dentalium shells. Caps were associated with the root harvest, the ritual gathering of the first roots being led by a senior woman wearing a cap. Lewis and Clark donated to Peale's Museum a "Cap, worn by the women of the Plains of Columbia," and "A Cap worn by the natives of Columbia River, and the Pacific Ocean."
SOURCES: Jackson 1978: 476, 478. On hats, see Wright 1991: 183.

Lone Dog's winter count, c. 1870

Lone Dog (Shunka-ishnala), Dakota
Bison hide tanned with hair on, pigment
77¼ × 106⅜
Courtesy of the National Museum of the American Indian, Smithsonian Institution, 010617
Gift of S. A. Frost

S. A. Frost purchased this artwork in around 1880 from the family of Captain Chichester. Lone Dog lived at Fort Peck when he gave the interpretation to Garrick Mallery, but his tribal ties were with the Yanktonai on the mid-Missouri River. Other winter counts from the Cheyenne River Reservation agreed with it. Although the first Sioux group to meet Lewis and Clark is usually identified as Yankton, they could have been Yanktonai.
SOURCES: Mallery 1893: 266–71, 273; McLaughlin 2003

CHAPTER 10
Filling up the Canvas

Letter from Lewis to James Madison, 1809

Meriwether Lewis
Ink on paper
7¾ × 6⅜
Missouri Historical Society, St. Louis, Meriwether Lewis Collection
Gift of Dr. Meriwether Lewis Anderson, 1936

SOURCE: Jackson 1978: 464–65

Meriwether Lewis, 1807

Charles Willson Peale
Oil on wood panel; gilded wood frame
21⅜ × 17½ (unframed); 26 × 22 (framed)
Independence National Historical Park, 13.161 (cat. 14096)
On loan from the City of Philadelphia

In 1854, after the demise of Peale's Museum, the City of Philadelphia purchased its portrait gallery. The frames are Peale's originals.
SOURCE: Jackson 1978: 492

Silhouette of Meriwether Lewis, 1803

Artist unknown
Ink on paper
Image: 2½ × 1⅜
Monticello/Thomas Jefferson Foundation, Inc., Charlottesville, Virginia, 1925-1-2
Gift of Mrs. Martin Littleton

This may be a tracing or copy from one of the etchings of Charles B. J. F. de Saint Mémin's Lewis portrait in the Missouri Historical Society. It is inscribed "Juin 20th 1803." Two illegible names appear to have been written at the top.
SOURCES: Miles 1994: 339; Jackson 1978: 593, 678n

William Clark, c. 1808

Charles Willson Peale
Oil on paper, backed with canvas on wood stretcher; gilded wood frame
20¼ × 16½ (unframed); 26 × 22 (framed)
Independence National Historical Park, 13.048 (cat. 11870)
On loan from the City of Philadelphia

SOURCE: Jackson 1978: 492

Camp chest, c. 1789

Biennais au Singeviolet, Paris
6½ × 19 × 12½
Chest: mahogany, brass, leather; contents: silver, porcelain, ivory, glass, wrought iron
Missouri Historical Society, St. Louis, 1955 108 0001
Gift of Stix, Baer & Fuller, 1955

From Clark the chest went to Meriwether Lewis Clark, then to his son Charles Jefferson Clark, then to his daughters Evelyn Clark Jones and Susanne Clark Houghton. They lent it to Jefferson Kearny Clark to display at Minoma, then to William Hancock Clark, then to the Society of the Cincinnati headquarters, Washington, D.C. In 1955 the department store Stix, Baer & Fuller purchased the chest from the Clark descendants for donation to the Missouri Historical Society.
SOURCES: McDermott 1948: 131; Lafayette to Clark, February 1, 1830, William Clark Papers, Missouri Historical Society

Robert Frazer, *Map of the Discoveries of Capt. Lewis & Clark*, c. 1807

Cartographer unknown
Black, red, and blue ink on paper
24¾ × 74¾
Library of Congress, G4125.1807
Purchase from Edward H. Curlander, 1921

The title continues, ". . . from the Rockey mountain and the River Lewis to the Cap of Disappointement . . . By Observation of Robert Frazer." This map came into the possession of John Henry Alexander, the Maryland cartographer, who died in 1867. The heirs to the estate of Alexander's son sold it to the Library of Congress in 1921. It was probably not drawn by Frazer himself; Moulton notes that one of the sources for the map appears to be the Mackay/Evans map, and the cartographer may have been French because of the French spelling given to many of the place-names. Beyond the Mandan villages, the names conform to Lewis and Clark's, suggesting the cartographer had access to Clark's route maps.

The only surviving prospectus for Frazer's book is at the Wisconsin Historical Society. It was found in letters from John Butler to his brother James. John Butler, an acquaintance of Frazer's from Rutland, Vermont, had moved to St. Louis to work at Christy's Hotel. There he recognized Frazer, who apparently gave the prospectus to him. It was of necessity manuscript, since there was no printing press in St. Louis at the time. The St. Louis origin of the prospectus may imply a St. Louis origin for the map.
SOURCES: Jackson 1978: 386; Wheat 1958: 2: 46–48, map 286; Library of Congress 1922: 69; Moulton 1983–2001: 1: 12, map 124

A Map of Part of the Continent of North America, 1807–14

William Clark
Ink on paper
29 × 51
Yale Collection of Western Americana, Beinecke Rare Book and Manuscript Library, WA Ms. 303
Gift of William R. Coe

This was owned by Julia Clark Voorhis in 1904, when Thwaites published it. It was in the part of her collection sold by her executor, Samuel Maguire, to William R. Coe.
SOURCES: Withington 1952: 170; Moulton 1983–2001: 1: map 125

Bibliography

Abel, Annie H. 1916. "A New Lewis and Clark Map." *Geographical Review* 1 (May): 329–45.

———, ed. 1939. *Tabeau's Narrative of Loisel's Expedition to the Upper Missouri*. Trans. Rose Abel Wright. Norman: University of Oklahoma Press.

Adams, Henry. 1890. *History of the United States of America during the Second Administration of Thomas Jefferson*. 2 vols. New York: Charles Scribner's Sons.

Adams, William Howard, ed. 1976. *The Eye of Thomas Jefferson*. Washington, D.C.: National Gallery of Art.

Albers, Patricia, and Beatrice Medicine. 1983. *The Hidden Half: Studies of Plains Indian Women*. Washington, D.C.: University Press of America.

Allen, John Logan. 1975. *Passage through the Garden: Lewis and Clark and the Image of the American Northwest*. Urbana: University of Illinois Press.

Ambrose, Stephen E. 1996. *Undaunted Courage: Meriwether Lewis, Thomas Jefferson, and the Opening of the American West*. New York: Simon and Schuster.

Ambrose, Stephen E., and Sam Abell. 1998. *Lewis & Clark: Voyage of Discovery*. Washington, D.C.: National Geographic Society.

American Journal of the Medical Sciences. 1828. 2d ed. Vol. 1. Philadelphia: Carey, Lee and Carey.

American Philosophical Society. 1809. *Transactions of the American Philosophical Society*. Vol. 6. Philadelphia: C. and A. Conrad and Co.

———. 1961. *A Catalogue of Portraits and Other Works of Art in the Possession of the American Philosophical Society*. Philadelphia: American Philosophical Society.

Anastasio, Angelo. 1975. *The Southern Plateau: An Ecological Analysis of Intergroup Relations*. Moscow: University of Idaho Laboratory of Anthropology.

Anburey, Thomas. 1789. *Travels through the Interior Parts of America: In a Series of Letters*. 2 vols. London: Printed for William Lane.

Anderson, Irving W. 1978. "Sacajawea, Sacagawea, Sakakawea?" *South Dakota History* 8, no. 4 (fall): 303–11.

———. 1980. "A Charbonneau Family Portrait." *American West* 17, no. 2 (March/April): 4–13, 58–64.

Anderson, Irving W., and Blanche Schroer. 1999. "Sacagawea: Her Name and Her Destiny." *We Proceeded On* 25, no. 4 (November): 6–10.

Anderson, Sarah Travers Lewis (Scott). 1938. *Lewises, Meriwethers, and Their Kin*. Richmond, Va.: Dietz Press.

Appleman, Roy. 1975. *Lewis and Clark: Historic Places Associated with Their Transcontinental Exploration* (1804–06). National Survey of Historic Sites and Buildings, vol. 13. Washington, D.C.: National Park Service.

Back, Francis. 1991. "The Canadian Capot (Capote)." *Museum of the Fur Trade Quarterly* 27, no. 3 (fall): 4–15.

Bakeless, John. N.d. Papers, microfilm 2580. The Albert and Shirley Small Special Collections Library. University of Virginia, Charlottesville.

———. 1947. *Lewis & Clark: Partners in Discovery*. New York: William Morrow and Co.

———. 1957. *Background to Glory: The Life of George Rogers Clark*. Philadelphia: J. B. Lippincott Co.

Barbour, Thomas. 1946. *A Naturalist's Scrapbook*. Cambridge: Harvard University Press.

Baumler, Ellen. 1997. "Masonic Apron of Meriwether Lewis." *Helena Independent Record*, September 17.

Beard, J. Howard. 1925. "The Medical Observations and Practice of Lewis and Clark." *Scientific Monthly* 20 (May): 506–26.

Beauregard, Nettie. 1923. "Clark Manuscripts." Typescript in Voorhis Accession file, Missouri Historical Society Archives, St. Louis.

Beckwith, Martha Warren, ed. 1938. *Mandan-Hidatsa Myths and Ceremonies*. Memoirs of the American Folk-Lore Society, vol. 32. New York: J. J. Augustin.

Bedini, Silvio A. 1984. "The Scientific Instruments of the Lewis and Clark Expedition." *Great Plains Quarterly* 4 (winter): 54–69. Reprinted without illustrations in Ronda 1998:143–65.

———. 1990. *Thomas Jefferson: Statesman of Science*. New York: Macmillan.

Beeman, Robert D., and John B. Allen. 2002. "Proceeding on to the Lewis & Clark Airgun." In *Blue Book of Airguns* (2d ed.), 50–77. Minneapolis: Blue Book Publications. Originally published in *Airgun Revue #6* (Ellicott City, Md.: Airgun Letter).

Bell, Michael. 1973. *Braves and Buffalo: Plains Indian Life in 1837*. Toronto: University of Toronto Press.

Bénétiz, E. 1999. *Dictionnaire Critique et Documentaire des Peintres, Sculpteurs, Dessinateurs et Graveurs*. Vol. 11. Paris: Gründ.

Benson, Guy Meriwether, with William R. Irwin and Heather Moore. 1995. *Exploring the West from Monticello: A Perspective in Maps from Columbus to Lewis and Clark*. Charlottesville: University of Virginia Library.

Betts, Jonathan. 1996. "Arnold and Earnshaw: The Practicable Solution." In *The Quest for Longitude*, ed. William J. H. Andrewes, 312–28. Cambridge, Mass.: Collection of Historical Scientific Instruments, Harvard University.

Biddle, Henry J. 1978. *Beacon Rock on the Columbia: Legends and Traditions of a Famous Landmark*. WPO Publication No. 3. Portland, Oreg.: Lewis and Clark Trail Heritage Foundation.

Black Elk. 1953. *The Sacred Pipe: Black Elk's Account of the Seven Rites of the Oglala Sioux*. Ed. Joseph Epes Brown. Norman: University of Oklahoma Press.

Boas, Franz. 1894. *Chinook Texts*. Smithsonian Institution, Bureau of American Ethnology, Bulletin 20. Washington, D.C.: Government Printing Office.

Bolz, Peter, and Hans-Ulrich Sanner. 1999. *Native American Art: The Collections of the Ethnological Museum Berlin*. Seattle: University of Washington Press.

Boss, Richard C. 1993. "Keelboat, Pirogue, and Canoe: Vessels Used by the Lewis and Clark Corps of Discovery." *Nautical Research Journal* 38, no. 2 (June): 68–87.

Bossu, Jean Bernard. 1769. *Nouveaux voyages aux Indes occidentales, contenant une relation des différens peuples qui habitent les environs du grand fleuve Saint-Louis, appellé vulgairement le Mississippi; leur religion; leur gouvernement; leurs mœurs, leurs guerres, & leur commerce*. 2 vols. Amsterdam: D. J. Changuion.

Boston Museum. 1847. *Catalogue of the Paintings, Portraits, Marble and Plaster Statuary, Engravings & Water Color Drawings, in the Collection of the Boston Museum*. Boston: Stacy, Richardson, Filmer, and Co.

Boswell, James. 1904. *The Life of Samuel Johnson*. 2 vols. in 1. Oxford: Oxford University Press.

Botkin, Daniel B. 1995. *Our Natural History: The Lessons of Lewis and Clark*. New York: Penguin Putnam.

Bowers, Alfred W. 1950. *Mandan Social and Ceremonial Organization*. Chicago: University of Chicago Press.

———. 1965. *Hidatsa Social and Ceremonial Organization*. Smithsonian Institution, Bureau of American Ethnology, Bulletin 194. Washington, D.C.: GPO.

Boyd, Julian, et al., eds. 1950–2002. *The Papers of Thomas Jefferson*. 29 vols. to date. Princeton, N.J.: Princeton University Press.

Boyd, Robert. 1996. *People of The Dalles: The Indians of Wascopam Mission*. Lincoln: University of Nebraska Press.

Brackenridge, Henry Marie. 1904. *Journal of a Voyage up the River Missouri in 1811*. 1816. 2d ed. Reprinted in *Early Western Travels, 1748–1846*, ed. Reuben Gold Thwaites, vol. 6. Cleveland: Arthur H. Clark Co.

———. 1962. *Views of Louisiana: Together with a Journal of a Voyage up the Missouri River, in 1811*. 1814. Reprint, Chicago: Quadrangle Books.

Bradbury, John. 1817. *Travels in the Interior of America, in the Years 1809, 1810, and 1811*. London: Sherwood, Neely, and Jones.

Brasser, Ted J. 1976. "Bo'jou, Neejee!": *Profiles of Canadian Indian Art.* Ottawa: National Museum of Man.

Brinkerhoff, Sidney B., and Pierce A. Chamberlain. 1972. *Spanish Military Weapons in Colonial America, 1700–1821.* Harrisburg, Pa.: Stackpole Co.

Brown, Jo Ann. 1999. "George Drouillard and Fort Massac." *We Proceeded On* 25, no. 4 (November): 16–19.

Brown, Joseph Epes. 1992. *Animals of the Soul: Sacred Animals of the Oglala Sioux.* Rockport, Mass.: Element Books.

Brown, Steven C., ed. 2000. *Spirits of the Water: Native Art Collected on Expeditions to Alaska and British Columbia, 1774–1910.* Seattle: University of Washington Press.

Brown, Stuart E., Jr. 1968. *The Guns of Harper's Ferry.* Berryville, Va.: Virginia Book Co.

Bullock, Steven C. 1996. *Revolutionary Brotherhood: Freemasonry and the Transformation of the American Social Order, 1730–1840.* Chapel Hill: University of North Carolina Press.

Burke, Edmund. 1958. *A Philosophical Enquiry into the Origin of Our Ideas of the Sublime and Beautiful.* Ed. J. T. Boulton. London: Routledge and Kegan Paul; New York: Columbia University Press.

Burroughs, Raymond Darwin. 1961. *The Natural History of the Lewis and Clark Expedition.* East Lansing: Michigan State University Press.

Bush, Alfred L. 1962. *The Life Portraits of Thomas Jefferson.* Charlottesville, Va.: Thomas Jefferson Memorial Foundation.

Bushnell, David I., Jr. 1909. "The Various Uses of Buffalo Hair by the North American Indians." *American Anthropologist,* n.s., 11:401–25.

Byron, George Gordon (Lord). 1933. *The Complete Poetical Works of Byron.* Boston: Houghton Mifflin.

Campbell, J. Duncan, and Edgar M. Howell. 1963. *American Military Insignia, 1800–1851.* Washington, D.C.: Smithsonian Institution Press.

Cappon, Lester J., ed. 1959. *The Adams-Jefferson Letters.* 2 vols. Chapel Hill: University of North Carolina Press.

Carey, Arthur Merwyn. 1953. *American Firearms Makers: Where, When, and What They Made from the Colonial Period to the End of the Nineteenth Century.* New York: Thomas Crowell Co.

Carrick, Michael F. 2003. "Meriwether Lewis' Repeating Air Gun." *The Gun Report* 48, no. 8 (January): 28–36.

Carter, Clarence Edwin. 1949. *The Territorial Papers of the United States.* Vol. 14. Washington, D.C.: GPO.

Carter, Edward C., II. 1993. *"One Grand Pursuit": A Brief History of the American Philosophical Society's First 260 Years, 1743–1993.* Philadelphia: American Philosophical Society.

Carver, Jonathan. 1956. *Travels through the Interior Parts of North America, in the Years 1766, 1767, and 1768.* 3rd ed. Minneapolis: Ross and Haines.

Catlin, George. 1866. *Illustrations of the Manners, Customs, and Condition of the North American Indians, with Letters and Notes Written during Eight Years of Travel and Adventure among the Wildest and Most Remarkable Tribes Now Existing.* 2 vols. London: Henry G. Bohn.

———. 1868. *Last Rambles amongst the Indians of the Rocky Mountains and the Andes.* London: Sampson Low, Son, and Marston.

———. 1954. *Indians of the Western Frontier: Paintings of George Catlin.* Ed. George I. Quimby. Chicago: Chicago Natural History Museum.

———. 1995. *Letters and Notes on the North American Indians.* 1841. Reprint, New York: Gramercy Books.

Century Magazine. 1904. "New Material Concerning the Lewis and Clark Expedition." 68, no. 6 (October): 872–76.

Chaky, Doreen. 1998. "Fossils and the Fur Trade: The Chouteaus as Patrons of Paleontology." *Gateway Heritage* 19, no. 1 (summer): 22–31.

Charbonneau, Louis. 1989. "Seaman's Trail: Fact vs. Fiction," *We Proceeded On* 15, no. 4 (November): 8-11.

Chatters, Roy M. 1977. "The Not-So-Enigmatic Lewis and Clark Air Gun." *We Proceeded On* 3, no. 2 (May): 4–6.

Chittenden, Hiram M. 1954. *The American Fur Trade of the Far West.* Stanford, Calif.: Academic Reprints.

Christensen, Lawrence O., William E. Foley, Gary R. Kremer, and Kenneth H. Winn, eds. 1999. *Dictionary of Missouri Biography.* Columbia: University of Missouri Press.

Chronister, Allen. 1999. "Bone Hairpipes." *Museum of the Fur Trade Quarterly* 35, no. 4 (winter): 13–14.

Chuinard, Eldon G. 1980. *Only One Man Died: The Medical Aspects of the Lewis and Clark Expedition.* Glendale, Calif.: Arthur H. Clark Co.

———. 1989. "The Masonic Apron of Meriwether Lewis." *We Proceeded On* 15, no. 1 (February): 16–17.

Clark, Ella E. 1966. *Indian Legends from the Northern Rockies.* Norman: University of Oklahoma Press.

Clark, William. 1826. Letter to James Barbour. March 1. William Clark Papers. Missouri Historical Society Archives. St. Louis.

Clark, William, and Meriwether Lewis Clark. N.d. "Catalogue of Indian Curiosities." William Clark Papers. Missouri Historical Society Archives. St. Louis.

Clifton, Gloria C. 1995. *Directory of British Scientific Instrument Makers, 1550–1851.* London: Zwemmer, in association with the National Maritime Museum.

Coe, Ralph T. 1977. *Sacred Circles: Two Thousand Years of North American Indian Art.* Kansas City: Nelson Gallery of Art—Atkins Museum of Fine Arts.

Coleman, Winfield. 1998. "Art as Cosmology: Cheyenne Women's Rawhide Painting." *World of Tribal Arts* 5, no. 1 (summer): 48–60.

Collot, Georges Henri Victor. 1826. *A Journey in North America.* Paris: A. Bertrand.

Colter-Frick, L. R. 1997. *Courageous Colter and Companions.* Washington, Mo.: Video Proof.

Conn, Richard G., and Mary D. Schlick. 1998. "Basketry." In *Plateau,* ed. Deward E. Walker, Jr. Vol. 12 of *Handbook of North American Indians.* Washington, D.C.: Smithsonian Institution Press.

Cook, James. 1784. *A Voyage to the Pacific Ocean.* Vol. 4 [atlas]. London: Printed by W. and A. Strahan, for G. Nicol, and T. Cadell.

Coues, Elliott, ed. 1893. *History of the Expedition under the Command of Lewis and Clark.* 2 vols. in 1. New York: Francis P. Harper.

———. 1965. *New Light on the Early History of the Greater Northwest: The Manuscript Journals of Alexander Henry and David Thompson.* 2 vols. 1897. Reprint, Minneapolis: Ross and Haines.

Craig, William D. 1971. *Coins of the World, 1750–1850.* 2d ed. Racine, Wisc.: Western Publishing Co.

Croce, George C., and David H. Wallace. 1957. *The New-York Historical Society's Dictionary of Artists in America.* New Haven, Conn.: Yale University Press.

Cutright, Paul Russell. 1963. "I Gave Him Barks and Saltpeter . . ." *American Heritage* 15, no. 1 (December): 58–60, 94–101.

———. 1964. "Lewis and Clark and Du Pratz." *Missouri Historical Society Bulletin* 21, no. 1 (October): 31–35.

———. 1967. "The Odyssey of the Magpie and the Prairie Dog." *Missouri Historical Society Bulletin* 23, no. 3 (April): 215–28.

———. 1968. "Lewis and Clark Indian Peace Medals." *Missouri Historical Society Bulletin* 24, no. 2 (January): 160–67.

———. 1969a. *Lewis and Clark: Pioneering Naturalists.* Urbana: University of Illinois Press.

———. 1969b. "Lewis & Clark: Portraits and Portraitists." *Montana: The Magazine of Western History* 19, no. 2 (spring): 37–53.

———. 1976. *A History of the Lewis and Clark Journals.* Norman: University of Oklahoma Press.

———. 1982. *Contributions of Philadelphia to Lewis and Clark History.* Portland, Oregon: Lewis and Clark Trail Heritage Foundation.

Davis, Leslie B., ed. 1979. *Lifeways of Intermontane and Plains Montana Indians.* Museum of the Rockies, Occasional Papers, no. 1. Bozeman: Montana State University.

Davis, Richard Beale. 1939. *Francis Walker Gilmer: Life and Learning in Jefferson's Virginia.* Richmond, Va.: Dietz Press.

Day, Richard. 1988. *Vincennes: A Pictorial History.* St. Louis: G. Bradley Publishing.

DeMallie, Raymond J., ed. 2001. *Plains.* Vol. 13 of *Handbook of North American Indians.* Washington, D.C.: Smithsonian Institution Press.

Denslow, Ray V. 1941. *Meriwether Lewis: Missouri's First Royal Arch Mason.* Trenton, Mo.: N.p.

Denslow, William R. 1959. *10,000 Famous Freemasons.* Vol. 3. Richmond, Va.: Macoy Publishing and Masonic Supply Co.

Densmore, Frances. 1918. *Teton Sioux Music.* Smithsonian Institution, Bureau of American Ethnology, Bulletin 61. Washington, D.C.: GPO.

DeVorsey, Louis, Jr. 1992. "Silent Witnesses: Native American Maps." *Georgia Review* 46 (winter): 709–26.

———. 1998. "American Indians and the Early Mapping of the Southeast." In *The Southeast in Early Maps,* ed. William P. Cumming, 65–98. 3d ed. Chapel Hill: University of North Carolina Press.

DeVoto, Bernard. 1947. *Across the Wide Missouri.* Boston: Houghton Mifflin Co.

———. 1953. *The Journals of Lewis and Clark.* Boston: Houghton Mifflin Co.

Dexter, Elias. 1862. *The St.-Mémin Collection of Portraits.* New York: Published by the author.

Dickson, Harold E. 1949. *John Wesley Jarvis: American Painter, 1780–1840.*

New York: New-York Historical Society.
Dictionary of National Biography. 1887. Vol. 9. London: Smith, Elder, and Co.
Diderot, Denis. 1762–72. *Recueil de planches, sur les sciences, les arts liberaux, et les arts mechaniques, avec leur explication.* 11 vols. Paris: Briasson.
Dippie, Brian W., et al. 2002. *George Catlin and His Indian Gallery.* Washington, D.C.: Smithsonian American Art Museum; New York: W. W. Norton and Co.
Discovery Writers. 1998. *Lewis & Clark in the Bitterroot.* Stevensville, Mont.: Stoneydale Press Publishing Co.
Dobkins, Rebecca J. 2000. "Honoring the Past, Embracing the Future: Native American Art at the Hallie Ford Museum of Art, Willamette University." *American Indian Art Magazine* 25, no. 2 (spring): 46–67.
Donaldson, Thomas. 1886. "The George Catlin Indian Gallery in the U.S. National Museum." Part 5. In *Annual Report for the Board of Regents,* 1885, pt. 2, ed. Smithsonian Institution. Washington, D.C.: GPO.
Douglas, Jesse. 1941. "Lewis' Map of 1806." *Military Affairs: Journal of the American Military Institute* 5:68–72.
Dover Stamping Co. 1971. *Dover Stamping Co., 1869: Tinware, Tin Toys, Tinned Iron Wares, Tinners' Material, Enameled Stove Hollow Ware, Tinners' Tools and Machines.* Princeton, N.J.: Pyne Press.
Dramer, Kim. 1997. *The Shoshone.* Philadelphia: Chelsea House Publishers.
Drucker, Philip. 1955. *Indians of the Northwest Coast.* Anthropological Handbook, no. 10. New York: American Museum of Natural History and McGraw-Hill.
Dunbar, William. 1809. "On the Language of Signs among Certain North American Indians." *Transactions of the American Philosophical Society* 6:1–3.
Duncan, Dayton, and Ken Burns. 1997. *Lewis & Clark: The Journey of the Corps of Discovery.* New York: Alfred A. Knopf.
Dunning, Phil. 2000. "Composite Table Cutlery from 1700 to 1930." In *Studies in Material Culture Research,* ed. Karlis Karklins, 32–45. Tucson, Ariz.: Society for Historical Archaeology.
Du Pratz, Le Page. 1758. *Histoire de la Louisiane.* 3 vols. Paris: L'Aine Chez de Bure, La Veuve Delaguette, et Lambert.
Durand, Paul. 1994. *Where the Waters Gather and the Rivers Meet (O-ki-zu Wa-kpa).* Faribault, Minn.: Paul Durand.
Edmondson, James M. 1993. *American Surgical Instruments: An Illustrated History of Their Manufacture and a Directory of Instrument Makers to 1900.* San Francisco: Norman Publishing.
Emerson, William K. 1983. "Cockades and Eagles." *Military Collector and Historian* 35, no. 3 (fall): 104–12.
———. 1996. *Encyclopedia of United States Army Insignia and Uniforms.* Norman: University of Oklahoma Press.
Engages, The. 1979. "Burning Glasses." *Museum of the Fur Trade Quarterly* 15, no. 4 (winter): 5–7.
Evening Fire-Side; or Literary Miscellany. 1806. "The Missouri Expedition." November 29, 1–2.
Ewers, John C. 1939. *Plains Indian Painting: A Description of an Aboriginal American Art.* Stanford, Calif.: Stanford University Press.
———. 1948. *Gustavus Sohon's Portraits of Flathead and Pend D'Oreille Indians, 1854.* Smithsonian Miscellaneous Collections, vol. 110, no. 7. Washington, D.C.: Smithsonian Institution Press.
———. 1954. "The Indian Trade of the Upper Missouri before Lewis and Clark: An Interpretation." *Missouri Historical Society Bulletin* 10, no. 4 (July): 429–46.
———. 1956. "George Catlin, Painter of Indians and the West." In *Annual Report for the Board of Regents,* 1955, ed. Smithsonian Institution, 483–528, with plates following. Washington, D.C.: Smithsonian Institution Press.
———. 1957. *Hairpipes in Plains Indian Adornment: A Study in Indian and White Ingenuity.* Smithsonian Institution, Bureau of American Ethnology, Bulletin 164. Washington, D.C.: GPO.
———. 1965. *Artists of the Old West.* New York: Doubleday.
———. 1966. "'Chiefs from the Missouri and Mississippi' and Peale's Silhouettes of 1806." *Smithsonian Journal of History* 1 (spring): 1–26.
———. 1967. "William Clark's Indian Museum in St. Louis, 1816–1838." In *A Cabinet of Curiosities: Five Episodes in the Evolution of American Museums,* 49–72. Charlottesville: University Press of Virginia.
———. 1968. *Indian Life on the Upper Missouri.* Norman: University of Oklahoma Press.
———. 1979. *Indian Art in Pipestone: George Catlin's Portfolio in the British Museum.* Washington, D.C.: Smithsonian Institution Press.
———. 1981. "Pipes for the Presidents." *American Indian Art Magazine* 6, no. 3 (summer): 62–66.
———. 1982a. "Artists' Choices." *American Indian Art Magazine* 7, no. 2 (spring): 40–49.
———. 1982b. "The Awesome Bear in Plains Indian Art." *American Indian Art Magazine* 7, no. 3 (summer): 36–45.
———. 1986. *Plains Indian Sculpture: A Traditional Art from America's Heartland.* Washington, D.C.: Smithsonian Institution Press.
———. 1997. *Plains Indian History and Culture: Essays on Continuity and Change.* Norman: University of Oklahoma Press.
Ewers, John C., with Marsha V. Gallagher, David C. Hunt, and Joseph C. Porter. 1984. *Views of a Vanishing Frontier.* Omaha, Nebr.: Center for Western Studies, Joslyn Art Museum.
Farnell, Brenda. 1995. *Do You See What I Mean? Plains Indian Sign Talk and the Embodiment of Action.* Austin: University of Texas Press.
Farnham, Thomas J. 1906. *Travels in the Great Western Prairies, the Anahuac and Rocky Mountains, and in Oregon Territory.* 1843. Reprinted in *Early Western Travels, 1748–1846,* ed. Reuben Gold Thwaites, vol. 28. Cleveland: Arthur H. Clark Co.
Faxon, Walter. 1915. "Relics of Peale's Museum." *Bulletin of the Museum of Comparative Zoology* 59:119–48.
Feder, Norman. 1980. "Plains Pictographic Painting and Quilled Rosettes: A Clue to Tribal Identification." *American Indian Art Magazine* 5, no. 2 (spring): 54–62.
———. 1984. "The Side Fold Dress." *American Indian Art Magazine* 10, no. 1 (winter): 48–55, 75.
———. 1987. "Bird Quillwork." *American Indian Art Magazine* 12, no. 3 (summer): 46–57.
———. 1995. *American Indian Art.* 1971. Reprint, New York: Harry N. Abrams.
Ferris, Warren A. 1940. *Life in the Rocky Mountains.* Ed. Paul C. Phillips. Denver: Old West Publishing Co.
Fielding, Mantle. 1945. *Dictionary of American Painters, Sculptors, and Engravers.* New York: Paul A. Struck.
Fischer, David Hackett, and James C. Kelly. 1993. *Away, I'm Bound Away: Virginia and the Westward Movement.* Richmond: Virginia Historical Society.
Fisher, William. 1813. *An Interesting Account of the Voyages and Travels of Captains Lewis and Clarke, in the Years 1804, 1805, & 1806.* Baltimore: P. Mauro.
Flayderman, Norm. 1990. *Flayderman's Guide to Antique American Firearms . . . and Their Values.* 5th ed. Northbrook, Ill.: DBI Books.
Fletcher, Alice C., and Francis La Flesche. 1911. "The Omaha Tribe." In *Twenty-seventh Annual Report of the Bureau of Ethnology, 1905–6,* ed. Smithsonian Institution. Washington, D.C.: GPO.
Foley, William E. 1989. *The Genesis of Missouri: From Wilderness Outpost to Statehood.* Columbia: University of Missouri Press.
Forrer, L. 1909. *Biographical Dictionary of Medallists.* Vol. 4. London: Spink and Son Ltd.
Forrest, Earle R. 1950. *Patrick Gass: Lewis and Clark's Last Man.* Independence, Pa.: Published by Mrs. A. M. Painter.
Fredrickson, N. Jaye, and Sandra Gibbs. 1980. *The Covenant Chain.* Ottawa: National Museums of Canada.
Furst, Peter T., and Jill L. Furst. 1982. *North American Indian Art.* New York: Rizzoli.
Furtwangler, Albert. 1993. *Acts of Discovery: Visions of America in the Lewis and Clark Journals.* Urbana: University of Illinois Press.
Gale, John. 1969. *The Missouri Expedition 1818–1820: The Journal of Surgeon John Gale with Related Documents.* Ed. Roger L. Nichols. Norman: University of Oklahoma Press.
Gallagher, Marsha. 1984. "An Exhibition at the Joslyn Art Museum: 'Views of a Vanishing Frontier.'" *American Indian Art Magazine* 9, no. 2 (spring): 54–61.
Garraty, John A., and Mark C. Carnes, eds. 1999. *American National Biography.* 24 vols. New York: Oxford University Press.
Gass, Patrick. 1810. *A Journal of the Voyages and Travels of a Corps of Discovery under the Command of Capt. Lewis and Capt. Clarke of the Army of the United States from the Mouth of the River Missouri through the Interior Parts of North America, to the Pacific Ocean, during the Years 1804, 1805 and 1806.* Philadelphia: Printed for Matthew Carey.
Gibbs, George. 1855. "Report of Mr. George Gibbs to Captain Mc'Clellan on the Indian Tribes of the Territory of Washington." In *Reports of Explorations and Surveys, to Ascertain the Most Practicable and Economical Route for a Railroad from the Missis-*

sippi River to the Pacific Ocean. 33d Cong., 2d sess., S. Doc. 78, vol. 1, 402–34. Washington, D.C.: Beverley Tucker.

Gibbs, Peter. 1982. "Duke Paul Wilhelm Collection in the British Museum." *American Indian Art Magazine* 7, no. 3 (summer): 52–61.

Gilkerson, William. 1993. *Boarders Away II.* Lincoln, R.I.: Andrew Mowbray.

Gill, Harold B., Jr. 1974. *The Gunsmith in Colonial Virginia.* Williamsburg Research Studies. Williamsburg, Va.: Colonial Williamsburg Foundation.

Gilman, Carolyn. 1982. *Where Two Worlds Meet: The Great Lakes Fur Trade.* Museum Exhibit Series, no. 2. St. Paul: Minnesota Historical Society.

———. 1999. "The Forensic Conservator and the Science of Lewis and Clark." *Gateway Heritage* 20, no. 3 (winter): 52–57.

Gilman, Carolyn, and Mary Jane Schneider. 1987. *The Way to Independence: Memories of a Hidatsa Indian Family, 1840–1920.* Museum Exhibit Series, no. 3. St. Paul: Minnesota Historical Society Press.

Gilmore, Melvin R. 1932. "Importance of Ethnobotanical Investigation." *American Anthropologist,* n.s., 34:320–25.

———. 1977. *Uses of Plants by the Indians of the Missouri River Region.* Lincoln: University of Nebraska Press.

Glassie, Henry. 1968. *Pattern in the Material Folk Culture of the Eastern United States.* University of Pennsylvania Monographs in Folklore and Folklife, no. 1. Philadelphia: University of Pennsylvania Press.

Goetzmann, William H. 1966. *Exploration and Empire: The Explorer and the Scientist in the Winning of the American West.* New York: Alfred A. Knopf.

———. 1988. *Looking at the Land of Promise: Pioneer Images of the Pacific Northwest.* Sherman and Mabel Smith Pettyjohn Lectures in Pacific Northwest History. Pullman: Washington State University Press.

Goetzmann, William H., David C. Hunt, Marsha V. Gallagher, and William J. Orr. 1984. *Karl Bodmer's America.* Lincoln: University of Nebraska Press, in association with Joslyn Art Museum.

Gould, Mary Earle. 1958. *Antique Tin & Tole Ware: Its History and Romance.* Rutland, Vt.: Charles E. Tuttle Co.

Grafe, Steven. 1999. "Nez Perce Decorative Art of the 1870s: Scientific and Souvenir Collections." *American Indian Art Magazine* 24, no. 4 (autumn): 60–71.

Greene, John C., and John G. Burke. 1978. "The Science of Minerals in the Age of Jefferson." *Transactions of the American Philosophical Society* 68, pt. 4.

Grinnell, Calvin. 1999. "Another View of Sakakawea." *We Proceeded On* 25, no. 2 (May): 16–19.

Griswold, Gillett. 1970. "Aboriginal Patterns of Trade between the Columbia Basin and the Northern Plains." *Archaeology in Montana* 11, nos. 2–3 (April-September).

Gun-That-Guards-the-House. 1908. "Story of a Medal, Related by Its Owner." In *Collections of the State Historical Society of North Dakota,* vol. 2. Bismarck: Tribune, State Printers and Binders.

Hague, Arnold. 1887. "An Early Map of the Far West." *Science: An Illustrated Journal* 10 (November): 217–18.

Hall, Robert L. 1997. *An Archaeology of the Soul: North American Indian Belief and Ritual.* Urbana: University of Illinois Press.

Hallowell, A. Irving. 1926. "Bear Ceremonialism in the Northern Hemisphere." *American Anthropologist* 28, no. 1:1–75.

Halsey, Ashley, Jr. 1984. "The Air Gun of Lewis & Clark." *American Rifleman* 132, no. 8 (August): 36–37, 80–82.

Halvorson, Mark J. 1998. *Sacred Beauty: Quillwork of Plains Women.* Bismarck: State Historical Society of North Dakota.

Hamersly, Thomas H. S. 1881. *Complete Regular Army Register of the United States: For One Hundred Years.* Washington, D.C.: T. H. S. Hamersly.

Hamtramck, Col. J. F. 1802. Standing Orders, Detroit, July 26. In Regimental Descriptive Book, 1st U.S. Infantry, 1801–14. RG 98. National Archives, Washington, D.C.

Hanson, Charles E., Jr. 1982. "Indian Trade Rings." *Museum of the Fur Trade Quarterly* 18, no. 4 (winter): 2–5.

———. 1986. "Trade Mirrors." *Museum of the Fur Trade Quarterly* 22, no. 4 (winter): 1–11.

———. 1987a. "The Scalping Knife." *Museum of the Fur Trade Quarterly* 23, no. 1 (spring): 8–12.

———. 1987b. "Butcher Knives." *Museum of the Fur Trade Quarterly* 23, no. 3 (fall): 1–4.

Harbinger, Lucy Jayne. 1964. "The Importance of Food Plants in the Maintenance of Nez Perce Cultural Identity." Master's thesis, Washington State University.

Harlan, Richard. 1824. "On a New Fossil Genus, of the Order Enalio Sauri (of Conybeare)." *Journal of the Academy of Natural Sciences* 3, pt. 2:331–37, pl. 12, figs. 1–5. Philadelphia: Printed for the Society by J. Harding.

Harless, Susan E., ed. 1998. *Native Arts of the Columbia Plateau: The Doris Swayze Bounds Collection.* Bend, Oreg., and Seattle: High Desert Museum and University of Washington Press.

Harper, J. Russell, ed. 1971. *Paul Kane's Frontier.* Austin: University of Texas Press.

Harrison, Julia D., et al. 1987. *The Spirit Sings: Artistic Traditions of Canada's First Peoples.* Toronto: Columbia and Stewart, Glenbow Museum.

Hart, Jeff, and Jacqueline Moore. 1976. *Montana—Native Plants and Early Peoples.* Helena: Montana Historical Society.

Haseltine, John W. 1885. *Catalogue of the Celebrated "Indian Collection" of the Late Mr. John H. McIlvain of Philadelphia.* Philadelphia: Thomas Birch's Sons. Source located at University of Pennslyvania Museum, Philadelphia.

Hawkes, Nigel. 1981. *Early Scientific Instruments.* New York: Abbeville Press.

Hill, Edward E. 1974. *The Office of Indian Affairs, 1824–1880: Historical Sketches.* The Library of American Indian Affairs. New York: Clearwater Publishing.

Himes, George. N.d. "Brief History of the Lewis and Clark Medal and Its Adoption as the Seal and Book Plate of the Oregon Historical Society." Typescript in accession file 84-84, Oregon Historical Society, Portland.

Hines, Donald M. 1999. *Tales of the Nez Perce.* Fairfield, Wash.: Ye Galleon Press.

Holland, Leandra. 2001. "Preserving Food on the L&C Expedition." *We Proceeded On* 27, no. 3 (August): 6–11.

Holloway, David. 1974. *Lewis & Clark and the Crossing of North America.* New York: Saturday Review Press.

Holmberg, James J. 2000. "Seaman's Fate?" *We Proceeded On* 26, no. 1 (February): 7–9.

———, ed. 2002. *Dear Brother: Letters of William Clark to Jonathan Clark.* Yale Western Americana Series. New Haven, Conn.: Yale University Press, in association with the Filson Historical Society.

Hornung, Clarence. 1972. *Treasury of American Design.* 2 vols. in 1. New York: H. N. Abrams.

Horse Capture, George, Anne Vitart, Michel Waldberg, and W. Richard West, Jr. 1993. *Robes of Splendor: Native American Painted Buffalo Hides.* New York: New Press.

Horse Capture, Joseph D., and George P. Horse Capture. 2001. *Beauty, Honor, and Tradition: The Legacy of Plains Indian Shirts.* Minneapolis and Washington, D.C.: Minneapolis Institute of Arts and National Museum of the American Indian.

Howell, Edgar M., and Donald E. Kloster. 1969. *United States Army Headgear to 1854: Catalog of United States Army Uniforms in the Collections of the Smithsonian Institution.* Vol. 1. Washington, D.C.: Smithsonian Institution Press.

Hunn, Eugene S., and David H. French. 1984. "Alternatives to Taxonomic Hierarchy: The Sahaptin Case." *Journal of Ethnobiology* 4, no. 1 (May): 73-92.

Hunn, Eugene S., with James Selam and Family. 1990. *Nch'i-Wána "The Big River": Mid-Columbia Indians and Their Land.* Seattle: University of Washington Press.

Hunt, Robert R. 1988. "Merry to the Fiddle: The Musical Amusement of the Lewis and Clark Party." *We Proceeded On* 14, no. 4 (November): 10–17.

———. 1990. "The Espontoon: Captain Lewis' Magic Stick." *We Proceeded On* 16, no. 1 (February): 12–18.

———. 1995. "Hoofbeats & Nightmares: A Horse Chronicle of the Lewis and Clark Expedition (Part 2)." *We Proceeded On* 21, no. 1 (February): 4–9.

Inglis, Brand, and Arthur Negus. 1980. *The Arthur Negus Guide to British Silver.* London: Hamlyn.

Jackson, Donald D. 1959. "Some Books Carried by Lewis and Clark." *Missouri Historical Society Bulletin* 16, no. 1 (October): 3–13.

———. 1966. "The Public Image of Lewis and Clark." *Pacific Northwest Quarterly* 57 (January): 1–12.

———. 1978. *Letters of the Lewis and Clark Expedition with Related Documents 1783–1854.* 2d ed. Urbana: University of Illinois Press.

James, Thomas. 1966. *Three Years among the Indians and Mexicans.* Ed. Milo M. Quaife. New York: Citadel Press.

Jarrell, Myrtis, trans., and J. N. B. Hewitt, ed. 1937. *Journal of Rudolph Friederich Kurz: An Account of His Experiences among Fur Traders and*

American Indians on the Mississippi and the Upper Missouri Rivers during the Years 1846 to 1852. Smithsonian Institution, Bureau of American Ethnology, Bulletin 115. Washington, D.C.: GPO.

Jefferson, Thomas. 1806. *Message from the President of the United States Communicating Discoveries. . . .* Washington, D.C.: A. & G. Way.

———. 1954. *Notes on the State of Virginia*. Ed. William Peden. Chapel Hill: University of North Carolina Press.

———. 1964. *Notes on the State of Virginia*. New York: Harper Torchbooks.

Kapoun, Robert W., with Charles J. Lohrmann. 1997. *Language of the Robe: American Indian Trade Blankets*. Salt Lake City: Peregrine Smith Books.

Kastor, Peter, ed. 2002. *The Louisiana Purchase: Emergence of an American Nation*. Washington, D.C.: Congressional Quarterly Press.

Kauffman, Henry J. 1960. *The Pennsylvania Kentucky Rifle*. Harrisburg, Pa.: Stackpole Co.

Kennerly, William Clark, and Elizabeth Russell. 1948. *Persimmon Hill: A Narrative of Old St. Louis and the Far West*. Norman: University of Oklahoma Press.

Kerber, Linda K. 1998. *No Constitutional Right to Be Ladies: Women and the Obligations of Citizenship*. New York: Hill and Wang.

Kimball, Fiske. 1944. *The Life Portraits of Jefferson and Their Replicas*. Philadelphia: American Philosophical Society.

King, Nicholas. 1799. "An Improvement in Boats, for River-Navigation." *Transactions of the American Philosophical Society*, 4:298–302, opp. p. 354.

Klein, Laura F., and Lillian A. Ackerman, eds. 1995. *Women and Power in Native North America*. Norman: University of Oklahoma Press.

Knight, Edward Henry. 1874–76. *Knight's American Mechanical Dictionary: Being a Description of Tools, Instruments, Machines, Processes, and Engineering; History of Inventions; General Technological Vocabulary; and Digest of Mechanical Appliances in Science and the Arts*. 3 vols. New York: J. B. Ford and Co.

Krieger, Herbert W. 1929. "American Indian Costumes in the United States National Museum." In *Annual Report for the Board of Regents, 1928*, ed. Smithsonian Institution. Washington, D.C.: GPO.

Kroeber, Alfred L. 1900. "Symbolism of the Arapaho Indians." *American Museum of Natural History Bulletin* 13:69–86.

———. 1983. *The Arapaho*. Lincoln: University of Nebraska Press.

Lamb, W. Kaye, ed. 1970. *The Journals and Letters of Sir Alexander Mackenzie*. Cambridge, England: Hakluyt Society.

Langdon, Helen. 1989. *Claude Lorrain*. Oxford: Phaidon Press.

Large, Arlen. 1995. "The Rocky Boat Ride of Lewis & Clark." *We Proceeded On* 21, no. 1 (February): 16–23.

———. 1997. "Captain Lewis Gets a Haircut." *We Proceeded On* 23, no. 3 (August): 14–17.

Lassey, Rod. 2000. "A Spontoon Tomahawk from the Upper Missouri." *Museum of the Fur Trade Quarterly* 36, no. 3 (fall): 7–9.

Lehmer, Donald J. 1971. *Introduction to Middle Missouri Archeology*. Anthropological Papers, no. 1. Washington, D.C.: GPO.

Lehmer, Donald J., W. Raymond Wood, and C. L. Dill. 1978. *The Knife River Phase*. Blair, Nebr.: Dana College.

Lentz, Gary. 2000. "Meriwether Lewis's Medicine Chests," *We Proceeded On* 26, no. 2 (May): 10-17.

Leonard, Kenneth O. 1995. Letter to North Dakota Historical Society, May 1, 1995. Correspondence File, State Historical Society of North Dakota, Bismarck.

Levine, Bernard. 1997. *Levine's Guide to Knives and Their Values*. 4th ed. Iola, Wisc.: Krause Publications.

Lewis, G. Malcolm. 1980. "Indian Maps." In *Old Trails and New Directions: Papers of the Third North American Fur Trade Conference*. Ed. Carol M. Judd and Arthur J. Ray. Toronto: University of Toronto Press.

Lewis, Waverly P. 1960. *U.S. Military Headgear, 1770–1880*. Devon, Conn.: Privately printed.

Libby, Orin G. 1906. "The Mandans and Gros-Ventres." *Collections of the State Historical Society of North Dakota*, 1:433–36. Bismarck, N.D.: Tribune, State Printers and Binders.

Library of Congress. 1922. *Report of the Librarian of Congress, 1922*. Washington, D.C.: GPO.

Lindert, Albert W. 1968. *Gunmakers of Indiana*. Homewood, Ind.: Published by the author.

Lindsay, Merrill. 1972. *The Kentucky Rifle*. New York: Arma Press.

Linn, Natalie. 1994. *The Plateau Bag: A Tradition in Native American Weaving*. Overland Park, Kans.: Johnson County Community College.

Loge, Ronald V. 1997. "'Two dozes of barks and opium': Lewis and Clark as Physicians." *We Proceeded On* 23, no. 1 (February): 10–15, 30.

Lowie, Robert H. 1909. "The Northern Shoshone." *Anthropological Papers of the American Museum of Natural History*, vol. 2, pt. 2. New York: American Museum of Natural History.

———. 1982. *Indians of the Plains*. Lincoln: University of Nebraska Press.

MacGregor, Carol Lynn. 1992. "The American Philosophical Society and Thomas Jefferson." *We Proceeded On* 18, no. 3 (August): 11–16.

———. 1997. *The Journals of Patrick Gass, Member of the Lewis and Clark Expedition*. Missoula, Mont.: Mountain Press Publishing Co.

Mackay, David. 1979. "A Presiding Genius of Exploration: Banks, Cook, and Empire, 1767–1805." In *Captain James Cook and His Times*, ed. Robin Fisher and Hugh Johnston. Seattle: University of Washington Press.

Mackenzie, Alexander. 1802. *Voyages from Montreal, on the River St. Laurence, through the Continent of North America, to the Frozen and Pacific Oceans; in the Years 1789 and 1793*. 2 vols. London: Printed for T. Cadell, Jr., W. Davies, Cobbett and Morgan, and W. Creech by R. Noble.

Madaus, Howard Michael. 1981. *The Warner Collector's Guide to American Longarms*. New York: Warner Books.

———. 1988. "The U.S. Flags in the American West, 1777–1876." *Raven: A Journal of Vexillology* 5:56–78.

Madsen, Brigham D. 1979. *The Lemhi: Sacajawea's People*. Caldwell, Idaho: Caxton Printers.

Mahan, Bruce E. 1926. *Old Fort Crawford and the Frontier*. Iowa City: State Historical Society of Iowa.

Mallery, Garrick. 1880. *Introduction to the Study of Sign Language among the North American Indians*. Washington, D.C.: GPO.

———. 1881. "Sign Language among North American Indians Compared with That among Other Peoples and Deaf-Mutes." In *First Annual Report of the Bureau of American Ethnology, 1879–80*, ed. Smithsonian Institution. Washington, D.C.: GPO.

———. 1893. "Picture-Writing of the American Indians." In *Tenth Annual Report of the Bureau of American Ethnology, 1888–89*, ed. Smithsonian Institution. Washington, D.C.: GPO.

Malloy, Mary. 1994. "'Boston Men' on the Northwest Coast: Commerce, Collecting, and Cultural Perceptions in the American Maritime Fur Trade, 1788–1844." Ph.D. diss., Brown University.

———. 2000. *Souvenirs of the Fur Trade: Northwest Coast Indian Art and Artifacts Collected by American Mariners, 1788–1844*. Cambridge: Harvard University, in association with Peabody Museum of Archaeology and Ethnology.

Marks, Lucy. 1797. Power of attorney, Lucy Marks to Meriwether Lewis. July 4. Lewis-Marks Collection. Special Collections, University of Virginia Library, Charlottesville.

Marr, Carolyn J. 1984. "Salish Baskets from the Wilkes Expedition." *American Indian Art Magazine* 9, no. 3 (summer): 44–51, 71.

Martin, Ned, and Jody Martin. 1997. *Bit and Spur Makers in the Vaquero Tradition: A Historical Perspective*. Nicasio, Calif.: Hawk Hill Press.

Masson, Louis R. 1889. *Les Bourgeois de la Compagnie du Nord-Ouest: Récits de Voyages, Lettres et Rapports Inédits Relatifs au Nord-Ouest Canadien*. Vol. 1. Quebec: A. Coté et Co.

Mathews, Alfred Edward. 1868. *Pencil Sketches of Montana*. New York: Published by the author.

Maurer, Evan M. 1992. *Visions of the People: A Pictorial History of Plains Indian Life*. Minneapolis: Minneapolis Institute of Arts.

Maury, Anne Fontaine, ed. *Intimate Virginiana: A Century of Maury Travels by Land and Sea*. Richmond, Va.: Dietz Press.

Mayer, Robert W. 1968. "Wood River, 1803–04," *Journal of the Illinois State Historical Society* 61, no. 2 (summer): 140–49.

McCracken, Harold. 1959. *George Catlin and the Old Frontier*. New York: Dial Press.

McDermott, John F. 1938. *Private Libraries in Creole Saint Louis*. Baltimore: Johns Hopkins University Press.

———. 1948a. "Museums in Early Saint Louis." *Missouri Historical Society Bulletin* 4, no. 3 (April): 129–38.

———. 1948b. "Dr. Koch's Wonderful Fossils." *Missouri Historical Society Bulletin* 4, no. 4 (July): 233–56.

———. 1951a. "How Goes the Harding Fever?" *Missouri Historical Society Bulletin* 8, no. 1 (October): 52–59.

———. 1951b. *Up the Missouri with Audubon: The Journal of Edward Harris*. Norman: University of Oklahoma Press.

———. 1954. "William Clark: Pioneer Museum Man." *Journal of the Washington Academy of Sciences* 44, no. 11:370–73.
———. 1960. "William Clark's Museum Once More." *Missouri Historical Society Bulletin* 16, no. 2 (January): 130–33.
McKenney, Thomas L., and James Hall. 1838–44. *History of the Indian Tribes of North America.* 3 vols. Philadelphia: F. W. Greenough.
McLaughlin, Castle. 2003. *Arts of Diplomacy: Lewis and Clark's Indian Collection.* Cambridge, Mass.: Peabody Museum Press; Seattle: University of Washington Press.
McWhorter, L. V. 1992. *Hear Me, My Chiefs! Nez Perce Legend and History.* Ed. Ruth Bordin. Caldwell, Idaho: Caxton Printers.
Meehan, Thomas. 1898. "The Plants of Lewis and Clark's Expedition across the Continent, 1804–1806." In *Proceedings of the Academy of Natural Sciences of Philadelphia 1898*, ed. Edward J. Nolan, 12–49. Philadelphia: Academy of Natural Sciences.
Meriwether, William, and Nicholas Lewis. 1786. Guardian bond. September 14. Albemarle County Records, Charlottesville, Va.
Merrell, Henry. 1876. "Pioneer Life in Wisconsin." In *Wisconsin Historical Collections*, vol. 7, ed. Lyman C. Draper. Madison: State Historical Society of Wisconsin.
Meyer, Roy W. 1977. *The Village Indians of the Upper Missouri: The Mandans, Hidatsas, and Arikaras.* Lincoln: University of Nebraska Press.
Miles, Ellen. 1977. *Portrait Painting in America: The Nineteenth Century.* New York: Main Street/Universe Books.
———. 1994. *Saint Mémin and the Neoclassical Profile Portrait in America.* Ed. Dru Dowdy. Washington, D.C.: Smithsonian Institution Press.
Miller, Alfred Jacob. 1951. *The West of Alfred Jacob Miller.* Norman: University of Oklahoma Press.
Miller, Angela L. 1993. *The Empire of the Eye: Landscape Representation and American Cultural Politics, 1825–1875.* Ithaca, N.Y.: Cornell University Press.
Miller, Christopher, and George R. Hamell. 2000. "A New Perspective on Indian-White Contact: Cultural Symbols and Colonial Trade." In *American Encounters: Natives and Newcomers from European Contact to Indian Removal, 1500–1850*, ed. Peter C. Mancall and James H. Merrell, 176–93. New York: Routledge.
Miller, Martin. 1978. *The Collector's Illustrated Guide to Firearms.* London: Barrie and Jenkins.
Moller, George D. 1993. *From the 1790s to the End of the Flintlock Period.* Vol. 2 of *American Military Shoulder Arms.* Niwot: University Press of Colorado.
Moore, Bob. 1994. "The Clothing of the Lewis & Clark Expedition." *We Proceeded On* 20, no. 3 (August): 4–13.
———. 1998. "A Closer Look at the Uniform Coats of the Lewis and Clark Expedition." *We Proceeded On* 24, no. 4 (November): 4–8.
———. 2000. "Pompey's Baptism." *We Proceeded On* 26, no. 1 (February): 11–17.
———. 2001. "Corps of Discovery Hats: What Did They Really Wear on Their Heads?" *We Proceeded On* 27, no. 2 (May): 20–27.
———. 2002. "Neatness Mattered: Hair, Beards, and the Corps of Discovery." *We Proceeded On* 28, no. 4 (November): 23–28.
Moulton, Gary E. 1983. "Another Look at William Clark's Map of 1805." *We Proceeded On* 9, no. 1 (March): 19–22.
———, ed. 1983–2001. *The Journals of the Lewis & Clark Expedition.* 13 vols. Lincoln: University of Nebraska Press.
Moulton, Gary E., and James J. Holmberg. 1991. "'What We Are About': Recently Discovered Letters of William Clark Shed New Light on the Lewis and Clark Expedition." *Filson Club History Quarterly* 65 (July): 387–403.
Mowbray, E. Andrew. 1997. *The American Eagle Pommel Sword: The Early Years, 1793–1830.* Lincoln, R.I.: Man at Arms Magazine.
Murphy, Robert F., and Yolanda Murphy. 1986. "Northern Shoshone and Bannock." In *Great Basin*, ed. Warren L. D'Azevedo. Vol. 11 of *Handbook of North American Indians.* Washington, D.C.: Smithsonian Institution Press.
Museum of the Fur Trade. 1967. "Collection Corner: Turlington's Balsam Bottles." *Museum of the Fur Trade Quarterly* 3, no. 3 (fall): 9–10.
Mussulman, Joseph. 2001. "Pomp's Bier Was a Bar." *We Proceeded On* 27, no. 1 (February): 39–40.
Nabakov, Peter, ed. 1978. *Native American Testimony: An Anthology of Indian and White Relations, First Encounter to Dispossession.* New York: Thomas Y. Crowell.
Neumann, George C., and Frank J. Kravic. 1975. *Collector's Illustrated Encyclopedia of the American Revolution.* Texarkana, Tex.: Rebel Publishing Co.
Newhouse, S[ewell]. 1867. *The Trapper's Guide; A Manual of Instructions.* 2d ed. Ed. J. H. Noyes and T. L. Pitt. Wallingford, Conn.: Oneida Community Press.
Nicandri, David L. 1986. *Northwest Chiefs: Gustav Sohon's Views of the 1855 Stevens Treaty Councils.* Tacoma: Washington State Historical Society.
Nichols, Roger L. 1969. *The Missouri Expedition, 1818–1820: The Journal of Surgeon John Gale with Related Documents.* Norman: University of Oklahoma Press.
Nolan, Marianne. 1991. "Searching for John Miles and His Lamps." *Rushlight* 57, no. 1 (March): 2–12.
Norfleet, Fillmore. 1942. *Saint-Mémin in Virginia: Portraits and Biographies.* Richmond, Va.: Dietz Press.
Olson, Lester C. 1991. *Emblems of American Community in the Revolutionary Era: A Study in Rhetorical Iconology.* Washington, D.C.: Smithsonian Institution Press.
Oman, Kerry. 2001. "Serendipity: A Newly Discovered Letter." *We Proceeded On* 27, no. 4 (November): 7–10.
Osgood, Ernest Staples. 1964. *The Field Notes of Captain William Clark, 1803–1805.* New Haven, Conn.: Yale University Press.
Osgood, Ernest S., and Donald Jackson. 1997. *The Lewis and Clark Expedition's Newfoundland Dog.* WPO Publication no. 12. N.p.: Lewis and Clark Trail Heritage Foundation.
Ottoson, Dennis R. 1976. "Toussaint Charbonneau, a Most Durable Man." *South Dakota History* 6 (spring): 152–85.
Outram, Dorinda. 1999. "On Being Perseus: New Knowledge, Dislocation, and Enlightenment Exploration." In *Geography and Enlightenment*, ed. David N. Livingstone and Charles W. J. Withers. Chicago: University of Chicago Press.
Paper, Jordan D. 1988. *Offering Smoke: The Sacred Pipe and Native American Religion.* Moscow: University of Idaho Press.
Peale, Charles Willson, et al. 1809–28. "Memoranda of the Philadelphia Museum." C. W. Peale Papers. Historical Society of Pennsylvania, Philadelphia.
Penney, David W. 1992. *Art of the American Indian Frontier: The Chandler-Pohrt Collection.* Seattle: University of Washington Press.
Pérez, Juan José. 2002. "A New Review of Spanish Dragoons' Swords." <http://bermudas.ls.fi.upm.es/~pedro/dragones_e.htm>.
Perrin du Lac, François Marie. 1807. *Travels through the Two Louisianas, and among the Savage Nations of the Missouri.* London: Printed for Richard Phillips by J. G. Barnard.
Peters, Virginia Bergman. 1995. *Women of the Earth Lodges: Tribal Life on the Plains.* North Haven, Conn.: Archon Books.
Peterson, Charles E. 1993. *Colonial St. Louis: Building a Creole Capital.* Tucson, Ariz.: Patrice Press.
Peterson, Harold L. 1965. *American Indian Tomahawks.* Contributions from the Museum of the American Indian, vol. 19. New York: Museum of the American Indian, Heye Foundation.
———. 1968. *The Book of the Continental Soldier: Uniforms, Weapons, and Equipment with Which He Lived and Fought.* Harrisburg, Pa.: Stackpole Co.
———. 1977. *The American Sword, 1775–1945: A Survey of the Swords Worn by the Uniformed Forces of the United States from the Revolution to the Close of World War II.* Rev. ed. Philadelphia: Ray Riling Arms Books Co.
Peterson, Jacqueline, with Laura Peers. 1993. *Sacred Encounters: Father De Smet and the Indians of the Rocky Mountain West.* Norman: University of Oklahoma Press.
Peterson, Mendel L. 1950. "American Epaulettes, 1775–1820." *Military Collector & Historian* 2, no. 2 (June): 17–21.
Plamondon, Martin, II. 2000. *Lewis and Clark Trail Maps: A Cartographic Reconstruction.* Vol. 1. Pullman: Washington State University Press.
Porter, Roy. 2002. *The Creation of the Modern World: The Untold Story of the British Enlightenment.* New York: W. W. Norton and Co.
Powers, William K. 1980. "The Art of Courtship among the Oglala." *American Indian Art Magazine* 5, no. 2 (spring): 40–47.
Preston, Richard S. 2000. "The Accuracy of the Astronomical Observations of Lewis and Clark." *American Philosophical Society Proceedings* 144, no. 2 (June): 168–91.
Preston, William. 1775. *Illustrations of Masonry.* 2d ed. London: J. Wilkie.
Prown, Jules David, et al. 1992. *Discovered Lands, Invented Pasts: Transforming Visions of the American West.* New Haven, Conn.: Yale University Press.

Prucha, Francis Paul. 1971. *Indian Peace Medals in American History*. Lincoln: University of Nebraska Press.
Pursh, Frederick. 1816. *Flora Americae Septentrionalis; or, a Systematic Arrangement and Description of the Plants of North America*. 2d ed. London: James Black and Son.
Quaife, Milo M., Melvin J. Weig, and Roy E. Appleman. 1961. *The History of the United States Flag: From the Revolution to the Present, Including a Guide to Its Use and Display*. New York: Harper.
Quimby, George I. 1954. *Indians of the Western Frontier: Paintings of George Catlin*. Chicago: Chicago Natural History Museum.
———. 1966. *Indian Culture and European Trade Goods*. Madison: University of Wisconsin Press.
Ray, Verne F. 1938. "Lower Chinook Ethnographic Notes." *University of Washington Publications in Anthropology* 7, no. 2 (May): 29–165.
Rees, John E. 1970. *Madame Charbonneau: The Indian Woman Who Accompanied the Lewis and Clark Expedition, 1804–6*. Salmon, Idaho: Lemhi County Historical Society.
Richardson, Edgar P., Brooke Hindle, and Lillian B. Miller. 1983. *Charles Willson Peale and His World*. New York: H. N. Abrams.
Riling, Joseph R. 1966. *Baron Von Steuben and His Regulations*. Philadelphia: Ray Riling Arms Books Co.
Ritchie, Roy, and Ron Stewart. 1999. *Standard Guide to Razors*. 2d ed. Paducah, Ky.: Collector Books.
Rockwell, David B. 1991. *Giving Voice to Bear: North American Indian Rituals, Myths, and Images of the Bear*. Niwot, Colo.: Roberts Rinehart Publishers.
Roehm, Marjorie Catlin, ed. 1966. *The Letters of George Catlin and His Family: A Chronicle of the American West*. Berkeley: University of California Press.
Ronda, James P. 1981. "Frazer's Razor: The Ethnohistory of a Common Object." *We Proceeded On* 7, no. 3 (August): 12–13.
———. 1984a. *Lewis and Clark among the Indians*. Lincoln: University of Nebraska Press.
———. 1984b. "'A Chart in His Way': Indian Cartography and the Lewis and Clark Expedition." *Great Plains Quarterly* 4, no. 1 (winter): 43–53.
———. 1997. *Thomas Jefferson and the Changing West: From Conquest to Conservation*. St. Louis: Missouri Historical Society Press.
———. 1998. *Voyages of Discovery: Essays on the Lewis and Clark Expedition*. Helena: Montana Historical Society Press.
Ross, Alexander. 1904. *Adventures of the First Settlers on the Oregon or Columbia River*. 1849. Reprinted in *Early Western Travels, 1748–1846*, ed. Reuben Gold Thwaites, vol. 7. Cleveland: Arthur H. Clark Co.
———. 1956. *The Fur Hunters of the Far West*. Ed. Kenneth A. Spaulding. American Exploration and Travel Series, no. 20. Norman: University of Oklahoma Press.
Ross, Marvin C. 1951. *The West of Alfred Jacob Miller*. Norman: University of Oklahoma Press.
Ruby, Robert H., and John A. Brown. 1976. *The Chinook Indians: Traders of the Lower Columbia River*. The Civilization of the American Indian Series, vol. 138. Norman: University of Oklahoma Press.
———. 1981. *Indians of the Pacific Northwest*. Norman: University of Oklahoma Press.
———. 1993. *Indian Slavery in the Pacific Northwest*. Spokane: Arthur H. Clark Co.
Rudd, Velva E. 1954. "Botanical Contributions of the Lewis and Clark Expedition." *Journal of the Washington Academy of Sciences* 44, no. 11 (November): 351–56.
Rulau, Russell. 1997. *Standard Catalog of United States Tokens, 1700–1900*. 2d ed. Iola, Wisc.: Krause Publications.
Russell, Carl P. 1967. *Firearms, Traps, & Tools of the Mountain Men*. Albuquerque: University of New Mexico Press.
Saindon, Bob. 1977. "The Lost Vocabularies of Lewis and Clark." *We Proceeded On* 3, no. 3 (July): 4–6.
———. 1981. "The Flags of the Lewis and Clark Expedition." *We Proceeded On* 7, no. 4 (November): 22–28.
Sapir, Edward. 1990. *Wishram Texts and Ethnography*, ed. William Bright. Vol. 7 of *The Collected Works of Edward Sapir*. Berlin: Mouton de Gruyter.
Sauter, John, and Bruce Johnson. 1974. *Tillamook Indians of the Oregon Coast*. Portland, Oreg.: Binfords and Mort.
Schama, Simon. 1991. "The Many Deaths of General Wolfe." In *Dead Certainties: Unwarranted Speculations*. New York: Alfred A. Knopf.
Schlick, Mary D. 1994. *Columbia River Basketry: Gift of the Ancestors, Gift of the Earth*. Seattle: University of Washington Press.
Schulze-Thulin, Axel. 1979. "Prairie and Plains Collections of the Linden-Museum Stuttgart." *American Indian Art Magazine* 4, no. 3 (summer): 52–55, 90.
Schuster, Helen H. 1990. *The Yakima*. New York: Chelsea House Publishers.
Scott, Jonathan. 1995. *Salvator Rosa: His Life and Times*. New Haven, Conn.: Yale University Press.
Seaman, Valentine. 1797. "On the Caustic in Urethral Obstructions." *Medical Repository* 1, no. 2: 179–80.
Sellers, Charles Coleman. 1947. *Charles Willson Peale*. Memoirs of the American Philosophical Society, vol. 23. Philadelphia: American Philosophical Society.
———. 1980. *Mr. Peale's Museum: Charles Willson Peale and the First Popular Museum of Natural Science and Art*. New York: W. W. Norton and Co.
Sellers, Frank M. 1983. *American Gunsmiths*. Highland Park, N.J.: Gun Room Press.
Smart, Charles E. 1962. *The Makers of Surveying Instruments in America since 1700*. Troy, N.Y.: Regal Art Press.
Smith, Dwight L., and Ray Swick, eds. 1997. *A Journey through the West: Thomas Rodney's 1803 Journal from Delaware to the Mississippi Territory*. Athens: Ohio University Press.
Snyder, Gerald S. 1970. *In the Footsteps of Lewis and Clark*. National Geographic Special Publications. Washington, D.C.: National Geographic Society.
Sorley, Merrow Egerton. 1991. *Lewis of Warner Hall: The History of a Family*. 1935. Reprint, Baltimore: Genealogical Publishing Co.
Spamer, Earle E., and Richard M. McCourt. 2002. "The Lewis and Clark Herbarium of The Academy of Natural Sciences: Part I, History." *Notulae Naturae*, no. 475.
Spier, Leslie, and Edward Sapir. 1930. *Wishram Ethnography*. University of Washington Publications in Anthropology, vol. 3, no. 3 (May). Seattle: University of Washington Press.
Spinden, Herbert J. 1908. "The Nez Perce Indians." *Memoirs of the American Anthropological Association* 2, pt. 3:165–274.
Starr, Eileen. 2001. "Celestial Navigation Basics." *We Proceeded On* 27, no. 4 (November): 12–18.
Steffen, Jerome O. 1977. *William Clark: Jeffersonian Man on the Frontier*. Norman: University of Oklahoma Press.
Stein, Susan R. 1993. *The Worlds of Thomas Jefferson at Monticello*. New York: Harry N. Abrams.
Stevens, Isaac I. 1860. *Narrative and Final Report of Explorations for a Route for a Pacific Railroad, near the Forty-seventh and Forty-ninth Parallels of North Latitude, from St. Paul to Puget Sound: Reports of Explorations and Surveys, to Ascertain the Most Practicable and Economical Route for a Railroad from the Mississippi River to the Pacific Ocean*. 36th Cong., 1st sess., H. Doc. 56, vol. 12, bk. 1. Washington, D.C.: Thomas H. Ford.
Stewart, Henry M., Jr. 1977. "The American Air Gun School of 1800." *Monthly Bugle*, Pennsylvania Antique Gun Collectors Association, no. 89 (February), 2–7.
Strong, Emory. 1959. *Wakemap Mound and Nearby Sites on the Long Narrows of the Columbia River*. Portland, Oreg.: Binfords and Mort.
———. 1960. *Stone Age on the Columbia River*. Portland, Oreg.: Binfords and Mort.
Swan, James G. 1870. "The Indians of Cape Flattery, at the Entrance to the Strait of Fuca, Washington Territory." In *Smithsonian Contributions to Knowledge*, vol. 16, article 8. Washington, D.C.: Smithsonian Institution Press.
Swanton, John R. 1911. *Indian Tribes of the Lower Mississippi Valley*. Smithsonian Institution, Bureau of American Ethnology, Bulletin 43. Washington, D.C.: GPO.
Taft, Robert. 1949. "The Pictorial Record of the Old West." *Kansas Historical Quarterly* 17, no. 2 (May): 97–121.
Tait, Frank A. 1999a. "The U.S. Contract Rifle Pattern of 1792." *Man at Arms* 21, no. 3 (June): 33–45.
———. 1999b. "Lewis & Clark and 'Short Rifles.'" *Man at Arms* 21, no. 6 (December): 7–8.
Taplin, William. 1803. *The Sportsman's Cabinet*. 2 vols. London: Printed and published for the proprietors by J. Cundee et al.
Taylor, E. G. R. 1966. *The Mathematical Practitioners of Hanoverian England, 1714–1840*. London: Cambridge University Press, in association with the Institute of Navigation.
Teitelman, S. Robert. 1983. *Birch's Views of Philadelphia*. 2d ed. Philadelphia: Free Library of Philadelphia and University of Pennsylvania Press.
Tesseract. 1998. *Early Scientific Instruments*. Catalog 61 (summer). Hastings-on-Hudson, N.Y.: Tesseract.
———. 1999. *Early Scientific Instruments*. Catalog 64 (summer). Hastings-on-Hudson, N.Y.: Tesseract.
Thiessen, Thomas D., W. Raymond Wood, and A. Wesley Jones. 1979. "The Sitting Rabbit 1907 Map of the Missouri River in North Dakota (Part 1)." *Plains Anthropologist* 24, no. 84 (May): 145–67.

Thomas, Davis, and Karen Ronnefeldt, eds. 1976. *People of the First Man: Life among the Plains Indians in Their Final Days of Glory*. New York: E. P. Dutton.

Thompson, Judy. 1977. *The North American Indian Collection: A Catalogue*. Berne, Switzerland: Berne Historical Museum.

Thwaites, Reuben Gold, ed. 1904–5. *Original Journals of the Lewis and Clark Expedition, 1804–1806*. 8 vols. New York: Dodd, Mead and Co.

Torrence, Gaylord. 1994. *The American Indian Parfleche: A Tradition of Abstract Painting*. Seattle: University of Washington Press, in association with the Des Moines Art Center.

Trigger, Bruce G., ed. 1978. *Northeast*. Vol. 15 of *Handbook of North American Indians*. Washington, D.C.: Smithsonian Institution Press.

Troccoli, Joan Carpenter. 1993. *First Artist of the West: George Catlin Paintings and Watercolors from the Collection of Gilcrease Museum*. Tulsa, Okla.: Gilcrease Museum.

Turnbaugh, Sarah Peabody, and William A. Turnbaugh. 1986. *Indian Baskets*. West Chester, Pa.: Schiffer Publishing.

Turner, Jane, ed. 1996. *Dictionary of Art*. Vol. 8. New York: Grove's Dictionary; London: MacMillan.

Tyler, Ron, ed. 1982. *Alfred Jacob Miller: Artist on the Oregon Trail*. Fort Worth, Tex.: Amon Carter Museum.

Tyrrell, J. B., ed. 1916. *David Thompson's Narrative of His Explorations in Western America, 1784–1812*. Toronto: Champlain Society.

Valentine Museum. 1941. *Exhibition of the Works of Charles Julien Balthazar Fevret de Saint-Mémin*. Richmond, Va.: Published by the author.

Van Ravenswaay, Charles. 1991. *Saint Louis: An Informal History of the City and Its People, 1764–1865*. St. Louis: Missouri Historical Society Press.

Vaughan, Thomas, and Bill Holm. 1990. *Soft Gold: The Fur Trade and Cultural Exchange on the Northwest Coast of America*. 2d rev. ed. North Pacific Studies Series, no. 14. Portland: Oregon Historical Society Press.

Vogel, Virgil J. 1970. *American Indian Medicine*. Norman: University of Oklahoma Press.

Von Steuben, Baron Friedrich Wilhelm Ludolf Gerhard Augustin. 1803. *Regulations for the Order and Discipline of the Troops of the United States*. Albany, N.Y.: Printed for Daniel and Samuel Whiting.

Walker Art Center. 1972. *American Indian Art: Form and Tradition*. Minneapolis: Walker Art Center, Minneapolis Institute of Arts, and Indian Art Association.

Walker, James R. 1980. *Lakota Belief and Ritual*. Ed. Raymond J. DeMallie and Elaine A. Jahner. Lincoln: University of Nebraska Press.

———. 1982. *Lakota Society*. Ed. Raymond J. DeMallie. Lincoln: University of Nebraska Press.

Wallace, Anthony F. C. 1999. *Jefferson and the Indians: The Tragic Fate of the First Americans*. Cambridge, Mass.: Belknap Press of Harvard University Press.

Warhus, Mark. 1997. *Another America: Native American Maps and the History of Our Land*. New York: St. Martin's Press.

Warner, Deborah Jean. 1998. "Telescopes for Land and Sea." *Rittenhouse: Journal of the American Scientific Instrument Enterprise* 12, no. 2 (April): 33–54.

Warre, Henry James. 1848. *Sketches in North America and the Oregon Territory*. London: Dickinson and Co.

———. 1970. *Sketches in North America and the Oregon Territory*. Barre, Mass.: Imprint Society.

Washburn, Wilcomb E., ed. 1988. *History of Indian-White Relations*. Vol. 4 of *Handbook of North American Indians*. Washington, D.C.: Smithsonian Institution Press.

Washington, H. A., ed. 1854. *The Writings of Thomas Jefferson*. Washington, D.C.: Taylor and Maury.

Weddell, Alexander W. 1930. *A Memorial Volume of Virginia Historical Portraiture, 1585–1830*. Richmond, Va.: William Byrd Press.

Wedel, Waldo R. 1957. *Observations on Some Nineteenth-Century Pottery Vessels from the Upper Missouri*. Smithsonian Institution, Bureau of American Ethnology, Bulletin 164. Washington, D.C.: GPO.

Wedel, Waldo R., and George B. Griffenhagen. 1954. "An English Balsam among the Dakota Aborigines." *American Journal of Pharmacy* 126, no. 12 (December): 409–15.

Wheat, Carl I. 1958. *Mapping the Transmississippi West, 1540–1861*. 5 vols. San Francisco: Institute of Historical Cartography.

Wheeler, Olin D. 1900. *Wonderland 1900*. St. Paul: Northern Pacific Railway.

———. 1904. *The Trail of Lewis and Clark, 1804–1904*. 2 vols. New York: G. P. Putnam's Sons.

White, Bruce M. 1994. "Encounters with Spirits." *Ethnohistory* 41, no. 3:369–405.

White, Gilbert. 1825. *The Natural History of Selbourne*. 2 vols. London: C. and J. Rivington.

White, Richard. 2000. "The Winning of the West: The Expansion of the Western Sioux in the Eighteenth and Nineteenth Centuries." In *American Encounters: Natives and Newcomers from European Contact to Indian Removal, 1500–1850*, ed. Peter C. Mancall and James H. Merrell, 541–61. New York: Routledge.

Wied, Maximilian, Prinz von. 1843. *Travels in the Interior of North America*. London: Ackermann and Co.

Wilkes, Charles. 1844. *Narrative of the United States Exploring Expedition during the Years 1838, 1839, 1840, 1841, 1842*. United States Exploring Expedition, 5 vols. Philadelphia: Printed by C. Sherman.

Wilkinson, Frederick. 1968. *Flintlock Pistols: An Illustrated Reference Guide to Flintlock Pistols from the 17th to the 19th Century*. Harrisburg, Pa.: Stackpole Co.

Will, Drake W. 1971. "Lewis and Clark: Westering Physicians." *Montana: The Magazine of Western History* 21, no. 4 (autumn): 2–17.

Williams, Lyle K. 1976. *Historically Speaking: Stories of the Men and Women Who Explored and Settled the Missouri River Headwaters*. Three Forks, Mont.: Williams.

Willoughby, Charles C. 1905. "A Few Ethnological Specimens Collected by Lewis and Clark." *American Anthropologist* 7 (October-December): 633–41.

Wilson, Alexander. 1808–14. *American Ornithology; or, The Natural History of the Birds of the United States*. 9 vols. Philadelphia: Bradford and Inskeep.

Wissler, Clark. 1904. "Decorative Art of the Sioux Indians." *American Museum of Natural History Bulletin* 18, pt. 3: 231–78.

———. 1907. "Some Protective Designs of the Dakota." *Anthropological Papers of the American Museum of Natural History*, vol. 1, pt. 2. New York: American Museum of Natural History.

———. 1912. "Societies and Ceremonial Associations in the Oglala Division of the Teton-Dakota." *Anthropological Papers of the American Museum of Natural History*, vol. 11, pt. 1. New York: American Museum of Natural History.

———. 1986. *A Blackfoot Source Book: Papers by Clark Wissler*. Ed. David Hurst Thomas. New York: Garland Publishing.

Withington, Mary C. 1952. *A Catalogue of Manuscripts in the Collection of Western Americana Founded by William Robertson Coe, Yale University Library*. New Haven, Conn.: Yale University Press.

Wollon, Dorothy, ed. 1952. "Sir Augustus J. Foster and 'The Wild Natives of the Woods,' 1805–1807." *William and Mary Quarterly*, 3d series, 9, no. 2 (April): 191–214.

Wood, W. Raymond. 1972. "Contrastive Features of Native North American Trade Systems." In *For the Chief: Essays in Honor of Luther S. Cressman*, ed. Fred W. Voget and Robert L. Stephenson. University of Oregon Anthropological Papers, no. 4. Eugene: University of Oregon Press.

———, ed. 1986. *Ice Glider 32OL110: Papers in Northern Plains Prehistory and Ethnohistory*. Special Publications of the South Dakota Archaeological Society, no. 10. Sioux Falls, S.D.: Sioux Printing, published in cooperation with the National Park Service.

Wood, W. Raymond, and Gary E. Moulton. 1981. "Prince Maximilian and New Maps of the Missouri and Yellowstone Rivers by William Clark." *Western Historical Quarterly*, no. 4 (October): 372–86.

Wood, W. Raymond, and Thomas D. Thiessen, eds. 1985. *Early Fur Trade on the Northern Plains*. Norman: University of Oklahoma Press.

Woods, William H. 1890[?]. "Historical Sketch of an Original Portrait of Governor Meriwether Lewis." Manuscript Collection 526. Oregon Historical Society, Portland.

Woodward, Arthur. 1979. *The Denominators of the Fur Trade: An Anthology of Writings on the Material Culture of the Fur Trade*. Rev. ed. Pasadena: Westernlore Press.

———. 1989. *Indian Trade Goods*. 2d ed. Portland, Oreg.: Binfords and Mort.

Wright, Robin K., ed. 1991. *A Time of Gathering: Native Heritage in Washington State*. Monograph/Thomas Burke Memorial Washington State Museum, 7. Seattle: University of Washington Press, in association with Thomas Burke Memorial Washington State Museum.

Yoder, Don, ed. 1976. *American Folklife*. Austin: University of Texas Press.

Zlatich, Marko. 1992a. "Hat, U.S. Infantry, 1801–1811." *Military Collector & Historian* 44, no. 1 (spring): 32–33.

———. 1992b. "Corps of Volunteers for North Western Discovery, 1804–1806." *Military Collector & Historian* 44, no. 4 (winter): 693.

Notes

FOREWORD

1. Jefferson to Lewis, June 20, 1803, in Jackson 1978: 61–62.
2. Adams 1890: 1: 215.

INTRODUCTION

1. Moulton 1983–2001: 5: 76–83. The Lemhi Shoshone accounts are in Ronda 1984a: 143.
2. James King to Banks, October 1780, in Mackay 1979: 29.
3. Jefferson to Michaux, April 30, 1793, in Jackson 1978: 669.
4. Jefferson to Lewis, Washington, D.C., June 20, 1803, in Jackson 1978: 61.
5. Lewis to Clark, Washington, D.C., June 19, 1803, in Jackson 1978: 57–60.
6. Jefferson to Lewis, Washington, D.C., November 16, 1803, in Jackson 1978: 137.
7. Outram 1999: 281.
8. Jefferson to Lewis, Washington, D.C., June 20, 1803, in Jackson 1978: 62.
9. Jackson 1978: 69.
10. Jackson 1978: vii.
11. Moulton 1983–2001: 5: 133, 9: 207.
12. Moulton 1983–2001: 8: 352.
13. Moulton 1983–2001: 4: 93.
14. Lewis to Jefferson, Fort Mandan, April 7, 1805, in Jackson 1978: 231.
15. Lewis to Jefferson, Fort Mandan, April 7, 1805, in Jackson 1978: 231.
16. Moulton 1983–2001: 5: 125–26.
17. Boswell 1904: 2: 227.
18. Jefferson to Adams, Monticello, June 10, 1815, in Cappon 1959: 2: 443.
19. Jefferson to Charles Bellini, Paris, September 30, 1785, in Boyd et al. 1950–2002: 8: 568.
20. Jefferson 1954: 13.
21. Jefferson to Michaux, April 30, 1793, in Jackson 1978: 670.
22. Lamb 1970: 417.
23. White 1825: 2: 39.
24. Cutright 1969a: 25.
25. Jefferson to James Cheetham, Washington, D.C., June 17, 1803, in Jackson 1978: 56.
26. Moulton 1983–2001: 8: 419.
27. Moulton 1983–2001: 4: 29.
28. The Robert Frazer Prospectus, October 1806, in Jackson 1978: 345.
29. Arthur Campbell to Jedediah Morse, Kentucky, November 20, 1806, in Oman 2001: 8.
30. Moulton 1983–2001: 11: 7.
31. The Patrick Gass Prospectus, March 23, 1807, in Jackson 1978: 390–91.
32. Lewis to the Public, Washington, D.C., March 14, 1807, in Jackson 1978: 385–86.
33. McKeehan to Lewis, Pittsburgh, April 7, 1807, in Jackson 1978: 399–407.
34. The Conrad Prospectus, Philadelphia, [April 1, 1807], in Jackson 1978: 394–97.
35. Conrad and Company to Jefferson, Philadelphia, November 13, 1809, in Jackson 1978: 469.
36. Clark to Jonathan Clark, St. Louis, October 5, 1808, in Holmberg 2002: 156.
37. Jefferson to Lewis, Washington, D.C., June 20, 1803, in Jackson 1978: 61.
38. Moulton 1983–2001: 2: 412.
39. Jefferson to William Dunbar, Washington, D.C., May 25, 1805, in Jackson 1978: 244.
40. Moulton 1983–2001: 4: 65–66.
41. Moulton 1983–2001: 2: 506.
42. Moulton 1983–2001: 8: 127.
43. Moulton 1983–2001: 7: 266.
44. Moulton 1983–2001: 4: 226.
45. Young quoted in Porter 2002: 308.
46. Moulton 1983–2001: 2: 346–47.
47. Lewis to Lucy Marks, Fort Mandan, March 31, 1805, in Jackson 1978: 223–24.
48. Moulton 1983–2001: 4: 108.
49. Moulton 1983–2001: 4: 266.
50. Moulton 1983–2001: 4: 205–6.
51. Moulton 1983–2001: 6: 33.
52. Moulton 1983–2001: 6: 33.
53. Moulton 1983–2001: 6: 67.
54. Moulton 1983–2001: 6: 104.
55. Moulton 1983–2001: 2: 215.
56. Moulton 1983–2001: 7: 238.
57. Larocque quoted in Wood and Thiessen 1985: 138.
58. Moulton 1983–2001: 7: 109.
59. McHenry quoted in Prucha 1971: 89.
60. Prucha 1971: xiii.
61. Moulton 1983–2001: 8: 314.
62. Coues 1965: 350.
63. Moulton 1983–2001: 8: 135.
64. Moulton 1983–2001: 5: 338.
65. Moulton 1983–2001: 3: 311.
66. Moulton 1983–2001: 3: 317.
67. Moulton 1983–2001: 3: 485.
68. Moulton 1983–2001: 3: 31.
69. Moulton 1983–2001: 7: 341.
70. Moulton 1983–2001: 5: 115.
71. Lewis to Lucy Marks, Fort Mandan, March 31, 1805, in Jackson 1978: 225.
72. Jefferson to the Indian Delegation, Washington, D.C., January 4, 1806, in Jackson 1978: 282.
73. Moulton 1983–2001: 8: 304.
74. Moulton 1983–2001: 5: 86n.9.
75. Moulton 1983–2001: 3: 219.
76. Moulton 1983–2001: 5: 91.
77. Moulton 1983–2001: 6: 169.
78. Moulton 1983–2001: 3: 219.
79. Moulton 1983–2001: 6: 74.
80. Moulton 1983–2001: 9: 105.
81. Boas 1894: 277–78.
82. Moulton 1983–2001: 3: 199.
83. Jefferson to Lewis, Washington, D.C., January 22, 1804, in Jackson 1978: 165.
84. Moulton 1983–2001: 11: 318.
85. Moulton 1983–2001: 5: 104.
86. Moulton 1983–2001: 7: 249.
87. Speech to the Oto Indians, August 4, 1804, in Jackson 1978: 205.
88. Moulton 1983–2001: 3: 29–30.
89. Moulton 1983–2001: 3: 31.
90. Moulton 1983–2001: 5: 118.
91. Moulton 1983–2001: 2: 218.
92. Wood and Thiessen 1985: 233.
93. Moulton 1983–2001: 9: 48.
94. Moulton 1983–2001: 5: 353.
95. Moulton 1983–2001: 9: 83.
96. Moulton 1983–2001: 4: 70.
97. Moulton 1983–2001: 7: 128.
98. Moulton 1983–2001: 5: 173.
99. Moulton 1983–2001: 7: 160.
100. Moulton 1983–2001: 9: 299–300.

CHAPTER ONE

1. Sapir 1990: 255–57.
2. First inaugural address, March 4, 1801, in Washington 1854: 8.
3. Hunn 1990: 241–51.
4. Allen 1975: 65.
5. Goetzmann 1966: 199.
6. Jackson 1978: 2, 12, 61; Ambrose 1996: 63.
7. Jackson 1978: 111; Jefferson 1964: 66n.
8. Here and below, see Allen 1975.
9. Ronda 1997: 15; Allen 1975: 97–103, 120; Jackson 1978: 12.
10. Jackson 1978: 320.
11. Allen 1975: 15, 39, 114, 137.
12. Jackson 1978: 59–60, 62.
13. Here and below, see Wallace 1999.
14. Jefferson 1964: 59.
15. Wallace in Ronda 1997: 17.
16. Wallace in Ronda 1997: 29, 30.
17. Ronda 1997: 38.
18. Jackson 1978: 62; Ronda 1997: 53.
19. See Kastor 2002: 1–10.
20. Miller 1993: 9.
21. Ronda 1997: 19.
22. Jackson 1978: 17–18.
23. Carter 1993: 12–22.
24. Richardson, Hindle, and Miller 1983; Sellers 1980.
25. Carter 1993: 20; MacGregor 1992: 14.
26. Jackson 1978: 13.
27. Jackson 1978: 32–33.
28. Jackson 1978: 22, 26.
29. Jackson 1978: 60.
30. Ambrose 1996: 45.
31. Jackson 1978: 57; Thwaites 1904: 1: xxiv–xxix.
32. Jackson 1978: 493; Steffen 1977: 3; Thwaites 1904: 1: xxvii–xxix.
33. Davis 1939: 361; Jackson 1978: 35, 117n, 180n.
34. Jackson 1978: 589–90, 592.
35. Jackson 1978: 111, 112.
36. Jackson 1978: 113, 116.
37. Moulton 1983–2001: 2: 510; Brown 1999; Holmberg 2002: 98–99.
38. Moulton 1983–2001: 2: 509–29; Jackson 1978: 58.
39. Jackson 1978: 146.
40. Holmberg 2002: 61.
41. Peterson 1993.
42. Ambrose 1996: 45; Jackson 1978: 151.
43. Jackson 1978: 108–9; Kastor 2002: 1–10.
44. Holmberg 2002: 76–77; see also Van Ravenswaay 1991: 118–20.
45. Jackson 1978: 165–66.

CHAPTER TWO

1. Jackson 1978: 64.
2. Jackson 1978: 176.
3. Jackson 1978: 163.
4. Moulton 1983–2001: 2: 240.
5. Moulton 1983–2001: 2: 233, 10: 8.
6. Moulton 1983–2001: 2: 249, 346.
7. Moulton 1983–2001: 2: 250, 289–90.
8. Moulton 1983–2001: 2: 455–56.
9. Moulton 1983–2001: 2: 306, 399, 492, 495.
10. Moulton 1983–2001: 3: 80–81; Jackson 1978: 223.
11. Moulton 1983–2001: 2: 377–78.
12. Moulton 1983–2001: 2: 501.
13. Moulton 1983–2001: 3: 71.
14. Moulton 1983–2001: 3: 53, 10: 36.
15. Moulton 1983–2001: 3: 83–84.
16. Jackson 1978: 205–6.
17. Moulton 1983–2001: 3: 29.
18. Moulton 1983–2001: 3: 23, 9: 33.
19. White 2000.
20. Jackson 1978: 166.
21. Moulton 1983–2001: 3: 124.
22. I thank James Ronda for providing this metaphor.
23. Ewers 1954.
24. Moulton 1983–2001: 5: 112. For a fuller treatment of European-Indian diplomacy, see McLaughlin 2003.
25. Washburn 1988: 185–87; Hall 1997: 48–58.
26. Moulton 1983–2001: 10: 45, also 11: 85.
27. Walker 1982: 25.
28. Ronda 1984a: 118.
29. Walker 1982: 24.
30. Ronda 1984a: 31.
31. Moulton 1983–2001: 3: 111, 112.
32. Walker 1982: 3, 6; Walker 1980: 205, 206, 218.
33. Walker 1980: 197.
34. Kinship terms were always slippery. A Lakota man might call all male relatives of his father's generation "Father." Though the Americans referred to the president as the "great father," when the Arikara translated the term back, it became "grandfather," which has a different emphasis. Moulton 1983–2001: 3: 165.
35. Ronda 1984a: 8.
36. Jackson 1978: 205; Moulton 1983–2001: 3: 118.
37. Moulton 1983–2001: 2: 215, 9: 67.
38. Moulton 1983–2001: 9: 47.
39. Moulton 1983–2001: 3: 113.
40. Walker 1980: 210.
41. Brown 1992: 98.
42. Here and below, see Moulton 1983–2001: 3: 118.
43. As recently as 1774, the Yanktonai performed a pipe ceremony identical to Clark's in all respects except for the inclusion of the mourning at the beginning; Peter Pond, a fur trader, was the participant who recorded it. Clark's description is too brief to be sure what happened to him. Hall 1997: 82.
44. Paper 1988: 28; Brown 1992: 98; Walker 1982: 12; Walker 1980: 75–76, 83 (quotation).
45. Hall 1997: 83; Walker 1980: 209, 220; Ewers 1979: 30, 32; Black Elk 1953; Walker 1982; Paper 1988.
46. Moulton 1983–2001: 3: 118, 9: 68.
47. White 1994.
48. Catlin 1995: 1: 257, 263.
49. Moulton 1983–2001: 3: 116.
50. Catlin 1995: 1: 276–77; Wissler 1912: 44, 80.
51. Walker 1980: 137.
52. Ronda 1984a: 27.
53. Moulton 1983–2001: 3: 113.
54. Moulton 1983–2001: 9: 71, 10: 47.
55. Moulton 1983–2001: 3: 124, 10: 47.
56. Jackson 1978: 235.

CHAPTER THREE

1. Coues 1893: 781.
2. Moulton 1983–2001: 3: 134, 145.
3. Ronda 1984a: 52–53.
4. Ronda 1984a: 49–50.
5. Moulton 1983–2001: 3: 158, 159, 162 (quotations); Meyer 1977: 48–54; Jackson 1978: 438.
6. Moulton 1983–2001: 3: 157.
7. Moulton 1983–2001: 3: 163.
8. Moulton 1983–2001: 3: 200.
9. Meyer 1977.
10. Bowers 1950: 24–25.
11. Moulton 1983–2001: 3: 204, 11: 105, 107.
12. Moulton 1983–2001: 3: 232; Coues 1893: 196.
13. Moulton 1983–2001: 3: 224–25; interview of Carolyn Gilman and Joseph Carlisle with Mike Cross and Amy Mossett, July 28, 1999.
14. In fact, all the way up the Missouri, Lewis and Clark had been noting the Euro-Americans who were already doing business on the river. They named twenty-one and mentioned at least as many without naming them. The names were Régis Loisel, Pierre Dorion, Sr., Mr. Fairfong, Pierre Dorion, Jr., Jean Vallé, Joseph Gravelines, Antoine Tabeau, Hugh McCracken, René Jusseaume, Toussaint Charbonneau, François-Antoine Larocque, Charles Mackenzie, Baptiste Lafrance, William Morrison, Joseph Azure, Baptiste Turenne, Alexis McKay, George Henderson, George Bunch, Hugh Heney, and Joseph Garreau.
15. Meyer 1977: 16.
16. Masson 1889: 304–6.
17. Masson 1889: 336.
18. Moulton 1983–2001: 3: 228.
19. Jackson 1978: 527 (other wife), 540 (sold as slave); Moulton 1983–2001: 4: 157 (fortitude), 171 (Bird Woman), 5: 120 (age); Coues 1893: 1184 (patience).
20. Moore 2000: 11; Brackenridge 1962: 202; Jackson 1978: 638–39. For summaries of the Sacagawea mythos, see Anderson 1978, 1980, and 1999.
21. Grinnell 1999; Rees 1970; interviews of Carolyn Gilman and Joseph Carlisle with Grinnell, Roseanne Abrahamson, and Snookins Honena, July 1999 and August 2000.
22. Moulton 1983–2001: 3: 488.
23. Gilman and Schneider 1987: 33.
24. Jackson 1978: 504; Moulton 1983–2001: 3: 117, 163.
25. Moulton 1983–2001: 5: 140, 289, 7: 291. For the Jefferson quotation, see Jefferson 1964: 57.
26. Moulton 1983–2001: 6: 168, 169. On preexisting stereotypes of Indian women, see Albers and Medicine 1983.
27. Moulton 1983–2001: 6: 168, 169.
28. Klein and Ackerman 1995: 232–38.
29. Miles 1994: 145–48; Peters 1995.
30. Moulton 1983–2001: 8: 305, 306.
31. Beckwith 1938: 23.
32. Here and below, see Gilman and Schneider 1987: 20.
33. Walker 1982: 42–43, 56.
34. Walker 1982: 40, 43.
35. Gilman and Schneider 1987: 116, 117; Peters 1995: 4.
36. Coues 1965: 344.
37. Jackson 1978: 44; Moulton 1983–2001: 3: 210; Coues 1965: 329.
38. Walker 1982: 43.
39. Peters 1995: 58; Bowers 1950: 62; Bowers 1965: 174.
40. Bowers 1965: 200–7.
41. Beckwith 1938: 232–33.
42. Walker 1980: 242.
43. Powers 1980; Brown 1992: 18.
44. Powers 1980: 41–42; Walker 1980: 107, 165–66; Durand 1994: 1.
45. Jackson 1978: 537.
46. Ronda 1984a: 62–64; Jackson 1978: 537; Moulton 1983–2001: 5: 121, 6: 142.
47. Moulton 1983–2001: 4: 266.
48. Kerber 1998: 11–15.
49. Bakeless 1947: 15–18; Ambrose 1996: 23–24.
50. Meriwether and Lewis 1786.
51. Marks 1797.
52. Here and below, see Bakeless 1947: 69, 195, 378, 383, 390–401; Jackson 1978: 388; Kennerly and Russell 1948: 14, 37. Julia's letters and her volumes of Shakespeare, mentioned below, are at the Missouri Historical Society.

CHAPTER FOUR

1. Jackson 1978: 63.
2. Bowers 1950: 107–8.
3. Moulton 1983–2001: 9: 106.
4. Moulton 1983–2001: 3: 266–67, 9: 107.
5. Masson 1889: 330.
6. Moulton 1983–2001: 3: 268; Bowers 1965: 451–63, quotation on 460. The italicized word is in the hand of Nicholas Biddle, the ghostwriter of the 1814 history of the expedition.
7. Moulton 1983–2001: 9: 103.
8. Moulton 1983–2001: 3: 276.
9. Moulton 1983–2001: 3: 244–47.
10. Moulton 1983–2001: 10: 71; Masson 1889: 330.
11. Moulton 1983–2001: 3: 269.
12. Ewers 1997: 184–85; Warhus 1997: 2, 157.
13. Ronda 1984a: 151, 160, 166, 225; Moulton 1983–2001: 5: 230, 7: 54.
14. Beckwith 1938: 303.
15. Ewers 1997: 187.
16. Ewers 1997: 182–84; Beckwith 1938: 304.
17. The discussion below is based on Lewis 1980, DeVorsey 1992, and DeVorsey 1998. See also Warhus 1997.
18. Ewers 1997: 185.
19. Moulton 1983–2001: 3: 301.
20. Sapir 1990: 219.
21. Starr 2001: 17; Benson 1995.
22. Preston 2000.
23. Moulton 1983–2001: 3: 180.
24. Bowers 1950: 184.
25. Thiessen, Wood, and Jones 1979: Warhus 1997: 43–52.
26. Thiessen, Wood, and Jones 1979: 151; Beckwith 1938: 133; Bowers 1965: 446–51 gives the Hidatsa version of the origins of buffalo-corral hunting.
27. Beckwith 1938: 129; Bowers 1950: 197–98.
28. Beckwith 1938: 18–20, 155–58.
29. Beckwith 1938: 7–17.
30. Beckwith 1938: 23–24.
31. Moulton 1983–2001: 3: 11, 299.
32. Moulton 1983–2001: 4: 285.
33. Furtwangler 1993: 23–51.
34. Burke 1958: 31–160, quotation on 59.
35. Moulton 1983–2001: 4: 266, 284, 285. Lewis was even more explicit in his wording when comparing two of the falls on June 14: "I determined between these two great rivals for glory that this was *pleasingly beautifull*, while the other was *sublimely grand*." Moulton

1983–2001: 4: 290.

36. Kroeber 1983: 110; Kroeber 1900; Coleman 1998; Torrence 1994: 249–50. The interpretations given to Kroeber before 1900 have been challenged by those who maintained that parfleche designs were simply decorative and had no meaning; in recent years, researchers like Torrence and Coleman have contradicted this assertion.
37. Moulton 1983–2001: 4: 294, 340, 362, 5: 112.
38. Moulton 1983–2001: 3: 238, 8: 308–9.
39. Moulton 1983–2001: 3: 268; Jackson 1978: 230; Ronda 1984b: 46.

CHAPTER FIVE

1. Densmore 1918: 96.
2. Moulton 1983–2001: 4: 9, 10.
3. Jackson 1978: 234.
4. Moulton 1983–2001: 4: 15.
5. Moulton 1983–2001: 4: 65, 101–2.
6. Moulton 1983–2001: 4: 67.
7. Moulton 1983–2001: 4: 152, 157, 171, 215.
8. Moulton 1983–2001: 4: 201.
9. Moulton 1983–2001: 4: 224–25.
10. Moulton 1983–2001: 4: 205, 10: 95.
11. Moulton 1983–2001: 4: 225–26.
12. Moulton 1983–2001: 4: 246, 248, 250, 269, 271.
13. Moulton 1983–2001: 4: 283.
14. Moulton 1983–2001: 4: 290–91.
15. Moulton 1983–2001: 4: 299, 301.
16. Moulton 1983–2001: 4: 328–29.
17. Moulton 1983–2001: 9: 173, 174, 179, 11: 211.
18. Moulton 1983–2001: 4: 342–43, 9: 176–77.
19. Moulton 1983–2001: 4: 333–34, 349.
20. Jackson 1978: 233; Moulton 1983–2001: 4: 354, 10: 105, 107.
21. Moulton 1983–2001: 4: 368–69, 10: 110 ("the Experiment").
22. Jackson 1978: 40.
23. Moulton 1983–2001: 4: 339, 340.
24. Moulton 1983–2001: 4: 67, 126.
25. Jackson 1978: 63.
26. See, for example, Susan Milius, "Should We Junk Linnaeus?" *Science News* 156 (October 23, 1999): 268–70.
27. The main sources on Lewis and Clark's work in natural history are Cutright 1969a, Burroughs 1961, and Botkin 1995.
28. Moulton 1983–2001: 4: 297.
29. Moulton 1983–2001: 4: 254, 294; Furtwangler 1993. Another example is his description of the eagle, who had "placed her nest . . . [where] neither man nor beast dare pass those gulphs which seperate her little domain from the shores." See Moulton 1983–2001: 4: 291.
30. Densmore 1918: 184.
31. The best examples are the Nez Perce stories—collected by Archie Phinney and reprinted in Hines 1999—in which the animals are constantly being warned to get ready for the arrival of humans. The same sensibility is found in the Mandan/Hidatsa stories of Beckwith 1938.
32. Densmore 1918: 172.
33. Walker 1980: 223.
34. Moulton 1983–2001: 10: 70–71, 11: 122.
35. The classic source on hunting attitudes and rituals is Hallowell 1926.
36. Walker 1980: 216; Brown 1992: 52.
37. Walker 1980: 214.
38. Walker 1980: 67, 68; Brown 1992: 14.
39. Brown 1992: 17.
40. Brown 1992: 32.
41. Densmore 1918: 188.
42. Densmore 1918: 268.
43. Moulton 1983–2001: 4: 31.
44. Moulton 1983–2001: 10: 108.
45. Rockwell 1991: 55.
46. Rockwell 1991: 56.
47. Rockwell 1991: 42, quoting Hallowell 1926.
48. Moulton 1983–2001: 4: 31, 85.
49. Moulton 1983–2001: 4: 113, 118.
50. Moulton 1983–2001: 4: 145, 292, 293.

CHAPTER SIX

1. Coues 1965: 352.
2. Moulton 1983–2001: 4: 319, 344.
3. Moulton 1983–2001: 9: 179.
4. Moulton 1983–2001: 4: 402.
5. Moulton 1983–2001: 4: 411.
6. Moulton 1983–2001: 4: 407. The phrase in italics is in the handwriting of Nicholas Biddle.
7. Moulton 1983–2001: 4: 416, 423, 430.
8. Moulton 1983–2001: 9: 190.
9. Moulton 1983–2001: 4: 436–37.
10. Moulton 1983–2001: 5: 9.
11. Moulton 1983–2001: 4: 436, 5: 18.
12. Moulton 1983–2001: 5: 7. The phrase in italics is in the handwriting of Nicholas Biddle.
13. Moulton 1983–2001: 5: 26, 30.
14. Moulton 1983–2001: 9: 196, 11: 257.
15. Moulton 1983–2001: 5: 59.
16. Moulton 1983–2001: 5: 74.
17. Moulton 1983–2001: 5: 74.
18. Moulton 1983–2001: 5: 68–69.
19. Farnell 1995 is a modern study of nonverbal communication in a Northern Plains tribe, the Assiniboine.
20. Here and below, see Moulton 1983–2001: 5: 69–70.
21. Kapoun and Lohrmann 1997: vii–ix; Fletcher and La Flesche 1911: 360–62.
22. Here and below, see Moulton 1983–2001: 5: 78–79.
23. Moulton 1983–2001: 5: 71, 79–80.
24. Moulton 1983–2001: 5: 79; Farnell 1995: 286–87.
25. Moulton 1983–2001: 5: 80.
26. Moulton 1983–2001: 5: 79, 80.
27. Moulton 1983–2001: 5: 81, 88; Dunbar 1809; Mallery 1880: 18–26; Farnell 1995.
28. Moulton 1983–2001: 5: 83.
29. The spellings of the names conform to Lowie 1909: 206, with additional information from Dramer 1997: 20; Madsen 1979: 24; and Murphy and Murphy 1986.
30. Ferris 1940: 90–91. Faro, the man quoted here, was identified as a Flathead; however, from the context, it is clear that he was living with the Shoshone at the time the quotation refers to.
31. Moulton 1983–2001: 5: 96.
32. Moulton 1983–2001: 5: 91, 114; Lewis here recounts in first person something that happened to Clark.
33. Moulton 1983–2001: 5: 105–6.
34. Moulton 1983–2001: 5: 91–92, 106.
35. Moulton 1983–2001: 5: 96.
36. Moulton 1983–2001: 5: 95, 103.
37. Moulton 1983–2001: 5: 104.
38. Moulton 1983–2001: 5: 96, 105, 106, 109.
39. Moulton 1983–2001: 5: 118.
40. Kapoun and Lohrmann 1997: 5.
41. Walker 1982: 27.
42. Moulton 1983–2001: 5: 159.
43. Moulton 1983–2001: 5: 160; see Davis 1979: 99–103 for a discussion of chieftainship among the Crow.
44. Wissler 1912: 15; Jackson 1978: 110; the patchbox is on Clark's rifle at the Missouri Historical Society, Acc. No. 1923 050 0016.
45. Densmore 1918: 176; Walker 1982: 34.
46. Horse Capture and Horse Capture 2001; William Cronon in Prown 1992: 199n.
47. Schama 1991.
48. Walker 1982: 32.
49. Walker 1980: 275 (quotation); Brown 1992: 92; Walker 1982: 36; Horse Capture and Horse Capture 2001.
50. Hamtramck 1802; Moore 1994 and 1998; Zlatich 1992b.
51. Wissler 1907: 47; Hunt 1990.
52. Moore 2001; Horse Capture and Horse Capture 2001: 53.
53. Moulton 1983–2001: 5: 159; Walker 1980: 270–71.
54. Moulton 1983–2001: 5: 150; Wissler 1907: 22–23.
55. Campbell and Howell 1963; Emerson 1996: 25–30, 119–21; Wissler 1907: 48.
56. Peterson 1950: 17.
57. Moulton 1983–2001: 3: 116; Jackson 1978: 517–18.
58. Walker 1982: 25, 29 (quotation), 31; Wissler 1912: 10 (quotation), 11–13, 23–25.
59. Walker 1980: 262 (last quotations), 269 (first quotation); Wissler 1912: 14–23.
60. Bullock 1996; Denslow 1959: 83–84; Preston 1775: 71–74; Denslow 1941: 4–12.
61. Wissler 1912: 16; Bushnell 1909: 414–19; Large 1997. Clark is shown in a queue in his portrait at the Missouri Historical Society, Acc. No. 1921 055 0001.

CHAPTER SEVEN

1. Coues 1893: 785.
2. Moulton 1983–2001: 5: 114.
3. Moulton 1983–2001: 5: 112, 114–15, 9: 206.
4. Coues 1893: 509, 510; Moulton 1983–2001: 5: 120.
5. Moulton 1983–2001: 5: 115, 159; Rees 1970: 8–9.
6. Moulton 1983–2001: 5: 88–91; Lewis is here rewording in the first person something that happened to Clark.
7. Moulton 1983–2001: 5: 92.
8. Moulton 1983–2001: 9: 212–13.
9. Moulton 1983–2001: 5: 138, 173, 8: 302.
10. Moulton 1983–2001: 5: 183, 9: 217–18.
11. Clark 1966: 130.
12. Moulton 1983–2001: 11: 300.
13. Moulton 1983–2001: 5: 188, 11: 301, 303.
14. Moulton 1983–2001: 5: 201, 9: 223.
15. Moulton 1983–2001: 5: 206, 207, 209 (Clark), 10: 143 (Gass), 11: 318 (Whitehouse).
16. Moulton 1983–2001: 5: 210–11.
17. Moulton 1983–2001: 5: 222.
18. Moulton 1983–2001: 5: 222.
19. McWhorter 1992: 17.
20. Moulton 1983–2001: 5: 226, 229.
21. Moulton1983–96: 5: 230, 258, 11: 329.
22. Moulton 1983–2001: 5: 232–33.
23. Moulton 1983–2001: 5: 226, 228n, 234, 11: 338.
24. Moulton 1983–2001: 5: 255–56, 9: 235.

25. Moulton 1983–2001: 6: 24.
26. Moulton 1983–2001: 5: 278, 304.
27. Moulton 1983–2001: 5: 278, 287, 289.
28. Ruby and Brown 1981: 19; Moulton 1983–2001: 5: 303, 305–6.
29. Moulton 1983–2001: 5: 298, 304, 11: 364.
30. Moulton 1983–2001: 5: 335.
31. Moulton 1983–2001: 5: 323, 7: 129.
32. Moulton 1983–2001: 5: 327.
33. Moulton 1983–2001: 11: 367.
34. Moulton 1983–2001: 5: 333.
35. Moulton 1983–2001: 5: 328, 333.
36. Moulton 1983–2001: 5: 339, 351.
37. Moulton 1983–2001: 5: 356.
38. Moulton 1983–2001: 6: 36, 187, 204–5.
39. Moulton 1983–2001: 5: 361, 362, 6: 9, 18.
40. Moulton 1983–2001: 5: 373, 6: 17–18.
41. Moulton 1983–2001: 6: 31–33, 10: 166.
42. Moulton 1983–2001: 6: 33.
43. Moulton 1983–2001: 6: 36, 38, 41, 47.
44. Moulton 1983–2001: 6: 81, 10: 171.
45. Moulton 1983–2001: 6: 50, 72.
46. Malloy 2000: 21.
47. Moulton 1983–2001: 3: 161, 5: 119, 303, 6: 188; Coues 1893: 623.
48. Williams in Ronda 1997: 68–69.
49. Boas 1894: 268–69; Ray 1938: 93–95; for discussion of a Shoshone wealth display, see Torrence 1994: 256–57.
50. Moulton 1983–2001: 6: 165, 214; Masson 1889: 331; Coues 1965: 356.
51. Ray 1938: 48–50; Ruby and Brown 1976: 47–48; Moulton 1983–2001: 5: 296.
52. Klein and Ackerman 1995: 79.
53. Moulton 1983–2001: 5: 371, 7: 254–55.
54. Griswold 1970: 32–36, 38–41.
55. Ruby and Brown 1993: 50–51 (first two quotations); Hunn 1990: 225 (last quotation). The first two quotations are from Sir George Simpson and Alexander Ross.
56. Moulton 1983–2001: 6: 75, 416.
57. Nabakov 1978: 164.
58. Moulton 1983–2001: 6: 199.
59. Wood 1972: 160.
60. Griswold 1970: 6; Spier and Sapir 1930: 224, 227; Anastasio 1975: 161; Ross 1904: 129–30. These are also the main sources for the previous three paragraphs.
61. Ross 1956: 146; Griswold 1970: 20–21.
62. Boas 1894: 277–78.
63. Brown 2000: 19–31; Wright 1991: 29–34.
64. Malloy 2000.
65. Moulton 1983–2001: 6: 187.
66. Moulton 1983–2001: 6: 434; Ruby and Brown 1976: 86.
67. Griswold 1970: 49; Ruby and Brown 1976: 67, 89.
68. Moulton 1983–2001: 6: 164–65.
69. Moulton 1983–2001: 5: 252; Anastasio 1975: 169.
70. Anastasio 1975: 170; Spier and Sapir 1930: 219.
71. Boyd 1996: 65, 66; see also Wood 1972: 163.
72. Harbinger 1964: 30–39.
73. Moulton 1983–2001: 6: 136.
74. Moulton 1983–2001: 6: 61, 123, 180; Griswold 1970: 47.
75. Moulton 1983–2001: 6: 168; Ruby and Brown 1976: 75; Griswold 1970: 46.

CHAPTER EIGHT

1. Vogel 1970: 63.
2. Moulton 1983–2001: 6: 79.
3. Moulton 1983–2001: 6: 85, 11: 398.
4. Moulton 1983–2001: 6: 97, 104.
5. Moulton 1983–2001: 11: 401.
6. Moulton 1983–2001: 6: 137, 9: 260, 262.
7. Moulton 1983–2001: 6: 151–52.
8. Moulton 1983–2001: 6: 157.
9. Moulton 1983–2001: 6: 267, 331.
10. Moulton 1983–2001: 6: 433, 436.
11. Moulton 1983–2001: 6: 164, 168.
12. Moulton 1983–2001: 6: 138, 166, 9: 272.
13. Moulton 1983–2001: 6: 143, 167–68, 171.
14. Moulton 1983–2001: 6: 182–83.
15. Ruby and Brown 1976: 43; Moulton 1983–2001: 6: 189. The Tillamook also killed a Portuguese sailor in 1788 (see Malloy 2000: 5).
16. Moulton 1983–2001: 6: 276, 309, 11: 420.
17. Moulton 1983–2001: 6: 421, 426. For a fuller treatment of the canoe incident, see Ronda 1984a: 211.
18. Moulton 1983–2001: 6: 429, 432n.
19. Moulton 1983–2001: 7: 8.
20. Moulton 1983–2001: 7: 57–58.
21. Moulton 1983–2001: 7: 105, 106.
22. Ross 1904: 126–27; Moulton 1983–2001: 7: 106. Here, Lewis was referring to the Watlala, but he also threatened the Wishram with death.
23. Moulton 1983–2001: 7: 133, 139–40.
24. Moulton 1983–2001: 7: 146, 148.
25. Moulton 1983–2001: 7: 156.
26. Moulton 1983–2001: 7: 180.
27. Moulton 1983–2001: 7: 179.
28. Moulton 1983–2001: 7: 212, 213.
29. Moulton 1983–2001: 7: 239–40.
30. Moulton 1983–2001: 7: 240.
31. Moulton 1983–2001: 7: 223–24.
32. Moulton 1983–2001: 7: 258, 268.
33. Moulton 1983–2001: 7: 244, 300–1.
34. Moulton 1983–2001: 7: 328, 347.
35. Moulton 1983–2001: 7: 267.
36. Vogel 1970: 69.
37. Vogel 1970: 63.
38. Moulton 1983–2001: 7: 212.
39. Moulton 1983–2001: 7: 244, 273.
40. Jackson 1978: 157.
41. Vogel 1970: 33.
42. On Lewis and Clark's medical methods, see Chuinard 1980; Will 1971; Cutright 1963; Beard 1925.
43. Jackson 1978: 64, 130.
44. Garraty and Carnes 1999: 19: 73; Vogel 1970: 57; *American Journal* 1828: 208; Jackson 1978: 54–55, 80.
45. Jackson 1978: 123n; Vogel 1970: 66, 114.
46. Moulton 1983–2001: 4: 278 (chokecherry), 7: 280 (onion), 336 (pine rosin), 8: 46 (cous), 58 (ginger).
47. Here and below, Moulton 1983–2001: 7: 283.
48. Walker 1980: 91, 92.
49. Beckwith 1938: 103, 106, 124; Vogel 1970: 14–19.
50. Harbinger 1964: 61; Hunn and Selam 1990: 193.
51. Hunn and Selam 1990: 241.
52. Boyd 1996: 121.
53. Boyd 1996: 135, 198.
54. Hunn and Selam 1990: 239; Boyd 1996: 79; Brown 1992: 62–63; Walker 1980: 92.
55. Harbinger 1964: 67; Boyd 1996: 127.
56. Walker 1980: 82–83.
57. Walker 1980: 83, 100, 104.
58. Wright 1991: 164–65.
59. Hunn and Selam 1990: 264–68; Schuster 1990: 36.
60. Wright 1991: 164.
61. Gilmore 1932: 321.
62. Jackson 1978: 17.
63. Vogel 1970: 71; Moulton 1983–2001: 12: 2.
64. Klein and Ackerman 1995: 94–96.
65. Harbinger 1964: 8, 23; Wright 1991: 158–59.
66. Harbinger 1964: 23, 42.
67. Harbinger 1964: 25, 28.
68. Hunn and Selam 1990: 193–98; Harbinger 1964: 71; Hart and Moore 1976: 3.
69. Hunn and French 1984.
70. Gilmore 1977: 29.
71. Moulton 1983–2001: 8: 14–16.

CHAPTER NINE

1. Masson 1889: 348.
2. Moulton 1983–2001: 8: 24.
3. Moulton 1983–2001: 8: 10, 22, 32–33.
4. Moulton 1983–2001: 8: 54, 57.
5. Moulton 1983–2001: 8: 68, 77.
6. Moulton 1983–2001: 8: 161, 167.
7. Moulton 1983–2001: 8: 172.
8. Moulton 1983–2001: 8: 174.
9. Moulton 1983–2001: 8: 179–80.
10. Moulton 1983–2001: 8: 184, 185, 187.
11. Moulton 1983–2001: 8: 209, 211.
12. Moulton 1983–2001: 8: 213–14.
13. Moulton 1983–2001: 8: 217, 277.
14. Moulton 1983–2001: 8: 280, 281.
15. Moulton 1983–2001: 8: 79, 88.
16. Moulton 1983–2001: 8: 104, 106.
17. Moulton 1983–2001: 8: 107.
18. Moulton 1983–2001: 8: 112, 122, 123, 127.
19. Moulton 1983–2001: 8: 128–29.
20. Moulton 1983–2001: 8: 113, 129, 130.
21. Wissler 1986: 36–37; Moulton 1983–2001: 8: 129.
22. Moulton 1983–2001: 8: 130–32.
23. Moulton 1983–2001: 8: 134–35.
24. Moulton 1983–2001: 8: 135. The medicine objects were later donated to Peale's Museum; see Jackson 1978: 477.
25. Moulton 1983–2001: 8: 135–36.
26. Moulton 1983–2001: 8: 138.
27. Ewers in Ronda 1998: 178.
28. Moulton 1983–2001: 8: 290.
29. Moulton 1983–2001: 8: 152.
30. Moulton 1983–2001: 8: 298.
31. Moulton 1983–2001: 8: 298, 301, 302–5.
32. Moulton 1983–2001: 8: 305.
33. Moulton 1983–2001: 8: 310, 329–31.
34. Moulton 1983–2001: 8: 346–47.
35. Moulton 1983–2001: 8: 363.
36. Moulton 1983–2001: 8: 367.
37. Moulton 1983–2001: 9: 366.
38. Jackson 1978: 591.
39. Jackson 1978: 326.
40. *Frankfort (Ky.) Western World*, October 11, 1806.
41. Jackson 1978: 350–51, 352.
42. Jackson 1978: 358–59; Ronda 1998: 236; Holmberg 2002: 119.
43. Furtwangler in Ronda 1998: 237–46, quotation on 241.
44. Jackson 1978: 394–96.
45. Jackson 1978: 490, 614.
46. Allen in Ronda 1998: 270–72; Cutright 1969a: 358–64, 386–87; Moulton 1983–2001: 12: 3–4.
47. Moulton 1983–2001: 3: 472; Preston 2000: 181–83; Jackson 1978: 418.
48. Jackson 1978: 200–1.
49. Ferris 1940: 92.
50. Discovery Writers 1998: 17.
51. Berkhofer in Washburn 1988: 529–32; Washington 1854: 8: 42.
52. Moulton 1983–2001: 5: 119–20.
53. MacGregor 1997: 39; Ronda 1997: 37.
54. Moulton 1983–2001: 3: 482–83.
55. I am indebted to Howard S. Miller

for pointing out the information about Linnaeus.

56. Steffen 1977: 56–57; Washington 1854: 42; Jackson 1978: 63.
57. Coues 1893: 57.
58. Ferguson is quoted in Ronda 1997: 68; Clark is quoted in Steffen 1977: 142.
59. Washington 1854: 42.
60. Clark is quoted in Steffen 1977: 133.
61. Jackson 1978: 35, 157–61.
62. Moulton 1983–2001: 3: 388–447; Jackson 1978: 62.
63. McLaughlin 2003: chapter 3.
64. Jackson 1978: 351.
65. Jackson 1978: 476.
66. Ronda 1998: 193; Jackson 1978: 539.
67. Hunn and Selam 1990: 250. A similar Nez Perce prophecy related by Otis Halfmoon is given in Clark 1966: 58.
68. Moulton 1983–2001: 7: 181.
69. Clark 1966: 57–59.
70. Clark 1966: 129–31; Discovery Writers 1998: 11–17.
71. Ferris 1940: 92–93; Farnham 1906: 273.
72. Moulton 1983–2001: 3: 209, 268, 5: 305, 8: 314; Coues 1965: 350. See also Ronda 1998: 196.
73. Abel 1939: 153.
74. Miller and Hamell 2000; White 1994.
75. White 1994; Black Elk 1953: 44.
76. Moulton 1983–2001: 3: 209; White 1994: 384; Walker 1980: 72–73.
77. Jackson 1978: 503; Ewers in Ronda 1998: 177.
78. Abel 1939: 200.
79. Gun-That-Guards-the-House 1908.
80. This is Lizzie Lowery's version, from Clark 1966: 57–58. Another version, by Nez Perce Chief Wottolen, is quoted in McWhorter 1992: 17.
81. Mallery 1893; see also Warhus 1997: 17–19.

CHAPTER TEN

1. Jackson 1978: 245.
2. Holmberg 2002: 216–18; Jackson 1978: 592; Ambrose 1996: 467.
3. Here and below, see Steffen 1977.
4. Clark 1826.
5. Foley 1989: 294; Steffen 1977: 155.
6. Holmberg 2002: 98–99; Anderson 1980: 62–63; Jackson 1978: 638–40.
7. Jackson 1978: 592.
8. Ronda 1998: 201, 268 (Allen quotation).
9. Goetzmann 1966: 3.
10. Grinnell 1999: 16; Williams in Ronda 1997: 49.
11. Jackson 1978: 547.

CONCLUSION

1. *New York Times*, December 22, 2002, sec. 2, p. 1.
2. To see more of Sally Thompson's interviews, go to http: //www.l3-lewisandclark.com.
3. *Indian Country Today*, April 26, 2000, and January 10, 2001.

APPENDIX

1. The inventory of this batch of materials is in Jackson 1978: 192–94. "Lewis and Clark's Map of 1804" is reproduced in Moulton 1983–2001: 1: map 6. For the other two maps, see the appendix entry in chapter 1, "Map of the Mississippi Country, 1804." They were published previously but were never associated with Lewis and Clark. On the sketch of the horned toad, see Jackson 1978: 277, 411.
2. Jackson 1978: 234–42, 253, 260, 263.
3. Jackson 1978: 323, 424; Moulton 1983–2001: 8: 418–19.
4. Jackson 1978: 260–61, 263, 267–68, 301–2, 411 (quotation), 418, 734.
5. Peale's original sketches are in his papers at the American Philosophical Society; Wilson's are at the Academy of Natural Sciences of Philadelphia and the Ernst Mayr Library, Harvard Museum of Natural History. Wilson's sketches were published in his book *American Ornithology*.
6. Jackson 1978: 439, 469, 476–79; McLaughlin 2003: chapter 4.
7. McLaughlin 2003: chapter 4; Boston Museum 1847.
8. Faxon 1915; Barbour 1946: 91–98; Sellers 1980: 323.
9. Willoughby 1905; McLaughlin 2003.
10. Ewers 1966.
11. Cutright 1976: 69–70, 110; Moulton 1983–2001: 2: 40–41.
12. Cutright 1976: 128–31, 138, 143.
13. Cutright 1976: 113.
14. Greene and Burke 1978: 29–33.
15. Moulton 1983–2001: 12: 3–7.
16. Moulton 1983–2001: 12: 5; Spamer and McCourt 2002.
17. Moulton 1983–2001: 2: 6, 9; Abel 1916.
18. Jefferson to Clark, September 10, 1809, William Clark Papers, Missouri Historical Society; Maury 1941: 187; Jackson 1978: 734.
19. Sellers 1980; McLaughlin 2003: chapter 6.
20. Holmberg 2002: 84, 89.
21. Cutright 1976: 145–47, 152–63.
22. Holmberg 2002.
23. Beauregard 1923: 4. The photograph is in the Missouri Historical Society photograph collection. Though it is labeled "General William Clark's living room," the styles of furniture and lighting are too late to show William Clark's home; the photograph must instead show the home of one of his descendants.
24. Cutright 1976: 118–21.
25. Beauregard to David R. Francis, July 6, 1921, and William K. Bixby, July 18, 1921, in Voorhis accession file, Missouri Historical Society Archives.
26. The internal discussion about the Coe collection is in the Voorhis accession file, Missouri Historical Society Archives.
27. Miles 1994: 339.
28. Cutright 1969b; *Century Magazine* 1904.
29. Wood and Moulton 1981.
30. Jackson 1978: 470–72.
31. Anderson 1938: 180.
32. Here and below, see Ewers 1967 (quotation on p. 54); McDermott 1948a; McDermott 1960. The accession register is in the William Clark Papers, Missouri Historical Society. It is undated but probably was started in about 1825. It does not contain many of the items described by visitors or anything identified as originating with the expedition.
33. Gibbs 1982.
34. McDermott 1948a: 133.
35. McDermott 1948a, 1948b, 1960.
36. Charles Stephens, a collector contemporary of Donaldson's, acquired some of the Catlin artifacts along with their Clark mythology, so some artifacts from his collection at the University of Pennsylvania Museum also must be treated with care.
37. Ewers 1967: 69; Thompson 1977: 147, 149–62.
38. Ewers 1967: 68.
39. McLaughlin 2003: chapter 6.
40. McDermott 1948a: 132; Ewers 1967: 65; Quimby 1954.
41. Cutright 1976: 114–15, 246.

Acknowledgments

CAROLYN GILMAN

A PROJECT AS LONG-LASTING and many-faceted as this one incurs a list of deep debts. It would be impossible to thank all of the hundreds of people in dozens of institutions who have helped us. But some stand out as having gone beyond the call of duty.

Our advisory committee has been with the project from the very outset, although the exact membership has ebbed and flowed. They have responded with wisdom and deep experience to endless outlines, plans, and presentations. Our most tireless and constant advisors have been the late Edward C. Carter II, Irene U. Chambers, Jeanne M. Eder, George P. Horse Capture, Gary E. Moulton, Castle McLaughlin, George Miles, James P. Ronda, Harry Rubenstein, Herman J. Viola, and Richard White.

The many institutions that have cooperated with us are listed elsewhere. But some of their staff members have earned special mention for making this project not only possible but pleasant. Because of the duration of the project, some have moved on; they are here listed at the institutions where they helped us: *Academy of Natural Sciences of Philadelphia:* Patricia Q. Connolly, Sean B. Duran, Richard M. McCourt, Tracy Meyers, Earle E. Spamer, Carol Spawn, Willard Whitson; *Alabama Department of Archives and History:* Robert A. Cason; *American Numismatic Society:* Michael L. Bates; *American Philosophical Society:* Beth Carroll-Horrocks, Edward C. Carter II, Robert S. Cox, Scott DeHaven, Roy Goodman, Valerie-Anne Lutz, Frank Margeson, Sue Ann Prince; *Athenaeum of Philadelphia:* Bruce Laverty, Roger W. Moss; *Beinecke Rare Book and Manuscript Library:* Jill Haines, George Miles; *Boston Athenaeum:* Sally Pierce, Richard Wendorf; *Chicago Historical Society:* Lonnie Bunch, Rob Kent; *Colonial Williamsburg:* David Blanchfield, Jay Gaynor, Carey Howlett, Martha Katz-Hyman, Pamela Randolph; *Columbia Gorge Interpretive Center:* Sharon Tiffany; *Denver Museum of Nature and Science:* Laura Brown, Liz Cook, Raylene Decatur, Richard K. Stucky; *Ernst Mayr Library:* Dana A. Fisher; *Filson Historical Society:* James J. Holmberg, Mark V. Wetherington; *Fort Canby State Park:* Evan Roberts; *Fort Clatsop National Memorial:* Curt Johnson, Cynthia Orlando, Don Striker; *Fort Ticonderoga:* Christopher D. Fox; *Grand Lodge A.F. & A.M. of Montana:* Dean M. Lindahl; *Harvard Collection of Historical Scientific Instruments:* William J. H. Andrewes, Martha Richardson, Sara J. Schechner; *Headwaters Heritage Museum:* Robin Cadby-Sorenson; *Huntington Library:* Dan Lewis; *Illinois State Museum:* Rick Purdue; *Independence National Historical Park:* Carrie Diethorn; *Joslyn Art Museum:* Marsha V. Gallagher, Larry Mensching; *Lewis and Clark College:* Doug M. Erickson; *Library of Congress:* Irene U. Chambers, Gerard W. Gawalt, Ronald Grim, James Hutson, Tambra L. Johnson, Cheryl Ann Regan, Winston Tabb; *Mariners' Museum:* Jeanne Willoz-Egnor; *Maryhill Museum:* Francine Havercroft, Betty Long-Schleif, Mary Dodds Schlick; *Massachusetts Historical Society:* Anne E.

Bentley; *Mercer Museum:* Cory Amsler, Daniel B. Reibel; *Montana Historical Society:* Kirby Lambert, Susan R. Near; *Monticello:* Elizabeth Chew, Daniel P. Jordan, Anne M. Lucas, Susan R. Stein, Carrie E. Taylor; *Museum of Comparative Zoology, Harvard University:* Douglas Causey, Alison Pirie; *Mütter Museum:* Gretchen Worden; *National Archives:* James D. Zeender; *National Museum of American History:* Judy Chelnick, Shelly Foote, James Gardner, Kathy Golden, Margaret Grandine, Kate Henderson, Harry Hunter, Donald E. Kloster, Doug Mudd, Sarah Reenders-Rittgers, Harry Rubenstein, Anne M. Serio, David Todd, Steven Turner, Deborah J. Warner, Diane Wendt; *National Museum of Dentistry:* John M. Hyson, Jr., Scott D. Swank; *National Museum of Natural History:* William T. Billeck, Deborah Hull-Walski, Johanna Humphrey, Marianne Keddington-Lang, Joseph Madeira, Theresa Malanum, Felicia Pickering, Heather Rostker, Robert D. Sullivan; *National Museum of the American Indian:* Bruce Bernstein, Douglas E. Evelyn, Emil Her Many Horses, Ann McMullen, Patricia Nietfeld, Erik Satrum, Lou Stancari, W. Richard West; *New-York Historical Society:* Jan Seidler Ramirez, Kimberly M. Terbush; *Nez Perce National Historical Park:* Bob Chenoweth; *North Dakota Lewis and Clark Interpretive Center:* David Borlaug, Kristie Frieze; *Oregon Historical Society:* Gloria Chernay, Jack Cleaver, Edward B. Kaye, Glenn Mason, Marsha Takayanagi Matthews, Beth Nelson, Chet Orloff, Norma Paulus; *Peabody Museum:* Genevieve Fisher, Susan H. Haskell, Castle McLaughlin, Anne-Marie Victor-Howe, Rubie Watson; *Rosenbach Museum and Library:* Karen Schoenewaldt; *St. Louis County Parks:* John D. Magurany; *State Historical Society of North Dakota:* Mark J. Halvorson, Timothy A. Reed, Jenny Yearous; *University of Pennsylvania Museum:* Marilyn Norcini, Melissa S. Wagner, William Wierzbowski, Lucy Fowler Williams; *University of Virginia Library:* Heather Moore; *Valley Forge National Historical Park:* Scott P. Houting, Michelle Ortwein; *Virginia Military Institution Museum:* Lt. Col. Keith E. Gibson; *Washington State Historical Society:* David Nicandri; *Western Historical Manuscript Collection:* James W. Goodrich, Nancy Lankford.

Just as crucial has been the generous help and advice we have received from Native American colleagues and advisors. I particularly wish to acknowledge, from the following tribes: *Chinook Tribe:* Tony Johnson; *Confederated Tribes of the Umatilla Indian Reservation:* Roberta Connor; *Confederated Tribes of the Warm Springs Reservation:* Eraina Palmer; *Eastern Shoshone Tribe:* Reba Teran; *Nez Perce Tribe:* Phill Allen, W. Otis Halfmoon, Diane Mallickan, Sam Penney, Allen V. Pinkham, Sharen Stevens; *Shawnee Nation:* Dark Rain Thom; *Shoshone-Bannock Tribe:* Rose Ann Abrahamson, Rosemary A. Devinney, Snookins Honena, Diana K. Yupe; *Standing Rock Sioux:* LaDonna Brave Bull Allard; *Three Affiliated Tribes of the Fort Berthold Reservation:* Gail Baker, Mike Cross, Glenda Embry, Calvin Grinnell, Tex Hall, Marilyn Hudson, Rose Marie Mandan, Amy Mossett, Tillie Walker.

The following people have given invaluable advice and assistance: John Logan Allen, Gerard Baker, Robert Beeman, Michael Bouman, Marsha Bray, Bud Clark, Katharine T. Corbett, Dayton Duncan, Steve Edwards, Dorinda Evans, J. Frederick Fausz, William E. Foley, Patricia and Meriwether Lewis Frazier, Sr., Jerry Garrett, Jack W. Gottschalk, Steven L. Grafe, Emma I. Hansen, Jane Henley, Tamilynn Holder, Landon Y. Jones, Kenneth W. Karsmizki, Peter J. Kastor, David Konig, Hartman H. Lomawaima, Howard Michael Madaus, Keith Melder, Bill Mercer, Beth Merrick, Ellen G. Miles,

Teresa M. Militello, Angela Miller, Howard S. Miller, Richard Molinaroli, Bob Moore, Jerry L. Ostermiller, Stanley Robertson, Simeon Stoddard, Frank A. Tait, Sally Thompson, Jane Weber, Anne Witty, Deborah A. Wood, Marko Zlatich.

Often we have felt that the project would never have gotten done without the interns and volunteers who have donated countless hours and creative thoughts. They were: Patricia Adams, C. Perry Bascom, Lara Boles, Elizabeth Chrastil, Julia Day, Katie Hunn, Cheryl Jett, Catherine M. Koziol, Rebecca Lawin, Elyse McBride, Elizabeth Shook, and Megan Styles.

The early stages of planning, research, and conservation were generously supported by a number of sources. I wish to thank the National Endowment for the Humanities (NEH), the National Park Service challenge cost-share grant program, the Lewis and Clark Trail Heritage Foundation, and the Lewis Family. Special thanks go to Clay Lewis and John D. Meredith of NEH; Ludd Trozpek of the Trail Heritage Foundation; Richard Williams and Gerard A. Baker of the Park Service; and Jane Henley of the Lewis Family.

The implementation of the project has been generously sponsored by Emerson. Major funding has also been provided by the U.S. Congress through the National Park Service and by the State of Missouri through the Missouri Lewis & Clark Bicentennial Commission.

The exhibit on which this book is based has gone through a long process of refining, selecting, and reorganizing of ideas. Crucial to this process, and to the way the exhibit eventually took shape, was the designer, The PRD Group. For the creative and intelligent way they took the show from idea to reality, I wish to thank Vicky E. Lewis, Daniel B. Murphy, Susan Petruccelli, and Lorraine H. Schmidt.

This book would never have come to be without the heroic efforts of the team working with Smithsonian Institution Press. I particularly wish to thank Caroline Newman for her vision and guidance, Suzanne G. Fox for a superhuman job of project management, Carol Beehler for elegant and sensitive design, Teddy Diggs for tackling a mindbreaking job of copyediting, and Gene Thorp for his beautifully rendered maps. They have made this book better than I ever thought possible.

Any group of people who work as a team on a huge undertaking like this become a sort of family, and so I have saved for last the staff and administration of the Missouri Historical Society. It is a rare institution that is willing to devote the staff time, budget, and administrative support necessary to pull off a project as ambitious as this one. Robert R. Archibald, President of Missouri Historical Society, had the vision of a national role for the institution in the Lewis and Clark Bicentennial, as well as the ability to inspire the governors and supporters of the Society, and allies across the country, to adopt his idea. This project would never have happened without his unwavering support.

Nicola Longford and Karen Goering, Vice Presidents of the Society, were the able executives in charge of organizing the staff, budgets, and operations to make the implementation of the project possible. Diane Ryberg, Vice President for Institutional Advancement, played the crucial role of selling the idea to funders.

The Lewis and Clark team were, besides myself: Benjamin Cawthra, Project Manager; Diane V. Mallow, Registrar; Timothy J. Grove, Educator; and

Jeff Meyer, Exhibit Researcher. Not to be forgotten is Joseph Carlisle, who worked as Exhibit Researcher for the first three years of the project. These people are totally awesome at what they do. They have brought endless energy, organization, diplomacy, creativity, and humor to the completion of the project. In particular, this book represents the work of Jeff and Joseph almost as much as mine.

The list of current and former Missouri Historical Society colleagues who have helped over the long course of this project is so long that I can mention only those who have exceeded all normal expectations: Susan Clifton Allen, Ken Anderson, Shannon Berry, David Bristol, Steve Call, Martha Clevenger, John Dalzell, Darlene Davies-Sugerman, Everett Dietle, Katherine Douglass, Myron Freedman, Tami Goldman, Becki Hartke, Jenny Heim, Chuck Hill, Cary Horton, Emily Jaycox, Donn Johnson, Vicki Kaffenberger, Marcia Kerz, Margaret Koch, Linda Landry, Caitlin McQuade, Lauren Mitchell, Kristina Perez, Kathy Peterson, Lee Ann Sandweiss, Carolyn Schmidt, David Schultz, Josh Stevens, Kathleen Strand, Tamaki Harvey Stratman, Andrew Walker, Anne Woodhouse, and Patti Wright. For everyone else who has fetched our books, paid our bills, vacuumed our offices, and let us in the building on countless evenings and weekends, you are the best!

Contributing Institutions

Academy of Natural Sciences of Philadelphia, Philadelphia, Pennsylvania
Afton Historical Society Press, Afton, Minnesota
Alabama Department of Archives and History, Montgomery, Alabama
American Antiquarian Society, New York, New York
American Museum of Natural History, New York, New York
American National Fish and Wildlife Museum, Springfield, Missouri
American Numismatic Society, New York, New York
American Philosophical Society, Philadelphia, Pennsylvania
Athenaeum of Philadelphia, Philadelphia, Pennsylvania
Beinecke Rare Book and Manuscript Library, Yale University, New Haven, Connecticut
Bernisches Historisches Museum, Bern, Switzerland
Boston Athenaeum, Boston, Massachusetts
Family of Owen Buxton
Chicago Historical Society, Chicago, Illinois
Collection of Historical Scientific Instruments, Harvard University, Cambridge, Massachusetts
Colonial Williamsburg Foundation, Williamsburg, Virginia
Columbia Gorge Interpretive Center, Stevenson, Washington
Denver Museum of Nature and Science, Denver, Colorado
Detroit Institute of Arts, Detroit, Michigan
Ernst Mayr Library, Museum of Comparative Zoology, Harvard University, Cambridge, Massachusetts
Mrs. Mary Johnston Evans
Dr. J. Frederick Fausz
Filson Historical Society, Louisville, Kentucky
Fort Canby State Park, Ilwaco, Washington
Fort Clatsop National Memorial, Astoria, Oregon
Fort Ticonderoga, Ticonderoga, New York
Gilcrease Museum, Tulsa, Oklahoma
Grand Lodge A.F. and A.M. of Montana, Helena, Montana
Grand Portage National Monument, Grand Marais, Minnesota
Mr. William H. Guthman
Harvard Museum of Natural History, Cambridge, Massachusetts
Headwaters Heritage Museum, Three Forks, Montana
Henry Ford Museum & Greenfield Village, Dearborn, Michigan
Huntington Library, San Marino, California
Illinois State Museum, Springfield, Illinois
Independence National Historical Park, Philadelphia, Pennsylvania
Jefferson National Expansion Memorial, St. Louis, Missouri
Joslyn Art Museum, Omaha, Nebraska
Lewis and Clark College, Special Collections Library, Portland, Oregon

Library Company of Philadelphia, Philadelphia, Pennsylvania
Library of Congress, Washington, D.C.
Mrs. Denise Stranahan Lowe
Mariners' Museum, Newport News, Virginia
Maryhill Museum of Art, Goldendale, Washington
Massachusetts Historical Society, Boston, Massachusetts
Mercer Museum, Doylestown, Pennsylvania
Minnesota Historical Society, St. Paul, Minnesota
Missouri Historical Society, St. Louis, Missouri
Montana Historical Society, Helena, Montana
Monticello, Thomas Jefferson Foundation, Charlottesville, Virginia
Musée du Louvre, Paris, France
Museo de América, Madrid, Spain
Mütter Museum, The College of Physicians of Philadelphia, Philadelphia, Pennsylvania
National Archives, Washington, D.C.
National Gallery, London, England
National Gallery of Art, Washington, D.C.
National Gallery of Canada, Ottawa, Ontario
National Museum of American History, Smithsonian Institution, Behring Center, Washington, D.C.
National Museum of Dentistry, Baltimore, Maryland
National Museum of Natural History, Smithsonian Institution, Washington, D.C.
National Museum of the American Indian, Smithsonian Institution, Washington, D.C.
National Portrait Gallery, Smithsonian Institution, Washington, D.C.
Newberry Library, Chicago, Illinois
New-York Historical Society, New York, New York
Nez Perce County Historical Society, Lewiston, Idaho
Nez Perce National Historical Park, Spaulding, Idaho
Nez Perce Tribal Committee, Lapwai, Idaho
North Dakota Lewis and Clark Interpretive Center, Washburn, North Dakota
Oregon Historical Society, Portland, Oregon
Mr. Everett Partridge
Peabody Museum of Archaeology and Ethnology, Harvard University, Cambridge, Massachusetts
Pennsylvania Horticultural Society, Philadelphia, Pennsylvania
Private Collection, Austin, Texas
Private Collection, Montgomery, Alabama
Public Archives of Canada, Ottawa, Ontario
Redwood Library & Athenaeum, Newport, Rhode Island
Rosenbach Museum and Library, Philadelphia, Pennsylvania
Royal Ontario Museum, Toronto, Ontario
Smithsonian American Art Museum, Washington, D.C.
Smithsonian Institution National Anthropological Archives, Washington, D.C.
St. Louis County Parks, Bissell House, St. Louis, Missouri
Stark Museum of Art, Orange, Texas
State Historical Society of North Dakota, Bismarck, North Dakota

Stewart Museum, Montreal, Quebec
University of Pennsylvania Museum of Archaeology and Anthropology, Philadelphia, Pennsylvania
Valentine Museum, Richmond, Virginia
Valley Forge National Historical Park, Valley Forge, Pennsylvania
Virginia Military Institute Museum, Lexington, Virginia
Walters Art Museum, Baltimore, Maryland
Washington State Historical Society, Tacoma, Washington
Washington State University Library, Pullman, Washington
Washington University, Olin Library, St. Louis, Missouri
Mr. Roger Wendlick
Western Historical Manuscript Collection, State Historical Society of Missouri, Columbia, Missouri
Wisconsin Historical Society, Madison, Wisconsin

PHOTOGRAPHERS

Art Resource
Rus Baxley Photography
Scott Berge Photography
Creative Photography
Rick Echelmeyer
Engstrom's by Mike Ridinger
Mark Gulezian, Quicksilver Photographers
Cary Horton, Missouri Historical Society
Harold Hutchinson, Ackroyd Photography
Frank Margeson, American Philosophical Society
Tad Merrick Photography
Melinda Muirhead, Missouri Historical Society
Edward Owen
David Prencipe
Stefan Rebsamen, Bernisches Historisches Museum
John Reddy Photography, with assistance by Rita Kauneckas
Sharon Silengo, State Historical Society of North Dakota
University of Texas Photography Services

Index

D

U

V

W

Y